Erratum

Please note, on page 382, that the Environmental Defense Fund has not accepted any payment for its advice to McDonald's and Johnson & Johnson, as the text incorrectly states. Future editions will be corrected. Also, the insurance company that EDF has advised is Prudential, not Mutual of Omaha, and EDF has not received payment from Prudential.

A MOMENT ON THE EARTH

☙ GREGG EASTERBROOK

A ☙
MOMENT
ON THE ☙
EARTH

The Coming Age of
Environmental Optimism ☙

VIKING
Published by the Penguin Group
Penguin Books USA Inc., 375 Hudson Street,
New York, New York 10014, U.S.A.
Penguin Books Ltd, 27 Wrights Lane,
London W8 5TZ, England
Penguin Books Australia Ltd, Ringwood,
Victoria, Australia
Penguin Books Canada Ltd, 10 Alcorn Avenue,
Toronto, Ontario, Canada M4V 3B2
Penguin Books (N.Z.) Ltd, 182–190 Wairau Road,
Auckland 10, New Zealand

Penguin Books Ltd, Registered Offices:
Harmondsworth, Middlesex, England

First published in 1995 by Viking Penguin,
a division of Penguin Books USA Inc.

10 9 8 7 6 5 4 3 2 1

LIBRARY OF CONGRESS CATALOGING IN PUBLICATION DATA
Easterbrook, Gregg.
A moment on the Earth / by Gregg Easterbrook.
p.   cm.   Includes bibliographical references and index.
ISBN 0–670–83983–3
1. Environmentalism.   2. Green movement.
3. Environmental protection.
4. Man—Influence on nature.   5. Social ecology.   I. Title
GE195.E18   1995
363.7'005—dc20   94–23411

This book is printed on acid-free paper.
∞

Printed in the United States of America
Set in Adobe Sabon
Designed by Kathryn Parise

For my father,
GEORGE EDMUND EASTERBROOK.
My hero.

For the realization of this volume I owe thanks to my friends, colleagues, and editors Michael Carlisle, Sandra Fine, Kevin Lamb, Maynard Parker, Charles Peters, William Rafferty, Connie Roosevelt, Al Silverman, Paul Slovak, Richard Smith, Stephen Smith, Andrew Sullivan, Evan Thomas, Toby Tompkins, Amanda Vaill, William Whitworth, and Dorothy Wickenden; and to my wife, Nan, who spent five years listening to me say "I've just thought of something else to add to the environment book."

Prior to publication, each chapter in this book was reviewed for accuracy by at least one academic expert or independent technical authority in the relevant field. For this service I am greatly indebted to Jesse Ausubel, Gordon Binder, Roger Blair, Rob Brenner, Donald Clay, Linda Fisher, Gordon MacDonald, Jonathan Martel, Alan Mearns, Michael Oppenheimer, Larry Reed, Milton Russell, Steven Seidel, Frederick Seitz, James Trefil, and Norton Zinder. These reviewers work at universities, government research agencies, or environmental advocacy groups; in reading the book they were representing themselves, not their employers. They are in no way responsible for the opinions expressed in these pages. Any errors that crept into the text despite their aid are mine alone.

CONTENTS ✍

PART THREE
THE GREEN FUTURE: PEOPLE AND NATURE
LEARNING TO THINK TOGETHER

Author's Note

BOOK READERS ENCOUNTERING QUOTATIONS ARE OFTEN CON-fused about the origin of the quoted words. Unfortunately there is no convention regarding identification of quote origins. Here is the proce-dure I follow. If a quotation comes from someone's writing, the attribu-tion says "has written." If a quotation comes from some material such as congressional testimony that is widely available to all researchers, the attribution reads "has said." If the quotation comes from an interview with another writer, the text says the person "told" the author or publi-cation cited. If the quotation comes from an interview with me, I say simply the person "says."

PREFACE:
WHY THE GOOD NEWS
SHOULDN'T SCARE YOU 🌿

IN THE AUTUMN OF 1992 I WAS STRUCK BY THIS HEADLINE IN the *New York Times:* "Air Found Cleaner in U.S. Cities." The accompanying story said that in the past five years air quality had improved sufficiently that nearly half the cities once violating federal smog standards no longer did so.

I was also struck by how the *Times* treated the article—as a small box buried on page A24. I checked the nation's other important news organizations and learned that none had given the finding prominence. Surely any news that air quality was in decline would have received front-page attention. The treatment suggested that the world was somehow disappointed by an inappropriately encouraging discovery.

American air is getting cleaner. Can this be happening on the same planet from which most current environmental commentary emanates? Vice President Al Gore has described the U.S. environmental situation as "extremely grave—the worst crisis our country has ever faced." The *worst:* worse than the enslavement of African-Americans, worse than the persecution of Native Americans, worse than the Civil War, worse than the Depression, worse than World War II. George Mitchell, till 1994 the majority leader of the Senate, has declared that "we risk turning our world into a lifeless desert" through environmental abuse. Gaylord Nelson, who as a senator in 1970 originated Earth Day and who is now a lawyer for the Wilderness Society, said in 1990 that current environmental problems "are a greater threat to the Earth's life-sustaining systems than a nuclear war."

And can this be the same planet from which most contemporary environmental writing emanates? *Silent Spring,* published by Rachel Carson in 1962, foretold such a widespread biological wipeout that today robins should be extinct, no longer greeting the spring with song. Instead the robin is today one of the two or three most prolific birds in the United States. Paul Ehrlich's *The Population Bomb,* released in 1968, predicted that general crop failures would "certainly" result in mass starvation in the United States by the 1980s. Instead the leading American agricultural problem of that decade was oversupply. The same book found it "not inconceivable" that some ghastly plague triggered by pollution would flash-kill half a billion people. Instead life expectancies have steadily increased, even in the overcrowded Third World. *The Limits to Growth,* a saturnine 1972 volume acclaimed at the time by critics in the United States, projected that petroleum would be exhausted by the 1990s. Instead oil prices hover near postwar lows, reflecting ample supply. *The Sinking Ark,* published in 1979 by the biologist Norman Myers, portrayed the vessel of nature as riddled with breaches and going under before our eyes, with thousands of species to become extinct during the 1980s. Instead there were at worst a handful of confirmed extinctions globally in that decade.

A Blueprint for Survival, a 1972 anthology that was a bestseller in the United Kingdom, decreed that environmental trends mean "the breakdown of society, and the irreversible disruption of the life support systems on this planet . . . are inevitable." *Green Rage,* a 1990 volume by Christopher Manes on "deep" ecology, spoke of humanity as engaged in a "lemminglike march into environmental oblivion." Other recent books and public-interest campaigns have proclaimed a mass "poisoning of America," general radiation calamities, catastrophic climate change, deadly drinking water, and exhaustion of the basic processes of life. Affairs are thought so unswervingly bleak that the writer Bill McKibben, in his much-discussed 1989 work *The End of Nature,* declared there is no need to wait for the worst. Nature has already ended: ultimately, irrevocably, horrendously.

Yet I look out my window and observe that the sky above the populous Washington, D.C., region where I live each year grows more blue. The sun not only continues to rise; it does so above a horizon that is progressively cleaner. Is everybody talking about the same world?

Let's contemplate smog for a moment. Findings like those described in the first paragraph hardly mean the battle against smog is over. But despite the impression given to the public by fashionably pessimistic commentary, underlying trends in air pollution were positive throughout the 1980s. In that decade ambient smog in the United States declined a composite 16 percent, even as economic output expanded and the number of automobiles increased rapidly. In the beginning of the 1980s there were about 600 air-quality-alert days each year in major cities. By the end of the 1980s there were about 300 such days annually. Air pollution from lead, by far the worst atmospheric poison, declined 89 percent during the 1980s; from carbon monoxide, also poisonous, went down 31 percent; ambient levels of sulfur dioxide, the main precursor of acid rain, declined 27 percent; nitrogen dioxide, another smog cause, went down 12 percent; in no smog category did ambient levels rise. In sum, American air was much less dirty in 1990 than in 1980, not more dirty as commonly believed.

Environmental Protection Agency figures from the 1990s show the improvement trend accelerating. In 1992, the number of Americans living in counties that failed some aspect of air-quality standards was 54 million—too many, but down from the 86 million people who lived in dirty-air counties in 1991, and only half the 100 million who lived in dirty air in 1982. In 1992 13 major cities, including Detroit and Pittsburgh, met federal standards for smog reduction for the first time, while no new cities were added to the violations list.

In 1993 I wrote an article for *Newsweek* presenting in detail the argument that the air grows cleaner. Later Senator Frank Lautenberg of New Jersey, chair of an important environmental subcommittee, waved the article before EPA administrator Carol Browner during a Senate hearing and declared himself "outraged" that *Newsweek* had printed such words. Senator Lautenberg did not challenge any of the factual material in the article. He appeared upset simply that positive environmental information was being reported. The good news scared him.

The good news should not scare anyone, particularly lovers of nature. Consider that recent improvements in air quality came mainly during a decade of Republican presidents—prominently Ronald Reagan, who labored under the garbled impression that trees cause more air pollution than cars. If a significant aspect of the environment got better even under Reagan, it sounds like something important is going on.

Something important *is* going on here: a fundamental, far-reaching shift toward the positive in environmental events. That shift is the subject of this book.

The volume you have opened is not an attack on environmentalism. Ecological consciousness is a leading force for good in world affairs. Without the imperatives of modern environmentalism—without its three decades of unstinting pressure on government and industry—the Western world today might actually be in the kind of ecological difficulty conventional wisdom assumes it to be in. Instead, the Western world today is on the verge of the greatest ecological renewal that humankind has known; perhaps the greatest that the Earth has known. Environmentalists deserve the credit for this remarkable turn of events.

Yet our political and cultural institutions continue to read from a script of instant doomsday. Environmentalists, who are surely on the right side of history, are increasingly on the wrong side of the present, risking their credibility by proclaiming emergencies that do not exist. What some doctrinaire environmentalists wish were true for reasons of ideology has begun to obscure the view of what is actually true in "the laboratory of nature." It's time we began reading from a new script, one that reconciles the ideals of environmentalism with the observed facts of the natural world. Toward that end this book will advance the following premises:

- That in the Western world pollution will end within our lifetimes, with society almost painlessly adapting a zero-emissions philosophy.
- That several categories of pollution have *already* ended.
- That the environments of Western countries have been growing cleaner during the very period the public has come to believe they are growing more polluted.
- That First World industrial countries, considered the scourge of the global environment, are by most measures much cleaner than developing nations.
- That most feared environmental catastrophes, such as runaway global warming, are almost certain to be avoided.
- That far from becoming a new source of global discord, environmentalism, which binds nations to a common concern, will be the best thing that's ever happened to international relations.
- That nearly all technical trends are toward new devices and modes of production that are more efficient, use fewer resources, produce less waste, and cause less ecological disruption than technology of the past.
- That there exists no fundamental conflict between the artificial and the natural.
- That artificial forces which today harm nature can be converted into allies of nature in an incredibly short time by natural standards.

- Most important, that humankind, even a growing human population of many billions, can take a constructive place in the natural order.

None of these notions are now common currency. It is possible to find yourself hooted down for proposing them at some public forums. A few years ago at a speech at a Harvard Divinity School conference on environmental affairs I was hissed merely for saying "People are more important than plants and animals." What better barometer is there of how nonsensical doomsday thinking can become?

But that is a passing situation. In the near future the propositions stated above will be widely embraced by society and even by the intelligentsia. Collectively I call these views *ecorealism.*

Ecorealism will be the next wave of environmental thinking. The core principles of ecorealism are these: that logic, not sentiment, is the best tool for safeguarding nature; that accurate understanding of the actual state of the environment will serve the Earth better than expressions of panic; that in order to form a constructive alliance with nature, men and women must learn to think like nature.

The coming wave of ecorealism will enable people and governments to make rational distinctions between those environmental alarms that are genuine and those that are merely this week's fad. Once rational decision-making becomes the rule in environmental affairs, the pace of progress will accelerate.

Essential to the ecorealist awakening will be the understanding that in almost every ecological category, nature has for millions of centuries been generating worse problems than any created by people.

Consider, for example, that today U.S. factories, power plants, and vehicles emit about 19 million tons per year of sulfur dioxide, the chief cause of acid rain. That level is far too high. Yet in 1991, the Mount Pinatubo eruption in the Philippines emitted an estimated 30 million tons of sulfur dioxide in just a few hours. Less spectacular, ongoing natural processes such as volcanic outgassing and ocean chemistry put about 100 million tons of sulfur dioxide into the atmosphere annually.

That nature makes pollutants in no way excuses the industrial variety. The comparison simply points to an important aspect of the environment, understanding of which is absent from current debate: that nature has spent vast spans of time learning to cope with acid rain, greenhouse gases, climate change, deforestation, radiation, species loss, waste, and other problems we humans so quaintly believe ourselves hurling at the environment for the first time. This knowledge suggests that environmental mischief by women and men will harm the Earth much less than popular culture now assumes. It further suggests that if people have the sense to stop the pollution they make today, and clean up that which they made in the past, the environment will regenerate in an amazingly short time by nature's standards.

Environmental commentary is so fogbound in woe that few people realize measurable improvements have already been made in almost every area. In the United States air pollution, water pollution, ocean pollution, toxic discharges, acid rain emissions, soil loss, radiation exposure, species protection, and recycling are areas where the trend lines have been consistently positive for many years. Yet polls show that people believe the environment is getting worse. Some of this can be explained by the new dynamic of fashionable doomsaying. Today many environmentalists and authors compete to see who can stage the most theatrical display of despair; public officials who once denied that environmental problems exist attempt to compensate by exaggerating in the other direction; celebrities whose lifestyles hardly reflect an ethic of modest consumption pause at limousine doors to demand that SOMEBODY ELSE conserve.

A peculiar intellectual inversion has occurred in which good news about the environment is treated as something that ought to be hushed over, while bad news is viewed with relief. Suppose a satellite produced evidence that ozone depletion was all a data error: some elements of the environmental movement would be heartbroken. Vice President Gore has written, in *Earth in the Balance,* that journalists should downplay scientific findings of ecological improvement because good news may dilute the public sense of anxiety. Gore has even said that scientists who disagree with the doomsday premise are "unethical" and must be ignored.

To the ecorealist, fashionable pessimism about the environment could not be more wrong, if only because it denies the good done already. In some vexing policy areas such as crime or public education it is difficult to imagine where solutions reside. On environmental affairs I can promise you—and will show you—that public investments yield significant benefits within the lifetimes of the people who make the investment. The first round of environmental investments did not fail; they worked, which is a great reason to have more.

I consider this glorious if only because as a political liberal I long for examples of government action that serves the common good. The extraordinary success of modern environmental protection is such an example: perhaps the best instance of government-led social progress in our age.

For this reason I have trouble fathoming why guarded optimism about the environment is politically incorrect. I have no trouble imagining that this situation will change. In the coming ecorealist ethic we will all be environmental optimists, citing conservation and pollution prevention as that rare area where government action and public concern lead promptly to results beneficial to all. Someday even Vice President Gore will smile when he talks about the ecology. Perhaps not tomorrow. But soon.

Let's note here three things that ecorealism is not.

First, it is not a philosophy of don't worry, be happy. The ecorealist must acknowledge there exists a wide range of human actions careless, selfish, or destructive to the environment. The point of ecorealism is that this equation can change, and it is much closer to that moment of transformation than all but a few people realize.

Second, ecorealism is not an endorsement of the technological lifestyle. In the past many foolish projections have been made about the course of technical events: from the thinkers of the Enlightenment, who believed that the perfectibility of humanity was at hand, to those daffy 1950s *Popular Mechanics* articles about how we'd all be flying personal helicopters by now. The epitome of this genre was a popular 1842 book by a writer named J. A. Eltizer called *The Paradise Within Reach of All Men, By Power of Machinery.* The title of the volume says everything you need to know about it. Ecorealism does not posit that technology is anyone's benefactor. It's just not necessarily bad, as is now fashionably assumed. Technology is a tool, and as a tool such as a knife can be used either to cause mayhem or carve a walking stick, technology may be used wisely or foolishly. It is up to us to decide which it will be.

Through the course of this book you will find many pages devoted to reasons for guarded optimism about the ecology juxtaposed against few detailing the evidence for ecological despair. There are passionate arguments for the latter position, the best expression of which can be found in McKibben's haunting *The End of Nature.* But the arguments for despair have received extensive explication. The arguments for optimism are rarely presented. So here I emphasize the story you haven't heard at the expense of the story you have heard. Through this book you will also encounter many passages in which the pessimistic aspects of environmental thought are generalized in ways that will fall short of reflecting the substantial range of opinions, some buoyant, that may be found within contemporary ecological mentation. By this I do not mean to suggest that the green movement is monolithic in its embrace of doomsday thinking; of course it is not. But pessimism is the main current in contemporary environmental thought, and its refutation is the main concern of this book. To those many nondoctrinaire environmentalists and environmental thinkers whose positions my paraphrases will not fully reflect, I apologize in advance.

Third and last in the inventory of what ecorealism is not, ecorealism has nothing to do with a minor fad called wise use. The phrase "wise use" once had a progressive meaning in environmental letters but in recent years has been expropriated by reactionary fundraisers. Today lovers of nature ought to have no use for wise use. The wise use crowd, for instance, is nearly psychasthenic in its opposition to the Endangered Species Act. The ecorealist ought to support strengthening of the act, for reasons we shall see.

One reason I propose ecorealism is to create a language in which environmental protection can be discussed without descending into the oratorical quicksand of instant doomsday on the left and bulldozer apologetics on the right. Ecorealism offers a guiding ideal for those who care about the integrity of nature yet hold no brief for the extreme positions on either side. People sharing those values—a group that I figure at about 90 percent of the American population—need a vocabulary and a platform for reasoned ecological debate. Ecorealism will provide it. Such debate will make environmental protection clearheaded and rational, and thus ultimately stronger still.

This book is divided into three sections: "The Long View: Thinking Like Nature"; "The Short View: Thinking Like People"; and "The Green Future: People and Nature Learning to Think Together."

The purpose of the first section is to suggest how nature might rank the problems humanity has caused in comparison to other problems faced by the natural world. This section is concerned principally with issues of natural philosophy and natural history and meant to be read in the conventional fashion, one chapter after the next.

The second section, the bulk of the book, concerns the specifics of current ecological problems—what's happening in the realms of air pollution, population, waste control, and so on. Each chapter is written as a self-contained essay on an environmental topic, with the essays arranged alphabetically by issue heading. Though I hope you will read them all, you may skip around if you wish. Chapters in the second section are individually self-explanatory.

The third section suggests how the long-term perspective of nature may be fused with the short-term perspective of human thinking. This section returns to the standard linear format in which each new chapter begins where the last left off.

Of course the problems we experience in our own lives concern us more than the perspective of the past or the promise of the future. But I am convinced that full understanding of environmental issues cannot be obtained from consideration of the present alone. Hence the book begins by thinking backward to ages gone by and ends by thinking forward to ages to come. Life is a river whose source is in the far past and whose delta—the point where the river suddenly spreads—may lie near at hand. We must attempt to fathom the entire expanse of that river to project where we will be carried on its currents.

There was a time when to cry alarm regarding environmental affairs was the daring position. Now that's the safe position: People get upset when you say things may turn out fine.

This book describes a possible sequence of events in which people, machines, and nature learn to work together to each other's benefit. Many, many things could go wrong with that vision. But why not set our sights on such a goal? Nothing makes more sense for our moment on the Earth.

ARLINGTON, VIRGINIA
June 1994

PART ONE

THE
LONG
VIEW

Thinking Like Nature

*Humankind has a highly inflated view of itself.
But then, somebody has to.*

THE DANCE OF THE AGES

THE VIEW IS AS IT HAS ALWAYS BEEN, STRETCHING BACK TO the unremembered dimness. Impossible distances, seen descending through the lens of instinct. Since sunrise the haphazard motion of many creatures has been observed. Most are of no concern, except for the target of antiquity. Suddenly all thought and purpose focus on a twitching shadow. There! On the ground, exposed to aerial view. A pigeon moving incautiously in search of its own ancient requirements. Above, everything becomes as it was and will be. The falcon dives.

Features of the cliffside pass in a blur. Diving, the falcon acts as a kind of machine, gears fashioned millennia ago. As the bird narrows its wings to accelerate earthward, promontories of lights throw irregular shadows, altering the silhouettes below. But the mechanisms that control this dive discard such distractions. Noises assail the bird's tiny ears, but these too are discarded: Rarely does the falcon show interest in sounds or sensations not directly linked to its cycles of predation and reproduction. The ground comes up, and views of other creatures proliferate. Small ones patrolling glades or rocky places at the feet of the many cliffs. Large ones, lumbering, oblivious. Discarded. All that matters is execution of the act that transfers life from one to another.

Nearing, nearer, taken. The struggle is brief: the victim old, the least fit always the favored mark of predators. Already the falcon feels the familiar ache that had been expanding through its body begin to subside. Clasping meat in its talons, the peregrine rises away.

Nearby creatures pay scant heed to what has transpired in their midst. Like the falcon, they will spend most of their lives disregarding nearly everything about the environment that does not concern them directly. They wander on searching out their own targets, evading their own predators.

What has happened in their midst is one small step in the dance of the ages, a polonaise performed by numbers of living things too great to contemplate, for periods difficult to fathom even in abstract terms. In the dance of the ages, marsh birds rise to greet the dawn; crickets call out to each other; the forests and grasses sway with the movements of breathing things; the ground hums with tunnels; the seas vibrate with warm things that swim; as far as the frigid poles and the arid deserts there is movement, there is renewal, there is the eternal longing of life.

In the one small step of the dance described above a falcon dives to kill a pigeon, part of the profound and terrible sequence by which the natural world sustains itself. But this step in the dance did not take place in some Edenic past or remote wilderness park. The example takes place in midtown New York City, in the present day. The bountiful natural world in which the falcon dwells is Manhattan.

A few decades ago falcon were near extinction in the northeastern United States, their eggs rendered unviable by residue from the pesticide DDT. After DDT was banned, some falcon bred in captivity were released near their old hunting grounds. Free to scout from the air a dwelling place of their choosing, several pairs took up residence in Manhattan, perhaps the most overdeveloped point on Earth. Skyscrapers apparently remind the falcon of the cliffsides on which their primogenitors evolved. The overfed, dull-witted pigeons of Central Park make tantalizing prey.

Falcon are living in Manhattan. To the squirrel in the suburbs of Atlanta; to the kangaroo rat in a housing development south of Los Angeles; to the sparrow in London; to the rabbit in a glade in Brussels; to most animals and plants, living on the overwhelming percentage of Earth's surface that has known no development; to most creatures of the ocean; and to most small life-forms such as insects, with whom man's interactions are incidental: the dance of the ages continues as it has since a boundless time ago.

People in their vanity wish to believe themselves already the be-all and end-all of the biosphere, a species of such power the natural world already bends to our whims. We are rather another set of characters come to a busy stage. As the prominent American biologist Lynn Margulis, of the University of Massachusetts, has said, "Humanity plays a relatively small part in the great phenomenon of life that transports and transforms the surface of the Earth. We accelerate but do not dominate the metabolism of the Earth system."

Consider that most sea life—the preponderance of earthly animation, since far more creatures live in water than on land—does not even "know" that humans have arrived on this planet. Most sea dwellers, either not being commercially harvested species or living below the surface waters where the nets dangle, have no contact with the dreaming ape. To their perceptions, nature is today precisely what it has always been.

Consider that for all the miles of road and rail laid by man, most of the acreage of Earth remains either wild or near-wild. For instance, although loss of tropical rainforests is today progressing at an alarming rate, the majority of the world's woodlands still exist in a mainly natural state. The worst-case estimate of global forest loss comes from the Club of Rome in its 1992 report *Beyond the Limits,* by Donella Meadows and others. Meadows thinks there were 14 billion acres of forest before the industrial era compared to ten billion acres now, netting a 29 percent loss. Otto Solbrig, a rainforest researcher at Harvard University, has put the worst-case estimate at 20 percent lost. Either figure represents a setback for the ecology; both are a long way from a rout of nature. The bulk of the world's forests remain, and in them the dance of the ages continues.

Not long ago I stood at a summer dawn in a mountain valley outside a rural town in the Colorado Rockies, watching prairie dogs go about their business. Till a few centuries ago that valley was devoid of human influence, and had been an unimaginable stretch of time. About a century back the valley was picked as the terminus for a narrow-gauge railway serving the mining boom of the time. The place grew chock with dirty, huffing engines, wooden buildings supported on planks, and grimy prospectors. By the time I arrived the railroad was gone, replaced by restaurants and trail-ride agencies. Any person would have said the valley had recently experienced rapid, dramatic changes. But to the prairie dogs it was all the same. They were living by their standards, not man's, smack in the midst of a machine-filled world.

As I stood watching the sunrise, a many-colored gondola balloon came floating down the valley, its hot-air torch occasionally emitting a soft roar that attenuated into the morning repose. A few of the prairie dogs glanced up at the intruder, the product of thinking vastly beyond their comprehension. Yet to the extent the expressions of animals are scrutable to humans, the reaction seemed a collective shrug. I suspect that flying craft of much greater sophistication will someday come down that valley, when its human use has changed again in some unknowable way, and that to the prairie dogs it will still all be the same.

Later I thought of that scene when reading a *Washington Post* dispatch by the journalist Phil McCombs. McCombs wrote of sitting at the mouth of a cave in Orogrande, New Mexico. Behind him he saw "whorls of tiny sea shells locked into the stone of the cliff, formed 300 million years ago under an ancient ocean." Now the fossil shells rest not beneath the seas but along a high-altitude desert, having moved there when the Rockies were upthrust perhaps 50 million years ago. In the distance McCombs beheld the uncanny flight of a Stealth fighter from a nearby air base, the aircraft skimming across the plain on a training mission. Behind him in the cave stood an archaeologist named Richard MacNeish, one of a growing number who suspect that human beings have lived in North America much longer than presumed.

In the Orogrande cave MacNeish has found evidence of a tool-using human culture at least 30,000 years old. That means people—giggling children, wizened grandfathers, fretful fathers and mothers—rode out many centuries of the last ice age in such caves. They did this a seeming eternity after the seashell creatures that once hugged the same rocks for protection had perished, the environment of their lost ocean "destroyed forever." They did this millennia before the advent of the peoples now called Native American, or the Europeans who followed, or the yuppie backpackers who follow anew. McCombs had found a spot where several great currents of the river of life were flowing backward and forward all at once. Yet to the animals that live there, I feel certain, Orogrande is as ever was and ever will be. To them the dance of the ages sways on.

Thinking Like a Mountain

In his 1948 book *A Sand County Almanac,* the most important work of American ecological philosophy, the naturalist Aldo Leopold challenged readers to "think like a mountain." But Leopold left the matter there, never fully specifying what thoughts a mountain might entertain.

Today environmental commentators often repeat Leopold's "think like a mountain" challenge, rightly saying the human gaze must learn to incorporate the views of the rest of the natural world. Learning the perspectives of nature may not only teach us new reasons why creation should be safeguarded; we may discover there is wisdom in the living world that can help us solve what now seem like intractable dilemmas of human culture.

Over the years I have occasionally pressed environmentalists to specify just what it is a mountain thinks. Usually the answer is that mountains think in a despairing one-dimensional manner; sedentary logic, perhaps. Mountains feel shock, anger, outrage, sorrow, horror, and other inclinations of pathos regarding human impositions on the land. Though these emotions are well-developed, mountains possess few other thoughts. They have no historical perspective and no interest in the good that people might accomplish along with the bad.

I suspect the thoughts of mountains are more refined. Women and men, groping to comprehend the world in which they find themselves, ponder the questions of nature in the manner appropriate to solving the problems encountered in daily life. We think short-term, devoting our attention to the events that will happen during our lifetimes. But such thought parameters hamper understanding of the environment. Nature is not a madhouse of short-term isolated events, rather an extremely long-lived whole in which all forces eventually interact with all others; in which small events in individual lives sometimes magnify to large consequences across spans of time and place too vast for the individual to envision.

If mountains think, this long term would be the leading issue of interest to them. And if there is a Larger Scheme, Earth's environment is the most significant portion of that enterprise men and women are so far able to experience directly. Thus the thoughts of the mountain may be more revealing than the thoughts of the seer sitting atop it. The first step in any attempt to create broader environmental understanding must be an exercise in imagining what mountains really think—in thinking like nature.

In order to think like nature we must address several matters: nature's sense of time; nature's perception of change; whether human influence on the ecology creates a special case; whether intellect is a desirable phenomenon or some departure from the intended flow of nature; whether nature has values; whether nature dreams; and where action by design—what humans do—might fit in a system that has maintained itself for astonishing spans of time by, so far as can be shown, spontaneous action alone.

We will start with the point at which human perceptions surely diverge most sharply from a hypothetical natural way of thinking— namely, whether humankind has yet had much effect on Earth. That is the question posed by the falcon in Manhattan.

Is Paradise Paved?

Human sprawl is ubiquitous on planet Earth. Cities both grand and dolorogenic dot six of the seven continents. Autos, trucks, and trains scurry everywhere. Mighty aircraft arc the skies; vessels larger than medieval towns course the seas; chandeliers of technology hang in space. Through human action whole provinces of Earth have been converted from forest or prairie to farms and pasture. Countless rivers have been dammed or diverted. And everywhere are man's machines, from the little motors that power handheld devices to the giant engines known as factories—machines spewing toxic chemicals, respiratory irritants, acids, greenhouse gases, water pollutants, caustic sodas, production slag, agricultural husks, cattle gristle, mineral till, "depleted" uranium, ash, polymer slurries, and products at times hard to distinguish from by-products. In parallel the homes of First World citizens have become little factories in their own right, generating heat or cold, ablaze with lights, pumping out wastes of every variety.

It's awful what people do to the Earth. And isn't it awfully grand? There is something perversely flattering in the thought that we quizzical primates have already brought an entire globe to heel. People fear tampering with the environment for a number of sound reasons, from the recurrence of folly to the nagging apprehension that by altering the face of Earth humanity does something that is better left undone. Yet there exists a contumacious satisfaction in the notion of ruining nature. In such formulations the human is a being of immense power and cunning. If you're writing your own press kit, you make yourself the star. The popularity of fashionable doomsaying partly reflects this self-aggrandizement from genus *Homo*.

From nature's perspective the picture is surely different. No one could dispute that genus *Homo* affects the Earth more than any other species. Humanity is resourceful and mischievous, assiduously engaged in environmental harm. But is nature really on the run? Several important indexes suggest that it is not.

First, the portion of Earth taken over by humanity is fantastically exaggerated in the popular imagination. The United States is the most growth-obsessed and machine-oriented of cultures. Yet so far only two percent of the U.S. surface area is "built up," according to the U.S. Geological Survey. This figure reflects the concrete footprint of cities, towns, roads, suburbs, homes, offices, factories, airports, and other artificial impositions upon American land. *Two percent.* If lakes formed by dams are thought of as built-up land, the figure rises to slightly over three percent. The comparable figure for Europe is about eight percent built-up. Europe has been in pursuit of the materialist lifestyle for several centuries longer than the United States. Yet even there only a small portion of the biosphere has been seized by people. North and west of New York City and London and Chicago, south of Paris and Bonn, east of San Francisco and Moscow, in all directions around Atlanta and Denver and Warsaw and Madrid, and in many similar locations worldwide, extensive tracts of habitat that have known only occasional human intervention abut centers of mechanistic human excess.

In his excellent history of the environmental movement, *A Fierce Green Fire,* Philip Shabecoff imagines what a traveler somehow able to soar across North America 500 years ago, as European colonization began, might have beheld. "Wherever our imaginary adventurer went he would see few indications of human occupation," Shabecoff wrote. Little more than "thin plumes of smoke from cooking fires [from] an Indian village in a small clearing in the woods" would have disrupted the beholding of a vast, calm, beatific wilderness. Today, however, "the continent has been changed almost beyond recognition . . . virtually all the landscape has been altered by human activity. . . . The mountains are scarred by mining and the clear cutting of trees . . . the wild rivers have turned brown and been tamed by locks and dams . . . much of the land is encrusted with cities and wide highways . . . the natural line of the horizon is broken with skyscrapers, radio and television towers. . . ."

That's the human perspective, to be sure. North America does appear a great deal different compared to how it must have looked five centuries ago. But what is nature's perspective?

At the small-scale level upon which most earthly creatures dwell, hardly anything has transpired. Does an insect care that the plants on which it feeds now grow in concentric circles, supported by farmers' irrigation wheels, rather than in random patches? Irrigation circles make the heartland of the United States look unnatural from the air. From the ground you can't even tell they are there.

Is any wild creature's existence adversely impacted by a "broken skyline"? Skylines get in the way of birds. So do mountains, occurring naturally at much greater mass and height. Shabecoff's premise that "virtually all the landscape has been altered" is an accurate reflection of what people *think* has happened, but it does not square with the observed facts of the natural world. Some wild American rivers are brown and tamed; most are blue and full of vitality. Cities and highways consume only two percent of America's land area, not "much" of it. Mining scars and forest clear cuts exist in distressing number, but there are a hundred wooded, placid acres for every one in the distressed category. The worst-case estimate for logging harm to U.S. forests in the past decade is four million to seven million acres damaged. That sounds like a horrifying expanse until you add that the United States has 728 million forested acres. Thus the most pessimistic statistical reading of that portion of America that Shabecoff calls "scarred . . . by clear cuts" is 0.5 percent to one percent of total woodland damaged.

Of course the fact that most land in the technological nations remains un–built upon hardly assures such land is pristine, that habitat conservation plans are adequate, that past development has been wise, that additional development would be justified. Like many arguments to be encountered in this book, the notion that most of the natural world has not been affected by human tampering is meant mainly as a device to shake readers out of the pessimistic mindset that controls current environmental debate. Think of it as something of a koan, a Zen puzzle used to liberate students from conventional pathways of thinking.

The anti-alarmism koans in this book are not intended to excuse the behavior of technological man toward nature, for that behavior is in need of reforms ultimately more sweeping than any common in public debate so far. But before society can understand what the environment really requires, the burden of false assumptions must be cast aside. Twenty years ago that meant rejecting the dogma that industrial growth is always good. Today it means rejecting the dogma of instant doomsday.

Trees: Headed Up

An important area in which human and natural perceptions differ is the forest. That portion of the world that remains wooded is a fine proxy for whether nature is in decline; for forests, even the tree plantations of the big lumber companies, are primarily temples of nature, not man.

Today most Americans would surely say that forests are in critical condition. Commentary on the 1990s dispute pitting loggers against the spotted owl in the Olympic forests of Oregon and Washington State was, for example, thick with the words "disaster," "destroyed," "ravaged," and "lost forever" in reference to American forests.

Deforestation is without doubt currently taking a toll on forests in many tropical nations. But in most affluent countries, forest cover has not been declining but expanding for at least several decades. The environmentalist's notion of a forest wipeout in progress is in the Western nations the reverse of the natural reality.

Western Europe today has nearly 30 percent *more* forest area than it had half a century ago, despite the fact that its human population has increased rapidly through that period. In the United States forests reached their nadir in the 1920s, damaged extensively by shoddy logging practices. But as the forestry analyst Roger Sedjo, of the Washington think tank Resources for the Future, has written, sometime around the early 1940s "forest growth nationally came into balance with harvests, and since that time growth has exceeded harvest." The total amount of forest has been *expanding* in the United States and Western Europe during the postwar era—the very period during which, environmental doctrine says, nature has been put to rout.

Deforestation caused by the white man began in the United States in earnest in New England in the seventeenth century, moved to the heartland and southeast about 100 years later, and around the turn of the century reached the Pacific coast. Aforestation is showing the same pattern, beginning in New England. In the mid–eighteenth century Vermont, Massachusetts, and Connecticut were only 35 percent wooded. Today these states are 59 percent forest, though their human populations have more than tripled, and large artificial landworks such as airfields have become commonplace. In the mid–eighteenth century New Hampshire was 50 percent woodland. Today the state is 86 percent forested, though portions of New Hampshire are now urban, whereas in the mid–eighteenth century, when forest acreage was smaller, the entire state was rural. In the mid–eighteenth century Maine was 74 percent forest. Today the state is 90 percent wooded, though it once was blissfully isolated and now attracts vacationers by the millions.

Similar progressions of forest recovery have begun to manifest themselves in the heartland, the southeast, and on the Pacific coast. Ponder this fact: Several U.S. states have more trees today than they did at the moment of the Declaration of Independence, when the white population of the country was but a few million. "Wilderness is a resource that can shrink but not grow," Aldo Leopold wrote in *A Sand County Almanac*. His sentiment reflects a central tenet of environmental doctrine—that things can only get worse, never better. Leopold set his words to page in the 1940s, the same decade the forest rebound began in the industrial world. Exactly at the moment Leopold was coming to the conclusion trees were doomed, a wilderness expansion was beginning.

At several points in the twentieth century, various environmental problems have seemed to reach a level at which they become irreversible. Forest loss, overuse of bioaccumulative pesticides such as DDT, and stratospheric ozone depletion are three examples. In each case commentators decreed hopelessness. In each case the irreversible problem promptly reversed itself. Forest acres in the developed world are now expanding; DDT was banished and its bioaccumulative effects are nearly gone from the U.S. biosphere; CFCs and other chemicals linked to ozone depletion are already in decline and will go out of production in most countries in 1996, with projections now showing ozone layer replenishment beginning early in the twenty-first century. Yet doctrines of pessimism somehow never get amended as the result of positive experiences.

At this writing two problems widely viewed as irreversible are loss of equatorial rainforests and the artificial greenhouse effect. But what if the developing world executes the same sequence of forest protection seen in the industrial world? A period of unregulated forest loss may be followed by a period of stabilization (deforestation rates have declined sharply in the last three years in Brazil, the country where the problem is worst) and after that a forest recovery. Aforestation of tropical woodlands might begin as soon as the early twenty-first century, a split second from now by the natural stopwatch. And what if nations learn to reduce greenhouse emissions through energy efficiency? That is already under way in many countries. Rather than steadily increasing as commentators consider inevitable, artificial greenhouse gases may begin to decline. Then the specter of global warming will recede as well.

Raw figures for items like wooded acres tell, of course, only part of a complicated story. Many growing forests in the developed world are not wilderness in the sense Leopold meant; they are not isolated from genus *Homo*. They may adjoin areas of development, exhibit unnatural features like gravel roads, be pruned by foresters and mucked with by everyone from campers to graduate students in botany. Yet no natural habitat, not even an island such as Madagascar, has ever won from nature any exemption from interaction with species as they unfold. If human beings wish to set aside patches of the biosphere as secure from interaction with people, fine. But we should do this because it seems like a good idea to us. Nature would not expect it.

Tree recovery statistics for developed nations include the "industrial forest," trees managed to maximize yield. Such forests are not wholly natural. Neither are they, as some ecologists would have it, dreary places. They teem with life: plants and animals going about their business oblivious to the presence of man. For instance, in northern California today there are more wild spotted owl living in "industrial" forests than in wholly natural forests, though managed forests constitute less than half the woodlands in that state. Thinking like nature, we'd rapidly come to the conclusion that what matters about forests is not whether trees are growing entirely on their own or under humanity's meddling eye; what matters is that forests are growing.

Population *and* Wilderness Increasing

Let's look closely at another forest measure. In a 1993 article in *The Atlantic Monthly,* the science journalist Charles Mann wrote about the six Hudson River counties an hour's drive from the World Trade Center in lower Manhattan. Mann noted, "When New York State surveyed itself in 1875, [those] six counties contained 573,003 acres of timberland, covering about 21 percent of their total area. In 1990, the date of the most recent survey, trees covered almost 1.8 million acres there, more than three times as much." Back in 1875, Mann continued, the six counties had 345,679 residents; by 1990 that number had risen to 924,075. In other words, while the human population of this heavily developed area near Manhattan was increasing threefold, its wooded portion—the zone where nature dominates—went up from 21 percent to 65 percent. How is this possible?

One explanation is that a century ago, when charcoal was a principal source of heat for New York City, forests in the nearby region were stripped for fuelwood without the systematic replanting that became integral to Northeast lumbering operations after World War I. Another is that till about the turn of the twentieth century, timber tracts near New York City were often cleared to create horse pasture. By the 1940s internal combustion had replaced horses, and clearing of forests for pasture ceased.

Most important, during the nineteenth century agriculture required much more acreage than it does today. Many complaints can be made against high-yield agriculture, including overuse of chemicals. But one overlooked advantage is that it consumes progressively less land. In the late 1930s, U.S. production of the 17 essential food and fiber products—wheat, corn, cotton, and so on—was 210 million metric tons from 77 million acres. By the late 1980s, U.S. production of the same commodities was 600 million metric tons from 72 million acres. Crops trebled while acres under cultivation declined. "Imagine what would have happened had we not had high-yield agriculture," asks Norman Borlaug, who won the 1970 Nobel Peace Prize for his work to increase farm production in the Third World. "Either people would have starved or the increases in food output would have been realized by drastic expansion of acres under cultivation—losses of pristine land 100 times greater than all losses to urban and suburban expansion combined."

Rather than claiming more land, Western agriculture claims progressively less. This development—often spun in the media as a shocking crisis of "vanishing farms"—is among the leading ecological success stories of the century. This development is also virtually unknown to the public and never remarked on by environmentalists.

When farm boundaries shrink even as output increases, nature smiles, because reduced acreage in production frees land for return to natural jurisdiction. Between 1980 and 1990, for example, U.S. cotton production rose 41 percent, corn production rose 20 percent, wheat production was up 17 percent—and total U.S. land under farm cultivation declined by 56 million acres. Fifty-six million acres works out to about 2.4 percent of the land area of the United States. Since about two percent of the country is "built up," the removal from cultivation of 2.4 percent of U.S. surface area means that in the past decade alone, more American land has been shifted away from artificial uses, handed back to nature, than is represented by the entire concrete footprint of all existing American cities and suburban sprawl.

Most land retired from farming by high-yield techniques is returned to forest or prairie, important natural uses. For instance, forest analyst Michael Williams has studied land-use patterns in Carroll County, Georgia. He found that between 1937 and 1974, 8,000 acres there were converted from forest to farmland. In the same period 90,000 acres were removed from agricultural use and returned to woodland, netting 82,000 acres reverting to nature. The returned land was not in a depleted state, and it reforested rapidly.

Another striking example of this dynamic comes from the Netherlands, where engineers recently began demolishing some of Holland's legendary dikes. Six percent of the country's land area, won in a centuries-long struggle of engineers versus the sea, will be returned from farming to its former status as wetlands and alluvial forest. Ever-higher yields on the Netherland's farms made this possible. Restoration of Dutch wetlands and alluvial forest will not only benefit the environment generally but create natural mechanisms for removing pollutants from the country's drinking-water supply, filtering of pollutants being a central role played by saturated soils in natural ecosystems.

If agricultural yield increases faster than the growth in population—as it has in the last few decades in most nations, even in the Third World—it is possible to have more people and less demand on land simultaneously. In this sense, a limited one to be sure, from nature's perspective some human impacts on the Earth have been decreasing during the twentieth century, the very century of population explosion and industrial excrescence.

Does Nature Like Manhattan?

Thinking like nature we might come to another heterodox conclusion: that factory-based economies may ultimately be the sustainable ones.

Consider that the metropolitan area around New York City has a higher population density than Bangladesh. New Yorkers live at the top of the resource consumption scale, doing practically everything via high-input mechanized means. Bangladeshis live at the bottom of the resource scale, doing most of what they do via the lowest-input means, namely manual labor. Yet today the New York area shows guarded measures of ecological improvement (rising forest acres, less smog, sewage being reprocessed for fertilizer rather than dumped in the ocean, increasing bird populations in the estuaries of the Hudson and East rivers, an upsurge in recycling) while in Bangladesh numerous measures of ecological health are veering toward the critical (filthy drinking water, topsoil loss through erosion, direct dumping of untreated human and industrial wastes into rivers).

Obviously America's economy and stable population base are the keys to this contrast. The United States has lots of capital to invest in pollution control, and its population is growing at a slow, manageable rate. By contrast Bangladesh is desperately poor, while its population expands at a stunning 2.8 percent per annum, at which rate it will double in just 25 years. Yet another factor may be this: Maddeningly enough, American existence, with its sordid addiction to resource consumption, may from nature's perspective be preferable to the hardscrabble way life is lived in Bangladesh.

In Bangladesh, deforestation is proceeding at a frightening clip because impoverished millions are felling trees for fuelwood, unable to afford the forms of energy used in the West. Rarely are the trees replanted. In the New York area, by contrast, trees are prolific in part because energy is extracted from the nonliving portion of Earth's crust as fossil fuels and uranium, using processes that alter hardly any land; or from the kinetic energy in falling water at hydroelectric plants, altering land but generating zero pollution.

In Bangladesh soil loss is proceeding at an alarming pace because farmers are too poor to practice conservation; most also work as sharecroppers, lacking long-term self-interest in the preservation of soil. Meanwhile overpopulation has forced many into low-lying monsoon areas where erosion control is nearly impossible. In the United States, farmers make enough income to care for their soils, and most own their farms, giving them incentive to keep the land whole. Most studies show that U.S. topsoil conservation is sound. In Bangladesh, impoverishment results in untreated human and factory wastes dumped into common water supplies, spreading disease to the human and animal worlds alike. In the United States, environmental regulation is bringing to an end the practice of discharging industrial and sewage waste into water.

Nature might prefer that women and men draw their energy from petroleum and uranium, extracted from geological strata of no concern to the biosphere, as against chopping and burning trees. Nature might prefer high-yield mechanized agriculture, with all its chemical drawbacks, to humble hand cultivation, if the effect is to allow significant amounts of land area to be returned to natural dominion. Certainly nature would prefer sewage treatment plants to open conduits running to the nearest stream. Nature might even feel that such technological approaches will *last longer* than romanticized peasant existence. In short, nature might consider the economies of the West the sustainable ones.

Mayan Resource Economics

But will Western economies inevitably exhaust the resources that make them possible? In recent years some historians and environmentalists have begun to assert that many past societies collapsed because they exceeded their resource base. It is now widely believed, for example, that disintegration of the Mayan culture of Central America, which flourished through the early centuries of this era only to disappear in just a few decades beginning in the year 761, was triggered by resource depletion. Mayans, the thinking goes, destroyed the fertility of their lands through indiscriminate irrigation, which can render soil saline. When crop yields plummeted, general warfare broke out among the Mayan states, each contesting for the remaining productive land. Under duress of environmental collapse the warfare ran wild, leading to a Mayan eclipse.

That societies collapse by exhausting resources was proclaimed a general theme of history in the popular 1987 book *The Rise and Fall of Great Powers,* by Paul Kennedy, a historian at Yale University who has since become a prominent doomsayer. Kennedy's interpretation is supported by some scientific research. For example Donald Ludwig, a zoologist at the University of British Columbia, wrote in 1993 in the technical journal *Science* that overexploitation of resources has been a common element of social policy for at least 3,000 years, citing failures of wheat crops in ancient Sumeria after excessive irrigation made the land saline. Resource exhaustion is particularly insidious, Ludwig and two coauthors wrote, as the problem may not be detected "until it is severe and often irreversible."

Yet such contentions mask a large omission: They emphasize a death of one society without mentioning the birth of the next. Resource collapse theories are like saying, "When the dinosaurs died, all life on Earth ended." While it may be true that some past societies have faltered from environmental exploitation, in nearly every case they were supplanted by new societies that are larger and use more resources.

Seven centuries after the Mayans fell, the Spaniards arrived in Central America and proclaimed the land lush beyond words. The ecology that to the Mayan perspective appeared "destroyed forever" was once again good as new. Spaniards and Mesoamericans began expanding on the former Mayan lands. Within one millennium of the year 761, significantly more people were living in the region than in Mayan days. Today perhaps ten times as many people dwell there, consuming far more resources than the Mayans ever dreamed of—even though lower resource consumption once caused a less populous ecology to crash. In short, the Mayan collapse was hardly irreversible. *Irreversible,* a favorite adjective of doomsayers, almost never conforms to the observed realities of the natural world. Extinction is irreversible. Otherwise nature reverses often enough to leave you dizzy.

Had human beings continued to live exactly as the Mayans did, the ecology would have known little hope. But they did not; commerce, agriculture, science, and many similar aspects of society changed. Similarly there is little chance Western life can be sustained exactly in its current manifestation. Fossil fuels, for one, are sure to become scarce eventually. It may take a decade, it may take a century; it will happen. But by the time current essential fuel resources become scarce they may already be worthless, because humankind will have moved on to other energy sources.

Today we cannot imagine a Western economy based on anything other than a whopping consumption of petroleum. But a century ago no leading intellectual imagined the world running on oil. Just as horses in nineteenth-century cities were certain to yield to some other mode of transportation, what the materialist lifestyle today depends on for its inputs is certain to change repeatedly through the centuries ahead.

Perhaps the most fundamental point of understanding about the biosphere is that it is a *living* system, not static but continuously reacting with itself and its circumstances. Human society is the same, alive and always in transition. If human society attempted to stand still by continuing to gulp petroleum at its current rate, fiasco would follow. But social change will not come to a halt, freezing current trends in place. Through the last 20 years, Western use of petroleum has begun shifting markedly in the direction of conservation. Such changes are partly driven by prices and government policies. But partly they may be seen as organic self-adaptation—society reacting just as nature would to self-correct a resource imbalance.

A Western energy economy based on hydrogen, solar-electric conversion, biomass from vegetation, and similar renewable power is not only not science fiction, it is odds-on to be realized in the lifetimes of some readers of this book. Currently many engineers scoff at the notion that hydrogen and solar-electric conversion will be useful on a commercial scale. But not much more than 100 years ago, gasoline and internal combustion were derided as nonsense. A century ago any sensible economist would have sworn that every dollar of capital in the world would be insufficient to construct the vast infrastructure necessary to create an auto culture: oil fields, refineries, pipelines, ubiquitous gasoline stations, automobile manufacturing facilities, repair shops, and so on. Yet Western society reinvented itself from no cars to all cars in 50 years.

It is well to remember that approaching the turn of the twentieth century, commentators called horse proliferation an "irreversible" peril to society—pasture land would crowd out farms, horse droppings would make cities unlivable, towns would run out of space to bury the horse carcasses, and so on. Just at the moment too many horses seemed an unresolvable environmental threat, the horse population began to drop drastically in response to the arrival of motor carriages. Running out of coal was a common refrain in the 1920s; the U.S. Department of the Interior and the British admiralty, charged with stocking the colliers of the English fleet, were among many authorities to declare coal would soon be gone forever. Within a decade a coal glut began, in response to new coal seam finds occurring at the same time that coal demand fell as the world's infatuation with petroleum commenced. In turn the imminent exhaustion of petroleum was universally decried in the 1970s. Shortly thereafter the price of oil began to plummet.

Here we may proclaim a law of environmental affairs: Whenever all respectable commentators believe a problem cannot be solved, it is about to be solved. Since respectable commentators now consider global warming unstoppable, this law predicts the greenhouse effect is about to become old news. And since respectable commentators now are "sure" that society can never wean itself from fossil fuels, therefore let's predict that the end of the fossil-fuel economy is near at hand.

Though a zero-polluting, renewable-energy economy is not practical at present, no improbable technological leaps are required to bring one into being. Today's fossil-fuel economy is already much closer in structure to a renewable-energy regime than the last century's energy economy was to today's. The Princeton physicists Joan Ogden and Robert Williams have suggested that within a decade or two, cost-effective solar-electric converters will become widely available. Large fields of such devices, placed in deserts where sunshine is intense and there are few living things to disturb,[1] would provide renewable power to separate hydrogen from water. The hydrogen would be piped back to cities for use as a gasoline replacement. In such an energy economy the basic fuel sources would be sunlight and water; the pollution output would be negligible, as hydrogen burns without meaningful air emissions or greenhouse gases.

Once an advanced energy economy is realized, petroleum might still be employed as a chemical feedstock and for other uses, but its political and social significance will conclude. Oil by and large will return to its former status of a murky nuisance that sometimes leaks from the ground; historians will come to consider the Oil Age a curiosity of less lasting significance than the Bronze Age. The industrial way of life may be irksome, but on several important fronts like this it is well ahead of the world's feudal cultures in pursuit of ecological transparency. Nature may love the citizens of the Third World but be rooting for the engineers of the First.

The Impermanence of the Permanent

Commentators further contend humankind has nature in check through the physical alterations made to Earth's surface. For instance Alan Durning, in his thoughtful attack on the materialist ethic, *How Much Is Enough?,* argues that "in 1990, mines scouring the crust of the earth to supply the consumer class moved more soil and rock than did all the world's rivers combined. [This] translates into global impacts that rank with the forces of nature." Others have put forth that by damming rivers to form power reservoirs, by diverting waters for irrigation and urban supply, by carving navigation channels, and by similar interventions, humanity has inflicted singular blows on the ecosphere.

Would nature be so impressed with the accomplishments of bulldozers and backhoes? Transplanting soil and rock is child's play to the natural world. During ice ages nature constructs glacial sheets several miles thick—ice so dense its weight causes continents to sink somewhat and may create cracks in the crust that give rise to volcanic action. All the skyscrapers of Tokyo do not come remotely close to this manner of impact on the topography. And those glacial ice sheets, weighing many quadrillions of tons, could *move*. Not even hydrogen bombs would enable genus *Homo* to construct something as large that moves.

Nature rearranges entire continents, a task people cannot imagine even in the abstract. For instance, the land mass on which North Americans live was not all that "long" ago situated near what is now the South Pole. And nature continuously draws huge amounts of underground materials to Earth's surface through volcanism and other processes, in far larger quantities than are displaced in mining. Mining projects may serve or harm, may be conducted wisely or carelessly; but there is nothing inherent in them that would raise the eyebrows of nature.

We are vain indeed if we believe human tampering with the waters of the world has yet to approach natural levels. In 1990, the *New York Times Magazine* published an article expressing outrage over the vast James Bay hydroelectric project in subarctic Quebec. Besides building reservoirs and diversion channels of unusual size, the article complained, this project had engaged in the hubris of modifying the flow of the Caniapiscau River. The Caniapiscau, a beautiful river in one of the world's hauntingly lonely spots, today empties west through some power turbines into James Bay, rather than northeast through some jumbled rocks into Ungave Bay, as the *Times* declared that it had "for eons."

For eons? Actually for 7,000 years. Farther back than that the Caniapiscau did not exist; the retreating Laurentide ice sheet had yet to carve it. Nature did not decree that the Caniapiscau must flow northeast. To nature, the existence and direction of this and all rivers are mere temporary expedients.

Hudson Bay, the Great Lakes, the Finger Lakes, the Niagara River, and many other magnificent features of North American hydrology did not come into existence until the close of the most recent ice age, a thaw that began approximately 14,000 years ago—yesterday to the geologic clock. Prior to that the portion of North America through which these rivers and lakes now course was for roughly 120,000 years lifeless and featureless, sealed under a glacial tomb. Flooding land to make the James Bay power reservoirs unquestionably kills a tiny percentage of the plants and animals of subarctic Quebec. The Laurentide ice sheet once killed 100 percent of the surface creatures that lived there.

Prior to the coming of that most recent ice cycle, subarctic Quebec contained numerous rivers and bays of unknowable configuration, all traces of them long ago crushed out of existence. Prior to that was another age of ice entombment; prior to that a third, equally unknowable lost arrangement of rivers and bays; and so on. Similar comparisons can be made for all human earthworks. The Panama Canal, the irrigation aqueducts of California, the dikes of the Netherlands, the Grand Coulee and Turukhansk and Itaipu and Raul Leoni and Gezhouba and other great dams are smaller in scale and ecological impact than many naturally occurring changes in water flows.

This is very different from saying that dams, canals, and hydro reservoirs are necessarily good ideas. Like any other human action they may be wise or foolish. An irrigation project attempted by the former Soviet Union at the Aral Sea backfired in dismal fashion, draining two-thirds of the sea's volume and ruining what was once a prime fishing area while increasing the salinity of local agricultural fields so much that they became worthless. The power obtained from the James Bay power complex may turn out to cost more than investments to displace electricity demand through conservation, which would render the project ill-advised from an economic standpoint. And the Cree, the (most recent) native population of the land where the project is being built, generally oppose further construction. It is an open question under both white and red man's law whether the Quebec provincial government has the authority to proceed in altering more rivers around James Bay, which might make the project unjust from a rights standpoint. But economic efficiency and political rights are concerns internal to humanity, not matters impinging on nature. From nature's perspective the James Bay project, known to the Quebecois is as *LaGrande,* is much less than grand. It's small potatoes.

Here to repeat a running caveat: Evidence that only a small portion of Earth has been altered significantly by men and women is only one aspect of a complex issue. Humanity may be executing many subtle forms of damage to the biosphere, damage that occurs far from developed areas or that is not yet apparent from our short-lived perspectives. The British biologist James Lovelock maintains that cities and factories are unlikely to be humanity's primary threat to nature. "When urban industrial man does something ecologically bad," Lovelock has written, "he notices it and tends to set things right again. The critical areas which need careful watching are the tropics and the seas close to the continental shores. There, where few do watch, harmful practices may be pursued to the point of no return before their dangers are recognized." The contention of this section is merely that few human activities have yet reached the natural scale. Such a level is sure to be reached someday: not, we may hope, before human understanding of the environmental system with which we tamper increases.

Unflattering Comparisons for People

As another proxy for the scale of human meddling with nature, consider emissions of the greenhouse gases that may cause global warming.

According to many environmental commentators, human-caused greenhouse emissions have already attained the point at which they alter the fundamental chemistry of the atmosphere. The chief manmade greenhouse gas is carbon dioxide. Releases of this compound have escalated dramatically during this century of industrial sprawl, so much so that the carbon dioxide content of the atmosphere is now about 25 percent higher than it was just 100 years ago. This certainly sounds like an area where even nature would experience alarm.

Global warming may indeed turn out to be real and injurious but surely not for reasons of scale, because on closer inspection human greenhouse activity is far from a level that nature would find impressive. Although the carbon dioxide content of the atmosphere has increased through the last century, the air contained only a tiny fraction of this gas when the increase began—about 290 parts per million about 100 years ago versus about 350 parts per million today. Something that exists in very small amounts may grow dramatically relative to itself yet remain tiny compared to the larger system, which is what is happening with carbon dioxide. In absolute terms human-caused emissions of carbon dioxide have only increased the gas by 0.006 percent relative to the atmosphere. It's quite common to hear alarmists express dismay over the 25 percent statistic, rare to find them bringing up the 0.006 percent side of the equation.

Global warming, in turn, is both natural and, within bounds, desirable. Without the natural greenhouse effect, Earth's surface temperature would be on average sixty degrees Fahrenheit lower. The standard estimate is that water vapor accounts for 99 percent of natural global warming. The remaining one percent of the greenhouse effect stems from carbon dioxide and other gases, which are themselves mainly products of nature, not man. Natural processes such as volcanic eruptions and the decay of plants add around 200 billion tons of carbon dioxide to the air annually, while human activity, mainly power production, automobile use and the burning of forests, adds about seven billion tons. The global rate of increase in artificial carbon dioxide emissions is at this writing running around one percent annually.

Let's perform some simple manipulation of those numbers. Carbon dioxide constitutes roughly one percent of the full greenhouse effect, with the human-caused component of the carbon dioxide cycle at roughly four percent and the rate of artificial carbon dioxide increase around one percent annually. This works out to the human impact on the green-house effect being roughly 0.04 percent of the total annual effect. That is, 99.96 percent of global warming is caused by nature, 0.04 percent is caused by people. The present rate of increase in human-caused green-house forcing, meanwhile, works out to about 0.002 percent per annum of the total effect. (These are simplified numbers. The basic range presented is correct.)

The smallness of such figures hardly renders them insignificant. The scales of earthly climate regulation are delicately balanced, and it well may be that a 0.002 percent annual addition is sufficient to tip those scales in favor of warming, especially if that alteration continues for many years unchecked by environmental reform.

The 0.002 percent figure is not a reason to dismiss global warming concerns, only another elementary measure of how an ecological effect may be perceived differently by people and by nature. People assume that the twentieth-century increase in artificial carbon dioxide emissions has an overwhelming impact on nature. From nature's way of thinking the impact may still be so minor it is difficult to detect.

Unflattering Comparisons Between People and Plankton

A relevant item here concerns James Lovelock, best known as a cofounder of the Gaia metaphor,[2] which holds that the biosphere behaves as if it were an organism. Lovelock is a scientist with credentials in the study of ozone depletion and other areas. During the 1980s, just as popular environmentalism was upshifting into autopanic, Lovelock changed his field of specialization from human environmental impact to marine biology. He did this, he said, because he had come to suspect that by virtue of sheer numbers, creatures of the sea have greater environmental impacts than men and women.

It might even be argued that in total environmental effect, humanity of the industrial era trails lowly marine plants, which produce most of the oxygen that keeps our atmosphere amenable to life. Oxygenating the atmosphere is a far more sweeping environmental impact than any yet attempted by humankind, deliberately or through negligence.

In Earth's primordial past the atmosphere probably had a nitrogen base, which probably could support only microbial life. Two billion years of toil by land and sea plants, breathing out oxygen, changed that. Today the atmosphere is about 20 percent oxygen, up from about one percent when animal life began perhaps 600 million years ago.

As oxygen is a reactive gas, it must continually be replenished by some living process or it will remove itself from the atmosphere via oxidation. Thus the oxygen level of the air is not an inheritance from prehistory but something maintained on a continuing basis by the flora of the present day. Compare the 20 percent of the atmosphere that is oxygen produced by land and sea vegetation against the 0.006 percent of the atmosphere that is carbon dioxide produced by human action. By this comparison today green plants put roughly three thousand times as much gas into the atmosphere as power plants.

2 ✍

THE GREEN FORTRESS ✍

IN THE AFTERMATH OF EVENTS SUCH AS LOVE CANAL OR THE *Exxon Valdez* oil spill, every reference to the environment is prefaced with the adjective "fragile." "Fragile environment" has become a welded phrase of the modern lexicon, like "aging hippie" or "fugitive financier." But the notion of a fragile environment is profoundly wrong. Individual animals, plants, and people are distressingly fragile. The environment that contains them is close to indestructible.

The living environment of Earth has survived ice ages; bombardments of cosmic radiation more deadly than atomic fallout; solar radiation more powerful than the worst-case projection for ozone depletion; thousand-year periods of intense volcanism releasing global air pollution far worse than that made by any factory; reversals of the planet's magnetic poles; the rearrangement of continents; transformation of plains into mountain ranges and of seas into plains; fluctuations of ocean currents and the jet stream; 300-foot vacillations in sea levels; shortening and lengthening of the seasons caused by shifts in the planetary axis; collisions of asteroids and comets bearing far more force than man's nuclear arsenals; and the years without summer that followed these impacts.

Yet hearts beat on, and petals unfold still. Were the environment fragile it would have expired many eons before the advent of the industrial affronts of the dreaming ape. Human assaults on the environment, though mischievous, are pinpricks compared to forces of the magnitude nature is accustomed to resisting.

The environmental torments cataloged above were not confined to the primordial eons. All are "recent" in geologic terms; most were endured by the primate ancestors of genus *Homo*. The bountiful natural world encountered by our forebears as they acquired self-awareness sprang not from gentle prelapsarian caresses but ceaseless defiance of calamitous duress.

Two more words conjoined in contemporary thought are "environmental abuse." Unlike the fragile environment, abuse of the environment is a genuine concept. But the scale by which humankind has abused the natural world is poorly understood, again handicapping society's ability to determine the truth or falsity of ecological alarms. All impertinent actions by genus *Homo* combined have yet to produce anything approaching the environmental damage nature inflicts on itself on a recurrent basis. Failed attempts to destroy the environment are among the great themes of the ages. What makes people think they can do any better?

The Living Fortress versus Killer Rocks

Let's first contemplate the fortress of life from the perspective of harm done to nature by nature. If we could ask nature how it might rank the environmental calamities that have so far occurred, surely all leading contenders would be natural, not artificial, events. The worst from the Earth's point of view is an asteroid or comet strike.[1] This is an extreme example, of course. But extreme environmental forces, not lesser matters like automobile emissions or Alar, are the first concern of nature.

Researchers now estimate that in the first several hundred million years of Earth's existence, when the solar system was still thick with debris from the planetary forge, so many asteroids and comets struck our primordial world that the heat generated from the constant impacts regularly sterilized the surface, obliterating any incipient life. James Kasting, a geologist at Pennsylvania State University, has calculated that the impact on Earth of a 60-mile-wide rock or comet, roughly equal to the object that caused the Orientale crater on the moon, would have heated Earth's atmosphere enough to "evaporate the top 30 meters [96 feet] of the ocean." Kasting believes there were many impacts of this ferocity during the period when life struggled to gain a toehold on Earth. Unspeakable as it would be, the simultaneous explosion of all nuclear weapons would not even come close to evaporating 30 meters of the world's oceans.

Till recently researchers thought that depredatory rock strikes were confined to the far past, probably ending about 3.8 billion years ago, when the coalescing of this solar system's planets seems to have ended and the amount of space debris is assumed to have declined sharply. The first self-replicating cells are thought to have appeared about 3.5 billion years ago, not that long after the celestial artillery barrage ceased, which to ecological optimists like me suggests that aspects of the natural world come prewired to favor life.

Discoveries of the past two decades indicate, however, that titanic rocks and snowballs plummeting from the sky are an ongoing problem for nature. For example, the hypothesis that dinosaurs were pushed to extinction by the aftereffects of a killer rock strike was proposed in the 1970s, when no crater large enough to satisfy the theory had been found. The notion of a killer rock strike as recent as 65 million years ago was, to many researchers who derided the theory, preposterous. Killer rocks and comets must have stopped falling on Earth in the far past—otherwise how could life possibly have endured? Then in 1983 remnants of a huge crater about 65 million years in age was detected by some petroleum geologists at Chicxulub, in the Yucatan region of Mexico. Later another large crater of the same age was found in Manson, Iowa.

Some researchers believe the craters in Mexico and Iowa were formed by asteroids that arrived in close succession, or perhaps by a single comet that split as it entered the atmosphere. In 1993 a team from the Lunar and Planetary Institute in Houston estimated the Chicxulub strike was an object as great as ten miles in diameter. This rock would have hit with a force equivalent to about 300 million hydrogen bombs, as compared to the roughly 60,000 that existed on all sides in the peak Cold War years, before strategic arms reduction began. The rock thus caused about 5,000 times the blast that would have been unleashed if all of man's Armageddon weapons detonated simultaneously.

In Mayan *Chicxulub* means the "Devil's Tail," and the name is fitting. Ronald Prinn, an atmospheric scientist at the Massachusetts Institute of Technology, has estimated the aftereffects. The shock wave compressed the air above Mexico to perhaps 3,000 degrees Fahrenheit, enough to ignite atmospheric nitrogen. (Horrible as they are, nuclear warheads do not create enough overpressure to ignite the atmosphere.) Billions of tons of dirt and dust were propelled into the air. The plume reached the stratosphere, higher than the mushroom clouds of nuclear explosions, distributing the dust worldwide. For several years and perhaps longer, this detritus blocked so much sunlight that the Earth fell into a perpetual frost. Perhaps several growing seasons were missed.

That's the mild part. Prinn believes the worst effects of a strike such as Chicxulub would be chemical. Atomized materials would fill the atmosphere with nitric and nitrous acids. When came the next rain, it would be a nightmare deluge as corrosive as battery acid. Two years might pass before the pH of global precipitation softened to the acidity of the worst man-caused acid rain. Meanwhile a sort of ultimate smog would form, causing many living things to choke to death. Seeds, Prinn thinks, would have had a better chance of survival than plants. How any animal life made it through the aftermath is anyone's guess. Yet if, as is estimated, 60 percent of the world's species were rendered extinct around the time of Chicxulub, that means the other 40 percent continued to breathe, eat, and reproduce during an incubus of unimaginable antibiotic properties.

The craters in Mexico and Iowa were not found until the 1980s because unlike on the moon, where no weather or plate tectonics smooth over geologic blemishes, the living environment of Earth gradually wipes away the marks of rock strikes. New techniques such as subsurface radar surveys conducted from orbit have begun to detect the subtle indicators in the planetary crust of craters whose primary features were long ago wiped away. The result of this research is chilling: Evidence of relatively recent killer strikes is being found across the globe. Analysis by the physicist James Trefil of George Mason University shows at least 120 large Earth craters made by impacts from space. That these craters are fresh enough to be detected means they represent "recent" strikes. Trefil's numbers suggest that throughout the existence of the environment, large rocks have fallen on our planet with depressing regularity.

In 1992 Wylie Poag, a researcher with the United States Geologic Survey, found evidence that a huge rock struck the Atlantic Ocean off New Jersey about 35 million years ago, causing a tidal wave perhaps 1,000 feet high: ample enough to wipe clean the ecosphere of the East Coast. Another recent find is of an asteroid that struck the Argentine pampas about 10,000 years ago, detonating with an estimated 18,000 times the power of the Hiroshima bomb. The Argentine impact obliterated a sizeable ecosphere and may have lowered temperatures around the globe. Those awful winters came about when our ancestors were preparing the first attempts at controlled agriculture along the banks of the Tigris River.

Drawing uncomfortably closer to the present is the huge explosion that occurred in 1908 above Tunguska, Siberia. This event is the subject of perennial speculation in the supermarket press as the self-destruct of an alien starcruiser or perhaps time travelers arriving ahead of schedule in their plot to spirit away Elvis. Researchers now believe the Tunguska blast was caused by a large comet that detonated in the air after entering the atmosphere at a shallow angle. Robert Park, a professor of physics at the University of Maryland, has noted that if this comet had exploded over Moscow or Tokyo rather than above Siberia, "it would have been one of the greatest disasters in recorded history." As it was, the explosion leveled hundreds of square miles of forest. The estimated force was ten megatons, or 715 times that of the Hiroshima bomb.

Uncomfortably closer still is the day in 1978 when a Pentagon early-warning satellite detected an unusual flash over the remote South Atlantic. The flash exhibited spectral characteristics of atomic fission. Since then this event has been variously described as a joint Israeli–South African atom bomb test or perhaps as the exhaust signature of Elvis's time chariot. Scientists now believe the flash was caused by a meteorite searing down into the lonely sea.

Was this flash a million-to-one fluke? In 1994 the Pentagon began to declassify historical readings from its early-warning satellites. Published in a technical volume called *Hazards Due to Comets and Asteroids,* edited by the astronomer Thomas Gehrels of the University of Arizona, the data show that from 1975 to 1992, military satellites detected 136 large explosions caused by asteroids or comets in the upper atmosphere. That is an average of eight per year. The typical explosive force was 15 kilotons, roughly the same as the Hiroshima bomb. Because the satellites see only about a tenth of the Earth at any moment, Gehrels projects that the true rate of upper-atmosphere comet and asteroid strikes may be 80 per year.

Many astronomers were stunned by the satellite data. The previous standard estimate had been that an asteroid or comet large enough to cause an atomiclike blast in the upper atmosphere would strike perhaps once a century. That such strikes actually may be happening several times per month is another indication that impacts of large objects from space are not a phenomenon of distant eons but have happened throughout the evolution of genus *Homo* and are likely to continue for eons to come.

Today Gehrels, the leading contemporary researcher into "near-Earth objects" and one of the few astronomers who regularly scans the skies for killer rocks, estimates that asteroids and comets large enough to cause a global environmental catastrophe strike Earth as often as once every 300,000 years. This suggests that the "fragile" environment has been battered a thousand times by hammer blows as strong as the one that wiped out the dinosaurs. It was Gehrels who in 1991 discovered a sizeable asteroid passing inside the orbit of the moon. Contrary to garbled press reports, that rock was never on a collision course with Earth. What if it had been? You might now be huddled in a cold, dim house where the power and water no longer work, trying to explain to your children that the perpetual murky pall outside might lift in a few years, assuming the world's food reserves last till then.

Here is the killer rock scorecard for the twentieth century: two major strikes on Earth, both doing the favor of impacting in isolated areas, plus one near miss. If you were nature, which would worry you more: killer rocks that can destroy the biosphere of entire continents; or parts per quadrillion of toxics that might cause a few additional cancer deaths per decade, the sort of issue that has taken over Western environmental debate?

That killer rocks and comets may be a regular event for the environment hardly means something gargantuan will descend from the heavens tomorrow. In 1992 there was a stir when an astronomer at the Smithsonian Institution calculated that a comet called Swift-Tuttle could strike the Earth in August 2126. Television played this finding prominently, and *Newsweek* put the killer comet of the twenty-second century on its cover. Immediately I relaxed. Readers may feel confident that any instant doomsday foreseen by a major media outlet is the one environmental disaster certain not to come to pass. Indeed, the prediction about a collision with Swift-Tuttle turned out to contain flaws and was withdrawn by the astronomer who made it.[2]

But don't relax over the general subject. Some researchers believe that large comets periodically may be thrown toward Earth by a wandering star whose gravity disrupts the solar system on a cyclical basis. This theory goes by the name Nemesis, for the wandering star that has never been glimpsed but whose existence can be inferred from gravitational wobbles of the outer planets. Beyond Pluto, the ninth planet, is believed to be a vast region of comets called the Oort cloud, a remnant of the formation of the solar system. One version of the killer comet theory holds that the passage of Nemesis perturbs the Oort cloud roughly once every 100 million years, sending down toward the inner planets a hail of comets that last perhaps a million years.

If a significant killer strike happens once every 300,000 years, that leaves a one in 4,000 chance that one will occur within any given person's lifetime. This is a low risk to be sure; yet the Environmental Protection Agency already regulates most cancer risks to the level of one chance in a million. Most European countries have or will soon have similar standards. Such policies may be prudent; why not try to eliminate even small cancer causes? But the contrast between human and natural environmental anxieties here is stark. Forms of ecological control have already reached the level of striving to contain small, conjectural risks. Meanwhile nature strives to withstand vast, horrifying, proven risks.[3]

Volcanoes: Not Just Special Effects

Almost everyone knows that whatever killed the dinosaurs brought along with it a mass extinction that wiped out many other species. Less well known is that there appear to have been at least ten mass extinctions in Earth's history, all caused by natural forces. The worst was the Permian extinction, which occurred around 250 million years ago, before the arrival of dinosaurs. During the Permian extinction the majority of land species, and an estimated 96 percent of marine species, vanished. Other major extinctions occurred 435 million years ago, 357 million years ago, and 198 million years ago, taking with them an estimated 30 to 60 percent of species alive at the time. Secondary extinctions at several points in the past ended the lines of 20 to 50 percent of the species of the time. All these totals are orders of magnitude greater than the worst possible outcome of current species extinctions caused by human malfeasance. Killer rocks were probably to blame for some natural mass extinctions. Unfortunately there are other candidates. One is volcanism.

The standard sci-fi movie scene of a landscape of volcanos framing the backdrop for a battle of roaring dinosaurs brings with it the assumption that widespread volcanism was a phenomenon confined to the primordial darkness. Volcanos, today's educated person might suppose, faded from the Earth eons ago, except for the occasional mighty eruption. Whatever fire once lit the globe with volcanic torches has long since been extinguished.

Today many scientists are beginning to believe volcanism an ongoing environmental influence. Were the powerful eruptions at Pompeii in the year 79, at Krakatau in Indonesia in 1883, or Mount Saint Helens in Washington State in 1980 weird exceptions for a world whose normal geologic condition has been placid since the dinosaurs? What if instead such events are nature's norm? The advance of humankind from disheveled hunter-gatherer to image-conscious bureaucrat has not only occurred during the short "interglacial" phase that falls between ice ages, but also during a period of what increasingly appears to be amazingly low volcanic activity.

Dewey McLean of the Virginia Polytechnic Institute and Michael Rampino of the Goddard Institute for Space Studies are two geologists who have noted that many mass extinctions appear to have coincided with floods of volcanic basalt—actual *floods* of molten rock, waves of the stuff covering not just the base of a volcano but tens or even hundreds of miles. "We tend not to pay much attention to volcanos as an environmental threat because for some reason unknown to us, volcanism has been unusually quiet during the Holocene," the 11,000-year period of human expansion, McLean says. "But throughout much of the past, volcanos have created environmental disturbances far worse than anything in human experience."

One geologic feature showing evidence of volcanic floods is the Siberian Traps, a vast area of the Eurasian subarctic where multiple sustained volcanic outflows created hundreds of miles of rock formations resembling stair steps. Rock formations suggest the magma outflow from the Siberian Traps eruptions was at least two million times as great as from the eruption of Mount Saint Helens. Researchers think sustained volcanic eruptions happened at the Siberian Traps for a period of about 600,000 years, or about 85 times as long as human civilization has existed. That period fell about 250 million years ago—right at the Permian extinction, the worst known silencer of life.

Another extended period of volcanism is represented to researchers by the Deccan Traps. The Deccan eruptions, which may have numbered into the many hundreds, covered much of what is now India with more than 1,000 feet of molten basalt. The advance of this liquid rock destroyed 100 percent of the ecosphere in its path, an effect incalculably worse than anything humankind has done to the Earth, except at the aim points of nuclear detonations.

Air pollution impacts would have been nearly unimaginable as well. Writing in *Scientific American* in 1993, the volcanologists Millard Coffin and Olav Eldholm estimated that a single flood-basalt eruption placed into the air 17 billion tons of carbon dioxide, about 2.5 times the current annual human-caused emission; 3.5 billion tons of sulfur, some 30 times current annual artificial emissions; and 28 billion tons of halogen gases, one hundred times more than total artificial release of these ozone-depleting chemicals. "The thousands of such [eruptions] that must occur in the accumulation of an individual large igneous province [such as the Siberian Traps] would modify the atmosphere in ways that would dwarf the effects of modern, human-generated pollutants," Coffin and Eldholm write. This suggests, among other things, that there have been past periods in which global rates of greenhouse gas emissions suddenly went up to a far greater degree than so far caused by human action—and that these periods lasted not a few decades or centuries but hundreds of thousands of years. On this comparison, even the worst-case estimate for human greenhouse malfeasance seems minor by nature's standards.

The sustained Deccan Traps eruptions came about 65 million years ago, coinciding with the end of the dinosaurs: Some researchers think the volcanos are linked to the dinosaur extinction. Michael Rampino has found evidence that extended periods of intense volcanism occurred at least 11 times in the past 250 million years, with most such periods falling close to a sudden increase in extinctions.

Severe volcano-caused ecological damage closer to our era occurred following the Toba eruption, an estimated 73,000 years ago in Sumatra. Toba is believed to have been among the largest volcanos ever. It erupted when our immediate forebears, the creatures researchers quaintly call "anatomically modern" humans, were alive and scrambling to exist. The anthropologist Stanley Ambrose has estimated that Toba pumped so much sun-blocking dust into the atmosphere that global temperatures fell by up to nine degrees Fahrenheit for several years—this when the world was already locked in the Pleistocene ice age.

Fantastic eruptions such as occurred at Toba might cause many of the environmental conditions ascribed to strikes of killer rocks. The 1991 eruption of Mount Pinatubo, a child's sparkler by the standards of Toba or the Deccan Traps, knocked global temperatures down by about one degree Fahrenheit for two years. Haze from a large series of volcanic eruptions might be sufficient to trigger a glacial phase; some researchers now believe an ice age occurred around the time of the Permian extinction. Along with volcano-driven cooling would come an era of ultimate smog. Sulfur dioxide and hydrochloric acid, two standard components of volcanic gases, would cause corrosive acid rain. Stinging ash, soot, and ozone would settle into the lower troposphere, attacking the lungs of animals in the same way as urban smog now harms the lungs of people, only on a more intense scale.

Somehow our forebears and the ecology survived the Toba aftereffects. Almost every species in the world today, including the desert tortoise and the pink-bellied Concho water snake, to cite two species now classified endangered, lived through the Toba eruption. And yet many alarmists today insist the desert tortoise and pink-bellied Concho have no hope of survival should California allow housing projects near the Mojave, or Texas allow operation of a water-supply reservoir at a place called Lake Ivie.

No one yet knows why some geologic epochs display intense volcanism and others do not. The molten regions of the mantle from which volcanic eruptions arise may respond to stimuli such as thermal or magnetic currents emanating from Earth's core. Or perhaps the causes are external to Earth. One theory making the rounds among scientists is that volcanic eras are triggered by strikes of killer rocks or comets: The impacts weaken Earth's crust sufficiently that pressurized lava can push through.

Should this hypothesis prove out it would mean the biosphere that some environmentalists today contend cannot resist so much as an oil spill or an overzealous crew of loggers has in the past survived the unimaginable multiple whammy of the atmosphere set on fire by a killer rock strike; followed by years of summer frost, megasmog, and acid rain from hell; followed by decades or centuries of continuous global volcanism set loose by the rock's effect on the crust.

This point is not made to rationalize oil spills or clear-cutting. No human environmental misuse should ever be justified on the grounds that the environment can recover, even if that is true. The point here is simply to compare the sorts of people-caused environmental insults that women and men today reflexively describe as "disasters" against the genuine disasters nature has survived in the past.

A billow of stagnant winter smog in London in December 1952 killed nearly 2,000 people, mainly senior citizens or young children with respiratory problems, in what we can hope will always remain one of the low points in human environmental mismanagement. Now try to imagine that sort of smog lasting not for a month, as it did in London, but for 600,000 years, as seemed to have happened during the Siberian Traps volcanic era. Again the notion invokes wonder: How did *anything* survive such environmental duress?

Does the Environment Grow Stronger?

One possibility is that creatures lived during the aftermath of killer rocks or eras of intense volcanism because evolution prepared them to do so. If throughout its history the environment has been subjected to global duress on a repeated basis, natural selection should have favored adaptations that brace living things against ecological disaster. Thinking like nature we might consider this an imperative.

Suppose the thick, nutty coatings of many seeds are not just a food source for birds or an evolutionary artifact but also serve as little time capsules that allow the seeds to survive such extremities as phases of extreme acid rain from natural causes. Such periods would be statistically improbable within the lifetimes of individual plants; but if they happen regularly over the long spans evolution seems to require for most adaptations, natural selection might push species to acquire genetic resistance to such episodes.

Today, contemplating the greenhouse effect, many commentators assume that two or three degrees of increase in Earth's temperature would lead to a devastating loss of species. This is certainly possible, though current global temperatures are actually somewhat low compared to most of the period in which mammals have lived. Now consider how nature might regard greenhouse anxiety. In the 1992 technical volume *Global Warming and Biological Diversity,* the biologist Russell Graham of the Illinois State Museum in Springfield, Illinois, pointed out that there have been "at least 63 different alterations between warm and cold climates in the last 1.6 million years." Most species that now exist are survivors of those ups and downs in climate. In the same volume Thompson Webb, a biologist at Brown University, noting that the lifetime of large vertebrate species is usually more than a million years, points out that to be alive today most creatures must have a lineage that has endured several large-scale climate swings and thus most current creatures probably possess genetic adaptability to at least some level of global temperature change.

Contemporary environmental orthodoxy discounts the likelihood that most species lines contain genetic adaptability to a range of habitat circumstances. Environmentalists often speak as if the typical creature is genetically hyperspecialized to precise conditions: Should those conditions change even marginally, death awaits. Yet scientific evidence increasingly suggests that frequent ecological alterations are the norm for nature. Thus it should be expected that natural selection has prepared the majority of creatures for this. This raises one of the most intriguing questions of evolution: whether the biosphere grows stronger over time, with each successive adaptation reinforcing the common heritage of life against future dangers.

Consider the advance from cold-blooded reptiles to warm-blooded mammals. Probably cold-blooded reptiles were Earth's dominant large life-form through the early dinosaur days. But because their bodies manufacture little heat, cold-blooded creatures have limited tolerance for climate vacillation and perhaps none for sudden climate swings of the type that may follow killer rock impacts or bursts of global volcanism.

Today most large life-forms are warm-blooded, which allows them to range over much greater areas of the ecosphere than could their cold-blooded ancestors. Not only can warm-blooded animals occupy the high and low latitudes of the world but they can also operate in the first few thousand feet of the sky, which is colder than Earth's surface. Warm-blooded animals are thus better equipped to survive everything from spates of poor weather to an epoch of global glaciation.

Many similar refinements, added to the common heritage as life evolves, can be seen in living things. For instance, locomotion represented an important advance for survival. The simple ability to move away from threats—or the more complicated ability to migrate, taking advantage of seasonal benefits of particular places—makes life more resilient. Once most plants employed a red chloroplast to make carbohydrates from water, air, and sunlight. Now plants use green chloroplast, which is more efficient for reasons of chemistry: This means more food both for the plants themselves and for the creatures that eat them. Adaptations such as long, articulated fingers help animals deal with the natural world. So do the stirrings of intelligence, hardly confined to genus *Homo*. Other examples, small individually but cumulatively powerful, could be cited to support the idea that the biosphere today must be the strongest so far to have existed on Earth, if only by virtue of what it has endured to reach this point. Perhaps the most telling of these arguments turns on diversity.

Researchers assume that the more diverse an ecosystem becomes, the more resilient it is against environmental stress. Having many creatures with different genetic allotments avoids the eggs-in-a-basket problem: If climate change or resource shortage or disease attacks one portion of the biosphere, in a diverse system other portions will deflect the attack. Scientists now believe Earth's ecosphere has become progressively more diverse, playing host to a greater range of species and gene lines as the ages have passed. Edward O. Wilson of Harvard University, a leading contemporary biologist, thinks that at present global genetic diversity is the highest ever, with perhaps as many as 100 million species walking the Earth. This does not mean we live in the best of all possible worlds. But from the standpoint of environmental resilience, we live in the best world so far.

Does Nature Get Better?

Many contemporary intellectuals are skeptical of this interpretation, implying as it does that nature is engaged in some progression from a lower to higher order. That the fortress of life is populated not by helpless waifs but creatures of proven resilience—each living thing today "higher" from the standpoint of genetic refinement than what it replaced—is the last thing many contemporary intellectuals want to hear. Also rejected is the idea of a biosphere growing more fully realized through the addition of new gene lines, as this suggests that nature would endorse genus *Homo* as a component of an advancing world. Today this view is derided in correct academic journals as "anthropocentrism," the misconception that men and women (*anthropos* in Greek) represent an important achievement for the natural world.

"Never use the words higher or lower," Charles Darwin once wrote in the margins on an evolutionary treatise. Darwin's concern was an assumption that arose in the late nineteenth century, among scientists as well as the public at large, that the natural selection hypothesis showed that nature strives to make organisms more complicated. Darwin believed that the goal of evolution was merely to make organisms better suited to their environment, for which simplicity may sometimes be superior to complexity. Darwin's concern, a technical one having to do with the mechanics of selection theory, soon became freighted with ideology. Theists such as Pierre Teilhard de Chardin declared the subtle logic of evolution to be proof that some lawgiver must stand behind the natural world. Philosophers such as Henri Bergson advanced a position known as "final causes," which essentially assumes that the entire convoluted, cataclysm-filled history of Earth was mapped out as a plan to call into being the present arrangement of people, animals, and natural vistas. On the opposite side the antireligion camp, personified by Darwin's nineteenth-century popularizer Thomas Huxley, declared that selection theory disproves the need for any sovereign standing above nature.

Today the suggestion there could be "higher" as well as lower existence has become impermissibly anthropocentric. Once, in *The Atlantic Monthly,* I summarized selection theory this way: "Good genes are preserved while bad ones are discarded; organisms become more sophisticated; thinking beings are eventually produced, and they figure it all out." The mail brought numerous letters from ecologists steamy with offense. How dare I suggest that "organisms become more sophisticated"! Natural selection is a neutral mechanistic process; complex creatures like people or whales represent no more to the vast meaninglessness of nature than pond scum. By suggesting otherwise I had gone beyond anthropocentrism to the more advanced sin of "speciesism," putting forth that people are better than bugs, which to factions of the ecological movement seems an inadmissible thought.

Actually what I asserted is that the modern horse is better than *Eohippus;* that *Homo sapiens* is better than *Homo hablis;* and so on. Nature may not have an ordained goal, as many religions believe. It unquestionably has a *result.* The result is our moment on the Earth, a moment no one should hesitate to proclaim as good, sophisticated, beautiful, and profound. This ought to be self-evident if nothing else because every contemporary species is the product (for the moment, the end product) of the most demanding ecological selection process ever set in motion. One reason the ecorealist ought to want to preserve the found world is that it's full of living things that are better than bugs—a lot better.

Guaranteed Environmental Destruction

A few other recurrent natural threats to nature bear mentioning. One is that strong cosmic rays periodically shine on Earth from outside the solar system. What causes this bombardment is a subject of debate among astrophysicists; suffice to say that cosmic radiation sometimes spikes upward for reasons not yet understood. Such episodes must have had a pervasive impact on the environment, perhaps causing bursts of mutations. Some researchers now believe that past episodes of cosmic radiation have, during relatively recent geologic eras, subjected the biosphere to a radiation bath approximately at the level of general nuclear war. If such horrible levels of cosmic radiation did occur, obviously they did not destroy life. We're here.

There is a related stellar threat to the environment. When stars explode into supernovas "near" our solar system, Earth may be bathed in ultraviolet rays. This is the same type of radiation routinely emitted by our sun and routinely screened away by the stratospheric ozone layer. A supernova explosion "near" Earth might, however, overwhelm the ozone layer with more ultraviolet radiation than it can resist. So far there is no indication of any such supernova ultraviolet barrage during the brief millennia of human civilization. But Neil Gehrels and Wan Chen, two NASA astronomers, and Giovanni Bignami, an Italian astronomer, believe a supernova detonated "near" Earth about 340,000 years ago, around the time our hominoid ancestors had graduated to the distinction of *Homo erectus.* One effect of the explosion may have been to blow off part of Earth's ozone layer, which is near the top of the atmosphere and thus vulnerable to physical forces from space. This would have allowed high levels of cosmic and ultraviolet radiation from the supernova, and additional ultraviolet radiation from the sun, to afflict the biosphere for many years or decades. Again this happened not in the primordial mists but to the immediate ancestors of women and men.

If the biosphere has been exposed to high levels of solar and cosmic radiation in the past, some encoded genetic response ought to be detectable in living things. Antarctic plankton is the life-form said most likely to be harmed first by artificial ozone layer depletion. Deneb Karentz, a researcher at the University of San Francisco, has found that this plankton manufactures molecules that shield its cells from ultraviolet wavelengths. Since this natural sunscreen is in the plankton gene pool, it probably represents an evolutionary adaptation to past ozone depletion occurring on a natural basis.

Botanists are now finding that most plants make substances called flavenoids that block ultraviolet radiation. Generally the more radiation from the sky a plant receives, the more flavenoids made. This does not mean plants are immune to radiation: it's still a danger, just as are many realities of life against which living things have partial defenses. Tests suggest plant flavenoids can resist significantly more ultraviolet radiation than would be caused by a worst-case reading of current stratospheric ozone depletion, but that the defense breaks down in the presence of high ultraviolet levels. This finding from botany shows that ultraviolet radiation is a genuine problem for the natural world, confirming that human actions depleting the ozone layer are a genuine concern. At the same time these findings suggest that what contemporary commentators call the "unprecedented" present-day effect of stratospheric ozone depletion is so far a pale version of something the environment has faced before on a natural basis.

Another natural threat to nature is polarity reversal in the Earth's magnetic fields. There are numerous points in the past when the "north" needle on a Boy Scout compass would have pointed toward the South Pole. Earth's polarity has flip-flopped many times, apparently in response to shifts in magnetic molten rock within the planet. On what cycle these shifts occur is unknown. Since many migratory birds navigate partly by flecks of magnetized substance in their brains that allow them to sense magnetic north, how such species survive years of a global polarity flip-flop seems quite mysterious. Some researchers think that during polarity flops, Earth's magnetic field falters. The magnetic field helps deflect cosmic rays; if it faltered radiation would stream down on the planet. It is possible, some scientists think, that moments of weakening in this natural radiation deflection system account for periodic mass extinctions. A period of magnetic-field faltering might represent a more drastic radiation impact on the environment than any humankind could cause short of maximal nuclear war.

Still another natural threat to nature is the post-glacial deluge. In 1992 Victor Baker, a geologist at the University of Arizona, suggested that when large ice dams crack at the end of glacial ages, they release "superfloods." In Siberia, Baker found evidence from around 15,000 years ago suggesting post-glacial inundations composed of walls of water as high as 1,500 feet and advancing at speeds of perhaps 275 miles per hour. If you've seen pictures of what the slowly developing 43-foot Mississippi River flood of 1993 did to the central United States—cracking reinforced levees, scouring away vegetation, drowning thousands of animals—try to imagine what a 1,500-foot wall of water moving like a rifle bullet might do to the biosphere. Try to imagine humankind exacting on the landscape any act remotely as violent. Yet the present-day ecology of Siberia, a lush taiga forest whose protection is rightly the subject of current international concern, flourished after being assaulted in this manner. Other currently thriving environmental niches may have survived superfloods as well.[4]

Still another natural threat to nature is the uplift of mountain ranges. Mountains are not just big, impressive items of surface relief; they are structures that interfere with Earth's winds, altering weather patterns. Some researchers, including Maureen Raymo of the Massachusetts Institute of Technology, believe that the Tibetan plateau on which the Himalayas sit disrupts climate more than any geological feature in Earth's history. Tibet began to rise about 40 million years ago, by happenstance sitting square in the path of a jet stream. Its transition from low ground to gigantic physical obstacle may have initiated a long series of weather alterations. Climate changes for which the Himalayas may bear some blame, Raymo thinks, include monsoons, ice ages, and rainfall distribution that brings too much water to places like Bangladesh and not enough to places like the Sahara.

Before the Tibetan plateau began to disrupt the climate, lush, easy-living ecosystems may have been the rule over most of the Earth. During the age of the dinosaurs, for example, the global climate was much warmer than today—probably by up to 12 degrees Fahrenheit on average, warmer than the worst-case projections for artificial global warming. Rainfall may then have been more evenly distributed, allowing a substantial portion of the globe to enjoy conditions approximately like those found in current tropical forests.

After Tibet arose the lushness of the Earth declined and the current phases of ice ages began. Most geologists believe there were glacial periods in Earth's far past when the sun was faint compared to now. Then ice cycles stopped for eons, including the warm interval enjoyed by the dinosaurs, which lasted more than 100 million years apparently without glacial interruption. Roughly 40 million years ago, around the time the Himalayas were upthrust, global ice began to come and go in what appears to be a tightly regulated cycle. Ice ages became a natural threat to nature of murderous proportions, cyclically wiping out perhaps a quarter of all life.

The Impermanence of the Very Ground

One last natural threat to nature bears mentioning: movement of the landscape itself. Today every schoolchild knows the once-ridiculed theory of continental drift, which stipulates that land masses are not anchored but float ever so gradually atop the crust of the Earth. Every schoolchild knows, in turn, that researchers believe the world's continents were once joined in a single mass known as Pangaea ("all lands") then broke apart and drifted to their current locations. This is why the east coast of North America looks like it would fit into the west coast of Africa on a jigsaw puzzle. The continents continue to drift and ages from now will rest in other, unknowable locations.

Continental drift brings with it environmental transitions of majestic gradation. They include climate change; the complete rearrangement of ecological niches, as what were once shores become mountains, what were mountains become seas; to the physical disassociation of resource areas that were once linked. For instance about 57 million years ago the drift between continents progressed to the point at which the Atlantic Ocean opened between Norway and Greenland. Some researchers believe that at that time a mass extinction occurred, coincident with a burst in formation of new species—ones adapted to the resources and climates of Scandinavia and northeastern North America as separate rather than cojoined entities. Pangaea seems to have begun its breakup somewhere around 250 million years ago. The poor creatures of the Permian extinction were thus subject to as many as three natural whammies of colossal scale: killer rock strikes, intense volcanism, and the splitting of the land upon which they lived. Given this, it may be no surprise that perhaps as few as four percent of Permian species survived.

What came before Pangaea? The geologists J. Brendan Murphy, of Canada's Saint Francis Xavier University, and Damian Nance, of Ohio State, have recently advanced a theory that there exists a "supercontinent cycle"—an environmental rhythm of Olympian magnitude. The crust of Earth, Murphy and Nance have written, may "follow an orderly pattern: every few hundred million years, all the continents congregate into a supercontinent," exist that way for a few hundred million years, then disassociate till the next congregation. Murphy and Nance think that before Pangaea, some 650 million years ago, was another supercontinent where the world's land was arranged in shapes entirely unrecognizable to the modern eye. Eons before that was still a third supercontinent, and so on. Eons in the future will come another supercontinent and then another breakup, resulting in an arrangement of ecological niches whose specifics no living person could guess at.

Whatever forces may cause supercontinent cycles—perhaps heat radiation from Earth's deep core, perhaps the gravitational effects of Earth's movement through the galactic plane—do not matter here. What matters is comprehension of the full scale of natural threats to nature. If the supercontinent cycle theory is true, then all habitats of Earth's ecosphere are automatically doomed and always have been.

Here then is one of the central tenets of thinking like nature: Environmental destruction is axiomatic. Even if humanity should magically vanish from the globe tomorrow, the environment would *not* be preserved. Forests would continue to fall and rise; creatures to disappear to extinction; the climate to change; lush lands to blow away into deserts, while deserts blossom into flowers; the land masses to rearrange themselves. The environments around us have not always been as we see them; throughout most of time they have been some other way. And they are guaranteed to be some other way in the future, because nature will always be in a transitional phase. No other condition is possible.

This ought not frighten us. It is the natural order that gave genus *Homo* being. The knowledge that all environments are fated to end ought to bring more clarity to our moment on the Earth: a deeper commitment to prolong it and renewed optimism about what may lie ahead.

Nature against Nature: Present Day

The sort of natural assaults against the environment described in this chapter may seem to readers abstract matters, because great natural upheavals have not occurred during our era and thus cannot be compared directly to human-caused pollution. Or can they? Perhaps natural assaults against nature happen all the time, even in the here and now.

On a spring day in 1992 I alighted from a helicopter on the crater of Mount Saint Helens in Washington State. Above me, shrouded in mystic fog, was a portal to the sort of power women and men can only guess at.

At Mount Saint Helens in May 1980, a vein of magma in a dormant volcano exploded sideways, incinerating the surface features of 200 square miles of land while tearing 1,300 feet of elevation off an entire mountain. Boulders weighing tons were thrown outward at 150 miles per hour. Local temperatures rose to more than 1,000 degrees Fahrenheit. Some 19 million old-growth Douglas firs, trees with deep roots, were ripped from the ground and tossed about like cocktail swizzles. A fan-shaped area more than 15 miles long was riven by the shock wave, pelted by boulders, then fried to black char. Researchers would later christen this sterilized vista "the pumice plain." Uncountable thousands of animals died. Fifty-seven people perished, including some who attempted to take shelter on the far side of a mountain nearly ten miles from the blast point.

Among the victims was David Johnston, one of the world's leading volcanologists, who had spent the previous week urging reporters and the curious who came to see the rumbling mountain to get away while they still could. At the time of his death Johnston had been publishing technical papers in support of his theory that volcanos play a much larger role in global air pollution than commonly understood. Today a small memorial stands near the point where Johnston screamed into a radio link to a research station in British Columbia his last words: "Vancouver! Vancouver! This is it!" No trace of Johnston's body was ever found.

The view I beheld from the crater of Mount Saint Helens, a dozen years after the detonation, still offered extensive panoramas of devastation—shorn trees, fields of rubble with little apparent life—yet much of the area was already back to normal or nearly so. I counted three herds of Roosevelt elk in the blast zone. Elk, the dominant large vertebrate of the Olympic forest, were expected to be wiped out by the aftereffects of the explosion, as it was widely believed that elk could not exist without old-growth woods; and in the Mount Saint Helens area today, thanks to nature there stands not a single old-growth tree. Yet the elk prosper, their young perceiving a world of fractured trees and black char the normal state of their environment.

Heat from the detonation of the mountain raised the temperature in streams below Mount Saint Helens to 90 degrees Fahrenheit for several days. Coho salmon, a native species, were thought unable to tolerate water warmer than 75 degrees; yet many lived through the experience and are running again. (There has also been some restocking.) Photos of the immediate blast aftermath at a place called Lower Shultz Creek show a moonscape of ash and inert stillness. Today Lower Shultz Creek is bright green again, lined with vegetation and wildflowers, its banks visited by thirsty small mammals. The blast zone was not cleaned up by work crews; this recovery is natural. Some photos taken by a local naturalist suggest Lower Shultz Creek began to recover on its own as early as 1983, just three years after the explosion.

One haunting discovery of the rebound of the Mount Saint Helens ecosphere concerns the heated streams. Even today Loowit Creek, which runs from a dome near the crater, emerges at around 175 degrees Fahrenheit, close to the boiling point of water at the local altitude. And there is life in the Loowit.

A form of simple blue-green algae grows in the Loowit, as do some single-cell organisms called archaebacteria. Archaebacteria are believed to number with the oldest continually living things on Earth: They metabolize sulfur and methane, substances more common in the primordial epoch. Tests suggest these determined organisms appeared in Mount Saint Helens streams less than two years after the detonation. It's hard enough to imagine how they thrive in such hot water. A simpler question: How did they get there?

Bacteria do not migrate, except over the long term as they ride in the guts of animals that die and decompose. So when something as terrible as the Mount Saint Helens detonation occurs, it would seem decades or even centuries would be required for enough creatures to stumble into the area to begin repopulation. This is one reason the standard gradual-ist interpretation assumes that very long spans of time must pass for nature to self-renew after an environmental insult. That, at least, was the prevailing view among scientists in May 1980. Many quoted in newspa-per accounts following the Mount Saint Helens explosion suggested the blast zone would remain lifeless well into the next century.

Instead the blast zone began to renew immediately. Today it is thought that the renewal of the Mount Saint Helens ecosphere was self-generated, not triggered by creatures migrating in. As Tim Beardsley wrote of the Mount Saint Helens reanimation in *Scientific American,* "Biologists have been impressed with how even the remains of dead organisms can spur recovery. One found that the leaves of a species of lupine [an edible seed plant] decompose to woody skeletons that serve as drift nets for organic materials and seeds. Likewise, downed trees stabi-lized soil that otherwise might have blown or washed away." It now seems roots of fireweed and pearly everlasting, two heroically stubborn plants that can sprout within hours of a forest fire, somehow survived the megatonnage of the detonation. And some animals that were under-ground during the worst survived. (A significant portion of the forest life-cycle occurs below the surface.) Where did the archaebacteria come from? One hypothesis holds it was there all along—a dormant species naturally "stocked" in volcanic areas, awaiting its chance.

Because nature is ancient, conventional wisdom posits that natural recoveries from environmental stress are exceptionally slow. Mount Saint Helens suggests the reverse: that natural recoveries happen very fast, along the same time horizons as human events. Thinking like nature we would consider this a logical expedient. If nature must resist great ecological duress not once every eon but over and over again, rapid-rebound systems would be the kind likely to evolve. We humans may not see much evidence of rapid natural recoveries of the past because the geologic and fossil records we study rarely are reliable to time blocks of less than 10,000 years. If Mount Saint Helens is any guide, that is far longer than required for natural self-renewal.

In an age when affairs of state are beginning to be driven by the conventional belief that human environmental interventions cause damage from which nature can "never" recover, doesn't this make the Mount Saint Helens blast zone seem a significant venue for study? Yet comparatively little research has occurred there. Congress has rejected several requests to fund Mount Saint Helens studies in the million-dollar range. At the same time the fiscal 1995 federal budget contains $1.5 billion to research the possibility of an artificial greenhouse effect. The Mount Saint Helens blast, which actually happened, is firmer ground for empirical analysis than the artificial greenhouse effect, something that only might happen and thus is studied mainly by the notoriously pliant technique of computer simulation. But the greenhouse effect fits the instant-doomsday fashion; work supporting this prospect is well funded. The recovery of Mount Saint Helens, being inconveniently optimistic, is deemed of little interest.

A living system able to withstand the detonation of Mount Saint Helens is a green fortress indeed. This does not rationalize any human assault on that fortress, for ingenious as the environment's defenses are, men and women may someday find a means to breach them. But understanding the strength and resilience of life helps us put the environmental issues of the day into a perspective larger than our own. Without such perspective humankind will not be able to make rational choices regarding which environmental alarms are genuine and which merely this year's fad.

3

TIME AS THE ULTIMATE RESOURCE

ONE OVERCAST DAY IN A RECENT WINTER I SAT ON THE ROOF of an expensive building at the center of Washington, D.C., watching the human organisms and their mechanized subordinates.

Through my lens, of intellect rather than instinct, I beheld the Rome of the modern era. Within my view were institutions backed by more wealth than any previous society could have imagined, by more armed force than could have been mustered by all previous nations of Earth combined. The women and men in seats of authority in the structures I espied commanded resources whose specifics would have left leaders of the Roman era breathless.

Below me, in the city's many office complexes, computers hummed with the knowledge of the ages. The machines conversed by nearly instantaneous means with Earth's expanding number of electronic cerebrums. Throughout the city exceptionally well educated men and women could call to their fingertips in a twinkling more information than a medieval monk encountered in a lifetime devoted exclusively to scholarship. Already the universal availability of information was so routine few paused to reflect on it.

In the distance I beheld an uninterrupted string of large flying machines descending into and climbing out of National Airport, their landing lights forming the beads of an endless necklace in the gray heavens. These creations functioned with utter precision, employing internal

46

complexity that would have stunned even the most farsighted scientist of a century before. Lower along the skyline, one helicopter after another made its determined beeline flight on some weighty business, seeming to defy gravity itself. It was easy to imagine for the near future of this society technical and material feats yet more grand than any embodied in the great metropolis of Washington; perhaps as inscrutable in their sophistication; perhaps as imposing in their appearance of permanence.

What might my forebears 40,000 years past have thought to look on this place? Shivering in the ice caves of what is now called France, scratching by the flickering light of crude fat-fueled lamps outlines of bison, reverie of which dominated my ancestors' spheres of insight: making pictures to lend their lives some purchase beyond the fleeting cycle of birth, struggle, decline, and death, a cycle then lasting less than half as long as it does now; perhaps hoping that one day some descendant exempt from the miseries of prehistory would find the drawings and pause to know that the progenitors of humankind had not just lived but dreamed. What would my blessed forebears think of the world their descendants had made?

Then I looked at my city and thought like nature. And I laughed.

Not a cruel laugh, an affectionate one. I knew that nature would like Washington. It just wouldn't be impressed.

Nature would like Washington because it is alive. If we can impute one motive to the natural world, surely it is that nature loves life; for when we observe the found Earth we see that nature wants the maximum extent of its territory to live. Penguins, murres, and bears that abide at the frigid poles; silver ants that sprint through the midday Sahara heat to snatch the bodies of other insects that have expired; microbes that survive in the roiling sulfur vents of the ocean floor; goats that pass their days clinging to mountainsides, bearing young on the impossible slopes; lodgepole pine whose nuts are designed to withstand forest fires, then burst open as they contract when cooling from the passage of the maelstrom, releasing seeds to begin the repopulation; there exist a thousand other examples.

For all the fashionably correct guilt many environmentalists attach to the human presence on Earth, I have no doubt nature looks on men and women with lasting affection, because we do what nature asks: We *live*. We honor the Earth's most basic injunction: Take of the inanimate, the vapid drone of vibrating atoms, take ye and show me life, this transcendent peculiarity that gives the whole of creation its meaning.

Thinking like nature, I quickly found myself pleased with an aspect of Washington that I and nearly all other people disdain: its population density. Hundreds of thousands of complex living things, including a surprisingly large number of animals, live with varying degrees of success or justice within the city's perimeter. The amount of life there is far higher than before genus *Homo*.

Nature seems to desire an upper-bound number of creatures within any habitat but is constrained by the availability of energy. Rainforests teem with life because in equatorial regions there is ample energy from nature's principal source, the sun. The farther north or south one ranges, the fewer large creatures per square mile because the energy available to support them, expressed as plants or prey, declines. Situated midway between the equator and a pole, the environs of Washington today are able to hold a much higher number of living creatures than they did before the human age because technology has added to solar energy other means of animation. Are those means sustainable? An open question. But thinking like nature I could not help being gratified that after eons of tying almost all life to the fortunes of the sun, experiments in other life-maintaining energy flows are now in progress. This is especially important because nature knows the sun will not last anywhere near as long as life might.

Thinking like nature, the seeming grandeur of Washington made me laugh a second time. I laughed because I knew the human world, which holds itself master of all it surveys, has not the slightest grasp of the greatest consideration in the natural world: time.

Humanity has not yet existed long enough for nature to pay much notice. Nature has made beetles that have lasted 200 million years. Compared to that, what's a can of Raid? Time, as used by nature, is so very large a resource that basic notions about it defy human comprehension. Probably you can conceptualize a billion dollars or a billion pounds. Can you conceptualize a billion years?

To nature time is a resource of colossal magnitude, perhaps even an infinite resource, inexhaustible in the literal sense. Roll the notion of inexhaustible time around in your frontal lobe a moment. Women and men stand in danger of drawing down the physical resources of Earth more quickly than they acquire the wisdom to forge societies based on sustainable economics. In contrast nature has at its disposal so much of its elemental resource, time, that what may seem to us problems of enduring proportions may seem to nature little more than passing irritations. Nature can use or even squander time in phantasmagoric amounts and yet still find itself with a stupendous quantity of this resource in reserve.

Nature requires time in vast amounts because time is nature's means to self-realization, from the manufacture of the firmament to the organization of the life within. And time is nature's measure of greatness:

Because for life to maximize, extension and survival through the vastness of time is far more important than expansion through the physical confines of any given place. Men and women will not begin to understand the larger implications of environmental issues until they have at least some ability to comprehend time in its meaning to nature.

The Magnitude of Natural Time

The cosmos is thought to be eight to 20 billion years old; Earth and its companion sun 4.5 billion years old; simple microbial life 3.8 billion years old; complex microorganisms perhaps 2.8 billion years old; animal life perhaps 600 million years old; mammalian life around 200 million years old. Given time in such vastness, researchers are prone to describing as "recent" events that occurred within the last few hundred million years. Recently, the land mass called North America was located at the South Pole. Recently, life was already very old.

By contrast, the world of intellect is in childhood. The lineage of genus *Homo* stretches perhaps 30,000 centuries into the past; toolmaking humankind may be 8,000 centuries old; *Homo sapiens,* the creatures that look like us, appeared around 350 centuries ago; civilization, defined by agriculture, is thought to have begun perhaps 80 centuries ago; technology may be said to have begun around 50 centuries ago, with Egyptian pyramids and sailing vessels; the human attempt to take over Earth's ecosphere began about two centuries ago, with the industrial era.

Tricks can be played with such expanses of time. Express the age of the Earth as a single year, as Carl Sagan likes to, and the first mammal draws breath on Thanksgiving Day. Our shaggy ancestor *Homo erectus* first beholds light on New Year's Eve. Anyone alive today is born as some blow-dried ninny cries out "two . . . one . . ." to the image of a gaudy ball descending toward inebriated Boeotians in Times Square.

Here is another device for conceptualizing what scientists call geologic time: State the comparison in multiples of generations. The period of human civilization encompasses somewhere around 320 generations. (Yes, it's that short.) The chambered nautilus, a creature that exists today in approximately the same form as it did near the beginning of animal life, has been alive in the neighborhood of 120 million generations. The whale has experienced somewhere around five million generations. Humanity has a long way to go before it can claim the kind of time-survival achievements already recorded by many "creeping and crawling things," as the Old Testament would say.

Natural processes that are central to environmental events often engage boundless spans of time. Perhaps the most important environmental event of Earth history, for example, was the conversion of the atmosphere to an oxygen base. Animal life is thought to have begun about 600 million years ago because it was at that point that the atmosphere first contained sufficient oxygen to support an oxidizing metabolic cycle, the kind animals and people use to "burn" carbohydrates in their cells; biological internal combustion based on oxygen liberates enough energy for a creature to be an animal and roam around, instead of standing still, as plants must. Oxygenating Earth's atmosphere from its primordial level to the level of today took around two billion years, about 250,000 times as long as civilization has existed.

Ice age cycles last around 20 times as long as civilization has existed. During the ice cycle much of North America, Europe, and Asia was glaciated for about 140,000 years. This means that merely the most recent glacial period, with persistent environmental conditions far worse than the worst man has created, was about 18 times longer than the period of civilization—and 700 times longer than the industrial era commentators now describe as an environmental force of unprecedented proportions. Cycles of extreme volcanism may last as long as two million years, or 250 times as long as civilization has existed. The mass extinction cycles that some researchers find in the fossil record may operate on frequencies of about 28 million years, or 3,500 times as long as civilization so far. The tectonic cycles by which the land masses of Earth rearrange themselves may last around 250 million years, or 31,000 times as long as civilization.

Some commentators have described the vastness of geologic time as a sort of natural wonder drug. Something dreadful like an ice age renders much of the globe hostile to life; or an asteroid or comet strikes Earth, triggering a "nuclear winter" and acid rain from hell. In the time-as-miracle drug view a catastrophic natural event transpires, immense numbers of years tick by, and then one morning everything is fine again, the birds sweetly singing and fair pastures of lilies turning their lineaments toward the sun. This view overlooks an elementary consideration: Between the catastrophe and the idyllic restoration, *life continues.* Nature has shown itself able to keep creatures alive through protracted periods when ecological conditions are horrible.

Many researchers believe the dinosaurs were rendered extinct by impacts of one or two asteroids striking with billions of times the explosive yield of the Hiroshima bomb. The aftereffects of that cosmic detonation ended the journeys of 60 percent of the species on Earth. Yet life continued everywhere on Earth, reduced in numbers but hardly wiped out. Over time uncountable numbers of living things must have been born into moments of environmental misery, living out their entire lives under such circumstances.

In the spring of 1992, as civil war broke out in the place called Bosnia Herzegovina, CBS Radio broadcast a remarkable report from a battle scene. A courageous correspondent, voice pumped with adrenaline, shouted above the horrible clatter of automatic weapons fire; yet clearly audible in the background were the bright mating songs of dozens of birds. In the midst of human battle, "intelligent" creatures using mechanized weapons to slaughter each other, the songbirds of Bosnia went about their annual rituals of renewal. This was happening not because the birds were insensible to the din. The birds sang above the tumult because nature has spent many eons accustoming its creatures to carrying on even through misery.

That nature can endure painful trials does not mean acts of human malfeasance against the ecology are insignificant. Any damage that occurs to the environment during each person's moment on the Earth frames that person's experience of the planet and diminishes his or her one chance at life, regardless of whatever corrections occur in the long run. And since your lifetime is all that matters to you, even a relatively small human environmental affront can be ample to inspire outrage. But your lifetime is not all that matters to the Earth. It is one of multiple trillions of considerations in an ongoing endeavor of astounding duration and complexity—an endeavor that, far from being on its last legs, may be just getting under way.

Could Humanity Be Found by Archaeologists?

Here is a thought experiment on nature's view of time. Suppose tomorrow humanity stepped into some ethereal Neverland, leaving behind its handiworks, from giant dams to those tasteful shopping malls. Could future archaeologists detect our brief and tarnished moment here? Suppose alien archaeologists came calling in 65 million years, the same span as between now and when the dinosaurs fell extinct. Such researchers might experience difficulty establishing that *Homo sapiens* had existed.

Many of the blotches that men and women leave on the Earth, and think cause permanent devastation, would disappear so quickly that seeking evidence of them would be pointless even a short time into the future. Consider Superfund toxic waste sites, areas many current commentators declaim as destroyed forever—as "environmental dead zones," in the words of Richard Fortuna, head of the Hazardous Wastes Treatment Council, a lobbying group. The worst of these sites will correct themselves naturally and return to life in less than a century, far too brief a span to leave any impact on the geologic record. Some Superfund sites have already recovered so much faster than anyone believed possible that they are being declared wildlife preserves. *Wildlife preserves.*

If humanity vanished, nearly all aspects of human-caused pollution would abate in periods long to you and me but essentially undetectable on the geologic clock. The remnants of cities would last many centuries, but would that be sufficient to catch the attention of a future dig team? Archaeologists consider the "resolution limit" of the sedentary fossil record to be at best about 10,000 years: Events lasting less than 10,000 years may be too minor to leave any fossil evidence of themselves. The entire civilized period of *Homo sapiens* could slip into one such notch unnoticed.

An immediate natural prospect will obliterate many cities, leaving nothing for future dig teams to unearth. That prospect is the next ice age, due in 1,000 to 2,000 years. If it is anything like the last, advancing walls of ice miles high will crush out of existence the high-latitude cities of North America, Europe, and parts of Asia. The unimaginable pressures will grind even the most sophisticated high-tensile alloy or carbon-fiber composite material into fine rubble.

In fact, unless humanity somehow learns how to manipulate the large-scale natural forces that trigger ice ages, the obliteration of most northern cities will occur whether or not humankind departs for Neverland. That is to say a complete natural wipeout and renewal of a significant portion of Earth's most developed area appears guaranteed *regardless* of what men and women do. If you think that the existence of Detroit or Berlin or any northern latitude city has "destroyed forever" what was once verdant wilderness, be aware that such locations seem fated to be verdant and pristine anew, and not that far into the future by the Earth's perception of time.

Beyond being crushed by ice, human handiwork faces many other foes. Over geologic spans of time, erosion and the chemical weathering effect of the mild acids naturally found in rain would dissolve away most construction projects. Chemical weathering by rain causes in nature a cycle of vast scope in which rock formations and eventually entire mountains are dissolved and flow to the sea. Cities have scant hope of outlasting mountains. Over the course of millions of years, cities would also be pulverized in slow collisions of tectonic plates as the continents rearrange themselves. Through tectonics some of humanity's creations would eventually be subducted back into the Earth's mantle, as happens regularly to parts of the crust, there to dissolve in the heat of molten rock.

Probably the human artifacts that stand the greatest chance of surviving to be discovered 65 million years hence are the landing craft and assorted detritus that NASA left on the moon, where there is no weather and no plate tectonics. Archaeologists with sensitive equipment might also be able to infer humanity's sojourn on Earth by detecting traces of radioactive elements that can be made in laboratories but are thought not to occur in nature. That's about it. Within a span of time at best intermediate to nature's way of thinking, all but the faintest echoes of the human intrusion on Earth may be no more.

So far the human presence in the biosphere is a fleeting thing. Our cities, waterworks, roadways, and factories have had much less impact on the ecology than many natural forces of the past and have lasted much less time than have those forces. Our generations, however threatening they have made themselves to each other, only begin to approach the low end of the numbers of generations in which nature thinks. Our walk along nature's path has barely begun.

Is Humanity a
Special Threat? ✍

SOME ECOLOGISTS WOULD OBJECT TO THE REASONING OF THE
previous two chapters on the grounds that natural harms to nature are
ones to which the environment has had eons to adjust. Artificial threats,
unfolding rapidly, may fall into a special category. Many contemporary
ecological commentators contend that humanity, in its hyperpyretic
quest for aggrandizement, contrives insidious new forms of environmental malice more quickly than nature ever could. If true, this is a disturbing notion.

Surely there are categories in which the velocity of human environmental abuse exceeds any comparable force in nature. But do artificial
impacts generally create warp-speed harms that nature cannot counteract? Let's explore a famous example.

In March 1989 the tanker *Exxon Valdez*, carelessly piloted, struck
Bligh Reef in Prince William Sound, releasing 11 million gallons of crude
oil into a place of pristine beauty and perpetual mists that might as well
have been named Brigadoon. Sea birds, otter, and other creatures died
by the thousands. Reports described the sound as the site of a "tragedy"
or "catastrophe." A judge, ordering the ship's captain jailed, compared
the harm done to the atomic bombing of Japan. The sound, it was commonly said, would never recover. Never, ever, ever. "Destroyed" quickly became the official verb for what had happened to the vast Alaskan
fiord.

Reaction ought to have been fierce. Both the negligence that caused the spill and arrogance of Exxon executives—the company adapting a position that may be summed up in two words that are not Merry Christmas—represented corporate unaccountability at its most offensive. But was Prince William Sound the site of a catastrophe? A few days after the spill, I wrote an article that included this sentence: "Ten years from now the sound will be so close to its former state that it will be impossible to determine where the spill occurred without resorting to navigation charts." Colleagues urged me not to publish that article, saying I would sacrifice my reputation. After all, the sound was destroyed. Forever and ever.

In 1992, I found myself bobbing through the choppy waters of Prince William Sound aboard the research vessel *Arctic Dream,* crewed by marine biologists under the sponsorship of the National Oceanographic and Atmospheric Administration, the agency with supervisory responsibility for investigating the spill. Quickly I learned my 1989 prediction had been wrong. It was just three years later, and already the sound was so close to its former state it was impossible to determine where the spill had occurred without resorting to navigation charts. This was true not only of the beaches that had been cleaned but the ones left untouched as well.

Dennis Lees, leader of the team aboard the boat and a researcher who has been studying Prince William Sound since a few days after the spill, used navigation charts to show me where the worst blotches of oil hit. From the deck of the *Arctic Dream,* no sign of oil was apparent anywhere in the sound. Nor could any degradation be seen close to the shore, when the crew disembarked in dinghies. Only by standing on the beach at various points was it possible to observe any residue of petroleum—usually traces below the surface in mussel beds, uncovered by shovel.

Studies clearly show some harm to wildlife in Prince William Sound. Colonies of murries, a bird similar to the penguin, have smaller populations than in 1989, and sightings of killer whales have fallen off in the sound since that year. Herring spawning has declined. But most indicators of life in Prince William Sound are robust. Sea otter, which in the nineteenth century were hunted to near extinction in Alaskan inlets by Russian trawlers, have repopulated the sound with a fervor since being placed under the Marine Mammal Protection Act in 1972. The otter's rate of increase was not interrupted by the spill. Prince William Sound had a record pink salmon catch in 1990, the year after being doused with crude. The salmon run in the sound was rich again in 1991, then declined in 1992 and 1993. Since pinks live just two years, the poor runs involved salmon that did not hatch until after the oil cleared, making some researchers think that the cold spring weather of 1992 and 1993, which reduced the plankton on which salmon feed, caused the drop.

It turned out that Lees's greatest concern about Prince William Sound was not wildlife loss, which he considered bad but a one-time effect; Lees's concern was that the cleanup did more damage than the spill. Under pressure from public opinion, Exxon and the Coast Guard committed themselves to a grand-scale cleanup operation that at its peak placed in the sound the greatest concentration of vessels engaged in a single operation since the Normandy landing. Hundreds of ships of all sizes anchored in the fiord, motors spewing exhaust and lubricants. Heavy helicopters thundered overhead; floatplanes and seaplanes darted everywhere. Navy landing craft were run ashore on beaches to act as dormitories for cleanup crews, crushing intertidal ecosystems beneath their bulks. In many ways these mechanized intrusions were of greater magnitude to the sound than one spill from a single vessel, even a spill of great proportions.

The *Arctic Dream* sailed to some beaches, at a place called Block Island, used by Exxon for the before-and-after pictures that grace its Prince William Sound brochures. The sand there looked as fine as the commercially processed sand found at amusement parks. Individual rocks had been scrubbed with hand brushes and even toothpicks; we found an old, oily toothpick in a ravine. We did not, however, find any animals, plant life, or sign of smaller organisms. "It's clean, and it's dead," Lees noted. In many places Exxon used high-pressure hot water to blast away oil. The hot water killed the microbial life on which the food chain is moored. The beaches that were left alone as experimental controls by and large cleansed themselves through wave action, microbic digestion, and other factors: the traditional defenses that nature has prepared against petroleum. The uncleaned beaches cleaned themselves while staying alive in microbial terms.

Lees, who once was Exxon-funded—the company dismissed his environmental consultancy after it questioned the cleanup—believes "the smartest thing they could have done after the spill is not one single thing." The two billion dollars Exxon spent on the cleanup would have generated more environmental benefits had it been used for energy efficiency, or to buy land to place in preservation status, or in any number of other ways. But because a sense of public panic was created regarding the "destruction" of Prince William Sound, this huge sum of money was expended in an enterprise that probably was unneeded and may have done more harm than good.

Why was there a sense of panic surrounding the *Exxon Valdez* in the first place? One reason is pictures. The spill occurred in March, and winter is the clear season for Prince William Sound. Television and news-magazine camera crews rapidly obtained spectacular footage of oil fouling the intertidal wilderness. Starting around June, the sound often fogs in and stays that way for months, socked in to the weather condition that pilots call flat—fog so close to the ground that long-range photography is out of the question. Had the spill happened during fog season, it would have been a page-six item. The ecological significance of the spill would have been the same, of course, regardless of whether pictures were available. But the significance of ecological events to the government institutions and news organizations that cross-pollinate each other's pantomime hysteria often is determined by factors unrelated to the ecology, such as the availability of pictures.

Why did so many commentators presume Prince William Sound the victim of an instant doom? Petroleum is a naturally occurring product. It "spills" from the Earth's crust continuously via seepage, though more slowly than happened at the sound. Because petroleum regularly enters the biosphere on a natural basis, some organisms long ago adapted to metabolizing it. Conceptually what Exxon did was reposition a naturally occurring pollutant from below Earth's surface to an ocean inlet, a place where wave action, sunlight, biology, and other factors immediately began operating in opposition to the intruder.

Of course the biosphere's self-healing ability does not excuse environmental abuses, any more than the regenerative powers of the human body excuse breaking someone's leg. Yet overall nature shrugged off the *Exxon Valdez* "disaster" as if shooing away a mosquito. Prince William Sound went from destroyed to almost like new in about three years, or in less than a single generation for the local large vertebrate species. This is standard operating procedure for the green fortress.

The Fortress against Man

Have I chosen an atypical instance of nature's ability to resist human assault? Let's run through a few less well known examples.

• In July 1991 several tank cars fell from a railway bridge into the Sacramento River in northern California. They ruptured, spilling 12,000 gallons of herbicide. Thousands of fish died in the 42-mile stretch between the derailment and Shasta Lake, where the river empties.

The spill, a photogenic event, was the lead story on network newscasts that evening. Showing dramatic photographs of a derailed train astride the river, CBS Television proclaimed the Sacramento River "destroyed." One newspaper account spoke of a "miles-long path of permanent destruction." By October 1991, three months later, fish and plant populations in the Sacramento were nearly back to normal, while no damage was apparent to the lake downstream. Steven Turk, a biologist at the California Department of Water Resources, told the *Washington Post,* "the river is recovering much more rapidly than we thought it could."

• In the 1960s lakes Erie and Ontario; the Potomac, Charles, Thames, and Chicago rivers; parts of Puget Sound; and other important water bodies were said to be on the verge of biological death. Chesapeake Bay, Lake Michigan, the Mississippi and Danube rivers, and many other bodies of water were widely considered locked in irreversible cycles of decline. Though problems remain, today all these water bodies have not only cheated death but several are once again safe for fishing and swimmers. A few are within hailing distance of their preindustrial quality levels. From dead to alive in about 25 years, a span far too short to leave any dent in the geologic record.

• During the 1920s in Pittsburgh, air pollution was so thick that automobiles ran with their headlights on at noon. Environmental organizations then had names like the Pittsburgh Smoke Abatement Society, smoke then begin the leading pollution concern, one worse from a health standpoint than all contemporary air emissions combined. Cleveland, Detroit, Memphis, London, the Birminghams of England and Alabama, most of the Ruhr Valley, and many other locations in the developed world were similar. I was raised in Buffalo; through the early 1960s, many mornings a child could draw his name in the haze of sulfur dust that had settled on the family car the night before.

Today all the cities mentioned above have urban air that is smokeless and contains ever-decreasing amounts of other pollutants. Reduced demand for heavy-manufactured goods is a factor in this change, but improvements have happened even where production continues. Pittsburgh, where steel mills and coke ovens hum still, is today considered among the most desirable places to live in the United States: clean, blossoming, a budding Paris. The conversation of Western industrial cities from beset by choking curtains of pollution to near-rural air-quality levels has happened in just half a century.

• Through the early 1980s the International Nickel smelting plant in Sudbury, Ontario, operating without pollution controls, was alone to blame for an amazing five percent of world air emissions of sulfur dioxide. Acid rain caused by the plant, combined with toxic heavy metals, left the area a moonscape in the literal sense: When NASA was planning its Apollo mission, the agency sent engineers to Sudbury to use the plant's denuded "footprint" to test designs for the lunar lander. By 1989 Sudbury emissions had been cut 90 percent. Today saplings sprout in the formerly lifeless ditchlines downwind.

• One of the worst pollution sites in the world is Foundry Cove, on the Hudson River near Cold Spring, New York, adjacent to a factory where for a century military munitions and then batteries were manufactured. In 1992 *Scientific American* declared that Foundry Cove contains "the highest concentration of toxic cadmium and nickel pollutants in the world." Yet despite a century of willy-willy dumping of cadmium, nickel, arsenic, and lead and other poisons directly into this small bend in the river, just 100 yards downstream sits an Audubon-protected sanctuary for migratory birds. The bird sanctuary has prospered adjacent to the cove for decades. Avian and aquatic life in the preserve show no ill effects. The spot is popular among bird-watchers, who arrive before dawn every spring to witness the dance of the ages enacted in its ancient splendor.

Jeffrey Levinton, chair of the Department of Ecology of the State University of New York at Stony Brook, has written that after studying the paradox of continuing life in Foundry Cove, he and a colleague concluded that even small creatures such as earthworms acquired genetic resistance to cadmium, the worst toxicant in the cove, over a much shorter period than biologists had guessed possible. Levinton wrote, "Rapid evolutionary tolerance for high concentrations of toxics seems to be common" in nature. This finding suggests two thoughts. First, though environmentalists rightly warn that insects and disease organisms may mutate to acquire resistance to man's pesticides and wonder drugs, they never discuss the flip side of this issue: that living things may mutate to resist pollution, rendering human ecological abuses less damaging than expected. Second, if small organisms *already* have genetic mechanisms that respond to toxics, they may have acquired this trait before the industrial era, by dealing with naturally created plagues of dangerous chemicals.

• Even the most extreme human failing, war, may seem to nature a manageable affront. Nuclear weapons, should they ever be used, would of course have disastrous environmental consequences. Chemical and biological weapons might do the ecology severe harm as well, though little is known with assurance about exactly how these substances would behave if released in significant quantities. These cautions aside, consider how rapidly nature has recovered from most bouts with war.

Europe and the western portions of the former Soviet Union were in the 1940s the scene of the most intense, violent combat in human history. Within two decades almost no ecological trace of that combat remained. Once-imperiled creatures have repopulated to the point that parts of Europe, like parts of the United States, now have too many deer, geese, swan, and other species. Today Europe has more forested acres than it had before World War II began. This is true despite the fact that a considerable amount of World War II European combat was tank warfare around forested areas—with shells, bombs, and fires not only destroying woodlands directly but the treads of armored vehicles ripping up the soil and flattening incipient plant life. The effects of this sustained assault on Europe's forests were wiped away by mainly natural action in a span of time too short for nature even to notice. Nevertheless the ground-chewing effects of the passage of logging vehicles, causing perhaps one one-thousandth of a percent of the environmental damage done by armored columns in combat, is said today by some commentators to insure irreparable damage to the forests of the Pacific Northwest.

Agricultural areas of the Korean peninsula were repeatedly bombed during the Korean War yet within a few years showed no ill effects. The earth itself around the former Stalingrad was "scorched" by retreating Russian soldiers in 1942 yet became living forest anew within a decade and with no help from the former Soviet regime in Moscow, perhaps the most antienvironmental government in history.

During the Vietnam War the United States spent years carpet-bombing the jungles of Vietnam and also dropping on them 19 million gallons of herbicides, including 11 million gallons of the infamous Agent Orange. Those jungles today are as lush as before the assault began, recovering with no assistance from various governments in Saigon and Ho Chi Minh City. In 1992 researchers found in a jungle near the Vietnam-Laos border the first new large mammal species detected on Earth in 50 years, a cow-goat dubbed the Vu Quang ox. In 1994 they found a second new large species, the giant muntjac deer. These creatures had been evolving, and surviving, in a jungle just 20 miles from the Ho Chi Minh Trail—the most intensely bombed target in military history.

Even at the time of the Vietnam defoliation effort, American soldiers complained that the herbicides did little to strip away the jungle cover their adversaries were using. Imagine millions of gallons of Agent Orange—the worst industrial alchemy could muster against nature—not only failing to wipe out the Vietnamese jungle "forever" but failing even to thrust it back over the short term of a military campaign.

This happened because the Agent Orange bombers were not attacking a fragile environment. They were flying against a green fortress.

The Polluted Parallel Universe

Researching this book I traveled the former Eastern bloc, where environmental insults from toxic dumping, shoddy nuclear waste disposal, unregulated coal burning, and other activities have left a depth of problems without peer in the industrial world. Because the woeful environmental state of the former Soviet bloc has been ably reported by others, I will not dwell on the subject, except to convey a few impressions of nature's tenacity.

One town I visited was Katowice, Poland, in the heart of the Silesian industrial belt. This entire region seemed a place that had taken a wrong turn in the year 1890 and traveled into a parallel universe where the worst excesses of heavy manufacturing were endlessly replicated, without any of the compensating virtues of material affluence. Some 300 coal mines, chemical plants, and steel mills interrupt the countryside around Katowice. Grim smokestacks dominate the horizons in every direction, pumping ash, toxics, sulfur, and nitrous oxides into the air.

The Silesian energy economy is based on lignite or "brown" coal, which has such a low BTU value coupled to high inherent pollution content that Western countries long ago ceased burning the substance. The anthracite or "black" coal combusted at most American power plants contains one to two percent sulfur, the source of haze and acid rain; the lignite coal burned in the former Eastern bloc is often 18 percent sulfur. The result is a madhouse of pollution. In Silesia lignite is combusted by the millions of pounds per year, with gross pollution ascending directly into the air through smokestacks that have no control mechanisms, not even turn-of-the-century ash traps. Most contemporary coal-burning power plants in the Western nations have multimillion-dollar systems to strip pollutants from emissions. What you see rising away from the smokestacks at such facilities is primarily steam and carbon dioxide. What rises from a power plant in Silesia is unadulterated pollution at its worst.

In Silesia, homes and offices are warmed in winter by the old system of central "district heating" plants that pipe hot water through neighborhoods. The district heating plants burn still more of the dirty coal; because such plants must be close to customers, many operate only meters away from housing projects, discharging their emissions directly toward the windows of residences. Owing to antiquated systems, energy waste in the former Eastern bloc is monumental. On the day of reunification, energy consumption per capita in the former East Germany was 25 percent *higher* than in West Germany, yet West Germans enjoyed a substantially better standard of living, benefiting from efficient machines, market-disciplined economic systems, and effective public pressure, all forces missing in the former Soviet bloc.

Extreme resource waste continues in the former Eastern countries. I was in Poland in April 1992, at a time outdoor temperatures were about 50 degrees Fahrenheit. In every home and office I visited windows were flung open wide yet the rooms were still stifling hot, because individual buildings lack thermostats and district heating plants were pumping out dead-of-winter heat. Calling at the Polish Foundation for Energy Efficiency, I found the officials there conversant in demand-side management, negawatts, and other up-to-date Western concepts. But the office windows were open to dissipate heat, the Foundation for Energy Efficiency lacking thermostats.

Walking through Katowice or any of its surrounding hamlets proved an otherworldly experience. Conveyor belts of coal mines and charging areas of steel mills sit inside the towns. Not near them, inside; there's no distinction between the residential and industrial areas of Katowice and nearby Chorzow, with housing projects and shops entwined with industrial structures. Along the main boulevards of Katowice are a series of giant mine wheels, an antiquated form of pump for removing water from coal seam operations. Endlessly they turn, as if the exposed gearing of the Underworld.

Creeks that flow through Silesian towns run jet black with factory wastes. My host offered to me a panoramic view of the Katowice area. To obtain it we went to a place called Kuda Slaka and climbed a 300-foot mountain of fly ash from a chemical plant, a dump that had sat for two decades directly between two housing projects. Children played on the ash mountain, hiding amongst the crags of hardened waste. Adjoining the fly-ash mountain was a vast lagoon of black gunk the thickness of power-steering fluid. Along the horizon I counted 27 large, active smokestacks.

The Katowice region does poorly on every index of health damage from pollution—with high rates of respiratory distress, incidence of lead poisoning in children, and low life expectancy. By any standard it is a Class A environmental disaster area. And smack in the middle is a thriving nature preserve.

Wojewodzki Park, bordered entirely by steel plants and coal mines, was opened in 1952 on degraded industrial land. "Back then the place was a moonscape," says Mieczyslaw Hojka, the park's director. Photos from the early days of park construction show workers with shovels and horse-drawn plows laboring on what appears to be the dark side of the planet Meepzor.

At first park managers planted evergreen trees, known for toughness.

But nature tells evergreens to replace their needles every seven years; within two years the needles of trees in Wojewodzki Park were so coated with pollutants they could no longer function. Deciduous trees that make leaves annually were substituted, and some took hold. Jan Palasz, a member of the Polish Academy of Sciences, describes what happened next: "By the middle 1950s, birds and mammals began to appear in the park on their own. We really have no idea how some of the wildlife got there, since there are no migratory corridors surrounding the park, only industrial facilities for many kilometers. Soon there were rabbit, deer, fox, pheasant, and about 30 bird species. There were so many jays we considered shooting some. To this day almost every year we record the arrival of a new species, and rarely do we know how it came to our park."

The park is not one your family would choose for a picnic. Its air, polluted by the surrounding impedimenta of industrial excess, can make the nostrils sting. Its foliage appears sickly, and the park's waters are uninviting. But Wojewodzki Park is alive and is a place where nature rules. This is happening at the epicenter of some of the worst pollution humanity has ever created—perhaps the worst men and women *ever* will create, if present reforms stay on track.

A few months after I left Katowice the Union of Concerned Scientists, an American organization whose work against nuclear arms proliferation was admirable, issued an environmental broadside above the signatures of 1,680 credentialed scientists, including 104 Nobel Prize winners. The document, titled *World Scientists' Warning to Humanity,* declared that "human activities inflict harsh and often irreversible damage on the environment." Absent rapid, drastic changes in man's behavior, the Union said, "the living world [may] become unable to sustain life in the manner that we know."

Rapid, drastic changes in man's behavior sound good to me. But the incentive should be optimism regarding the gains that might be realized, not melodramatized gloom. An instructive contrast is the *Heidelberg Appeal,* another scientists' broadside. Signed by some 2,600 credentialed researchers, including 72 Nobel winners, among them Peace Prize laureates Linus Pauling and Elie Wiesel, it draws approximately the opposite conclusion from the Union statement. "We are worried," the Heidelberg statement says, "[about] the emergence of an irrational ideology opposed to scientific and industrial progress. . . . We contend that a Natural State, idealized by movements with a tendency to look toward the past, does not exist and probably has not existed since man's first appearance in the biosphere. . . . The greatest evils that stalk our Earth are ignorance and oppression, not technology and industry." The *World*

Scientists' Warning to Humanity, being pessimistic, received extensive recognition in the American press. Ever heard of the *Heidelberg Appeal?* I didn't think so.

Examining issues from the perspective of nature teaches that the word "irreversible" has no place in the environmental debate. Extinction is final. Every other form of environmental harm not only appears eminently reversible: So far most natural recovery processes observed directly by humanity, or inferred from the geologic record, have happened more rapidly than even optimists deemed possible. Long before genus *Homo* appeared in the scene, the natural world was already set up to aid humanity in undoing the damage humanity would eventually do—should we only become aware of how much we are capable of accomplishing and the speed with which those accomplishments may arrive.

Is Humanity a Mistake?

One of the strangest notions that has arisen in environmental debate is that humanity's existence represents a vile distortion of nature, or at best some kind of cosmic bureaucratic blunder. "Man is fallen, nature is erect," Emerson declared, pronouncing during a time some historians call the Age of Optimism a seditious thought that would become the embodiment of safe, status quo opinion in the Age of Instant Doomsday.

David Foreman, who in the late 1980s enjoyed a phase as a media darling when running the purported ecological-sabotage organization Earth First!, was fond of calling humanity "a cancer on the Earth."[1] Foreman once said the onset of a new ice age would be a welcome event because it would kill billions of people, returning the human population to its Pleistocene level. Such statements did not cause Foreman to be treated as a crackpot, for depicting the arrival of genus *Homo* as the darkest hour of Earth history is today a broadly accepted convention of environmental philosophy. The biologist Edward Wilson has said that "the human species is an environmental abnormality. It is possible that intelligence in the wrong kind of species was foreordained to be a fatal combination for the biosphere." Thomas Berry, a featured writer of the Sierra Club Press, said in 1991 that humankind is "an affliction on the world . . . [a] violation of Earth's most sacred aspects." The low point of any contemporary environmental conference is invariably reached when someone takes the podium to deliver a litany of fashionable guilt over his or her own existence.

Humanity's vogue for culpability regarding its own existence must be exceptionally difficult for nature to fathom. To reject the human presence as unnatural evinces fundamental misreading of the character of the living world. Humankind springs from the natural scheme just as does any beast or plant. Our sprawl across the globe, however excessive, is in strict accord with the behavior patterns of other species, most of which attempt to expand to fill the maximum area available to them. Our interventions with the environment, though greater in scope, are no different in principle from those of the beaver that floods a meadow habitat when it dams a stream, amending the environment to its needs at the expense of other species; the tall, old-growth climax trees that take over a forest, blocking out smaller plants' access to sunlight; the territorial predators that drive other predators away, monopolizing a prey range; and so on. To reject the human presence as unnatural is to fail to understand what nature has been up to all these eons, for it is scarcely a mystic reading of evolution to say that nature has been striving for nearly four billion years to bring some creature like *Homo sapiens* into being.

Either a divinity made humankind and gave us a prominent role in nature, or nature made us and did the same. That notion bears reiteration because it is essential to understanding the possibility of constructive relations between people and their environment. *If God made humankind, then women and men must be central to nature. If God did not make humankind, then women and men must be central to nature.* Regardless of whether the environment was called forth by some higher power or was self-generated, genus *Homo* received a prominent role.

Here is another inescapable either/or proposition that bears on whether humanity is integral to the natural scheme: Either nature has meaning or it does not. If not, then the environment has no "sacred aspects" to violate. Such ethics as may exist are the product of human dreaming and may be whatever we deem them. If yes, then women and men share in the sacredness that arises with life, since our species awoke to the same summons as all others. We may falter or prosper, seek wisdom or abscond in ignorance, but we are not an offense to the natural world. We are a component of that system—potentially the most important component.

Nature, Fearing the Natural in Man

To people it seems man's ability to construct artificial implements is what would frighten nature the most. But thinking like nature we quickly come to the realization that nature would fear most in people their natural tendencies.

Surely the worst thing that could happen to the Earth would be for humankind to continue to behave in an entirely natural manner, doing no more or less than other creatures would do if competitors did not stop them—that is, expanding to the maximum extent. Perhaps via resort to technology, a form of interaction with the ecosphere unavailable to other living things, an expanding human population will always be able to stay one step ahead of its resource needs, staving off the Malthusian cataclysms that have been predicted repeatedly throughout the industrial era. Perhaps even an expanding humankind will learn to use resources on a vast scale while keeping the Earth clean. After all, preventing the planet from becoming inhospitable is in our own interest. And if nothing else, humankind has demonstrated a true gift for self-serving action.

But the world that might emerge from an entirely natural human expansion would be one in which the pristine elements of nature stand little chance. "Nature can't take any more animals as successful as man," the naturalist Farley Mowat has written. Thus when we think like nature, we realize nature would want women and men to behave artificially—to impose self-restraint not from programmed instinct but because their intellects tell them it is wise. Either God or natural selection gave genus *Homo* the power to cause great mischief—and also the awareness that doing so is wrong. The human track record of forsaking the doing of wrong is wretched, but at least the awareness of moral thinking is now present in our genus line. Most people know they should not wrong their fellows, or nature. What they do not know is how to achieve this ideal. In this light, we dreaming apes do not seem a cancer or affliction, merely offspring in search of a proper relationship with the rest of our family.

For instance, to find that proper relationship it will be essential that people learn to restrain their naturally imbued inclination to expand population. That humankind continues to expand its numbers at a dramatic pace, and still produce the food and resources necessary to keep that population alive, suggests that stabilization of human population growth is more likely to be achieved by artificial self-restraint than by the natural retaliations of starvation or pestilence. Therefore nature will root for men and women to come to terms with the synthetic aspects of their species character. Nature fears in genus *Homo* what is natural and looks to what is artificial as the resolution.

Hyper Speed versus Gradualism

Nevertheless the idea is deeply embedded in environmental orthodoxy that human access to artificial technology creates a special threat to nature. This notion traces most prominently to Rachel Carson, who via the masterpiece *Silent Spring* became the Athena of contemporary ecology; Vice President Al Gore, for example, has called Carson the greatest influence on his thought. Carson acknowledged that nature often transforms environments, sometimes in ways antithetical to the interests of species. But, she wrote, human environmental transgressions are fundamentally different because they occur with great speed. In nature, Carson maintained, rapid environmental changes are not observed. Carson's notion that only technology can produce rapid impacts on nature has become a tenet of pessimistic doctrine. "It's not the absolute amount of change being caused by humans but the pace that is so frightening," says Stephen Schneider, a climatologist at Stanford University and a leading contemporary ecological pessimist. Schneider allows, for example, that even current worst-case projections for artificial global warming fall within the range of natural increases that Earth has experienced in the past. But natural temperature swings of such magnitude required centuries if not many millennia, Schneider says.

This is the core of an argument, made by several contemporary environmental thinkers, that however constrained human action may seem in relation to the grand stresses found in nature, genus *Homo* has entered into the ecological equation a new stress with no natural analogue: hyper speed. Natural adaptability mechanisms that serve ably over long spans of time cannot handle assaults staged at the frantic human pace.

There may be weight to this argument. Knowledge of the biosphere is at present too rudimentary for anyone to know whether the pace of human change does indeed represent a singular threat to nature. But increasingly there are reasons to suspect that nature itself often catalyzes extremely rapid environmental change and thus must have some ability to resist rapid forces. This evidence comes from a research area generally known as "nonlinear effects." Theories of nonlinear effects contrast in several respects with a century-old scientific idea that natural transitions happen only at a crawl. The older hypothesis, called gradualism, is essential to understanding why many prominent thinkers came into the current decades inclined to think that human-induced rapid change had no counterpart in natural history.

The founder of modern geology, Charles Lyell, proposed in the mid–nineteenth century the principle of uniformitarianism, which holds that natural forces have in Earth's past been identical to the forces observed today. To the contemporary high-school student this sounds like a statement of the obvious, but only because Lyell's arguments were persuasive; in earlier centuries, many scientists assumed that the physical forces of nature had not been consistent in the past. The great benefit of

Lyell's premise was that if past physical forces were the same as current ones, then people can reason backward from the present condition to imagine what Earth might have been like long ago.

At about the same time as Lyell's theory came one of the primary discoveries of the nineteenth century, the age of the Earth. As researchers began to realize humankind's home was thousands of times older than supposed, fundamental assumptions about the role and significance of humanity were drawn into question. People had assumed themselves the purpose for which the Earth, if not the entire cosmos, had been called forth into being; and most religions assumed that the temporal period of humankind would be brief, to be supplanted by a timeless realm of divine justice. Suddenly genus *Homo* seemed no more than the latest minor item in a natural world that had existed for billions of years before humanity and seemed constructed to endure for billions of years more into a purely temporal future.

The dawning of awareness of the age of the Earth was both a breakthrough for nineteenth-century science and the beginning of the period, which continues to the present, in which science and religion were placed at odds, with science, consciously or subconsciously, assigning itself the task of disproving God by showing that all circumstances of nature can be explained without recourse to the supernatural. Today this is called the "materialist" or "naturalist" perspective: Materialism in this sense means that material forces account for everything; naturalism in this sense means that nature contains no more or less than meets the eye. The form of science-versus-church antagonism that began around the time of Charles Lyell turns out to have surprising significance to current environmental debates.

A Gradual Explanation of Gradualism

Findings about the age of the Earth arrived at a time when religious and secular authorities spoke of creation as young. In 1625, the Irish bishop James Ussher issued his famed proclamation that the Earth was made in precisely the year 4,004 B.C. For two centuries afterward the notion of Earth as newly formed was taught at Oxford. Genus *Homo* was assumed to have come into existence either coincident with the formation of the Earth or a very short time thereafter—since what would have been the point of the planet without Adam?

When in the nineteenth century geologists began to demolish the young-Earth premise, the belief in an ancient natural world became the mark of a progressive intellect. To support the progressive intellectual idea of an ancient Earth, scientists began to focus on ideas suggesting extremely slow natural processes. Lyell and those who followed him grew deeply suspicious of those who claimed to see in the geologic record any fast-happening or "catastrophic" events. By the turn of this century all credentialed scientists were gradualists, conceptualizing nature as the sum of very deliberate effects.

The acceptance of gradualism as the reigning intellectual idea about the natural world happened in part because it is so difficult to conceive of time passing in multiple millions of years. The best image most people can conjure of geologic time is some sort of smooth, changeless continuum. That presumes away an environment in which the unexpected constantly occurs. How could there have been millions of centuries chock with natural action? Gradualists came to view nature as essentially static because this seemed the only manner in which an enterprise of unfathomable age could be administered.

The bias toward belief in gradual natural forces was enforced by the fact that the fossil and rock-strata records essential for clues to the past have "resolution" only to blocks of time many thousands of years long. Events happening on a more rapid basis—such as, say, the entire historical period of humanity—can slip through the cracks of such analysis. Since rapid natural effects are by definition short-lived, they would be unlikely to leave much evidence of themselves—at least not evidence of the traditional kind, found by hammer, chisel, and whisk. Ecologists throughout this century may have labored under the subconscious presumption that because science only possessed evidence of gradual natural forces, gradual forces are all that exist.

The concept of a living world governed by languorous forces was entrenched by the general acceptance of evolutionary theory. The Charles Darwin–Alfred Wallace explication of natural selection turns on the notion that evolutionary changes are excruciatingly slow, this premise fashioned in part because when Darwin and Wallace formulated their theory neither knew of the existence of genetics, not to be discovered by Gregor Mendel till decades later. Without genetics it was hard to imagine how the mutations that drive natural selection came to be. Many ideas that now sound like half-witted conceits were entertained by Darwin and Wallace. For reasons that can be skipped here, they both resolved the problem by assuming imperceptibly slow natural change.

Geology and evolution were a potent counter to religious convention. Findings suggesting the Earth unimaginably ancient could be used to argue against the likes of Bishop Ussher and more generally against the idea that Earth was forged for the accommodation of man. Findings on evolution could be used to argue against the Garden. The antireligious applications of these new disciplines worked best if gradualism were assumed. Hundreds of millennia for minor evolutionary changes seemed to show that Adam and Eve could not have been plunked down in Eden within the immediate genealogical sphere of those named in the Bible.

Many scientists had an emotional stake in the disproving of religion, if only in retaliation for religion's past intolerance of science; soon gradualism became not just a hypothesis but an article of faith to the research world. This bias on the part of many researchers is now found in the environmental community as well, where there exists a subconscious desire to view all natural processes as extremely slow-moving in order to throw rapid human action into a more negative light. Gradualism may indeed prove out as the most important of natural rhythms, but recent findings have begun to undermine its status. Soon gradualism may be seen as sharing significance with nonlinear or rapid-acting natural effects.

Nonlinear Nature

During recent decades new research techniques have produced inferences about the past calibrated to shorter time scales than the multiple-millennia units of conventional fossil and rock-strata investigations available to scientists when the assumptions of gradualism were developed. Ocean sediment analysis; ice-core readings; molecular clock studies, in which rates of evolution are calculated backward; radioactive dating techniques more accurate than carbon 14; and other developments are being used to break down knowledge of the ecosphere's past into data blocks a few decades in length or smaller. Within them researchers now find considerable evidence suggesting nonlinear events are common occurrences in natural history.

Nonlinear, as researchers use the term, means a sudden jump to a condition that is not a direct (or linear) consequence of the previous condition. Obviously there are natural events that involve such transitions: The eruption of a volcano is about as nonlinear as existence can get. Yet however important these events may be, naturalists tend to view them as one-time haphazard mischances offering no larger insight into the rhythms of the natural system. If nonlinear events are integral to the natural world, they should be found in some recurrent aspect of nature—in physical cycles and evolutionary patterns. That is exactly where contemporary researchers are beginning to find them.

One focus of recent study is a moment from the recent past with an odd name, the Younger Dryas. Toward the end of the latest ice age, around 13,000 years ago, glacial sheets were in retreat from most of North America and Eurasia. Most plant and animal life had rebounded to approximately what it is today, helped by global temperatures thought to have been rising gradualistically for a few thousand years. Then, suddenly, temperatures fell off the cliff. New evidence suggests that air temperature in Europe declined by 11 degrees Fahrenheit in less than a century, causing an essentially instantaneous return to ice-age climate. Oak trees and similar mild-weather vegetation vanished from Europe in fewer than 200 years, replaced by vast fields of dryas, a glacial flower from which the period draws its name.

Thus a nearly global-scale, natural environmental disaster injurious to innumerable species occurred in about the same amount of time, two centuries, as the period of the industrial era—the period current commentators persist in describing as the unprecedented peak moment of environmental stress in Earth history. And this fast, naturally driven disaster happened not in the primordial mists but at a time when our immediate ancestors walked the Earth, behaving much like us in many respects, except that they were far more vulnerable to fluctuations in the environment. This naturally driven environmental disaster also happened at a time when most current plants and animals existed in approximately their present forms.

Surely if oak forests and their attendant life-forms began disappearing from Europe at anything remotely like the speed with which they died during the Younger Dryas, contemporary commentators would proclaim an ecological catastrophe of hyper-mega-ultramagnitude. Yet even the worst-case interpretation of human-induced deforestation does not remotely approach the significance of the Younger Dryas weald wipeout.

What triggered the Younger Dryas? No one knows; the cause is among the keenly debated mysteries of natural science. Cyclical variations in the Earth's axis and orbit around the sun, presumed to be the principal on/off switch of ice ages, could not have been the explanation, since at the time these variations were tending to warm the Northern Hemisphere. Some oceanographers have supposed that the oceans, which shift heat north toward Europe from the tropics, might hold the key to understanding the Younger Dryas. They may, but in a highly nonlinear way.

In 1992 Scott Lehman, a researcher at the Woods Hole Oceanographic Institute, shocked the climate-study business with a study suggesting that at the moment the mysterious cooling of the

Younger Dryas began, sea surface temperatures in the North Atlantic Ocean dropped by nine degrees Fahrenheit in less than 40 years. A climate swing of nine degrees in less than half a century represents roughly three times the fastest rate of temperature change projected by the most pessimistic computer models for an artificial greenhouse effect. It is roughly 20 times the highest claimed observed (actual, as opposed to computer-projected) global temperature change to have occurred during the last century, supposedly the century in which genus *Homo* has caused unparalleled climate mayhem. Aside from killer rock impacts, a nine-degree temperature change in 40 years may well be the fastest environmental alteration ever to have occurred on Earth. Lehman called this nonlinear effect a "climate collapse."

Climate collapse. It's just a descriptive term coined by a researcher, who may or may not be right about what he believes he has found. But what happened to the environment during the Younger Dryas was much worse than any effect so far caused or threatened by human malfeasance. The primary ecology of much of the globe was swept away—we'd say "destroyed forever"—in just two centuries, as temperate forests were replaced by glacial flowers and their accompanying cold-weather life-forms. Then, in just a few centuries more, the Younger Dryas switched off. The boreal forests of North America and Eurasia were un-destroyed, returning to their previous expanse and magnitude. At this point any environmental commentator of the time would have proclaimed the glacial flower ecology "destroyed forever" and would no doubt have lamented that without the environmentally vital dryas plant, the European ecology could never again be the way nature intended it to be.

Just as the cause of the Younger Dryas is mysterious, the mechanism of ocean-triggered climate collapse is unknown. Lehman speculates that fresh meltwater returning to the seas as the continental ice sheets thawed may have altered global ocean currents in such a way as to slow the movement of warm water normally pumped northward from the tropics. When the ocean "pump" that sends warm waters north shut down, a boreal big chill followed. Eventually, this speculation continues, the ocean balance between salt and fresh water was restored. Warm water once again flowed north from the tropics. The planetary warming in progress before the Younger Dryas resumed its course.

Nonlinear Norms

Lehman's "climate collapse" is just one of many recent discoveries pointing toward rapid effects in the natural ecology. Other scientists have recently uncovered what they believe to be evidence of nonlinear natural cycles whose velocity rivals that of human-caused environmental change. The geologic period at issue is that in which most of Earth's current plants and animals have lived, suggesting that for the denizens of the living world rapid environmental change is not some appalling new imposition of the wayward genus *Homo* but a standard environmental challenge.

Since the 1980s, Maureen Raymo of MIT, Wallace Broecker of Columbia, and George Denton of the University of Maine have been producing evidence that during the last 2.7 million years, Earth's temperature has bounced up and down enough to render any gradualist motion sick. "The rapidity of the transition to warmer climates at the end of the last glacial age seems to demand the presence of a nonlinearity or a threshold within the climate system," Raymo has written. "Rapid [climate] terminations, characteristic of the last half million years, seem to reflect an almost catastrophic instability in a climate system able to flip suddenly between two 'stable' modes."

The Raymo-Broecker-Denton hypothesis has been controversial within the science world, partly because it suggests that nonlinear ecological oscillations are a norm, not a rarity. Further, if these researchers are correct, the stability of temperatures during the Holocene, the most recent 10,000 years of Earth's history, may be a strange and pleasant gift bestowed by some offices at which we can only guess—a fantastic ecological favor to the prospects of men and women. When Raymo, Broecker, and Denton proposed their ideas, other scientists questioned whether the three possessed sufficient evidence to back the notion of rapid natural climate change. Many felt any verdict should wait until results were produced by two teams drilling ice cores in the glaciers of Greenland. Analysis of the ice in Greenland glaciers, much of it millennia old, is thought to provide the most accurate inferences about past temperatures. In July of 1993 the two Greenland teams, one led by scientists from the Niels Bohr Institute in Copenhagen, the second a consortium of French, Icelandic, and American universities, announced their findings. The cores appeared to confirm the idea of regular nonlinear effects in nature.

The Greenland analysts found evidence that between about 115,000 and 135,000 years ago, during the interglacial period previous to ours (the temperate era just before the most recent ice age), sudden, nonlinear climate transitions occurred many times. In one, Earth's average temperature seems to have fallen about 25 degrees Fahrenheit in just 70 years, a drop of greater speed and magnitude than associated with "nuclear winter" predictions.

The authors of the Greenland study do not speculate about what might have caused this astonishing temperature decline; they merely report evidence that it seems to have occurred. During the past interglacial, the Greenland studies further suggest, rapidly rising temperatures melted so much polar ice that sea levels rose 30 feet, roughly 50 times the rise currently projected by pessimistic greenhouse-effect studies. England became so warm that hippopotamuses wallowed along the banks of what is now the Thames. Even worst-case projections for artificial global warming do not include hippo in London. Reporting their findings in the technical journal *Nature,* the two Greenland teams noted that in light of apparently nonlinear climate norms in past interglacial periods, the Holocene period of human suzerainty has been "strangely stable."

Some analysts have found inconsistencies among the apparent climate clues of ice cores drilled in different places on Greenland glaciers, causing them to wonder whether the ice sheet may have compacted over time in a way that nullifies its value as a Rosetta stone to the climate of the past. At this writing, the accuracy of the cores was not resolved. But if the recent Greenland findings of rapid climate swings are upheld then the immediate ancestry of humankind, and of most current plants and animals, survived not only an ice age but at least two rapid nonlinear climate transitions far more profound than worst-case projections for climate changes caused by human action.

This does not mean that the prospect of human-caused climate changes is not a serious one. In a sense the Greenland findings may make artificial global warming more worrisome. If nonlinear climate "flips" are the norm, any artificial global warming may not transpire in a gradual fashion, giving warning of itself and many decades for society to react; but rather it may occur suddenly, perhaps after a period during which it appears there is little about which to worry.

Findings about nonlinear climate effects from Lehman, the Raymo group, and the Greenland teams hark back to an idea advanced in the 1970s by Hermann Flohn, a German climatologist. Flohn said that in the South Pole ice-core record he saw evidence that at the outset of the most recent ice age, global air temperatures fell about nine degrees Fahrenheit in less than a century. Flohn's work was scoffed at by most scientists: At the time gradualism was a rigid canon within academic Earth science departments. Nevertheless it was Flohn's notion of a "snowblitz"—that global glaciation may start rapidly, not gradually— that fueled the great instant-doomsday fad of the 1970s.

The 1950s and 1960s were cold decades, and temperatures remained low in the 1970s, with the winter of 1976–77 being the coldest on

record in North America. That year was so frigid 29 people died in a single blizzard in Buffalo, New York, a metropolis well accustomed to win-
try climes. From this many environmentalists proclaimed an ice age at
hand. A book called *The Cooling,* which forecast imminent glaciation of
northern society, was published to general acclaim. Several important
analysts who currently warn of global warming then warned of global
cooling. (Colder, hotter—it's got to be one or the other. Unless it's neither. But nobody's going to get funding to study the idea that nothing in
particular is happening.)

Immediately after an instant ice age was proclaimed in the 1970s, the
Earth warmed. Through the 1980s global temperatures rose. Alarmists
dropped their ice age predictions cold, as it were, and began to proclaim
global warming. Newspapers ran frightening bar graphs showing the
1980s warmer than the previous decade, not mentioning that the 1980s
was being contrasted to an unusually cold decade. One reason the
warmish winters of the 1980s so disquieted the baby boomers running
the U.S. media is that their generation awoke to the world in the 1950s
and 1960s, cold years with historically high snowfall rates in most of the
country. The low-snow winters of the 1980s did not conform to childhood memories of what winter ought to be. The generation born into
the low-snow 1980s, in turn, perhaps will be spooked into another ice
age scare whenever the twenty-first century has its first sequence of
harsh winters, since deep snow will not correspond to that generation's
adolescent recollection.

Nonlinear Evolution

Rapid natural action-reaction seems increasingly apparent in the biological as well as physical aspects of the environment. One twentieth-
century supplement to Darwin is the notion that evolution does not
necessarily occur in gradualist fashion but may happen in bursts that
some researchers call "punctuated equilibria." When theories of "punctuated" evolution were proposed about 20 years ago, researchers admitted they did not know what caused the bursts. Since then the emerging
notion of an environment in which naturally driven nonlinear events
happen fairly often has begun to dovetail with the predictions of punctuated evolution.

A standard objection to conventional Darwin-Wallace mechanics is
the scarcity of missing links. Paleontologists often find ancestor and
descendant species in the fossil record but rarely unearth evidence of the

intermediate creatures bridging the two. Gradualist thinking says the intermediaries should have been alive for very long periods and thus should have left fossils. If, instead, the environment is often subject to sudden changes through nonlinear natural effects, fast changes from ancestor to descendant species might be expected, explaining the paucity of missing links. Transitional creatures would still exist but be hard to find, since they would not be around long by nature's way of thinking. Various theories, backed by strong but not conclusive evidence, now hold that the gene heritage of most species is reasonably stable when the environment is stable, alters rapidly when the environment begins a phase of rapid change, then stabilizes anew when the environment calms. Many contemporary plants and animals appear to be the product not of strict gradualism but of such evolutionary bursts.

If nonlinear effects are fairly common in natural history, this might explain another common objection to Darwin. Before the rise of gradualism many researchers, such as the early nineteenth-century American zoologist Louis Agassiz, assumed species extinctions had been quite common throughout the past. At the time Agassiz and others thought past extinctions were driven by "catastrophes," a word that later fell into disrepute among scientists; the current term of choice, nonlinear effects, means about the same thing but has the bloodless, high-tech tone now in fashion.[2] As Ernest Mayr, a contemporary biologist and defender of Darwin, has written, Agassiz's ideas about frequent extinctions caused by natural catastrophes was "unpalatable to [Charles] Lyell," who insisted that extinctions, like everything else, could only happen very slowly. Darwin, an exemplary gradualist, embraced this premise. But that created a paradox in his theory. If species are acted upon only by very slow forces, why don't most have ample time to modify themselves in response to gradual environmental change, avoiding extinction?

Numerous tumescent monographs have been written on this question, which is far from resolved. As the study of the past increasingly produces evidence of fast-happening natural environmental stress, the chances increase that evolution is driven in no small part by various nonlinear influences. This would suggest that by the time humankind and its impertinent inventions appeared, the living world had already been elaborately prepared by nature to endure high-velocity environmental assault. The pace of man's attacks on the environment, though still a problem for nature, would no longer seem unprecedented.

Suppose evolution does not grind along in gradualist fashion but stages fast transitions in response to rapidly evolving environmental circumstances. What is the mechanism for fast evolution? One puzzle of the new science of molecular genetics is that most DNA appears to be inactive. Some 90 percent of the genome of the human being currently is considered "junk genes," meaning DNA that so far as researchers can tell does nothing. In other creatures the junk gene percentage appears higher still. Some biologists now speculate that rapid ecological responses can happen because within the junk genes reside switched-off instruction sets for dealing with ecological circumstances that the creature's lineage encountered in the past. When the circumstances recur, these genes are activated in some unknown manner and passed to offspring. Should this speculation prove accurate, it would demonstrate an important avenue by which the biosphere becomes stronger and more resilient as the millennia pass: Each succeeding generation would possess in its genetic library more information than the last regarding how to resist environmental assaults.

Recently some researchers have found indications that species can respond rapidly to environmental changes that involve behavior. In a 1993 article in *Nature,* a researcher from the University of Heidelberg reported that a bird called the European blackcap had altered its migratory pathways, apparently in response to patterns in urban development. Through the first half of this century the blackcap wintered in Spain; now it winters in southern England, using a new migratory route that avoids urban development raised along its former path. The researcher, A. J. Helbig, found that this was not just acquired behavior but has already, somehow, been transmitted into the blackcap gene pool. Offspring of the birds that winter in England, if raised in isolation from their parents, promptly fly toward England.

This item of knowledge not only bears on the question of rapid transitions in nature but also on other concerns. Environmentalists sometimes concede that genus *Homo* has only taken direct hegemony over a tiny portion of Earth's surface; yet they assert that one devastating effect of human development is that the traditional breeding grounds and migratory pathways of seasonal animals are disrupted much more rapidly than the creatures can acclimate themselves to new areas and pathways. This may be a substantial concern; that the European blackcap successfully adapted its migration hardly insures other species will do the same. But the rapid behavioral response of the blackcap suggests that the worry about disrupted migratory routes may be overblown— that birds have faced rapid naturally driven alterations in their migratory pathways in the past, since the blackcap apparently entered the industrial era already bearing the genetic codes necessary for fast response to route changes.

Loud Spring

The notion that natural selection may already have developed means of responding to rapid ecology stress ought to be reassuring. Instead environmental orthodoxy finds it offensive. In the orthodox view, genetic mechanisms are assumed capable of menacing mutations that will destroy the lush nature women and men love, but incapable of protective reactions. For example environmentalists often warn that insects exposed to pesticides and microbes exposed to drugs might not be wiped out but rather mutate in ways that make the chemicals ineffective. This would leave the pests and pathogens stronger than before, owing to human meddling. In 1993 Al Meyerhoff, an official of the Natural Resources Defense Council, said that in the race between insects and pesticides, "the bugs are winning." That same year Mike Toner of the *Atlanta Journal-Constitution* won a Pulitzer Prize for a series on pesticide resistance that warned of "strains of monster bugs resistant to nearly everything in our arsenal. The outlook is dismal. And it is getting worse."

Situation dismal—and getting worse! The perfect distillation of instant doomsday locution.

Warnings about resistance mutations contain an element of truth. Medical researchers agree that the staphylococcus, enterococcus, and tuberculosis bacteria (the first two infect wounds) have mutated to acquire resistance to standard antibiotics, including the potent antibiotic vancomycin, sometimes the last resort of current pharmacology. A common estimate holds that at least a dozen types of insects that attack commercial crops are now resistant to current pesticides, while perhaps 500 other insects and 150 fungi that plague farms have partial immunity to agricultural chemicals. Then again, there are at least thousands and perhaps millions of insects and fungi that prey on commercial crops. The English researcher R. N. May estimates, for example, there are five to ten million insect species in the world. If that number is right, hundreds of thousands of them live within snacking distance of U.S. croplands. So while some pest species have developed a vexing resistance to man's chemicals, most have not; the resistant portion may be far less than one percent. This is a cause for concern but not for slamming society's fist down on the panic button.

The year 1994 saw the republication of Carson's *Silent Spring*, by acclamation the most influential work of American environmental commentary. It was Carson's thesis that the unique speed of human actions, combined with the introduction of synthetic chemicals for insect control, would accelerate the occurrence of resistance mutations to such a degree that invincible insects would swagger across the Earth. Industrial alchemists would then fashion ever-stronger potions in a frantic attempt to stop the superbugs. Armed with mutated immunity the superbugs would defy the new poisons; as farmers grew desperate, pesticides would be sprayed indiscriminately. The superbugs would escape unharmed, but indiscriminate spraying would wipe out the crops, flowers, and "friendly" insects farmers hoped to encourage. The battle would end in less than a human generation, with favored species vanquished at every turn. Once the earthworm, a key friendly species, fell extinct from excess spraying of poisons, the food chain of songbirds would be destroyed forever. The next year would come a silent spring.

A dismal scenario indeed. Yet nothing Carson forecast in *Silent Spring* came to pass.

"The robin seems to be on the verge of extinction," Carson wrote. When she put those words on paper in 1962, the robin was the most common bird in North America. The notion that the most prolific avian was about to fall extinct was the most eye-catching assertion in *Silent Spring* and brought the book considerable publicity. The prediction never reached the general zone of true. The robin remains ubiquitous at backyard feeders. In 1994 it was still among the most prolific birds in America, the robin population having risen steadily since Carson wrote.

Though some counts of neotropical migratory birds such as the northern oriole and Canadian warbler show a downward curve probably related to deforestation of the birds' wintering grounds in Mexico and the Caribbean, and some migratory birds of the Southwest have been harmed by the drying of marshes and agricultural pollution of the Kesterson National Wildlife Refuge in California, most avian species have grown in number since Carson projected their decline. Each Christmas the National Audubon Society stages a nationwide bird count. Data from the count are compiled by the North American Breeding Bird Survey. I asked Bruce Peterjohn, chief analyst for the Breeding Bird Survey, to assemble statistics on population trends among the birds Carson suggested are in danger of extinction. The figures cover 1966, the first year for which full compilations are available, through 1993. In each category where Carson used a common name for bird types, figures are for a representative sampling of subspecies. Bird types are the ones mentioned in Carson's chapter "And No Birds Sing."

POPULATION TRENDS, 1966–93,
for birds described as likely to become extinct in *Silent Spring*

American robin: up 1% annually

brown creeper: population stable

cardinals: population stable

catbirds: population stable

black-capped chickadees: up 1.9% annually
boreal chickadees: down 4.6% annually
Carolina chickadees: population stable
mountain chickadees: population stable

bald eagle: up 5.4% annually

Fulvous tree duck: population stable

eastern king bird: population stable
eastern wood pee-wee: down 1.6% annually
great crested flycatcher: population stable
western king bird: up 1.5% annually
western wood pee-wee: population stable

brownhead nuthatch: population stable
pigmy nuthatch: up 2.2% annually
red-breasted nuthatch: up 2.5% annually
white-breasted nuthatch: up 1.9% annually

black phoebe: up 1.9% annually
eastern phoebe: population stable
western phoebe: population stable

screech owl: population stable

starling: down 1% annually

bank swallows: population stable
barn swallows: up 1.1% annually
cliff swallows: population stable
purple martin: down 4% annually
rough-winged swallows: population stable
tree swallows: up 3.1% annually

tufted titmouse: population stable

Carolina wren: up 1% annually
house wren: up 1.6% annually
rock wren: down 1.7% annually

downy woodpecker: population stable
hairy woodpecker: up 0.9% annually
pilliated woodpecker: up 1.2% annually
red-headed woodpecker: down 1.8% annually

red-bellied woodpecker: population stable
yellow-shafted flicker: down 2.8% annually

Scorecard: of 40 birds Carson said might by now be extinct or nearly so, 19 have stable populations, 14 have increasing populations, and
seven are declining. That means half of the birds Carson thought could
fall extinct have shown no change; 35 percent are going up, about 15
percent are going down. This sounds like business as usual for nature.

None of the other major conjectures of *Silent Spring* have been realized. Insects have not taken over the Earth. Though the poundage of
agricultural chemicals used in the Western world has increased since
1962, it has increased at a lesser rate than farm output, meaning pesticide application relative to farm production has declined. Use has grown
more judicious, not indiscriminate as Carson anticipated. Carson
thought routine aerial pesticide bombardment would become commonplace even in urban areas, partly because in the early 1960s many cities
employed aerial sprays to kill mosquitos. Instead mosquito abatement in
the Western world is now accomplished mainly without general spraying. Spraying in populous areas has become so rare that the two times
this has happened in the U.S. in the last 20 years, during California's
medfly outbreaks, it was headline news. Carson further thought pesticides would grow ever-more poisonous. Instead most new pesticides are
less toxic than those they supplant. Carson thought that pesticide
buildup in the ecosphere would continue indefinitely. Instead new pesticides receiving certification in the U.S. are ones that break down after
use, rather than bioaccumulate. In general crops, flowering plants, and
worms are doing quite nicely—so much so that nearly all commercial
food, fiber, and flower products are in chronic oversupply throughout
the industrial world.

If chemical-use trends had continued forever exactly as they were in
the 1960s, then the severe ecological harm Carson foretold would have
come to pass. But trends almost never continue uninterrupted. Much
doomsaying is based on the Fallacy of Uninterrupted Trends: taking patterns for carbon dioxide production or water pollution or other problems and projecting them out into the future as if they could never, ever
change. But change is nearly assured. Projecting trends as if there could
be no change is what led so many smart people during the 1970s to proclaim that oil prices could "never" decline.

As an ecorealist, I find it marvelous that the premise of *Silent Spring*
turned out to be unfulfilled. Society heeded Carson's warning, enacted
the necessary reforms (like bans on bioaccumulative pesticides such as
DDT and chlordane), and realized such a prompt environmental gain

that the day of reckoning Carson foresaw never arrived. This shows environmental reform works—and can work in time for nature's regenerative properties to provide the Earth with a margin of safety.

Why *Don't* Bugs Win?

Therefore Rachel Carson performed an important public service by being wrong. But why was she wrong?

First, Carson assumed synthetic toxics to be the main poisonous compounds found in the environment. In the early postwar era, when the study of ecology was in its infancy, most ecologists operated on this assumption. Bees and scorpions might have venom; only genus *Homo* made antibiotic compounds in quantity. In recent years researchers have begun to amend this view. Plants make, in fantastic quantities, a wide range of toxins for protection against competitors. The plant kingdom is not a serene green backdrop against which the drama of the animal kingdom is staged but the first great chemical manufacturing complex, busily inventing wicked potions just as do Monsanto, Dow, and the rest.

Poisonous plants such as some mushrooms and herbs are dangerous because they contain toxins fashioned by evolution to prevent those plants from being eaten by rabbits, caterpillars, and similar foragers. Arsenic, a natural toxin, is found in small amounts in many plants and poses a problem for insects and fungi. Several tree species make a toxin called terpene, designed to kill pine beetles. Tobacco has nicotine in its leaves because this toxin kills most caterpillars and makes rabbits and other small foragers nauseous. Similar examples of "natural pesticides," researchers are finding, are nearly ubiquitous throughout the plant kingdom. In evolutionary terms this makes considerable sense. Since plants cannot protect themselves by flight they require static defenses; toxins fit the bill. Carson made a far-reaching error by embracing the notion that the unleashing of toxics was without precedent in natural history. As she wrote, "For the first time in the history of the world, every human being is now subjected to contact with dangerous chemicals, from the moment of conception until death." Today research suggests that from time immemorial, people have been exposed to dangerous chemicals from birth forward. Many such dangerous chemicals are natural insecticides, now understood to be ubiquitous in the biosphere. If the presence in the biosphere of insecticides were going to trigger a burst of mutations creating invincible superbugs, this would have happened millions of years ago.

Second, Carson erred because she saw the struggle between plants and insects selectively. She presumed that living things would mutate quickly in ways inimical to human interests but not that the reverse could happen—no mutations positive to human interests would occur. Pest insects would become more aggressive, but "friendly" insects and birds that eat the pests would not respond by, say, multiplying in the presence of what would for them represent an enhanced food supply. Pests would acquire more resistance to sprays, but crops would never acquire more resistance to pests. Carson assumed such things although most actual examples of the balance of nature show that mutations and countermutations occur in roughly equal proportion.

Such selective awareness of the balance of nature continues to flavor current writings about the battle between pesticides and bugs. Today environmentalists describe as utterly frightening that bugs mutate in response to pesticides; pesticide designers must then mutate their chemicals; then the bugs mutate again; then products are altered again; and so on ad infinitum. To environmental commentators this is ominous. To me it sounds exactly like a standard evolutionary relationship.

Similarly, bacteria that attack mammal bodies mutate in response to antigens, whether natural or synthetic; the antigens are then altered, either by the body's genes or pharmacologists; the bacteria mutate again; and the antigens are altered again. In nature, biotic and antibiotic competitors rearrange themselves continuously. This process has been ongoing since the dawn of life. True, entering into that process substances rearranged in laboratories alters the character of the contest somewhat, but the ground rules continue as before. What's especially odd about those who fret today about the continuing conflict between bugs and chemists is that at bottom they seem frightened by the fact that the chemicals don't win. Instead of wiping out their targets, man's toxic potions gradually lose effectiveness. This is not frightening. It's great. It is much healthier to have bugs and pesticides engaged in an inconclusive running duel—that is, interacting the way living things are supposed to interact—than to have any chemical actually succeed in obliterating a pest. Somehow the doomsday line on pesticides has been twisted around to the point that the fact that the pesticides are not as deadly as they sound is supposed to frighten us. It should reassure.

An intriguing discovery regarding the running battle between antibiotics and microbes was published in 1993 in the technical journal *Antimicrobial Agents and Chemotherapy*. A research team led by Anne Summers of the University of Georgia found that an apparent reason some bacteria now resist penicillin is the mercury used in tooth fillings. Tiny amounts of mercury seep from filled teeth and reach the intestines, where the metal encounters bacteria normally resident there. The traces of mercury are in a form not toxic to human cells but dangerous to some creatures of the micro world; they cause the bacteria to mutate to resist the metal. It turns out the genes that help bacteria resist mercury often occur in coincidence with genes that increase resistance to penicillin.

If Summers's hypothesis is confirmed, mercury in tooth fillings may explain why bacteria, especially those that cause human urinary tract infections, now shrug off some wonder drugs. Materials used in tooth fillings will be changed in response, with, perhaps, whatever is chosen as a substitute for mercury serving as the trigger to some unanticipated new microbial mutation. Then filling materials will be changed again, and microbes will change again. This does not demonstrate that science is out of control or that the bugs are winning. It demonstrates action-reaction action-reaction action-reaction, an eternal rhythm of life.

Finally, when writing *Silent Spring*, Rachel Carson imagined that mutations by pest insects could happen very quickly, in nonlinear fashion, but that countermutations by plants and friendly species could only grind along governed by the principles of gradualism. This is an example of the practice I call selective doomsaying: citing the arguments for trepidation but not the countervailing arguments for equanimity. Selective doomsaying, constructively employed by Carson to emphasize important points about an unusual ecological area where a true emergency existed, has become a central tenet of contemporary environmental commentary, now applied to almost every topic whether called for or not.

How Woody Allen Confused Environmental Policy

A quirk of contemporary intellectual affairs accounts for an especially annoying instance of selective doomsaying. The quirk is that a few decades ago several prominent Western philosophers and writers became entranced with a principle of physics called the second law of thermodynamics. This is the entropy law: It holds that all isolated energy systems inevitably change "order," represented by the wood that stokes the fires, into "disorder," represented by the smoke that rises away. The law says that isolated systems must have zero or positive entropy values, entropy meaning the disordered state in which the potential of something has been used up and cannot be restored without fresh energy from outside the system.

At one level the second law of thermodynamics only states the obvious—you can burn a lump of coal but once. At other levels the law suggests that energy-dependent systems cannot sustain themselves: They must either run down or receive a continuous infusion of energy. But from where would the universe itself receive an infusion of energy? Because of that question, some readings of the second law hold that the firmament is fated to wheeze into a slurry of blah nothingness. This reading is not necessarily correct, for reasons too detailed to note here. But because this reading can make the very structure of the universe sound nihilistic, the second law has become a darling of intellectuals anxious for faux-scientific proof that life lacks meaning.

Pop intellectuals from the novelist Thomas Pynchon to the former comedian Woody Allen have used second-law references to buttress fashionably vacuous contentions that everything inevitably falls apart. Pynchon's novel *The Crying of Lot 49* employs as a controlling metaphor the inescapable descent of existence into entropy. In one of Allen's movies, an angst-driven intellectual is paralyzed by fear that the universe is expanding into an entropic dull gray. A leading European pop music group of the 1970s, Nektar, based a best-selling album, *Recycler,* around some second-law mumbo jumbo about how energy was escaping from the universe and only recycling could prevent the ultimate rundown of everything. A 1976 doomsday volume, *The Poverty of Power,* by Barry Commoner, the most influential American ecologist of the 1970s, employed garbled but appropriately pop-intellectual misunderstandings of the second law to decree the oil shortages then in effect as a herald of both Western economic collapse and even the eventual expiration of the universe itself.

Commentators continue to employ misunderstandings of the second law to suppose that environmental degradation signals an unstoppable descent into a lifeless final condition that represents a sort of ultimate doomsday for the entire cosmos. This ain't necessarily so. Earth's living history is a drama of defiance of the second law, as the biosphere has proceeded not to disorder but to ever-greater complexity. The arrival of a thinking creature accelerates the pace at which complexity is added to the living world. In some very distant future the destiny of the universe may be entropic enervation, but so far the biosphere of Earth has won victory after victory over disorder and decline. Perhaps one purpose of humankind is to expand complexity in defiance of the second law—a prospect we will raise again toward the end of this book.

The Runaway Mind

There is one sense in which men and women do bring an entirely new force to bear on the environment. People have adaptive intellect. Should you care to view intellect as a mutation, the mind is perhaps the first genetic development with the potential to become a runaway.

Ponder for a moment the final days of the woolly mammoth, a dominant large mammal of North America for millions of years, surviving such natural onslaughts as the rise and fall of ice-age cycles. The mammoth fell extinct approximately 12,000 years ago, as Paleo-Indians began to proliferate on this continent.

For many millennia natural competition existed between the mammoth and its predators, including another species that vanished around the time of the Paleo-Indian expansion, the saber-toothed tiger. Through the generations tigers might grow a little faster or fiercer, which unchecked could lead to the end of the mammoth. But mammoths might grow a little more imposing or wary, maintaining an action-reaction balance with predators. At some point a band of Paleo-Indians discovered that the mammoth had an Achilles heel: If you stampeded the creature toward a cliff, it kept right on going. Researchers have found several New World escarpments where fossil piles of mammoth bones line the base, dating roughly to the same period as human bones, stone-cutting tools, and cooking-fire remains found adjacent. At these places Paleo-Indians may have lived for extended periods from the meat and fur of mammoths that hunters herded off into space.

Perhaps there were times when a saber-toothed tiger frightened a mammoth toward a precipice, saw the prey fall, made its way to the cliff base, and dined. Competitive pressures on the mammoth would have increased slowly as a result of this discovery, because other saber-toothed tigers would have exploited this new hunting technique mainly to the extent the behavior could be spread to offspring via incorporation into the tigers' gene pool. In contrast, once Paleo-Indians discovered the mammoth's flaw, pressures on the species must have increased immediately. Preserved by adaptive intellect, this knowledge was transferred rapidly from tribe to tribe and to the hunters' offspring.

The full cause of mammoth extinction is unknown; hunting by Paleo-Indians may have been only one factor. This example, however, suggests two relevant points. First, suppose that Paleo-Indians did hunt the mammoth to its demise. Those tribes doing the hunting would have lived well, with an oversupply of meat and fur awaiting them at the cliff base. The tribes might have grown cocky about their mastery of nature. Perhaps some members of the tribes warned that the hunting was not sustainable, declaring that the red man was killing the goose that laid the golden egg, or whatever metaphor was current then.[3] One day the mammoth was gone. From the Paleo-Indian perspective the environment that succored the tribe would have crashed, with no hope that future generations would find the resources needed to survive. Yet Paleo-Indians prospered for another hundred centuries, until Columbus. The pre-European period of Native American ecology—a time many environmental commentators now look back on wistfully as "an Eden of astonishing plentitude," in the words of the ecotopian Kirkpatrick Sale—came *after* Native Americans of mammoth-hunting days would have perceived the environment as destroyed forever.

The second point that this example suggests is that human minds are much more significant to the long-term prospects of the environment than human machines. Paleo-Indians wrought havoc on the mammoth and perhaps other species without the use of technology or chemicals or recombinant DNA. They did it solely with hand tools and their minds.

Since in these chapters we're thinking like nature, the long term is what concerns us. We (nature) have seen that man's mechanical interventions with the Earth, though damaging, pose no unprecedented environmental threat. In contrast, nothing like the human mind has ever assaulted the environment. And though by the 1990s the machines are already being tamed—made to run on fewer resources, emitting fewer pollutants—the minds are expanding in number and power. Electronic cerebrums, we (nature) hear, have recently been invented, furthering this mutation. Someday may come electronic consciousnesses that have expectations of their own.

Perhaps machines are peaking as threats to nature. Minds, on the other hand, are a long way from their peak. But then minds have been around for some time longer than technology. Can it be that when our age began the mind had *already* destroyed the correct form of nature? Or was there ever any Correct environment?

THE END OF NATURE:
NOT A MOMENT TOO SOON

SUPPOSE ONE MORNING HUMANITY DECIDED TO DEVOTE ITSELF to preserving the correct form of the environment. The idea has certain attractions. There is also a drawback: It would be impossible to determine what the Correct environment might be.

For instance, in the United States a current political cause is the preservation of Adirondack forests, under a banner called "forever wild." The forever-wild movement sounds great to me: I love the Adirondacks, and hope developers can be kept away from them for a long, long time. But even a highly successful forever-wild campaign for these forests will not protect them in any natural "supposed to be" sense. Many of the tree species that today populate the Adirondacks are transplants from Europe. Many of the animals that roam the Adirondacks as part of what is widely presumed its "traditional" ecosystem are recent arrivals by nature's way of reckoning, having lived there only a few millennia or less. None of this alters the fact that the Adirondacks are a place of beauty where nature, not people, has the upper hand: ample reason to protect them. But what would be protected is not any Correct Reality. It's simply the reality that happens to exist at this moment. And it is guaranteed not to last, whether man leaves the Adirondacks alone or not.

Perhaps you say, then to preserve the Adirondacks as they are supposed to be, we should first restore them to the condition that existed before Europeans began to alter the species mix there. Today, in many places, environmentalists are pressing hard on the notion that species transplanted by deliberate or inadvertent human action must be eradicated in order to restore local ecospheres to the Correct state. Unfortunately, stepping back before Europeans came to the Adirondacks does not help us discover the Correct state for these lovely hills. For at least ten thousand years prior to the white man and perhaps much longer, indigenous Americans altered the landscape and ecosystems of the Adirondacks.

Must we then push back earlier than the Paleo-Indians? Before them the Adirondack ecology was frozen stiff during the Pleistocene ice age. Lifelessness doesn't sound particularly Correct. Back then several million years, before the onset of cyclical ice ages? That gets us to the Oligocene Era, when much of North America was arid: Water-dependent boreal forests like those in the Adirondacks probably did not grow. Back to the Cretaceous? Now we're in the era of dinosaurs, when global temperatures were substantially higher—too high for the tree types the Adirondacks host today. Another complication: The Adirondacks did not exist, the Earth's tectonic plates not yet having thrust these mountains up.

Back to the Triassic? In that age all current continents were joined. Nature looked nothing like it does at present: The needle on our Environmental Correctness meter would not register a thing. Searching for the way the Adirondacks are "supposed" to be our gaze will travel backward through the salt deposits of the Silurian to the evolutionary explosion of the Cambrian to the age of blue-green algae to the formation of the Earth from cosmic whorl and we will never know which environment was Correct.

Environmentalism today labors under the Fallacy of Environmental Correctness—that if only left to its own devices, the environment will find some abstractly proper alignment of species and life cycles, one that is right where others are wrong. There no such thing as Environmentally Correct. The human fixation on this chimera would be exquisitely enigmatic to nature.

Earth's ecosphere is ever in flux, knowing no fixed or proper alignment. A scant 12,000 years ago the North American rivers and lakes we now fret about preserving did not exist to preserve; the retreating glaciers had yet to hew them. Turn back a few pages and none of the rain forests or wilderness tracts we fear losing existed to lose, nor did most current plants and animals, nor did the current climate, nor did even the current continents.

When commentators say that human meddling causes ecospheres to be lost forever, strictly speaking that is correct, since no degree of restoration could ever bring back *exactly* the alignment of plants, animals, and vistas that existed when the meddling began. But then nature offers no hope of preservation for any exact alignment of plants, animals, and vistas either.

That every specific manifestation of the environment will someday pass away does not justify any action hastening the day. Every person reading this book will die someday. Knowledge of certain eventual death is no reason any reader should drive like a maniac, smoke cigarettes, or engage in any other act that accelerates demise.

Exactly because their moment on Earth must someday draw to a close, most people take prudent steps to prolong it. The same thinking ought to apply to environmental protection. Knowing that all ecosystems are fated to pass away, human beings should treat the natural world with extreme care, to avoid hastening the inevitable.

Let's Blame the Aboriginals

It has become standard for commentators to assert that nature is receding because people now play a significant role in environmental affairs. Perhaps this formulation is correct, but if it is—if the environment becomes irrevocably impure at the point at which human involvement grows significant—then nature ended millennia ago. In this formulation it was too late for the environment long before Columbus sailed to Hispaniola, long before the Norse sailed to Greenland, long before Alexander sailed to Egypt. The real bad guys in the drama of environmental degradation are not petrochemical manufacturers and shopping mall developers but the Paleo-Indians of the late Pleistocene, the Paleo-Europeans of our distant Cro-Magnon ancestry, perhaps even the Paleo-Africans of the Olduvai Gorge.

The orthodox environmental and academic-left view of human ancestry is that until very recently genus *Homo* had no meaningful effect on the environment. In *The Conquest of Paradise,* a 1991 book, Kirkpatrick Sale wrote that before Columbus, indigenous Americans lived "in balanced and fruitful harmony" with nature, in "an untouched world, a prelapsarian Eden of astonishing plentitude." In *Seeds of Change: Christopher Columbus and the Columbus Legacy,* an anthology published in 1991 by the Smithsonian Institution, North America before 1492 was described as "a First Eden, a pristine natural kingdom" where humans were "transparent on the landscape, living as natural elements of the ecosphere." The phrase "transparent on the landscape" is today often invoked by environmentalists to describe the way in which people related to nature before the arrival of industrial society and its technological monstrosities. Increasingly research suggests this view is wishful thinking.

A 1990 collection of technical studies, *The Earth as Transformed by Human Action,* edited by B. L. Turner, a geologist at Clark University, cites significant artificial irrigation as having been in progress along the Euphrates River at least 6,000 years ago. By around 3,700 years ago, parts of the Euphrates basin became infertile because poor irrigation methods left them excessively saline. Thus the Euphrates basin lost its Correct Reality (at least, its most recent Correct Reality) long before technology was conceived.

Environmentalists have asserted that the central highlands of Mexico were Edenic till the arrival of Spanish colonialists in the early sixteenth century. Since then, it is said, Mexico's highlands have suffered extensive topsoil erosion owing to high-intensity agriculture. This assertion of past human "transparency" on the landscape took a fall in a 1993 study published by Sarah O'Hara of the University of Sheffield in the United Kingdom. O'Hara found evidence of topsoil erosion caused by farming in the Mexican central highlands stretching back at least 3,500 years. She also found that erosion rates since the early sixteenth century have been about the same as or lower than historic rates.

In his book *Fire and Civilization,* the Dutch sociologist Johan Goudsblom recounts that arriving off the shores of Australia in the year 1644, shortly after the first known European sighting of the island continent, a sailor named Abel Tasman was amazed to discern "smoke and fire all along the coast." Aboriginal peoples had been burning Australia to make rangeland long before European influence.

Today many environmentalists say it is both an environmental affront and a terrible danger to the soil that what was once the vast, wavering prairie of the Great Plains has been converted to the breadbasket of American agriculture. Farmers in the Midwest grow mainly annual crops planted each spring and harvested each fall. Annuals, environmentalists say, deplete the soil at a rapid pace. To restore the environment of the Midwest to its Correct Reality, a substantial portion of the Great Plains should be returned to its pretechnological condition of grassland. The perennial grasses typical of prairie ecologies, plants with multiseason growth cycles placing lower demands on soils, will save the Great Plains environment, according to this thinking. Once the restoration of a Correct prairie ecology for the Midwest has been accomplished, then there can be widespread reintroduction of wild buffalo and other prairie species, returning an important part of North

America to the way it is "supposed to be." An ecologist named Wes Jackson who has carried the argument for returning the Great Plains to grasslands currently is a leading hero of American environmentalism.

Here is the Fallacy of Environmental Correctness writ large. Growing more perennials and reintroducing buffalo may well be wise policy for the Midwest but would hardly restore any Correct ecology, since the Great Plains are not naturally plains. The Midwest was prairie when whites first laid eyes upon it. Much of that grassland had, however, been generated by Native Americans.

After the Laurentide glaciers withdrew from North America, much of what are now called the Great Plains became forests, not prairies. Probably the Great Plains would have remained woodland had it not been for Native Americans, whom we will also call by the unavoidable misnomer Indians. At least five thousand years ago, Native Americans began burning the forests of North America, particularly in the Midwest. This was done to create grazing areas for the animals the Indians hunted, increasing the supply of game; to make hunts more productive, by decreasing hiding places for the prey; and to render travel more practical, since it's easier to traverse prairie than forest. Left to their own devices, grasslands usually evolve into timber. They must be burned periodically to vanquish trees, an order that has adapted itself to besting smaller plants by depriving them of access to sunlight.

Perhaps then a fair way to approximate the Correct Reality for the North American environment would be to restore as much as possible to the condition that existed just before Columbus. To many contemporary environmentalists, this would sound sensible. Yet good luck figuring out what even the Native American version of a Correct Environment might be.

You would have to bar Native Americans from hunting game with rifles. Would you also take away the Indians' horses? The modern horse came to North America from Europe. Within about a century, most Native American nations considered horseback their "traditional" means of travel and hunting. Within about the same period some horses escaped and sufficiently adapted to local conditions that mustangs are now considered by most environmentalists an "authentic" aspect of the ecosphere of the American West. Federal law grants wild horses special protection, though they are not an endangered species. So would it be Correct to round up all mustangs and ship them back to Bavaria and Coventry? Would Indian nations vote for such a plan?

Earlier in the book it was noted that most American forests have been increasing in size in the past century, not decreasing as conventional wisdom holds. One reason forestland began to expand in places in the

United States late in the nineteenth century is that the Native American practice of periodic prairie fires had been ended by the persecution of the Indian. Too few Indians remained to burn the grasslands, as had been the cycle of North American ecology for many centuries.

Burning by genus *Homo* often is necessary to keep prairies from progressing to forest stage. In turn burning by nature destroys many forests so created. Thus when the red man stopped burning the U.S. prairie at about the time the white man began fighting forest fires, an extensive program of ecological alteration was inadvertently set in motion. One human intervention counteracted another, returning many tens of millions of acres of land to woods: a status that, if not abstractly Correct, was at least the condition nature seemed to favor in its most recent reiteration of much of North America.

Let's Blame the Indians

Prairie creation is far from the only effect pretechnological American Indians had on the environment. Recent research suggests that far from being "transparent on the land," many Native American nations pushed the ecology as far as they could, given their means and knowledge.

In his 1983 book *Changes in the Land: Indians, Colonists and the Ecology of New England,* William Cronon points out that Native American burning practices were harmful to the prospects of some forest species but increased the fortunes of elk, deer, beaver, rabbit, turkey, quail, and ruffled grouse: the game animals Indians favored. These were taken by arriving colonists as the "natural" fauna of the New World. Don't waste any time wondering which are, then, the "natural" fauna of North America. The species groups that dominated New World forests when the Indians began deliberate burning were themselves comelatelies who followed the glacial retreat. Before that another set of species displaced an existing alignment when the preglacial cold cycle began. And so on.

Writing in 1992 in the *Annals of the American Association of Geographers,* William Denevan of the University of Wisconsin, a leading authority on the Americas before the whites, shredded what he called the "pristine myth" of pre-Columbian North America. Denevan showed that "by 1492 Indian activity throughout the Americas had modified forest extent and composition, created and expanded grasslands, and rearranged microrelief through countless earthworks. Agricultural fields were common, as were houses, towns, roads and trails." Denevan thinks that in addition to burning forests to create prairies, Indian action before the year 1492 caused many woodlands to convert from mixed tree species to single-species dominant stands. In the romantic image of the Edenic forests of the New World, groves of oaks, pines, sequoias, or maples stretched to the horizon in all directions, their magnificent canopies unfolding to the sky in alignment. To the extent the early colonists did encounter such autochthonous glories, Denevan thinks, they were finding forests where Native Americans had taken a role in seed dispersal. When human involvement is not a factor, forests often exhibit essentially random mixtures of tree types, heights, and characteristics. Such purely natural woodlands are not what the early white arrivals in the New World reported encountering.

Denevan notes that early in the sixteenth century the de Soto party, a long train of people, horses, and livestock, was able to move through much of what is now the Southeast without notable difficulty. This could not have been possible if the New World before the arrival of Europeans was the pristine forest of ecological imaginings—if it had been what the forestry expert Michael Williams, author of the 1989 book *Americans and Their Forests,* has called with irony "the vast, silent, unbroken, impenetrable and dense tangle of trees beloved by many writers in their romantic accounts of the wilderness." The de Soto party was able to move in a continent lacking roads because prairies burned by Indians were available.

In the plant kingdom, Denevan thinks that Indian forest burning practices were a boon to species such as strawberries, which were then available for picking both by Native Americans and by the animals that thrive on berries. Indian-caused alterations in the indigenous plant life were another factor that pushed the North American species mix in the direction of game animals such as elk, deer, turkey, and similar creatures at whose abundance the early colonialists marveled.

Denevan goes so far as to propose that the Amazon rainforests, the paragon of pristine nature to contemporary environmental orthodoxy, "are largely anthropogenic in form and composition." Research now suggests that Paleo-Indians of South America have been burning the rainforests for millennia, as well as scattering seeds in ways that alter the tree and plant species mix. A significant percentage of Amazonian soils show traces of ancient charcoal: an evidence of burning caused by people, since lightning rarely ignites fires in the moist woodlands of the tropics.

Another aspect of research into pre-Columbian North America concerns Indian populations. Historians have long assumed that when Europeans came to the New World its indigenous population was low, perhaps a few million people scattered from northern Canada to what is now Panama. As the Indian rights advocate Ronald Wright shows persuasively in his book *Stolen Continents,* low estimates were favored because white historians wanted to minimize the sense that genocide had been conducted. Wright believes that the North American population when Columbus landed may have been as high as 100 million, with most of this number living in Central and South America.

By the year 1600, the Native American population had fallen through disease and persecution to perhaps just ten million. By the founding of the United States in 1776, a mere 125,000 Indians were living east of the Mississippi. These statistics reflect profound human tragedy. If the Indian population dropped in one century from as much as 100 million to as little as ten million, the New World carnage for which Europe and the young American government was responsible has no peer in history—even if the majority of deaths were caused by Indian exposure to Old World diseases.

Conflicting estimates of prewhite America's population are politically charged. Native American advocates favor high-end estimates, since these numbers make white action against the Indian seem even more horrible. Environmentalists favor the low-end estimates, since unless Indians were few in number, it is unlikely they could have lived "transparent on the land." If there were 100 million people in the Americas when whites first glimpsed the continent, there already must have been extensive environmental impacts; and the desire to expand population must be seen as something rooted even in indigenous peoples, not a perversion of human nature brought on by the excesses of industrial society, as current orthodoxy would have it. Wright believes that in the year 1500 the Aztec capital of Tenochtitlan (Mexico City) had a population of 250,000, making it larger than London of the time. Aztec society in the year 1500 was busily engaged in imperialist campaigns against neighbor states, in deforestation, in artificial irrigation, in wide-scale exploitation of mineral resources. In sum the Aztecs were behaving "naturally," attempting to fill the maximum ecological niche they might occupy.

Let's Blame Cavemen

Following the trail of human disruption of the biosphere backward, we find continuing evidence of significant impacts. In his book *The Diversity of Life,* Edward Wilson notes that approximately 12,000 years ago there appears to have been a "collapse of diversity" as Paleo-Indian hunting societies expanded through North America. Wilson estimates that nearly 75 percent of the large mammal and bird genera of the late ice age era were gone from North America by the time Europeans arrived, with some of these extinctions hastened along by Indians in the sort of hyperspeed fashion now presumed an exclusive feature of industrial society.

Similar extinctions caused by preindustrial man have occurred throughout the world, Wilson thinks: Early humankind "soon disposed of the large, the slow and the tasty." Perhaps 70 percent of large mammals fell extinct in Australia about 30,000 years ago, when indigenous peoples first traveled there, probably from Indonesia. Eighty percent of large mammal genera disappeared from South America about 12,000 years ago, also as Paleo-Indians arrived. All the flightless birds of Madagascar became extinct about A.D. 500, again probably at the hands of nontechnological peoples arriving from Indonesia.

The fate of mammoths, mentioned in the previous chapter, is revealing. Mammoths were an important creature of the New World for at least two million years, represented by three species: the Columbian, the imperial, and the woolly. Mammoth were robust enough to survive several ice ages. But when Paleo-Indians began to expand, Wilson writes, "within a thousand years all the mammoths were gone." Worst-case biodiversity loss estimates for the present run as high as 20 percent of species worldwide lost by the early twenty-first century. Imagine instead that 75 percent of major animal and bird genera, a much larger grouping than species, had disappeared during the industrial era. Compared to the (bad enough) worst-case estimates of species loss today, rates of species loss during Paleo-Indian times seem like a wipeout of unimaginable gravity. Yet this wipeout came in a North America conceptualized as Edenic, untouched, an entirely Correct version of nature.

There is an intriguing possibility suggested by statistics such as the dramatic rate of species loss of 12,000 years ago: namely, that the animal kingdom completed the most painful portion of its adjustment to the human presence thousands of years before the industrial era began.

It may be that toward the end of the last ice age, as *Homo sapiens* began to reach significant numbers, our forebears slaughtered those species that for whatever reasons lacked evolutionary preparation to defend themselves against the sort of environmental pressures caused by intellect. Once this dirty work was done, the species that remained were those that did have some power to resist or evade man. These species then traveled with genus *Homo* into the contemporary world. There men and women mistakenly view them as frail victims being tested for the first time, when in fact they are survivors of an earlier, bloodier onslaught. Perhaps by the time the industrial era began, the species resident on Earth were already, by genetic process of elimination, the ones best prepared to endure human malfeasance. Thinking like nature, that would have been a wise arrangement to make.

An evidence of this possibility comes from Africa. Since approximately 125,000 years ago to the present, less than 20 percent of Africa's large animal genera have fallen extinct in ways that might link to human activity, a much lower rate of large species loss than researchers are detecting on the five other populous continents. This may have happened because most early human evolution occurred in Africa, meaning animals there have been interacting with genus *Homo* the longest. Perhaps animals in Africa had, in natural-selection terms, an advance warning on the coming development of intellect and thus more time to evolve responses to human-caused pressures.

The Horror of Change

A central reason contemporary environmentalists fall into the trap of imagining that there exists some ephemeral Correct Environment is fear of change—even of constructive change, in which living things successfully react to new circumstances. This is an important area where human and natural perspectives differ.

To nature, change is a companion of timeless stature. Change is essential to the environment's sustenance, to its everlasting process of self-renewal. The physical portion of the ecosphere—its land masses, rainfall patterns, climate conditions, and so on—changes endlessly. The living portion of the ecosphere must change endlessly in response. That makes change nature's most powerful ally.

Men and women, in contrast, may view ecological change as a trapdoor under the carpet that conceals instant doomsday. Peruse most contemporary environmental commentary and encounter an endlessly reiterated theme: that the environment can only get worse. Any new land use would be horrifying. Any atmospheric change would be horrifying. Any new genes would be horrifying. Any species realignment would be horrifying. Systems can only run down; renewal is impossible; the sun can only set.

It's hard to imagine a view more myopic. Without ecological change not only would humanity not now exist, neither would the very ecosphere we now revere. For living creatures to alter their ecology is not an offense; it is integral to the process of self-renewal.

The original ecosphere of Earth was inanimate. When replicating molecules formed, they immediately began to amend that ecosphere to reflect their needs and conveniences. Primordial plants spent two billion years converting Earth's atmosphere from a nitrogen to an oxygen base. To the metabolic systems of living things today, oxygen is the manna of the natural world: beneficent, sustaining. To draw a breath of it after the briefest interruption is among life's sweetest sensations. But to life-forms of the primordial past, oxygen was a menace. Oxygen is a reactive gas capable of corroding iron, employed in such dangerous substances as rocket fuel and artillery propellant. Oxygen is a close molecular relation of fluorine, an unstable element chemistry students are taught to fear. Unless a life-form has been elaborately prepared to handle the reactive and corrosive aspects of oxygen chemistry, this vapor is a sure poison.

Thus as the atmosphere of Earth became oxygenated, mass extinctions occurred among earlier living things whose respiratory functions were anaerobic. The fossil record of the Archean Era—the period from the formation of the Earth till the advent around 700 million years ago of life recognizable to the modern eye—is slight, so no scientist can be certain what happened then. But it is likely that the arrival of oxygen, the first significant life-driven environmental change, poisoned to extinction thousands or millions of species that had struggled for unimaginable spans of time to win their place on the Earth.

Imagine how any nightly newscast of the time would have treated this news flash. Imagine, say, the cable Archean News Network, supported by advertisements for anaerobic fitness videos. News personalities would have spoken in horror of the oxygen pollution being pumped headlong into the atmosphere by the inappropriate technology of the unregulated new photosynthetic plants. Oxygenation of the atmosphere would have been labeled an unmitigated ultra-hyper-megadisaster that would destroy the environment forever and ever.

Consider a secondary effect of oxygenation: formation of the stratospheric ozone layer. Natural forces could not have created the ozone layer until the atmosphere had been sufficiently altered by green plants that there was plenty of "standard" oxygen available for conversion to the radiation-blocking ozone variant of this element. The level of sufficient atmospheric oxygen for ozone creation in the stratosphere is thought to have first been reached about a billion years ago. By somewhere around 600 million years ago, the ozone layer had thickened enough to acquire a significant ability to screen out harmful solar and cosmic wavelengths.

That point is one paleontologists are beginning to call the Big Bang of Evolution, since then in a relatively short time all known animal phyla (basic body plans) sprang into existence. Prior to the 600-million-year line, it seems likely that ambient solar and cosmic radiation levels were so high on Earth's surface that complex life was not possible. Life beyond the multicellular stage may have existed only in the seas, where water provided a radiation screen. After the ozone layer thickened at about the 600-million-year line animal life began to appear on land, either evolving there or moving out of the seas or both. Thus the first life-generated global environmental disaster was the poisoning of millions of primordial life-forms with oxygen, in order that green plants and then animals could take sway over the Earth. The second life-generated global environmental disaster was the creation of the stratospheric ozone layer.

How could that be, when today any damage to the ozone layer is considered an emergency of the first order? By protecting Earth's surface from radiation, the ozone layer was in every respect a boon to *Homo sapiens,* the California condor, the California gnatcatcher, and the myriad other living things whose DNA malfunctions in the presence of strong ultraviolet and cosmic rays. But the coming of the ozone layer spelled doom to the radiation-resistant life-forms that once dominated the land ecologies of Earth. It is thought that before the ozone layer most land life was specialized to resist radiation and perhaps even use it for metabolic purposes. Once the ozone layer came into being, new, more energetic, more sophisticated creatures were made possible. They wiped out the old, rudimentary land life-forms in short order. If, as environmental doctrine now posits, ecological change is invariably awful, then the coming of the ozone layer was among the most awful events of all time.

Imagine how the Archean News Network would have reported the discovery of ozone accumulation: "Satellite measurements revealed today that a menacing stratospheric ozone layer is forming above the Earth. This ecological nightmare will block out life-giving ultraviolet radiation from the sun. It will cause uncontrollable mutations among the bizarre, genetically inappropriate life-forms researchers call mammals. 'The environment will be destroyed forever and ever,' the Multicellular Defense Fund said at a hastily called press conference. . . ."

In Praise of Extinction

Deeply vested in the hearts of human beings is the desire to preserve nature for as long as possible in the condition which humanity knew during the childhood of its genus. The alignment of animals, flowers, forests, rivers, grasslands, estuaries, and other natural components that existed when the human race first began noticing the world will always hold for people the nostalgic pull and associations of rightness that every child finds in the particulars of whatever the world was like when he or she awoke to it for the first time. And as the significance of the sights and smells of childhood increase when the adult ages, as genus *Homo* passes out of adolescence, the ability of future generations to walk with the creatures of humanity's youth—to walk with them through the same forests and glades where our dreaming ancestors once walked—will grow in power and value.

I want my children and their children and children of every generation that awakes to this Earth to experience as I have the echoes of the ages that may be heard at dawn deep in the Gallatin National Forest of Montana, or below North Brother Mountain of upper Maine, or near Honeymoon Lake in the Alberta Rockies, to name some wondrous locations I happen to know; to hear those echoes in any of the hundreds of similar natural habitats that still exist worldwide and still may be preserved. I want every generation to see these places much as they were when our forebears first looked on them. Without this, humanity will surrender a portion of its collective childhood. Sheer selfishness ought to tell us that would be a stunning error. To think that people should preserve salamanders or trout or eagle or forests or swamps or tundra simply because we *like* them is a value judgment many environmentalists reject, as it begins with the human perspective. But the strongest conservation policy will always be that which appeals first to self-interest, since this is the leading motivator in human affairs.

Yet easy as it is to compose reasons why human beings should protect individual species, it is as difficult to imagine reasons why nature would do so. Nature may find humankind's nostalgic affection for species and habitats enigmatic, as nature exhibits none of this sentiment. Ninety-nine percent of the species ever to have come into existence are now extinct—ended by the hand of nature, not man.

The greatest known loss of Earth life was the Permian extinction that occurred roughly 250 million years ago. At that time as many as 96 percent of the life-forms on Earth fell extinct. If you believe the current ordering of nature gloried and worthy of reverence, then you must believe the Permian extinction was a splendorous event. Without it the species and ecological wonders we now seek to preserve would never have come into being. Some other set of creatures and wonders would exist, to be sure. But there might be, say, no dolphins or whales: The Permian extinction was particularly hard on aquatic life. There might be no bear, no frogs, no otter, no songbirds, no flowering plants, no old-growth forests, no taiga, no Madagascan lemur.

Other mass extinctions reflect the same paradox. For instance had not the dinosaurs died there might today be no spotted owl, a creature that can trace its genetic lineage to those lost reptiles. Thus as genus *Homo* decides to devote ever more of its resources to the preservation of species and habitats, many members of that genus may be pleased: I certainly will be. But bear in mind: This action by men and women will be fundamentally unnatural.

The Illusion of Stop-in-Place

At many points along the way environmentalists have in effect declared that they could live with whatever changes man has wrought so far, but whatever is due next will be the last straw. However flawed the present may be, this reasoning holds, additional change can only make things worse. This is the Illusion of Stop-in-Place, a corollary to the Fallacy of Environmental Correctness.

Had environmental change somehow been banned, say, two million years ago, no thinking creature would now exist to worry about this. Thinking creatures have their pluses and minuses. But can it really be that Earth is worse off with them than it would be if environmental change had been banned two million years in the past? And can we really say that were it possible further change should be banned now, precluding the realization of whatever the environment may advance to in the next two million years?

Some environmental commentators allow that change is inherent in nature. But to most, only naturally occurring change ought to be permitted. Any alteration caused by women and men is flagitious, a wicked corruption. When holding such views environmental doctrine takes common cause with, oddly enough, political conservatism, whose hallmark is the desire to repeal whatever century is in progress.

The founding of contemporary American conservatism came in the mid-1950s, with the publication of William F. Buckley's favorite book, *The Conservative Mind,* by Russell Kirk. Kirk held the modern industrial state to be a horror because it caused rapid change. A booming industrial economy creates development, income shuffling, social mobility—all upsetting the conservative view of a stable social order. The intense aversion to change found in conservative writings of the 1950s would by the 1960s echo in the writings of ecologists, as would the desire to fix one's gaze backward toward an imaginary serene past. The romanticized bygone times depicted in the writings of some ecotopians—strife and hardships nonexistent, people "transparent on the landscape"—bear about as much resemblance to the actual past as does the imaginary world of the fancies of political conservatives.

Like many contemporary environmentalists, the conservative Russell Kirk felt the solution to the disagreeable change he found around him was stop-in-place. For centuries, if not longer, men and women have believed that society, which was ordered and blissful in their youth, can be saved only by the banishment of new changes invariably described as unprecedented, unbearable, and sure to destroy life forever. Some of the most ancient writings that survive to our day complain of cultures being afflicted with adulteration from inventions, from other lands, and, worst, from new thoughts. Around the world today are numerous political movements that assert the same: They want to stop Western ideas from influencing Islamic cultures, to stop democracy from penetrating China, to stop social justice concepts from creeping into capitalism, and so on.

All these movements overlook the self-deceit of stop-in-place: that the cultures or places they seek to preserve were themselves products of change bearing down on earlier cultures, in most cases only very recently causing the form that stop-in-place advocates consider traditional. For instance the "traditional" Middle East many Muslims now wish they could barricade away from change has existed for only half a century, since independence from Britain.

Similar self-deceit can be found in environmental assumptions about how the Earth should be fixed in some idealized Correct Reality, about how nature's past was serene and pure, about how present problems can be addressed by erecting a barrier to change. Such sentiments do not arise from the study of the natural world. They are baggage we check with us into ecological debates.

Does Nature Have a Soul?

Since our pre-adamite forebears began to speculate on the world around them, they have imputed to the Earth both volition and consciousness—viewing nature as a spirit, as a god or a confect of gods, as the collective yearnings of living creatures. From the animist origins of theology to the panlogism of the Greeks to the pantheism of Native American faiths to the deist groundings of the European Enlightenment to the cosmic theism of Whitman ("with the twirl of my tongue I encompass worlds") to modern environmental lobbying, people suppose that nature has sensibilities that may be pleased or offended. Even urbane skeptics commonly speak of nature as a spirit or a She.

But of course we don't mean it. This way of talking about the natural world is just a pleasant artifice, a poetic construct. Few modern commentators actually believe the living world possessed of spirit. It's just a deterministic matrix of carbon compounds, plate tectonics, and thermodynamic transfer equations. Mindless proteins, enzymes, and helixes.

But suppose nature does have a soul. Perhaps the founders of Native American religions were wise to speak of the living world as holding a collective consciousness, and perhaps we would be wise to employ such thinking today with renewed ardor.[1] Conceiving of nature as a spirit helps us to think like nature, a plateau that must be reached to place environmental claims into useful perspective. Presuming nature does in truth possess some ineffable nonmaterial presence helps us understand the natural scheme and humankind's proper role in it.

Who can say that nature does not contain Larger yearning? Anyone can see that nature breathes, that it strives, that its offspring great and small can be made happy or sad by each other's actions. The indomitable heartbeat of life could not be possible without some form of spiritual longing: Mere chemistry could never account for this wonder. In the field of astrophysics—the ultimate environmental topic—cosmologists currently suppose that at the moment our universe was created gravitational fields projected in all directions, creating a useful void into which blazing substantiality from the primordial fireball could advance. I think that at the moment the spark of life was first struck on the young Earth, *longing* spread in all directions, creating a useful essence into which the hopes of life could pour. That spirit, no more ethereal than a gravity field and in some ways less fantastic, has since held nature's dreams. It holds them today.

How can society treat nature as a spirit in any manner that satisfies rationalism? One step might be a revival of the Native American concept of granting to the natural world legal standing: allowing judges to consider the interests of voiceless creatures when deciding cases. Today judges generally cannot do this except in certain lawsuits arising under the Endangered Species Act.[2] Some commentators have long anticipated the development of standing for nature. Leopold wrote in *A Sand County Almanac* of an "ethical sequence" in Western law. Rights, he said, were first granted to the aristocracy, then the merchant classes, then the poor, then children, then minorities. Leopold believed the inevitable next step would be a "land ethic" that "enlarges the boundary of the community to include soils, waters, plants and animals or collectively, the land."

Rights for plants—preposterous? Hardly. Leopold's sequence has already been activated. In 1992 there was an elaborate enactment of doomsday melodrama regarding the United Nations Earth Summit in Rio de Janeiro. Environmentalists, commentators, and politicians competed to see who could express the most theatrical horror over the centerpiece of the conference, a treaty to reduce greenhouse gas emissions. Supposedly that treaty was an empty farce: Actually it will create notable greenhouse gains, as chapter 17 will show. Relevant here is a little-noticed portion of the compact, a few stunning paragraphs I call the "green rights" title.

In those paragraphs the Western capitalist states acknowledge that the global environmental commons has legal standing regardless of what a country's internal laws specify. Countries that ratified the greenhouse treaty—America among the first—agreed to submit to the authority of the United Nations for the purpose of regulating global-warming gases, surrendering any claim that greenhouse emissions are a matter of internal economic policy. Capitalist economists have for decades resisted the notion that nations be required to factor international "externalities" such as the global environment into their policies. Yet because of Rio, George Bush, John Major, Helmut Kohl, Kiichi Miyazawa, and other captains of the capitalist system affixed their signatures to this very thought.

The green-rights premise of the Rio treaty may within a few decades be a conspicuous influence in international decision-making. According to the prominent environmentalist Jessica Tuchman Mathews, a fellow at the Council on Foreign Relations, the green-rights clause has "more potential to cause governments to change their ways of doing business than any international agreement other than the Helsinki Accords."

Mathews's reference to Helsinki is astute. Premises in international law often start small then gradually acquire great force. In 1975 leaders of the world gathered at Helsinki to insert the vague, nonbinding phrase "human rights" into international law. At the time the Helsinki Summit was dismissed by pundits in the same terms later used to denounce the Earth Summit: as a sham exercise in windy speechifying. Yet by 1989, just fourteen years later, Soviet-bloc governments began to fall. Eastern democracy movements reported that a leading factor was the vague, nonbinding phrase human rights. The concept held that fundamental freedoms have legal standing regardless of what a country's internal laws specify. Once these words were on the books in the old Communist states, they created a logic of reform impossible to stop. The green-rights premise may have a similarly profound effect on American and European law, driving environmental reforms yet to come.

Of course if we suppose nature has a soul that should be granted recognition, we must wonder what it is we will be recognizing. This raises the question of whether people and nature are antithetical.

People: Doomed to Themselves

A puzzling antagonism has arisen in thinking about the soul of nature. Today we presume the artificial irrevocably at war with the natural, the duplicitous human prefrontal cortex the sworn adversary of nature's innocent spirit. This point of view is relatively new and relatively Western. In ancient times the Greek philosophers thought matter and intellect inseparable: human beings merely a different manifestation of the same underlying phenomena found in animals, rocks, or plants. That notion was developed independently by the ancient Eastern religions, which carry the idea forward to the present day.

As society grows more capable of meddling with nature, commentators increasingly assert that the very notion of human interaction with the environment offends the sensibilities of creation. As Mark Sagoff, a philosopher at the University of Maryland, has written, pessimistic environmental thinkers such as Edward Abbey, Annie Dillard, and Bill McKibben "regard nature and humanity as utterly separate." For instance McKibben laments, "We have ended that thing that has, at least in modern times, defined nature for us—its separation from human society. We have deprived nature of its independence, and that is fatal to its meaning. Nature's independence is its meaning. Without it there is nothing but us."

In this view, nature exists to the extent that it is not human. Now, merely by our presence, humanity robs nature of its soul. Deprived of independence nature somehow ceases to be, preferring oblivion to the slightest brush with a thinking creature. For the sin of ending nature, men and women must suffer an ultimate punishment: imprisonment with our own selves, in a place where "there is nothing but us."

Surely McKibben is correct, at least regarding the way people feel. Some aspect of the suspicion he gives voice to is vested in every heart. But whose way of thinking is this? The notion that humankind is a curse on nature comes from human beings, not nature—just as the notion that human minds are the enemies of nature's spirit comes from those very minds, sadly renowned for their determination to read conflict into every situation.

When contemporary environmental thinkers lament the end of nature what they mean is the end of a spontaneous world, in which physical and biological arrangements are derived solely from autonomous self-alignments of elements randomly distributed and haphazardly perturbed. Once all aspects of the living world had a random origin; all life-forms were in essentially equal competition; all results were value-free. Clearly these standards no longer apply. And unless there is an extinction of intellect, they will never apply again.

The altered, values-attached environment that replaces a purely spontaneous nature may be good or bad, of course; but can it really be such an offense to the soul of nature? Once, at an environmental conference, I listened to a speaker discourse on the horror of the "managed" forests timber companies create. Yes, the speaker said, when loggers fell trees they now replant, and what rises differs little from what would have arisen on its own after a natural forest-clearing event such as a lightning fire. But the new trees, the speaker said, will ascend in regimented rows where man's empirically oriented management systems plunk them, rather than rise spontaneously. Even if the forest remains primarily a realm of nature, the placing of trees in straight lines means the woods no longer possess "separation from human society." The spirit of nature is thereby exorcised.[3]

People may find a neat, meticulous stand of planted trees nowhere near as interesting as a glade scattered into random clumps. But that is a human aesthetic judgment. Thinking like nature, I doubt we'd care one way or the other whether the trees stood in lines. And if we (nature) were to see some benefit in a system that gets lots of young trees growing quickly, we'd embrace the idea in an instant.

No sensible person would fail to recognize that nature has through spontaneous action created majesty of a measure exceeding everything humankind has created via design. But that scarcely proves spontaneity is essential to the ecology. Until the arrival of intellect, spontaneity was the only mechanism available to the natural world: Nature had no choice but to proceed on these terms. And since the natural world has been running a spontaneity engine for many millions of times longer than the period in which action by design has been possible, in a sense it's only to be expected that spontaneous nature so far has all the really impressive achievements.

At some levels the contention is irrefutable that intrusions on spontaneity render the environment unnatural. If nature is defined as an environment knowing only autonomous action—as a place where seeds are never planted, only tumble upon the ground—then nature has indeed ended. But by this standard the battle to save the environment was lost along the banks of the Tigris and Euphrates, in the morning hours of human ambition. By this standard an utter destruction of the entire majesty of the biosphere, a totality that had resisted forces at the very level of the cosmos for nearly four billion years, was achieved essentially instantaneously when a few paltry tribes not yet able to write decided some crops would grow better here as opposed to there. This act shattered a metaphysical protective shield around the environment by introducing the heresy of action by design. It's been downhill ever since.

In this light some environmental commentators almost evince relief to have reversed the view of the ancients, no longer supposing humankind and nature are one but rather that they are antagonists. This notion creates pessimism by definition. If mere failure to wall off the human and natural realms causes some palpable harm to the biosphere, then bad news is guaranteed no matter how modestly women and men might learn to live. Today humankind is the foe of most species, assiduously sabotaging their hopes. But that's today, with human knowledge of the environment and our proper role in it at a miserably low level. Who's to say that as time passes human wisdom will not increase to the point at which people become agents for the preservation of life? Environmental thinkers who contend that only unplanned, autonomous outcomes are valid for nature are preparing in advance to be dissatisfied even on the day that men and women achieve full enlightenment regarding natural protection.

Can Carbon Dioxide End Nature?

McKibben makes the flight of nature's soul disturbingly current, saying it has come in his lifetime: during the postwar era in which the expansion of manufacturing and the delivery of millions of private automobiles began to alter in earnest the chemistry of the atmosphere, by adding carbon dioxide. Previously, McKibben says, little ends of nature happened here and there as habitats were lost to human meddling, but these were locally confined—the deep jungles and far Tortugas spared. As the altered atmosphere now spreads everywhere on Earth, no aspect of the biosphere can any longer remain "separate" from man. Thus the spirit of nature is destroyed as if struck by a cosmic mallet.

This line of thought has a little defect and a big defect. First the little defect. McKibben assumes more carbon dioxide in the air acquires an almost mystical (or perhaps antimystical) power when it results from action by design—of the starting of cars in the morning—rather than from spontaneous natural forces such as plant decay. This sequence of logic is difficult to follow. Strictly speaking, carbon dioxide is not even a pollutant. Substances like DDT and trichloroethylene are pollutants; when people spill or release them, we put into the environment compounds not normally there. Carbon dioxide is normally found in the environment in colossal quantities. Natural cycles move CO_2 back and forth from the atmosphere to the seas, back and forth from the atmosphere to plants, forth from volcanos to the atmosphere and back from the atmosphere to Earth's crust at a rate of around 200 billion tons per year, versus about seven billion tons annually added to the cycle by artificial means.

McKibben, Vice President Al Gore, and other believers in a greenhouse emergency have noted that human activity has through the past century helped push the carbon dioxide content of the atmosphere to its highest level in 160,000 years. This is said to confer on CO_2 a sort of honorary pollutant status. Current airborne carbon levels may indeed bring unhappy consequences. But the 160,000-year high becomes less shocking once context is added.

The CO_2 records generally accepted by scientists come from ice cores drilled into glaciers: These cores provide the inference that the carbon content of the air is today the highest in 160,000 years. Gore regularly mentions ice-core data as supporting his notion that global warming poses "the worst crisis ever faced by humanity." Unfortunately the usefulness of ice-core study now ends at about 160,000 years in the past; older ice appears too compacted for meaningful analysis. But what was happening during the last 160,000 years? Through most of that span *Earth was in an ice age.* When a comparison is made between current airborne CO_2 levels and historical records from an ice age, it would be amazing if current levels were not high.

What was atmospheric carbon like earlier than 160,000 years ago? No definitive proxies exist, but recently Dutch researchers lead by Johan Van Der Burgh of Utrecht University broached this question by studying the stoma (roughly, the breathing passages) of fossil leaves. Leaf stoma are believed to shrink or enlarge in response to atmospheric CO_2. Writing in the technical journal *Science,* Van Der Burgh reported that typical airborne CO_2 levels of the past ten million years have varied from 280 to 370 parts per million. The current CO_2 level is about 355 ppm.

This suggests that in the past ten million years—overall a relatively cool period for global climate—the carbon dioxide content of the atmosphere has at times been higher than today's on a purely natural basis. Current atmospheric CO_2 levels may still be a problem, as at present rates of increase they will sometime in the next century exceed the "recent" natural peak found by the Utrecht team. But nature would giggle at the current idea that by raising the carbon level of the air, men and women do something shockingly "unnatural."

Farther into the past, CO_2 estimates become speculative. Some paleoclimatologists believe there have been many points when the CO_2 content of the atmosphere was appreciably higher. During whole bygone eras such as the appropriately named Carboniferous, when dinosaurs and insects were developing, atmospheric CO_2 may have been above 500 ppm, higher than worst-case projections for artificial greenhouse levels for the late twenty-first century. Kenneth Caldeira of Pennsylvania State University has estimated that around 120 million years ago the naturally occurring carbon dioxide level may have been as high as 5,000 ppm, some 15 times the current level that alarmists call unprecedented. And points in the past when atmospheric CO_2 concentrations were higher lasted far longer than the current people-induced CO_2 bulge. The Carboniferous era was about 80 million years, two million times longer than the period of industrial emissions of carbon. Through that entire span the carbon dioxide level of the air was dramatically higher than today, without triggering any instant doomsday.

Here, then, is the little defect in McKibben's contention that greenhouse emissions caused by humanity are antithetical to nature: The condition those gases has generated is so far much *less* pronounced than greenhouse conditions nature previously made of its own accord. Of course, it may be that species of the present do not profit from greenhouse air as much as did species of the Carboniferous; fair reason for carbon emissions controls, which would be a sound idea. But the notion that humankind is committing some sort of unprecedented outrage against the environment by adding carbon dioxide to the air is shot down by understanding of Earth's natural history.

The big defect in McKibben's premise about the repugnance of carbon emissions stems from a related consideration. Artificially emitted carbon dioxide is chemically identical to naturally emitted carbon dioxide. It may be foolish for human beings to put CO_2 into the air unnecessarily. Currently the climate is to humankind's liking, to the liking of our fellow creatures, and to the liking of the agriculture upon which billions depend for sustenance. Why take chances with something as important as the climate conditions necessary for agriculture? But when people act in ways that put extra carbon dioxide into the air, all they do is confront nature with a bit more of a substance that would have been in the air man or no.

To suppose, as do McKibben and other commentators, that some metaphysical horror is engendered by the fact that the increased percentage of CO_2 in today's air stems from action by intellect rather than autonomous natural spontaneity—and to suppose this horror is so bottomless as to cause the soul of nature to flee the Earth in anguish—is an incredible stretch of reasoning.

Thinking like nature, we would rapidly conclude that the effects of CO_2 added to the air by design are indistinguishable from the effects of CO_2 added by spontaneous natural processes. Such effects may be good or bad. But if they are bad we are merely left with a practical problem, a management screwup requiring energy-production technology that lowers carbon emissions, conservation systems that reduce energy demand, and lifestyle changes that eliminate energy waste. We are not left with an assassination of nature's spirit. Nature would certainly consider that one a hoot.

Why Environmental Collapse Is Reassuring

In a strange way it can be comforting to suppose, as does current environmental doctrine, that until recently everything was fine but now the world is falling apart. The sentiment that till recently everything was fine grants high standing to nostalgia, one of the strongest human emotions, while the idea that everything is suddenly falling apart is among the oldest of human sentiments. Women and men who lived in every age seemed to believe they just missed being born into a better time and instead were cursed to exist among unprecedented tumult. Socrates complained that since he was a boy, people weren't serious anymore; Plato griped that since his youth academic standards had gone to hell; Thomas More, beheaded in 1535, believed that society, which knew the power of reason in his youth, had in his adulthood lost that power forever. Throughout history the wisest and the most learned have believed everything to be coming unglued. It must be a habitation of the human heart to suppose the world was once proper in some vague romanticized way but now unravels. Today this notion is applied to environmental affairs and distorts understanding of them.

For some, current ecological events constitute nothing less than a second Fall. Men and women, who once cast themselves out of the Garden via spiritual transgressions, now destroy the Garden itself with physical assault. Variations on the second loss of Eden are a common metaphor in environmental rhetoric. This raises the question of what role the Garden plays in subconscious assumptions about nature's soul.

The psychologist Carl Jung once supposed that parables of the Fall are reinterpretations of the journey from childhood to maturity. To young children, at least those born into secure circumstances, all the world at first seems sweet and ordered. There is unlimited abundance; food, shelter, and amusement are had through no effort on the child's part; parents seem infinitely wise regarding matters about which the child has not the slightest grasp.

Then comes Jung's version of the Fall: adolescence. Forbidden knowledge is acquired, the cloak of innocence removed. A world that cooed warmly to the child grows judgmental to the adolescent. Where the child was surrounded with plentitude, the adolescent pines keenly for things beyond reach. It begins to dawn on the adolescent that the years of play will end, followed by a lifetime of hard work. And suddenly those demigods, the parents, regularly are angry with their offspring on complex matters a quick, charming smile will not resolve.

This dynamic, Jung believed, plays out in our thoughts about a historical Fall from a time when people knew divine dispensation and perfect harmony with nature. The parable of the Garden arose from attempts to project conflicted thoughts about the loss of the limitless world of childhood onto a narrative of expulsion from a place of perfection.

The same dynamic asserts itself in contemporary environmental pessimism, which projects inner torment from the adolescence of human society onto a new parable of destruction of a place of perfection, the environment; a place that once loved genus *Homo* unconditionally but now rages against its former favorite. The psychological dynamic here may be particularly strong if, as this book supposes, genus *Homo* is beginning its passage from childhood to adolescence relative to the Larger Scheme: men and women knowing enough to make mischief, impatient regarding their many desires, but well on the south side of wisdom. Conflicted thoughts about the passage may manifest themselves in an active wish for news of environmental destruction—for the reverse-psychology reassurance that compared to today's screwed-up world, there was once a Garden.

Of course the fact that many previous generations believed the world was falling to pieces does not guarantee the world will not, finally, fall to pieces. But knowledge of natural history surely falsifies the vague premise that nature's soul has fled the Earth in horror over matters as small as parts per million of carbon dioxide. If nature has a spirit it dwells with humankind today. That raises the next question: Does nature have values?

DOES NATURE HAVE VALUES?

HERE IS SOMETHING I CALL THE MISSING-SPARKLE PROBLEM. Get out your test tubes, your electron microscope, your spectrometer, your magnetic-resonance imager, your neutrino tomograph, and any other instrument you may wish to withdraw from the wizard's pouch of high-priced science. I will present you with three sets of water molecules and challenge you to tell me which set came from a coho salmon, which from a stream in Amazonia, and which from the condenser coils of a power plant in Indiana. That is, I will challenge you to say which substance was lately biological, which natural, and which technological. You won't be able to.

Now let's alter the thought experiment such that you are able to train your instruments on the cells of, say, a gray timber wolf as it walks a forest path in Yellowstone National Park, without the wolf being aware of your crafty intrusion.[1] Examining this wild creature through your sophisticated gizmos you would find that at the elemental level its cells, like those of any person or animal, are made from mundane materials such as carbon, nitrogen, and minerals. Your detectors would find identical materials all around the wolf in the ground, the air, the rain: where, after all, the constituents of the wolf's body originated, via intermediary stops inside other living things. Within the wolf these bland materials acquired life and became sacred. But fiddle with the dials of your detectors all you like and you will not be able to discern any physical difference between individual elements in the wolf's body and the same substances in the adjacent inanimate environment.

You will discern important operational differences: materials in the wolf's body are reacting with each other at high rates, can form copies of themselves, and so on. But as to the basic stuff that makes up the wolf, there's no detectable difference between it and the basic stuff of the nearest Buick. Animate particles do not display any known special feature compared to inanimate particles, which is why I call this the missing-sparkle problem. We think that because our bodies are alive they must be made up of substances that have some sparkle or glimmer or unique property about them. We're not. We're just made of the same stuff as hills and vales.

The missing-sparkle problem is the starting point for understanding that the distinction between artificial and natural, which means a great deal to people, means nothing whatever to nature. Since in these chapters we attempt to think like nature, we must consider whether from nature's point of view the human mind and the material impedimenta it creates are offensive to nature. At one level the debate is about technical matters—the difference between artificial and natural, for example—but in the end the question hinges on something much more important: values. Let's take the easier issue first.

The Horrors of Peanut Butter

As Helen Hiscoe, a retired medical researcher at Michigan State University, wrote in 1983 in the *Journal of the American Medical Association,* "The underlying assumption of those who value things because they are natural is the belief that nature is a benign force whereas human power is evil." When the words *artificial* and *natural* are used to convey the senses of "made by people" and "made by nature," they carry informative content. But in their concocted modern cultural senses of *tawdry* or *false* (artificial) and *genuine* or *beatific* (natural), these words break down to meaninglessness, at least when we think like nature.

The standard debate regarding artificial and natural substances turns on the content of food products. Many processed foods contain substances not found in raw foods, and this clearly renders the product artificial in the sense of made by people. But then even purely organic foods are also artificial in the sense of made by people. Ever seen all-natural yogurt growing wild in a field? And under no circumstances does natural mean absence of chemicals. Current law in most Western countries requires food labels to cite only what is *added* to a food product. If labels were required to list chemicals naturally present in oranges or potatoes or anything else, the list would run on for several paragraphs of polysyllabic, creepy names.

All-natural bread would be listed as containing formaldehyde, the ultimate preservative. All-natural peanut butter would be listed as containing aflatoxins, a family of potent fungal poisons. All-natural apple juice would be listed as containing as many as 137 natural "volatiles," organic compounds that are primary ingredients in urban smog; three are known rodent carcinogens. Various foods ingested daily would be listed as containing on a purely natural basis arsenic, heterocyclic amines (a rodent carcinogen group), lead, and other scrumptious stuff. Any food containing vitamin A would bear a large-type all-caps warning label, since when given to lab animals vitamin A appears powerfully carcinogenic.

Each cup of coffee would be labeled as containing up to ten milligrams of naturally occurring rodent carcinogens. Ten milligrams equals the estimated *total* annual consumption of synthetic pesticide residues per American. That's right—a single cup of coffee may contain, by weight, as much carcinogen as your entire year's exposure to pesticide residues. (Some synthetic carcinogens are stronger than some natural ones, fuzzing this comparison slightly.) We feel comfortable with the coffee, peanut butter, and bread because they are natural; we fear the pesticide residues because they are artificial. This is like standing confidently in an open field during a thunderstorm because lightning is natural but quaking with dread when asked to hold a flashlight battery.

The craze for all-natural products has in many respects been a fribbling exercise. My favorite frivolity was the recall of Perrier after it was revealed the touted natural source of that water contains minute quantities of benzene, a carcinogen. Pulling bottles off shelves, Perrier's purveyors complained loud and long that the benzene level was so tiny even someone drinking their product by the gallon would face no elevated risk. Perhaps so. But which water seller had spent millions on advertising designed to persuade the public its product had mystic purity? To lull consumers into believing the scientifically null premise that even minute impurities generate a worrisome health risk? To restore its status quotient, Perrier now uses filtering devices that remove benzene from the output of its "fissure in the Earth." In other words the natural product employs artificial means to remove a naturally occurring substance, creating the artificial impression the product is more natural than could be found in nature. Imagine explaining to nature why people care about this.

None of this means that allowing chemicals in food is necessarily

wise. Some pesticides and food additives are harmless; some offer benefits greater than risks; some are hazardous; some merely dispensable.
The fribble of the natural-products craze has created important lessons,
one being that foods may do quite well freed of their additives. An evidence of this concerns the apple pesticide Alar, banned in 1989. The case
against Alar, made mainly by the Natural Resources Defense Council, is
now generally considered by scientists to have been severely exaggerated. Pantomime panic about this chemical, from weeping Hollywood
celebrities to newscast faux-hysteria, was a low point for rational discourse on environmental affairs.

Yet the outcome of the Alar flap was positive: Apples remain plentiful and delicious, prices remain low, and growers continue to make
money. The primary use of Alar was to keep apples extra shiny: Who
cares if apples are extra shiny or only sort-of shiny? I would rather my
children eat unshiny fruit in exchange for even a tiny reduction in risk.
The crusade against Alar is an example of what the social critic Mickey
Kaus calls "framing the guilty"—creating an unfair case against a target
that deserves indictment. Framing the guilty has become a central operating tactic of environmentalism, and is sometimes defensible.

Much of what presents itself in public debate as an artificial-versus-
natural environmental argument is really about aesthetics. For instance
a home made of lumber as opposed to pressboard has greater value
because the connotation of quality is higher, the emotional satisfaction
of ownership higher, the visual beauty enhanced.[2] These are appropriate
concerns for people but quite abstract and irrelevant to nature.

This logic applies to most forms of the phony artificial-natural distinction. An artificial creation such as a high-rise apartment tower may
be a good idea or a bad one depending on a wide range of factors: But
nature would find it absurd to suggest there is something objectionable
about the tower merely because it is made of processed materials
assembled by cranes, pulleys, lifts, and other devices. Nature itself manufactures bulk materials through such processes as igneous and sedi-
mentary rock formation and often fashions very large dwelling places,
such as lakes, using engineering practices far more ambitious than those
employed in apartment construction. Some of nature's creatures spend
a good deal of their time forging the inanimate. For instance, the light-
ness and strength found in some marine shells is so impressive
researchers now study how the substances might be duplicated. Shell
materials made by a scallop are natural; the same substances fabricated
in a factory would be artificial. Would any meaningful difference separate the two?

Natural and Artificial Genes

An important current artificial-natural dispute concerns whether governments should allow the marketing of food and fiber products containing genes placed into plants and animals through laboratory engineering. Current genetic structures are natural in the sense of made by nature; future structures will be partly artificial in the sense of made by people. Will there be a consequential distinction?

Until about two decades ago it was believed that genes did not cross species lines in nature. Had this belief been upheld, it might have created a strong basis on which to object to "transgenic" engineering like, say, the recent experiment in which DNA from fish was inserted into a strain of tomatoes in an attempt to make the tomatoes frost-resistant, as many types of fish can tolerate near-freezing water. Scientific findings have shown, however, that genes do jump between species in nature, probably carried aboard viruses. In nature many different species share common DNA coding, suggesting there is nothing inherently dangerous about genes that originated in one animal ending up in another. Human and chimpanzee DNA so far appear to differ by only around one percent; people have some DNA strands in common with laboratory flies and worms. It is assumed that once more is known of genetics, most species will turn out to have gene material shared with other species, either through common ancestry or natural gene jumps.

So transgenic engineering is not artificial in the sinister sense; it is natural. That does not necessarily make genetically engineered products good ideas. There are sound reasons to be suspicious of this technology and for governments to regulate it closely. But the guiding rule should be what is in the product, not by what technique the product is fashioned. That is, when fish genes are inserted into tomatoes do the resulting tomatoes contain anything that could hurt anyone? (So far it seems not.) And do the tomatoes taste good? (So far they taste rather like red, squishy fish.)

The first genetically engineered product to engender a public howl was bovine somatotropin, a hormone some dairy farmers give cows to increase milk output. Traces appear in the milk. This caused numerous activists to attack the substance, some dairy lobbyists to call it a threat to small farmers, and many supermarket chains to decline to stock milk from cows that receive the hormone, fearing consumer boycotts. Nobody wants that awful artificial BST in their pure, natural milk.

The trouble is that all cow's milk is "tainted" with BST. Codes for somatotropin occur naturally in bovine DNA. Bovine somatotropin was not invented by mad scientists; scientific knowledge of DNA is far too crude for any researcher to devise genes from scratch, although perhaps this will happen someday. At present, researchers only try to rearrange genes nature has already field-tested. The BST hormone was found in cows and copied from it. Because BST is natural, traces of the substance appear even in the milk of cows grazed entirely on organic feeds and never given any drug.

When in 1994 BST was certified by the Food and Drug Administration for sale in the United States, the fashionable Ben & Jerry's ice cream company began affixing cartons with labels boasting that the firm will not buy milk from dairies that inject cows with BST. Curious, that lawyerly passive wording. The labels do not say Ben & Jerry's ice cream does not contain BST: All ice cream has BST traces, as does all cow's milk. Meanwhile Ben & Jerry's "super premium" ice creams, made from whole milk and cream, contain dozens of grams per dish of one of the most potent known carcinogens: fat. Studies show high-fat diets more closely associated with cancer than any factors other than cigarette smoking and, perhaps, heredity. High-fat diets are also a leading cause of heart disease and hypertension. But milk fat is natural. So Ben & Jerry's pushes fat, a severe confirmed health risk, while boasting that it shuns BST, which during years of clinical trials produced no evidence of even mild carcinogenicity—probably because unlike fat, BST and a related compound called insulin-like growth factor break down in the stomach into harmless constituent chemicals. Because neither BST nor insulin-like growth factor has any adverse health effect detected after a decade of testing, even the American Academy of Pediatrics calls milk from BST-treated cows safe. Embracing fat in large amounts while fearing BST in tiny amounts is not even close to rational, yet is in keeping with contemporary environmental orthodoxy.

Given that humans have had long-term exposure to natural BST, if anything about BST is dangerous the human "germline" of DNA would by now have had an opportunity to mutate in the direction of resistance. On the other hand, initial studies of hormones have not always turned up what later seem clear problems. The side effects of the original high-dose birth control pills, based on hormones, are an obvious example. So unusual caution about products like BST is well justified. But the cause of caution should have nothing to do with engineered versus natural, as the public debate is now phrased. The cause should be the question of good versus bad. Suppose further studies do show that ingested BST engages some health risk. In that case genetic engineers may someday be assigned the task of removing the natural BST coding from the natural cow DNA germline. The fact that BST was first found in milk naturally would not constitute a defense. Bad is bad, and naturally occurring bad substances ought to be vanquished just as bad synthetic substances ought to be.

What something *is*, is a far more important question than how it was made. In deciding whether to eat a mushroom we don't care one whit about the evolutionary history of its phylum, we care only about whether what is in those little stumps is nutritive or poisonous—what the mushroom is. Environmental standards based on what is natural may work occasionally, but in the main will be as futile as trying to figure out the Correct Reality for any given ecosphere. For instance when forest preserves or wildlife refuges are declared, the typical tactic is to take the area's existing border and guard it against change. Yet in nature the boundary zones of habitats move constantly in response to small changes in the climate, species competitions, and surely other factors of which people are presently unaware. Enforcing a boundary around a preserve may be a good idea, but it is an entirely artificial idea, contravening nature. So do it because it's good, not because it's natural. Only standards based on what is good or bad will have universal applicability to environmental decision-making.

Free of Preservatives, and of Values

Good and bad—what could be more artificial, more distressingly human judgments? Once values are injected into a system two worrisome things happen. First, wrong values may be chosen. Second, whatever happens no longer just happens. The outcome is the responsibility of genus *Homo*. When we think like nature the first failing, wrong values, worries us considerably. The second, accountability, is splendid news. From nature's perspective it is about time somebody took responsibility for the condition of the world.

This is another area where the human and natural perspectives are reversed. Nature would be likely to desire that there at last exist accountability for outcomes; ecological dogma is deeply disturbed by the idea that the accountability would rest with people. Some environmental thinkers concede that most human actions differ only in scale, not in principle, from those found in nature. Yes, they might allow, reservoirs created by a hydroelectric dam may vary only slightly from natural lakes, and such reservoirs may brim with life. But human environmental interventions come about because someone decides that a lake ecology is a better use of a particular chunk of land than a riverine ecology. Nature, this line of thinking continues, never imposes any judgment. It simply responds to deterministic physics in a value-neutral way. Any human attempt to impose judgments on the ecology is a heterodoxy.

Reasoning of this sort can lead to paradoxes. Sometimes the same commentators who wish nature viewed as possessing consecrated rights simultaneously want the core of nature to be free of values, hostile to the evolution of thought. Nature is seen as a hallowed entity far more deserving than humankind and yet utterly bereft of feelings, priorities, and aspirations. Nature is going nowhere for no purpose yet has an inviolable nonnegotiable right to be left alone forever.

These sorts of mutually contradictory thoughts can be found below the surface of most contemporary environmental discourse. Such contradictions arise partly because lovers of nature have been unable to come to terms with the cruelties found there. Daily in nature living things die by the millions through violence. Starvation is a standard means of population control; creatures ill or injured have no hope of release from suffering; whole species seem to arise to be chased and swallowed. This portrait does not sync with the natural world found on environmental fund-raising calendars: calico sunsets, gracefully paddling swans, mother animals tenderly caring for cubs.

In nature swans do paddle and mother animals do cuddle cubs. But many of those mother creatures have fangs and claws they would employ without an instant's hesitation to rip open the carotid artery of the offspring of some other animal, feeling no remorse as that other mother's cute little cub dies squealing in pain and terror. Rather than attempt to reconcile the nature of grandeur with the nature in which creatures kill, many environmentalists simply embrace contradictory views of the subject.

The two realities can be reconciled—we'll try to do so in a moment. But to most environmental thinkers any attempt at reconciliation is considered bad for business, in the same manner that religious organizations would just as soon steer the conversation away from the silence of God. And so the matter of how nature can be at once consecrated and cruel often is dismissed by environmentalists as some sort of unfair trick question. Merely asking about values in nature displays a hopeless anthropocentric bias, environmentalists may assert by way of changing the subject. It may not be pretty to watch wolves maul Bambi but nature, some environmentalists will say, makes no judgments. Therefore humankind should make no judgments about nature.

Reasoning that "wolves must eat, therefore make no judgments about whether they are merciful to deer" is fallacious. We might as well say "people must have energy to cook food to avoid trichinosis, therefore make no judgments about that plume of noxious gases rising from the power plant." Judgments about values are exactly what both nature and human society need more of, in order to combat the bad and preserve the good.

Make-no-judgments thinking about nature is sufficiently widespread that it is among those rare notions shared by thinkers of the left and right. From the left John Livingston, a York University professor and author of *A Natural History of Human Arrogance,* has written, "In speaking of ethics in a nonhuman context, we are jabbering into a void. Nature does not need ethics; there is no one to hear." From the right Richard Posner, a federal judge and prominent legal scholar, writes approvingly, "The majority of educated Americans believe that nature is the amoral scene of Darwinian struggle." To the left envisioning nature as a "void" is a device for evading loaded questions about values. To the right envisioning nature as an "amoral scene" is a device to excuse human excess; better to subjugate such a brutal landscape.

A significant problem with value-free thinking is that if no one can say what is good or bad, meaning in life becomes elusive. One finds philosophy on a Teflon-coated slope leading downward. Once the natural world is conceptualized as bereft of meaning, the entire span of the universe can be made to seem hollow with surprising ease. Steven Weinberg, a Nobel Prize physicist, wrote a popular book in 1977 about the creation of the cosmos, *The First Three Minutes.* In his final paragraph Weinberg concluded, "The more the universe seems comprehensible, the more it seems pointless." This is the perfect distillation of modern liberal thought on meaning in nature.[3]

The Convenience of Pointlessness

To a point fear of values is sensible. Values may be wrong, wrong values may become entrenched in culture, and entrenched wrong cultural values can go haywire in horrible ways. But at some level the fear of values becomes a handy excuse for occupying a comfortably hypocritical role in society. In the contemporary United States and Europe, some of the most strident environmental bravado emanates from the favored few—stage and screen celebrities, lawyers, physicians, network television anchors—people whose lives hardly represent an ethic of modest consumption.

Bernard Weinraub of the *New York Times* recounted in delightful fashion a 1991 Hollywood environmental awards dinner at which Robert Redford, Jane Fonda, the pop singer Sting, and others arrived in stretch limousines to applaud themselves for listening to unctuous speeches about how SOMEBODY ELSE is ruining the environment. "There wasn't a car pool in sight," Weinraub reported. Of the gas guzzler in which he arrived the actor Ted Dansen, who has promoted his career by testifying before Congress about how deeply troubled he is that OTHER PEOPLE don't protect the environment, told Weinraub, "I tried to find a car that got thirty miles per gallon, but just couldn't." There are of course dozens of models that do as well or better, but none of them self-propelled phallic symbols. The moment of absurdity for this sort of sanctimony was reached at the Earth Summit in Rio, when the actress Shirley MacLaine proclaimed at a dinner that she was "considering" renouncing material possessions.

Of course celebrities are famous for hypocrisy; it is practically a guild requirement. And of course only a few people live at the Hollywood level of material narcissism. But a substantial number of people in the industrial world live at the level of affluence, and in recent years it has become not uncommon for the same sorts of well-to-do Americans and Western Europeans who declaim that horrifying environmental abuse is destroying the planet to consume, themselves, more resources than whole villages of the developing world. For instance, annual per capita energy consumption in the United States is seven times that of Mexico and 33 times that of India. Per capita meat consumption in the U.S. is 58 percent higher than in Brazil and 88 percent higher than in Egypt. Per capita auto ownership in the U.S. is 3.5 times higher than in Japan and 74 times higher than in Cameroon. This book supposes that advanced economies can find an equilibrium between environmental protection and high resource consumption. Yet most affluent environmental pessimists of the Western world profess to believe no such balance can exist. They profess to believe high resource consumption inherently awful, while continuing merrily along that track.

This is where the assumption of a pointless, value-free natural world becomes convenient. A subconscious reason many celebrities and opinion makers in the Western countries have a fondness for instant doomsday thinking is that they would just as soon life be seen as beyond redemption. In a pointless world the favored few might as well go ahead and enjoy. Opposing propositions—such as that every instance of material deprivation is an outrage—rapidly lead to the conclusion that the riches of the world are not equitably divided. This is an item the favored of the affluent nations, even the liberal classes, do Not Not Not wish to discuss.

The Spectacular Exception of the Tiger

Here is as good a place as any to raise the Gaia metaphor, first advanced during the 1970s by the biologists James Lovelock and Lynn Margulis. The notion has two central elements, one widely discussed in the popular press, one rarely addressed.

The widely discussed idea is that the biosphere of Earth behaves as if it were a single organism. Lovelock and Margulis often are misrepresented as thinking the biosphere actually is an organism. What they say is that the biosphere behaves *as if* it were an organism, in the same way that when Newton described the mathematics of celestial motion, he said planets move around the sun *as if* bound by some invisible force.[4]

Nature behaves as if a single organism in many ways. Life adapts the environment to its liking by oxygenation. Plants help regulate climate by influencing the rate at which carbon dioxide is added to and subtracted from the air. Microbes and worms break rocks into soil where plants grow and are eaten by animals; the animals die and are decomposed for food by microbes and worms. Birds are attracted to the fruiting bodies of plants. The fruits—designed to nourish the birds, not the plants, in order to draw customers—contain seeds birds cannot digest. Birds eat, fly off, and later excrete the undigested seeds to take root. Thus does the plant distribute itself on the landscape. Bird and plant behave as if they were engaged in a single enterprise.

The second, overlooked element of the Gaia metaphor flows from the bird-plant example. It holds that symbiosis, not competition, is the dominant interaction system of the environment.

Symbiosis has a limited definition in popular understanding, suggesting those statistically rare arrangements in which two life-forms are formally linked to each other, such as the tickbirds that perch on the backs of rhinoceroses, eating parasites for their nutrition and thereby protecting the host from disease. But to Lovelock and Margulis, symbiosis is not the exception to the rule. It's the rule.

Margulis's major contribution to biology is something called the "serial endosymbiosis theory," which holds that most cells did not develop out of cutthroat competition with other cells but rather from cooperation in primitive microbial communities. Components such as the mitochondria of mammal cells (the parts that transform carbohydrates to biological energy) were once autonomous in the microbial community, Margulis believes, but gradually joined forces with other cells to form the complex structures that exist today. Living close together, devoting resources to mutual gain rather than attacks on neighbors, processing each other's wastes, the cells of prehistory prospered.

This lesson can be expanded into a larger premise about the environment. Biological cooperation, Lovelock and Margulis believe, is far more common than warfare. Predator species are the minority. Most species find evolutionary success by expanding into safe niches that complement rather than challenge other life-forms. Most plants, for example, don't try to evolve ways to wither the trees that block their access to sunlight; they try to find ways to live in the shadows of trees, making use of tree by-products. Most animals don't try to find ways to kill off the predators that threaten them; they try to find life-cycle patterns that avoid predators. Even most predators do not attempt to savage the natural world around them. Rarely do they slay more than necessary for their own survival.

Suppose that symbiosis, not "amoral" competition, is in fact the governing principle of the natural world. We human beings observe the spectacular exception of the tiger that stalks the antelope, falsely presume this to be the way of all flesh, and emulate the tiger in everything from personal relationships to statecraft. We falsely believe nature the scene of a merciless struggle of killed or be killed, when in fact if we would only pay heed to the least of the creatures at our feet, we would see that nature is setting an important example for humankind: that cooperation pays.

Nature further shows us that the meek do inherit. Cooperative species are far more numerous than combative species and usually have larger populations, for instance deer greatly outnumber wolves. The numerical success of nature's meek is true in the present and appears to have been true throughout the past. For every one animal that lives by predation there are a thousand that live cooperative lives, attacking no one and avoiding confrontations. If only humanity could do half as well.

As it pertains to symbiosis the Gaia metaphor would amend Darwin, at least as he is commonly understood. In the Gaian view most living things pursue mutual goals of expanding the living sphere and overcoming the natural drawbacks of nature. The natural world is not a war of all against all, with the weak cruelly swept away, as is typical in depictions of Darwinian mechanics. Plants and animals do kill each other and do fall extinct; bad things happen to good creatures. But the bad outcomes result from imperfections of life, not from any drumbeat of death at the center of the system.

"Occasional attempts are made to derive social norms from nature so construed, but they are not likely to succeed," Judge Posner has written. Under the standard apprehension of Darwinism, Posner is correct: Every species is trying to drive every other species to extinction, making human social institutions positively chivalrous by comparison. No useful lesson could be derived from such a system. But what if this way of viewing nature is fundamentally wrong?

How Clarence Thomas Confused Environmental Debate

In 1991 there was extended controversy regarding the nomination of the appeals judge Clarence Thomas to the Supreme Court. Whether Thomas was a sage choice is not a subject for this book, but one aspect of his nomination bears closely on the topic at hand. In his writings, Thomas had declared the highest human aspirations may be obtained from the realization of "natural law." For this belief Thomas was treated by pundits as some member of a crank secret society, like the Moose Lodge. Hardly anyone in the United States seemed to know what natural law was. Those who did recognize the words seemed to view them as an antiquated concept from the days when people believed in alchemy and phlogiston. The notion that natural-law thinking would seem to the enlightened classes of today a quaint eccentricity would have shocked the enlightened classes of two centuries past: for in the late eighteenth century, natural law was considered the most progressive of philosophical concepts. How natural-law thinking came to be, fell into discredit, and will soon be revived is a key to the subtext of current ecological affairs.

Most of the American Founding Fathers, along with most of the great thinkers of the European Enlightenment, such as Beccaria, Hume, Kant, Rousseau, Smith, and Voltaire, subscribed to some aspect of natural law philosophy, the manifesto of which is contained in a few words that are among the most beneficial in world history: *We hold these truths to be self-evident.*

Essential to natural law is the notion of self-evidence: that some truths arise from nature and require no proof beyond declaration. Ernest contemplation of the state of nature was thought by Thomas Jefferson and others to lead any open-minded person to the principles of democracy: that people should be free, as are the denizens of the wild; that basic rights are inalienable, conveyed by the state of nature itself; that rulers must obtain the consent of the governed, as social animals appear to "choose" leaders; that property and happiness ought to be available to anyone, as they seem available to all in nature.

Natural law was popular during the Enlightenment partly because the religious convictions of the leading rationalist minds turned on the concept of deism. Deism holds that God is not absent from the Earth but manifest in the glory of nature. Thus the study of nature is both the proof of God and the path to God. Deists were suspicious of claims of direct contact with God or of miracles, because revelations are not subject to rational confirmation. Nature, on the other hand, is everywhere and undeniable. No one can doubt that nature exists and is majestic beyond human powers of understanding. If the study of nature shows the natural world contains wisdom of an order higher than known to humankind, there to the deists would reside tangible proof of the divine.

Do not think this is an historical footnote. This background bears on the present-day arguments concerning species protection, climate change, and a host of other issues. The social critic Garry Wills devoted an exceptional book, *Under God,* to his contention that current Western politics cannot be understood except in light of long-term trends in religious belief—beliefs that to the eternal consternation of the chattering classes underlie the value systems of most citizens of Western nations. Wills protests that most modern intellectuals and journalists write about Western politics as if religion was at best a curiosity. This, Wills said, guarantees faulty understanding of contemporary politics. His premise applies to contemporary environmentalism as well. Environmental debates have a much stronger religious aspect than most participants like to let on.

The eighteenth-century deists believed that in the state of nature, living things behaved nobly; therefore human society should become as much like nature as possible. Such views were considered quite advanced at the time, standing in apposition to the conventional view of nature, that pronounced by Thomas Hobbes in the mid-seventeenth-century work *Leviathan,* named for the shadowy beast about which God warns humanity at the end of the book of Job.

Hobbes was that lighthearted fellow who pronounced existence "nasty, brutish and short." To Hobbes, the monstrous Leviathan was a metaphor for the natural condition. The normal condition of what is now called the environment, Hobbes asserted, was fratricidal war of all against all. Men and women should submit to civil governments, however repressive, to escape the universal violence of nature. Hobbes did his writing toward the end of the Thirty Years' War, a conflict demented even by the grim standards of human combat. Nevertheless Hobbes believed people were better off slaughtering each other under the banners of Gustavus or Maximilian than they would be in the unspeakably backward state of nature.

Deists and natural-law thinkers strove to overturn this joyless assessment, partly because Hobbes's view was used to rationalize the divine rights of kings. Kings may sometimes be depraved, Hobbes allowed, but better to bow down in dignity before an enfeebled monarch than howl in the jungle like an animal. Later Ronald Reagan, as president, would refer to "the law of the jungle" awaiting society if production and order were not sustained. Reagan's was very much a Hobbesian view.

In contrast, natural-law thinkers believed humankind would enjoy a superior existence if society were modeled on the jungle—or perhaps, the pasture. Social institutions must be deeply corrupt, natural law argued, because only a depth of corruption could impel people to behave in defiance of their naturally good instincts. The deists further rejected most trappings of formal churches, holding them as insidious as monarchy. Jefferson, for example, wrote worshipfully of Jesus. But Jefferson opposed organized religion so openly he was dogged throughout his presidential campaigns by accusations of atheism.

Deists and natural-law thinkers believed the more that was known about nature, the more women and men would find evidence of a guiding hand. Deists were ardently proscience, convinced rational inquiry would uncover the rules by which God administers the firmament. In the quest for divine law, rational minds would find many self-evident truths; these truths, the deists felt sure, would be progressive and liberating. Eventually humanity would construct a civil order patterned on the inherent goodness of nature. In that order social repression and general war, ills never observed in nature, would at last be cast aside.

How Nature Switched from Blissful to Awful

Instead the course of nineteenth-century science established the reverse of what the deists anticipated. The geologist Charles Lyell seemed to show natural forces were not guided by higher powers but merely blundering along, goin' nowhere. Darwin seemed to show nature a heartless realm where the most gentle creatures could be rendered extinct without a second thought. After Lyell and Darwin, nature seemed again a brutal void. All species were continuously trying to render all others extinct. The very continents were mindlessly slamming each into the next. Attrition in the war of all against all was even worse than Hobbes dared guess.

Findings of nineteenth-century science caused sophisticated thinkers to retreat in consternation from natural law. Some intellectuals thanked their stars that liberty by argument from nature, an idea that suddenly seemed like a flight of fancy, had been cemented into the U.S. Constitution before it could be exposed by the very rational inquiry on which the deists had pinned their hopes. By the turn of the twentieth century, benevolent natural-law thinking had been supplanted by social Darwinism, which argued that life's losers deserved to lose, just as the losers of nature deserved their fates.

This background sets the stage for contemporary environmentalism. By the beginning of the modern ecology movement, deism and similar optimistic notions about nature had been discarded. No longer seen as benefiting from any guiding hand, the living world was conceptualized as weak, vulnerable, fragile. If nature was no more than random permutations of deterministic chance, soulless and exposed, how could the environment resist an onslaught from man?

Today the intellectual prejudice against natural-law and deist thinking is sufficiently entrenched that so far as I know, nobody has pointed out a far-reaching implication of Lovelock's and Margulis's work: If cooperation, not competition, is the driving force of biology, then the warm and welcome premises of natural law and deism may turn out right after all. Perhaps nature is a moral realm, operating on principles that have progressive implications for human society. Perhaps nature creates wisdom as well as amino acids. Perhaps nature has family values.

Does Nature Have a God?

RECENTLY IT HAS BECOME AN OFT-HEARD VIEW THAT ENVI-ronmentalism is a new religion. Watermarks of organized faith are present: transcendentalism, claims of revelation, dogma. On the positive side, like religion environmentalism demands of its adherents a high behavioral standard. On the negative side, like religion environmentalism sees its believers as sanctified and chosen, others coarse and damned. The environmental faux-faith is expressly fundamentalist. Frederick Turner, a professor of history at the University of Texas, has suggested that if you take the creeds of traditional monotheist beliefs, cross out *God* and insert *the Earth,* no further changes are necessary to create a new catechism.

Suppose we call the new denomination Earthianity. Here is its founding mythos. Women and men are born in a fallen state, as their ancestors committed transgressions against nature. The Earth, a benevolent creator, once offered unlimited milk and honey in a perfect Garden. Flushed with self-importance, men and women thought they could improve on creation by altering the Garden and to that end grasped for forbidden knowledge. Humanity became a curse upon the land. Now all humans live in a state of sin, defiling the Garden they were given to tend.

As punishment the Earth will send environmental collapse as the new Deluge. This apocalypse is due at any moment. Suffering will be universal; even the righteous will know misery. The Earth will exact the fullness of a great fury but even so take pity on humankind, stopping short of extinguishing the offender altogether. Those who have sought environmental enlightenment will be spared to continue the race. Their efforts will bring about an End of Days in which technology and science are swept away. Through this terrible destruction and self-denial, innocence will be regained. The human race will once again live as well-behaved children who never dare to question the Earth, their benefactor.

The most important shared emphasis between traditional religion and its new environmental variant is presumption of an original sin. In some interpretations of Christianity there is no ablution the individual can perform that washes away such sin. No matter how righteous a person becomes, no matter the sacrifices endured or services performed, she or he is Fallen at birth and remains Fallen through life. Similarly in some current interpretations of environmentalism, no matter how modestly humans might live, no matter how clean their machines might grow or how respectful of nature their governments may become, people dwell forever in a Fallen state of sin because their mere presence on the Earth has "ended nature." Only the coming environmental collapse can restore grace by wiping the slate clean.

Perhaps the strangest aspect of some interpretations of Christianity is the outright yearning for cataclysm. At services of what are generally called premillennial Christian denominations, one hears weirdly expectant talk that soon, very soon, Armageddon will occur. One of the best-selling books of publishing history, a "premil" tract called *The Late Great Planet Earth,* concerns how the author wishes Armageddon would hurry up and arrive. In a standard premillennial vision of the coming eschatology, holy fire rains on man's cities, all of which are accursed and wicked; the final battle between good and evil is staged; a handful of chosen survivors rebuild a world in which time ends and the Kingdom begins. The parallels between this sort of thought and the fringes of instant-doomsday yearning are obvious.

Premil fundamentalism is an extreme, of course. Most Christians do not look forward to Armageddon any more than most environmentalists look forward to global warming. But as there is a faction of every religion that harbors a yearning for horrifying turns of events (visited, of course, upon others), there is a faction of the environmental movement that feels the same way.

At its margins, Earthianity can be downright goofy. For instance, a faction of the environmental community advocates a return to animist attitudes. Nature should be "resacramentalized," in the awkward made-up verb now heard. The ecology journal *Annals of the Earth* reported a 1990 appearance by Kirkpatrick Sale at New York City's Church of Saint John the Divine, which is the Vatican of Earthianity, a church essentially dedicated to environmental ceremonies. (Al Gore once appeared there dressed in a priestly stole.) In his talk Sale complained that water was "no longer thought of as holy or sacrosanct," as it was under Aztec, Celtic, and Persian lore. "Water is even, I blush to say it, regarded as a commodity," he continued, assailing the "secularization of water." Sale told his audience that if water were once again deified, no one would dare propose such outrages as trading of water rights.

Thanks, I'd rather wash my pots in secular water. Among other things most environmental economists think market pricing is the best tool for reducing water waste in the western United States. Sentiments like Sale's indicate the extent to which converts to Earthianity, like converts to extreme versions of other religions, prefer to live in a dream world, assuming away the inconvenient verities of actual life.

Was "Dominion" a Favor?

Increasingly, environmental doctrine holds mainstream religion accountable for ecological decay. The book of Genesis, scripture to Judaism, Christianity, and Islam, states that humankind was granted "dominion" over the Earth, its creatures "delivered unto your hands." Environmental commentators show increasing distress regarding "dominion over the Earth," asserting this phrase demonstrates that the monotheist religions indoctrinate toward environmental abuse. Recently they have been joined by the Goddess theorists, who believe ancient religions began with a benign Earth-centered female panoply. To some Goddess theorists the dominion verses are an evidence of the collusion by which communal maternal religions were displaced by authoritarian faiths based on a single He.

Contentions about anthropocentric bias in the Bible, Torah, and Qur'an contain a degree of truth but are not fully persuasive. For instance the Bible, though sometimes harsh in reference to the Earth, and often harsher in reference to people, offers many admonitions regarding the sanctity of nature. Ecclesiastes summarizes the dance of the ages with these perfect words: "One generation passes away, and another generation comes, but the Earth abides forever. The sun also rises." In Genesis, Job, and elsewhere, God cautions men and women not to tamper with natural forces they do not understand.

Important organizations of the monotheistic faiths, such as the National Council of Churches in the United States and the World Council of Churches on the international scene, have since the 1970s usually cast their lots with environmental alarmism, the National Council for instance avowing the greenhouse effect ranks among the leading "spiritual" crises of our age. In 1993 the National Council, U.S. Catholic Conference, Evangelical Environmental Network, Jewish Life, and other organizations formed a National Religious Partnership for the Environment, which issued an appeal that declared, "The cause of environmental integrity must occupy a position of priority for people of faith." For Earth Day 1994 this partnership distributed to 53,000 churches and synagogues readings in which leaders were to intone such thoughts as "We are responsible for massive pollution of Earth, water and sky." Congregations were to respond, "We are killing the Earth, we are killing the waters, we are killing the skies." At my church, of the liberal Presbyterian U.S.A. denomination, we read responsively such thoughts from the packet as, "In the name of 'progress' and 'development' we have raped the countryside . . . until we have come to threaten life itself with extinction."

This hardly suggests organized religion is brainwashing its adherents to anthropocentric arrogance. If anything the brainwashing flows in the opposite direction, attempting to persuade congregations the environmental situation is much worse than the facts show. Nonfundamentalist denominations have in recent decades encountered considerable resistance from their flocks against the preaching of sin doctrines, as many baby boomers reject the notion of prostrating themselves before God. Prostrating before nature is in the current political milieu more acceptable. Anxious to keep the notion of inherent sin alive, church organizations may find transferring that guilt to environmental issues a useful stratagem.

Another objection to the dominion critique is that careful reading of Genesis suggests God assigned Adam and Eve "dominion" not for human grandeur but human discomposure. The comments God makes to Adam and Eve as they exit the Garden are taken by biblical scholars not as the passing out of entitlements but as censure. For example, God tells Eve that as punishment for biting the apple, "In pain shall you [women] bring forth children." What's going on here is a demotion of humankind, not the announcement of special privileges. As Adam and Eve leave, God gives them permission to kill cattle and fowl for food; apparently in the state of innocence, the first humans were vegetarians. Adam's and Eve's descendants are thus fated to centuries of backbreaking labor raising stock, rather than picking fruit from heaven-tended trees. God pronounces that henceforth "the fear and dread of you shall be in every beast," whereas in the Garden, all animals loved Adam and Eve and attended to their requirements.

Such a bitter send-off hardly seems designed to exalt humanity at the expense of nature. But then exalting humanity is not what the parable of the Fall is about. Thus what the dominion verses really suggest is that one of humankind's quests ought to be the renewal of harmonious relations with the planet, reestablishing a symbolic condition of the human childhood. There is no reason in principle at least why humankind cannot eventually fashion a world in which no beast fears any man or dreads any construct of technology.

Environmental Antireligion

The notion of Earthianity makes for an interesting semiotic plaything, but only a small segment of the environmental movement subscribes to this creed. In the main environmentalism is not a new religion: It is a new guise of antireligion.

Because most environmentalists are products of the liberal intellectual milieu, which conceptualizes a natural world in which outcomes have no meaning, most rarely invoke nature's soul, the dream of the Earth, or any such piety. Invocations of a sacramental nature come mainly from New Age types and from believers in "deep ecology," an amorphous faction that mixes laughable ideas with abstemious calls for ethical progress. (Some deep ecologists maintain that disease viruses have a right to life. Some also say humanity will never be happy on the Earth until it finds a nonmaterialist lifestyle, a proposition that seems to me eminently defensible.) To the environmental mainstream at the forefront of state and federal lobbying, nature is viewed mainly as a victim. Nature's rights are being trampled. We should protect those rights without making any judgment on how they will be used. Such thinking tacitly asserts that God cannot protect the rights of nature because God does not exist. If God did exist then how could the end of nature be tolerated? Since nature is older than humanity and enfolds far larger populations, in some ways injustices against the environment might seem to God more offensive than injustices visited upon people. So the Lord's apparent complicity in the ecological instant doomsday may be seen as yet another evidence that God does not exist.

This is not in the front of the minds of most environmentalists. But it is at the back; and if the back of the mind sometimes dominates the front, this sheds light on some of the reverse-religious fervor of contemporary environmentalism. Through the twentieth century a goal of intellectual liberalism has been to assert a final disproof of God. Perhaps this impulse is well-grounded: God may not exist. But the prevalence in liberal thought of the desire to disprove God colors environmental thinking toward bleakness. As Garry Wills has shown that U.S. politics cannot be understood without religion, ecological disputes cannot be understood without this factor either. And to anyone hoping for a final disproof of God, dismal environmental news is wonderfully satisfying.

In the realms of Western academia and letters, the standard sherry-hour view now holds that Darwin proved there was no discrete moment in which living things were lowered down to Earth by a sovereign; Freud proved that men and women are mired in infantile sexual compulsions no high-minded God would insert into the psyche; Einstein proved that God need not have been present at the creation of the cosmos. Twentieth-century political history adds another powerful disproof of God, with human suffering advanced to a fearful scale in sheer numbers. By the 1960s, theologians of the God-is-dead movement were proposing that God had passed to another plane of existence or in some other way been dissembled. Around that time contemporary environmental consciousness began. If it could be shown that forces as minor as the local municipal landfill send Earth careening toward destruction, surely another argument would be forged that the firmament is not administered by any providential plan.

Of course ideologies often exaggerate the gravity of whatever might advance their world views. In the postwar era the right has been guilty of such tactics more often than the left. Communists running the State Department, fluoride in the water, nuclear weakness—these are just a few of the doomsday notions that the right pushed with cheap theatrics. Thinkers of the right often tried to press home farfetched notions about these subjects with feigned urgency, knowing the desired advantage must be gained before the notions were discredited, as they were sure to be. Today the same feigned urgency is often displayed in environmental thought. Some environmental thinkers must have sensed early on that although ecological problems are real, most are open to ready solutions. For instance restraining pollution, mainly an engineering problem, is much easier than making advances in intractable fields such as racial discrimination or social equity. To derive the maximum gloom-producing potential from environmental alarms, it would be necessary that environmental calamity be promoted rapidly, before that inconvenient day when undooms were set in motion.

How soon is undoom coming? A decade ago I thought the onset of environmental recovery would occur during my lifetime. Now the rate of ecological progress in the developed world has accelerated to such a degree that I believe the discrediting of instant doomsday will happen by the turn of the century. Conventional wisdom will reverse: environmental protection will be seen not as a realm of disasters and decay but as the great success story of postwar government activism. Liberals will boast—and rightly—of having saved capitalism from itself by curbing environmentally destructive aspects of the market system and compelling corporations to become resource-efficient. Liberal thinkers who today go on about environmental gloom will become ecological happy-talkers, in the same way that conservatives of a decade ago, who drummed endlessly on the notion that the former Soviet Union was an evil empire, are now the primary advocates of foreign aid to the same land.

Though the coming outbreak of ecological optimism will reflect well on the achievements of Western liberalism, it may not be entirely to the liking of those who deserve the credit. Political and intellectual liberals will realize that by compelling industry to grow clean and resource-efficient, they have secured the prospects of capitalism into the next century. And the academic left will find God's prospects rebounding along with nature's. Whoops!

God and Nature Both Decline to Expire

One of the little surprises nature has in store is that God will survive the twentieth century, and not just in the sense that some people will continue to practice the religions of their birth regardless of what the evidence may show. God will survive, at least as a contingency, because increased knowledge of the natural world, coupled with recognition of the astonishing velocity of environmental recovery, will swing the pendulum back toward the sentiments of natural law and deism.

Often it is asserted that an ache in Western culture is the absence of connections between the typical person, lost in material pursuits, and the ancient rhythms of life. Rene Guenon, a French philosopher, said in the 1930s, "Sooner or later excessive material development will destroy the West if it does not seriously consider a return to the source." Guenon was correct. Yet the restoration he sought will be found not in walling off nature from genus *Homo* as environmental orthodoxy now proposes but in the realization that the two were together once and will be together again.

Soon nature will be seen not as fragile and corroded but as more robust than women and men ever dared guess. Nature will be seen not as a pile of chance permutations ready to collapse with the addition of a grain of sand but as a construct of sublime geometry. Nature will be seen not as an amoral realm of kill or be killed but as a paragon of constructive values, should we only stop to heed the smallest creatures that crawl at our feet.

New scientific findings about the resilience of the environment throughout natural history; about its preparation for the kinds of current abuses people today think unprecedented; new knowledge of the success of most ecological protection programs; and the establishment of environmentalism as a core political value; will all be aspects of a great triumph for nature. They will cause men and women to realize that the living world is as subtle and radiant as the natural-law thinkers once dreamed. This will renew people's faith in their abilities to bring about "impossible" advances of social progress, should they only turn their minds and hearts to the task.

Whether nature is wise owing to some higher Maker or whether its wisdom was self-generated by autonomous force does not matter here. Nature may or may not have a design; it unequivocally has a result. Nature may or may not have been vested at the outset with meaning. But if nature did not begin with meaning it can *acquire* meaning as it goes along. No matter what you may believe about the initial condition of the firmament, it is certain that nature has in some manner acquired qualities of glory and subtlety. By extension human life has glory and subtlety—is sacred, regardless of whether the origin of life was divine or spontaneous. It would be nice to think that meaning was present in the Big Bang or on the day Earth coalesced from the ethereal lint. But if meaning was lacking then, human beings can make it now.[1]

Recently I listened as a friend, a prominent Washington liberal who describes himself as both a cynic and atheist, related the sense of wonder he experienced watching ultrasound images of his first child developing in his wife's womb. If you've ever seen a fetal sonogram, you know the images themselves are hardly wondrous: just a bog of squiggly lines that might as well be radar weather maps of central Ohio. But the squiggles inspire reverence because they announce the approach of new consciousness.

My friend remarked on how even top obstetricians find confusing the data outflow from ultrasounds, fetal MRIs, and similar high-tech womb scanners: The process of creating a child from nothing more than two cells is so complicated the best human minds still barely grasp what's going on. Consider, I replied, that the wondrous process is entirely governed by a six-billion-point string of amino acid bases too tiny to read without an electron microscope.

My friend's cynicism wavered. He really wanted to believe nature a void, life a coincidence: He had been raised to believe that, taught it in one of the leading universities in the land. I pointed out to him that the bases aligned along the DNA strands forming his child may have been assembled with the help of a divine sovereign. Or they may across the eons have assembled themselves. In either case it is impossible to ponder what DNA does when it makes a new child or owl or otter and not conclude that those acids have been invested with *meaning*.

Life is gloried beyond the power of words to express; life is here; no matter how that happened, we are surrounded with magnificence. The debate over the existence of a God or Goddesses may not be settled for centuries, or ever. Regardless of that, the natural world from which life springs will soon renew its standing as a source of the kind of constructive inspiration for which our species longs. When the majesty of nature seemed to waver under the fallacy of the "fragile" environment, women and men were justified in wondering what might be left in which to believe. Once it is understood that the living world is undiminished and perhaps undiminishable, faith in nature can be restored. Perhaps after that faith is given new lease, faith in ourselves and in that which is larger than ourselves will be renewed as well.

Nature and Values

If nature is the product of celestial power—of a "divine watchmaker," in the metaphor of William Paley, an eighteenth-century deist and author of *Natural Theology*[2]—then it is incontestable that people should look to the living world of nature for guidance. Or if nature has created itself, then humanity has immediately before its eyes the fullest store of knowledge, logic, and ethical systematics known to our senses. Again we would be fools not to look to nature for guidance.

Whether terms like natural law and deism will make a comeback is impossible to say. The term I propose is "natural values." Recognition that natural values exist will be an intellectual breakthrough in several respects, not least of which that the concept has something to offend everyone: And traditionally, those notions that tweak every established point of view are the ones with staying power.

Natural values will displease the political right because it will show that the biosphere has inherent significance and deserves not just scattershot conservation but general legal protection of the type Aldo Leopold once proposed. Natural values will displease the political left because men and women will be forced to deal with not being contemptible perversions of nature after all. To some factions of the liberal world, that would be the ultimate guilt trip.

Anyone proclaiming that nature has values had better list them. Here they are:

- Cooperation is better than competition.
- The arrow points up. Setbacks occur but by and large creatures, ecologies, and people get better with the passage of time.
- All environmental mistakes are reversible, except extinction.
- The artificial and the natural were meant to be allies.
- No temporal arrangement, including any environment, is permanent. This may be sad but otherwise does not matter.
- Most change is good for living things.
- Whatever increases or protects life is good.
- All the physical objects of the universe combined are not as interesting or important as the lowliest living creature with the slightest glint of self-awareness.
- The longing of life is more powerful than all physical forces of the universe combined.
- Life has such power because life is sacred.
- Life is sacred because life has meaning.

Once it is understood that the old presumptions of natural law and deism were right, there will be a new dawning of hope for the human prospect. Women and men will see themselves not as lonely miscreants in a crumbling ecology of null purpose but as offspring of a system that is rational, pacific, and in for the long haul. Of a system that cares; that wants to help; that has taken eons preparing itself for this moment.

There was a time when sophisticated people thought the study of nature was the path to God. Today sophisticated people think nature a frail, meaningless void. Soon they will again believe.

And now, having praised nature, let's slam it.

THE CASE AGAINST NATURE 🌿

IN THE YEAR 1992 A GRAPHITE TUBE RUPTURED INSIDE A Chernobyl-type reactor vessel at the Leningradskaya nuclear plant near Saint Petersburg, releasing some radioactive gas. The leak measured about 0.2 roentgens immediately downwind of the plant, according to the International Atomic Energy Agency. This is about one-fifth the radiation of a chest X-ray. The accident was banner headline news internationally. Four months later the heads of state of the G-7 nations pledged $700 million in emergency aid to former Eastern bloc countries to improve reactor safety.

Also in 1992 a tsunami struck the Pacific coast of Nicaragua, killing an estimated 2,500 people. When the wave reached the Nicaraguan shoreline it was about 65 feet tall and possessed of enough energy to move 1,000 yards inland, obliterating everything in its path. The deaths caused were sudden and horrible. Many peasants must have died trying desperately to cling to their children as waters strong enough to shatter concrete ripped apart all shelter. In addition to the loss of human life the ecology at the impact area was essentially wiped clean. The tsunami merited a blip box in the news-update sections of newspapers. Later that year another tsunami hit Indonesia, killing an estimated 1,000 people and causing extensive environmental destruction. This event also made no impression on the world's consciousness.

There are clear reasons to worry about nuclear power plants, especially those of the ill-designed Chernobyl class. Sixteen of these plumber's nightmares continue to make power in the former Eastern bloc: Investments in their safe operation represent money well spent. It is also sad but indubitable that reactors proximate to white Europeans are of greater concern to Western leaders and editors than any force imperiling the brown masses of the developing world. But the disparity in reaction to these two categories of 1992 stories—an inconsequential artificial environmental event harming no one is widely viewed as a shocking horror, while natural environmental events killing thousands and leaving behind vast swaths of devastation are greeted with a collective ho-hum—reveals much about how human beings perceive the living world.

Today environmental problems caused by people are considered a maximum-priority concern, while environmental problems caused by nature are simply acts of God. This last is a curious phrase if ever there was one. It suggests that though God declines to intercede on Earth to prevent the sufferings and injustices of the world, the Maker does regularly act to hurl disasters at the innocent. Most people who use the figure of speech "act of God" do not, of course, believe that God wills the occurrence of tidal waves and similar calamities. They believe such things happen for no reason at all. In a limited sense, that will always be the best explanation. But somehow the popular understanding has come to hold that naturally occurring damage to the ecology does not count as an environmental problem: It's just something that happens. Only men and women cause environmental problems. Which events of the year 1992 were more likely to be troubling to nature, the gas leak at Saint Petersburg or the tsunamis at Nicaragua and Indonesia?

In order to highlight the transgressions of people, in contemporary environmental thought nature is depicted as a utopia. An occasional environmental slogan is "Back to Eden." This motto implies that if only humankind ceased its meddling the living world would revert to a previous condition of unlimited abundance and general bliss. Who's kidding who? The notion that nature absent man would be an Eden doubtless appeals to the fund-raising imperatives of environmental lobbies, and to modern humankind's inner need for self-opprobrium. But it is certain nature does not see itself as an Eden.

It is not inconsistent to assert that nature is learned and inspirational and also riven with faults. In a bureaucracy as monumental as the entire living world, failings are inevitable. People or institutions can be sublime at many levels yet flawed at others. Democracy is the best known form of government, but nobody pretends it does not have maddening faults. Wine is the most wonderful beverage; it's also full of calories and causes harm ranging from headaches to chronic degenerative illness. Shakespeare was a superb writer; he also penned plays and sonnets that fell to the ground with a loud clunk. And so on.

"Nature does not know best," said Rene Dubos, a pioneer of modern environmental thinking. Dubos, who died in 1982, was an advocate of wetlands conservation and originated the slogan "Think globally, act locally." He composed many works fiercely critical of human ecological abuses. But Dubos was also critical of nature. Dubos thought many natural systems wasteful or plagued by shortcomings. For example, he thought species such as deer that exhibit cycles of overpopulation and die-off demonstrate nature can be just as immoderate as humanity. Dubos felt veneration of nature a foolhardy distraction.

Because Dubos was critical of nature, today many in the environmental movement speak of him as having been some kind of double agent. A custom is developing in which saints of environmentalism are reclassified as demons if they criticize nature or fail to be adequately frenetic in condemnation of people. James Lovelock, once the leading science figure to environmentalists, became persona non grata when he began to say the biosphere was so resilient not even nuclear war could destroy it. The toxicologist Bruce Ames, a hero to environmentalists in the 1970s when he proved the fire retardant Tris carcinogenic, is now intensely detested because his last 20 years of research convinced him naturally occurring food-chain substances are more dangerous than additives or pesticide residues. Richard Doll, a British epidemiologist who established the link between cigarette smoking and lung cancer, was for a time an angelic figure to environmentalists. Now he's Lucifer incarnate, because his last two decades of research weigh against the notion that synthetic toxics in the environment are a leading cancer cause. Another former environmental hero whose name has been slipped down the memory hole is the oceanographer Roger Revelle, founder of modern greenhouse science. In his book *Earth in the Balance,* Vice President Al Gore cited Revelle as the great tutor who convinced him global warming was a threat of unspeakable urgency. But Revelle himself did not describe the greenhouse effect in the apocalyptic terms favored by Gore. Before his 1991 death, Revelle cautioned against greenhouse alarmism. Gore doesn't talk about Revelle any longer.

One ecological orthodoxy that has arisen in recent years is the notion that since human involvement with nature is invariably negative, the only constructive relationship people can establish regarding the biosphere is to leave it alone. There are times and places when people ought to leave nature alone: partly to preserve, partly to acknowledge our poor understanding of how the environment operates. A principle of wisdom holds: We don't know what we don't know. Not only is human understanding of the environment rudimentary but we don't yet know enough to guess where the worst gaps in our knowledge fall. Until such time as we do, people should interfere with the environment as little as possible.

But if people leave parts of the environment alone, we can be sure nature will not. Nature will keep changing, not in some pointless eternal vacillation but seeking refinement. Dubos believed that nature was engaged in a long-term undertaking of self-improvement and thought human beings might be able to assist nature. Before turning to the idea of people helping nature, let's review the case against the environment. It may be summarized in these words: People should not worry that they will destroy nature. It is more likely nature will destroy us.

Nature: Not Frolicsome

Green sentiment currently holds that nature ought to be revered because natural arrangements are metaphysically superior to their artificial counterparts. There are many reasons to love nature. This is not one of them.

Physically the natural world is magnificent compared to most human concoctions. But metaphysically? It is easy for humans to impute sanctity to the natural scheme, since we sit at the pinnacle of the food chain. No species preys on us, no organisms save diseases challenge us. But to those of Earth's creatures that live to be chased and eaten, it is doubtful the natural scheme suggests Eden. What does an antelope experience, dying in terror and agony as it is gored by a tiger—blissful oneness with the spheres? Nature may shrug at this, considering cruel death an inevitability of a biological system. Perhaps people should respect such an order. We should not offer it blind allegiance.

Nature may be a place of transcendence, but it is also a domain of danger. Danger may take the form of large-scale natural assaults such as asteroid strikes, ice ages, and eras of global volcanism. What might be called everyday natural badness can be as distressing. Consider a representative end of life under the natural scheme. Often in subarctic regions migrating caribou drown in large groups when they ford rivers that were safe to cross the year before but now are not, the water volumes and speed of wild rivers varying unpredictably. Should you think nature absent man is utopia, try to imagine drowning in a roaring subarctic river. You are seized with panic as icy water slops into your lungs. You flail helplessly, the world falling away under your feet. This is not some peaceful end to a gentle, contented cycle of birth and renewal. This is a horror.

As the animal expert Vicky Hearne has written, "The wild is not all that frolicsome a location." Hearne has noted that among wild lion cubs of Africa, 75 percent die before reaching their second year of life. This high level of mortality is what happens to the fiercest of predators—imagine what happens lower on the food chain. A statistic of significance to the debate on human population has been cited by the zoologist Ernest Mayr: In the wild on average only two of any mammal's offspring ever themselves reproduce. To people, this figure may suggest that population stability attained by replacement fertility rates would be in keeping with balancing mechanisms of nature. To animals that may bear dozens of offspring of which but two exist long enough to reproduce, this figure suggests the extreme cruelty of the natural world. Next time you coo over a litter of domesticated puppies whose secure lives are assured, reflect that if the litter were born in the cold and hungry wild, nearly all the pups would be dead in fairly short order.

Environmentalism has not come to terms with the inherent horribleness of many natural structures, considering recognition of this point to be poor public relations. For instance the Norwegian philosopher Arne Naess, inventor of the phrase "deep ecology," in his 1989 book *Ecology, Community and Lifestyle* danced around the fact that much of the natural order is based on violent death. "The ecological viewpoint presupposes acceptance of the fact that big fish eat small," Naess wrote. Deep ecologists are supposed to believe that in moral value human beings are the same as animals: no better or worse, just another creature. So if it's okay for animals to kill each other is it okay for people to kill each other? Naess waffles: "It is against my intuition of unity to say 'I can kill you because I am more valuable,' but not against that intuition to say 'I will kill you because I am hungry.' " Then would Naess object if a poor man who was hungry killed Naess to take his wallet? Because orthodox environmentalists feel they must pretend that there is nothing—not the slightest little thing—wrong with nature, they can easily be trapped, as Naess trapped himself, into declaring that it's okey-dokey to kill to eat.

Deep ecology can go even further than that, at its extreme asserting people are no more valuable than rocks. For a time after its founding in the mid-1960s the American wing of the deep ecology movement, led by Bill Sessions, a professor at Humboldt State University in northern California, said it advocated "biocentrism," or the importance of life above technology. Believe it or not the term biocentrism was attacked in politically correct ecological writing, as it dares imply that living things are more important than inanimate objects. Today some deep ecologists say they endorse "ecocentrism," which purports to grant rocks and plains the same ethical significance as living things. "Let the river live!" is a phrase now found in some deep ecology tracts.

So it's not only fine for a tiger to gore an antelope and a hungry robber to gun down a passerby, it's fine for all these people and animals to drown in a river since the river is only expressing its right to flow. If the question of whether it is bad to be killed confounds environmental philosophers, small wonder they have such trouble coming to grips with the practical flaws in nature.

Nature as Pollution Factory

Now let's expand the indictment against the environment. Nature makes pollutants, poisons, and suffering on a scale so far unapproached by men and women except during periods of warfare.

For example if the greenhouse gas carbon dioxide is considered a pollutant, as environmentalists say it should be, then nature emits an estimated 200 billion tons of this pollutant annually, versus a human-caused emission total of about seven billion tons per year. Nature makes huge quantities of the precursor chemicals for acid rain. The 1991 eruption of Mount Pinatubo alone released an estimated 60 percent more sulfur dioxide, the primary cause of acid rain, than all United States emissions that year. Lesser eruptions, and the many volcanos that release gases without erupting, add to annual natural output of acid-rain chemicals. Natural processes, mainly the photochemistry of tree leaves, place into the air volumes of volatile organic chemicals, the same class of substances that evaporate from petroleum and help form smog. Though Ronald Reagan was wrong to say that trees cause more air pollution than cars, his concept was not entirely fallacious. Pristine forest areas often exhibit palls of natural smog caused by tree emissions interacting with sunlight. Thomas Jefferson's beloved Blue Ridge Mountains are so named because even in preindustrial times they often were shrouded in a bluish haze.

Nature generates toxins, venoms, carcinogens, and other objectionable substances in far larger quantities than do people, even considering the daunting output of man's petrochemical complexes. Current research is demonstrating that a significant percentage of plants make dangerous compounds for defense against environmental competitors; and that since the living quantity of plants is substantially greater than that of fauna, plants may be the principal toxin factories of the world. Recently an important topic of public discourse has been the need to preserve rainforests, in part so that drug companies can prospect for pharmaceuticals. Rainforest preservation is a good idea. But why do pharmaceutical companies find rainforest plants of such interest? Because they are rich in natural toxins that kill living cells—what many medications, especially cancer drugs, are asked to do.

In recent years researchers have begun to understand that over eons of evolutionary time, plants have acquired sophisticated chemical defenses against being munched by animals and insects, including in some cases active "immune responses" that dispense toxins when competitors arrive. For instance researchers have found that when some pines are attacked by mountain pine beetles, the trees direct to the affected bark chemicals called terpenes that make pine beetles ill. Potatoes and tomatoes make toxins that interfere with the digestive systems of their perennial competitors, the caterpillar. When the coyote tobacco plant is nibbled on, its "immune system" directs an increase in nicotine, a powerful toxin, to the affected leaves.

The discovery that plants manufacture far more toxins than once assumed has led toxicologists such as Ames and Lois Gold, both of the University of California at Berkeley, to estimate that the typical American diet contains 10,000 times more naturally occurring carcinogens than those of the synthetic variety. Natural toxins comprise five to ten percent of most plants by dry weight, Ames and Gold think. Thus natural toxins are "by far the main source of toxic chemicals ingested by humans," Ames says.

People and animals must in turn have evolved resistance to natural carcinogens or their ancestors would have keeled over from consuming plants long ago. If people and animals carry some natural resistance to toxins, this hardly means consuming chemicals has no cost, any more than people who have natural resistance to certain diseases can be assured they will never get sick. But here the finger of badness points at nature more than people. For example, it may eventually be shown that natural chemicals are a leading cause of cancer. After all, if natural toxins outnumber the synthetic variety 10,000 to one in the typical diet, then nature is a more likely cancer cause than synthetics. In turn, if natural carcinogens in foodstuffs are an important cancer cause, the way to get rid of them would be through genetic engineering, a technology environmentalists oppose.

Next: Which would you say causes more deaths per year, industrial accidents or natural disasters? The answer is nature by a substantial margin. Theodore Glickman, Dominic Golding, and Emily Silverman, researchers at Resources for the Future, a Washington, D.C., think tank, compared significant natural disasters to significant industrial deaths for the postwar period. The study concentrated on immediate deaths, not long-term health degradation. The authors found that on average natural badness kills 55,786 people per year worldwide, while industrial accidents kill 356 people annually. Natural badness took forms such as these: 700,000 dead in a 1976 earthquake in China; perhaps 500,000 dead in a 1970 cyclone in Bangladesh; another 110,000 dead in a 1948 earthquake in the former Soviet Union; another 57,000 dead in a 1949 flood in China; at least 100,000 dead in a 1991 cyclone in Bangladesh. Industrial accidents through this same period often have been frightful, taking forms such as the death of about 4,100 innocents at Bhopal in 1984 or the loss of an estimated 2,700 lives in a 1982 fuel-truck explosion in a mountain tunnel in Afghanistan. All told, nature has consistently outdone man in generation of noncombat misfortune.

Environmental orthodoxy responds to figures like the ones above by saying that if the human population were lower there would be fewer deaths in natural disasters; that far too many people live in dangerous places like the coastal plain of Bangladesh, where the likelihood of natural badness from cyclones is high, or in the fault zone of California, where the natural threat of earthquakes is high. Such points contain measures of truth but are deceptive, skipping over the effects of natural disasters on the nonhuman ecology—effects that would be awful whether people existed or not. During cyclones and similar natural badness there is tremendous loss of plant and animal life, plus destruction of the ecosphere generally. Environmentalists sometimes fudge this counterpoint by saying that the ecosphere usually recovers rapidly from catastrophic "acts of God." Usually that is the case. But if the environment routinely recovers from cyclones and tidal waves, events substantially more destructive than human action, why is it that we are in panic mode regarding human ecological impacts? And if there were fewer people, fewer would die in any natural disaster. But if there were fewer snow leopards or sandhill cranes fewer of them would die at nature's hand as well. Has anyone ever heard an environmentalist argue that therefore there are too many animals?

Meanwhile the occupation of dangerous areas such as the coastal plain of Bangladesh usually occurs out of desperation on the part of the impoverished. That genus *Homo* has built a society in which many millions of the impoverished have no choice but to live in places vulnerable to disaster is an inculpation of human social institutions, but is not out of accord with the behavior patterns of nature. Countless species populate ecological niches where exposure to natural badness is above the norm. For instance, every plant and animal that lives near an active volcano is crazy from a detached point of view. Nature, being flawed, puts creatures in such places nonetheless.

Nature's Leading Defect: Disease

The comparison for natural versus manmade disasters does not include deaths from routine events such as traffic accidents and, more important, does not include wars. As many as 60 million people have died as a result of twentieth-century warfare, a much larger total than killed by natural disasters. But in turn, many more people have been killed by nature through diseases than have been killed by warfare. The World Health Organization estimates that each year about 33 million people die prematurely owing to disease. (This figure excludes deaths from degenerative illnesses at the end of a long life.) In the last decade alone roughly five times as many people have been killed by diseases than by all twentieth-century warfare. Disease is distressingly easy to overlook as an ecological issue. Yet it is the world's worst environmental problem by a wide margin.

A straightforward place to compare the badness of nature to the badness of people is disease from food. A wide range of foods carry naturally occurring salmonella, *Trichinella spiralis,* and other germs or parasites. Even in the contemporary United States, food poisoning is common: For instance in 1992, 20 Americans died after eating oysters containing a bacterium called *Vibrio vulnificus* that attacks the liver.[1] The federal Centers for Disease Control estimate that around 9,000 Americans die each year from natural food poisoning. By contrast, worst-case estimates for U.S. annual deaths from pesticide residues ingested in food run at a few thousand, with most estimates placing the figure much lower.

Social patterns such as crowding in cities or intravenous drug use may spread contagion or accelerate mutations that make pathogens virulent. Such factors mean men and women share some of the blame for the severity of diseases. But in the main blame for diseases must be laid squarely at nature's doorstep. Malaria, smallpox, measles, plague, influenza, meningitis, dysentery, and dozens of other illnesses arose from the natural scheme and have killed millions of human beings. Naturally occurring disease has killed many trillions of animals and plants, causing widespread deaths probably since life began.

AIDS, a disease for which people are partly responsible, is rightly considered a nightmare. How bad is AIDS compared to disease nightmares entirely natural in origin? So far AIDS has killed an estimated four million people worldwide, according to the International AIDS Program of the Harvard School of Public Health. Sorrowful as it is this figure pales in comparison to naturally driven disease events, for instance the global influenza pandemic of 1918 to 1919, which killed an estimated 25 million. Crowding in military barracks and refugee centers, malnutrition, and poor health care associated with World War I contributed to the virulence of the pandemic; but nature, not man, was its root cause. Ponder for a moment the magnitude of 25 million deaths. This is three times the present population of Sweden, all dead within a few months from one of nature's day-to-day operational flaws. The flu pandemic of 1918 and 1919 killed far more people than all human environment abuses combined through the course of history. Nevertheless in environmental orthodoxy people are fallen and evil; nature is uplifted and beneficent.

Some researchers have wondered whether diseases evolved to perform an ecological role of which genus *Homo* is not yet aware. It is possible there is something to this. Most likely, however, diseases are simply flaws in the natural system. The best evidence of the fault character of disease is that nature has devoted incredible energies to the mounting of defenses: immune systems, predators to the insects that transmit disease, disease-resisting life cycles.

Dubos spent his professional life studying disease pathology. A bacteriologist, his chief accomplishment was the discovery of gramicidin, which kills the gram-positive bacillus strains associated with strep throat and similar infections. Dubos thought that the fight against disease would be the first important place where humankind could repair a rend in the fabric of the natural world. It was this belief—that however they may stumble, women and men ought to tamper with the natural world toward constructive ends—that started Dubos down the path of being rejected by the modern environmental movement.

Nature: Self-Destructive

There is a final, centrally consequential way in which nature is structurally flawed: the matter of self-destruction.

Restricted to operating in a deterministic manner, nature has destroyed virtually everything it has made, with the exception of life itself. Fashioning new species and habitats, nature acts like a Renaissance artist, painting the most recent work over an older one already on the canvas. In nature's case this painting-over has happened countless times, with the previous works not recoverable by stripping away the subsequent. The knowledge that nature loses everything it gains—except life itself—is central to thinking like nature. From this knowledge several lines of speculation can arise.

One speculation is that species extinction in itself simply does not mean much. Ecorealists should consider the preservation of biodiversity a priority issue. But to understand the hard-edged as opposed to fuzzy arguments for preserving species, it is necessary to acknowledge the cold realities of nature. Present human misbehavior may be pushing some species toward extinction at an alarming pace, but people are only speeding up what was already written on the wind, since historically nearly all species have proven expendable. The full measure of the environment's toughness is how little it needs us, the spotted owl, the sea otter, or any particular creature.

Another speculation is that we're living on borrowed time. It is not reductionist to say that humanity evolved during a period in which circumstances were favorable for human evolution. For the past 14,000 years or so Earth's climate has been temperate, rainfall has been plentiful, volcanic activity has been low, no killer rocks have fallen, the ozone layer has been stout, and so far as is known no cosmic radiation storm front has moved through the solar system. Any of these conditions could change in the time it takes for a grain of sand to descend through nature's hourglass. Understanding that human proliferation was aided by favorable Earth conditions is a key to ecological caution. For instance, though it is unclear whether the greenhouse effect is increasing, governments ought to bear in mind that climate change appears the principal factor in most past extinctions. By tampering with the climate, people play with exactly that aspect of nature experience suggests most likely to do them in. Even if the odds of an artificially triggered climate emergency are low, prevention is amply justified.

Should the conditions that now favor humankind end, life will go on. Nature will simply raise up new creatures that thrive on murky greenhouse air or dine on compounds that human metabolisms find toxic. Nature might feel some sense of regret to see humanity pass. Ultimately all nature would care about is that life continues, allowing perhaps another chance that another thinking creature, more judicious, will rise and avoid man's mistakes.

That nature may destroy humankind may seem a droll jest to some readers, especially those persuaded by the current fashionable view that awesomely powerful human beings already have the living world in helpless retreat. But since 99 percent of past species have been rendered extinct by natural forces, it is hardly wild speculation to suppose that genus *Homo* will someday face the same fate. In 1993 J. Richard Gott, an astrophysicist at Princeton University, used something called the Copernican Principle to calculate the possible life span of genus *Homo*. Gott estimated humankind will walk the Earth for an additional 200,000 to eight million years, then fall extinct. Needless to say, the statistical means by which he reached this estimate involve a great deal of conjecture. But writing in the technical journal *Nature,* Gott pointed out the primary implication of his estimate: "It [is] a mistake to assume that we occupy a privileged position in the universe. . . . [The odds are that] we will indeed be like all other species on Earth," ticketed for eventual elimination by natural forces.

Lastly we may speculate that nature, having destroyed nearly everything it has made in the past save life itself, would be willing to surrender much of what exists if, in exchange, it received a more secure, less harsh environment. Even knowing some actions taken by people will be ill-advised, nature might be quite content to accept human meddling with the natural world in return for assistance in the expansion of life.

Of course today it is hard to think of many areas beyond disease control where men and women are more likely to aid nature than to damage it, because human understanding of the environment is rudimentary. Here are just a few entry-level issues on which ecologists are divided at this writing: Are there more plant and animal species alive now than in past eras, or fewer? Was there ozone depletion before CFCs? Would a warmer climate be wetter or drier? Are disruptions in weather-makers such as the El Nino currents an omen of coming climate change, or have such disruptions been happening since time immemorial and are only now being documented? Is smog caused mainly by volatile organics or mainly by nitrous oxides, two entirely different groups of compounds? Why are songbirds diminishing in the eastern United States when the eastern forests are expanding? Are frog species in decline worldwide because of human action or were frogs on the path to extinction before man appeared? And just how many species are there? Three million? Ten million? Thirty million? One hundred million? In 1992 *Scientific American* quoted Robert May, an Oxford University researcher, as saying, "Scientists know vastly more about, and spend vastly more time studying, the systematics of stars than the systematics of earthly organisms. They have as good a knowledge of the number of atoms in the universe, an unimaginable abstraction, as they do the number of species of plants and animals on Earth."

It may seem that a scientific establishment now able to perform such feats as counting the neutrinos released by supernova explosions thousands of light-years away—researchers did this in 1987—ought to be able to answer such basic questions as whether a warming climate would be wetter or drier. Yet in some respects, distant supernovas are easier to study than the local landfill. Understanding the biosphere of Earth may prove more challenging than understanding the far cosmos because the environment is a *living* system. That is deceptively easy to overlook. In astronomy, geology, physics, and other disciplines, natural forces are explicit, large-scale, and uniform across extended periods of time. In the biosphere change is continuous and often happens quickly, so that what a researcher studies today is not the same the following day and never will be the same again. Alexander Pope wrote: "All nature is but art unknown to thee, all chance, direction which thou canst not see." Science is only at the initial stages of attempting to discern the direction in what looks like the multiple chance movements of natural systems.

But how long will that state of affairs last? A few decades? A hundred years? Environmental research was not an important concern for the world's science community until roughly the 1970s. With the ecology now a scientific priority, human understanding of the biosphere will begin to progress. Within a span of time that may be no more than another grain through nature's hourglass, women and men may begin to grasp the inner rhythms of the natural world.

When we think like people we shudder at this prospect, imagining global-modification projects gone hideously wrong. That could happen. Most environmentalists say that increasing levels of human knowledge about the environment will not prevent repetitions of folly such as the Soviet irrigation fiasco at the Aral Sea. As the deep ecologist Christopher Manes phrased it in his book *Green Rage,* the notion that people can improve the natural world "chalk[s] up the blunders of human history to some grandiose mission not otherwise apparent to this author."

But when we think like nature, perhaps we would be enticed by the prospect of men and women becoming wise enough not only to stop harming the environment but also to begin helping it. Human intellect has countless faults, yet from nature's perspective intellect and its corollary, the ability to act by design, surely must be the most interesting environmental developments since the first animals 600 million years ago. If all environments are always fated to end then the old, purely spontaneous form of nature was always fated to end, too. To nature our young species may be making extraordinary progress—especially considering how very little of nature's most important resource, time, we have so far used up.

Moral Evolution

How people may someday modify nature in ways of which nature would approve will be the subject of the third section of this book. To close this first section, let's consider that in order for human knowledge someday to increase to the point at which constructive tampering with the the natural order becomes possible, nature must root for two entirely artificial developments. One is everyone's least favorite: technology. The other is everyone's least well developed: morality.

Nature may have values, which can be inherent and self-evident; but nature lacks morals, which are artificial systems requiring forethought. The tiger does not recognize such concepts as right or wrong; it kills by rote, feeling no compunction as it ends the life of the antelope. Tigers as a group would experience no moral doubt if they slaughtered enough antelopes to render that group extinct. Men and women have, at least, developed the spark of conscience that holds that such behavior is wrong.

That spark has yet to light any blaze of virtue. But that's today. By nature's way of reckoning the very notion of morality is brand-spanking-new: yesterday's mutation. Integrating into the natural scheme new concepts far less challenging conceptually than morality—concepts such as eyes, ears, warm blood, wings—required tens of millions of years. Morality has only been under development for a few thousand years.

Many women and men consider the promise of virtue discredited by centuries of injustice. But to nature's way of thinking the advance of morality may be stunningly rapid. To nature, morality is only a few millennia old and already almost kind-of sort-of working. For all the powerful criticisms contemporary environmental pessimists such as Thomas Berry, Herman Daly, Bill Devall, Annie Dillard, Paul Ehrlich, Al Gore, Oren Lyons, Bill McKibben, Carolyn Merchant, Jeremy Rifkin, and others make regarding humanity's abuse of the globe, I am constantly amazed they seem to care so little that the arrival of genus *Homo* has at least entered into the natural equation something never there before: the new, innovative and entirely artificial idea of morality—that sufferings and cruel death ought to be opposed.

By gaining access to technology, a form of interaction with the biosphere unavailable to other living things, people are the first creatures to broach the possibility of existing without killing, by rote or otherwise. Today we slaughter animals for food and our fellows for distressingly trivial reasons. But though the tiger cannot think its way out of needing to prey on the antelope, the person can think his or her way out of both reliance on other species for nutrients and materials (with a technical solution) and of persecution of his or her own for gain or politics (with a moral solution).

Sound like wishful thinking? Let's outline a possible technical alternative to drawing the sustenance of life from killing. Confounded by the requirement that biological creatures must consume biological substances, today even the most morally conscious human beings swallow foods whose production requires that animals experience brief, miserable lives in confinement then die horribly in automated abattoirs. Suppose that biological substances could instead be manufactured at the cellular level, without engaging the use of stock or fowl. If biological nutrients (and biological materials, such as leather) could be made without any involvement of animals, this would have no effect on the killing that occurs between animals in nature. But at least it would get human beings out of the killing cycle, an important step in the right direction. (How animal-free meat production might happen will be suggested in section three.)

Technology might someday help human beings escape the cycle of killing each other as well. One of nature's admirable values, reflecting the wisdom imaged by the deists, is that species do not slay their own. In nature lethal attacks among members of the same animal group are extremely rare: Some species fight over mates, but rarely to the death. No Earth creature save the human being methodically preys on its own.

Why don't species other than *Homo sapiens* kill their own? This does not just happen. A physical regulatory mechanism must be at work, one powerful enough even to restrain the primal urge to eat. So far as is known, animal behavior patterns—instinct—emanate from DNA. That suggests animals carry in their genes some code that enjoins them from attacking their like. Given that a goal of natural selection is to increase the survival prospects of genes related to the ones you carry, a DNA instruction that forbids attack against members of your own species—your genetic peer group—would be logical.

For some unknown reason, perhaps simply a flaw of nature, the code that prevents creatures from attacking their genetic peers seems absent from genus *Homo*. Suppose that code could be isolated from some other animal and inserted into the human germ line through genetic engineering. Some animal in the primate order may possess a no-kill gene code, perfected by nature, that will function or "express" when recombined to human DNA. Perhaps the mild-mannered, vegetarian mountain gorilla of Africa would be the place to begin searching for such a gene. Many things could go wrong with genetic engineering; there exist plentiful reasons to be cautious about this technology. But if there is an identifiable DNA sequence in animals that confers on them an instinct not to kill their own, and that sequence can be transferred to people, imagine the moral new age that might dawn.

Supervised Evolution

Regrettably, the above sentence employs the term "new age." Placing any New Age concept into favorable context may be a breach of intellectual protocol. But there is a point at which New Age notions and the revival of deism may conjoin, and the key to that possibility is Pierre Teilhard de Chardin.

Teilhard was a paleontologist, an adherent of Darwin, a spiritualist, and a Jesuit priest. He spent much of his life on archaeological digs in China, working on the team that found Peking Man, the first specimen of *Homo erectus*. When Teilhard began to insist that Darwin was right about evolutionary mechanics, he was barred from teaching or writing as a Jesuit. Among other things Teilhard found it impossible to reconcile original sin with physical evidence that humanity evolved over long periods. According to Catholic doctrine, original sin was acquired by Adam and Eve, progenitors who had no antecedents. If the fossil record shows instead that human life was not created de novo in a single act, Teilhard reasoned, then the Garden must be a parable and there cannot be original sin, at least in the way the Church describes that burden. This belief was not a recipe for career success in the Jesuit hierarchy.

Teilhard came to think that the purpose of human intellect was to serve as a "steward" over a coming phase of evolution. His view was that deterministic, chance-based evolution has gone over four billion years about as far as it is likely to go. Action by design is required for the next phase of evolutionary advancement. Help in this regard, Teilhard believed, is something nature intensely desires.

Today Teilhard is sometimes depicted as a daffy New Age oracle, babbling on about higher orders of existence. Yet around the middle of this century, he represented to intellectuals the sweetest hope of the human prospect. Teilhard was a person of reason, relentlessly insisting that empirical findings of science take precedence over dogma. He also felt sure the spiritual realm is as real and significant as the temporal world, despite our inability to observe it directly. Most of all Teilhard believed that the arrow of existence is pointed up. Flaws in nature and in people are not eternal curses from on high but errors intellect can resolve. And compared to the four billion years expended to get this far, Teilhard thought, correction of the flaws of nature and humankind may come about with blinding speed.

Teilhard's thoughts once held wide appeal to intellectuals because until recent decades, most of the world of letters maintained guarded optimism about the human prospect. Today that optimism is gone. The shift to environmental pessimism has come at a time when shifts to pessimism are the vogue in all quarters of academia and the arts. In the current received wisdom of liberal thought, humanity is such a lost cause—bumbling, bellicose, dependent on repressive social structures, wasting resources, pointless in the cosmic sense—that the idea women and men might not only help nature but serve as "stewards" over a beneficial coming phase of evolution makes the academic and literary set gag. But fortunately in these chapters we can think like nature and allow ourselves, ever so cautiously, as did Teilhard de Chardin, to begin to show a smile.

What Does Nature Want?

This book now departs from the long-term perspective of nature to address the environmental problems that today plague the short terms of human and animal life. Before moving to the book's second section, let's derive these general principles from the exercise in thinking like nature:

- Absent nuclear war, no environmental threat humanity causes or is likely to mount is unprecedented. Nature has dealt with worse many times. This does not excuse human environmental malfeasance. It simply indicates that nature is already prepared, both in physical properties and from the standpoint of evolution, to recover from the sorts of ecological wrongs men and women now commit. Given the chance, nature will in most cases recover with surprising rapidity.
- Interactions between intellect and nature may go well or poorly, but there is no reason to fear them in principle. In principle the arrival of intellect is encouraging to nature.
- Even when they entail high rates of resource consumption, technological lifestyles do not in themselves imperil nature. Done poorly, technological life is a menace to the environment. Done properly, a high-consumption technological existence actually may be less taxing to the environment than a subsistence lifestyle.
- "The fragile environment" is a nonsensical phrase. Nature is around for the long haul. The question is, are we?
- Nature has problems too. Maybe human beings will keep mak-

ing nature's problems worse. Maybe we can learn to solve them.

- Exactly as the Enlightenment philosophers once supposed, nature is a source of wisdom and values.
- Either nature was created by something larger than men and women or has autonomously made itself into something larger. Whichever the case, directly before our eyes every day is proof that there exists a Larger Scheme, welcoming women and men to join its enterprise.

Human perceptions of nature form a tumultuous chronicle. Long ago our dim and frightened ancestors, huddled in the ancient night of ignorance, saw the natural world as a lurking adversary. Gradually some measure of understanding developed: People began to perceive nature as a stern but not uncaring parent. Philosophy arrived, and people wondered if they and nature were not consubstantial in essence. An Enlightenment followed, in which people dared to dream that nature could light the way to freedom and moral virtue. Then came an age in which nature was made to seem a thrumming automaton, heartlessly driven by blind chance. Finally came the present day in which nature is imagined as some sort of fading ideal—beautiful but doomed, unable to put up a fight.

Soon the view of nature will again be transformed. Humankind and the natural world will be seen as identical in essence: both full of promise, both plagued by flaws. Nature and humanity will be seen as two travelers seeking the same destination—that place where life is assured and where sufferings end. Perhaps, as travelers that can share each other's burdens.

🌿 PART TWO

THE 🌿 SHORT VIEW

Thinking Like People 🌿

It is time to reconcile the sentiments of environmentalism with the observed facts of the natural world.

This will allow society to distinguish ecological alarms that really matter from those merely passing fads.

Reconciling the sentiments of environmentalism with the verities of nature will result in environmental optimism. It will also strengthen the rational grounding of environmentalism as a lasting social cause.

ACID RAIN 🌿

Depending on where you stand on grandfather Mountain, a gentle peak that rises from the Blue Ridge hills near Linwood, North Carolina, you can imagine the twentieth century did not transpire. An access road ascends, a microwave relay tower juts from an adjacent peak, and a trading-goods store below the summit sells the full inventory of contemporary souvenir kitsch. But across most of the mountain the hush of nature prevails. In every direction graceful ridges are crowned with a seamless canopy of Fraser fir and old-growth red spruce. Within the glades dwell in a wild state nearly every animal and plant that called the Carolinas home before the arrival of Europeans. In 1992 Grandfather Mountain was certified as a part of the United Nations Biosphere Reserve program, the first private land in the world so designated. Among the swaying trees of the mountain, some four centuries old, echo strains of the melody to which the dance of the ages is stepped.

But near the top of the mountain something is wrong with the regal scene. Stark trunks denuded of needles pepper the green expanse. Many high-elevation trees on Grandfather Mountain are in various stages of dying, and not from senescence. Robert Bruck, a professor of plant pathology at North Carolina State University, began studying the Blue Ridge around Linwood in 1983. At that time about five percent of high-altitude trees were "showing mortality," as foresters say, versus the typical two percent for a healthy Appalachian forest. By the 1990s the sick-tree figure was 60 percent for high-elevation trees on Grandfather Mountain and 90 percent on nearby Mount Mitchell, at 6,684 feet the highest point east of the Mississippi. Near the summit of Mount Mitchell an 11-mile ridgeline of lush trees has since the 1960s turned into an eerie stockade line of lifeless gray spikes. "The tops of the Blue Ridge mountains are becoming tree graveyards," Bruck says. This is ground zero of American acid rain.

Well as any issue might, acid rain exemplifies the flummoxed state of the modern environmental debate. When acid rain first came to general public attention in the late 1970s, it was declared an instant doomsday of epic proportions. Acid from raindrops would cause "a new silent spring," environmentalists asserted; die-offs of forests and lakes would be ubiquitous; the number of lakes too acidic for fish would double by the year 1990, the EPA projected in the 1970s; it was commonly predicted that lake acidity even in wilderness areas would soon reach 100 times the preindustrial level. Acid rain became an important item in American, Canadian, and European politics, engaging the attention of heads of state.

Then around 1990 an acid rain backlash set in. An extensive government study of the question, the most methodical environmental assessment ever conducted on any issue, found only a few American lakes and forests, not a huge number, imperiled by air pollution. "60 Minutes," the country's most popular television show, devoted an episode to taunting acid rain claims.[1] Conservative call-in shows began to go into earnest depth about the acid rain hoax and how the devious pinks were using it to shut down industry.

A problem cannot be at once a threat to life as we know it and a hoax without grounding. But the prism of environmental perception is today machined to polarize debates into such extremes. When an issue splits to polar extremes, the chances are that both sides have lost sight of the real world. That has happened with acid rain. It is a genuine environmental problem, but its significance has never been as important as claimed. Meanwhile the cures, some already being put into effect, are effective and for the most part affordable.

The above description can be applied to nearly all current environmental problems: genuine but exaggerated, subject to correction surprisingly quickly at reasonable cost. Thus understanding acid rain provides a model for understanding the reality, as opposed to the hype, of most environmental issues facing humankind.

Acid Expectations

The carbon that nature has for eons cycled into the atmosphere by the billions of tons naturally combines with moisture to form carbonic acid, which falls as rain. Rain downwind of deserts may be mildly alkaline, because desert dust contains minerals that neutralize carbonic acid. Most other natural rain is mildly acidic. Acidity and alkalinity are measured on the pH scale, which runs from zero (peak acid) to seven (neutral) to fourteen (peak alkaline). Before the industrial era most rain falling on North America and Europe is thought to have had a pH of 5.0 to 5.6, roughly as acidic as tea.

Because mildly acidic rain has been falling on the world since time immemorial, nature has long since adapted to resist it. Life, indeed, has learned to resist acid rain of frightening power. As noted in part one, past impacts of asteroids and comets unleashed periods of acid rain from hell. Global downpours at a pH of 1.0 or lower, as corrosive as battery acid, are thought to have followed killer rock strikes. Volcanos emit sulfur dioxide and nitrogen compounds, which may mix with cloud moisture to form sulfuric and nitric acids of harsh pH. Natural acid rain with a pH of 2.0 to 3.0, about the same as the worst industrial acid rain, often occurs for weeks downwind of large eruptions such as happened in 1991 at Mount Pinatubo. During past periods in which global volcanism was more substantial than it has been throughout humankind's walk on Earth, much of the world's rainfall may have lingered at low pH for centuries or longer.

Past bouts of natural acid rainfall mean the living world was not unprepared when artificial acid rain began. Raindrops at a pH of 4.0 or even 3.0 appear to have no harmful effect on the skins of most animals or surfaces of most plants: The outer coverings of most living things are perhaps not by coincidence composed of cells that resist acid. In turn, because mild acids are common in rain, many plants make use of them. A wide range of flowers and trees are acid-loving, employing corrosive compounds as fertilizer; many commercial fertilizers are designed to be slightly corrosive. Gardening-tips columns recommend throwing used coffee grounds around azaleas, to lower the pH of soil. Azaleas bloom in thanks. If gardeners go out of their way to put mild acid on plants, why did we think mild acids in raindrops would create an instant doomsday?

Of course, just because the environment is adapted to mild natural acid hardly means adding more is a good idea. Your stomach has a natural acidity of around 1.5, but if you swallow any substance more corrosive you're in big trouble. Similarly, because the environment has survived episodes of severe acid rain in the past hardly means another go-around would be welcome, any more than having malaria once and recovering would leave the patient agreeable to a relapse. But the basic fact that most rain is acidic to begin with was almost immediately lost when the acid rain controversy began. It's this point, the sort that would seem obvious to nature, to keep in mind as you read along.

Everybody's Downwind of Something

Like most pollution, artificial acid rain stems primarily from combustion of fossil fuels. Factories and power plants fired by coal emit a great deal of sulfur dioxide and nitrous oxides, "precursors" that cloud moisture and sunlight convert to sulfuric and nitric acids. Of the fossil fuels coal contains most sulfur and hence its combustion is the worst acid rain cause. Oil contains moderate amounts of sulfur and natural gas contains very little, making these fuels secondary and tertiary acid rain causes. Widespread combustion of coal began shortly before the turn of this century,[2] with widespread combustion of petroleum following a few decades later. Thereafter came the first human-caused acid rain.

By the 1960s, Western oil companies had become sufficiently proficient at "cracking" petroleum that cars and trucks ceased being important sources of sulfur dioxide, though vehicles continue to make the secondary acid rain precursor, nitrous oxides. Substandard refining remains an air pollution plague in the Third World, with many developing nations still burning gasoline thick with sulfur and other contaminants long since banished from U.S. fuels.

For both technical and political reasons, power plants and factories did not make the kind of progress against sulfur made by gasoline refiners. By the year 1970 the U.S. was putting 28 million tons of sulfur dioxide into the air annually, more than two-thirds of that from coal-fired power plants. Demand for electricity was growing at around three percent per year, suggesting many new power plants would be built. And following the 1973 Middle East war and the first OPEC oil shock, governments in the United States and Europe encouraged industry to substitute coal, a high-sulfur fuel, for oil, a moderate-sulfur fuel. From 1970 to the present day, coal would grow from supplying about 38 percent to about 56 percent of U.S. electricity; use figures went up similarly in most Western European nations. Such trends suggested sulfur emissions would expand exponentially, with rain becoming increasingly acidic in forests situated to the lee of power plants. In the U.S. this meant problem areas were likely to be the Adirondacks, the Blue Ridge Mountains, the Great Smokies, the White Mountains, and other woodlands downwind of the numerous coal-fired power plants built near the seemingly inexhaustible mines of Illinois, Indiana, and Ohio.

By the mid-1970s, rain had become unnaturally acidic in many parts of Europe. German foresters began to speak of *Waldsterben*, forest-death, especially in areas where the prevailing winds blew from the colossal coal-driven forge complexes of the Eastern bloc. A few lakes in the Adirondacks and along the Blue Ridge dropped under a pH of 5.0, too low for fish such as trout. Conservationists noted with alarm that New York's Lake Colden, where as a lad Teddy Roosevelt caught trout by the bucketful, had acidified and could no longer support game fish. Canada, whose southern regions lie in the footprint of upper Midwest American power plant emissions, began to assert that it was the victim of a cross-border pollution assault, claiming 42,000 dead lakes, most small. Foresters even in the remote northern timberlands of Maine reported unhealthy trees.

Acid rain soon advanced from an unknown concept to a political catchphrase. News organizations ran four-alarm stories accompanied by stark photography of bare trees, suggesting this would soon be the fate of all forests. In 1980 the National Academy of Sciences issued an acid-rain report that lent a blessing to the concept of a "new silent spring" by employing the phrase in its executive summary. The bulk of the NAS report, though gloomy, was less alarmist than the summary. But the summary is the only portion of a science document any journalist or politician ever actually reads—an important factor to keep in mind when the subject turns to global warming. Once the NAS work was published, an official instant doomsday scare was on.

Ronald Reagan took office shortly after the NAS report was released. He came to the presidency persuaded that the environmental alarms were left-wing propaganda. In this view Reagan mirrored the generational politics of the ecology. When Reagan's generation encountered the world, nature was still an adversary needing to be "conquered"—a hostile source of disease, crop failures, and Dust Bowls. The sight of an electricity generating station rising from the countryside, fierce with power and belching sulfurous plumes, was a welcome vision of human self-assertion. An imperfect assertion, of course, since no one from any generation ever liked the belching plume. But to many from Reagan's peer group, that was the price to be paid for freedom from cold and want. In the view often endorsed by thinkers of Reagan's choosing, either society enjoys the benefits of industrial production and accepts the environmental damage without any mawkish whimpering about the poor birdies and fishies (the "better them than us" school of thought) or factories and power plants are shut down by impossibly idealistic demands, and we all go back to living in teepees.

Based on this sort of analysis Reagan instructed his first EPA administrator, Anne Burford, to ignore acid rain. But the president continued to have his ear bent about the issue by Congress and by Canada. So Reagan opted for the time-honored dodge of further study, ordering the expansion of a federal survey to assess the extent of acid rain. Though detached science is something environmental affairs need more of—

repeatedly this book will call for increased scientific reasoning on the ecology—in Reagan's case the primary purpose of the National Acid Precipitation Assessment Program was to generate delay. Reagan announced the expanded NAPAP with Rose Garden pomp. But White House aides saw to it the study's organizational structure was so convoluted NAPAP would be unlikely to yield results during the Reagan presidency. Ultimately it did not.

Early in the acid rain maneuvering, as in many areas of environmental conflict, conventional ideological lines were drawn. Most important acid rain pessimists, such as Michael Oppenheimer, chief scientist for the Environmental Defense Fund, were political liberals; most who denied the problem, such as Reagan and Burford, were political conservatives. This ordering is in keeping with the preferred world views of ideological camps. Liberalism presumes industrial activity to be flagitious, and so by-products such as sulfur dioxide must cause horrible harm to the defenseless Earth; all who claim otherwise must be insidious servants of the corporate conspiracy. Conservatism presumes material economics to be human destiny, and so by-products must fit into the divine plan; all who claim otherwise must be clandestine agents of the socialist one-world cabal. Neither ideology has space in its catalog of preconceived notions for formulations that are ecorealistic—for instance that acid rain is a problem but one that can be fixed rapidly without notable pain.

Reasons to Doubt

Today up on the Blue Ridge the worst fears of doomsayers seem realized. Some clouds that float across Mount Mitchell have a pH of 2.2, almost as corrosive as lemon juice. Typical clouds are 3.1, lower than any contemporary natural acid rain except that which occurs after a volcanic eruption. In the spring young fir needles sometimes shrivel as though dipped in acid. In 1985, Bruck of North Carolina State estimated that "stressed" trees atop Mount Mitchell would last only ten more years. Three years later nearly all were dead. "I cannot prove beyond doubt that pollution is killing these trees, in the same way you cannot prove beyond doubt that cigarettes cause lung cancer," says Hugh Morton, who owns Grandfather Mountain and sells tickets to its summit both as a living and to finance conservation programs there. "But anybody who seriously believes the tree deaths are a purely natural coincidence is a damned fool."

Faltering trees along the Blue Ridge clearly are a problem, but do they represent an emergency? To understand the scene atop Grandfather Mountain it is necessary to engage in an essential ecorealist exercise: the separating of exaggerated from genuine environmental claims. Here, first, are some reasons for moderating the alarm.

One is that acid rain conditions at the tops of many Blue Ridge peaks, and at many similar mountains along the Appalachian backbone, are made abnormally severe by altitude. Acid in clouds can only harm life if it falls back to Earth's surface; much acid rain does not fall until the acid-bearing clouds have floated out over the Atlantic. There it appears to cause no harm, since the top layer of the ocean easily dilutes rain to a standard pH level. But mountaintops that sit within clouds may be exposed to acidity that does not rain out. Because of the placement of the Appalachians in the prevailing U.S. weather structure, clouds tend to stall there. Owing to cloud-stall, Mount Mitchell gets 84 inches of rain per year, versus 35 inches per year for Seattle, widely viewed as the country's precipitation capital. According to Bruck, clouds that envelop Mount Mitchell, shrouding trees without releasing precipitation, create the equivalent of 240 inches of annual rainfall.

Owing to such factors all sides of the acid rain debate agree that high-elevation forests receive much more acid "deposition" than other woodlands. Thus it might be expected that acid rain damage would be worse near the tops of East Coast mountains than at lower altitudes, where the bulk of the forest resides. Lower-altitude forests might show only minor damage. This is exactly what the NAPAP survey found.

NAPAP was a ten-year, $540 million effort that sent researchers to sample 7,000 lakes and hundreds of woodlands. Environmental policy is fraught with computer projections, extrapolations, guesstimates, and projections based on extrapolations of guesstimates. Thorough studies of the actual condition of the natural world are quite rare. NAPAP, compiled by credentialed scientists and peer-reviewed by academics with no stake in the outcome, was groundbreaking in this regard. In 1991 it concluded that "there is no evidence of a general or unusual decline of forests in the United States or Canada due to acid rain." NAPAP found dangerous acidity in four percent of eastern lakes, not 50 percent as widely predicted. The study found high tree mortality in three percent of eastern forests, not 100 percent as widely predicted. The worst effects, NAPAP showed, were on high-altitude spruces in places like the Blue Ridge.

The NAPAP findings caused unease in the environmental community, and not just because they took most of the air out of a dandy doomsday issue. Some environmentalists privately worry that too many of their predictions are based on computer models, not empirical study of the actual world. If NAPAP, the largest systematic attempt to obtain real-world ecological data, found the situation nowhere near as baneful as projected, would reality checks determine other pessimistic pronouncements as flawed?

A second reason to question acid rain emergency claims is that rain is only one of many influences that may cause a forest to decline. In the 1930s, when industrial sulfur emissions began in earnest, Fraser firs of the eastern U.S. also began to be plagued by the balsam woolly aphid, a parasite. "A lot of what people claim is acid rain damage is really from the aphid," says William Anderson, an economics instructor at the University of Tennessee at Chattanooga, whose campus sits near the Great Smokies. "Growing Fraser firs for Christmas trees is a big industry in the same parts of Tennessee and North Carolina where acid rain damage is said to be wiping out the Fraser fir. The Christmas tree crop does fine because it's sprayed with lindane [an insecticide], which kills aphids. Wild trees in the national forests are not sprayed."

A third objection to acid rain alarmism turns on the beneficial effects of nitric acid. To the tree and plant species that have learned to use naturally occurring acids, nitric acid in rain acts as a fertilizer, supplying the nitrogen required by green plants. Industrial activity that puts excess nitrous oxides in the air may offend believers in pure autonomous nature but may not offend trees and plants that benefit.

Many critics of the acid rain scare jumped on this point. Suppose sulfur emissions do hurt some trees, they said; nitrous oxide emissions help other trees. Maybe it all comes out in the wash. John Sununu, who before becoming White House chief of staff for President Bush was governor of New Hampshire, an acid rain target area, often said the reason some fir trees in his state displayed "burned" needles was not from low pH rain. Instead, Sununu maintained, extra nitric acid in the air extended the normal tree-growing season through a fertilizing effect, causing still-growing needles to "burn" in the first frosts of autumn. Some studies supported this interpretation.

And a chemist named Edward Krug maintained that the basis of scientific understanding of acid rain is erroneous. Krug, whose work has been published in peer-reviewed technical journals—more than can be said for many acid rain alarmists—believes that most acid in eastern lakes and forests originates not in raindrops but from the soil, set free by plant action. Krug thinks lake-bottom core samples show most water bodies of eastern North America have been acidic since the end of the Pleistocene ice age. "When acid in lakes and forests was found we automatically assumed rain acid to be the cause, without stopping to wonder if maybe it was there all along," Krug says. The average acidity of eastern lakes, Krug hypothesizes, is today no different than what core samples suggest it was 200 years ago.

Saying there are 240 eastern lakes that became "critically acidic" since the 1950s, as the NAPAP study did, is a half-truth, Krug believes: There are about as many eastern lakes that became *less* acidic during the period. NAPAP's findings included puzzling ones such as these: Most of the "critically acidic" lakes are in Florida, yet Florida is not in the downwind footprint of Midwest power plants. Meanwhile Ohio, where record acid rainfall has been recorded, has no critically acidic lakes. To Krug such enigmatic results mean that acid from rainfall, though sometimes damaging, cannot be the primary explanation for acid in forests and lakes.

In fact Krug thinks that to the extent some eastern lakes have become in recent years too acidic for trout, they are not being degraded but rather returned to a previous natural condition. Lake Colden, Krug suggests, probably knew no trout when Europeans arrived in North America. Iroquois lore speaks of the lake as a poor fishing ground, which would be strange if the tasty trout were present. In the nineteenth century, when slash-and-burn timbering was common, the hills around Lake Colden were logged bare. In this state they experienced the worst effect of irresponsible logging: uncontrolled erosion. Erosion washed topsoil into the lakes. While the earth a few feet down may be acidic most topsoil is alkaline, so erosion reduced the waters' natural acidity. Fish that don't like acidic water then proliferated; Teddy Roosevelt enjoyed a fisherman's dream boyhood. Slash-and-burn logging was banned by Congress in 1915. As the trees above Lake Colden and other eastern lakes grew back, erosion declined. Alkaline topsoil stopped being washed into the waters; the lakes' natural acidity returned. A natural antitrout equilibrium was restored, upsetting environmentalists and the sports-fishing industry, both of which then blamed acid rain.

Krug's ideas enjoy the same status as nearly all other ideas about acid rain: unproven. At the current level of human understanding of the biosphere, no one really knows such basic items of information as whether acid in eastern North American lakes comes mainly from the ground or mainly from the rain.

Reasons to Believe

The above inventory of acid rain objections does not rule out alarm. Here, in turn, are reasons for continued concern. The first is the miner's-canary hypothesis. In bygone days miners took caged canaries into the underworld because the birds are sensitive to oxygen deprivation, carbon monoxide, and methane. A canary's sudden expiration would trigger an evacuation. Suppose, some environmentalists argue, only a small percentage of American forests and lakes are damaged by acid rain today. Perhaps they are miner's canaries, warning of what is about to happen to the ecology generally.

Miner's-canary analogies are prevalent in contemporary green theory. They serve environmentalism from an institutional standpoint, lending a reason to stay in autopanic mode even when the evidence counsels calm. Yet this analogy cannot be dismissed. I have little doubt that lurking out there is at least one true miner's canary: an ecological issue where alarms that now seem overmuch will turn out distressingly real. Acid rain has as good a chance as any to be that issue.

Another reason to continue worrying about acid rain is that the woolly aphid cannot alone account for what has happened at the summits of Mitchell and Grandfather mountains. Only about a third of the Fraser firs in those places are infested with the aphid; two-thirds are sickly. The red spruce, sickly along the Blue Ridge, is immune to the aphid. Bruck of North Carolina State notes that the aphid arrived in the United States in 1936, inadvertently carried from Europe as part of a Forest Service experiment to transplant the silver fir on American soil. For the next 30 years foresters considered the bug insignificant. Around the mid-1960s—the same period when acid rain emissions were beginning to accumulate—aphid outbreaks increased. It is possible that Fraser firs weakened by air pollution became more susceptible to the aphid, meaning the mortality ascribed to this pest is a pollution by-product. Similarly it may be, as Sununu maintained, that fertilization from airborne nitric acid tricks trees into growing late into the autumn, at which point the first frost damages needles. But isn't this a problem caused by pollution, even if nature delivers the blow?

Another cause for continued concern about acid rain is its effect on soil. Though nitric compounds from acid rain are a plant nutrient, in some places they are deposited at three times the level trees require. In high concentration the acid becomes a toxin, just as the human body benefits from small amounts of salt but reacts adversely to large amounts. Sulfuric and nitric acids tend to release from soils calcium and magnesium, two nutrients required by green plants. Commercial foresters sometimes compensate for such loss by dusting with powdered rock, but so far few public forest preserves have been dusted. High acidity liberates aluminum, a toxic metal found naturally in soils but chemically bound to other minerals. Liberated aluminum is uptaken by trees, initiating a condition similar to mercury poisoning. Some researchers believe the liberation of soil aluminum is the ultimate cause of death for the dead trees of the Blue Ridge.

Finally several researchers, including Paul Steudler of the Woods Hole Oceanographic Institute, think excess nitrogen deposited in soils by acid rain promotes an organic chain reaction that leads to increased natural emissions of methane. Methane is the most powerful greenhouse gas, 20 to 30 times more potent than carbon dioxide. Thus a link between acid rain and methane emissions, which would not register on standard tests of forest health or lake acidity, may nonetheless be of importance to environmental policy.

Such a link suggests the most important reason to believe that acid rain really is a problem: holistic thinking. Despite the mangled pop-cultural usage of this term, holistic thinking remains essential to environmental understanding. Here the essential holistic insight is that trees and lakes are not just exposed to acid rain; they are exposed simultaneously to other airborne pollutants: carbon monoxide, dust, chlorine, and ozone,[3] the primary ingredient in smog.

Tree-ring studies of some wild eastern species suggest that annual growth began to decline in the 1960s, when both acid rain and smog were increasing. The 1960s were not a period of drought or other natural factors that might slow wild tree growth, so the likelihood is strong that pollution explains the growth decline. Lance Kress, a researcher at Duke University, has found that the loblolly pine, a common southeastern tree, today grows about 20 percent less quickly in the air of Duke's home city of Durham than control trees grow in filtered air. Acid rain harms trees only when it rains, which is only a small portion of the time. Ozone and other air pollutants harm trees continuously, creating cumulative damage.

Such findings raise the question of whether acid rain damage to forests should be assessed in isolation or holistically. The political and media worlds tend to address environmental issues in isolation, obsessing on this or that for a while then moving on to the next fad. Most environmental policy has been forged this way. To nature such thinking is childish. If everything is part of everything else—an environmentalist's motto well spoken—then the whole of pollutant effects, not their individual parts, are what matter.

In some areas holistic environmental thinking will reduce the seriousness of doomsday claims by showing that the effects caused by women and men are but tiny influences in the totality of nature. But in areas such as air pollution, holistic thinking escalates alarms. Then it becomes important to know how political systems respond.

Acid Rain Politics: The Backdrop

The law governing the air above the United States is the Clean Air Act, first passed in meaningful form in 1970 and made more strict in 1977 and 1990. This statute is among the most complicated and expensive tools of modern government, its language and regulations now running to many thousands of pages and perhaps costing as much as an estimated $50 billion per year, about what the federal government spends annually on aid to education. The Clean Air Act regulates acid rain, CFCs, smog, and toxic emissions from cars, trucks, buses, factories, offices, power plants, and businesses as small as bakeries; creates multiple hierarchies of federal, state, and local planning; and around 1995 will be extended to regulate emissions from lawn mowers, outboard motors, chain saws, paints, and consumer products such as charcoal lighter fluid.

Sulfur dioxide, the primary acid rain cause, was among the first air pollutants subject to U.S. federal regulation. Since the 1970 Clean Air Act, every new fossil fuel–fired power plant built, and most new factories, has incorporated sulfur controls. The most common controls are switching from high-sulfur coal to low-sulfur coal or to natural gas; washing coal chemically before combustion, to remove sulfur; and installation of expensive devices called stack scrubbers, which strip sulfur from exhaust gases ascending the smokestack to exit the plant. Today new power plants and factories emit about 90 percent less sulfur per unit of fuel input than facilities built in the 1970s. By the late 1990s the figure will be about 95 percent.

Because action against sulfur pollution began in the United States more than two decades ago, the emission of acid rain precursors has long been in decline. Between 1970 and 1991, U.S. emissions of sulfur dioxide fell by 27 percent annually, even as coal use increased by 45 percent. Ambient levels (the measure of pollutants actually in the air) of airborne sulfur fell by 53 percent through that period; ambient levels of nitrous oxides, the lesser acid rain cause, fell by 27 percent.[4] This means that during the very period when the public was becoming convinced acid rain was growing much worse, the problem was trending steadily down—a fact almost never mentioned in coverage of the issue.

While the U.S. took early action against acid rain, other Western nations dragged their national feet. For all the outraged rhetoric Ottawa directed against Washington regarding Canada's complaints of U.S. acid-rain output, Canada did not install its first stack scrubber on a coal-fired power plant until 1992, decades after the first American scrubber. This fact, too, was never mentioned in press coverage of acid rain, which depicted Canada as a helpless victim of U.S. indifference. Most European Union nations were slow to adapt sulfur controls; the United Kingdom did not begin its crackdown till the late 1980s. Only Germany, where the forest has a revered standing in the national psyche, and France joined the U.S. in taking early action against acid rain. France's form of action was not, however, to the liking of environmentalists. By national policy France is the most nuclear-dependent nation, now generating 75 percent of its electricity from the atom, with zero air pollution output.

Politically, the first Clean Air Act adapted a common compromise of imposing strict standards on new power plants or factories but allowing "grandfather clause" exemptions for existing facilities. The expediency here is obvious: It's always easier to impose new rules on future action than to change something that already exists. Yet focusing strict antipollution controls on new versions of anything may create a situation in which new clean technology goes unbuilt while the dirty old way of doing things is preserved. The cost of contemporary air-emission controls has played a role in making new power plants so much more expensive than continuing to run old plants—what utilities call "embedded capacity"—that construction of new generating facilities has been put off throughout the country. This has happened despite the fact that construction of new power plants is in society's general interest, since new plants are invariably both cleaner and more energy efficient.

Because the grandfather clause effectively encouraged old power plants to remain open, by 1989 just 49 of the country's power stations, all built before 1970, were emitting fully half of U.S. sulfur dioxide. Most of the dirty stations are in the Midwest. Midwestern power plants tend to be dirty both because they number among the country's oldest and because they are linked to midwestern mines that produce relatively high-sulfur coal. The sprawling Gavin power plant in Chesire, Ohio, the largest coal-fired electricity installation in the country, burns some 300 railroad hopper cars of coal daily, all from mines within a ten-mile radius. Gavin also emits more than a ton of sulfur dioxide daily, which drifts on prevailing winds toward the Appalachians. Power plants along the East Coast generally run more cleanly because many are modern facilities built after 1970. Power plants in the Rocky Mountain states and along the West Coast usually run cleanly as most are both new and burn low-sulfur coal from Wyoming.

When the Clean Air Act was amended in 1977, one title seemed to require that older power plants reduce acid rain emissions by shifting to low-sulfur coal, a product that came to be known as "compliance coal." But as the Yale law professor Bruce Ackerman has shown in his fine book *Clean Coal, Dirty Air,* the 1977 rules were twisted by lobbyists to create a sort of federally protected status for high-sulfur coal. Most high-sulfur coal comes from Appalachian and midwestern underground mines where hourly personnel belong to the United Mine Workers, an old-line constituency of the Democratic Party. Low-sulfur coal comes from open-pit or "surface" mines west of the Mississippi, where few workers belong to unions. Members of Congress from underground-mine states such as West Virginia flipped when they realized the 1977 law would inspire utilities to switch to Western compliance coal. Interest groups aligned with underground mines managed to have the 1977 regulations written in such a way that many utilities were in effect required to continue burning high-sulfur coal, while adding stack scrubbers. This did cut emissions but was often the most expensive means to achieve the goal.

At the same time the federal government embarked on a program of finding ways to make high-sulfur coal burn cleanly. The Department of Energy's clean-coal office has since expended billions of dollars—$694 million in fiscal 1992 alone—on a quest for a practical means to make high-sulfur coal behave like low-sulfur coal. These expenditures have sacred-cow status to the congressional delegations from states that produce high-sulfur coal. On Capitol Hill coal, the dirtiest fossil fuel, does well politically because it has a single-minded champion in Senator Robert Byrd of West Virginia, whereas natural gas, the cleanest fossil fuel, has not had a politically prominent champion since Lyndon Johnson.

Acid Rain Politics: The Foreground

When George Bush took office in 1989, acid rain alarm stories continued to be common in the news. Democrats, controlling both houses of Congress throughout most of the 1980s, felt embarrassed that they had been unable to compel the White House to accept new acid rain controls. George Mitchell of Maine, then Majority Leader of the Senate, made the issue a personal cause. Maine is leeward of Midwest power plant emissions, and some studies suggest its forests show early effects of the sort of damage more readily visible along the Blue Ridge. Scorecards from environmental groups are important in Maine politics. Green lobbyists let Mitchell know they would rate him poorly unless he pushed acid rain reductions through the Senate.

Mitchell was amenable; he had tired of pronouncements from industry lobbyists that new controls would cause economic disaster. The basic ways to address acid rain are to add smokestack scrubbers or switch from high-sulfur coal. "Every year," Mitchell told me, "the utilities would count up capital costs as if every power plant in the country installed scrubbers, and the unions would count up mining jobs lost as if every power plant in the country switched fuels. Then they would combine these figures and come up to Capitol Hill yelling 'Oh my God!' "

On the flip side of environmental predictions of instant doom for the Earth if pollution is not controlled are business predictions of instant recession for the economy if pollution is controlled. As Forest Reinhart, a professor of economics at the Harvard Business School, says, "The cost of environmental controls is consistently less than half of what corporate trade associations say it will be." A law of motion of eco-politics seems to be that for every improbable claim of coming environmental disaster, there is an opposite and equally improbable claim of coming economic disaster.

Environmentalists interpreted the appointment of John Sununu as the Bush chief of staff as a bad portent, given Sununu's status as a fierce conservative. But on acid rain Sununu was a progressive, having signed as governor of New Hampshire one of the first state laws restricting sulfur emissions from power plants. "The acid rain pronouncements were exaggerated, but that did not mean there was no underlying problem," Sununu says. "It was a fixable problem from an engineering standpoint."

The fix advocated in 1990 by EPA Administrator William Reilly was a cut of about 50 percent in sulfur emissions, from the 1990 level of 19 million tons to nine million tons per year by the year 2000. The 2000 amount would thus be only a third of tonnage of sulfur emitted in the United States in the peak year, 1970. Reilly further advocated that nitrous oxide emissions from power plants be cut 15 percent by 2000. And in an unnoticed clause with important long-term implications, Reilly suggested that once sulfur emissions decline to the year 2000 level they be capped there permanently. This cap provision, whose existence was missed entirely by commentators, represented ecorealist environmental thinking at its finest: a mechanism to insure that future economic growth could occur without future pollution growth. Under Reilly's proposal the coupling between economic growth and pollution growth would be broken; utilities would know they could expand only if they did so cleanly. The idea that more of anything (in this case, electricity) inexorably means more pollution would be laid to rest.

Once the control proposals were on the table, there ensued what Reilly called "hardball lobbying at its most primitive." Labor interests fought the Reilly proposal, fearing job cuts at the underground mines;

jobs would be created at surface mines, but they would likely not be union jobs. (Labor lost.) The National Coal Association fought the new rules. (Big coal lost.) Western representatives such as Senator Alan Simpson of Wyoming lobbied to exempt their utilities, arguing that western power plants already run much more cleanly than midwestern plants. (Western states lost.) Midwestern states lobbied for federal subsidies to help their utilities meet the new rules. (Midwestern states lost.) Underground-mining states fought for subsidies for displaced workers. (They lost.) Conservative ideologues attacked Reilly as some sort of glassy-eyed dreamer. (Conservative ideologues lost.) Conservatives in the White House attacked Reilly as a closet Democratic liberal. (Conservatives in the White House lost.)

Indeed all entrenched lobbying interests lost their fights regarding acid rain controls. Who won? High-altitude spruce trees. In a profound display of the power of environmentalism, acid rain controls moved through Congress almost to the word as Reilly had written them. Mere trees defeated an armada of traditionally indomitable interests: the coal lobby, the labor lobby, the business lobby, the utility lobby, the old-line Senate lobby, the conservative antigovernment lobby.

Success for Reilly's rules came only a few months after NAPAP had at long last tendered its findings. The new regulations were premised on the notion that acid rain is an emergency; NAPAP concluded that acid rain is a secondary concern. But by the time NAPAP finally reported, the outlines of the acid rain deal had been cut. Few in Congress, the EPA, or the White House were inclined to reopen the issue. This was just as well by environmentalists, who did not want to have to explain why the "new silent spring" seemed on inspection considerably less frightful than expected. The right-wing talk-show circuit would later grant frequent hearing to the notion that a conspiracy existed to hush up NAPAP's conclusions. The actual explanation, a prosaic one, was less entertaining: NAPAP finished late.

The Right to Pollute

When the trees beat the business lobbies on the 1990 acid rain rules, were environmentalists happy? A few were. Yet many condemned the legislation, and not just because environmental lobbyists are genetically programmed for gloom. Reilly had arranged that the sulfur cuts be achieved not through traditional binding regulation but an experimental system of emissions trading. Utilities would be allowed to sell each other a right to pollute. This market-based approach was found vulgar by the movement's orthodox wing.

Here in simplified form is how acid rain trading works. Each power plant receives a sulfur emission allowance, reflecting an overall national reduction of about 50 percent. Utilities can meet their limits either by reducing emissions or by purchasing credits from utilities below their limits. Generally a utility that cuts emissions below its allowance is free to sell the credit thus created at whatever price the market will bear.

The emissions-trading idea does formally sanction some pollution. "But the worst way to sanction pollution is the way we used to do it, by having regulations that sounded great on paper and could not be enforced," says Timothy Wirth, at the time of the 1990 vote a senator from Colorado. Wirth and the late Pennsylvania Senator John Heinz were leaders in advancing the idea of pollution trading as a form of environmental regulation; Dan Dudek of the Environmental Defense Fund, Robert Hahn of the American Enterprise Institute, and other economists also worked on development of the idea.

Emissions trading rests on the notion that "performance" standards are better than "process" standards. Traditionally antipollution initiatives have worked through process standards, under which government agencies go into elaborate detail specifying what devices companies may use under what circumstances. At their best process standards are cumbersome. At their worst they are prone to hijacking by lobbyists, as happened with the 1977 acid rain rules.

When performance standards are employed government simply says, "Here's the level you must cut to, how you do it is your business." Officials need not peer over the shoulders of engineers. Government only monitors compliance, an increasingly straightforward task with modern modem-linked sensors that report factory emissions directly to regulatory agencies in "real" time, that is instantaneously. Nearly all academic economists, and an increasing number of environmentalists such as Dudek, believe performance standards coupled to emissions trading are the future of environmental regulation. Cheaper and faster than any action government might take, these systems encourage free-market creativity. If market efficiency can be brought to the campaign against pollution, positive trends are sure to accelerate.

Acid rain has now become the test case for market-based approaches to environment protection, and early returns are promising. Wisconsin Power and Light started the trading of acid rain by selling some permits to Duquesne Light of Pittsburgh; analysts were surprised by how low the price was. The right to emit a ton of sulfur was expected to sell for $600 to $700. Instead acid rain permits are trading at around $150 per ton. So far the highest price paid for an acid rain permit was $350 by Resources for the Future, a Washington think tank that wanted a single certificate to hang on its office wall. The permits are now traded on the Chicago Board of Options Exchange, which offers an instrument similar to a pollution futures contract.

The low price of permits means that once utilities finally had no choice but to reduce acid rain, they discovered the task could be accomplished more cheaply than anticipated. Acid rain permits are selling at about $150 per ton because this, not $700, is roughly what utilities are spending on controls. The low price suggests that when the acid rain control system is in full effect in 2000 the cost to society will be only $1.3 billion a year, not $6 billion as widely projected when the rules were enacted. Further, the acid rain market exhibits a preponderance of sellers over buyers. This means utilities are cutting their emissions more than the law requires, creating excess allotments for sale. A best of all worlds arrangement is realized: voluntary overcontrol at a low price. Sound impossibly pleasant? As this book will show, environmental protection, far from being a dismal subject where futility rules, is one where pleasant outcomes are common.

The experiment in market rules for acid rain controls has not been without foibles. Environmentalists in New York were less than enthusiastic when Long Island Lighting sold acid rain vouchers to American Electric Power, owner of the Gavin generating station. This means sulfur once rising from power plants on Long Island and drifting out to the ocean will instead emanate from Ohio and drift eastward over the Adirondacks. This realization led a faction of New York state environmentalists to call for repeal of the new law. Forgotten in the process: Though credits are being shifted from Long Island to Ohio, net emissions from Ohio will fall dramatically, by 81 percent in the case of the Gavin plant.

Twists such as shifting emissions from New York to Ohio are inevitable: All government initiatives create results no one anticipated. But unintended consequences are not always untoward. Conservationists realized any private party might buy an acid rain certificate on the open market and simply rip it in half, annulling forever a right to emit sulfur. Several environmental groups, and some green businesses such as the Working Assets investment fund, are now purchasing allowances in order to retire them. According to market logic, that's grand.

Widely misunderstood is that the permits are temporary. They do not, as many reports have asserted, confer an indefinite right to emit sulfur to the sky; nor do they create any property rights regarding emissions. The value of each allowance declines annually, until it becomes worthless in the early 2000s.

In 1992, shortly before the Earth Summit in Rio, I sat in the office of Carlo Ripa di Meana, then chief environmental official of the European Union, the Western European metagovernment. Ripa was at the time engaged in an oratorical campaign accusing Washington of every manner of environmental perfidy. "The very notion of legally sanctioning pollution is an outrage to civilized minds," Ripa said. "I can't imagine it—converting pollution into property rights, allowing industrialists to trot off to court boasting of the right to pollute." I mentioned to Ripa that the permits did not confer rights but were self-cancelling instruments, that progress against acid rain was more rapid in the United States than in Europe partly because of the new system. "The permits go down in value? The industrialists do not get to keep them?" he asked, taken aback. At the time Ripa was one of the world's most important environmental officials, and he did not know basic information about the hottest idea in pollution control. Or perhaps Ripa did not wish to know, since the reality of the U.S. acid rain–control program confounds cherished preconceived notions about instant doomsday.

Acid's End

All the carefully spun theories about sulfur, soil leeching, woolly aphids, and the rest may someday give way to some unknown, entirely different understanding of the problem. "Though I am furious about air pollution," says Bruck, who sat on a NAPAP review board, "I cannot tell you for certain that pollution is what is killing the Blue Ridge trees. It is impossible to construct a control set for the effects of pollution—an entire mountain where everything is the same except no artificial compounds in the air. Until we know more, it's all opinion."

Nor is it possible to say that the roughly 50 percent acid rain reduction now in progress is the "correct" level in any scientific sense. In a world where the only thing we know about the environment is that we don't know what we don't know, the notion of scientific certainty in ecological policy is a chimera. The goals William Reilly chose for the U.S. acid rain effort are essentially arbitrary ones, selected because they seemed attainable politically and bearable economically. They may or may not do the job; they were the best possible under the circumstances. That is, they are reasonable. Reasonableness, not ideology or wish fulfillment, should be a guiding ideal of the new ecorealism.

Some commentators have argued that acid rain reduction is foolish because shortcuts exist. Robert Crandall of the Brookings Institution says the price of the new controls is "ridiculous" when, "for hundreds of times less money," the acidity of eastern lakes could be neutralized by adding powdered limestone, a common quarry material. Liming has been tried in Sweden, with good results. But liming is merely a stopgap. Cutting emissions at the source imposes a solution, and any environmental problem worth addressing is worth solving.

But as the acid rain solution goes into effect it is important to bear in mind how extravagantly society misjudged this peril. Not only did the controversy proceed in ignorance of a basic fact of the natural world, that rain is naturally acidic, but pundits declaimed an imminent doomsday for forests *at the very time when American forests were expanding.* At the height of the late-1970s acid rain scare, one television documentary spoke of the Adirondacks as "a ragged landscape of dead and dying trees." At the moment those words were being spoken the Adirondack forest had just reached its largest acreage in more than a century and was still expanding, as it continues to expand today.

Indeed the very Blue Ridge summits now threatened by acid rain are prime examples of nature's ability to recuperate from human assault. Mount Mitchell, the hardest-hit peak in North Carolina, has changed in the last two decades from a dense primeval forest to a plateau of sick trees. But just a few ticks farther back Mount Mitchell was much worse off. Around the turn of the century, Cornelius Vanderbilt constructed a tram railway up the peak so that loggers could take out the valuable old-growth trees. The mountain was clear-cut and left for dead. By the 1950s Mount Mitchell was once again biologically vibrant. Its dense, primal form is not a leftover from pre-European times, but a recent arrival. Today death knocks anew along the Blue Ridge. Soon, within your lifetime, the mountain will again live.

AIR POLLUTION

LIFE IS SHORT, AND CITIZENS OF LOS ANGELES SPEND A DIS-
heartening portion of that brevity stuck in traffic. One hot summer
morning in 1992 I watched an L.A. rush hour from a hill above the city.
Along the highways of the city crept a profluence of vehicles so extensive
it seemed difficult to believe all the factories in the world could create
such a mechanical outpouring, setting aside whether genus *Homo* made
a wise choice dedicating so much of its production base to that task. But
as I watched a different subject came to mind. Sometimes important
news is concealed in that which does not occur. What was not occurring
that sweltering morning was a smog advisory.

Rising from the automobiles engaged in the city's daily ritual of creep
was nowhere near as much pollution as in years before. As recently as
1988, Los Angeles experienced air-quality or ozone warnings 148 times,
essentially on every hot day. By 1992 the number had fallen to 42.
(Calculations in this chapter adjust for a difference between California
and federal ozone standards and for new standards that took effect in
1980.) In the 1950s, according to the South Coast Air Quality
Management District, an antipollution agency with the regrettable
acronym SCAQMD, peak summer ozone concentrations in the Los
Angeles basin hit 57 times the level at which a current federal advisory
would be declared. Since then peak summer ozone readings have
declined continuously. During this same period the human population
of Los Angeles tripled; the population of automobiles, the primary
source of smog, has quadrupled. There are several ways of calculating

181

overall ozone exposure. By the simplest Los Angeles ozone has fallen about 40 percent overall since 1970, a period during which the car population of the city almost tripled.

If smog can be bested in Los Angeles—the city with, for reasons of prevailing winds and basin geography, America's worst conditions for smog—then air pollution would seem a surmountable problem almost everywhere. That is exactly what statistics show. National air pollution emissions have been declining on an almost uninterrupted basis since the 1970s, even as the population increases, more cars are driven more miles, and the economy grows.

In 1970, when the first Earth Day was celebrated, by consensus the most troubling form of air pollution was lead. Lead is a poison to mammals and causes IQ loss in children. In 1975, Los Angeles had 100 days in violation of the federal standard for airborne lead. By 1988 the number had dropped to zero, where it has stayed since. With the advent of unleaded gasoline and restrictions on lead from industrial sources, lead is for intents and purposes now gone from the Los Angeles sky. Nationally airborne lead levels have declined 96 percent since 1975. From a standing start, airborne lead was eradicated in less than two decades.

The composite national ozone decline since 1970 is about 27 percent, also during a period in which ever-more cars were driven ever-more miles. In 1988 there were 915 days of worst-case ozone "exceedance" in U.S. cities; the number has been declining since, to 232 total days in 1992. In the 1970s, Los Angeles violated federal standards for carbon monoxide, which causes respiratory distress and headaches, around 40 times per year. Now the average is down to about ten days per year. In 1992 the state of California passed the year without a carbon monoxide violation for the first time. Nationally, carbon monoxide levels fell 57 percent from 1975 to 1991. In 1990 there were 113 days nationwide with a carbon monoxide violation recorded in a U.S. city; by 1992, the number was just two days. New York City averaged about 70 days above federal carbon monoxide levels in the mid-1980s. The number has been falling since, to two days in 1991 and no days in 1992.

Another air pollutant is nitrous oxides, which form acid rain and smog. In the mid-1970s Los Angeles violated standards for these gases about 15 days per year; by 1990 the figure was down to two days. Nationally, nitrous oxide levels fell about 24 percent through the same period. National emissions of "volatile organics," smog-forming chemicals that evaporate from paints and the aromatic compounds in gasoline, declined 39 percent from 1970 to 1990. Los Angeles has not violated federal standards for sulfur dioxide emissions, the primary cause of acid rain, since the early 1970s. Nationally sulfur dioxide emissions fell 20 percent during the 1980s, even as the combustion of coal for power, the main cause of this pollutant, increased.

Still another air pollutant is particulates, or soot. Gross soot caused by the unfiltered burning of coal was common in the U.S. roughly through the 1920s. Gross soot had severe respiratory effects, sometimes killing the elderly or young. Gross soot has all but been eliminated in the developed world, where the concern today is fine soot. Such particles have a diameter of ten microns or less (human hair is about 75 microns in diameter) and are known to regulators as PM10.

Fine soot pollution comes mainly from industry, agricultural tilling, and from driving on unpaved roads. Unpaved roads put some 14 million metric tons of PM10 into the U.S. air in 1991, versus about five million from factories. Dust blown by natural wind erosion added another nine million metric tons of PM10. These statistics mean that fine-soot pollution caused by people has fallen sufficiently that natural emissions now constitute a third of the problem. National levels of PM10 in the air have declined by about 26 percent since 1975; today most cities rarely violate the federal standard for this pollutant, though some researchers have begun to believe the federal standards for PM10 should be lowered, as new research suggests even low levels of fine soot in the air can cause premature deaths among those with asthma.[1]

Fine soot, sulfur dioxides, and nitrous oxides all contribute to that wavy, translucent pall that cuts visibility on smoggy days. The EPA monitors urban visibility: It has been improving for a decade in cities such as Pittsburgh and Chattanooga. Notable gains in visibility are expected to come to Los Angeles, Denver, and other perpetual-haze cities by the late 1990s.

One unsettling scientific discovery of the 1970s was a pall of air pollution forming over the Arctic Circle, thousands of miles from the nearest Oldsmobile. North Pole smog was widely decried by environmentalists as proof the entire globe inexorably would be blanketed in air pollution. In 1993, researchers from the National Oceanographic and Atmospheric Administration announced studies showing North Pole smog peaked in 1982 and has been declining since. The 1970s was the decade when several forms of air pollution peaked in the United States; the rapid decline of subsidiary smog over the Arctic suggests the speed with which nature can recover once pollution is controlled.

Should present trends continue, early in the next century smog for intents and purposes will be history in the United States. This is especially encouraging because air pollution is an environmental issue from which there is no escape. The affluent can drink bottled water, retreat to mountain homes, invest in Canada if there's global warming. But we've all got to breathe the same air. Air pollution is the great equalizer.

Heat Wave, No Smog

The introduction to this book cites the significant jump in air-quality figures during 1991 and 1992 and how little attention these statistics received, since they failed to reinforce prevailing notions of ecological despair. When I asked several Washington environmentalists what they made of the 1991 and 1992 numbers, each called the figures meaningless because the summers of 1991 and 1992 were mild.

Smog forms when pollutants react photochemically with sunlight; the hotter the weather, the more smog. The air-pollution figures that really count, environmentalists said, are those for 1988. That was the worst smog summer in history, as a sustained heat wave put the prospect of global warming into the news. Los Angeles violated air standards on 148 days; Philadelphia exceeded the federal ozone standard on 23 days; Washington, D.C., had 12 violation days; other cities had similarly high numbers. Today environmental pronouncements about air pollution, and news reports decrying smog, invariably cite statistics from the summer of 1988 as if they were typical. Apparent improvements in 1991 and 1992, environmentalists assert, were a fluke caused by moderate weather. As soon as the heat returns, so will the appalling smog.

But in the summer of 1993 the heat returned and the appalling smog did not. A prolonged weather structure caused cold, extreme rain and flooding in the Mississippi Valley, coupled with high temperatures and stagnant air from Raleigh to Boston. New York City exceeded 100 degrees Fahrenheit for four days running for the first time since 1948.[2] Washington, D.C., was favored by eight consecutive days at 95 degrees or more. Between this heat and the stagnant front, conditions were ideal for smog. Yet during the boiling 1993 summer Washington had an ozone advisory zone just twice, versus 12 times in 1988; Philadelphia seven times, versus 23 times in 1988; other East Coast comparisons were similar.

A revealing statistic in this regard might be called the smog batting average, the number of days over 90 degrees that trigger ozone advisories. In this system the lower the average, the better. In 1988 in major East Coast cities, 39 percent of days above 90 degrees resulted in smog warnings. In 1993, just 14 percent did. Thus the smog batting average had fallen to less than half its previous level in a mere five years. Yet the absence of air pollution during the heat wave of 1993 was a nonstory, barely remarked on by media organizations, environmentalists, or politicians.

True Killer Smog

Air pollution and material life have been partners. As early as the year 1306, the British throne issued a proclamation forbidding the burning of coal within London, because of the mineral's noxious fumes. As industry expanded in the nineteenth century, coal and then petroleum were combusted in vast quantities for decades with no restrictions on pollution output. By the turn of the century heavy-industry towns like Birmingham (U.K. and U.S. both), Buffalo, Chattanooga, and Pittsburgh regularly experienced air so murky street lights were turned on in daylight. At that time plain old smoke, an awful pollutant, was the leading threat. Prototype environmental organizations with names like the London Smoke Abatement Society sprang up in response.

What may always be the global low point for air pollution occurred in postwar London. British industry was running full-tilt without stack controls; with the economic recovery, autos were beginning to take over the streets and discharge pollutants uncontrolled. Most dwellings in London were then warmed by an antiquated system of district heating: coal-fired boilers located every few blocks, making hot water piped to flats. The plants ran without controls, disburdening acrid plumes directly into residential neighborhoods. Air pollution in the British capital became unbearable. Gross soot at around 500 micrograms per cubic meter of air was common; the worst recent levels in the United States averaged one-tenth that. Schoolchildren and the elderly were kept indoors during winter heating season. Early postwar photos do not show the magical London of childhood stories, rather a town swathed in a hellish billow under which miserable humans scurried.

In December of 1952 a prolonged temperature inversion trapped stagnant air above London for most of the month. Pollution thickened to a degree now unimaginable. Some 4,000 Londoners died of respiratory distress, about as many people as perished in the 1984 Bhopal chemical disaster. The worst comparable U.S. air pollution happened in October 1948, when 20 people perished from lung failure during a five-day coal-smog inversion above Donora, Pennsylvania.

After the horrible smog of 1952, Britain began closing coal-fired district heating facilities, replacing them with boilers powered by clean natural gas and with individual oil-fired home furnaces. It is useful to recall that oil, which today seems such a font of pollution, as recently as the 1960s was promoted as a "clean-burning" fuel, its smoke output so much lower than that of coal or wood. London's smoke and gross soot problems were brought under control. But other forms of air pollution began to increase there and throughout the industrial world. Emissions of sulfur from coal-fired power plants rose as Western society was electrified. Emissions of air toxics increased as petrochemicals became ubiquitous. And the automobile proliferated. Soon oil was understood to be not so clean after all.

Taming the Automobile

Until the 1960s, air pollution control consisted primarily of local ordinances regarding smoke. In 1907 Chicago passed an ordinance requiring that new factories conform to generally accepted engineering practices for smoke abatement. In the 1940s the American Society of Mechanical Engineers began publishing guidelines for reduction of gross air pollution; many localities mandated that for new factory construction the ASME rules at least be consulted. But such mild strictures produced at best a rear-guard action preventing air pollution from getting entirely out of hand. Calls for serious reduction of smog inevitably were met by claims that the economy would go bust.

By the 1960s, air pollution had grown sufficiently obvious, while prosperity seemed sufficiently secure, that the political dynamic changed. Beginning in 1965, a state law imposed smog controls on cars sold in California. The first restrictions were not effective, but a precedent had been set. Pressure mounted in Washington for national action, which came in the form of the 1970 Clean Air Act. Not only did this bill set in motion the cleanup that, just two decades later, manifested itself in dramatic reductions of air pollution, but enforcement of the act would demonstrate that environmental cleanup and economic prosperity are not antithetical. The U.S. gross national product has increased by 73 percent in real terms since the act was passed: Economic production has headed steadily up while air pollution has gone steadily down.

The Clean Air Act had both successful and failed provisions. The most successful was tailpipe controls for automobiles. Today new automobiles produce some 99 percent less pollution than cars built before 1970. The next time you take a drive, glance at the tailpipes of the cars ahead. Only older models in poor repair will be emitting any visible pollutant.

A measure of how far American society has come in incorporating

environmental protection as a core political value is that today not even
the right wing challenges the notion that auto exhaust should be tightly
restricted. Yet in the 1960s, when cars on local streets were spewing
blackened contaminants willy-nilly, the idea of regulation was extensively controversial. "Federal Standards Impossible, Automakers
Declare" was a standard headline as the 1970 legislation approached
passage in Congress. Executives of the Big Three repeatedly told
Washington significant pollution reductions either were a technical fantasy or, alternatively, could be accomplished only at prohibitive cost:
$1,000 per car was a common estimate, at a time when the typical new
car cost about $3,000.

Congress rejected such tales of woe and enacted strong restrictions.
Thereby three important lessons were learned. The first is that predictions of calamity, for auto sales or the environment or anything else, are
inherently implausible. The more extreme a coming problem is forecast
to be, the less credible the prediction.

The second lesson is *never* believe Detroit. Tailpipe emission controls
were supposed to be impossible and soon were working fine. Better fuel
economy was supposedly out of the question, too: In 1974 Ford told
Congress that if federal fuel standards were enacted the largest car the
company could ever make again would be a subcompact. Today Ford
still manufactures the Crown Victoria and Lincoln Town Car, and these
land yachts comply with fuel standards.

The rule of never believe Detroit is important because self-serving
claims that the limits of antipollution technology have been reached continue to be a common automaker theme. After the 1990 Clean Air Act
passed, states began debating whether to mandate an extra round of
emission controls that is optional under the legislation. In 1991 Al
Weverstad, a General Motors official, declared that the extra standard
would cost at least $1,000 per car. A few months later a Ford executive,
Michael Schwarz, told the Maryland state legislature the new rules
would be a nightmare because "there are no cars in existence" that
could meet the standard. The Maryland legislature voted down the
added requirement. Just three weeks after Schwarz spoke, Ford unveiled
a production car that did meet the standard, at an added cost of $100.

The third lesson of auto tailpipe controls is that pollution reduction
is usually cheaper than expected. The predicted $1,000 cost per car to
meet 1970 air emission standards works out to nearly $4,000 in current
dollars. Yet new cars meet today's much stricter standards at a cost of
about $400 per vehicle.

Corporations cry wolf regarding environmental controls partly
because cost estimates are based on technology existing at the time a cut-

back is proposed. "Before a regulation exists, industry has little incentive to invent control technology," says David Doniger, a former air pollution analyst for the Natural Resources Defense Council. "Once regulations arrive industry finds better and cheaper ways to meet the goal, so actual costs are nowhere near the dire predictions." In 1970, when gloom forecasts were made regarding auto controls, no one had ever heard of the catalytic converter. Once this device was invented, rapid and cost-effective reductions in auto emissions were realized.

In Praise of the Arbitrary

A reason auto tailpipe controls worked is that they were drawn as performance standards, not process (sometimes "command and control") rules. Instead of attempting to dictate to auto manufacturers what sort of antipollution technology should be installed on cars, the 1970 Clean Air Act simply decreed that auto tailpipe pollution must be cut 90 percent. How carmakers met the target would be their concern. The selection of a 90-percent performance standard "was a back of the envelope calculation," says Philip Cummings, who was at the time counsel to the Senate Environment and Public Works Committee, where parts of the act were drafted. "We just picked that number because it sounded like a good goal."

A continuing sand trap for environmental policy is the longing for scientific certainty—an exact, numerically elegant determination of what effect on the environment particular human actions will have. Yet neither the EPA nor any environmental analyst has ever been able to prove exactly what levels of emissions are bad, any more than any industrial researcher has ever been able to prove exactly what levels are safe. A tenet of ecorealism is that for the moment all we have to work with is reasonable guesses about human effects on the Earth. And a reasonable pollution reduction executed immediately is infinitely preferable to delay in search of hypothetical perfect reforms.

In this sense arbitrariness can be a virtue in environmental affairs. Many civic presumptions are fundamentally arbitrary. No one can prove, for instance, that 55 miles per hour is the "right" speed limit for highways, although everyone agrees that somewhere around that number falls the reasonable range. When Congress picked 90 percent as the target for auto emission goals, its decision was arbitrary but reasonable. Had Congress instead directed the EPA to convene panels of worthy personages to debate the ideal, scientifically certain level of auto emission reductions, those personages would still be meeting today—probably in a basketball arena, to accommodate all the lawyers—and cars would continue to spew mephitic exhaust.

The Infuriatingly Clean Car

The pace of improvements in tailpipe emission controls creates an annoying verity: The modern American automobile is the cleanest system of transportation ever devised. Cleaner, certainly, than cars sold in the Western European nations that U.S. environmentalists depict as models of ecological enlightenment. Catalytic converters did not begin to appear on Western European cars until the late 1980s, versus 1975 in the United States. They did not become mandatory in the United Kingdom till 1993 and are still not mandatory in several European Union nations. Unleaded gasoline did not appear at the first Western European pump until 1988, versus 1977 in the U.S.

New American cars run much cleaner than buses. The diesel engines of buses emit up to 70 times more particulate pollution than comparable gasoline engines of automobiles. A typical urban commuter bus may discharge as much total pollution as 150 new cars. Thus, though bus transportation does save fuel, from a pollution-control standpoint the riders of a city bus might do better for the Earth by all being the sole occupants of new cars. Buses traditionally received exemption from clean air regulations, urban governments pleading, don't impose on us poor cities the antismog costs you impose on suburbanites. By the time the 1990 clean air bill was enacted that argument had outlived its heart-tugging appeal. Emission standards for buses began in 1994. In 1993 federal law began to require refiners to reduce the sulfur content of diesel fuel, which will cut the pollution output of buses and heavy trucks. Additional California state regulations require refineries to remove from diesel fuel most of the "aromatic" chemicals that contribute to smog; this rule will become nearly universal throughout the country in the late 1990s. As of 1992, catalytic converters were mandated for pickup trucks and "sport utility vehicles" (Jeeps and their upscale cousins) for the first time outside California, meaning these vehicles, increasingly popular with suburbanites, will soon run as cleanly as cars.

Because the state had an antismog agency, the California Air Resources Board, in place before the 1970 federal legislation passed, the act imposed uniform standards on all states except California, which was granted approval to seek waivers from EPA rules. California has consistently applied for the waivers, requiring cleaner cars than are sold in the nation as a whole. This practice infuriates automakers, forcing them to design two versions of vehicles—a California car and a 49-state car. In the 1990s a movement began to build among environmentalists to get other states to match California standards. At this writing California's superstrict auto standards for the late 1990s have been matched by Massachusetts and New York. California, Massachusetts, and New York represent a quarter of the American auto market. If a few more states match California, automakers may find economies of scale in offering superclean autos to the entire U.S., accelerating the pace of progress against smog.

How clean is superclean? Today new cars emit about one percent as much pollution as 1970 models. Beginning in 1997 cars sold in California and in matching states will drop to about 0.5 percent of the 1970 level. In addition, in 1998 two percent of cars sold in California and matching states must be zero-emission; zero-emission vehicles must rise to ten percent of sales by 2003.

Electric cars are the likely candidates for the California zero-emission program, with the Big Three, fearful of losing position in the nation's largest auto market, developing electric prototypes with a 1998 market date in mind. There is also a possibility natural gas will emerge as the zero-emission winner. School buses in Columbus, Ohio, and service trucks of the utility Brooklyn Natural Gas, have been running successfully on this fuel for several years. In 1993 the utility Southern California Gas placed a substantial bet on natural gas locomotion, announcing a factory that will convert General Motors vehicles to natural gas power.

A decade ago automakers were swearing to Congress that practical zero-emission cars were a physical impossibility. They now concede electric cars or cars running on natural gas or methanol are feasible. What remains to be seen is whether anyone will buy such cars. There may be little demand for, say, an electric car that can only carry two people 120 miles before needing an overnight recharge. How to gauge zero emissions is another question. An electric car releases nothing to the air, but production of the juice to charge its battery may be a different story. Most electric cars will be powered by fossil-fired generating capacity that shifts emissions from the city, where most voters live, to outlying areas.

The 1990 Clean Air Act further specifies that the government agencies and buyers of fleets begin purchasing significant numbers of vehicles that run on natural gas, methanol (an alcohol that can be made from natural gas or from trees), and similar fuels. In theory, vehicles using these fuels could operate with emissions only marginally above zero. Proposals for cars burning alternate fuels have spawned a minor industry of engineering studies regarding which combination of liquids, gases, and perhaps even powdered metals would make for optimum performance. What matters most is that the federal initiative will solve the chicken-or-egg dilemma that plagues proposals for nonpetroleum fuels, causing an alternative fuel infrastructure to come into existence. Then it will become possible to sort out which alternative fuel ideas work in the only way such ideas ever are sorted out effectively, through market forces and actual trial and error.

Dismay Over the Clean Car

Advanced antismog features only apply to new cars. Today one auto from before the model year 1970, when there were no tailpipe controls, can neutralize the controls on 100 new cars. One car from before the model year 1980, when catalytic converters became more effective, can neutralize the antipollution gains from 50 new cars.

In 1992 the California oil company Unocal offered $700 to anyone signing over a pre-1971 car to be scrapped; Unocal ended up with 8,300 takers. Too few to be more than a public relations exercise? This purchase offset the pollution caused by roughly 700,000 new cars, equal to some eight percent of that year's new-car purchases nationwide. Bizarrely enough, the Unocal "cash for clunkers" program was roundly condemned by Los Angeles environmentalists, who complained that people who swapped their old cars for the $700 would use the cash to buy new cars, perpetuating the cycle of auto ownership. Yet "by far the most important factor in reducing smog is turnover of the auto fleet," says Kay Jones, a former official of the federal Council on Environmental Quality during the Jimmy Carter Administration. "The sooner people buy new cars and retire their pre-1980 models, the sooner smog will end."

Advanced antismog systems are also only effective if in working order. A standard estimate is that today 60 percent of smog comes from 20 percent of cars, either precontrol models or vehicles in which antipollution devices are not working properly. The new Clean Air Act ordered the EPA to impose stringent inspection programs on both cars and taxis. In 1991, EPA Administrator William Reilly told states they could accomplish more at a smaller investment by tightening inspection programs than by matching the California standards for new cars. Governors, Reilly found, did not want to hear that they ought to tighten auto-inspection programs that are infamous with voters. No governor wants to announce the inspection lines will get longer. Following opposition by governors to the EPA's strict-testing plan, Reilly drafted new standards under which auto tailpipe inspections would become only somewhat more strict. For this he was widely denounced in Congress, including by then-senator Al Gore, and sued by the Natural Resources Defense Council. To settle the lawsuit Reilly proposed a testing regime stricter than the first one. Reilly's plan would have required that most major cities test all cars in new inspection facilities equipped with $150,000 chassis dynamometers. In 1994, in a move that somehow attracted no public notice, the Clinton Administration backed away from Reilly's strict-testing plan, telling California that only 15 percent of its vehicles need be checked in central inspection stations.

The pain-in-the-rear aspect of antismog inspections has inspired some entrepreneurial innovation. For instance a University of Denver engineer named Donald Stedman has been advocating automated roadside stations that would use infrared sensors for random checks of cars driving by. If a car's exhaust registered as dirty, a camera would photograph the license plate. A fine would then be mailed. Smog inspections along highways would become continuous, catching cheaters; yet no motorist would have to take time off from work to idle in line at an emission inspection center.

Tests in Denver suggest that Stedman's system is effective. Environmentalists and state pollution-control agencies are resisting the remote-sensing idea, on the grounds that it cannot assess auto exhaust as fully as a dynamometer, which is true. But Stedman thinks the real objection is that his system is cheap, costing about 50 cents per car checked, versus perhaps $15 per car at a drive-in station, plus the loss of the owner's time. Some researchers think the whole subject of emissions-testing regulations will soon become moot, as improvements upon Stedman's idea allow highly accurate automated roadside check stations to replace central emissions testing with continuous checks that are cheap and simple. This is the type of clean-tech advance happening throughout pollution control.

Because the environmental community is unable to come to terms with the fact that most people like cars, some enviros are disappointed by clean-car progress. Increased cleanliness of cars has decreased driving guilt; the enviro hard core wants the guilt of driving to rise. From the ecorealist perspective it is delightful to think that while there are 60 percent more cars on the road today than in 1970, each driving nearly twice as many miles annually, smog continues to decline. From the orthodox environmental perspective more driving with less pollution is a disastrous turn of events. At times I have heard "deep" ecologists argue that federal mpg standards were a horrible mistake, because mileage improvements made driving more practical. Falling oil prices and better fuel economy result in cars steadily cheaper to operate; adjusted for inflation, today the typical new car's fuel expense per mile is 40 percent lower than in 1970. Some deep ecologists have said tailpipe emission controls were a horrible mistake as well, because if cars were still as dirty as they once were, smog would by now be so hideous cities would have no choice but to ban the automobile altogether.

Nefariously, clean cars continue to be tolerable. But when most environmentalists say cars are venal what they mean is that OTHER PEOPLE'S cars are venal. A few admirable ecologists travel only by public transportation. The influential environmental lobbyists of Washington and Sacramento would not recognize the interior of a metro bus: They carry their press releases denouncing the car culture in the waybacks of late-model imports, and would never dream of doing otherwise.

Evil Bakeries

Though cars, trucks, and buses are the cause of most urban air pollution—about two-thirds of smog originates with vehicles—they are not the only source. Federal strictures are beginning to control almost every air emission that originates anywhere.

For instance in 1991 a consortium of utilities that owns the Navajo generating station, a large coal-fired power plant in Page, Arizona, signed an agreement with the EPA to install $430 million in new pollution-control devices, though the plant already met Clean Air Act standards. Navajo station is near the Grand Canyon, and many people feel the misty haze that has descended on the canyon frequently in the past two decades results from the plant's emissions. This notion has caused an extended technical controversy, including the release of a tracer chemical in Navajo stack emissions to determine if the tracers turned up in the air above the Grand Canyon. Most did not, because Navajo station is *downwind* of the park; a fair number of researchers believe that Grand Canyon haze is a by-product of Los Angeles smog, the L.A. basin being upwind. Nevertheless the new control devices at Navajo station will render it one of the cleanest-running power plants in the world.

This is the first enforcement of a 1977 law that allows regulators to impose special restrictions on pollution that lowers visibility in a national park. Power plants near Shenandoah National Park, in the Virginia Appalachians, are in the process of agreeing to special requirements to cut that park's haze, too. Such action is great news for parks but worth pondering for a moment. Clear vistas in places of natural beauty are an obvious social good. But consider $430 million spent at a power plant on the off chance it will reduce haze slightly. In an age when such conservation expenditures have become routine it is absurd to say, as environmentalists still do, that the United States does not make ecological protection a social priority.

In rural areas where smog is rare, new factories had been required to install only moderate levels of pollution controls, on the theory that emissions would attenuate harmlessly. Beginning in 1991 that exemption essentially ended. New emission sources in rural areas are required to install what regulators call best-available technology, meaning the latest antipollution engineering, to insure that pristine air is not degraded by avoidable emissions. What constitutes best-available technology is defined in smog zones like Los Angeles. Whenever new control devices are perfected they become defined as "best-available technology" and now will be extended for use in all parts of the country.

For instance, for technical reasons control of nitrous oxides ("NOX") lags behind other forms of pollution reduction. In the 1980s some engineers believed there would never be a practical means to cut NOX from coal-fired power plants. In 1992, however, Long Island Lighting Company sponsored a project in which urea, an inexpensive fertilizer component, was added to the boilers of a power station at Port Jefferson, New York. By tinkering with the way in which the urea entered the boiler's flame path, engineers found they could cause combustion by-products that would otherwise have formed nitrous oxides to rearrange themselves into pure nitrogen. Pure nitrogen is not a pollutant; 79 percent of the atmosphere is pure nitrogen. By 1994 a chemist named Robert Farrauto had perfected another process that cuts NOX from power plants. Using a catalyst of palladium oxide, Farrauto created efficient boiler combustion at a temperature lower than that at which NOX forms. Such experiments mean NOX controls will soon be considered "best-available technology" and required of most industrial facilities. Similar advances are in progress in other pollution categories.

In the worst smog cities regulators have begun to impose restrictions on dry cleaners, bakeries, paint shops, and other small businesses. Believe it or not, baking of your daily bread may result in evaporation of volatile organic chemicals. In chemistry "organic" means carbon-based, not alive; many carbon-based commercial chemicals break down into compounds similar to automotive hydrocarbons, then react with sunlight to form smog. For example the solvents that liquify paint evaporate when exposed to air, so that paint cures to a solid. Traditional paint solvent is made from volatile organic compounds. In Los Angeles, paints based on high-solvent formulas can no longer be sold; paint shops must report their paint use, employing bar-code scanners to document that the cans they open contain approved formulations. This is the level of detail at which air-pollution officials now find themselves working. Under a federal court order that requires Los Angeles to eliminate nearly all smog-forming emissions by the year 2010, California state officials are in the early stages of imposing antismog regulations on lawn mowers, chain saws, outboard motors, and other currently unrestricted engines, and on such consumer products as hair sprays and charcoal lighter fluid, which emit volatile organic compounds. Eventually the EPA will extend such strictures to most of the country.

This is not an exercise in regulatory overkill. The chain saws and lawn mowers of California, for instance, annually emit smog precursors equal to the pollution output of 3.5 million new cars. Making small motors nonpolluting is simply the next step in clean tech. In 1992 a spokesman for Toro, the home-tools manufacturer, said his company was resigned to emission controls on lawn mowers, which run in the smoggy summer season, but hoped the EPA would not require controls on snowblowers, which by definition operate only when hot sun is not an issue. This is the level of awakening Corporate America had reached by just 1992, a mere two decades since the first Earth Day—conceding that even lawn mowers must be emissions-controlled. This concession, arrived at so soon in historical terms, means it will not be long until business acknowledges that all products in all categories must be pollution minimizing.

Conservative reaction to pollution controls on devices as small as lawn mowers may be summarized in the word *HARRUMMPPHHHH!* But stopping pollution is not a wearisome, negative, restrictive chore, as the right so often suggests. It is an exciting technical challenge. The next generation of clean-tech machines will be at once more sophisticated and less intrusive, easier on the ecology and also on everyone's nerves. For instance a likely replacement for the gasoline lawn mower is a new electric mower with rechargeable batteries that eliminate the tangled cord. Rechargeable mowers are not only much cleaner than gasoline mowers and easier to use; they run with hardly any noise.

Pollution output aside, the incessant roar of the gas mower is unpleasant for the person walking behind it and antisocial toward the community. Noise can be a form of pollution, as pervasive as any humankind makes. One of nature's abiding virtues is that most of its operations are soothingly quiet. Humankind's first impact on an ecosphere is to add unwelcome noise: *Homo sapiens* might better have been designated *Homo clatterus*. Thrumming mechanical noise may someday seem as intolerable to our descendants as horse dung in the streets, a commonplace of the nineteenth century, seems to us today. In the coming clean-tech era daily life will recover much of the stillness typical to natural life. This will soothe modern nerves, including the nerves of conservatives, which clearly require extra soothing.

Reformulated Gasoline

One of the first major products of the coming clean-tech world is already on the market in Los Angeles: reformulated gasoline. This substance, whose existence is little known even where sold, plays an important role in accelerating progress against smog.

When the Clean Air Act of 1990 was being debated, it was expected the final bill would contain strong provisions mandating alternative fuels. A possibility raised by Reilly was that ten percent of cars sold by the year 1998 would run on something other than gasoline. This provision received a serious hearing because at the time most pollution engineers assumed that no matter how effective automobile antismog devices became, some portion of the inherent pollution content of gasoline would always exit the tailpipe. That George Bush, a former oil man nominally from the petroleum state of Texas, was lending serious consideration to Reilly's alternative fuels proposal was a loud wake-up call to oil interests. In Los Angeles an even more aggressive proposal was advancing. The South Coast Air Quality Management District released a plan that specified that after the year 2007, petroleum could no longer be sold in the Los Angeles basin. The Southern California car culture is a gold mine to oil companies. Suddenly that mine seemed in danger of being reclaimed.

Faced with such reform initiatives oil companies were expected to respond in the time-honored way: Put the squeeze on members of Congress, channel funds through political action committees, and rev up deceptive public-relations campaigns. This time something clicked in the boardroom at Arco Petroleum. The company instructed its chemists to reduce the inherent pollution content of gasoline. In just 90 days they devised a formula that reduced smog precursors in gasoline by 37 percent. In 1989 Arco started selling the reformulated gas at its Los Angeles stations.

"Until we began discussing an alternative fuels mandate at the White House level," Reilly says, "I had never even heard the term reformulated gasoline. No oil-company executive had ever given the EPA the slightest hint it could be done." Suddenly it was done. And the beauty of reformulated gasoline is that the gains are not confined to new automobiles, as with each round of new tailpipe restrictions; benefits spread to every car on the road. Arco's first reformulated gasoline was intended for pre-1980 cars, the worst smog contributors. Soon the company had a low-pollution grade for all models. Arco published a description of reformulated gasoline in open technical literature, waiving patents. This placed pressure on other oil companies to match; most did, at least for Southern California. Arco found ways to bring the added refining cost of reformulated gasoline down to just 4.3 cents per gallon. A break-through had been realized with amazing speed and at a reasonable price.

It was hard to know whether to laud or vilify the company. James Morrison, an Arco vice-president, told me the company could have invented reformulated fuel years before: "But we were already selling all the gasoline we could make and there was no government requirement for a low-pollution product, so where was our incentive?" When Arco finally made reformulated gasoline the company's goal was not so much smog prevention but blocking the alternative-fuels legislation. "Good deeds are wonderful," Arco CEO Lodwrick Cook told Bruce Piasecki, who runs an environmental study program at Rensselaer Polytechnic Institute in Troy, New York, "but I like good numbers [profits] more."

Just as it matters not what motivates charity, environmental gains inspired by corporate self-interest are as welcome as any other kind. Arco began to lobby for national gasoline reformulation, in return for softening of alternative-fuel mandates. Oil companies such as Texaco opposed the initiative: Texaco's canny plan was old-fashioned arm twisting as oil interests have practiced it for decades. Texaco failed. A national gasoline reformulation clause ended up in the new EPA rules, coupled to the softer alternative fuels rule for which Arco hoped.

Federal gasoline reformulation regulations have triggered a series of successful antipollution initiatives that has drawn almost no public attention, owing to its inappropriately positive character. The first action was a 1990 EPA decision to impose a lower volatility standard on gasoline. Gasoline volatility governs how much fuel evaporates when a car's gas tank is opened at a service station; the component that evaporates is rich in volatile organics, a smog cause. Since the 1970s, cities have tried to combat gasoline evaporation with those cumbersome vapor-recovery nozzles that frustrate everyone who patronizes self-service gas stations. The direct solution is to lower the tendency of gasoline to evaporate by lowering its volatility. Refinery companies had long sworn this impossible on a practical basis. In 1990, after a lobbying fight involving eye-glazing technical arguments—position papers on a subject as obscure as "reid vapor pressure" ascending all the way to the Oval Office—the EPA imposed a strict antievaporation standard. Oil companies suddenly discovered they could make gasoline less prone to evaporate after all. Lately slender, easy-to-use vapor-recovery nozzles for gas pumps have been invented, adding another tool against evaporation.

The second fuel formula change was the debut of "oxygenated" gasoline, designed to control carbon monoxide. Carbon monoxide pollution is produced mainly by winter weather; as ozone is the smog bane of summer, carbon monoxide is the smog bane of winter. Analysts have long supposed that by putting oxygen into gasoline, usually through an additive called methyl tertiary butyl ether, carbon monoxide could be reduced. In the late 1980s Denver, whose combination of cold air and prevailing weather structure renders the city prone to carbon monoxide buildup, passed a local ordinance requiring oxygenated gasoline. Results were promising. Based on Denver's experience the 1990 Clean Air Act required that gasoline distributors in cities doing poorly on the EPA carbon monoxide scale offer only oxygenated gasoline during winter.

Petroleum companies registered the usual protests about how this was utterly impossible. Nevertheless by the fall of 1992 oxygenated gasoline was at pumps in most big cities. Oxygenated gasoline was among the reasons New York City, which experienced 71 days above the EPA standard for carbon monoxide in 1985, ended 1992 with zero violation days. New York's city council had been considering such measures as no-drive days to combat winter smog. Now it appears further action against carbon monoxide will be unnecessary in that city. National levels for carbon monoxide fell to record lows in 1992, with only a handful of violations nationwide. Preliminary results suggest that 1993 carbon monoxide levels will be even lower.[3]

The most important change in fuel chemistry is the spread of reformulated gasoline out of Southern California to the rest of the country. By 1995, reformulated gasoline will be sold in Baltimore, Chicago, Houston, Milwaukee, Philadelphia, New York, San Diego, and south-suburban Connecticut—the nation's smoggiest areas other than Los Angeles. Other cities are likely to require this clean fuel in the late 1990s. David O'Reilly, a vice president of Chevron, says that "Eventually reformulated gasoline will be universal." Once reformulated gasoline becomes widely available, the pace of smog reduction will accelerate.

Some environmentalists considered the reformulated gasoline provisions a defeat because the law did not require clean gas to be universal immediately. But in another respect the reformulation rules were groundbreaking: Final terms were arrived at by a regulatory negotiation or "reg-neg."

For years environmental policy in the U.S. has been made following a tormented sequence in which Congress passes a law, industry uses technicalities to evade compliance, the EPA becomes hopelessly bogged down in legal detail, environmentalists sue to force action, and ultimately a bewildered federal judge imposes a decision unsatisfactory to all parties. In a reg-neg, the sequence of lawsuits is assumed to be inevitable: So why not get the parties together before the courts take over? In the gasoline reformulation reg-neg, representatives of major environmental organizations and Big Oil met for informal talks on details of gasoline reformulation. The goal was to hammer out a rule that would fend off the customary lawsuits and interminable delay. The EPA acted as a mediator, not as a policy-making body. The arrangement represented a stark admission of the current American political reality: that arm wrestling between interest groups, not detached contemplation in regulatory agencies, is how law is shaped.

Reg-neg on the reformulated gasoline rules took place in the office of William Rosenberg, then EPA's chief air pollution official. The parties met at a table beneath a favorite painting belonging to Rosenberg, one depicting medieval Talmudic scholars remonstrating over a single word. An oil company official who attended the sessions told me, "We went into this thinking we could snow the enviros under and were amazed at how sharp they were." Ultimately the oil companies accepted most of what environmentalists wanted for reformulated gasoline content; environmentalists made concessions on matters such as flexible performance standards. As the negotiations concluded, the parties signed pledges not to sue each other—a first for two participants, the Natural Resources Defense Council and Sierra Club, whose litigation departments have long been their policy-making arms. Because of the no-lawsuit pledge, implementation of reformulated gasoline rules is proceeding apace, without judicial intervention or make-work for lawyers.

Smog Trading

Some environmentalists left the gasoline reg-neg feeling uneasy that they had met privately with The Enemy and emerged with a nonconfrontational agreement. Yet such voluntary approaches to pollution control are the wave of the future. Market innovation and nonlegalistic mediation are infinitely preferable to judicial review and bureaucratic rule making, since even when the latter are successful they are agonizingly slow and expend resources on process rather than on results. But the idea of genial meetings that lead to voluntary agreements runs counter to the cultural norms of environmentalism. The Natural Resources Defense Council practically exists for the purpose of litigation: It sues the EPA and industry so often that, one federal lawyer in environmental affairs says, "They might as well open a branch office in the Justice Department." All bureaucracies resist change; environmental bureaucracies are no different. Any switch from confrontation to mediation will be difficult for the green movement, even if the results are promising.

Aspects of flexible thinking are reflected in other new efforts against air pollution, and again Los Angeles is the leading example. After the South Coast Air Quality Management District startled Los Angeles with its plan to go so far as to regulate lighter fluid, infuriating the political right, the SCAQMD then infuriated the political left by announcing a system of smog-permit trading. Previously the SCAQMD had dictated to companies technical specifics: the cumbersome exercise of process controls. Now, the district declared, companies would be governed by performance standards, simply given reduction targets and allowed to meet the targets as they wished. Companies cutting emissions beyond their targets would be allowed to sell smog credits on an open market.

Soon Allied Signal, Northrop, Shell, and other Southern California firms were trading smog offsets to each other, a practice against which environmentalists regularly inveighed but which the SCAQMD believed was accelerating smog control. In what must have been a first, the SCAQMD even got a military installation, March Air Force Base, east of Los Angeles, to purchase $1.2 million worth of smog credits when the base needed to expand its power boilers.

James Lents, director of the SCAQMD, says, "If I had been the one who had the idea for reformulated gasoline, it would have taken me five years to get the first regulation into the field. If instead I can persuade a company to do something like that voluntarily, emission reductions begin more rapidly and process costs are lower." Lents grew interested in pollution trading partly because he feared that SCAQMD rules were on the verge of becoming self-defeating. Aerospace manufacturers, an important part of the Southern California economy, began to complain that paint solvent restrictions would prevent the application of as little as a single quart of specialty aircraft coatings. In one instance the Los Angeles–based Douglas division of McDonnell-Douglas, which builds the MD11 jetliner, flew a new transport out of California merely to apply paint, then flew the plane right back. Pollution from that avoidable trip outweighed any paint-solvent reductions, jet exhaust being among the few unregulated emissions sources remaining in the U.S. "All it takes is one red tape horror story like that to undermine hundreds of legitimate rules," Lents notes. Pollution trading reduces the likelihood of horror stories.

Daddy, What Was Smog?

Shortly after the new Clean Air Act passed the National Academy of Sciences released a dispirited study that concluded, "Despite the major regulatory programs of the past 20 years, efforts to attain the national ambient air quality standard for ozone largely have failed." Taking this into account, the states and cities that implement air pollution directives were told to expect the situation to grow much worse.

Instead smog numbers began declining. "When you adjust for meteorology, the underlying trends are almost entirely positive," says Jones, the air pollution analyst. Had the National Academy of Sciences adjusted its figures for the 1988 heat-wave summer, its conclusions would not have been pessimistic, Jones thinks. Members of the National Academy smog research team in 1993 published an update that was decidedly more upbeat than their first work, basing mild optimism mainly on the advent of reformulated gasoline. The depressing 1991 National Academy report was front-page news across the country. The encouraging 1993 update was, so far as I could determine, not mentioned in any major newspaper.

Atmospheric chemists have long assumed that hydrocarbons and volatile organics (collectively VOCs in the regulatory acronym) are the primary cause of smog, with nitrous oxides a secondary factor. Because the 1991 National Academy study found that smog was not falling as quickly as the decline in VOC emissions, the study suggested that perhaps the entire premise of modern air pollution regulation is faulty. Perhaps nitrous oxides, not VOCs, are the core problem.

Developments of this sort are testaments to the uncertain state of human understanding of the environment. In lab tests the relationships among VOCs, NOX, sunlight, and smog formation appear straightforward. But the atmosphere of the living Earth is not a laboratory beaker. In it pollutants mix unpredictably with hydroxyl radicals, a natural antipollutant. The mixing occurs under unpredictable circumstances of wind, humidity, and cloud cover. In the unpredictable atmosphere, NOX compounds sometimes appear to absorb VOCs, one pollutant counteracting another. At other times NOX appears to increase the smog potential of VOCs. Sometimes NOX forms smog by itself; sometimes NOX blows away harmlessly; sometimes NOX converts to nitric acid and contributes to acid rain. In the end the National Academy of Sciences was left to admit it really does not know what causes smog. Maybe it's VOCs. Maybe it's NOX. Maybe it's phases of the moon.

Jones, who has an exceptional track record at predicting smog incidence, believes that VOCs really are the true cause of most smog, as assumed. He has studied the ozone patterns in Louisville. That city cut its VOC emissions 36 percent in the last decade. Adjusting for weather, Louisville ozone has declined 36 percent in the same period, Jones finds. All this raises the possibility that smog, far from being an intractable problem that will haunt society well into the future, will be nearly gone as soon as the turn of the century. Already the number of cities plagued by what the EPA delicately calls "air-quality nonattainment" has declined by almost half since the late 1980s. Jones believes that "if present trends continue cities like Baltimore and Washington will meet the EPA standards in two or three years, even if government takes no additional action." Only Houston and Los Angeles are likely to remain seriously smoggy past the turn of the century, Jones thinks. And even Los Angeles now projects that it will banish smog around the year 2015. On the day that clean air comes to Southern California, modern industrial life will have placed itself firmly on a course toward a green future.

Environmentalists offer two arguments against such hopefulness. The first is that the greenhouse effect may warm the climate, in which case increased ozone formation during hot weather would cancel gains from reductions in emissions. This possibility cannot be counted out. The second objection to the good news about smog is that current ozone standards are being met because the standards are not strict enough. Today a smog violation is recorded when any monitor in an urban area registers more than 12 parts per billion of ozone for one hour; until 1980, the standard was eight parts per billion. President Carter's EPA relaxed the standard on the basis of studies suggesting that 12 ppb is safe. Since then other studies have suggested it is too high. At this writing the American Lung Association is suing the EPA, asking courts to reimpose the eight ppb standard. Should this happen dozens of cities instantly will violate federal standards, and it will seem like a sudden smog pandemic has been triggered.

On the premise that all pollutants should be driven to the lowest practical level, the eight ppb standard sounds like a good idea: though such a definitional shift would forestall the day when children ask their parents, What was smog? For the moment let's consider the remaining major category of air pollution: airborne toxics.

The Paranoid Number

One day in 1989 I stood in a rail yard across from the USX Clairton Coke Works, among the largest factories in the United States. The Clairton Works sprawls across a bend in the Monongahela River south of Pittsburgh. Through a light haze of soot I could discern batteries of three-story metal ovens stitched with rail spurs, power boilers, "bag houses" designed to capture ash, pyramids of coal and other raw materials, dilapidated slag towers, and caked-brown service roads. Alongside ran the tired channel of the Monongahela. In the distance, well within the haze bubble of the factory, lining the river's banks and escarpments were houses, homes to laborers of the Clairton Works for close to a century. Men, faces flushed red from the heat, walked atop the ovens, side-stepping jets of flame and tongues of yellow sulfur. Occasionally they would strike the ovens with crowbars, to whack metal plates into alignment. Various automated systems had been tried for this purpose. Hardened men walking the ovens and whacking them with crowbars proved more capable.

The Clairton Works is a vast organism that makes coke, the carbon feedstock for steel. The organism also exhales: sulfur, nitrous oxides, PM10. Clairton exhales toxics and carcinogens, air pollutants that conjure more worrisome images than smog. In the late 1980s, the factory was releasing about six million pounds a year of toxic chemicals into the Pennsylvania sky. "We do put up big numbers," Philip Masciantonio, a USX vice president, told me. "But every one of those pounds going into the air is in total compliance with the law." Indeed: That was the point.

Much as any place might, Clairton symbolizes plodding progress against air pollution. Beginning in the 1970s, USX management invested more than $200 million in emission controls at the factory, dramatically cutting its releases of sulfur and soot. But emissions of toxics remained. Although laws gave regulators powerful tools against smog, toxics perfectly legal when put into the sky included chloroform, formaldehyde, phosgene (used as a nerve gas in World War I), butadiene, and butane (carcinogens).

When the 1970 Clean Air Act was passed, Congress instructed the EPA to impose regulations on 320 industrial air toxics. In the 20 years between the presentation of that charge and the new Clean Air Act of 1990, the EPA managed to publish regulations on precisely nine. The other 311 remained uncontrolled. In 1985 Rep. Henry Waxman of California, a leading congressional environmentalist, issued a report estimating this nonregulation caused 80 million pounds of toxics to be released to the air each year. Waxman says, "Industry went haywire. They denounced the figure as wildly irresponsible environmental paranoia." Later Congress passed a bill requiring corporations to disclose their toxic output, the first compilations being published in 1989. Confessed toxic air pollution added up to 2.7 billion pounds—34 times Waxman's paranoid number.

In 1970, Congress imagined that the EPA could charge through the inventory of 320 chemicals devising a precise, infallible safety level for every compound. Each of the 320 suspect chemicals was to be assigned rules on a case-by-case basis. This early drive for scientific certainty was appealing to the young EPA. It would christen the agency, founded in 1970, with academic objectivity, abjuring mere political calculation. Thus the EPA set about generating mountains of paperwork to prove that toxics are bad for you. However easy this may sound, done formally it is pulling teeth. Agency life came to be dominated by droning committee sessions, courtroom-like hearings, and excruciating debates over minutiae. The EPA began to miss statutory deadlines by years. Unable to reach agreements on fundamentally unknowable questions such as what level of a chemical is safe, the EPA issued documents with goofy names like "preliminary draft proposal" or, my favorite, the "interim final regulation."

Because the EPA claimed to be seeking a scientifically precise basis for regulations, corporate lawyers found they could stall almost any decision by trotting out an expert to testify that more study was required. Federal rules generally are blocked by judges if found "arbitrary or capricious." A monster was soon created as courts began to hold essentially that whenever EPA attempted to define a scientifically certain level for emissions, any regulation about which there existed scientific doubt was capricious and must go back to the drawing board.

Meanwhile emissions continued. In 1986 came passage of the disclosure law, called the Community Right to Know Act. Under the bill plenary emissions of toxic chemicals remained legal but companies had to report how much they released. The EPA would then publish directories listing emissions by factory name. Corporate America lobbied arduously against this bill. It's amazing to consider that as recently as the middle 1980s Congress affirmed that billion-pound-scale emissions of toxic substances are permissible, while corporations had the temerity to complain that merely disclosing the specifics somehow trampled their rights.

However meek the Community Right to Know Act seemed in premise, its effect was as pronounced in practice. "As soon as that law passed I knew there would have to be a total transformation in the way industry conducted itself," Richard Mahoney, CEO of Monsanto, says. Petrochemical companies are the country's leading producers of toxic emissions. Mahoney continued, "The public is clearly terrified of toxic emissions and has let it be known these will no longer be tolerated. Might as well get on with fixing it." Thus on toxic air emissions industry began to be dragged into the clean-tech age by public pressure: a faster and more flexible mechanism than any government action.

Roughly through the early 1980s, the public either did not know or did not care about toxic emissions. In petrochemical zones such as the Monongahela Valley, the Kanawha Valley of West Virginia, and "cancer alley" between Baton Rouge and New Orleans (in 1990, factories around Baton Rouge emitted about 200 pounds of toxics for each nearby resident), bravado had always been the attitude toward toxic pollution. Pollution means people are working, those around chemical factories would say. Fumes? The stuff can't hurt you as long as you can smell it. Then public tolerance of toxic pollution transformed. Part of the cause was increasing information, part was scare stories: Rolled together the two represented a powerful force. The same month it made its first toxic disclosures, Monsanto committed itself to a voluntary 90-percent reduction in toxic air emissions. DuPont, Hoffmann LaRoche, Union Carbide, and other big emitters of toxics soon made similar commitments. Some, like Monsanto, have since advanced to a promise of zero toxic emissions.

When Reilly became EPA Administrator in 1989, he believed that voluntary pressure on business would have a faster effect than reworking the agency's rule-issuing apparatus. With this in mind Reilly started an initiative with a corny name, sounding like something a bunch of white males in suits would come up with at a Chamber of Commerce session: the 33/50 Program. Under 33/50 corporations were asked voluntarily to cut emissions of 17 high-priority toxics such as benzene, cadmium, and mercury by 33 percent by the year 1992 and 50 percent by 1995. For reasons ranging from enlightenment to craven fear of liability, 1,135 companies joined. Lacking adversarial drama, the 33/50 Program attracted no attention. I've never seen an article mentioning it in any nontechnical publication. The corny program's results: From 1989 to 1992, emissions of the target chemicals fell 34 percent. Through the period releases of the 17 chemicals posing the greatest known risks to human and environmental health fell a total of 501 million pounds. This is hardly a cure for chemical pollution but represents, in just four years, more progress against toxic emissions than had been realized throughout the entire previous span of the postwar era.

Overall toxic air emissions have declined about a third since the disclosures began. This still leaves two billion pounds of toxics, now a mere 22 times Waxman's paranoid number, wafting into the U.S. atmosphere annually. In 1994 the EPA, having abandoned scientific certainty, published approximated rules covering 112 more toxic air compounds, such as benzene and chloroform. The 1994 regulations will cut U.S. toxic air emissions by another one billion pounds annually, reducing total pollutants in this category to far less than half the level of the mid-1980s: an amazing record achieved rapidly, especially considering growth and profits in the petrochemical sector have remained robust.

No fair appraisal of progress against toxic air emissions could reach any conclusion other than that industry and government took the issue too lightly too long. But consider that pollution in this category had been marching steadily upward since the beginning of the industrial era until 1988. In that year emissions began a precipitous decline that has accelerated since. It is all but certain toxic air emissions will never start back up again. Unlike some forms of environmental abuse that can be restrained but not eliminated, there is no reason why toxic emissions cannot be zeroed out in perpetuity; and in all likelihood this reform will be completed during the lifetimes of readers of this book.

The Maximum Exposed Individual

Critics of the industrial state often protest that whatever technology becomes possible, becomes inevitable. There is weight to this complaint. In environmental affairs a counterbalance is developing: Whatever antipollution technology becomes possible, becomes inevitable. For example the new Clean Air Act requires that factories install the "best-available" controls for toxic emissions. Such a rule can never be entirely inoculated against red tape: There will be tedious legal arguments turning on what technology is "best." But henceforth whenever one company invents a toxic-emission control other companies will eventually match it, voluntarily or at the business end of a lawsuit. A logic of continuous pollution reduction is created. Best-technology rules are being applied in many areas of environmental controls; they are a potent force for a new clean-tech order. Such rules are ecorealistic, requiring that regulators and engineers do the best job on what is known today, without wasting time arguing imponderables.

An example of what can happen when the system becomes obsessed with arguing out imponderables—and hence an example of the dying style of environmental regulation—came during an attempt to write risk standards for the 1990 air legislation. Environmental lobbyists wanted the air-toxics title written in a way that defined an acceptable risk as no more than one additional cancer in a million people downwind of a factory. Business wanted the standard set at one additional risk in 10,000. A flurry of computer models and statistical paradigms were created to support competing notions on both sides, including the Maximum Exposed Individual: a hypothetical person who lives an entire 70-year life within spitting distance of the plume of a factory smokestack.

The dispute between cancer risks of one in one million or one in 10,000 is a running theme in contemporary U.S. environmental politics. At congressional hearings, at scientific symposia, during speeches and interviews I have heard players in the environmental debate hold forth at great length on the statistical motes and jots of the two positions. Environmentalists say that even one additional risk in a million is too much for society to tolerate. Industrialists counter that since of among one million people 250,000 will develop cancer anyway, it is ridiculous to spend billions to fend off a single additional cancer in that large group. Usually one in a million prevails as the regulatory premise: Currently it governs pesticide residue and Superfund cleanups, for instance. In the case of air toxics one in 10,000 prevailed, in part because computer models could not demonstrate that even the hapless Maximum Exposed Individual would get cancer.

Does a legally tolerated risk of one additional cancer in ten thousand seem to you heartless? It might be, except that the formulas employed by the EPA to compute this risk are extremely conservative. The toxicologists Bruce Ames and Lois Gold of the University of California at Berkeley calculate that exposures engaging a one-in-10,000 risk of cancer according to the EPA's usual method of computer modeling include drinking a glass of orange juice every other week (orange juice contains a suspected carcinogen called d-limonene); consuming one head of lettuce every second year or one carrot per week (both contain caffeic acid, a suspected carcinogen); eating three ounces of mustard annually (mustard contains the carcinogen allyl isothiocyanate); or drinking one glass of wine every three years (wine contains ethyl alcohol, known to cause a range of health problems).

For the ecorealist both ends of one in a million versus one in 10,000 dispute seem mired in the postulatory. When researchers don't yet know what causes cancer, who can hope to make a judgment to exacting decimal places about exactly what toxic chemicals might or might not do? But anyone can agree in an instant that toxics cannot possibly be good for people or the environment. Then the question becomes simpler: How much protection can we afford?

Declining Clean-Air Costs

During the lobbying fracas over the 1990 Clean Air Act, estimates of the cost of the new rules ran from a White House figure of $19 billion per year (about what the federal government spends on housing aid) to an estimate from William Fay, head of an industry-funded lobby called the

Clean Air Working Group, of $50 billion a year (about what the federal government spends on pensions for retired civil servants). Fay declared the bill would throw 600,000 people out of work. The EPA projected a net employment gain of 15,000, as some jobs were lost but others created. Fred Smith, a former EPA official who heads a libertarian think tank called the Competitive Enterprise Institute, said the bill would trigger a "clean air recession."

One reason estimates land all over the map is that provisions of the new Clean Air Act do not involve direct government expenditures voted on by Congress, which must be itemized. Instead strictures are imposed on industry and consumers; toting up such costs involves guesswork. That most pollution-control regulations entail costs imposed on the economy, rather than direct government expenditures, is a reason Congress finds them relatively painless to enact during a period of federal budget deficits.

Cost figures, in turn, hold little meaning unless weighed against benefits. Benefit estimates run as broad a range as cost estimates and are inherently more difficult to derive since the exact health effects of many pollutants cannot be determined with surety. And some abstract ecological benefits defy quantification. What's the value of wilderness, of solitude, of being able to see vistas of forest, prairie, or savannah little altered from those seen by your ancestors? Of merely knowing such vistas exist, regardless of whether you personally behold them?

Aspects of the ecology can be assigned benefit estimates, but the figures are squishy at best. Game animals and cash crops, for example, have a money value. Genetic material does too, though future values in this category are largely unknowable. A decade ago the Pacific yew would have been assigned a negative value in cost-benefit analysis, since the tree was considered by foresters a weed species. Then the yew was found to contain taxol, which may inhibit cancer. Suddenly people scoured forests of the Northwest looking for the yew. Some bacteria or mold in someone's forest or garden is certain in decades to come to be considered priceless.

With such notions in mind it is possible to take a rough look at the benefit side of air pollution control. The American Lung Association estimates that air pollution costs the country $40 billion per year through increased medical expenses and lost work days on the part of those with respiratory problems. The Lung Association figure, compiled in the late 1980s, was derided by many conservative commentators as excessive. Then a 1992 study by the impeccably respectable National Research Council lent weight to the previously pop-science notion that pollutants may mildly suppress immunological responses. The NRC found that severity of asthma cases has been increasing since about 1970, partly owing to the cumulative impact of smog; this tended to support the Lung Association estimate. Should the Lung Association number be close to correct, control of air pollution would pay for itself by offsetting health-care expenditures.

Perhaps the keenest analysts of environmental cost-benefit relationships is Paul Portney, an economist at Resources for the Future, a nonpartisan think tank in Washington. Portney believes the 1970 Clean Air Act cost about $6 billion a year but created $36 billion annually in benefits. "In a few areas such as elimination of lead, even classical tools of market-oriented economics demonstrate a positive benefit-cost ratio for environmental controls," Portney says. But Portney is less sure about current rounds of pollution control. He thinks the 1990 Clean Air Act will cost about $35 billion per year, with benefits below that level. Should Los Angeles go through with its most ambitious plans to eradicate smog, Portney estimates industry and consumers in that city alone might spend $13 billion a year to receive $3 billion in benefits. The benefit side of the equation would go up, Portney acknowledges, if such disputed notions as smog damage to crops are proven.

Calculations such as those Portney makes have an unseemly aspect, involving money numbers assigned to suffering. For instance Portney places a benefit value of $25 on each asthma attack averted by smog regulation. Asthma sufferers would surely assign a higher value, especially if the tab were being picked up by society generally. Supporters of more regulation trot out studies with equally debatable numbers. The South Coast Air Quality Management District commissioned a study that concluded the ambitious Los Angeles smog-control plan would produce tens of billions of dollars worth of annual benefits. But to reach a large benefits number the study employed such techniques as assigning economic value to the satisfaction people get from jogging, which is more pleasant in clear air. Jogging does offer a wholesome satisfaction. But are good jogging conditions really a social priority?

Certainly it is possible to become oversensitive to environmental protection and spend more than necessary, given society's other needs: Superfund cleanups are the leading example. And certainly it is possible to go about a valid conservation goal in a manner that wastes money. Some proposals for the control of greenhouse gases fall into that category, supposing that developed countries ought to spend many billions of dollars to wring small amounts of emissions out of their production facilities, when much larger reductions could be obtained at lower cost through Western support for Third World economic modernization.

But in the main environmental initiatives ought to be considered worth the price unless proven otherwise, with the burden of disproof upon opponents. Here is why: Most environmental initiatives of the past seemed expensive and questionable at the time, and today every one of them appears a bargain in retrospect. Looking back on the present a few decades hence, society will consider every environmental program running now to have been a bargain, and wish more programs had been started sooner.

CASE STUDY:
THE SPOTTED OWL

On a fine autumn day in 1993 I rather casually did something that according to environmental orthodoxy is inconceivable: Hiking through the woods, I saw lots of spotted owls.

Spotted owls are supposed to be so rare that even an experienced forester spends weeks trying to catch a glimpse of one. I saw four in just a few hours. The owls were living wild in a habitat where it is presumed impossible for them to exist: a young woodland, not an old-growth forest. And they were living in a place, California, where environmental doctrine holds spotted owls are rare birds indeed.

In the evolution of political issues often comes a sequence that runs like this: First a new concern arises. For a while the system attempts to deny the claim's validity; eventually, some action is taken. By then advocates have become an interest group, fighting as much for the preservation of their cause as anything else. The fight takes on a life of its own. The specifics of the original issue are discarded.

In the 1990s this sequence was recurring in the matter of the spotted owl. A decade before, researchers warned the bird was declining toward extinction. Legal gears were set spinning. First came a 1991 court-ordered suspension of most Northwest logging, at the cost of thousands of high-wage jobs. In 1994 the Clinton Administration filed court documents that unless overturned will make permanent most job losses. By the time the Clinton White House began contemplating its owl plan, the issue had become a standard Washington lobbying jangle in which environmental and business constituencies competed to see which could shout the phrase "screw you" with most resonance. The original question of whether the owl is endangered isn't even discussed anymore.

Legal and political maneuvers continue on the assumption that 1980s studies hypothesizing an owl extinction were correct. They may not be. Today research suggests the spotted owl exists in numbers far greater than assumed when the extinction alarm was sounded. Whereas a headline-making 1986 National Audubon Society report said that 1,500 spotted owl pairs throughout the United States was the number necessary to prevent extinction, it now seems as many as 10,000 pairs may exist. David Wilcove, a biodiversity expert for the Environmental Defense Fund, says, "It appears the spotted owl population is not in as bad shape as imagined ten years ago, or even five years ago." Clinton's plan to shut down most Washington and Oregon logging may not only be unnecessary, it may be resting on an illusion.

The notion of a pending owl extinction is a parable of modern environmentalism: illustrating both its manifest virtues and the internal faults that, uncorrected, could bring the movement down. The owl fixation has many political virtues for green sentiment: It's an issue easily understood by the public; it has graphic appeal for television, an essential of contemporary politics; graphically what is represented is a genuine need, that of forest preservation; it has allowed conservationists to win many battles against government and industry.

In all these areas, the environmental movement has its heart in the right place. Its head is another matter. To environmentalists the spotted owl dispute is a proxy for the goal of preserving old-growth forests. In private many environmentalists acknowledge owl extinction claims have been extensively pressurized with hot air. They justify this on the grounds that a valid goal, old-growth forest preservation, is served.

Old-growth preservation is important for the protection of biodiversity, for conservation of what remains of America's pre-European heritage, and against the prospect that ancient forests may someday be understood to play an irreplaceable ecological role of which men and women are not yet aware. These are strong reasons that logging in the Pacific Northwest should be closely regulated.

Yet an argument based on forest preservation for its own sake would in the long run be stronger than specious species arguments. After all if conservation rules are based on an owl extinction claim that research someday disproves, why shouldn't hell-bent logging resume? Whether spotted owls are really endangered is also the issue of whether forest conservation can be placed on a secure, rationalist foundation that out-lives alarmist fads.

Environmentalism has accomplished many wonders, and ought to become a gilt thread in the American social fabric. For that to happen, what environmentalists wish were true for reasons of ideology must no longer obstruct their view of what actually is true in "the laboratory of nature." In no area is this reconciliation more urgent than the issue of the spotted owl. There the instinct of environmentalism, to preserve ancient forests, is correct; while the specific claim of an instant dooms-day for the owl may be removed from actuality.

Assumptions of an Illusion

"I know they're here. I know it," said Lowell Diller as he and I stood in the gathering dusk in a redwood glade outside the forest town of Eureka, California. We had hiked to a spot where Diller previously marked a nest. For 15 minutes Diller hooted to summon the owl pair that lived there. Though we could see no shadows moving in the near-dark, Diller was convinced the owls were observing the intrusion by genus *Homo*.

Suddenly, no more than 15 feet away, furry outlines resolved out of the dark. A spotted owl pair had conducted their flying approach through a dense forest understory without making any sound audible to us. The owls, who doubtless had heard our clumsy footsteps a mile off, regarded us, perhaps wondering, *How can these bipeds survive when they make so much noise in the forest? Why doesn't something eat them?*

The owl-extinction alarm is premised on two notions: that spotted owls live only in ancient forests and that a last, fragile, dwindling popu-lation of the northern spotted exists mainly in Oregon and Washington. Current research suggests neither premise is true. California does not end at the Golden Gate: Between there and the Oregon border lies a 300-mile corridor of mostly Sierra Nevada forest. This vast young woodland, ignored in the owl debate, may contain a profusion of spot-ted owl.

Diller is a biologist employed by the firm Simpson Timber. In 1990 he began to survey a California tract of second-growth, "managed" tim-berland owned by that company. Since then Diller has found and band-ed 603 spotted owls. Federal documents assume only 653 owl pairs exist in the whole of California and that essentially none live in private timberland. Diller's 603 owls were found by inspection of a small snippet of California's Klamath range. Most California woodlands have never been surveyed for owls. The primary federal document on which the Northwest logging ban is based projects there exist in the United States "somewhere between 3,000 and 4,000" pairs of spotted owls. Research such as Diller's now suggests as many spotted owl may roost in California alone.

Some residents of Pacific Coast woodlands—those who spend their days among its trees, rather than drawing up legal papers in San Francisco or Washington—for years have felt these forests contain a notable number of owls. So have some researchers. For instance Thomas Cade, a cofounder of the Peregrine Foundation, which helped reverse the expected extinction of the North American falcon, says, "Biologists have long suspected there are a lot more spotted owls out there than assumed."

Federal owl research has concentrated on Oregon and Washington, states with the mature, monocultural Douglas fir stands traditionally presumed the exclusive habitat of spotteds. Diller is among the first to look for spotted owl in successional or nonancient California forests, not beginning his work until the bird was "listed" under the Endangered Species Act. Diller thinks that "if research had started in California rather than in Oregon, the spotted owl would not now be considered endangered. It would be seen as a prolific, genetically secure bird."

In 1993 Steve Self and Thomas Nelson, researchers employed by Sierra Pacific, a California timber company with a progressive reputation, projected spotted owl populations for the majority of California forests that have not been surveyed for the bird. They estimated the state home to 6,000 to 8,000 pairs of spotted owls, comfortably more than the 1,500 pairs the 1986 Audubon report said were needed to preserve the species. If Self and Nelson are even close to correct, the spotted owl population is not in the zone of an extinction emergency.

Of course Diller's research and the Sierra Pacific study are backed by industry, which has a stake in debunking owl alarms. But then works of owl pessimism such as the Audubon report have been backed by advocacy groups with a stake in advancing the same alarms. Nevertheless such studies are granted wide credence, including by federal courts.

A significant aspect of Diller's work is that he finds spotted owl reproducing in young woodlands managed by foresters: places environmental doctrine presumes the bird cannot abide. "The northern spotted owl rarely if ever successfully fledges young from any habitat except old-growth," the Aubudon Society declared in 1988. Most of Diller's 603 owls are living their entire life cycles outside old-growth. One active nest

Diller showed me was not only in a tree glade of medium height and age but within sight of a logging road where trucks rumble past daily.

Though Diller's work lends support to the industry point of view, it has backfired on his employer. Because Diller has turned up so many owls, Simpson Timber has had to file plans that place about 50,000 acres of its land into pure-preservation status and restrict company logging in other ways, since tree harvests that might "take" a spotted owl are essentially forbidden even on private land. Meanwhile Diller's findings have inspired others to begin systematic owl surveys of the vast northern California forest. Already researchers from such agencies as the California Department of Fish and Game have found spotted owl living and reproducing in several types of nonancient woodlands, including oak savannas—low-tree habitats unlike any in the Cascade Range of Washington and Oregon.

Owls and Rats

How can the spotted owl thrive in California forests that are not ancient? One reason may be that young woods are more alive than old ones. Serene old-growth regions of Washington and Oregon are places of stirring beauty and abiding ecological significance. But they have a drawback environmentalists would rather not discuss: Though high in biological diversity, the floor of an ancient forest is low in overall level of life. When tall trees close the "canopy" of a mature Douglas fir stand, direct sunlight ceases to reach the forest understory. That means plants grow slowly; in turn they produce fewer of the seeds that sustain small mammals; in turn there are limited numbers of small mammals for predators such as spotted owls to eat.

Spotted owls in Washington and Oregon prey mainly on a relatively small population of flying squirrels. In California, spotted owls prey mainly on the dusky-footed wood rat. California managed woodlands have sunlight on the forest floor, because foresters space and trim trees for access to light: Ample sun maximizes tree yield. The warm climate of California further encourages plant growth. The result is forests with lots of food for small mammals and lots of wood rats to be devoured by spotted owls.

Records suggest California woodlands of past centuries did not have the lush understory now observed. A 1900 Interior Department survey describes wholly natural northern California forests as "timber rarely if ever dense . . . a characteristically open forest." Though green orthodoxy calls human-tended forests "managed deserts," contemporary

California timberlands have understories so heavily vegetated they're hard merely to hike through. This may benefit the spotted owl in another way.

It's an owl-eat-owl world: Spotteds are preyed on by the larger great-horned owl. Within the understory of managed California forests, the spotted can maneuver to pursue rats but the great-horned cannot maneuver to pursue spotteds. Some researchers think spotted owls have evolved a preference for habitat where the mean distance between tree branches is sufficient for their wings but too small for the wings of the great-horned. Diller believes California forest practices, from tree spacing to suppressing forest fires (fewer fires mean more clutter), produce timberlands with exactly the desired branch openings. "It's possible there are now more spotted owl in California than before the white man arrived," Edward Murphy, a forester for Sierra Pacific, notes.

Environmentalists reject such thinking on two grounds. First they say owls in young California forests are "packed"—driven there by logging of old-growth, living for the moment but sure to die prematurely. This is possible yet seems unlikely given that current California owl surveys did not commence until half a century after the timber industry became entrenched in that state. If owls packed by logging expire rapidly, then the spotted of California should have passed to oblivion by now. Second, environmentalists assert that spotted owls are an old-growth "obligate"—genetically hyperspecialized to the upper canopy of mature forests. Even with plenty to eat, the owl will eventually die in anything other than tall, old timber.

Again this is possible, but it contradicts most of what is known about natural selection. A few vertebrates such as the panda have become so specialized they exist solely in a narrow habitat. Most creatures have some genetic ability to adjust to changing conditions, since throughout their evolution, environmental conditions constantly changed. The old-growth forests of the Cascade Range did not pop into existence, complete with hyperspecialized owls. Those forests evolved from earlier forms. For millennia, some spotted owl must have existed in conditions other than serene old-growth. After all, nature "logs" too, through lightning-caused fires that take down mature trees and replace them with saplings, much as timber companies do.

Pessimists portray the spotted owl as an old-growth obligate because under this analysis the bird is a fragile waif, unable to adjust to the slightest variation in ecological circumstance. But species that cannot adjust to habitat change usually fall extinct anyway, protected by federal law or not. In the more likely case that the spotted owl has some genetic ability to adapt, the bird lives but the doomsday claims die.

Many wildlife biologists are uncomfortable with claims of a thriving spotted owl cohort in California. For instance Ralph Gutierrez, a biologist at Humboldt State University, in Arcata, California, thinks the reason spotteds are being found in California timberlands is that most "contain a remnant of ancient forest, which sustains the owls. Once those remnants are logged out, the owls will die." Gutierrez has also examined the statistical assumptions used by the Steven Self study. Applied to one of the few portions of California subjected to federal owl study, a preserve called Willow Creek, these assumptions predict 108 spotted owls. Gutierrez's surveys show Willow Creek home to 72 owls. "This means the optimists are too optimistic by a third," Gutierrez says. But suppose Gutierrez is right. Reducing the optimistic estimate by a third still leaves northern California with 4,000 to 5,400 spotted owl pairs, giving that state alone more of the birds than Endangered Species Act documents presume exist in the entire country.

Owls and Clearcuts

In 1976 an Oregon State University graduate student named Eric Forsman published a master's thesis saying his field work showed that spotted owls of Oregon were "declining as a result of habitat loss." The study caused a sensation in the green community.

The Endangered Species Act had just become law, in 1973. Supporters were eager to find a test case. Also in 1976, in a bonehead decision of epic proportions, clear-cutting was made legal on Forest Service land. (Clear-cutting, a technique for razing large areas of forest without causing erosion, had long been employed on federal lands under hazy legal circumstances; the National Forest Management Act of 1976 imposed a few controls on clear-cutting but by legalizing the technique opened the door for greater use.) Clear-cutting meant rapid reductions of the "unharvested old-growth conifer forests" where Forsman found most spotted owl. Pitting the mediagenic image of the soft, cuddly-looking bird against rapacious clear-cutters was ideal as an Endangered Species cause.

Environmentalists were right to be incensed about clear-cutting, which is not only poor ecological policy but often economically foolhardy. The Forest Service uses tax funds to subsidize money-losing clear-cutting on public lands while private timber firms harvest their lands at a profit, without subsidies, using selection logging or the related shelter-cutting, ecologically responsible practices that generate more jobs than clear-cutting. Though clear-cutting can be defended as a nature-mimicking practice in some circumstances (the Douglas firs of the Pacific Northwest seem genetically designed to rise in open fields following lightning-caused natural fires), in the 1980s many Northwest loggers showed themselves unable to clear-cut without running wild.

Forsman's notion of an owl drop in Oregon is unassailable. Although Oregon and Washington today contain about seven million acres of primal old-growth forest, an area larger than several states, from roughly the 1940s to the 1980s ancient forests there were "slicked off" by loggers much faster than such forests can regrow. Fewer forest acres inevitably means fewer forest creatures, including owls.

Yet while Forsman's paper is now celebrated as a founding text of owl doomsaying, he did not assert the spotted was falling extinct. Indeed Forsman found some of what Diller has found—the birds prospering in young timberlands, suggesting "owls could tolerate harvest activity" so long as clear-cutting is regulated. Spotted owl may be plentiful in California in part because for reasons of climate and tree type, clear-cut forestry is not practiced in most of the state. Can it be coincidence that the Oregon owl drop detected by Forsman began about the same time clear-cutting on public lands became widespread there? A fair reading of Forsman's early papers suggests that if clear-cutting were restricted and Northwest logging rationalized, owl populations would rebound naturally as forest acres rebounded.

This reasonable avenue of escape from the owls-versus-loggers mess—timber commerce reduced to the sustainable rate, followed by a rapid natural rebound of the Northwest forest and its creatures—is depicted by green orthodoxy as a sham. Orthodoxy holds the sole hope for the Northwest forest to be nearly zero commercial activity. The seemingly powerful relationship between an Oregon owl decline detected beginning in the mid-1970s, and the federal approval for clear-cut forestry in the same place at the same time, makes the species conservation problems of the Northwest sound merely a correctable government-policy blunder. Can't have that! To doctrinaire elements of the green movement the idea that people-caused problems can be corrected relatively easily via improved government policy and reformed behavior is a scurrile, heterodox notion.

Yet rapid forest rebounds in the midst of commercial activity have been the pattern throughout the United States and Western Europe. Serious deforestation commenced in the United States roughly two centuries ago in New England, as timber was cut or woods burned for cropland. About a century ago, destructive logging practices began to end in New England, while cropland began to be returned to forest as the first stirrings of high-yield agriculture meant fewer acres needed to be cultivated. As chapter four noted, New Hampshire was 50 percent forest in about 1850 and is 86 percent forest today, though its human population has expanded sixfold. Massachusetts was 35 percent forest in about 1850 and is 59 percent forest today. Figures throughout New England are the same.

In a similar progression the Southeast began to be deforested about a century ago then to reforest about half a century ago. Today the Southeast has far more forested acres than prewar, despite a population boom. Deforestation peaked in Western Europe before World War II then was supplanted by aforestation. Today the European Union nations have more forest than prewar, though their human population has nearly doubled. Because the Pacific Northwest was the last place in the continental United States to which determined logging spread, its deforestation trough was not reached until the 1980s, at the low point for sanctioned clear-cutting. But in that decade Northwest timber firms also began planting far more trees than they cut. The reforestation cycle commenced. So long as future logging is held at sustainable levels, the Cascade forest will exhibit the rapid recovery observed everywhere else in the developed world.

Formal warning of spotted owl extinction was not tendered until the 1986 Audubon report. In the wake of that report conservation groups sued to have the northern spotted listed under the Endangered Species Act. In 1990 this happened. Coincident to the listing a government science panel headed by the biologist Jack Ward Thomas concluded that 3,000 to 4,000 spotted owl pairs exist in the U.S. and that to provide a margin of safety over the 1,500-pair extinction number, a minimum of 3,000 owl pairs must be protected. In 1991 William Dwyer, a federal judge in Seattle, banned most logging in Washington and Oregon to carry out measures the Thomas report called necessary to assure survival of 3,000 owl pairs. At this point the notion of an owl doomsday was locked in legally.

Shortly after taking office in 1993, Bill Clinton staged an "owl summit" in Portland. Later Clinton proposed a plan that would allow some resumption of logging in Washington and Oregon for a few years—basically through the president's 1996 reelection bid—then eliminate most Northwest timber commerce in perpetuity. Forsman's studies, the 1986 Audubon warning, the 1990 Thomas report, the 1991 judge's ruling, and the 1994 Clinton plan have something important in common: They all assume Oregon to be the center of the spotted owl universe, with California containing hardly any of the birds. Environmental orthodoxy makes this assumption too. It must: otherwise the rationale for an owl doomsday collapses.

In 1993 Thomas, whose owl gloom brought him national standing among environmentalists, was named by Clinton as the first biologist to head the Forest Service. Placing a biologist in charge of the agency is an excellent idea, since today protection of biodiversity should be a higher government priority than the felling of trees. But will gloom orthodoxy make for any more reasonable a guiding ideal for the Forest Service than its previous adoration of chain saws? "It may well be that there are a significant number of spotted owls on private lands in California, but so what?" Thomas said in an interview at Forest Service headquarters. "The injunction controls the issue now." Dwyer's injunction discusses the need to preserve old-growth habitat generally, but its legal power derives from the presumption of an owl emergency, a notion neither green orthodoxy nor the Clinton Administration wished to disturb with inconveniently positive findings from the field.

Further Forgotten: The "California" Spotted Owl

Also sidestepped in the debate is the existence in California of hundreds and perhaps thousands of birds called "California" spotted owls. As the California spotted owl is not considered endangered it has never been surveyed for in methodical fashion, leaving its population not well known. Estimates place the bird's numbers in the low thousands of breeding pairs.

According to environmental doctrine, the fact that the Golden State contains thousands of birds called California spotted owls has nothing to do with the "northern" owl extinction alarm, because the breeds are disjunct. Yet the birds live in proximity—California spotteds can be found roosting not far from the northern spotted populations Diller studies—and appear so nearly identical even ornithologists have difficulty telling them apart. Some observers have long wondered whether there is really any meaningful difference between northern and California spotted owl.

In 1990 George Barrowclough, an ornithologist at the American Museum of Natural History in New York, and Gutierrez of Humboldt State compared proteins from the northern and California spotted owls. "No genetic difference was found" between the two, their report states. The researchers further found no statistically significant genetic differences between the northern and Mexican spotted owls, Mexican spotteds being another bird strikingly similar to their Cascade Range kin. The Mexican spotted roosts in woodlands adjacent to the deserts of the Southwest and Mexico: habitat utterly different from the moist old-growth forests doomsayers describe as the sole imaginable habitat for northern spotted. Because differences in DNA may be surprisingly small, the protein-coding genetic test is considered inconclusive by some researchers. In 1994 Barrowclough began using genome sequencing, an advanced test, to determine whether there exist subtle DNA distinctions between northern and California spotted owls missed by the first assay. It's worth noting that Barrowclough calls both bird types "Pacific Coast" spotted owls, reflecting a feeling the two soon may be seen as one and the same.

This seemingly abstract point of ornithology has tremendous bearing on the owl debate. All biologists concur that small, isolated populations are more prone to extinction than large populations spread over a range of habitats. If the spotted owl of Washington and Oregon is a lonely, isolated breed, then the odds of peril rise. But if those birds belong to a large genetic family existing in a range of habitats spread the 1,500 miles from Vancouver to Mexico, then it becomes unlikely any local owl population downtrend will lead to an unstoppable descent. And if the northern and California owls are not distant relations but really both Pacific Coast spotteds, there may be 10,000 or more pairs of these raptors in the United States—4,000 to 6,000 northern owls in California, 2,000 to 3,000 northern owls in the Northwest, a few thousand California owls in California.

Does a figure such as 10,000 pairs of spotted owl still sound perilously small? Not only is this far more birds than environmentalists once described as necessary to assure spotted-owl survival, it is significantly greater than the population nadirs of similar raptors that avoided extinction. The bald eagle was down to 417 known nesting pairs in the lower 48 states in 1963 and now has recovered to about nine times that number; in 1995 the American bald is expected to be "delisted" from endangered status. The peregrine falcon was down to about 1,000 breeding pairs in North America two decades ago and now has bounced back to an estimated 5,000. Delisting of the falcon subspecies that lives in Alaska and Canada is anticipated. The banning of DDT was essential to both birds' comebacks. Recent Forest Service decisions to reduce the level of clear-cutting should have a similar positive effect on the owl.

And if there are today in the neighborhood of 10,000 pairs of spotted owls of the general Pacific Coast type, this number may not differ materially from the level that existed before the white male. Many territorial or top-chain predators such as owls or grizzly bears are few in number under natural circumstances because they require a wide prey range. Biologists believe that Oregon and Washington ancient forests can support at most one spotted owl pair roughly every 1,000 to 7,000 acres.

This means that even if no Northwest old-growth tree had ever been cut by people, the region's spotted owl population might be only a few thousand pairs higher than the current number, as the natural owls-per-acre factor would impose a low limit on total owl numbers.[1] In turn it may be that human alterations in the forests of California have caused spotted owls to become more numerous there. Added together these factors suggest that before whites came to the Pacific Coast, spotted owl populations may have been only somewhat higher than today: cause for concern, but not for sennets of instant doomsday.

Perhaps anticipating that findings about California owls will be substantiated, pessimists are shifting their rhetoric. Up to the 1991 logging ban, enviros spoke mainly of total owl numbers, repeatedly asserting the funereal 1,500-owl-pair level was at hand. Now many assert that owl numbers are less important than the demographic trend: That is, actual birds counted in "the laboratory of nature" mean less than prospective birds projected by computer model. The Dwyer logging ban accepts this logic, essentially declaring computer-projected trends more important than actual owl numbers. This is a quizzical judgment. Since the late 1970s, pessimistic owl studies have been projecting population trends averaging around minus-five percent annually, suggesting total spotted owl numbers should have fallen drastically by now. Yet actual field surveys continue to find more birds than previously counted. Todd True, an attorney for the Sierra Club Legal Defense Fund, says that "numbers of owls in the woods aren't the issue. Inevitably as researchers look for owls they will find more than we knew about before anyone was looking. If the demographic trend is negative the species is still in trouble."

True's point has merit. A species might be imperiled even if its population seems profuse, as the human species has uncountable troubles despite robust numbers. But here comes another problem for owl orthodoxy: The northern spotted owl is not a species.

An Endangered Species that Isn't a Species

Perhaps the most curious aspect of the owl debate is that even under the worst-case analysis, there is no evidence that the spotted owl faces extinction as a *species*.

According to the American Ornithologists' Union, which certifies bird types, the northern spotted owl is a subspecies, not a species. Only spotted owls generally are a species, *Strix occidentalis* to taxonomists.

As a species the spotted ranges from northerns that live as far north as British Columbia to Mexicans roosting south of the Rio Grande. Thus even if spotted owl ceased to exist entirely in Washington and Oregon, the species line would go forward in other places.

Yet for the purposes of the Endangered Species Act, the spotted owl of Washington and Oregon is treated as if it were a species. The act mandates protection not only of species but also of habitats and of "locally distinct" populations, a phrase courts and federal agencies have interpreted to mean everything from subspecies with local variations in genetics or morphology to subspecies simply living in a manner different from how kin live elsewhere. Dogma therefore holds that even if lots of spotted owls thrive in northern California, logging bans must continue in Washington and Oregon because the owl populations there are locally distinct. There owls dwell in cool habitats not found in California or the Southwest, feeding on arboreal squirrels, a "distinct" Northwest delicacy.

This is an accurate reading of the language of the Endangered Species Act as written, but it points to a deep logical fault in environmental orthodoxy. By the theory that local variations in climate and diet convert creatures into different species, a black man who lives in Seattle, gets rained on, and eats salmon would be a different *species* from a white man who lives in stifling humidity in Louisiana and dines on gumbo. By this theory the human race contains hundreds of entirely distinct species. The typical northern and California spotted owls appear more alike than the typical American and Asian. But according to orthodox doctrine, the different people are identical while the similar birds are drastically different.

People have mobility and interbreed from region to region, refreshing their gene pools and making genus *Homo* "panmictic" to biologists. Creatures such as spotted owl rarely leave the region of birth, genetic isolation rendering them more likely to "speciate," or form local ecotypes by breeding with near kin. This, some environmentalists will say, is a reason the genes of animals and plants require special protection that the human DNA pool does not. But if continuous mixing is good for the human germ line (that's what researchers call your DNA heritage), why then is isolation from change what environmental orthodoxy recommends for animals and plants? It can't be that people profit genetically from endlessly having their living circumstances shaken up while owls and other creatures can only profit from being placed into preservation zones where their genes would be isolated against change.

Contradictory logic about what's good for species is important to political environmentalism because sometime in the mid-1990s Congress must reauthorize the Endangered Species Act. If the most-noted contemporary candidate for extinction is not dying after all, how will the lobbying be kept correctly pessimistic? Two poles of possibility exist for the act. Reactionaries hope to eviscerate the law. Progressives would switch the act from its cumbersome creature-by-creature approach to a rationalized system in which blocs of habitat are pre-served but species vacillations within those blocs do not trigger legal panics, since species vacillations happen in nature anyway. Orthodoxy wants the act renewed much as is, in its effective but panic-oriented form. For this a continuing owl emergency is a political essential.

Spotted owl resilience further can seem distressing to political envi-ronmentalism because the movement has found the alluring visage of the bird an effective tool for fund-raising. That's fine with me: I'm glad that today's environmental advocates have substantial resources. But money colors the ability of interest groups to see issues clearly. Institutional environmentalism must come to terms with the fact that by the 1990s it had been a long time since greens took any important position that ran counter to their own financial interests.

Finally there exists a visceral reason environmentalists are disap-pointed by indications the owl is declining to die. The notion of pending owl extinction is one on which environmentalism has defeated business at every turn, up to the Oval Office of Republican and Democratic pres-idents. Putting the rout to the opposition can become to political move-ments an end in itself. Business lobbyists often bash environmentalists for no clear reason beyond self-satisfaction. Environmentalists are not exempt from the temptation to repay in kind.

Missing Victims

Could it be that spotted owls are not endangered but other old-growth species are? This is an important concern. Often it is argued that the spotted is a bellwether for other creatures presumed locked in decline. Perhaps the postwar replacement of many old-growth Northwest forests with young, managed timberlands has caused a wipeout among crea-tures harder to count than owls. After all, current environmental theory holds that deforestation is the worst form of human activity from the standpoint of biodiversity loss. And there is no doubt that until roughly the past decade, Northwest timber companies slicked off the Cascade Range with scant regard for conservation.

Since the 1991 logging suspension, alarmist legal maneuvers have concentrated on expanding the scope of the ban to include some 1,400 non-owl species presumed imperiled old-growth obligates. At one point in 1991, a Jack Ward Thomas study said that Northwest timber commerce need be reduced only to about half the 1980s peak rate in order to safeguard the spotted owl. By the time the Clinton plan was finalized in 1994, allowable logging had been reduced to a much lower proportion of the 1980s rate. This happened because environmental lobbyists asserted that additional timber restrictions were necessary to prevent the 1,400 other species from meeting the same fate as the owl.

Yet with the exception of Pacific Coast salmon, whose 1990s runs were unequivocal disasters, only a handful of the supposed 1,400 additional dying Northwest old-growth species has shown worrisome population trends in studies. Just one, a bird called the marbled murlet, has been classified threatened under the Endangered Species Act, despite the act's increasingly lenient standard for listing. About a half dozen plants in the region are "missing in action"—not observed recently, though known to prosper elsewhere. It certainly is possible that species other than the spotted owl are imperiled in the old forests of the Northwest. Yet the strongest scientific evidence of imperilment involves the spotted owl, and that evidence is far from conclusive.

Perhaps, pessimists assert, evidence of old-growth species in decline is hard to come by partly because large numbers of creatures have already been wiped out by development and logging. This claim is often repeated in press reports with a curious omission: no specifics.

So far in the postwar era there are *no* known extinctions of animals or vascular (loosely, green-stemmed) plants in the Pacific Coast forests, according to the Nature Conservancy, the Environmental Defense Fund, and other sources. Several mammals, among them the red vole and the fisher, are believed in decline. But so far zero known extinctions. This in a habitat range that has not only been subjected to extensive logging, which according to environmental doctrine is the human action that causes most harm to biodiversity, but also numbers among the most intensely studied in the world, and thus is a place extinctions are likely to be detected.

Zero known postwar extinctions in the Pacific Coast forest belt. Combined with the prospect that there exist many more spotted owl than previously estimated, this raises the question of whether the owl instant doomsday, which has cost thousands of honest people their livelihoods and occupied the attention of presidents, is at heart a false alarm.

The Case for Forest Preservation

In contrast the need to preserve the old-growth is not a false alarm. Poorly regulated Northwest logging left forests of Washington and Oregon "fragmented"—containing lots of trees but in blocks chopped into checkerboards. Many studies suggest that moderate numbers of spotted owls and similar creatures in contiguous forest "clusters" would be more secure than twice as many living in fragmented checkerboards. This alone is reason for strict regulation of Pacific Northwest logging.

But the clear need for strict regulation of Northwest forestry should be argued on its own merits, not by resorting to dubious claims of owl peril. And the clear need for strict regulation of Northwest logging can be met without the extremes of the Clinton plan.

Consider that Jerry Franklin, a University of Washington researcher and the leading proponent of "New Forestry," drove timber companies to distraction in the 1980s by saying that to protect biodiversity and achieve sustainable yield, Northwest logging must decline to one-half the 1980s peak rate. Until quite recently, Franklin was the left wing of the debate. By 1994, responding to the hypothesized owl emergency, Clinton proposed to reduce Northwest logging to 20 percent of the 1980s peak. (Franklin signed the Clinton plan; he told me extinction claims helped convinced him Northwest logging must be driven to a very low rate.)

As soon as Clinton formalized his plan the National Audubon Society sued to block it, asserting even its modest logging quotas were too high.[2] A group of credentialed researchers produced a study suggesting that the Clinton plan "will not prevent the extinction of the northern spotted owl." Yet Clinton's plan puts an area of primal forest the size of Vermont into preservation status, walled off against any human action much beyond back-packing. If an exclusive domain the size of Vermont is not enough to save the spotted owl, aren't we forced to conclude that nature has targeted this creature for extinction anyway?

Consider that to the extent U.S. timber production declines, demand for foreign timber escalates. Countries will buy wood from nations like Malaysia and Brazil, where forestry practices may be summarized by the cry TIMMM-BURRR! Today Japanese firms are slicking off the lush Sarawak rainforest of Malaysia to feed a global wood market energized by logging bans in the United States. In the Sarawak there are no niceties about species preservation or sustainable yield, no well-funded environmental litigators. Moving logging from Oregon to Malaysia may move the problem out of sight, out of mind. It is not much of a deal for the environment.

Consider that current antilogging sentiment, born in the desire to protect old stands requiring centuries to restore, now spills over into activism against logging in young forests easily restored. For instance in 1990, California, via a ballot initiative that lost narrowly, nearly banned most logging even on tree plantations. Yet to the extent commercial forestry produces ample harvests, the pressure to log out the old growth declines. "High-yield forestry can work in concert with old-growth preservation," says Michael Oppenheimer, chief scientist of the Environmental Defense Fund.

Consider that from 9,500 (the White House's own number) to 85,000 jobs will be abrogated by the Clinton owl plan. The lost jobs are skilled, high-wage employment of the sort that real-world Americans who aren't lawyers or consultants need to send their children to college. Lumber prices have also nearly doubled since the 1991 ban, adding roughly $5,000 to the price of a new home. This increase is regressive, hitting the working class harder than the Sierra Club set.

The owl illusion represents both a peril and an opportunity for environmentalism. The peril is a coming loss of face that could be devastating to the many achievements of the movement. The opportunity is to sustain and strengthen the movement before that loss occurs.

If it is eventually understood that affluent environmentalists with white-collar sinecure destroyed thousands of desirable skilled-labor jobs in order to satisfy an ideology and boost the returns on fund-raising drives, a lasting political backlash against environmentalism may set in. There is time to prevent this turn of events. Ancient forests can be protected, additional timber jobs restored, and the constructive political power of environmentalism sustained. Disengaging the doomsday alarm about owls could be a beginning.

CHEMICALS

In December 1982 the Meramec River crested its banks near the little town of Times Beach, Missouri. A sample of the flood waters showed local soil contained some 1,000 parts per billion of dioxin. The EPA safety limit for dioxin in soil is one part per billion. A Times Beach contractor named Russell Bliss had sprayed waste oils on the town's dirt roads to suppress dust. The oils contained dioxin. Flood waters percolating into the tainted earth began picking up the chemical and transporting it into people's basements. Within a day of the discovery the situation was headline news around the world.

Dioxin—a synthetic compound few people had heard of before its 1978 discovery beneath a schoolyard at Love Canal, New York—had at the time become a subject of public fascination, regularly described as "the most deadly substance ever devised." Dioxin was said to be both hypertoxic and a sort of warp-speed carcinogen, capable of causing cancer overnight. Loosed on the world in the name of progress, dioxin seemed to exemplify a new class of chemical horrors spreading unrestricted. The late Senator Philip Hart of Michigan declared that the existence of the dioxin may "portend the most horrible tragedy known to mankind."

The Times Beach flood not only came after Love Canal; it came just after public health alarms regarding a similar chlorinated organic compound, polychlorinated biphenyls (PCBs), and regarding asbestos. By 1985 *Time* magazine had declared "The Poisoning Of America" on its cover. Around the same time Ralph Nader and two coauthors published

Who's Poisoning America? Other prominent books of the time included *America the Poisoned* and *Laying Waste: The Poisoning of America by Toxic Chemicals.*

It was against this backdrop that dioxin was discovered at Times Beach. State and federal officials urged the 2,240 residents not to return to their homes as the flood receded. Warning signs (ENTERING TOXIC EMERGENCY ZONE) and roadblocks were posted. The Saint Louis County Police announced that no squad cars would patrol Times Beach, for fear of contamination. Men in moonsuits came to take soil samples, sometimes arriving and departing by helicopter, seeming to want to be in contact with the town for as few seconds as possible. Journalists from around the world appeared, some wearing gas masks and plastic gloves.

Eventually Times Beach was evacuated; the federal government later bought out homeowners. The evacuation was staged as insensitively as possible. Irreplaceable personal belongings such as family photographs were destroyed without warning by government bulldozers. Basic information—what people need most in time of crisis—was denied to town residents till long after avoidable panics began. Housing buyouts for the working-class residents were penurious, while unlimited millions were showered on consultants and lawyers who did little but generate delay. In the end Times Beach became a modern ghost town—to this day unoccupied, its name removed from Missouri state maps, the warning signs posted still.

Was this trip necessary? Today there is a body of science suggesting that dioxin, though clearly dangerous, is not hypertoxic or hypercarcinogenic. Studies conducted by the Missouri Department of Health and the federal Centers for Disease Control have failed to find any statistically unusual disease incidence among former Times Beach residents. Vernon Houk, an official of the Centers for Disease Control, who in 1983 ordered Times Beach evacuated, said in 1991 that "it looks as though the evacuation was an overreaction." Houk, who died in 1994, was widely denounced for that statement by environmentalists and accused of being an apologist for industry—even though he spent most of his public-health career being denounced by industry, as Houk supported research proving that lead paint was dangerous and that open-air atomic testing during the 1950s had harmed veterans.

That the evacuation probably was unnecessary does not mean all former Times Beach residents are in good health. Activists attach great significance to the fact that three former Times Beach families were struck by childhood cancers or mothers having more than one miscarriage. In any such instance tragedy occurs. But cases of childhood cancers or multiple miscarriages are found throughout the country, even in wholly pristine areas. In the United States roughly one pregnancy in five ends in miscarriage, regardless of environmental circumstances. Roughly one person in four contracts cancer, regardless of environmental circumstances. Cancer, far from being unknown among the young, is the number-two killer of children. Childhood cancers and multiple miscarriages have struck families since preindustrial days; their occurrence in a place such as Times Beach does not in itself demonstrate an emergency.

Studies of most substances about which there has been extreme public fear show that while asbestos, Alar, dioxin, DDT, PCBs, and other products of industry are dangerous, they are no more hazardous on balance than substances found in nature, such as arsenic and cadmium. Linda Fisher, a former assistant administrator of the EPA for toxic substances, notes that, "The more we learn about chemicals like dioxin, the more we realize they are less of a problem than once thought. The more we learn about lead, the worse it sounds. Yet we can never get people as concerned about lead exposure as about dioxin." Lead is a natural substance that has caused public health problems at least since the Romans reported that drinking wine from lead flagons addled the mind. Though environmental groups do pressure for programs to reduce lead exposure (federal drinking water standards were revised in 1990 to reduce lead in city pipes), lead as a health threat has never drawn the attention granted dioxin or PCBs. Yet estimates hold that one American child in nine has a worrisome level of lead in the blood—a number hundreds of times more significant than the worst-case projection for children with exposure to dioxin or PCBs.

On the right-wing talk-show circuit, two false ideas have arisen in recent years about the risks posed by synthetic compounds. One holds that dioxin, DDT, and the rest are actually harmless. This view is nonsense. The second is that panic about chemicals indicates an antiscientific hysteria at work in the public at large. Far from it: Public fear of chemicals is an entirely rational reaction.

Most people have no recourse but to rely on news reports for basic judgments about what is safe. In the past 20 years such reports consistently have been alarmist. A television newscast may present a perfectly accurate report stating that people who live near a place where toxic chemicals have been handled are frightened: The report then skips over the slow-moving subject of whether there is a logical basis for fright. Peter Sandman, a former professor at Rutgers University who has studied how television depicts chemical issues, says, "Nearly all on-camera time is devoted to emotional images of fear, with little mention of risk data." In turn, the presence of reporters often engenders the very emotions reported on. If a journalist in a gas mask descended from a helicopter into your street, thrust a microphone toward you and said, "Are you scared?" who wouldn't answer, Yes!

Television viewers react to images as much as words spoken. In coverage of the risks of chemicals, the imagery is always negative—lifeless wastelands, ominous test tubes. Such news treatment is not necessarily bad; it has forced government and industry to reexamine the belief that new chemicals automatically mean progress. Today's standard is that chemicals are assumed dangerous and must be elaborately tested before introduction, with the burden on the manufacturer to establish safety rather than on critics to establish a threat. This is a positive reform.

But now that this important adjustment has been made, it is time for general dread of synthetic compounds to be reexamined. Some doctrinaire environmentalists assert that chemicals invented by men and women are inherently bad and should no longer be pursued. Surely nature would never think like this. Nature experiments constantly with chemicals, making some beneficial ones and some awful ones. People do likewise. The challenge for the ecorealist is to discard the bad chemicals while keeping the useful. Closer understanding of chemicals such as dioxin will suggest how such judgments might be made.

Missing Fly Corpses

Dioxin is a collective term for a group of chemical by-products caused mainly by manufacturing of pesticides and paper; the most dangerous dioxin goes by the acronym TCDD. Most dioxins form when chlorine is heated. Dioxin is found primarily in manufacturing wastes, though it also was present in some herbicides, including the notorious Agent Orange.

In the 1970s, studies began to associate dioxin with diseases ranging from chloracne, a skin condition, to cancers, mainly non-Hodgkin's lymphoma and a soft-tissue sarcoma. Animal testing was performed: Dioxin showed itself a potent carcinogen among laboratory rats. The discovery of dioxin at Love Canal came in the wake of the animal tests and of increasing concern from Vietnam War veterans about chronic health problems that might relate to Agent Orange. Establishment publications, prominently the *New Yorker,* ran articles suggesting dioxin represented an entirely new class of synthetic compound, able to cause cancer with exceptional speed in tiny quantities. A San Francisco television station told viewers dioxin was so hideous "an ounce could wipe out a million people." Ralph Nader later amended the estimate slightly, declaring "three ounces of dioxin could kill more than a million people."

Claims that an ounce of anything might kill an entire city are at some levels too preposterous for words, if only because the world's military establishments have invested billions in the search for actual hypertoxics, discovering many dreadful substances but none with properties like those attributed to dioxin. Huge amounts of dioxin were released around soldiers during the Agent Orange defoliations of Vietnam, and the worst-case reading favored by veterans' groups is that the chemical has caused a few hundred deaths so far and may cause a few hundred premature deaths in the future: horrible, but nothing like what should happen if a mere ounce of dioxin could "wipe out a million people."

But events do not occur in isolation. Through the 1970s the public heard many reports that PCBs and asbestos had suddenly been discovered as hypercarcinogens. Through the same period the general credibility of government declined. Thus when officials declared the residents of Love Canal not endangered, how could such blandishments be believed? "Trust is essential to the way people perceive risk," says Vincent Covello, a researcher at the University of California at Berkeley, who studies risk perception. "Most people start off more frightened of statistically tiny risks such as toxic wastes than powerful everyday risks like smoking or driving. If trust is missing—if people are assured that some chemical is safe by a company or government agency that has a track record of lying—the perception of risk will shoot upward as much as an additional two thousandfold."

It is common among risk analysts to attribute heightened fear of lesser threats to the difference between risks people assume of their free will and risks forced upon them. "I used to be a three-pack-a-day smoker," says David Chittick, who in 1994 retired as AT&T's vice president for engineering, and who in the 1980s campaigned successfully for his company to stop using CFCs ahead of the legal timetable. "But when I smoked I was in control. When it came to the air and water, industry was in control. So I would get more worked up about chemicals than about smoking, though I knew perfectly well which of the two was more dangerous."

To this equation add a reality of human nature: that many people would rather believe distant villians are to blame for any sickness they may contract. Studies constantly suggest that lifestyle choices—smoking, excessive drinking, overeating (especially of fats, strongly linked to breast and other cancers), and lack of exercise—account for 70 to 80 percent of preventable deaths in the United States. But people do not want to hear that. Once illness begins, they may prefer to view themselves as victims. For the sick to be victims, there must be a villain.

Also important is the real-world calibration test. People have common sense understanding of risks such as driving: Not everyone may drive with sufficient care, but everyone does know what sorts of behavior on the road are likely to increase risk. This form of everyday calibration is lacking from the realm of chemicals. Though in the long run something like a few parts per billion of trichloroethylene may represent less peril than the cigarettes and beer for sale in the local 7–11, most people feel they have no commonsense way of coming to terms with this.

Yet there are commonsense ways to approach claims that the world is now plagued by the arrival of hypertoxics. One might be called the Fly Corpse Factor. If we're all supposed to be dropping like flies, where are the fly corpses?

Epidemiology conducted since the 1960s has failed to show any acute patterns of disease among people living near petrochemical factories or toxic waste sites. There are a few terrible exceptions: one is elevated cancer incidence in "Cancer Alley" between Baton Rouge and New Orleans. Another is a toxic waste site in Woburn, Massachusetts, where a petrochemical plant and other factories polluted municipal wells. In the surrounding community rates of childhood leukemia are four times that for similar towns in the region.

But nothing like a widespread poisoning of America has ever manifested itself in epidemiological data. In 1991, the National Research Council published an exhaustive interdisciplinary study of the health effects of chemicals at Superfund and spill sites, including Times Beach and Love Canal. The study found scattered harm at places such as Woburn, but no general public-health effects. On the key question of whether synthetic chemicals are fundamentally good or bad the NRC wrote, "Based on review of existing literature [scientific studies], the committee finds it is impossible to answer that question." If a public health wipeout from toxic chemicals were in progress, some hint of this should appear in the epidemiology of toxic waste sites. So far it does not.

Most public health categories for the postwar era show not deterioration but improvement. Heart disease, hypertension, stroke, and some forms of cancer have been steadily declining in the American population for half a century. Life expectancy has been rising steadily for a century. Only in a few areas such as lung cancer, breast cancer, and AIDS are public health trends alarming. James Enstrom, a cancer epidemiologist at the University of California at Los Angeles, has calculated that if the mortality rates of the year 1940 had applied to the population of the year 1988, four million Americans would have died that year. Instead

2.2 million people did. This represents a spectacular net public health improvement during the very period when the manufacture, use, and disposal of toxics and radioactive substances increased exponentially.

Perhaps public health would have improved further were it not for pollution and toxic wastes. This may be all the argument that is required to justify more environmental reform. But it cannot be true that Americans are being poisoned and growing healthier simultaneously. If we're all being poisoned by sinister hypertoxics, our bodies have a funny way of showing it.

Reckless use of toxics peaked roughly in the 1960s, with indiscriminate spraying of "hard" pesticides such as chlordane. Reckless disposal of toxics peaked roughly in the 1970s, around the time of discoveries of Love Canal, the Stringfellow Acid Pits of California and similar monuments to irresponsibility. If the poisoning of America was going to occur, it should have come when use and disposal of chemicals was reckless. It did not, which suggests that the poisoning of America will never occur. In the Western world the peak moment of danger from chemicals passed at least a decade ago.

In the Parts per Quadrillion

Vernon Houk, who said the evacuation of Times Beach was an overreaction, has also said it was understandable at the time. In 1982 animal tests lent good reason to suspect dioxin to be exceptionally dangerous. But other evidence inclined in the opposite direction. In 1976 there was an explosion at a chemical plant in Seveso, Italy. The blast exposed several hundred people in a nearby town to a cloud of dioxin. Some victims registered blood levels of 27,000 parts per trillion of TCDD, 50 times more than the worst exposure among Vietnam veterans. Because the Italian government covered up what happened at the plant, a full 17 days passed between the explosion and the first public warning of toxic release—meaning the exposures of many Seveso victims were prolonged. Little-known in the United States, the Seveso blast was viewed in Europe as an event of profound horror, widely called "the Hiroshima of Europe." It was assumed most of the exposed would die. Instead none died.

Seveso residents have been extensively studied. Many developed chloracne and some have shown somewhat increased incidences of cancer. A 1993 study by University of Milan researcher Pier Bertazzi, published in the journal *Epidemiology,* found mildly elevated incidence of leukemia, lymphomas, and gallbladder cancer among Seveso victims.

But overall, the Seveso group's cancer rate was about the same as that of people living in uncontaminated areas in the same part of Italy. Other studies published in the *Journal of the American Medical Association* and the *American Journal of Epidemiology* detected slightly higher rates of cardiovascular problems among Seveso victims but nothing like mass poisoning. Cancers take up to three decades to develop, so Seveso diseases may still be coming. But since it is nearly two decades after the explosion and the illnesses among Seveso victims are by the worst-case analysis only slightly worse than in the Italian public at large, the contention that dioxin is a hypercarcinogen seems put to rest.

Other studies support this conclusion. One, published in the British medical journal *Lancet* in 1991, found that German workers exposed before the year 1950 to pesticides containing dioxin—workers now old enough to have developed cancer—were somewhat more likely to suffer cancers than similar workers not exposed. This study supports the notion that dioxin, if not a hypercarcinogen, is dangerous. A second important study was published in 1991 by the National Institute of Occupational Safety and Health. Examining 5,000 American workers exposed to dioxin, NIOSH found only a "slight" excess rate of cancer.[1] A third study, released in 1993, was conducted by the Institute of Medicine, an affiliate of the National Academy of Sciences. The IOM reviewed all published technical literature on the effects of Agent Orange on Vietnam veterans—an amazing 6,420 articles. The committee found dioxin associated with chloracne, soft-tissue sarcoma, non-Hodgkin's lymphoma, Hodgkin's disease, and a rare liver disorder. The researchers further noted "limited or suggestive" links between dioxin and other cancers but "inadequate or insufficient evidence" tying dioxin to birth defects.

General scientific views of dioxin began to change when it was discovered that people and laboratory rodents have fundamentally different responses to the compound. Mice are not men: Different species respond differently to different chemicals and diseases. The insecticide clausenvafus, for example, kills rats in tiny doses. But rabbits tolerate moderate amounts, and dogs seem positively impervious to the stuff. Mice and rats are used as test subjects for most chemical assays because these rodents are small, breed quickly, and don't live long, meaning "lifetime" results may be observed in a practical span. From a metabolic standpoint, pigs are much more like human beings than are mice. But pigs are large, breed slowly, and they live many years, rendering them impractical subjects for lab tests.

In 1991 a committee formed by Kenneth Olden, director of the National Institute for Environmental Health Studies, declared that many standard assumptions of rodent-based health studies "do not appear to be valid." Olden told Keith Schneider of the *New York Times* that lab-animals studies should never be the basis of environmental policy, since such studies can be misleading. This statement was especially telling because Olden's agency conducts hundreds of rodent assays per year. In criticizing them Olden was implicitly criticizing his own funding, which is thin ice for any government official.

Rats, it is now known, store dioxin in their liver, which is a cancer-prone organ. People store dioxin in their lipid (fatty) tissues, not normally a genesis site for cancer. By 1984 the Council on Scientific Affairs of the American Medical Association had concluded that dioxin is a potent toxic to lab animals "but has not demonstrated comparable levels of biological activity in man."

When doubts began to grow about dioxin emergency claims, former EPA Administrator Lee Thomas proposed, in 1987, to conduct a technical review. The proposed review was intensely opposed by a range of interests. Environmental lobbyists did not want dioxin reviewed because it is among the ecological areas where everyone is scared to death, and keeping everyone scared to death has become for institutional environmentalism an agenda item. The small industry of consultants and lawyers involved in the Superfund program to clean up toxic wastes opposed the dioxin review, having a stake in preventing news that makes waste sites less threatening. Vietnam veterans opposed a review because they were at the time locked in a bitter fight to compel the Veterans Administration to certify dioxin exposure as grounds for military disability payments. There were also interest groups in favor of a review: mainly paper manufacturers, who have engaged in a variety of lobbying and public-relations gimmicks to make it seem as though dioxin is harmless, a position no respected researcher holds. But in 1987—even under a Reagan presidency hostile to environmentalism—groups with an interest in keeping dioxin seen as deadly prevailed over those with the opposite stake. Thomas put the dioxin review in limbo.

When William Reilly took the EPA post in 1989, he pledged to improve scientific standards in policy-making. One of his first decisions was to restore the dioxin review. Veterans by that time were acquiring Agent Orange disability rights directly through an act of Congress, changing the lobbying balance such that the review became politically tenable. Reilly was dismayed that what he planned as a pure-science effort was freighted with ideology. "I sometimes think I'm being had by both sides of the debate," he says. "One side says that dioxin is a threat to all life as we know it, the other side says the stuff is practically harmless." At this writing the EPA had just released in draft form some 2,000 pages of the dioxin review. The review documents, boldly stamped Do NOT CITE OR QUOTE, were being widely cited and quoted in research circles. The draft review concludes that dioxin is a "probable" human carcinogen—a much less powerful claim than was being made about the substance by pessimists a decade before—and that dioxin is a confirmed toxic, though of uncertain potency. The draft review further supposes that even a few parts per trillion of dioxin in human cells—about the level most Americans probably have in their bodies normally—"may" cause reproductive harm. This last contention was the most controversial among specialists, because it was arrived at using computer models, not actual health data. The computer model employed assumes (essentially) that a cellular level of five parts per trillion of dioxin is extremely dangerous, despite evidence from Seveso and the NIOSH study suggesting that levels drastically higher have done only small amounts of harm. All told the EPA draft review, begun under the Bush Administration but published by Bill Clinton, depicts dioxin as a danger, but nothing like the hyperthreat once assumed.

Not expected to be settled by the dioxin review is one of the most animated contemporary disputes among scientists, environmentalists, and policy-makers: the "threshold" question. Is there a safe threshold of exposure below which chemicals do not cause cancer? Or are some chemicals so dangerous they harm in any quantity, even a single molecule? Countless technical papers have been written on the topic of thresholds, which most researchers consider unresolved. This question became relevant to the dioxin debate when Robert Gallo, a scientist at the Robert Wood Johnson Medical School in New Jersey, demonstrated that dioxin causes harm by binding to certain receptors on cells. In order to trigger a reaction, Gallo calculated, several thousand receptors must be occupied. This finding, contested by other researchers, suggests that dioxin does have a threshold and that the threshold is high enough that incidental contact is unlikely to be dangerous.

By the 1990s regulation of dioxin had become the strictest ever imposed on any substance, stricter in some ways than regulation of plutonium. Benefits are beginning to show. In the early 1970s, Americans randomly tested for dioxin typically showed 11 to 13 parts per trillion in their cells. By the 1980s, the Centers for Disease Control were finding the typical cell level at four ppt. Children exposed to the dioxin cloud at Seveso averaged 19,100 ppt in cells; the most-exposed workers in the NIOSH study had 3,600 ppt; soldiers who handled Agent Orange had around 400 ppt. Michael Gough, a toxicologist for the federal Office of Technology Assessment, thinks the dioxin background concentration, the amount that occurs in cells naturally, is about two ppt.

Some researchers think there is a natural cell background level because dioxin is made naturally, mainly by lightning-caused forest fires; some tests find in the smoke from such fires a strong dioxin called PCDD. At this writing the question of whether there is dioxin in nature in is dispute among scientists, however. Some believe that there is no natural dioxin; were it not for industrial activity, cell levels of this substance would be zero. We shall soon find out, since new emissions of dioxin are already nearly eliminated from society, just 15 years after Love Canal. Similar progress is seen in levels of other chemicals. Since 1979, DDT residues in the body fat of randomly sampled Americans have declined on average 79 percent; PCB residues in human cells are down 75 percent.

Dioxin is now generally regulated to the smallest discernable amount—the "limit of detect," in regulatory parlance. Steadily reducing legal levels of a pollutant have the paradoxical effect of creating the impression that a substance is running amok even as its actual occurrence shrinks. For instance readers of the Athens, Ohio, *Messenger* awoke one morning in 1989 to the apparently shocking headline that fish with "double the legal limit for dioxin" had been caught downstream of a paper mill in Chillicothe, Ohio. Far into the story was the detail that the Ohio state limit for dioxin in fish was then one part per trillion; the fish caught contained 2.1 ppt. Twenty years ago laboratory analysis of fish would not have turned up anything in concentrations as tiny as 2.1 parts per trillion. Today such a concentration is regulated.

In many categories of toxic chemicals, some factions are pressing for "limit of detect" regulation in part because advances in detection create an endless sense of unresolved crisis as violations occur at steadily lower standards. From the standpoint of fund-raising, unresolved controversies are the best kind. As the limit of detect for some toxic chemicals approaches the parts per quintillion—about one grain of sand on the beach at Waikiki—activists will be able to express horror that practically everything will be shown to contain some trace of a "deadly" synthetic substance.

As dioxin production has declined, remaining trace emissions from paper mills have become a green cause. Greenpeace, for example, has staged protests around an International Paper plant in Georgetown, South Carolina. Greenpeace literature hit hard on the fact that the plant was "violating state and federal standards" for dioxin. This claim is true but glosses over the complicating factor that in 1990, process water leaving that mill contained about 0.64 parts per trillion of dioxin: an infinitesimal amount but greater than the limit of detect. If the naturally occurring background level of dioxin in human cells is as some researchers think around two parts per trillion, the shocking pollution emanating from the Georgetown plant held less dioxin by proportion than the cells of the people who were shocked. Today the EPA national standard for dioxin discharge to water is 13 parts per quadrillion. (A part per quadrillion is a thousand times less than a part per trillion.) At the 13 ppq level, I roughly estimate that U.S. papermills will release about eleven ounces of dioxin in 1994, less than was dropped by a single pass of an Operation Ranch Hand aircraft during the Agent Orange defoliation of Vietnam. Total dioxin releases from all U.S. sources in 1994 will be about 30 pounds, according to the EPA, most as smoke-stack emissions, most of which do not enter the food chain.

It is possible to make such figures sound like absurd regulatory overkill. Yet developments like dioxin restrictions at 13 ppq are wonderful to the ecorealist. In just 15 years papermakers have been able to drive dioxin emissions down to a level that is zero in all except the literal sense, while paper remains high in quality and low in price. This is the sort of advance in store for nearly every category of pollution.

The Dose

There are two essential rules for understanding why the stunning toxic output of modern industry does not create the havoc so widely predicted. One is that the dose makes the poison. The other is that exposure must precede harm.

The second of the two propositions is easiest to grasp. Large amounts of dangerous compounds may be present at a petrochemical complex or a hazardous waste site. But if you're not exposed to them, you are not harmed. Exposure requires proximity. How many times in your life have you actually walked inside a petrochemical complex? Walked onto a Superfund toxic waste site, bent down, and held a hand-ful of earth to your nose? For that matter can you name one Superfund site you have ever seen with your own eyes?

That most people have never been to a place where toxics are con-centrated does not, of course, mean people or the ecology are safe from such chemicals. Toxics may waft far on the air or seep into groundwa-ter, a serious concern wherever groundwater is used for drinking. But the basic point should not be overlooked: Exposure must precede harm. Moving trains are dangerous; motorboat propellers are dangerous; sew-ers are dangerous; waterfalls are dangerous; grizzly bears are dangerous; the majority of the Earth's surface that is underwater is, to mammals, extremely dangerous. The way people protect themselves from these dangers is by avoiding contact with them. The mere existence of locations containing danger, whether that danger is a waterfall or a spilled chemical, is not in itself any cause for alarm.

On the point that the dose makes the poison, important work has been done by Alice Ottoboni, a former staff toxicologist for the California Department of Health, whose technical book *The Dose Makes the Poison* has steadily gained influence among researchers and regulators. She argues that dose and exposure time, not degree of toxicity, determine the body's response to chemicals. Vitamin D, Ottoboni notes, is highly toxic in large doses but essential to life in small doses. One hundred cups of coffee contain a lethal dose of caffeine, but the dose is only lethal if taken at one sitting. Twenty pounds of spinach, Ottoboni continues, contains a lethal dose of oxalic acid, while 400 pounds of potatoes contain a lethal dose of solamine. Smaller amounts of these vegetables are not only not harmful but beneficial. "The effects of all chemicals are dependent on how much chemical is involved (the dose) and how long the exposure occurs," Ottoboni writes. This is true regardless of whether the chemical is synthetic or natural, Ottoboni believes, as the body has no mechanism for distinguishing between the two. The body distinguishes only between biochemical (useful to life) and xenobiotic (not useful).

The Maximum Dose

A staple of "Tonight Show" jokes is the laboratory rat given thousands of times the human dose of a substance. Such tests are not fraudulent exercises. Effects on cells must be stimulated somehow: Exposing lab animals to large doses is the best idea anyone has come up with so far. But in recent years the assumptions of the "rodent assay" have come under criticism within scientific circles. Leading the criticism are Bruce Ames and Lois Gold, toxicologists at the University of California at Berkeley.

Ames was once a hero to environmentalists. He is the inventor of the Ames Test, a device for screening carcinogens, and in the 1970s proved that the synthetic material Tris, added to children's pajamas, may cause cancer. Then Ames's research took an incorrect turn. Americans, Ames concluded, are exposed to far more natural toxins than synthetic toxics: perhaps 10,000 times as many natural toxins by weight. Ames began to believe that society has essentially tricked itself into assuming synthetic chemicals to be the main cancer trigger, because rodent assays are constructed in ways that make them likely to find the tested chemical dangerous. "But we were only testing synthetic chemicals," Ames says. Researchers were finding a high percentage of synthetic chemicals test out as carcinogens, without asking themselves what would happen if natural chemicals were subjected to the same analysis.

Ames and Gold began to do just that. To the chagrin of environmentalists, in lab animal tests natural chemicals ring the bell as carcinogens almost exactly as often as synthetic chemicals do. Juice made from apples grown without Alar contains, Ames estimates, 137 varieties of natural toxin. Five have been subjected to animal testing, and three registered as carcinogenic. The three were alcohol, found in apples and many fruits in tiny amounts; acetate; and acetaldehyde. Each of these carcinogens occur naturally. The latter two would inspire supermarket panic if injected into foods by processing companies. Ames and Gold have compiled a database on 1,117 chemicals subjected to rodent assays, and find that 52 percent register as carcinogens. "This suggests that either half the chemicals in the world are carcinogenic, which seems unlikely since then cancer should be universal, or that the methodology of the tests is suspect," Gold says.

Synthetic chemicals are tested in order to win the government permits required to market them. Since there are no restrictions on the chemicals that occur naturally in foods, there is no incentive for producers to spend money to determine whether natural compounds in foods are safe. Ames notes most consumer exposure to synthetic toxics comes from eating fruits and vegetables—often sprayed with more agricultural chemicals than grains and other foods, then delivered to the consumer in unprocessed form, which increases the odds of residues. Yet studies consistently show people who eat lots of fruits and vegetables are less likely to contract cancer. How can it be that eating more of the food groups that contain the most synthetic carcinogens reduces the odds of getting cancer?

A wag might say: Obviously because synthetic carcinogens prevent cancer. Two additional explanations present themselves. One is that the rodent tests and similar protocols used for current classifications of carcinogenic properties produce numerous false positives. The other is that the tests are right and thousands of chemicals, natural and synthetic, really are carcinogens. In the latter case people and animals must have some inherent ability, attained through natural selection over long periods of exposure to natural toxins, to resist carcinogens in small doses. Presumably this resistance would cross over to most synthetic carcinogens, which might help explain why some forms of cancer have fallen through the postwar era, even as the prevalence of synthetic compounds has risen.

Peanut Butter Logic

A central instrument in rodent testing is the Maximum Tolerated Dose. This is the most of a chemical that a mouse can stand without simply dropping dead. An objection to the main study cited in the campaign against the pesticide Alar is that the Maximum Tolerated Dose was exceeded. So much of an Alar breakdown product was given to test mice that many died immediately, poisoned: as table salt or aspirin or other common substances will cause quick death by poisoning in large enough amounts. There were, however, other tests of Alar considered credible because the Maximum Tolerated Dose was calculated correctly. These tests entailed mice being injected with the equivalent of 65,000 times the expected human exposure to the pesticide. To researchers the use of the 65,000 times the human dose is not as strange as it sounds, since the objective is to create in an artificially short time a disease response such as tumor formation. Further, the tests seek to develop tumors that exceed the control rate: That is, if a quarter of rodents would naturally develop cancer over a lifetime, chemical tests must cause tumors in more than 25 percent to reach a finding of carcinogenesis. Under such circumstances high doses are unavoidable.

What Ames and Gold object to is not the high doses but the assumption that if lab animals do develop tumors, this proves the test substance is a carcinogen. They believe that the Maximum Tolerated Dose often triggers a condition just short of poisoning, in which there is widespread cell mortality near the injection point. Normal cell replacement then goes awry causing a neoplastic tumor, but not the kind arrived at through standard cancer process. The test ends with the chemical acting like a carcinogen, though it might not cause tumors in quantities less than a Maximum Tolerated Dose.

Gold notes that by the reasoning of Maximum Tolerated Dose, "calories are the most striking rodent carcinogen ever discovered." Feeding rats just 20 percent more food than needed reduces lifespans and increases incidence of endocrine and mammary tumors. Far higher doses of synthetic chemicals are usually required to trigger cancers. In people, obesity is associated with endometrial and gallbladder cancer, heart disease, stroke, and arteriosclerosis. Based on what happens in standard rodent assays calories should be classified as carcinogenic—at which point it could truly be said that Everything Causes Cancer.

Ames and Gold have given their analysis of rodent tests the dead-weight label "mitogensis is not carcinogenesis." This means the cell damage caused by the local-poisoning effect is different from the cell damage associated with cancer. Many researchers disagree. For instance, Bernard Weinstein of Columbia University believes that the sort of mutations Ames and Gold presume unique to Maximum Tolerated Dose circumstances are sometimes observed in "normal" cancer development. Lester Lave of Carnegie Mellon, Gilbert Omen of the University of Washington, and Phillippe Shubik of Oxford University are among the prominent researchers who have sided with the Ames-Gold premise. Shubik further believes that animal test interpretation standards of the International Agency for Research on Cancer, an affiliate of the World Health Organization, are biased in ways that exaggerate the number and seeming potency of carcinogens. The EPA and other federal agencies generally employ IARC standards when regulating synthetic compounds, and so may be passing an exaggeration along.

Ames and Gold have developed a larger critique of the role of chemicals in the environment. First, they say, cancer risks from common foods and everyday activities are much greater than from synthetic chemicals, for the simple reason that exposure to common foods and everyday activities is higher. In *Science*, Ames and Gold published what has come to be known as the "peanut butter chart," because it used a sandwich made from all-natural peanut butter as the standard against which to assess risks. The typical PCB exposure of an American, the chart declared, is substantially less likely to cause cancer than the natural toxin in one peanut-butter sandwich. A glass of herb tea, one raw nonpoisonous mushroom, or one can of diet soda are all more dangerous than a glass of tap water from the Woburn, Massachusetts, wells found to contain trichloroethylene. A glass of wine, containing sulfates, ranks as much more carcinogenic than a glass of Woburn water; a sleeping pill containing phenobarbital as hundreds of times more carcinogenic than a glass of Woburn water. People who would pronounce themselves horrified by the notion that PCBs or TCE are sitting in drums hundreds of miles away merrily place phenobarbital directly into their bodies on a regular basis.

Given the imprimatur of the world's most prestigious technical journal, the peanut butter chart has since been misinterpreted by conservative commentators as proving synthetic chemicals to be inconsequential. The chart expresses nothing of the sort. On it can be found clear danger rankings for synthetics: For instance the chart shows the pesticide EDB very hazardous. By peanut butter reasoning PCBs, EDBs, and the rest are bad news—just less bad than mythology has it.

The second part of Ames and Gold's general critique has another deadweight name, the "human exposure dose to rodent potency dose" scale, or HERP. This tool attempts to take into account the fact that different substances have different effects on different species. A running environmental controversy near the researchers' home in Berkeley is the presence of industrial solvents leaked into some aquifers from computer chip manufacturing in Silicon Valley. Using the HERP scale, Ames and Gold rated the 35 most contaminated wells of Silicon Valley as safer than Berkeley tap water. Why? Partly because TCE appears dangerous mainly in the lungs. When swallowed in water, TCE does not contact the lungs; its toxicity to people declines. Meanwhile Berkeley tap water, like three-quarters of U.S. tap water, is chlorinated. Chlorination is a known cause of bladder and rectal cancers, leading to an estimated 10,700 cases per year. Chlorine seems to do most damage when swallowed, obviously what happens with tap water. Like nearly all scientists and environmentalists, Ames and Gold believe chlorination of drinking water is a good idea, because the benefits of preventing waterborne disease far outweigh the additional cancers.[2] Their point is simply that chlorine, a chemical with a well-known downside, is widely accepted while compounds like TCE are regarded with hushed terror, though they may cause much less harm.

Finally Ames and Gold are critical of a common feature of environmental literature, something called the "linear dose response." Linear dose response, Ames says, "has been the dominant assumption in regulating carcinogens for many years, but it may not be correct."

The Modeled Dose

Suppose, to employ a mildly simplified example, 100 units of a chemical can kill ten people. If ten units are then presumed capable of killing one person, a linear dose response has been assumed. The EPA, for example, has found that six parts per million of formaldehyde will cause tumors in one percent of lab rats. So the agency assumes that six parts per billion, or a thousandth of the dose, will cause one additional cancer in 100,000 people, or one-thousandth as often. This assumption is then used in setting emission regulations. Yet one one-thousandth of anything may not necessarily have one one-thousandth the effect of the whole. A quart of whisky contains enough ethanol to kill a 200-pound adult. One one-thousandth of the quart—about a thirtieth of an ounce, less than the alcohol in a tablespoon of pediatric cough syrup—has no discernible effect.

Agencies such as the EPA do not use linear dose assumptions because they are unaware of the drawbacks; rather, because where low exposures to chemicals are concerned, all analysis involves guesswork. But many scientists feel the linear dose presumption exaggerates the seeming potency of chemicals. The linear dose assumption used in formaldehyde regulation, if applied to alcohol, would lead to the immediate ban of light beer as a hypertoxic.

Many EPA and environmentalist estimates of the carcinogenic potential of substances are based not on empirical data—studies of the cause of death, for example—but on computer models in which the risks of low exposure are extrapolated from high exposure. This is a notoriously tricky business, partly because high-exposure data may involve extreme conditions inapplicable to low-level doses. For example, some EPA estimates of the dangers of radon gas were computer-modeled from the exposure suffered by uranium miners. Radon is dramatically more intense in uranium mines than homes. Extrapolating from miners' exposure, an EPA radon model predicted in 1988 that Iowa would be the most dangerous state for this gas, with 1,600 radon-caused lung-cancer deaths there per year. But in 1988 the actual number of lung-cancer deaths in Iowa, according to the National Cancer Institute, was 1,420— with most of these deaths caused, of course, by cigarette smoking.

Extrapolations in toxicity models sometimes include a statistical process called "stepwise regression," which some mathematicians question. Studies that seek to show the relationship between illness and exposure to a chemical usually include data on a number of independent variables that change within the study group, such as environmental exposure, age, gender, and so on. In a stepwise regression, researchers eliminate independent variables that link to the disease no better than chance, then assume that whatever is left must be the cause. There are several problems with this approach. One is that through manipulation of the model a researcher can essentially define in advance that which he or she expects to find, then train the computer to reject whatever fails to satisfy the expectation. Another fault is that stepwise regressions may record false positives, pinpointing apparent relationships between sets of numbers that have nothing to do with each other, or were even chosen at random. When the small apparent relationship is multiplied back across some huge group such as the population of the United States a high estimate for deaths may result, though it is impossible to know whether the risk is real or a statistical artifact.

"Stepwise regression is a fishing expedition," says Paul Meier, retired chairman of the department of statistics at the University of Chicago. "There's nothing wrong with fishing through numbers, but you must understand that what you find is not necessarily credible, and certainly unlikely to be a basis for sound government policy." Yet this form of analysis is a common tool in environmental gloom studies.

To guard against random number associations taking over a regression study, statisticians use a mathematical formula designed to filter out coincidence. The standard is that any claimed relationship between cause and effect must not have more than a five percent likelihood of resulting from chance. Called "five percent confidence," this is an established principle of academic statistics.

Increasingly, however, environmental studies use a ten percent level as the filtering device. For example EPA studies supporting the claim that 20,000 people die each year from radon gas in their homes—nearly half the number killed each year in U.S. highway accidents—were arrived at using relaxed statistical assumptions. Analysts first ran radon exposure studies at five percent confidence level and found nothing. They increased the parameter to ten percent: Suddenly the computers spit back what appeared to be a nationwide epidemic of radon death. The EPA then declared radon an environmental threat of major significance, a notion rapidly embraced by environmentalists. But did the radon study have meaning? "It is irresponsible to claim statistical significance in a finding arrived at using ten percent confidence," Meier says.

Cancer Up or Down?

A look at cancer trends can help put the fear of chemicals into perspective. Richard Doll, the British researcher who in the 1960s proved that cigarette smoking causes lung cancer, and his colleague Richard Peto of Oxford University believe that if cancer statistics are adjusted for increasing longevity, most forms of cancer are in decline. To reach this conclusion Doll and Peto omit figures for lung cancer, estimated to kill 395,000 people annually in the United States, on the grounds that most lung cancer is caused by cigarette smoking and thus is a self-imposed illness that tells nothing about underlying trends.

For several years Doll and Peto have engaged in a public conflict with Devra Davis, currently senior adviser to the U.S. Department of Health and Human Services, who believes that in the developed world most cancer rates, adjusted for age and smoking, are trending slightly up. In 1992 the National Cancer Institute, which previously had leaned toward the Doll-Peto position, began to incline toward Davis.

The statistical artillery exchanged between the Doll-Peto and Davis camps is thunderous, and too technical to broach here. Doll and Peto assume it now proven that environmental exposures are only a small factor in carcinogenesis, causing one to five percent of cancers, rather than 70 to 90 percent as was commonly assumed through the 1970s when the culture of chemophobia was building. Polls of the public show the reverse: that people do know smoking is dangerous but believe 70 to 90 percent of cancers come from environmental problems.

In 1993 an important study buttressed the Doll-Peto position. Writing in the *Journal of the American Medical Association* two physicians, Michael McGinnis and William Foege, reviewed cause-of-death studies published in U.S. technical journals from 1977 to 1993. Rolling these studies together, McGinnis and Foege found that tobacco is the leading killer in the United States, causing 19 percent of preventable or premature deaths through cancer, heart disease, lung failure, and other conditions. High-fat diet and "activity patterns" (sedentary behavior) was the number-two killer, at 14 percent. "Toxic agents," McGinnis and Foege estimated, killed three percent of Americans, with workplace exposures and secondary cigarette smoke, not trace pesticide residues or Superfund sites, accounting for most toxic-agent deaths. Thus this study found that deaths caused by pollutants and synthetic chemicals are indeed real, but the number of such deaths is nowhere as high as conventional wisdom assumes.

Davis has produced studies suggesting that toxic chemicals will someday be shown to account for more cancers than the work of Doll and Peto or McGinnis and Foege suggests. She says she expects environmental exposure to synthetics "will eventually be shown to account for between ten and 20 percent of cancers, cautioning that this is a guess because too little is known about cancer to speak with assurance." Davis occupies the leftmost range of credentialed scientific debate on cancer numbers. It is significant that her best guess for environmentally caused cancers, though higher than the Doll-Peto estimate, is still far lower than the figures widely assumed in the 1970s.

Davis objects that although studies such as those conducted by Ames and Gold can show, say, that the odds of TCE hurting someone are extremely small, TCE is hardly the only synthetic chemical to which people are exposed. People are exposed to dozens of toxics, and next to nothing is known about what they do in combination: The constraints of control groups mean chemicals invariably are studied singly. Surely Davis is right: Synthetic toxics must do more harm in combination than in isolation. But if this is true then natural toxins must also do more harm in combination than in isolation. If natural toxins outweigh synthetic toxics by 10,000 to one for the typical person, then combination natural effects would far outpace combination synthetic effects.

In recent years the Western press has devoted zillions of words to real but exaggerated threats from Alar, dioxin, and PCBs; to speculative threats such as brain cancer from cellular phones; to tertiary threats such as computer-screen emissions. Somehow through this doomsday wish fulfillment cigarette smoking, by a huge margin the leading cause of preventable death, remains old news. Newspapers and magazines, including my publication, *Newsweek,* avoid the subject for fear of offending advertisers. But even television rarely emphasizes lung cancer as a subject of public concern, and television is barred by law from accepting cigarette advertising. It is bizarre indeed to think that low-order cancer threats are now being regulated down to the parts per quadrillion with cost no object, yet 395,000 lung cancer deaths from smoking occur each year with the underlying cause, the content of cigarettes, exempt from regulation.

Legal observers expect that sometime in the 1990s Lorillard, a major tobacco marketer, will become the first cigarette company to pay a liability judgment over a lung cancer death. This is because in the 1950s Lorillard marketed its Kent cigarette as tipped by a miraculous Micronite filter. The secret ingredient in the Micronite filter was asbestos. For pushing the asbestos, a secondary carcinogen, Lorillard may pay, principally because federal law now formally calls asbestos a hazard. For pushing the tobacco, the worst carcinogen by a fantastic margin, the company will not pay. This is the current state of rationality in U.S. environmental policy.

Finally on the question of environmentally triggered cancers there is the time-lag factor. The latency period for cancer can run to 30 years. Mass production of synthetic toxics began in the postwar era. Through the 1950s and 1960s, use and disposal of synthetic toxics expanded essentially without regulation. In the 1970s that began to change. By 1990 uses of synthetic toxics were tightly regulated; releases and disposal were declining fast.

This suggests that to the extent toxic chemicals are a source of cancer, the bill is coming due today, as the latency period from exposures in the 1950s and 1960s expires. Once that bill is paid there may be no further invoices. Future generations will have been exposed to far fewer toxics then the current over-65 generation. "Somehow no one ever picks up on this," Devra Davis notes. "Cancer rates are up but that is basically a cohort effect from exposures in the 1950s and 1960s. As early as the end of the 1990s we should see rates start to fall. Cancer increases of the present are real and provable. But the problem of environmental toxics has already peaked and won't repeat."

Alar

In 1989 the Natural Resources Defense Council, working with the television show "60 Minutes," proclaimed the apple pesticide Alar an extraordinary threat to children, who eat more apples than adults. The EPA promptly declared Alar a "probable" carcinogen, and its manufacturer, Uniroyal, withdrew the substance. Later the EPA banned Alar. Since then the statistical methods used by the NRDC and the images employed by CBS (skull and crossbones imposed on an apple) have been roundly denounced by scientists. Today the EPA's formal classification of Alar rates it only about five percent as likely to cause cancer as assumed at the time of the ban. The World Health Organization does not consider Alar as a carcinogen.

Much has been written about the Alar tiff, yet a few observations remain. First, society is better off without Alar. Alar was used mainly to make apples extra red instead of only sorta red, and who really cares about that? Lawrie Mott, the NRDC's Alar specialist, may have overloaded her statistical case but is on the money when she asserts that eliminating Alar did society no harm. Some apple growers lost value in the crops they were taking to market when the Alar controversy was swirling. But the following year's crop set records for bushels and revenue, showing apples could be grown quite well without Alar.

Next, the Alar flap shook up government and industry in a useful way. "The EPA became much more responsive to the public after Alar," says Linda Fisher, the former EPA chief for toxics. "So did the Department of Agriculture. Before Alar we constantly contradicted each other in public about pesticide safety and nobody much cared. After Alar it became important that our policies coordinated." This development laid the groundwork for the 1993 announcement by President Clinton that the EPA, the USDA, and the Food and Drug Administration would write cohesive pesticide standards, replacing a hodgepodge of overlapping rules.

A similar unintended but constructive consequence of Alar was that pesticide manufacturers, fearing publicity, became more cooperative with the EPA. When the Alar controversy broke, Fisher's office had been working to restrict parathion, a pesticide with much more troubling health estimates than Alar; though the main risk was to farm workers, not photogenic schoolchildren. "We expected to have a horrible time, to be dragged to court over every word," Fisher says. "Instead the manufacturers were cooperative." Parathion companies realized they were better off making peace with the EPA than listening for the tick-tick-tick of the "60 Minutes" introduction theme.

Asbestos

In the 1960s an epidemiologist named Irving Selikoff began to notice that dock workers and asbestos factory laborers were suffering from a cancer of the lung lining called mesothelioma, a disease not known before this century. By the mid-1970s Selikoff had proved that asbestos in insulation, ship-fitting materials, and factory dust was the cause. Data Selikoff collected from the 1960s suggested between 1,000 and 3,000 mesothelioma deaths per year could be attributed to asbestos. There was reason to fear that since cancer may take decades to incubate, people exposed to asbestos, the manufacturing and use of which took off around World War II, would not begin to exhibit symptoms till the 1970s or 1980s. Since asbestos was then commonly used in building materials, meaning everyone came near the stuff at some point, Selikoff began to predict that mesothelioma could surpass lung cancer as a health threat. By 1978 Joseph Califano, Secretary of Health and Human Services for the Carter Administration, said mesothelioma would soon kill about 85,000 Americans per year, more than the current annual death toll for breast cancer.

Selikoff's work set in motion a chain of events that led to the end of asbestos mining and manufacturing, followed by an EPA ban on almost all asbestos use; to the bankruptcy of several asbestos manufacturers; to perhaps the most complex tort litigation in history, an ongoing class-action liability trial in Philadelphia in which some 26,000 lawsuits handled at one point by several hundred full-time attorneys (no kidding) working under a Supreme Court case-consolidation directive are being brought against the remains of U.S. Gypsum and other asbestos firms, with about two-thirds of the funds expended going to legal costs rather than to victims; to the 1986 Asbestos Hazard Emergency Response Act, passed in response to stories about asbestos in schools; and to a number of local ordinances, prominently one in New York City, enacted in the wake of the federal law and requiring that asbestos be removed from many buildings regardless of whether a risk is shown.

The last two steps in this progression of events are now generally considered by scientists and by students of public policy to be blunders committed under the pressure of alarmism. There is no doubt that asbestos fibers in large concentration in factories posed a grave risk to workers. But the numbers of deaths from mesothelioma has never approached the emergency estimates. Ten thousand mesothelioma cases per year is the current worst-case estimate; most estimates are much lower, at 1,000 cases per year or fewer. With most asbestos use now banned, it is unlikely the doomsday number ever will be realized.

Moreover, research since Selikoff's original alarms has shown that the type of asbestos used in building materials is not particularly dangerous; and to the extent that it is dangerous it is better off left in walls, inert. Ripping asbestos shingles and insulation out of walls, in contrast, causes the fibers to become airborne, creating the very harm the Asbestos Hazard Emergency Act sought to avoid.

In the early 1980s Malcolm Ross, a minerals specialist at the U.S. Geological Survey, began to say that Selikoff made a fundamental error by assuming all asbestos has equal properties. Ross believed that only a rare form of asbestos called amphibole attacks the lungs. The primary form of asbestos, called chrysotile, is close to benign, Ross thought. Only about five percent of the asbestos used in the United States was the dangerous kind. When Ross began propounding these views, he was widely derided. Environmental lobbyists labeled Ross's work pseudo-science; congressmen who favored more asbestos regulation, such as Rep. George Miller of California, denounced Ross. By 1990, Ross's idea had gone from crackpot to standard throughout the science world. A pathologist named Brooke Mossman at the University of Vermont led a team of researchers that documented the distinction between the types of asbestos, upholding Ross.

About the time in 1989 that Mossman began to publish her doubts on asbestos risk, a large panel of international asbestos and cancer experts issued a thick report, *Asbestos in Public and Commercial Buildings,* concluding, "The available data do not support the concept that low-level exposure to asbestos is a health hazard in buildings and schools." The study had been directed by Congress and organized by the Institute of Medicine, an independent academic group. It found that so long as asbestos is left in wall panels, such that it does not become air-borne, all asbestos in U.S. schools would cause one additional cancer for every ten million students. The panel criticized health damage estimates used by the EPA and environmentalists to press for passage of the 1986 emergency act. The estimates, the committee noted, were not based on actual disease incidence; rather they were extrapolations generated by computer models.

Yet this transformation of scientific understanding of asbestos, being inappropriately positive, had no impact on the public-policy world. In 1993, the start of the New York City school year was delayed by an asbestos scare. Investigators discovered that survey teams inspecting New York City schools for asbestos had faked documents. Schools closed while emergency teams redid the inspections. Reinspection was necessary. But as what New York newspapers and politicians called the "asbestos crisis" picked up steam, there was essentially no discussion of whether asbestos fears were grounded in fact. The driving considerations were that parents had been made to shudder at the word *asbestos* and that the success of tort litigation claims involving impossibly small quantities of asbestos exposed New York City to lawsuits filed for the purposes of seeking settlements, regardless of whether any harm had been done.

Images and media presentations about asbestos were uniformly fearsome during the New York "crisis." Even the somber *New York Times* ran a prominent photograph of an inspector holding a sealed vial of asbestos fibers in a rubber-gloved hand, as though the contents would kill on contact. A group of 17 credentialed asbestos researchers, including Mossman, Bernard Gee of Yale's School of Medicine, and Catherine Skinner of Yale's Department of Geology, issued a statement saying "there is virtually no risk to schoolchildren from asbestos in the city's public schools," and that "the doses of asbestos fibers which may have caused cancer to workers [in asbestos factories] *vastly* exceed those to which schoolchildren ever will be exposed" (Italics original). The only way New York schoolchildren might be harmed, the scientists wrote, is if panic caused a removal program. "Unnecessary asbestos removal," they said, "is a real concern since it has the ability to release substantial quantities of asbestos into the air. Post-abatement fiber levels in schools are occasionally so high that they approach levels to which asbestos workers were exposed 50 years ago." This scientists' statement was by and large ignored by New York political leaders and news organizations. The New York school asbestos "crisis" caused at least $119 million to be spent on emergency inspections and removal, money that might have been invested in health care, better education, or any number of areas where the needs of the city's poor are painfully real.

So far an estimated $6 billion to $10 billion has been spent ripping asbestos from buildings, with a likelihood that most of that expenditure was pure waste. Asbestos can still be found in a few products such as replacement brakes for older cars, but new vehicles use nonasbestos linings. Asbestos has also been banned in fireproof materials such as firefighter's clothing. Whether this degree of anti-asbestos obsession is wise is a matter being tested in the courts. In 1991, the federal appeals court in New Orleans suspended some asbestos bans. The court essentially said the EPA failed to take into account how the lives that might be saved by removing asbestos from brakes and firefighters' clothing would compare to the lives that might be lost by increased brake failures or firefighters' gear that does not protect as well. At this writing the federal appeals ruling is unresolved.

Looking at the EPA's reasoning in the New Orleans case Supreme

Court justice Stephen Breyer, then an appeals judge, expressed amazement. The EPA estimates that a total asbestos ban will save at most 15 lives per year. Breyer has noted that twice as many people die annually from swallowing toothpicks. Yet while billions have been spent to counter an assumed asbestos doomsday, anyone suggesting a single dollar be spent to prevent toothpick ingestion would be laughed out of town. This, Breyer says, is an example of a regulatory "vicious circle" in which bans takes on lives of their own, divorced from common sense.

Does Breyer's example seem overstated? Consider that the economists Maureen Cropper of the University of Maryland and George Van Houtven of East Carolina University estimate that asbestos regulation costs up to $49 million per premature death avoided. This sum adds a hypothetical few years to the ends of a few people's lives, when the money might be invested in education, health care, crime prevention, or other social needs with much better paybacks. Between the fashionability of environmental scares and the fact that the $49 million per death avoided is invisible spending—buried in product costs, litigation fees, and lost employment—there is no public opposition to such initiatives. Yet if preventing early deaths is a priority, as it ought to be, consider that studies have shown the simple expedient of requiring auto and truck headlights to be on at all times (as is already required in Canada) would reduce highway deaths by 3,000 to 5,000 per year by making it easier to see oncoming traffic. A lights-on regulation would be just shy of free. Yet while costly asbestos restrictions that save at most a handful of lives march forward protected by doomsday orthodoxy, simple expedients to save thousands of lives on the highway remain undone. Are these rational priorities?

PCBs

Two classes of chemicals about which there now exists general consternation were viewed as welcome developments when invented because they were thought benign. One class is the chlorofluorocarbon, which till its ozone-depletion effects became known was used partly because CFCs passed toxicity tests with flying colors, causing no harm even at Maximum Tolerated Doses. The other class, polychlorinated byphenyls, or PCBs, came into wide use as an electrical insulator because they seemed wholly inert.

By the late 1970s, animal tests had begun to suggest that PCBs were not inert but rather hypercarcinogens. Manufacture of the compounds was banned in the U.S. in 1978. Soon PCBs began showing up in the toxic waste sites. PCBs were also found at the bottom of rivers such as the Hudson, in the mucks of harbors, and along the floor of the Great Lakes. The EPA classified PCBs as a "group B2 carcinogen," meaning one assumed to have no threshold—dangerous even as a single molecule. Disposing of PCBs legally, even in modern hazardous-waste facilities, became nearly impossible. Estimates for long-term PCB cleanup costs began to run as high as $100 billion.

But PCB exposure in people has not upheld the frightening predictions of rodent tests. Follow-ups on workers exposed to high levels of PCBs from the 1950s till the 1970s—the people most likely to become ill and who are now old enough that diseases should manifest—have led to "no known cases of cancer," Philip Abelson wrote in *Science* in 1991. Abelson holds a senior position with the American Association for the Advancement of Science and has won its Public Welfare Medal for his work in exposing the unhealthy conditions faced by uranium miners during the 1950s. Abelson speculated that a basic misunderstanding about PCBs arose because early animal tests were on a version of the compound, called Alaclor 1260, that was very high in chlorine. Most forms of PCBs were not high in chlorine. When tested later, low-chlorine PCBs did not trigger alarms as hypercarcinogens. Unreasoned fear of PCBs has led to such near-comic acts as a 1993 decision by the Port Authority of New York–New Jersey to stop dredging its harbors because trace levels of PCBs were found in the muck. Only the dread-inducing character of the term PCBs, and the legal consequences of any misstep, explain such decisions.

Recently evidence has begun to show that PCBs do not represent an indefinite bioaccumulative threat to the ecology. A group of researchers at General Electric found that natural microorganisms in the Hudson River have "learned" through mutation to decompose the low-chlorine forms of PCBs and are now using them as a food source. General Electric has a corporate interest in this finding. The company dumped some 500,000 pounds of PCBs into the Hudson between 1946 and 1975, from factories in Fort Edwards and Hudson Falls, a problem General Electric has spent many millions trying to fix. But the G.E. research report has been peer-reviewed by scientists not affiliated with the company and found accurate. While the multinationals, the EPA, and state agencies continue to argue among themselves about what to do with PCBs in the Hudson, microbes too small to see may be resolving the problem for them, subsisting on a synthetic compound supposedly hyperdeadly in the tiniest amount. This does not make PCBs excusable. It's just the way nature handles problems we humans imagine cannot be handled.

Though less directly toxic than once feared, chemicals such as PCBs may someday be shown to have unsuspected damaging properties, especially in reproductive health. For instance in 1993 Devra Davis and some colleagues published a series of studies suggesting that some compounds found in pesticides are transformed in the body into chemicals that act like hormones. These false hormone intermediaries might trigger breast cancer (thought to be linked to the hormone estrogen) or depress sperm counts (sperm counts have declined in much of the Western world in this century, for reasons not yet understood).

In 1994 the New York State Department of Health published a preliminary study suggesting that breast cancer rates were high among postmenopausal women who during the 1960s and 1970s lived close to two poorly regulated chemical factories on Long Island. Breast cancer rates are elevated throughout Long Island, even for women who have never lived near industrial facilities; the federal Centers for Disease Control has studied the island extensively and been unable to find an environmental cause for high breast cancer incidence there. If the 1994 state study withstands peer review (incomplete at this writing) it would be the first in the United States demonstrating a clear link between breast cancer and synthetic toxics.

The Zero-Emission Future

That finding hit home to me with some force. My mother, Vimy, died of breast cancer at age 58. During World War II she worked at Hooker Chemicals in Niagara Falls, New York, the very factory that made the wastes buried at Love Canal. I visited the plant as a child and vividly recall that my head was set reeling within minutes by airborne chemicals: probably benzene, which has a fierce aroma. Through the 1940s, 1950s, and 1960s, toxic pollution from Hooker and two other petrochemical complexes in Niagara Falls was essentially unregulated. Yet studies of the area do not show any general epidemic of cancer, despite the passage of the latency period. Evidence such as this suggests that synthetic compounds cannot be the unstoppable hyperpoison environmental orthodoxy makes them out to be. But that is entirely different from saying they can be handled carelessly without a human cost, perhaps including my own mother's life.

The fact that death estimates for synthetic chemicals are oversold has nothing to do with the desirability of reducing to zero all forms of toxic discharges to the environment while cutting wherever practical chemical uses in manufacturing, in products and in the home. Toxics cannot possibly be good for us or the ecology. That's all we really need to know to justify a goal of zero toxic discharge.

Within a decade, zero toxic discharge will be the standard for developed nations. Developing nations will follow early in the next century. Once this level of ecological protection has been achieved the typical person—including the typical rapacious businessperson—will be amazed to think that it was ever otherwise.

CLEAN TECH 🌿

RECENTLY I HELD IN MY HANDS ONE OF THE MOST ADVANCED materials in existence, a spun-filament thread similar to silk. The substance was so thin as to be barely visible, yet gram for gram possessed higher tensile strength than many specialty steels. The strand had been manufactured to a standard of zero toxic emission. All wastes from the manufacturing were biodegradable. No petrochemical feedstocks were employed; the raw materials were common commodities that might be found lying on the ground. Manufacturing was accomplished at standard one-bar air pressure and at about room temperature. Only tiny amounts of energy were employed, less than a watt per meter of product. No acrylic glues, industrial acids, bulk alkaloids, or polychlorinated compounds were used; all intermediary chemicals were water-soluble and harmless to most living things. Yet there it was, a thin line of glistening fiber of incredible strength.

I was holding a strand from a spiderweb.

Today the manmade spun-fibers most similar to spider's silk cannot be manufactured without great heat, high pressure, and large quantities of acid. Spiders make fibers without any technological gizmos and their product is superior in ease of use, simply hardening when exposed to air. The mundane spiderweb represents the future of human industry: clean technology, the coming successor to high technology.

The clean-tech revolution is already afoot in products and manufacturing processes that use substantially fewer resources and less energy than those they supplant. In 1976 the best-selling sedan, the Chevrolet

Caprice, weighed 4,424 pounds and went 16 miles on a gallon of gasoline. By 1993 the best-selling sedan, the Ford Taurus, weighed 3,420 pounds and recorded 29 miles per gallon. By the turn of the century the typical sedan is expected to be down to about 3,000 pounds and up to 35 mpg. Fax machines and modems are high tech compared to the postal van yet are also clean tech, able to send messages essentially unlimited distances with almost no expenditure of resources. New jetliners such as the Boeing 757 and Airbus 320 burn 30 percent less fuel per passenger-mile than jetliners of a decade ago, while not emitting the ear-splitting thunder of earlier transports. Coming jetliners such as the Boeing 777 will burn 50 percent less fuel per seat-mile and radiate still fewer decibels. Twenty years ago 164 pounds of metal were expended during the manufacture of 1,000 soda cans. Today the figure is 35 pounds. By 1992 some 38 percent of aluminum beer and soda cans were being recycled, with the percentage rising each year; fashioning a new soda can from recycled aluminum requires about 90 percent less energy than manufacturing a virgin can from bauxite. Suspicious of the new plastic grocery sack? One thousand paper grocery sacks contain 140 pounds of material. Plastic sacks holding about the same amount require 40 pounds of material.

Pessimists assume machines become ever more dangerous and more voracious in use of resources. There is no reason this need be so: Already most trends are in the opposite, clean-tech direction. It's hard to think of any important current product that requires significantly more resources than what it supplants or creates significantly more waste.

The current transition to less resource-intensive products represents only the initial stage of what will eventually become a sweeping conversion to an industrial order based on clean technology. Two important factors, neither yet understood in public discourse, are at work here. The first is the end of the age of materials. The second is the beginning of the age of knowledge—by which I don't mean lots of computers (everybody knows about that) but an age in which women and men learn to make what they need using the simultaneously advanced yet simple techniques perfected by nature and embodied in the spider's silk.

Beyond the Age of Materials

First World countries "are leaving the age of materials and moving into an era in which the level of materials use will no longer be an important indicator of economic progress," says Eric Larson, a researcher at the

Center for Energy and Environmental Studies of Princeton University. Larson continues, "Since the industrial revolution, a hallmark of economic growth has been ever-increasing consumption of materials. In recent years there has been a fundamental change in this pattern. The markets that expanded rapidly during the era of materials are now by and large saturated. New markets tend to involve products that have a low materials content."

An important example of this transition is declining per-capita use of steel in the developed world. Through the year 1920, steel consumption in the United States grew much faster than the gross national product. From the 1920s to the 1950s steel use grew less rapidly than the GNP but per-capita consumption continued to increase with the postwar boom in auto manufacturing. Then per-capita consumption stopped increasing; it has been declining since. By the 1980s, steel use per dollar of GNP had fallen to 40 percent less than its 1920 peak. Today U.S. steel consumption per GNP unit is about what it was when Grover Cleveland was president. The trend line continues to decline backward toward the pre–Civil War level.

Per-capita use of wood, cotton, specialty metals, lime, phosphorus, ammonia, minerals, concrete, potash, rubber, plastic (yes, even plastic), and many other materials has been falling for a decade or more, Larson's figures show. Per-capita use of aluminum is up, but with the jump in recycling, consumption of virgin aluminum has declined through the same period. There is but one major materials category in which per-capita consumption continues to rise in the developed world. The material is paper. For good or ill the United States now leads the world in per-capita paper consumption.

One example of how technical advances result in lower, not higher, materials consumption can be found at the Empire State Building. In the early 1980s engineers replaced girders in the building that were showing metal fatigue. The replacement girders contained only about one-third as much steel. "New metals are stronger, so less weight was required," Larson explains. "Knowledge of architectural engineering has improved, so designers now do more with less. New theories of how to build and manufacture using fewer materials are spreading to the Third World, meaning that at least in principle, developing countries should find they do not need to duplicate the enormous levels of material consumption we had here, to achieve about the same standard of living."

Another sign the Age of Materials is drawing to a close is that the depletion of natural resources, repeatedly predicted throughout the industrial era, has yet to occur in any important category.

Twenty years ago absolutely everyone was convinced that the exhaustion of petroleum would be the world's dominant problem by the 1990s. Today governments argue about the political entanglements and pollution caused by fossil fuels, but questions of supply are forgotten. At current consumption the world has proven reserves of about 35 years of oil, 70 years of natural gas, and 300 years of coal. Undiscovered deposits should at least double those figures: In natural gas and coal there may be as much as thousands of years of supply. David O'Reilly, a vice president of Chevron, says, "There exists at least another decade of global oil supply around $20 a barrel, and there may be several decades more of global supplies at low prices."

As the resource analyst Jerry Taylor of the Cato Institute in Washington, D.C., points out, in 1939 the Department of Interior declared that the U.S. would run out of oil by 1952. In 1947 the Department of State announced that no oil remained to be discovered on U.S. territory. In 1951, State projected that all petroleum supplies worldwide would be exhausted by 1964. In 1979 the International Energy Agency announced that then-current world reserves of 645 billion barrels would be exhausted by 1985. "By the year 1990," Taylor says, "not only had oil not run out but the global reserves figure had risen to 1,000 billion barrels."

Perhaps some rude surprise awaits, but it appears that no important resource is in danger of exhaustion. Jane Shaw, an economist with the Political Economy Research Center, a Bozeman, Montana, think tank, says that "no nonrenewable resource has ever actually disappeared, because in a market system whenever prices of materials rise, people start looking for substitutes."

Shaw's statement is not entirely true. For instance when the Spanish began to break up bat guano deposits in Mesoamerica in the sixteenth century for shipment to Europe for fertilizer that resource, nonrenewable over the time scale of human lives, rapidly depleted. But in the main Shaw is correct. Wood, coal, rubber, oil, copper, tungsten, chromimum, platinum, and other resources have been subject to pronouncements of imminent exhaustion during the industrial era: All now exist in greater supplies, selling at lower real-dollar prices, than when they were supposedly about to exhaust. This has happened because people have found ways to conserve or have switched to substitutes. The rubber shortage of World War II, for instance, helped inspire the creation of the plastics industry, the discovery of rubber substitutes, and the invention of products such as the radial-belted tire that make rubber last longer. The rubber tree, overtapped and considered a candidate for extinction 50 years ago, is now in some parts of the world just a tree once more.

The Age of Knowledge

I use the term Age of Knowledge in a limited sense. I do not mean the coming century will be ordered around knowledge as the Greeks or ancient Egyptians used the term. For that we must await an Age of Wisdom. But readers of this book stand a reasonable chance of living to see knowledge become the principal commodity embodied in commerce. Both people and nature will benefit from such a turn of events.

Obviously knowledge is a prime ingredient in software and similar electronic sector products. Less understood is its potential application to manufacturing. An Age of Knowledge in manufacturing will dawn with the realization that present ways of making things—requiring large inputs of raw materials, heat, and pressure—are hardly the only means by which to create products. Far from it: Present manufacturing processes are but transitional systems, stopgaps to be used until human understanding can increase to the level of nature.

Nature makes incredibly sophisticated, rugged, complex, and specialized products—living things and their appurtenances—with hardly any energy and no gigantic stamping presses or reaction vats, generating almost no waste that cannot be employed by some other living thing. John Cordingly, a researcher at the University of Wyoming, has pointed out that abalone shells, an extremely durable yet lightweight substance, are formed using mere calcium carbonate (chalk) as their raw material, held by a biological polymer glue into a matrix whose mathematical precision is only now yielding to analysis. Similarly walnut shells, also strong for their weight, contain hardly any material. They are made strong by virtue of sophisticated matrix patterns: the same class of molecular arrangements that convert graphite, a loose material, into diamonds.

That nature can make sophisticated substances using small amounts of materials and energy is a reflection of the vastness of knowledge incarnate in the natural system. Consider a vogue subject of the 1990s: cooking. Cooking is mainly a knowledge pursuit. All cooks work with approximately the same ingredients, the same pans, and the same heat. Yet by knowing exactly how and when to combine materials, different cooks achieve spectacularly different results.

Lacking knowledge of such matters as the mathematics of the matrix in walnut shells, human beings have fashioned materials with brute-force techniques. As women and men realize that nature is a reserve of enormous volumes of knowledge, they will abandon the brute-force approach to manufacturing and make the transition to the natural approach. This idea—called by some researchers "biomimetics" or the mimicking of biology—will increasingly be employed if only because manufacturing with low energy and resource inputs and little waste will be more profitable than the brute-force approach. While some biological processes are too slow for commercial scale, biomimetics need only work in a few areas to depress the trend lines of materials and energy use even farther downward.

The Age of Knowledge in manufacturing will also bring with it a shift away from hard materials toward soft ones. Yoshihito Osada and Simon Ross-Murphy, two accomplished researchers of gel-based materials, point out that "current industrial products are generally made of metal, ceramic or plastic. Biological materials consist mostly of soft gels, sometimes without a rigid frame." Today researchers are seeking to duplicate the behavior of such "intelligent gels" in commercial applications. One possibility is a class of materials that normally is soft but becomes rigid by application of an electrical charge; it might form a useful, low-input new category of construction and manufacturing materials. A similar possibility is "frozen smoke." Some rigid structures found in biological cells appear to contain almost no materials, as if smoke had frozen in place. Researchers are now pursuing the industrial analogue to frozen smoke: gases that could be blown into position then frozen with a shift in their molecular matrix, leaving behind a strong shell that weighs just this side of nothing.

A Clean-Tech Sampler

• The typical toilet today uses five gallons per flush. As of 1994, federal law restricted new toilets to 1.6 gallons per flush. New shower heads and faucets will also be required to employ conservation flow rates. Most states now require that new factories and power plants recycle process water. Taken together, these measures are expected to cause U.S. water use per capita to begin declining by the late 1990s. Energy use for the treatment of wastewater and for water heating will decline proportionately.

• Plastics recycling, considered hopelessly impractical just a decade ago, is beginning to catch on, with plastic the fastest-growing recycling category. Most plastics are now produced with symbols or bar codes that make them easier to sort for recycling. Recycled plastics can be found today in such products as Dunkin Donuts packaging and 3M desk organizers.

• One reason tall old-growth forests are targeted by loggers is that long, thick lumber milled from large trees in a single piece is traditional-ly considered necessary for the rafters and joists of homes. New glues and forming techniques have begun to allow sturdy rafters and joists to be made from pressboard, for which the raw material can be anything from wood chips to the loblolly pines that in humid Georgia grow more than twice as rapidly as trees in the Northwest. Improved pressboard for rafters and joists cuts the requirement for whole-log lumber from 10,000 to 3,000 board-feet for the typical new home.

• As recently as 1992, special battery management programs were being enacted in New Jersey and other states, in order to keep the toxic mercury thought essential to battery manufacturing out of the house-hold waste stream. By 1993 Eveready and Duracell had reduced the mercury in batteries to less than one part per million. Regulatory pres-sure sparked the reform; clean technology leapfrogged the special collec-tion programs and made them unnecessary.

• AT&T has replaced the industrial solvent tricholoethane, used in cleaning silicon chips, with n-butyl butyrate. A swap of one god-awful chemical for another? N-butyl butyrate is a synthetic version of a sub-stance found in cantaloupes. Similarly Arm & Hammer now markets a version of baking soda for industrial degreasing. The solution replaces degreasers based on methylene chloride.

• Methyl chloride was eliminated from consumer products so rapid-ly there wasn't even time to turn it into a scandal. Once common in hair sprays, this compound was discovered in 1988 to deplete stratospheric ozone. By 1993 3M of Minneapolis had invented a substitute. The com-pany and virtually all other manufacturers dropped methyl chloride vol-untarily, even as international negotiators were debating whether the chemical should be banned starting in 2000 or 2005.

• Paint is stripped from aircraft using high-pressure solvents that run off the airport tarmac into sewers. Some airlines and the Canadian military are converting to paint stripping using "ice blast"—ice particles that strip paint via impact energy, with water as the runoff.

• The solvents that evaporate when paints dry contribute to smog; solvent-free paints were long considered a technical impossibility. Now two solvent-free brands are on the market, costing only a bit more than standard paints. The first, from Glidden, bears the amazing name Lifemaster 2000. A bonus: no paint-odor migraines.

• Ozone is a problem in smog, because as a reactive gas it harms lung tissue. But a reactive gas sounds good for cleaning. Ozone com-pounds may eventually replace laundry detergents; tests suggest washers using ozone would need about half as much water and less energy. In water ozone dissolves, meaning no smog emission after the wash. Ozone may also replace the toxic and smog-forming chemical "perc" used by dry cleaners.

• Coming sooner to your clothes: a washing machine that loads from the front rather than the top. Tumble washers consume far less water and electricity than the top-loading models. By the time strict national appliance-efficiency standards become U.S. law in 1999, Maytag, Whirlpool, and other washer manufacturers may sell nothing but tumblers.

• Some water districts are experimenting with ultraviolet radiation to replace chlorine for killing microorganisms in drinking water. Ultraviolet radiation is not radioactive in the manner associated with nuclear products; once it passes through water there is no lasting effect.

• In 1952 a researcher named W. O. Schumann showed that the ground is negatively charged owing to iron in Earth's core, and the atmosphere is positively charged owing to the effect of cosmic rays. Because of this people evolved with an electrical charge difference between the head and feet. Metal structures from modern buildings to cars and aircraft shield out charge differences, eliminating this natural effect. Between the negative ground and positive sky are also five natural frequencies now called Schumann resonances. One of the five, 7.83 cycles per second (7.83 hertz), turns out to be an internal frequency of the human brain. Probably the match stems from the fact that brains evolved in the presence of Schumann resonances. The metal in contemporary buildings blocks natural resonance cycles, while the buildings hum to 60 hertz, the cycle used by U.S. electric current. Some researchers believe these factors account for the headaches, low productivity, and stress reported by workers in modern office buildings.

Of course modern life may alone be sufficient to explain headaches, low productivity, and stress. But there are two implications here for the Age of Knowledge. One is that you really might be better off working in a wood-framed home that does not shield out Schumann resonances or head-to-toe charge differences—or in any small, human-scale wood-framed structure—than in the wide selection of contemporary architectural nightmares. Another implication is that architecture can be amended in ways that allow natural resonances and charge differences to prevail in the interior of buildings. Some of the oppressive feel of modern buildings may thus be found to have a basis in ecological science and be resolved.

• In 1993 Wal-Mart, that institutional monument to packaging flow-through, built a store in Lawrence, Kansas, designed from the bottom up for environmental quality. Recycling bins are positioned so that customers can use them conveniently. Plumbing fixtures have controlled flows. Energy features, designed with the aid of conservation advocate Amory Lovins, cut power use to less than 50 percent that of comparable Wal-Marts. Half of the store is day-lit, saving power and ameliorating that artificial feel. Workers prefer assignments on the day-lit side; customers gravitate there, with sales per square foot higher. *The customers like the environmental features.* When customers like something, it spreads.

• "Antinoise" devices are becoming practical. By generating sound waves identical to the waves of noise but opposite in phase, they cancel out sound as two opposite swells, meeting in the ocean, combine to produce calm water. Soon lawn mowers, leaf blowers, chain saws, and similar earsplitting contraptions may make little sound, allowing society to move back toward the hush that is the natural condition. In principle, antinoise devices may eventually cancel out the sounds of engines and tire friction from cars, buses, and trucks, leading to noiseless highways; create a silent subway car; dampen most of the controlled thunder of the airliner, sparing the ears of those who live near airports and allowing normal conversation within planes.

• Bellcore Laboratories in Red Bank, New Jersey, has shown it is possible in theory to make transistors that effectively contain zero materials, only electron spin states controlled by magnetism. This could lead to computer chips that are extremely small, requiring little in the way of raw materials or energy. In a similar development Texas Instruments had found a theoretical way to make "quantum dots," subatomic particles confined at specific mathematical points. These may prove useful in the manufacture of extremely low-input materials.

• Researchers at the Rensselaer Polytechnic Institute have devised a synthetic ivory that pianists find indistinguishable from elephant ivory. The new substance has the same perplexing quality of simultaneous smoothness and stickiness. Once in general use, this product should reduce population pressure on African elephants.

• Researchers at Penn State University in 1993 converted graphite into a substance that is almost a diamond—employing only the heat of a kitchen oven. This discovery may lead to affordable diamondlike paints for buildings and aircraft, making surfaces extremely hard with little additional use of materials.

• Industrial ceramics continue to improve. Eventually they may replace metals in applications where heat transfer is important, such as in automobile engines. This would result in metals, which are high-input materials, being replaced by low-input clays plus knowledge.

• Various researchers have found that simple dyes and benign compounds such as quinic acid may replace mercury, silver, and benzene as intermediaries in the manufacture of complex chemicals.

• Methanol, a petroleum substitute with low inherent pollution content, may soon be formed cheaply from natural gas by use of a recently discovered catalyst. Huge amounts of natural gas are found in places such as the North Slope of Alaska, too far from users to have value. If such gas can be converted cheaply to methanol for shipment, a long-term low-pollution alternative to petroleum might be realized.

• For decades researchers have first invented new chemicals, then tested the chemicals for dangerous properties. In 1994 the EPA began a program with the American Chemical Society by which researchers hope to learn how to predict, in advance, what new chemical chains will be hazardous, then design safety into compounds from the start. Nicholas Bodor, director of the Center for Drug Design at the University of Florida, is investigating a similar subject. He believes a process called "retrometabolic" engineering will soon enable designers of pharmaceuticals to remove side effects from many drugs by fiddling with chemical chains to attach active features to the parts of molecules that do not cause side effects.

• John Craven, a former submarine designer for the U.S. Navy, has for about a decade been extracting cool deep-ocean water in a pilot plant off Hawaii. In theory any temperature difference, such as between cool deep waters and warm surface waters, can be used to make electricity. Craven not only has begun to make zero-pollution electricity and air-conditioning at his pilot plant but has also found that cool, microbe-free ocean water grows gigantic, unusually delicious fruits and vegetables. There appears to exist more cool, deep ocean water than humanity could exhaust in thousands of years of determined waste. Coastal areas may soon tap this resource for power and low-input agriculture.

You Did *What?*

Many things could go wrong with the clean-tech vision, as many past technological promises have gone unrealized. A century ago H. G. Wells believed that by today human beings would live in a benign technical paradise; and there was that business about how we'd all be flying personal helicopters.

The ecorealist should not think technology offers any sort of salvation for society. Technology has always created as many problems as it has solved; surely it will continue to create many problems in the future.

It's just that the environment is one area where technology has finished a phase of creating problems and now enters a phase of solving them.

Looking at old photographs of today's factories—surrounded by mountains of crushed ores, chemical drums, and powdered coal; pulsing with pressure and heat; toxic wastes being carted out the back in containers emblazoned with Day-Glo death's heads—our near descendents will say "You did *what?*" just as we express shock when confronted with photographs of turn-of-the-century sweatshop production. Our near descendents may think of a factory as a place that makes no noise, causes no emissions, and requires little in the way of raw materials and lots in the way of knowledge. A place that generates products the way nature does: intelligently and sustainably.

Clean tech will not be a settling for less or a manifestation of an age of limits. Rather it will enrich life by offering a form of material prosperity compatible with the long-term requirements of the Earth. Creating a clean-tech world will be exciting: the sort of challenge to which Western researchers and economies have risen before.

A new challenge is needed. For 200 years the central concern of Western economics has been to increase production. The new challenge is to make production benign so that material prosperity can be enjoyed indefinitely. Sophisticated machines don't pollute. Only crude ones do. And the age of the crude machine is nearly over.

CLIMATE I:
GLOBAL COLD

AFTER AN ETERNITY OF COLD, SOME FLIGHT OF MERCY MADE the gods send warmth. Humanity, which lived a frightened childhood in a numb world of perpetual frost, now found the Earth a temperate and welcoming parent. Glaciers receded; what was planted bloomed. The long night of human ignorance and innocence began to end about 14,000 years ago, when arrived the first true global spring in more than 100,000 years.

With the warmth came for good or ill the onset of civilization. The advance of genus *Homo* from querulous shaper of sharp stones to a being capable of systematic building, writing, pondering, and warring was made possible by—or at least was coincident with—a strange interlude in Earth's environment: a warm spell descending into an ecology that has over the past few million years known mainly unstinting cold. Other species prospered as well, with billions more living things able to exist in the warm interlude than had lived in the frozen ages before.

By the decade of the 1980s genus *Homo* had developed an intense paranoia that a warming ecology would be catastrophic. Yet whether a greenhouse effect is coming is speculation; that more ice ages are coming appears a finality. Therefore before contemplating the prospect of a greenhouse age we must consider its antipode, the ice age. There is not the slightest doubt another ice age will have awful consequences, including the loss of far more plant and animal life, and millions more acres of habitat, than could happen under the worst-case projections for all human ecological abuses combined. People worry about the Earth becoming too warm. Nature worries about the Earth becoming too cold. If natural history is any guide, Earth started back downhill toward deep cold nearly 9,000 years ago.

The Slide into Deep Cold

First, a sketch of what researchers think they know about Earth's climate history:

Roughly from its formation around 4.4 billion years ago till about three billion years ago, the surface of the Earth was probably far hotter than today—often hot enough for the oceans to boil. Just why Earth was so hot in its dawn ages is not well understood, because the young sun was "faint," producing perhaps 30 percent less heat than today. Carl Sagan has calculated that if the faint solar energy available in the ancient eons shined on Earth today, even the tropics would freeze.

One line of speculation holds that the ancient Earth was hot because the atmosphere then contained substantial amounts of ammonia, which is no longer found in the air: The ammonia functioned as an ultimate greenhouse gas. A related theory suggests that the Earth's store of carbon dioxide, today mostly held in rocks and the oceans, was once mainly in the air, again creating a super–greenhouse effect. A third idea is that when freshly formed, the Earth was notably radioactive, with heat from radioactive decay compensating for a faint sun. A fourth notion is that so many asteroids and comets struck the Earth in the ancient eons that regular explosions pumped heat into the atmosphere. The least exotic explanation for the heat of the ancient climate is that the early Earth had few clouds. Today cloud cover bounces about a third of the sun's heat back into space. If there were no cloud cover global temperatures would soar.

Around two billion years ago the climate of Earth began to moderate. This was also the time when plants made the first life-driven alteration of the ecology, transforming the atmosphere toward an oxygen base. Probably as the atmosphere oxygenated it became more amenable to water vapor, which forms clouds. Rain became more frequent, aiding the spread of plants. Increased cloud cover bounced away a portion of the increasing heat from the sun, which burned slightly hotter each millennium. Yet the climate moderated at temperatures much higher than today's. From about two billion years in the past till around 40 million years ago, Earth's typical temperature probably ran ten to 22 degrees Fahrenheit higher than current readings.

To put that range into perspective the global temperature increase for the present century—an increase environmental doctrine holds to be a disaster of shattering proportions—is slightly less than one degree Fahrenheit. The "best-guess" estimate of the Intergovernmental Panel on Climate Change, a United Nations affiliate whose greenhouse predictions were used to justify the aura of pessimism that pulsated around the 1992 Earth Summit, is an eventual people-caused temperature rise of 4.5 degrees Fahrenheit. Such an increase surely would be significant but would still leave the Earth starkly cooler than has been its condition for most of the span in which mammals have existed.

A perspective: Did the hot 1980s seem hot to nature? No, the decade was chilly by nature's standards and even somewhat cool by the standards of recent history. The interglacial period prior to ours, called the Eemian, appears to have peaked at global mean temperatures about four degrees Fahrenheit higher than current readings, according to estimates by the Greenland Ice Core Project, a multinational effort to obtain past climate information by drilling into old ice. Our interglacial period, called the Holocene, appears to have reached peak warmth between 9,000 and 6,000 years ago, also with global mean temperatures about four degrees Fahrenheit higher than today. It was around this time that women and men began to think controlled agriculture might be preferable to a hunter-gatherer existence.

Another perspective: Around 1,000 years ago came several centuries during which northern latitudes were perhaps a few degrees warmer than today. During this warm spell the Vikings may have been able to sail to North America because they could stop en route at Greenland to rest and hunt. A thousand years ago Greenland was alive: probably the place Viking records call "Vineland," blooming in the warmer temperatures of the time. All but the most pessimistic forecasts for an artificial greenhouse effect call for no more global heat than was common during the days of Vineland, a period that occurred just a wink of the eye ago to nature.

Back to the past: Through the Jurassic Era, beginning some 195 million years ago, Earth's climate was so warm that coal deposits were being laid down by dying ferns at what is now Mount Weaver near the South Pole. Antarctica was at the time somewhat north of its present position but not far enough north to account for a lush climate. Dinosaurs roamed as close to the poles as the southern tip of Australia, then south (the cold direction in the Southern Hemisphere) of its present location. These creatures may have lived a life without parallel before or since: enormous reptiles and their budding mammalian competitors existing in a place of temperate climes but, because of its near-polar location, months of uninterrupted darkness.

As "recently" as about 100 million years ago, midpoint of the Cretaceous, the Earth was so warm that dinosaurs fed on tropical ferns in Montana. Alligators hunted in what is now the icy Canadian province of Labrador. The great age of reptiles, lasting at least one million times as long as the industrial era of humankind, almost certainly was consistently much hotter than the current climate.

Then somewhere around 40 million years ago the environment slid downhill precipitously toward cold. Let William Ruddiman, a geologist at the University of Virginia and one of the world's leading authorities on past climate, take up the story:

"The world climate that people consider normal is a geologically recent development," Ruddiman says. "Prior to 40 million years ago most of the world was warmer and wetter. Rainfall tended to be evenly distributed throughout the year, and evergreen and deciduous forests covered much of the globe. Grasslands and deserts were rare. Because of the lack of cold, northern spruce forests and tundra regions were small. The sea ice that now covers the Arctic Ocean was either limited or absent. Immense glaciers like the ones that now cover Greenland did not exist." In other words until a point in time relatively near, most of Earth's ecology was what the Eden stories imagine it to have been: a warm, lush forest. Ruddiman: "Somewhere around three million years ago the Earth grew so cool it began to experience periodic ice ages. All recorded history has taken place during a brief, mild interlude in what is essentially a glacial era."

For the past three million years the Earth has been in an ice-age stage about 85 percent of the time and in an "interglacial" stage like the current one only 15 percent of the time. Ice ages have come cyclically and predictably through this period—brief warmth, followed by extended deep freeze. Because the cold phase predominates, many ice masses never finish melting during warm eras: Antarctica, once home to crocodiles, has throughout the existence of genus *Homo* been imprisoned under an ice block most researchers think has not thawed for at least 4.3 million years. Human beings acquired self-awareness, and began to contemplate the ecology, in a small channel broken into an icy sea.

If the observed cycles hold, Earth will descend toward its next deep freeze sometime between 1,000 and 2,000 years from now.[1] Incidence of sunlight falling in summer on the high-latitude glaciers of the Northern Hemisphere, a key natural influence acting in opposition to ice sheets, peaked about 9,000 years ago, when our ancestors were peering at the flood cycles of the Euphrates River basin and wondering if they might be put to some use. Summer sunlight falling in the north has been declining since.

During the last ice cycle glaciers a mile thick extended as far south as Des Moines and Copenhagen. Should that pattern repeat Boston, Cleveland, Chicago, Detroit, Montreal, Oslo, Saint Petersburg, Stockholm, Toronto, and many other current cities will be ground to fine dust. Most northern forests—the largest global ecosystem, much larger than the tropical rainforests—will cease to exist. Hundreds of billions of creatures will die while unknowable numbers of species fall extinct, with extinctions occurring in the oceans as well as on land, since ocean temperatures will fall as currents and salinity patterns change.

Today the world's heads of state ought to worry first about a greenhouse effect, as one is possible within the lifetimes of their children. But nature worries about the reverse. An ecological ice disaster is due on a schedule quite pressing by the way nature measures time.

Cycles within Cycles

That the Earth has undergone recent ages of ice was first suggested in the early 1800s, as students of minerals began to question how it was that smooth, polished boulders were found in the midst of the open fields of Europe, far from the nearest mountain from which they might have rolled. When this question was first asked church authorities responded: Why, the boulders were deposited by Noah's flood. But how could boulders, which sink, move via flood? In 1837 the naturalist Louis Agassiz showed by studying extant glaciers of the Alps and their polishing effect on rocks that the boulders had been rolled by sheets of ice that once covered northern Europe. Once this proposition was accepted, the search was on for the mechanism that causes ice ages. That search continues today.

During the 1940s a Serbian astronomer named Milutin Milankovitch demonstrated that Earth's orbit has three periods of "eccentricity" in the orientation of the planet's axis, polar wobble, and the path Earth transcribes about the sun. These periods of 22,000, 41,000, and 100,000 years, Milankovitch showed, cause cycles in the intensity of sunlight falling during summertime on the northern latitudes. Researchers now call this factor the "solar insolation." Milankovitch was concerned with solar insolation in the north because ice ages are primarily a Northern Hemisphere phenomenon. This is so, first, because most of the world's land mass lies in the north. Second, the subarctic regions of North America and Eurasia physically adjoin those continents, allowing ice sheets to flow south unimpeded. In contrast Antarctica lies far from the southernmost tips of South America and Africa. Ice sheets that begin at the South Pole probably cannot reach adjacent continents.

Milankovitch came to believe that summertime sun in the high northern latitudes is the key to ice ages. A certain amount of solar insolation would be required each summer to melt back ice from the previous winter. When orbital cycles cause that sunlight to decline, the northern glaciers grow from year to year. As this happens they cover additional portions of Earth, converting dark-colored ground and dark forests that normally absorb sunlight into white glaciers that reflect heat back to space. At some point the expanding glaciers become their own "feedback mechanism," reflecting so much heat the climate begins to cool. Now an ice age is in progress, and sheer cold allows the glaciers to extend their range. Later when the orbital cycles revert, increased solar insolation switches the ice age off.

What is now called the Milankovitch cycle theory competed with other ice-age explanations, most prominently a proposal that periodic outbreaks of multiple volcanic eruptions block sunlight for extended periods. The global-volcanism and Milankovitch-cycle theories were in roughly equal competition until the early 1970s. Then a group of researchers led by John Imbrie of Brown University analyzed marine mud cores believed to contain chemical isotope variations related to the temperatures of past air. Imbrie's team found that global temperatures appear to rise and fall along curves divisible by 22,000, 41,000, and 100,000 years. That seemed to lock down Milankovitch cycles as the explanation of ice ages.

But in the 1990s the consensus has unraveled. Calculations now show there simply isn't enough energy difference in solar-insolation fluctuations to deactivate a worldwide freeze. The increased sunlight that falls on the northern glaciers when Milankovitch cycles end works out to only a few watts per square meter, about the heat of a penlight. "The solar radiation changes in Milankovitch cycles are just so tiny they cannot be anything more than one of many factors," says Gifford Miller, a paleoclimatologist at the University of Colorado.

In 1992 a team lead by Isaac Winogard of the U.S. Geological Survey discovered, in a cave called Devil's Hole in Nevada, some calcite materials that may hold more precise clues about past temperatures than the ocean-floor sediments Imbrie's team had used. The Milankovitch theory says that the second most recent ice age ended 128,000 years ago; Imbrie's work supported that timing. The Devil's Hole evidence says that ice age ended 140,000 years ago, a mark on the time line that has no significance to Milankovitch cycles. Separate tests conducted in 1992 at the California Institute of Technology put the end of the previous ice age at 135,000 years ago, also contradicting Milankovitch.

Ice from Fire

Into the uncertainty about the Milankovitch theory have come several new ideas with immediate bearing on humanity's relationship to the environment. The first is the notion developed by Maureen Raymo of the Massachusetts Institute of Technology that the uplift of the Tibetan plateau altered the climate in a way that caused long-term cooling. Tibet began to rise about 40 million years ago. It reached its present altitude about eight million years ago, "shortly" before glacial cycles began. Raymo and other researchers who have studied the Himalayas think, first, that these mountains have caused long-term changes in the Earth's prevailing winds, preventing the jet stream from circulating heat from the equator as evenly as it once did; second, Raymo thinks the new wind pattern causes more rain to fall in the area of the Himalayas, the lee side of which is now a monsoon region. Among other things, Raymo suspects these forces accelerate the natural rate at which carbon dioxide cycles out of the atmosphere. This would weaken the natural greenhouse effect and trigger a gradual Earth cooling.

If Tibet is not the cause of Earth's cooling trend, perhaps volcanos are. David Rea, a paleoceanographer at the University of Michigan, has found in the North Pacific thick ash deposits, apparently from 2.6 million years ago, roughly when cyclical ice ages began. If there have been outbreaks of global volcanism during the past few million years this bodes ill for humankind and the environment both, as it suggests that ecological destruction by widespread volcanic action, which has not occurred during recorded history, might return at any time.

The most surprising recent proposed explanation of ice ages comes from Miller of the University of Colorado and Anne de Vernal of the University of Quebec at Montreal. By studying fossils of microbial life in sea beds, they believe they have found evidence that global temperatures went up as the last ice age began. "In high school they teach you that when the world gets cold an ice age begins," Miller explains. "The geologic record says this is not so. At the beginning of the last ice age things got a little warmer, just as they are doing now." How could warmth cause an ice age? Snow is the raw material of glaciers. But snow rarely falls in very cold climates because the air can hold significant humidity for snow only when warmer than zero Fahrenheit. Today, for example, glaciers cover most of southern Greenland. The ground is bare in north Greenland because it is colder there, making snow uncommon.

Suppose, Miller and de Vernal think, when the climate grows a little warmer more snowflakes descend in the northern latitudes. If at the same time Milankovitch variations reduce the summer sunlight that melts back snow accumulation, glaciers would begin to grow. At some point they might grow large enough to reflect a significant amount of sunlight back into space, setting off the feedback loop that starts a climate crash. "The best way to cause glaciation may be to begin with a cool era, like the one we live in, then warm it up slightly," de Vernal says. The Miller–de Vernal study has an ominous implication: that ice ages do not necessarily require millennia to build but may "strike" over a time span of perhaps only centuries. "We're just beginning to understand that the natural system is capable of changing with extreme rapidity. Very rapid ice age effects are at least possible," Miller says.

Announced in 1991, the Miller–de Vernal finding shook up the ice age business. Old-liners considered the notion that mild warming preceded glaciation to be, as scientists delicately say, "counterintuitive." Some researchers declared there must be a flaw in the study. In July 1993, however, the Greenland Ice Core Project, a multimillion-dollar effort, caused jaws to drop around the academic world when it released data suggesting that during the Eemian, the warm period prior to ours, global temperatures bounced up and down dramatically. "The last interglacial period was characterized by a series of severe cold periods which began extremely rapidly and lasted from decades to centuries," the team's report says. In contrast, "the climate of the past 8,000 years has been strangely stable."

Among other things, the ice data suggested that the rapid Younger Dryas cooling of 11,000 years ago, in which North American temperatures seem to have fallen nine degrees Fahrenheit in just 40 years, was not some weird anomaly but a fairly standard event in recent Earth history. Try to imagine what it must mean to nature if it is fairly common for global temperatures to vacillate nine degrees Fahrenheit in a few decades. This would create regular ecological havoc vastly worse than all human actions so far.

What might have caused the fast-moving natural temperature changes inferred by Miller and de Vernal and the Ice Core Project? Many theories involve ocean currents. "If the Greenland ice core findings are right the mechanism would almost have to be some ocean superconveyor effect we don't know anything about," says Wallace Broecker, a paleoclimatologist at the Lamont Doherty Observatory in New York.

The scientific value of ice-core studies is in dispute, as Broecker's phrasing suggests. There are parallel Greenland ice projects run by European and American consortiums. Initial results from the American bore hole do not support the climate-swing notion. At this writing, scientists were divided on which team's ice reading is true. Additional cores will be drilled in an attempt to resolve the discrepancy.

In the interim the causes of ice ages remain at root a scientific unknown. Researchers cannot yet explain what is by far the most significant environmental force of the "recent" past—deep cold—or why deep cold is temporarily absent today. Broecker puts it this way: "We don't know why the Earth experienced climate swings during the last interglacial, and we don't know why Earth is not causing those swings during the Holocene, our period. Another way of saying that is that we don't know why agricultural cultivation has been feasible during the historical period of humanity."

Don't Touch that Dial

Though it is unlikely an onset of glaciation will be detected during the lifetimes of anyone reading this book, the more that is learned about the rapidity of climate swings the more troubling this prospect sounds. James White, a geochemist at the Institute of Arctic and Alpine Research in Boulder, Colorado, notes that current civilization has been assembled "at perhaps the only time when climate was stable enough to let us develop the agricultural infrastructure required to maintain an advanced society. We don't know why we have been so blessed, but we are beginning to know that the climate is capable of changing dizzyingly fast. If the Earth had an operating manual, the chapter on climate might begin with this warning: Don't touch that dial."

As will be shown in the coming pages, current alarms about global warming appear exaggerated. But even if there exists but a slight chance that artificial greenhouse emissions will engage the geologic gears that summon the next ice age, it is in society's urgent interest to prevent that day.

CLIMATE II:
GLOBAL WARMTH ✍

No more, it seemed, would winter be punctuated by the crunch of snow underfoot. Global temperatures reached record highs. Farmers feared their crops would wilt in the sun. Coastal cities braced for a modern-day deluge with a rising of the sea. The worst seemed confirmed when a renowned climatologist took the podium at the staid Royal Meteorological Society to declare that the greenhouse effect had begun.

Disaster scenario for the twenty-first century? No, historical footnote: This happened 60 years ago. There was a global-warming scare in the 1930s. Then, as now, temperatures rose for several years running. Then, as now, artificial gases, especially carbon dioxide, were assumed the culprit. Spencer Weart, a historian for the American Institute of Physics, says that greenhouse effect rhetoric of the 1930s was "exactly what would be heard again in the 1980s"—of irreversible damage, of humankind overstepping its bounds in horrifying fashion. In 1938 G. C. Callandar, a prominent climatologist, told the Royal Society that because of greenhouse gases the future could only be hotter.

Immediately it got cold. From 1940 through the 1970s global temperatures declined, hitting bottom during the frigid winter of 1977, coldest in a century in North America. Some environmentalists declaimed a new ice age. Congress held hearings into the looming global cool-off.

Immediately it got hot. Through the 1980s one warm year followed another. Some of the same voices that had cried ice age began to proclaim global warming, and this time the idea stuck. By the end of the 1980s polls showed that most Americans believed scientists had stated with certainty that an artificial greenhouse effect was in progress. By 1986 Senator Al Gore would declare "there is no longer any significant disagreement in the science community that the greenhouse effect is real and already occurring." Gore would contend that 98 percent of the science world concurs that a greenhouse emergency has begun.

Yet much as the greenhouse effect exists in the popular imagination, there is no scientific consensus on whether it has manifested in "the laboratory of nature." In February 1992 the Gallup Organization polled members of the American Geophysical Union and American Meteorological Society, the two professional groups for climatologists. Only 17 percent said warming trends so far convinced them an artificial greenhouse effect was in progress. That same year Greenpeace surveyed climate researchers using a poll whose questions were worded such as to elicit alarm. Some 47 percent of respondents said a runaway greenhouse effect is either impossible or highly improbable.

Many proclamations of greenhouse doom, including most spoken at the 1992 Earth Summit in Rio, are buttressed by the report of the Intergovernmental Panel on Climate Change, a committee of prominent scientists formed under the auspices of the United Nations. The IPCC report's executive summary does contain quotable expressions of alarm. But what follows in the four-volume document is hundreds upon hundreds of pages of credentialed skepticism. For instance, from page 254: "It is not possible to attribute all, or even a large part" of twenty-century temperature trends to artificial greenhouse gases.

By several measures an artificial greenhouse effect is the most disturbing ecological prospect of our moment on the Earth. I hope to show that while the prospect is a serious one against which women and men are well advised to take immediate steps, the chances of runaway global warming are extremely small. This makes the greenhouse effect a perfect issue for ecorealists: one where reasoned discourse leads to the conclusion that reforms are justified but also that end-of-the-world rhetoric may be dispensed with.

First let's run through a few points of interest about greenhouse science and politics:

• Eight of the last 14 years have been warm. "The year 1990 was, of course, just the latest 'warmest year on record,'" wrote Vice President Gore in *Earth in the Balance*. Warm compared to what? "The record" goes back only to the 1880s, when systematic preservation of weather data began. It turns out that the late 1800s was a cold period. Earth could experience "record" warmth relative to the 1880s and remain cool compared to the bulk of its past.

As the previous chapter detailed, it appears the Earth has spent hundreds of millions of years in conditions environmentalists would call a global-warming disaster, with typical temperatures higher than today's by ten to 22 degrees Fahrenheit. A temperature rise in this range would surely render the Earth inhospitable to genus *Homo* and thousands of other present species; but not even worst-case projections anticipate warming of such magnitude. The Intergovernmental Panel on Climate Change says its "best guess" is that a doubling of the atmospheric level of carbon dioxide, likely to take about a century at present rates, would increase global temperatures 4.5 degrees Fahrenheit. Should it occur, this increase would surely disrupt climate patterns but still leave the land environment notably cooler than through most of the planet's history.

• Starting about five centuries ago, Northern Hemisphere temperatures declined in an event researchers call the Little Ice Age. From about 1500 to the late 1700s winters were harsh and harvests uncertain. Paintings from the period show skaters on the canals of Holland, a rare joy for skaters alive today. Starting around 1850 global temperatures began to recover, seeming to seek the level that prevailed before the Little Ice Age. Thus when dawned this century of industrial sprawl, the climate was already warming on its own. Robert Balling, a climatologist at Arizona State University, has supposed that most of the mild warming observed in the twentieth century may be the tail end of natural recovery from the Little Ice Age.

• Many studies of temperature trends, including those by the Goddard Institute of Space Studies in New York, an important center of greenhouse true believers, show that global temperatures have increased by about one degree Fahrenheit through the past century. The same studies show that most of that one-degree increase came *before* 1940— before artificial greenhouse gas emissions were substantial.

• Artificial greenhouse gases did not become significant until the postwar industrial boom of the late 1940s. According to greenhouse theory, sharp heat increases should have followed. Instead the warming rate slowed down. According to Patrick Michaels, a climatologist at the University of Virginia, "Every annual high since 1950 falls below the trend of natural increase established during the 1880 to 1950 period, when industrial carbon emissions were not significant."

• The studies that find a global warming trend during the 1980s rely on surface-temperature readings taken near cities. Researchers know that the urban "heat-island effect" distorts such readings, and they adjust data to compensate. The degree of adjustment required is controversial, however. The Goddard Institute, whose greenhouse studies are downbeat, subtracts about 0.1 degree Fahrenheit. Other researchers maintain that about 0.3 degrees must be subtracted to remove the heat-island effect. If the Goddard Institute adjusted by 0.3 degrees, this would cancel out the entire claimed global temperature increase of the 1980s.

• Studies of the total heat in atmospheric air volumes conflict with studies confined to ground temperatures. National Aeronautics and Space Administration data from atmospheric satellites show a small global temperature decline during the past decade. John Christy, a University of Alabama at Huntsville scientist who heads the NASA air temperature study, says, "We don't see any global warming in our data, and our satellites monitor the entire world, not just urban areas like the ground-temperature studies."

• Readings from another major source of global temperature information, the oceans, do not resolve the dispute. Studies of global ocean surface temperatures performed by the Meteorological Office of the United Kingdom found a slight warming during the 1980s. Studies of sea-surface temperatures performed by the National Oceanic and Atmospheric Administration in the U.S. found a slight cooling during the 1980s. No ocean temperature data is considered conclusive.

• Trees grow more in warm years than cool. Among the most long-lived trees is the *Fitzroya cupressoides* or alerce of southern Chile; some are 3,620 years old. Antonio Lara of the University of Arizona and Ricardo Villalba of the University of Colorado have studied the rings of old alerce trees. Lara and Villalba found evidence of prolonged cold from 1490 to about 1700, roughly corresponding with the Little Ice Age in Europe. But in the tree rings they detected "no evidence of a warming trend during the last decades of this century that could be attributed to anthropogenic causes."[1]

• In the United States, six of the ten years of the 1980s were indisputably warm in urban areas. This was taken in many quarters as proof that an inexorable global warming had begun. Then the trend dissipated, with 1991 and 1992 being slightly cool for American cities. Greenhouse true believers attributed this decline to the 1991 eruption of Mount Pinatubo, which ejected large amounts of sun-filtering aerosols into the stratosphere. Tests showed that by late 1992 most Pinatubo effects had washed out of the air, suggesting that if an emergency global warming were in progress it ought to resume in 1993. But global temperatures recorded by NASA satellites for 1993 remained slightly below the 1980s average.

• A net world increase of about one-third of one degree Fahrenheit is what made the 1980s the hottest decade "on record." Richard Lindzen, a meteorologist at the Massachusetts Institute of Technology, computes one-third of one degree as the standard deviation, or natural variability, of the weather. In other words the warm 1980s might be an omen. Or mean nothing whatsoever.

Grownups with Models

Global warming has already struck hundreds of times in the foothills of the Rocky Mountains, at the National Center for Atmospheric Research (NCAR) in Boulder, Colorado. The center operates one of the world's leading "general circulation models" (GCMs), computers that simulate the effects of human trespass on the atmosphere. When scientists run the Boulder GCM, usually they get bad news. Simulations predict that doubling of the atmospheric content of carbon dioxide—a strong possibility for the next century, given the rate at which humankind is burning fossil fuels and forests—will warm the Earth by between three and nine degrees Fahrenheit. The low end of this range could be an annoyance. The upper end represents the same net temperature difference between today and the end of the Pleistocene ice age.

Temperature increases of up to nine degrees Fahrenheit from doubled carbon dioxide are almost exactly what was predicted in 1896 by Svante Arrhenius, the Swedish chemist who first postulated that fossil fuel combustion would engender an artificial greenhouse effect. Arrhenius did his calculations with a slide rule. Since serious work with GCMs began in the late 1970s, supercomputers have been coming to approximately the same conclusion.

Many scientists who work with GCMs are greenhouse true believers. Today the climate modelers John Firor of NCAR, James Hansen of the Goddard Institute, and Stephen Schneider of Stanford University are the most influential greenhouse-emergency advocates on the Washington policy circuit. In turn, the studies of Intergovernmental Panel on Climate Change rely principally on computer models. When news reports say there is a scientific consensus that the Earth will warm, what they mean is that computer models concur in predicting a warming. There are half a dozen major GCM projects in the United States and Europe and none forecasts anything other than warmer years to come.

This is quite different, however, from saying that experts believe global warming will happen. In 1988, Hansen told a congressional committee he was "99 percent certain" that summer's heat wave stemmed in some manner from greenhouse emissions. The technical journal *Science* promptly ran an article titled "It's Hansen against the World," reporting that numerous other prominent climatologists felt Hansen should not state as fact something the science mainstream considers unproven. Hansen's "99 percent certain" statement was prominently reported as confirmation of a greenhouse disaster in progress. The science world's reaction drew less attention.

Nor was much attention drawn by this fact: Though it surely was hot in North American in summer 1988, at the same time central Asia experienced a cold wave. The cold Asian area was roughly equivalent in size to the warm North American region. It turns out to be common that cold spells in one part of the world are offset by warm spells elsewhere. But in 1988 environmentalists and news organizations engaged in selective doomsaying, rolling the drums for disquieting numbers about the part of the world that was warm while deleting any reference to reassuring numbers about the part of the world that was cool.

Climate versus Weather

The most basic distinction in global warming research is between weather and climate. Weather is what happens over weeks; climate is what happens over centuries. It is a fallacy to assert, as some greenhouse zealots do, that the rising temperatures of the 1980s prove the Earth is warming. It would be equally fallacious to argue that the cool summers of the early 1990s show that a greenhouse effect is not due. Neither trend proves either case, both being too brief to bear statistical significance. The day after Christmas 1993 the coldest-ever football games were played in stadiums in Buffalo and Green Bay, two places accustomed to low digits; on the same day Juneau, Alaska, had shirtsleeve weather. Together such facts reveal nothing other than that weather is changeable, known to Benjamin Franklin. Most weather variations are essentially meaningless oscillations with no bearing on longer-term climate trends.

Current weather computers can forecast highs and lows about three days in advance and developments such as storm fronts out to about five days. When weather computers attempt to forecast more than ten days in advance, their output devolves to darts on a board. The atmosphere of an entire planet contains so many variables acting in such dimly understood ways that no computer can take everything into account, especially given that variables may interact in ways that defy prediction. In *Chaos: The Making of a New Science,* James Gleick detailed the "chaotic" or nonpredictable interactions in the atmosphere now believed by some researchers to render long-range weather forecasting essentially impossible, even positing a hypothetical computer with unlimited processing power and information.

How then can computers be trusted to say what the temperature will be decades from now? In most computer projections, emergency greenhouse increases do not begin for 30 to 50 years. The GCM at Hansen's Goddard Institute does not project an emergency increase until the late twenty-first century, nearly a century away. This is heady stuff considering that the weather-forecasting computers cannot project trends for more than a week.

In recent years the belief among greenhouse thinkers that the future may be viewed based on computer projections has gotten out of hand. For instance in 1992 in the footnoted letters column of *Science,* Stephen Schneider, Michael Oppenheimer of the Environmental Defense Fund, William Nordhaus of Yale University, and other prominent players in the greenhouse controversy debated in somber tones a computer projection Nordhaus made regarding economic impacts of global warming. About what did the letter writers syllogize? Whether Nordhaus could assume that cumulative U.S. GNP growth will be 450 percent or 470 percent *by the year 2105.* It turned out this choice determined whether Yale's computer predicted a gloomy or rosy result. These are the sorts of environmental data points, earnestly debated today by intelligent and conscientious souls, that are 100 percent guaranteed to be wrong.

The limited track record of weather forecasting does not disqualify computer models from assessing the long-term climate. In statistics it is often impossible to say exactly what a number will be, while possible to deduce general trends. For instance analysis of the 1993 football season would allow computers to predict that if the best team, the Dallas Cowboys, played the worst team, the Cincinnati Bengals, a dozen times, the Cowboys would emerge from that experience with the better record. But it would be a complete waste of everyone's time for the computer to attempt to predict the exact final score of any one of the games. In greenhouse studies the same obtains. Projections of a global warming trend might well turn out correct, even though the fanciest greenhouse computers would be at a loss to forecast the temperature in Houston or Florence next week.

The challenge faced by greenhouse GCMs is much greater than would be faced by a sports computer, however. Statistics from sports are hard numbers; climate statistics involve guesstimates. Because the data fed to climate models contain approximations, GCMs are vulnerable to the "garbage in, garbage out" problem—punching fuzzy numbers into a computer, running them through precise mathematical formulas, then treating the results as if they were precise. The farther out into the next century that computers churn imprecise numbers, the more magnified distortions grow. "It is a failure of logic to believe that a GCM, loaded with approximated data and using assumptions about nature that may be wrong, can produce a statistically significant forecast for another century," Lindzen, of the Massachusetts Institute of Technology, says.

Next, because the biosphere is vast, even advanced computers deal with it only in approximations. When the climate model at NCAR prints out an image of the globe, Japan and the United Kingdom are absent. These nations are too small to fit under the model's "resolution limit."

Michael Schlesinger, a climate modeler at the University of Illinois, notes that most GCMs subdivide Earth's surface into blocks about 300 miles in the horizontal. Schlesinger says, "A computer model with three-hundred-mile data grid boxes has only one point for Oregon. But within Oregon there is a coastal ancient forest, followed by mountains, followed by a high-altitude valley, followed by a desert. Today's climate computers don't know that; they see Oregon as a dot in a grid box. They produce for Oregon an averaged result that may bear no relationship to actual conditions anywhere in the state." Schlesinger thinks that improving the size of greenhouse computer blocks to 30 miles—enough to show the existence of the Finger Lakes, Wales, and similar topography—would make projections more reliable. But even with the fastest current computers, 30-mile data boxes would increase computation times of greenhouse models around a thousandfold. Today the best GCMs require two weeks of round-the-clock computing to complete a projection. If block resolution were improved to 30 miles they would require three decades.

As more powerful computers are developed, greenhouse models will become able to accept more refined data. For now their projections form a tenuous basis on which to analyze a greenhouse effect that so far is at worst only slightly larger than the margin of error embedded in the numbers. Even Schneider of Stanford, a prominent greenhouse believer, acknowledges, "It's possible that everything in the last 30 years of temperature records is no more than noise." *Noise* is statistician's slang for little numerical fluctuations that don't add up to a hill of beans.

All of which leads to a substantial objection to the use of GCMs in greenhouse policy: When global climate models run from the past forward, they fail to predict the present. Researchers who have set GCMs to conditions of the nineteenth century find the models conclude that global temperatures should have risen about five degrees Fahrenheit by now. But the actual increase that has occurred is at most one degree.

This leads to an obvious speculation that greenhouse forecasting techniques are simply biased toward warmth.

Hansen says that the GCM used at the Goddard Institute has been sufficiently tuned that, run in "reverse," it now predicts only twice as much warming as has actually been observed, rather than five times as much as it once did. This is a significant step toward a model that can be trusted. Hansen says further that when he sets the Goddard GCM to the conditions of 1958, the year in which recordkeeping of atmospheric carbon levels became sophisticated, the computer predicts a present only slightly warmer than it should. "So perhaps the models are too sensitive to warming, but each time we tune them they become more accurate," Hansen says.

Paleoclimatologists often snicker at GCMs because greenhouse computers are stumped by ice ages. When Pleistocene conditions are plugged into climate models, no ice sheets appear. The precise causes of ice ages are unknown and therefore hard to simulate. But the lack of glaciers in ice-age simulations leads some researchers to believe that climate models contain fatal biases in the direction of warmth. In 1993 Schlesinger of the University of Illinois announced the first greenhouse model able to "grow" glaciers. When Pleistocene conditions are plugged into his computer simulation the world cools, just as happened in the laboratory of nature. And when conditions of the present are plugged into Schlesinger's GCM the world warms, but more slowly and to a lower peak than predicted by the Goddard and NCAR models that have received the most attention in Congress and in the media.

Perhaps then it is no coincidence that Schlesinger is a greenhouse-effect moderate, having produced in conjunction with the Rand Corporation studies that suggest the prospect of artificial warming is real but that claims of an emergency are not. In 1990, after the University of Illinois completed a study saying gradual fossil-fuel use reductions over the next several decades would be sufficient to avert an artificial greenhouse effect, then-senator Al Gore called Schlesinger "irresponsible." By this standard Gore himself has since become irresponsible, as he now sits in a White House that advocates gradual fossil fuel reductions carried out over the next several decades.

Declining Highs

Because climate is complex, it is unavoidable that the work of computer modelers contains assumptions that will eventually be shown in error.

For example in 1989 the greenhouse GCM of the British Meteorological Office was predicting that doubled carbon dioxide levels would cause global temperatures to increase by ten degrees Fahrenheit. Then British researchers realized their model assumed all water vapor in the atmosphere occurs as a liquid. It does not; some forms ice crystals having different heat-trapping properties. When the British computer was adjusted to reflect this distinction its predicted worst-case warming declined to about 3.5 degrees Fahrenheit. Similarly a GCM operated by the Max Planck Institute in Germany predicted during the 1980s that doubled CO_2 would raise global temperatures about eight degrees Fahrenheit. But then researchers at the Planck Institute began to incorporate the moderating effects of oceans into their model. The German worst-case estimate declined to about four degrees Fahrenheit.

As climate-simulating computers become more sophisticated, most worst-case predictions become less worrisome. In 1979, the National Academy of Sciences convened a panel of climate modelers who projected an up to nine-degree Fahrenheit warming from doubled CO_2. For years this was the favored doomsday number of greenhouse believers. When in the late 1980s preliminary studies by the Intergovernmental Panel on Climate Change endorsed the nine-degree number, the IPCC's became the doomsday prediction of choice. After the 1992 Rio conference broke up, the IPCC amended to its "best guess" two to 4.5 degrees Fahrenheit from doubled carbon dioxide—a range that could hold nasty surprises for the ecology but is nothing like the emergency numbers that dominated Rio rhetoric. The IPCC's lowered forecast stems from the increased sophistication of models such as those of the British Meteorological Office and Planck Institute. Since 1990 the National Academy of Sciences has backed away from the high end of its 1979 forecast, though the number is still cited by doomsayers as an "official" prediction. In 1992 Martin Hoffert of New York University and Curt Covey of the Lawrence Livermore Laboratory attempted to test global-warming projections by comparing GCM forecasts against past climates both warmer and colder than the present, then averaging the results. Using this technique they predicted that doubled carbon dioxide would increase world temperatures about four degrees Fahrenheit. This falls in line with the trend toward lower greenhouse-effect estimates—a trend that has received little media attention and caused no political stir, being nonalarming.

In early 1993 Hansen revised downward the forecast of the Goddard Institute GCM, which is the most influential computer in greenhouse politics, given that the Goddard Institute is an affiliate of the U.S. government. Through the 1988 to 1992 Earth Summit period in which greenhouse alarmism was building, the Goddard computer predicted that global temperatures would rise five degrees by the year 2030. Today Goddard's computer predicts such an increase will not be realized until the late twenty-first century: cause for concern but not cause for doomsday theatrics.

Greenhouse projections are being revised downward partly on the basis of evolving knowledge about the climate. For instance as recently as 1990 CFCs, the chemicals that deplete the ozone layer, were considered a potent global-warming agent. CFCs were estimated to generate perhaps a fifth of the artificial greenhouse effect; some researchers had supposed CFCs might someday be injected into the atmosphere of Mars, to warm that planet to habitability. Then in 1991 it was found that CFCs appear to have different greenhouse functions depending on altitude. At some altitudes they trap heat; at others they reflect sunlight back into space. Taken together the effects form a sort of zany equilibrium: CFCs may be bad for the ozone layer but now appear neutral to climate.[2]

This discovery alone knocked one or two degrees out of greenhouse doomsday predictions. It also complicated political planning for the Rio summit. Environmentalists were pressing for the summit's main goal to be a declaration that Western nations would by the year 2000 restrict greenhouse emissions to the level of the year 1990. Michael Deland, George Bush's director of the Council on Environmental Quality, announced in 1990 that the U.S. would honor the goal, known by the ponderous bureaucratic appellation "1990 stabilization." Western nations initially thought stabilization would be a snap because they had already agreed to abolish CFCs, assumed to be potent greenhouse gases. Then it was shown CFCs might have no net warming effect. "The CFC discovery really threw us for a loop," Deland says. It can be argued that this esoteric academic finding helped undo the Bush presidency, since Bush was blitzkrieged with bad press when he reversed himself and decided not to endorse the stabilization goal. Bush's poll numbers began to decline in May 1992, just when he was being ridiculed for failing to embrace the global-warming treaty.

"Masked" Warming

Through the 1980s many researchers assumed that sulfur dioxide, the chief cause of acid rain, was a minor greenhouse gas. But in the late 1980s Thomas Wigley of the University of East Anglia in the United Kingdom and Robert Charlson of the University of Washington proved that sulfur pollutants instead have a cooling effect. Wigley and Charlson showed that as sulfur drifts upward it forms aerosol particles that increase Earth's "albedo," the percentage of sunlight the atmosphere reflects back into space. Under some circumstances sulfur also forms cloud-condensation nuclei, the droplets around which clouds establish. Most clouds have a net cooling effect, reflecting sunlight to space. That sulfur dioxides may help cool the Earth is not a reason to like acid rain. Balancing one pollutant against another is no solution, not least because acid rain emissions are coming under control.

Today Charlson estimates that sulfur pollutants roughly cancel out the greenhouse gases put into the air so far by human action. This is the "masked greenhouse" theory—holding that an artificial global warming actually is taking place but is masked by a simultaneous artificial cooling. Charlson says, "The greenhouse gases will win" because society's output of carbon is increasing while its output of sulfur declines. Wigley and Sarah Raper of the University of East Anglia project that without sulfur cooling and lesser masking effects caused by smog, Earth's temperature would have increased several degrees Fahrenheit over the past century.

Other researchers are less convinced. There exists "a great range of uncertainty" in estimates of the cooling effects of pollution, Thomas Karl, an atmospheric scientist with the National Climatic Data Center in Asheville, North Carolina, has written. Sulfur dioxide washes out of the atmosphere rapidly, usually with the first good rain. So if sulfur aerosols have been masking the greenhouse effect, global temperatures should have taken off in a spectacular way when sulfur pollution began its sharp deline in the 1970s. This did not occur.

Karl also points out that throughout this century there has been little sulfur pollution in the Southern Hemisphere, where industrial activity is much lower than in the North. Greenhouse gases are a global issue because they remain in the atmosphere for years, distributed around the world. Acid rain, on the other hand, is a local issue because sulfur washes out of the air before it can be blown to another hemisphere. Karl reasons that sulfur pollution might mask a greenhouse warming in the Northern Hemisphere, where there are lots of coal-fired power plants; but since the atmosphere of the Southern Hemisphere has greenhouse gases but little sulfur, masking would be absent there. Thus Southern Hemisphere temperatures should be rising relative to the North. Records do not show this. In this century "the difference between temperatures in the hemispheres seems to shift at random," Karl has written, displaying no relationship to trends in sulfur aerosols.

Solar Variations

Till recently astronomers thought the primary energy output of the sun, driving force of climate and benefactor of all Earth life, varies only over millions of years. Reflecting this belief, researchers referred to the sun's production as "the solar constant." The notion of a solar constant was grounded more in psychological assumptions about the permanence of the heavens than in observational data, however. Through the last two decades satellites have begun to compile empirical data about solar output: Indications are that Earth's star is not entirely constant. Since the late 1970s the sun's production has varied about 0.1 percent annually, says Judith Lean, an astronomer at the Naval Research Laboratory. One-tenth of a percent may not sound like much, but it represents roughly the same range of annual climate energy variations assumed by most greenhouse models.

Attempting to cross-check findings of moderate variability in Sol, Earth's sun, in the 1980s astronomers turned their instruments on other nearby stars about the same size, color, and age. Findings from this research so far are equivocal. Some astronomers think that nearby sunlike stars exhibit no more than the 0.1 percent annual variation noted by Lean. But Richard Radick, an astronomer at the Phillips Laboratory, who has been observing 33 sunlike stars for a decade, thinks they exhibit short-term luminosity variations up to 0.3 percent annually. This would be sufficient to overturn many assumptions of greenhouse GCMs, which treat incoming energy levels from Sol as invariant.

In the late 1980s two credentialed scientists, Robert Jastrow of Dartmouth College and William Nierenberg, president emeritus of the Scripps Institution of Oceanography, began to argue that the newly discovered solar variations explain temperature trends. Temperatures have been up a little because the sun throttled up a little, they suggested; temperatures will fall a little when the sun throttles down. This idea, dubbed the "solar fix," had considerable influence on the Bush White House. Doomsayers were beside themselves about the solar fix, as it would void most human culpability. Yet even Hansen of the Goddard Institute assumes solar fluctuations must have something to do with climate trends. "I wouldn't be surprised if solar variability turns out to have been involved in the global cooling that occurred from 1940 to 1960," he says.

As the solar fix grew popular with former White House chief of staff John Sununu and other conservatives, researchers led by Hansen demonstrated that a variation higher than obversed in any sunlike star would be necessary to counter the worst-case temperature increases some greenhouse models predict. Besides, solar variability can cut two ways. Advocates of the solar fix assumed temperatures would decline when the sun's output eased off. What if instead solar luminosity ramps up? That little complication threw solar variability out of fashion as a greenhouse cure. By 1991 it seemed a dead argument.

Then in 1992, Eigil Friis-Christensen and Knud Lassen of the Danish Meteorological Institute published some graphs of sunspot measurements that, overlaid with twentieth-century temperature trends, blend with amazing precision. Researchers were stunned. The graphs seemed to say that global climate trends could be explained by trends in sunspots.

Scientists were instantly suspicious of the study. One of the first assignments handed to young graduate students in statistics is to find an overlay between sunspots and some entirely Earthbound phenomenon. Any enterprising student of statistics can seem to discover relationships between sunspots and batting averages, hemlines, the stock market, you name it. This initiation rite is supposed to make students of statistics aware that it is common for chains of numbers to overlap more closely than chance would appear to allow. Thus for working scientists to exclaim, as the Danish researchers did, "Eureka! The explanation is sunspots!" struck some scientists as if an apparently serious person had exclaimed that power blackouts are caused by UFOs. Still the Danish finding was sufficiently striking to put solar variability back into play as a possible greenhouse influence. Since 1992 Sallie Baliunas, an astrophysicist at the Harvard-Smithsonian Center for Astrophysics, has compiled extensive evidence suggesting a closer link between solar activity and observed temperature trends than between those trends and greenhouse gas emissions. Baliunas told a congressional committee in 1994, "If not caused by the buildup of greenhouse gases, then what changes the Earth's climate? There is evidence the sun does."

The Wild Card

Another important climate unknown is the role of oceans. Karl, of the NCDD, calls oceans "the wild card" of greenhouse theory. As known to followers of the ever-popular El Nino, stuff of local weather forecasting legend, ocean currents pump warmth from one region to another. The main pump takes warm water from the equator toward the poles; without that system moderation the global climate might fail. A second system carries warm, oxygen-rich surface waters down into the depths, bringing back cool, nutrient-rich waters upon which sea life depends.

Oceanographers have long assumed sea currents to be stable, but they now find this is not necessarily so. For example James Kennett, a researcher at the University of California at Santa Barbara, has found evidence that 57 million years ago the main north-south conveyor belt shut down for unknown reasons, stopping the flow (or "fall," as oceanographers say) of polar waters toward the tropics. Patterns of ocean nutrients and saltiness changed; perhaps 50 percent of sea microbe species fell extinct. This happened, Kennett thinks, during a phase when the world was warming.

Early greenhouse models paid no attention to currents on the presumption they were invariant, like the solar constant. Such models effectively assumed away the vastness of the oceans—though the oceans are the largest "object" on Earth, an object that by virtue of the greater mass of water than air has more thermal storage capacity in its uppermost ten feet of depth than is found in the entire atmosphere. When research of the late 1980s began to show sea currents capable of rapid alterations, assumptions changed. Newer simulations that take oceans into account, called "coupled ocean-climate models," produce less ominous predictions. For instance when the NCAR computer model in Colorado was "coupled" to an ocean model, its predicted global warming from one type of carbon doubling declined from seven degrees Fahrenheit to three degrees.

Because they are massive compared to the air, oceans may lag behind atmospheric temperature trends, moderating the early portion of climate swings. When it was cold from the 1940s to the 1970s the oceans probably were still relatively warm from the 1930s, and moderated the cold. When it was warm during the 1980s the oceans probably were still relatively cool from the 1970s, and moderated the heat. An obvious concern presents itself: Are the seas accruing a "heat debt" to be paid in the next century when their relative coolness is exhausted and the oceans stop moderating global temperatures? The Intergovernmental Panel on Climate Change has phrased this concern with these detached words: "Realized global temperatures at any given time are between 60 and 80 percent of the committed temperature rise."

Today's greenhouse computers also do not acknowledge the effects of the living world on climate trends. Ocean plankton, which exist by the trillions, gobble carbon dioxide as part of their life cycles, and probably prosper in warmer climates, providing some natural greenhouse counterbalance. Trees "sequester" carbon in their cellulose, and grow faster in warm years. Such biological impacts are absent from greenhouse GCMs. Current greenhouse models take into account only one biological effect—the negative human action of generating carbon dioxide through combustion.

In this respect the models are severely unrealistic, regarding the Earth as if it were a flattened, inanimate billiard ball whose sole surface activity is greenhouse gases rising from industrial facilities, when in fact the Earth is an irregular mainly water-covered object that teems with life-forms both adding and subtracting gases from the air. The Meteorological Office in the U.K., the Planck Institute in Germany, NCAR, and the Laboratory for Modeling of Climate in Paris are now at work on computer models that "couple" the atmosphere to the vegetation of the land and the plankton of the sea.

Sea Levels

Greenhouse theory posits that a dire effect of a warmer world would be elevated sea levels, as melting glaciers return their water to the oceans. Coastal cities might be inundated, while some Pacific islands would disappear from navigation charts. One of the breakthrough moments in greenhouse doomsaying came in 1980 when Stephen Schneider, then of NCAR, produced with a colleague some computer graphics depicting the Washington Monument partially submerged by rising seas. This converted greenhouse claims from an abstract scientific dispute to pictures communicating a panic message that would resonate regardless of the couch-words attached to the graphic. The flooded monument graphic endures as a favorite of greenhouse alarm documentaries.

Scientific support for the notion of a drastic rise in sea level has waned rapidly, however. A decade ago, sea-level increases of ten feet were commonly projected for the twenty-first century. Now the worst-case estimates are two to seven feet. The IPCC report, in one of its thick-type technical sections, gives an ocean-rise "best guess" of just 29 centimeters through the end of the next century, or about 11 inches. The highest observed actual sea-level rise in this century is a mere one inch.

Why isn't the sea rising if temperatures are rising? Because many glaciers are growing, not melting. Some of the world's glaciers are retreating, visibly smaller each year. But many retreating ice sheets are in mountains of the tropics or are relatively small European glaciers. These ice sheets may have been melting for centuries, since the end of the Little Ice Age.

The situation appears different for many large northern glaciers, the ones that matter. One of the largest studied northern glaciers is the Bering Glacier, a vast ice sheet that extends through central Alaska. During the late 1980s the Bering Glacier was retreating several yards annually; environmentalists cited this proof of an encroaching greenhouse doom. Congressional hearings were held, surely the first time the margins of a glacier have been the subject of formal Capitol Hill debate. In 1993 the Bering Glacier reversed course. By December 1993 it was advancing up to 300 feet per day, growth so rapid scientists called the movement a "surge." Faced with word of the misbehaving Bering Glacier, environmentalists began to say that yearly vacillations in glacial growth or retreat are too minor to reveal much about long-term climate trends. This is probably true, but it is much different from what environmentalists claimed just a few years before.

Though the science of longer-term glacial behavior is uncertain, there are indications trends point away from the conspicuous melting asserted by greenhouse theory. A NASA researcher named Jay Zwally surprised the climate business in 1990 by showing with satellite images that the central glaciers of Greenland expanded during the very 1980s years when North American temperatures were high. How could glaciers be growing if temperatures were up? For the reasons stated in chapter 16: that mild warmth might cause snow in places otherwise too cold for precipitation.

It's haunting to think that Greenland, a bleak and unforgiving island, is today the focus of passionate scientific debate. But Greenland is believed to have been ground zero of the last ice age; to greenhouse theory, Greenland may be the most important place on Earth. Since Zwally's surprise finding, researchers have begun to study in earnest the counterintuitive idea that mild warming increases glacial size. One of the first things they found was that Zwally made a mathematical error; his original paper has been replaced by a new study offering less spectacular claims. Yet other researchers have come to conclusions along the same lines. In 1992 David Jacobs of the American Museum of Natural History and Dork Sahagian of Ohio State University showed that past warm epochs on Earth might have known noticeably *lower* sea levels, as increased humidity in the air caused more rainfall over land, shifting significant amounts of water to glaciers, lakes, and underground aquifers. Jacobs and Sahagian have found a gigantic dry basin in China, called the Tarim, that in past ages of greater rainfall may have held water equivalent to 3.5 feet of world sea level.

Recent studies are also tending to hold that the largest mass of ice on Earth, the Antarctic ice cap, is not melting and has not melted in a long time. Often alarmists include a collapse of the eastern Antarctic ice shelf on the inventory of doomsday events due shortly in a greenhouse world. If the eastern Antarctic ice shelf thawed enough to fall into the ocean, sea levels might rise as much as 25 feet. The notion of an impending ice-shelf collapse is not, however, supported by science. George Denton of the University of Maine, a leading ice researcher, thinks that the eastern Antarctic shelf has little susceptibility to temperature swings lasting less than thousands of years. David Marchant, also at the University of Maine, believes the Antarctic ice shelf has been stable for the last 4.3 million years, though mean air temperatures at the South Pole have been at least five degrees Fahrenheit higher during that period. "One implication," Marchant has written, "is that the collapse of the east Antarctic ice sheet due to greenhouse warming is unlikely, even if global temperatures rise."

For his part Stephen Schneider thinks there is a straightforward explanation for the expanding glaciers some researchers think they see in Greenland—that it's simply gotten colder in Greenland lately. Indeed, some records suggest that it has.

It's getting colder in Greenland? Isn't the Earth supposed to be warming?

Hot Nights

Temperature shifts are not uniform. There's nothing strange, except to our sensibilities, about a mild winter in Minneapolis while a blizzard shuts down Jerusalem, two conditions that conjoined in 1992. But this would seem a strike against greenhouse theory, which holds that artificial warming should center in the high and low latitudes, as equatorial regions seem historically insulated against climate swings. Greenland, a high-latitude northern location, is not warming notably; neither is the north generally. Any warming that may be in progress appears roughly uniform globally.

For reasons like this, just where and when global warmth manifests itself has become a pivotal issue of greenhouse analysis. Karl, of the National Climatic Data Center, has demonstrated that U.S. midsummer and daytime highs have changed little during the postwar period. Public perceptions aside, summers of the 1980s were not unprecedented scorchers. P. D. Jones, a prominent British climatologist, reinforced this conclusion in 1993 when in the technical journal *Holocene* he wrote, "Summers are no warmer now than they were in the 1860s and 1870s." But, Karl finds, 1980s winters were indeed mild, and nighttime lows were less low. Greenhouse alarmists say artificial warming will peak on summer afternoons: the worst time, as summer daytime highs kill crops and push up energy demand. Karl's work suggests that any warming in progress is instead arriving in winter and in the dark.

When Karl's studies were first published, some global-warming proponents thought their theory had taken a killer hit. But thought through, Karl's work may lend greenhouse theory new impetus. The pollutants and carbon human activity puts into the atmosphere must be doing *something*. Perhaps they are warming the Earth: But during the day, the smog mirror caused by sulfur pollution "masks" the warming by reflecting extra sunlight into space, netting no change. At night the gases continue trapping heat, but now, there being no sunlight to reflect, the masking effect is deactivated. The world would warm, though more slowly than the computer models predict: exactly what Karl has found.

Clouds are an important factor in day-night warming trends. During the day clouds are coolers, blocking the sun; at night they cause warming, holding heat near the ground. As there is at present total disagreement within scientific circles regarding whether a greenhouse world would know more or less rainfall, there is similar total disagreement on what would happen to clouds. Some researchers think that during global warming clouds would decline, creating a feedback that would make the Earth progressively warmer. On the other hand, William Collins and Veerabhadran Ramanathan of the Scripps Institution have proposed that clouds are a primary climate self-regulation system. Warmer weather, they think, makes for more daytime clouds, preventing the Earth from ever slipping into a runaway greenhouse effect. Studies by Michaels, the University of Virginia climatologist, find that Earth's cloud cover has increased about four percent in the past four decades, possibly as a natural self-regulatory response to carbon emissions.

The Missing Carbon

A common misconception is that artificial gases dominate the greenhouse effect. In fact natural gases are far more significant. Without the natural greenhouse effect, global mean temperatures would be some 60 degrees Fahrenheit lower. A runaway ice age, similar to the one that seems to have occurred on Mars, would lock the planet in glaciers forever.

Nearly all of the natural greenhouse effect, about 99 percent, is driven by water vapor. Carbon dioxide provides the final one percent of the natural greenhouse effect, shuttling among the atmosphere, the seas, and the biota in a cycle of majestic scope. About 200 billion tons of carbon are emitted to the air each year by volcanic eruptions, plant decay, and natural forest fires and the oceans, which hold vast amounts of dissolved

CO_2, according to estimates by the Oak Ridge National Laboratory. Almost exactly the same amount cycles out of the air each year. How is it removed? About 100 billion tons of CO_2 is breathed in ("uptaken," in the researcher's favored term) by land plants, primarily trees. Another 100 billion tons or so is withdrawn from the air by ocean plankton and algae or via the chemical weathering of rocks. The remaining CO_2 is absorbed by desert soils. At any moment, Oak Ridge estimates, only two percent of the CO_2 active in the natural carbon cycle is in the air.

In contrast to the magnitude of the natural carbon cycle, human-caused carbon dioxide levels seem positively puny. Most artificial CO_2 comes from combustion of fossil fuels; tropical forest clearing by fire is the other important source. Artificial CO_2 emissions are currently seven to eight billion tons annually. This means that natural carbon dioxide entering the atmosphere today outnumbers the artificial variety about 29 to one.

That does not excuse greenhouse emissions. The natural carbon cycle is in an approximate equilibrium state. Sometimes even tiny additions to a system in an equilibrium state can cause big consequences. Greenhouse believers often cite the equilibrium state of the natural carbon cycle to justify an assertion that even tiny human-caused additions of carbon dioxide will cause big problems.

Certainly this is possible. But in making the assertion doomsayers leave out a key modifier: The natural carbon cycle is in an *approximate* equilibrium state. Ice-core records are clear on the point that natural CO_2 levels bounced up and down long before the first flint struck steel. Into the *approximate* equilibrium of the natural carbon cycle comes such natural perturbations as periods of global volcanism, ice ages, droughts that reduce carbon dioxide subtractions by land plants, weather vacillations that cause rainy seasons and increase carbon dioxide subtractions by land plants, and many other natural carbon-altering events. In environmental orthodoxy, before the arrival of men and women the Earth dwelled in a sort of Golden Era when all natural forces ideally balanced. Surely there were individual centuries when this was so; perhaps there were millennia. But at least in the most recent four million years of Earth history, the period of cyclical ice ages, the biosphere could hardly be described as a placid equilibrium state.

Early in the century, some scientists thought observed CO_2 buildup might stem from some natural influence causing the oceans to release more carbon. Even a small increase in ocean CO_2 emissions would swamp the entire human output. This idea was disproved, however, by an oceanographer named Roger Revelle. Revelle also disproved an idea, popular among conservatives, that the oceans through their mass could absorb almost any human output of CO_2. Revelle showed that ocean absorption of human-generated carbon dioxide appears limited to about the level the world economy exceeded early in the postwar era. Revelle further devised the first global system for precise monitoring of atmospheric carbon levels. For his work Revelle was dubbed by Dr. Greenhouse by *Scientific American*. Remember his name for a few pages.

When in 1958 Revelle produced the first precise atmospheric CO_2 data, he was immediately struck by something: Half of artificial production was missing. Seven or eight billion tons of carbon dioxide are put into the air each year by human action, but when researchers test the atmosphere, only about three billion tons read as present. Where does the missing carbon go? This missing-carbon problem has haunted greenhouse science since.

"The evidence for a terrestrial sink for the missing carbon is growing," says Edward Rastetter, a researcher at the Woods Hole Oceanographic Institute. "Sink" is the techno-term for whatever absorbs carbon dioxide; the primary "terrestrial sink" is trees. Gordon Bonan, a scientist at the National Center for Atmospheric Research, has estimated that forests of the Northern Hemisphere may be uptaking far more greenhouse gases than once thought, essentially eating the missing carbon.

Though deforestation continues at an alarming pace in the tropics, in the developed world aforestation is the rule. Growing trees absorb substantial amounts of carbon dioxide. The expanding boreal forests of North America and Eurasia are much larger than the rainforests of the tropics. Within the boreal forests are tens of millions of acres of "managed" woodlands in which trees aided by people grow faster than natural forests. In 1993 a team of Harvard University researchers led by Steven Wofsy examined carbon dioxide transactions in a Petersham, Massachusetts, woodland that was denuded of trees by a 1938 hurricane, then replanted by people. They found the trees to be pulling from the air about 50 percent more CO_2 than assumed by standard studies: about 3,500 pounds of CO_2 per acre annually.

About 3,500 pounds of carbon dioxide happens to be roughly what the average car emits annually. Though smog emissions have been nearly eliminated from the exhausts of new cars, for reasons of physics it today seems nearly impossible to invent affordable devices that would strip carbon dioxide from auto exhaust or the smokestacks of power plants burning fossil fuels. The only currently practical means to reduce society's carbon output is fuel-conservation technology that reduces the volume of fuel combusted. This suggests that to establish a proper carbon balance with the atmosphere, each automobile in the world would require its own acre of young forest: a stark way of stating the green-house control challenge.

Methane

A final unknown of global warming is exactly what role methane plays in the process. Because carbon dioxide is the leading greenhouse gas, political attention focuses on it. But methane has greenhouse properties as well: by some estimates 30 times the warming potency of CO_2.

Methane, the primary constituent in natural gas, has a natural cycle based on emissions from volcanos and from wetlands, where some forms of decay result in methane to the air. People cause methane emissions via exploration for oil; by "flaring" of gas found in conjunction with oil; by leaks from natural gas pipelines; by growing rice (creating artificial wetlands in the form of paddies); and, in a manner that has caught the popular imagination as a punchline of jokes but is neverthe-less real, through emissions that let's just say originate with the world's substantial herd of dairy and beef cattle.

Researchers generally believe that airborne methane levels in prein-dustrial times were about 650 parts per billion; today the figure is 1,700 ppb. Some researchers think crops overtreated with nitrogen-based fer-tilizers cause the soil to absorb less methane, leaving more to float in the air. Others believe the hydroxyl radical, a class of molecule that serves as a natural antipollution agent, in preindustrial times extracted significant amounts of methane from the atmosphere. During the postwar era levels of hydroxyl radicals in the air have fallen as these molecules are con-sumed by interactions with smog precursors. This may expend the hydroxyl radicals before they can disarm methane, helping the methane accumulate. Because methane is so potent as a heat-trapping gas, it may be as responsible as carbon dioxide for any recent warming. F. Sherwood Rowland, the University of California scientist best known for the basic equations of ozone depletion theory, says, "If we are really serious about the greenhouse effect we would go after methane first."

One reason methane could be the focus of greenhouse policy is that most emissions have no economic utility. Emissions of carbon dioxide may be bad, but based on current technology it is difficult to imagine how society could function without placing some of this gas in the air. In contrast it is easy to imagine that methane emissions could be cut with-out economic consequences. Improved oil-drilling techniques and better natural-gas pipeline maintenance alone could drop methane emissions substantially.

Researchers from the National Oceanographic and Atmospheric Administration found, in a study published in a 1994 issue of *Geophysical Research Letters,* that global methane accumulation in the atmosphere actually slowed during the 1980s, a period when orthodoxy assumes greenhouse output was rising at a shocking rate. Better yet, by mid-1992 the rate of methane increase in the air of the Northern Hemisphere, where most industrial activity occurs, had dropped to zero. As no antimethane regulations took effect in any country during this period, this finding is not yet fully understood. The leading possible explanation is efforts in the former Soviet Union to plug wasteful leaks in the huge natural-gas pipeline that stretches from Siberia to Western Europe.

If the rate of increase in atmospheric methane could be halted merely by leak-plugging in a country experiencing economic turmoil, imagine what might be accomplished by a program of methane emission controls run by market forces in the Western world. Merely burning for electric power the natural gas now flared from the world's oilfields would cause global methane emissions to begin to decline, while creating power from a fuel source currently wasted. And many activists may not wish to hear this, but new bioengineered substances such as the controversial bovine somatotropin might reduce greenhouse methane emissions. Use of BST causes cows to give about 15 percent more milk. This means 15 percent fewer cows are needed, and in turn a 15 percent decline in, let's say, bovine output.

One reason environmentalist locution focuses on carbon dioxide rather than methane is that the United States is the leading per-capita source of the former gas, the American energy economy being coal-dependent. Greenhouse effect claims emphasizing CO_2 can be used to bash the United States, satisfying a primal instinct of orthodoxy. Many European economies are natural-gas dependent, with much of their supply coming from the former Soviet Union. The Netherlands, a country often praised by U.S. environmentalists because official statements by its government are heavy on green guilt, is also the leading per-capita source of methane emissions, using considerable amounts of natural gas for such purposes as round-the-clock heating of the greenhouses that grow tulips.

At the 1992 Earth Summit, European negotiators, including the Dutch representatives, fervently condemned the United States for its insufficient commitment to carbon dioxide control, while maneuvering behind the scenes to have methane restrictions deleted from the greenhouse treaty. "Arguing in the alternative" like good lawyers, Dutch negotiators asserted that carbon emissions are a horror but methane emissions should not be restricted because—get this—global-warming science is uncertain. Eventually at Washington's insistence the treaty was amended to cover all greenhouse gases. For this strengthening of the global-warming reform plan the United States received no credit, the development being an unwelcome departure from the desired doomsday script. In 1994 a panel of the IPCC formally declared that methane is a more substantial greenhouse gas than had been understood at the time of the Earth Summit. This inconvenient revelation, again making the U.S. position on greenhouse gases seem thoughtful, also went unremarked upon.

The Gopher Tortoise Factor

Terry Root, an ecologist at the University of Michigan, has documented the changing winter range of the eastern phoebe, a songbird that in recent decades has moved somewhat north, suggesting it is retreating from warming. Root points out that while birds, being flighted, may respond readily to climate trends, the trees and vegetation essential to their life cycles cannot. She thinks present trend lines for warming may soon accelerate ahead of the ability of plants to "migrate" via distribution of seeds, leading to a prolonged period of ecological disruption.

That prospect cannot be dismissed. Yet it is currently impossible to know whether the eastern phoebe would be ranging north regardless of the greenhouse situation. Plants and animals have moved among ecosystems since time immemorial, responding to numerous pressures. Russell Graham, a paleontologist at the Illinois State Museum, has shown that when the world warmed at the end of the Pleistocene ice age, a species called the gopher tortoise began to range south, rather than north as would be expected for a cold-blooded animal. Root's studies of the northward movement of the phoebe are often cited by environmentalists to suggest that this fact alone indicates disaster in progress. All they really indicate is another unknown of nature, one whose underlying cause may be good, bad, or neutral.

Movement of plants and animals may or may not have larger significance, but there is a clear short-term concern: that migratory changes may undo some current efforts to preserve endangered species. The Smithsonian Institution's Thomas Lovejoy, a prominent advocate of species protection, has pointed out that U.S. federal efforts to save the Kirtland's warbler, an endangered songbird that today lives in the forests of upper Michigan and Minnesota, could falter if a warming trend inspires the bird to migrate just a few miles north to Canada. Yet such concerns ultimately flounder on the stop-in-place fallacy—the notion it would be desirable, to say nothing of physically possible, to freeze the ecology in its present state, preserving forever what is imagined to be Correct alignment. The Kirtland's warbler may transit to what women and men call Canada regardless of what the climate does. Surely the gopher tortoise will resolutely march in the wrong direction, confounding the best-laid preservation plans.

The Case for Warming

Here's an aspect of the greenhouse controversy that drives environmentalists to distraction: Is global warming bad? The high range of doomsday predictions for a warmer Earth would be fearsome. But mild warming is probably in society's interest, particularly if present trends hold and the warming comes in wintertime or on summer nights.

No one contends that the warming of the past century has done the slightest harm. The prime results of that mild warming, higher crop yields and lower energy consumption, are powerful pluses. What was the economic bottom line on the 1980s, the "hottest years on record"? Agriculture was strong throughout the world. Most developing nations produced sufficient food for domestic consumption. In 1986 India— India!—briefly entered the food export market. Energy consumption was soft, winter peak demand being a key variable in power needs. In turn, energy prices declined. By 1994, in real-dollar terms gasoline cost less in the United States than during the 1950s, a period enshrined in collective memory as Energy Heaven. High agricultural yield and soft energy demand are especially important to the Third World. Farm yields stave off malnutrition, while most developing nations are fuel importers whose populations suffer when oil prices rise.

"I have a hard time following why longer growing seasons, lower energy use and fewer subzero days in North Dakota are the new apocalypse," says Michaels, of the University of Virginia. He argues that up to a global increase of around three degrees Fahrenheit, an artificial greenhouse effect will be benign. Pessimists try to wave away such arguments. Paul Allen of the Natural Resources Defense Council has said that mere discussion of benefits from global warming is "preposterous." Yet the notion of gains from warming is not without respectable backing. The Intergovernmental Panel on Climate Change has estimated that a 3.5-degree Fahrenheit warming would increase agricultural yields in the former Soviet Union by 40 percent, in China by 20 percent, in the United States by 15 percent. Even at this point, global temperatures would remain below their level for most of Earth's history.

If it were certain current temperature trends were natural, we might now be reading stories about the wonderful global warming. But the idea that clumsy tinkering with the atmosphere inadvertently has done something useful—that we benefit from pollution!—is almost too peculiar for polite discourse. Spencer Weart, the historian at the American Institute for Physics, has suggested that people feel this way because their ancestors assumed changes in the weather to be portents. Harsh storms, eclipses, and other phenomena were considered omens. Today, Weart thinks, emotions that once expressed themselves as dread of lightning have been transferred to technology: The notion that human action might change the weather evokes ancient fears of evil augery, even if that change seems for the moment beneficial.

Of course future warming may not follow the present pattern. It may come at noontime in summer, searing crops and driving up power consumption for cooling. It may alter weather in ways that deprive presently fertile regions of rain.

The prospect that a warming world will be one of disastrous storms has caught on in popular culture. In pop depictions of the greenhouse effect, such as the 1993 CBS television miniseries *The Fire Next Time,* it is asserted as fact that greenhouse warming will create hyperstorms. So far this notion is unsupported by research. Severe twentieth-century hurricanes occurred mainly in cool years. For instance Hurricane Andrew came in 1992, during the mild post-Pinatubo summer. There have been two maximum-category hurricanes in the United States in this century. One which struck Florida in 1935, when storms were unnamed, arrived long before significant emissions of greenhouse gases. The second, Hurricane Camille, came in 1969, a cool year. So far research suggests that warm years tend to produce more storms of low intensity, cool years fewer storms of higher intensity.

The CBS miniseries depicted a man and boy attempting to travel the Mississippi in an ecologically ruined United States of the year 2007—a world of searing warmth, sustained droughts, hyperstorms, and dangerous exposure to bad dialogue. Conservative critics were aghast at the film, saying it indoctrinated mass audiences with greenhouse scenarios far worse than any projected by the most pessimistic computer model. My reaction was the opposite. By trivializing the greenhouse effect into a subject as ludicrous as the premise of a television miniseries, *The Fire Next Time* served mainly to convince audiences the prospect of global warming is just another Hollywood gimmick, which unfortunately it may not be.

The low point of the miniseries came when the real Stephen Schneider, playing himself as an aging scientist, declared the reason global warming got out of control was that "very little was done" at the 1992 Earth Summit in Rio. That was the conventional doomsday line when *The Fire Next Time* was being filmed. By the time the movie was shown this statement had become nonsensical, the United States having ratified the Rio global-warming treaty and voluntarily strengthening it, as will be explained later in this chapter.

The Greenhouse–Cheap Oil Link

Richard Benedick, a fellow at the World Wildlife Fund, argues that "the very existence of scientific uncertainty about global warming should lead us to action rather than delay." This sentiment is common in the orthodox environmental community, where it is often said scientific uncertainty about the greenhouse effect is merely a ruse to forestall reforms. Government and industry do sometimes collude to put off needed actions, and to the extent science can be induced to join in the foot-dragging by promises of funds for further study, stalling may have broad-based appeal to the pillars of the establishment. But can "the very existence of scientific uncertainty" really be an argument for reform? After all there was, in the 1970s, a great deal of scientific uncertainty regarding that decade's fashionable notion that an ice age was beginning. Had Congress acted then in advance of scientific consensus, it might have legislated a crash program of *increased* carbon dioxide emissions.

Rational environmental decision-making is possible within a context of scientific uncertainty. The ecorealist need only concentrate on those actions that are justified in and of themselves, regardless of what later research might show. In greenhouse matters ample opportunities exist for the most important reform: increased efficiency in the use of fossil fuels. As the economics of the greenhouse will show, reasonable energy efficiency reforms justify themselves, whether global temperatures are going up, down, or sideways.

"Cure for Greenhouse Effect: The Costs Will Be Staggering," read a 1989 headline in the *New York Times*. Estimates then being batted around the White House for greenhouse gas reductions ran from $100 billion per year to a mind-bending $3.6 trillion annually, nearly the gross national product. Such calculations contained an astonishing omission. The primary way to control carbon dioxide is to make energy use more efficient. The big money numbers took into account the capital costs of new conservation investments, but not the value of the fuel saved. Factor in the value of fuel savings, the conservation analysts Amory and Hunter Lovins showed in a landmark 1990 study, and the cost of global-warming control not only falls, it becomes possible to imagine cutting greenhouse gases at a profit.

This finding has since been upheld by a landslide of studies. An EPA analysis determined that U.S. greenhouse-gas emissions could, by the year 2000, be stabilized at the level of 1990 at essentially zero net cost, when the value of saved energy is taken into account. The federal Office of Technology Assessment found that "moderate" carbon dioxide reduction could be achieved at zero net cost, noting that reductions in smog and acid rain would be realized as a premium. The National Academy of Sciences projected that greenhouse emissions could be reduced by about 25 percent at a price equivalent to about 11 cents per gallon of gasoline.[3] By 1992 even internal White House documents projected that U.S. carbon dioxide emissions could be cut by about 11 percent with little economic impact.

Fuel cost savings from greenhouse-gas control would not be confined to the specific coal, petroleum, or natural gas reductions at any factory, office, or automobile that became more efficient. They would spread broadly to all energy prices, by reducing demand.

A central reason world energy prices remain pleasingly low is that consumers have become more efficient. The United States now uses about 28 percent less energy per dollar of economic output than it did two decades ago, a change made possible by everything from high-mileage cars to smart thermostats. Somehow the economic payoff of fuel efficiency goes unappreciated. Everyone is keenly aware that in 1974 and 1979 fuel prices rose enthusiastically in response to reductions in supply. Overlooked is that fuel prices also follow the second half of the supply-and-demand equation, falling faithfully in response to reductions in demand. World equilibrium oil prices have been soft since the early 1980s because the United States, the main player in marginal demand for oil, consistently buys less than once expected. The U.S. balance-of-payments deficit for world trade would be awful had oil prices climbed to $100 a barrel, as was widely projected in the mid-1970s, rather than tumbling to $15 a barrel by 1994, a lower real-dollar cost than when the first oil shock occurred in 1973. Oil costs have virtually dropped off the political radar: an unheralded benefit of fuel efficiency.

When Iraq invaded Kuwait in August 1990, oil prices spiked on the expectation that supply would be disrupted or demand would rise through panic buying. Oil companies looked longingly toward a repeat of the 1974 and 1979 windfalls. Yet the price spike vanished in less than two weeks. There was extensive, gloomy public reaction to the brief price increase but hardly any notice of the decline, though the latter was far more significant. No panic oil buying occurred in August 1990 because society, by virtue of energy efficiency gains, was less obsessed about oil supplies than the last time around. A similar example involves the cold snap of January 1990. Prices of fuel oil for home heating rose for two weeks in the Northeast, suppliers anticipating a windfall from a buying panic. The increase was front-page news nationwide, the phrase "energy crisis" trotted out by headline writers for the first time in a decade. Congressional hearings were held; Michael Dukakis, then governor of Massachusetts, declared with full gravitas, "Somebody is making money here—big money." In February 1990, one month later, fuel oil prices recorded their sharpest *decline* in 55 years, as improved energy efficiency prevented the price panic from taking hold. This development, being inconveniently positive, was relegated to the inside financial pages.

Today new frontiers in fuel efficiency are in prospect. For instance the National Academy of Sciences has said that federal auto fuel economy standards could be increased from the current 27.5 mpg level to 35 mpg without sacrifice in safety, comfort, or affordability. If automobiles averaged 35 mpg, an ecorealistic goal, the United States could import no oil from the Middle East, while U.S. emissions of carbon dioxide would decline about 18 percent. Cheap energy used efficiently is a best-of-both-worlds situation for everyone except an assortment of desert princes. Viewed this way, insurance against global warming looks like an attractive buy.

California is the best example. Various California state regulations enacted in the 1980s have made that state the national leader in fuel conservation. California requires efficiency in commercial appliances, industrial motors, and many other categories. Amory Lovins calculates that if the United States as a whole merely achieved in the 1990s the same rate of fuel efficiency realized under real-world circumstances in California during the 1980s, net U.S. energy consumption would fall by two to three percentage points per year, even as economic production rose.

In addition there are two global arguments for a new commitment to energy efficiency, both having to do with where the world is headed. The first turns on competitiveness. Stephan Schmidheiney, the Swiss industrialist who heads the Business Council on Sustainable Development, notes that Germany and Japan, two of the world's most competitive economies, each have poor domestic energy supplies and much higher energy prices than the United States. Gasoline sells for about $1.30 a gallon in the United States, about $2.90 per gallon in Germany, and about $3.30 per gallon in Japan. Schmidheiney says, "These countries do well not in spite of their energy situations but because of them." German and Japanese firms must be efficient in their use of resources. The sorts of efficiencies that serve well in controlling energy costs spill over into other aspects of manufacturing, resulting in general competitiveness. By this logic a new national commitment to energy efficiency in the United States would not harm the competitiveness of American industry but improve it.

Finally, inexorably, there are the efficiency requirements necessitated by global population growth. Consider an example offered by William Lee, CEO emeritus of Duke Power, a North Carolina utility. Suppose that over the coming decades world population stabilizes around the low end of United Nations estimate: at 5.4 billion souls today, it expands to nine billion. Next suppose that the majority of the world's residents will reach a standard of living equal to one-half that enjoyed by Americans, as measured by per-capita income. Reaching this level alone represents an immense challenge; but anything less would leave a morally unbearable gap between the comfort of the First World and the deprivation of the Third. Finally suppose that all energy uses become twice as efficient as they are today. Lee calculates that under these optimistic assumptions, the world in the twenty-first century will need to generate three times as much power. Using the even more optimistic assumptions favored by Lovins, the twenty-first-century power requirement drops to a mere double that of today's.

Considering that energy is the world's leading pollutant; that energy efficiency saves money; that fossil fuel supplies, while today robust, are nevertheless finite; the sorts of fuel efficiency strictures that would buy greenhouse-effect insurance will soon be seen as a global priority regardless of the thermostat.

Carbon Costs

For years the standard assumption among environmentalists has been that the best way to inspire fuel-use reduction would be through a carbon tax, a fee per ton of carbon dioxide emitted to the air. Carbon taxes would strongly discourage the use of coal, the fuel richest in CO_2; discourage somewhat the uses of oil and natural gas; and encourage renewable, nonfossil power forms such as wind, biomass (fuel from trash or plants), solar conversion, and hydropower. Such taxes would also encourage nuclear power, which produces radioactive waste but no greenhouse emissions. Early in the Clinton Administration the White House proposed a variation on the carbon tax, a BTU fee that would have mildly taxed the heat content in fuels. This initiative differed from a carbon tax mainly in that it would have deleted the favor to nuclear power, since uranium can be measured by BTU content. After Clinton's BTU tax failed in Congress, discussion of an eventual carbon tax resumed.

Business groups invariably predict that carbon taxes would have a catastrophic effect on the U.S. economy. The National Coal Association, whose constituents would be losers under the tax, has estimated that even a low carbon tax of ten dollars per ton would cost the economy $41 billion per year. Yet many appraisals of carbon taxes are optimistic. Paul McCracken and Martin Feldstein, former chairs of the federal Council of Economic Advisors (Feldstein a Reagan appointee), favor moderate carbon taxes. Three of the leading environmental economists—Robert Crandall of the Brookings Institution, Robert Hahn of the American Enterprise Institute, and Robert Stavins of Harvard University—have endorsed aspects of carbon taxation, provided the system is revenue-neutral. This means levies on carbon would be offset by reductions in corporate and personal taxes, so that the system would merely encourage fuel efficiency, not shift social resources to government. Stavins says, "In America today we tax labor and capital, both of which are socially beneficial. We should shift toward taxing pollution and resource consumption, activities that harm society, while lowering taxes on labor and capital."

An even better means of controlling greenhouse gases may be a system of marketable trading permits, modeled on the acid rain trading permits. "Tradable carbon permits would allow for complete market flexibility, not involving government bureaucracts in the specifics of business and personal decisions," says Dan Dudek, an economist at the Environmental Defense Fund. Tradable permits could evolve into a world system, creating a financial incentive for developing countries to control greenhouse emissions, while shifting some resources from the First to the Third World, since there would be many cases in which First World companies found they could achieve carbon reductions in developing nations much more cheaply than in the developed.

Some businesses have already found this to be so. New England Electric System, a Massachusetts utility, has a pilot project in Malaysia aimed at carbon reductions through improved rainforest logging practices. The company is offsetting carbon emissions at about one dollar a ton, drastically less than the lowest proposed U.S. carbon tax. Mark Trexler, an Oregon energy consultant, estimates that carbon reduction projects in the developing world will average around five dollars a ton for Western investors: still much less than carbon taxes, yet a large enough sum that significant assistance would be transferred to the Third World in the process.

Here again the greenhouse issue defies current orthodoxy in both directions. Probably the problem is nowhere near as distressing as assumed. Yet reforms will be cheaper than expected, with benefits like lower energy prices and increased Third World investment provided essentially free. So why don't global-warming politics reflect such positive considerations? Let's see.

Pleasingly Nebulous Domestic Politics

Inaction on the greenhouse effect would be a catastrophe, according to the Sierra Club. The hour may already be too late, according to the Club of Rome. Global warming is even "a spiritual crisis," according to the National Council of Churches.

The greenhouse effect is a trumped-up environmentalist's power play, according to former Office of Management and Budget Director Richard Darman. It's a disguised plan to shut down the industrial state, according to the coal lobby. The global warming treaty signed at Rio represents "Greenpeace in our time," according to the libertarian Cato Institute.

Global warming can inspire such polar positions because the subject is so pleasingly nebulous. Crime, welfare, health care—most issues are anchored in the muck of the real. The greenhouse effect is a blank screen onto which partisans may project whatever they wish to behold.

Reactions to the greenhouse issue fracture along the fault lines of conventional politics. Such divisions are found in the science as well as political worlds. In the United States, the most prominent greenhouse true believers—John Firor of the National Center for Atmospheric Research, James Hansen of the Goddard Institute, and Stephen Schneider of Stanford—are political liberals. The most prominent greenhouse naysayers—Robert Jastrow of Dartmouth, Richard Lindzen of MIT, and Patrick Michaels of the University of Virginia—are political conservatives.

In the overheated atmosphere of global warming politics, science is subject to more than the usual misuse. Lindzen's work is often described by right-wing commentators as establishing that global warming will not happen, something Lindzen himself has never said: He says only that the artificial greenhouse effect is an unproven hypothesis. By the same token but from the opposite perspective, Vice President Gore attributes to the late Roger Revelle, "Dr. Greenhouse," the notion that global warming means certain doom, something Revelle did not say.

In *Earth in the Balance,* Gore waxes on at length about his associations with Revelle, from student days at Harvard, when he met the great researcher, to Revelle's appearances before congressional subcommittees chaired by Gore in the House and Senate. It was Revelle, Gore has said, who persuaded him that the greenhouse effect is a dire emergency. Yet before his death in 1991, Revelle coauthored a paper that concludes, "The scientific base for greenhouse warming is too uncertain to justify drastic action at this time. There is little risk in delaying policy responses."

Revelle advocated fuel efficiency and a transition from fossil fuels to clean energy, both as greenhouse insurance policies and as sound ideas on their own merits. But Revelle also thought that moderate greenhouse increases might provide a carbon fertilization effect for agriculture and that nuclear power, with its zero greenhouse output, should be reconsidered as a clean energy candidate. Such views being insufficiently bleak, Gore and other environmentalists who cite Revelle's pioneering work in establishing the seriousness of CO_2 emissions always skip over the parts about carbon benefits and nuclear alternatives.

A subtle factor in greenhouse political theater is fund-raising on the left and right. Conservatives can assail their mailing lists with claims of socialist central planning masquerading as climate protection. Environmental groups have found scary direct mail essential to financial well-being. But with toxic wastes having failed to pan out as a general threat, and CFC bans already in place, end-of-the-world issues are in short supply. Thank goodness for the greenhouse effect! Similarly, in elective politics, global warming affords for Republicans an opening to paint the other side as eager to clamp unneeded regulations on the economy. For Democrats, there is the chance to depict the opposition as playing fast and loose with the very future of the Earth.

Privately some environmentalists admit greenhouse rhetoric has gone too far. They defend this with what might be called the Benevolent Big Lie theory: So long as the direction in which society is being pushed is positive, make-believe hysteria is justified to grab the public's attention. But there is, as well, the danger that a Benevolent Big Lie may backfire by distracting the world's attention from more important issues. This is what happened to greenhouse politics at the Earth Summit in Rio.

International Greenhouse Politics

For two years negotiations progressed at the highest levels of government over the greenhouse treaty to be signed in Rio. Countless threats, inducements, and double-crosses were exchanged at Earth Summit "prepcons" at the United Nations, sessions attended by hundreds of negotiators from nearly every nation: So many attended that some prepcons had to be held in the cavernous General Assembly hall. The European Union (then called the European Commission) staked its nascent prestige on its ability to make the climate treaty happen. The Japanese, normally circumspect about diplomacy, trumpeted themselves as greener-than-thou on greenhouse controls. As the June 1992 opening of the conference approached, world headlines were dominated by the issue of a greenhouse treaty. Through this period global warming became, as least as judged by news inches and by the behavior of heads of state, the leading issue in the world. Never had great nations devoted so much energy to addressing an entirely speculative problem.

Two principal issues existed for the Rio global warming treaty. One was whether it would come into existence at all, for it required that nations (on paper at least) subjugate domestic economic decisions such as fuel-use policies to the authority of the United Nations. The second principal issue was what action would be taken. The European Union, representing most states of Western Europe, wanted a binding treaty requiring stabilization of carbon dioxide at the level of 1990 by the year 2000—"1990 stabilization." Denmark, Germany, Japan, the Netherlands, and other nations announced their eagerness to approve binding stabilization. European officials declared that the nations of Western Europe would accept a strict carbon tax in order to assure sweeping action. Among Western leaders, George Bush was alone in opposing binding stabilization.

The U.S. position was vilified by commentators and diplomats as a shocking affront to humanity. The Brazilian newsmagazine *Veja* called the U.S. "Uncle Smoke" and the "Earth Summit enemy" because of its stance against a binding stabilization clause. Carlo Ripa di Meana, the chief E.U. environmental official, boycotted Rio in protest of the U.S. position. Kamal Nath, India's environment minister, declared that the American opposition "outrage[s] the world." Genevieve Pons, a senior E.U. official, told me as the conference approached, "Traditionally Europe looked to America as the environmental forerunner. Now America grows timid. It is embarrassing to watch."

At Rio the U.S. position prevailed; the Rio greenhouse treaty became nonbinding. The Western European nations then held a self-

congratulatory ceremony in which they vowed to go it alone with binding 1990 reductions. For their noble promise the Western European
nations were widely praised. World reaction was universally hostile to
the United States. Then this story of the century vanished. Reporters
invariably treated Rio as if treaty maneuvers came to a conclusion there:
Actually they began. All that occurred at the Earth Summit was that
world leaders initialed declarations of sentiment. Treaties do not come
into being until they are ratified. What happened after Rio?

The U.S. Senate ratified the greenhouse treaty almost immediately,
by voice vote. Bush was still president; he, a Republican, sent to the
United Nations the formal letter acknowledging international authority
in greenhouse matters. After replacing Bush, Bill Clinton unilaterally
bound the United States to 1990 stabilization. Meanwhile the European
Union countries stalled for nearly two years before approving the Rio
greenhouse agreement.

Western European nations seemed quite happy to let this little exercise in doublespeak disappear from world consciousness. Meeting in
Copenhagen in June 1993, on the first anniversary of Rio, the E.U.
Council of Environmental Ministers quietly tabled so much as discussing when they might propose ratification of the greenhouse accord.
German environment minister Klaus Topfer acknowledged the situation
made the Europeans appear "foolish, if not actually devious." And
Western Europe's theatrical promise to go it alone with a binding 1990
stabilization program was discarded as soon as the CNN cameras
panned elsewhere. At this writing, not a single Western European nation
had matched the United States in drawing up a binding policy to hold
carbon emissions at the 1990 level. Several have perfunctorily noted
they will no longer even attempt to meet the goal. The Netherlands—
warmly applauded at Rio for declaring that its 2000 carbon output
would not only be stabilized but lower than the country's 1990 emissions—quietly announced in late 1993 that, er, ahem, actually Dutch
carbon emissions in 2000 will be as much as ten percent higher than in
1990.

Considering that pundits, diplomats and environmentalists hyperventilated about the greenhouse treaty when Europe seemed the hero
and Washington the scoundrel, why did silence descend when roles
reversed? One explanation is that the pleasure of bashing the United
States vanished from the equation. Another is that turns of events made
Bush's Rio position seem reasonable; and institutional environmentalism cannot abide the notion that anything Bush did at Rio was reasonable. Clinton and Gore, having campaigned on the theme that Bush was
an ecological charlatan, had no incentive to acknowledge that a major

environmental policy decision by the former president seems in retrospect not so bad. Bush deserves credit for what should be reinterpreted as his progressive position on the Rio global warming treaty; Clinton and Gore deserve credit for advancing that position to the stabilization commitment. Between them they transformed the United States from Uncle Smoke to the world leader in action against the greenhouse effect.

Carbon Stabilization: Worthless but Well Advised

In the uncountable words written and spoken about the Rio Earth Summit, no mention was made of a bedrock question: Will the goal of the treaty, stabilization of carbon emissions at the 1990 level, prevent global warming? The answer is: Not a snowball's chance in, well, Alberta, should the warming occur.

Policies announced by President Clinton to hold U.S. greenhouse emissions at the 1990 level in the year 2000 should prevent, according to the White House, 100 million metric tons of carbon releases that year. Depending on who does the calculating, that represents 1.2 to 1.4 percent of world industrial carbon emissions expected in 2000. Since naturally occurring carbon emissions outnumber human-caused emissions roughly 29 to one, the U.S. cut will dilute to a reduction of just 0.03 to 0.05 percent of total carbon entering the atmosphere. In turn, since carbon dioxide accounts for only about one percent of total greenhouse effects, the U.S. reduction will further dilute to a drop of just 0.0005 percent of combined greenhouse influences on the atmosphere. Since the natural carbon cycle is roughly in an equilibrium state, relatively small human-caused additions may do harm. But numbers such as these are far too small to offer any meaningful impact on climate trends.

Nevertheless Clinton was wise to bind the United States to the 1990 goal, because if an artificial greenhouse effect is developing, society must start learning the art of carbon reduction. Long journeys begin with small steps: The knowledge gained in realizing a 1.4 percent reduction in world carbon output might lead to breakthroughs that would make possible significant controls. Clinton also saw that since carbon emissions have declined slightly in some recent years anyway, there exists an opportunity to create a positive momentum for greenhouse reform. Global carbon emissions from industry and vehicles climbed rapidly through the 1950s to 1970s and hit a mini peak in the year 1979 at 5.3 billion metric tons; then fell through the early 1980s; then rose again through the late 1980s and have remained roughly steady at about 5.8 billion metric tons since that time.[4] Finally Clinton's decision to bind the

United States was wise because carbon reductions will be realized mainly through conservation of fossil fuels, a good idea in any case.

Clinton's plan includes the beginnings of a carbon trading system: credits to U.S. companies for net carbon reductions in the Third World, an idea proposed by Susan Tierney, an assistant secretary in the Department of Energy. Many environmentalists fought the Tierney plan, known by the clumsy term-of-art "joint implementation," saying it would violate the letter of Clinton's promise to reduce *American* emissions. But what was the goal of Rio: progress against a greenhouse or ceremonial guilt-tripping by the industrial powers? If the former, all that matters is tons of carbon emissions avoided, regardless of the country of origin. Western involvement in preventing carbon emissions in the developing world will grow increasingly significant in the next century, because greenhouse reductions realized in the First World will rapidly be swamped by the Third.

Since greenhouse-effect concerns arose, commentators have hammered endlessly on the notion that the First World is the global menace: Through the 1980s the United States, the former Soviet Union, and Europe produced slightly more than half of world carbon emissions. Projections were that the balance would not shift toward the developing nations till the twenty-first century. Instead this happened in 1992. That year the Third World produced 52 percent of global carbon emissions, supplanting the First World as the greenhouse malefactor. Since 1970, Third World carbon emissions have increased nearly three times as rapidly as First World emissions. Yet environmental lobbying pressure remains focused on the United States, where the guilt-tripping payoff is.

Of course growth in Third World greenhouse gases does not mean there should be no progress against the gases in the United States. As the plump have more pounds to shed than the slender, wasteful systems such as the U.S. energy network will be healthier and happier once greenhouse reductions are realized through energy efficiency. But even as the Western world strives for greenhouse cutbacks, Third World output of carbon dioxide will continue to soar—*should* soar at least through the short run, as industrialization brings to the impoverished of developing lands some measure of material comfort.

China, which now emits 13 percent of world greenhouse gases, possesses an essentially unlimited supply of low-grade carboniferous coal. The Intergovernmental Panel on Climate Change has estimated that at current rates of increase in Chinese coal-power production, by the year 2025 China alone will emit more greenhouse gases than Canada, Japan, and the United States combined. Alan Manne of Stanford University and Richard Richels of the Electric Power Research Institute in Palo Alto,

California, have estimated that if all First World countries reduce their greenhouse output by 20 percent—a more ambitious goal than so far contemplated by any nation—while Third World nations merely continue on their current rate of increase in power output, early in the next century the net global carbon dioxide output will increase 15 percent.

Such gloomy scenarios can be averted, though this will require among other things a renewed commitment to international aid on the part of affluent countries. The developing world can have the increased prosperity that is its due, without repeating Western levels of energy waste. Though the short-term outlook says world greenhouse emissions are certain to rise, there is no reason why the rise cannot be intercepted before it becomes catastrophic, by a combination of fuel efficiency reforms in the First World and the bringing of clean technology to the Third. Then the carbon doubling projected by James Hansen's computer will recede further, perhaps into the twenty-second century—meaning it will never happen, because society will have kicked the fossil fuel habit by then.

But before you start to feel good . . .

Eight Million Dead

In 1992 the World Health Organization published a thick volume of analysis of global environmental health damage. The book contains paragraphs here and there about issues that occupy the attention of the affluent in industrial lands: the greenhouse effect, skin cancer from sunbathing, trace pesticide residues. It goes on for hundreds of pages about the environmental issues that matter daily to the majority of the world's population. For example, according to the WHO, 3.2 million children died in 1991 from diarrheal diseases. (By 1993, that figure would rise to 3.8 million.) Most of the deaths could have been avoided by safe drinking water and controlled sanitation.

Another three million Third World children died preventable deaths in 1991 from acute respiratory distress brought on by living in unventilated huts where heating and cooking was done with wood or even dung, causing smoke damage to the lungs. (By 1993 that figure would be up to four million.) Most of these deaths could have been prevented by electrification, or even simple propane stoves. Total 1993 preventable childhood deaths from gross water and air pollution in the Third World: 7.8 million.

Nearly eight million children dead each year versus someday, maybe, one more degree Fahrenheit. On the runup to the Earth Summit at Rio, instant-doomsday hyperbole caused the world's attention to focus on the hypothetical threat of global warming to the exclusion of environmental menaces that are real, palpable, and awful right now—but which only affect the abstract legions of the distant poor and which have no PC quotient, since waterborne diseases or dung smoke cannot be blamed on corporate plutocrats.

This is the powerful example of the way in which the Benevolent Big Lie thinking on global warming has veered out of control. The Earth Summit should have been about environmental issues that are confirmed emergencies, such as drinking water purity and dung smoke. But the emotional satisfaction and fund-raising quotient of America bashing is missing from these issues, so locution honed in on the greenhouse effect. There is something faintly indecent about the world's heads of state gathering, as they did at Rio, to bestow many tens of billions of dollars on the greenhouse effect, a speculative concern, while lifting not a finger to assist 7.8 million children dead each year from drinking infected water and breathing dense smoke. Yet this ordering of priorities is in sync with contemporary environmental doctrine.

A little-reported part of Rio was a proposed agreement by which the First World would increase environmental aid to the developing world, for purposes such as water sanitation. Western nations ended up rejecting this proposal, pleading, *We'd love to help, but we just committed ourselves to big investments in fighting the greenhouse menace.* Even Sweden, the world's most generous state in foreign aid, turned down the water-purity initiative, pleading new greenhouse commitments.

Among some Third World intellectuals there is growing suspicion that for all the First World hand-wringing about how painful greenhouse controls will be, developed countries suddenly care about this issue for selfish reasons. Global warming might affect property values on Cape Hatteras; raw sewage in drinking water in Bangladesh will not. Energy efficiency, supposedly a terrible sacrifice for industries of wealthy nations, will help prepare them for twenty-first-century competition with the developing world. As Mabubul Haq, an official of the United Nations Development Programme, has noted, "Although global warming has yet to kill a single human being and may not do so for centuries, it has received enormous attention and resources. The silent emergencies that are killing people every day do not attract the screaming headlines and well-funded action plans."

Hasn't anybody wondered why a delegation of corporate CEOs, including Kenneth Derr of Chevron and Frank Popoff of Dow, met with George Bush a few weeks before the Rio conference to ask him to back the climate treaty? Because they realized greenhouse control is in their self-interest. Ultimately all environmental protection is in everybody's self-interest. The dawning of this consciousness, once complete, will drive great environmental reforms yet to come. Till that happy day, the First World can recover some perspective by approaching global warming from an ecorealist point of view: as another environmental problem to be fixed in a rational and cool-headed manner, not as an instant doomsday.

And women and men everywhere can recover some perspective by considering the issue of greenhouse gases from the point of view of nature. Nature would be unlikely to care much about an urban warm spell or even decades of high fossil-fuel use. The prospect of high fossil-fuel use continuing indefinitely would, however, give nature pause. Not because nature would "end": the biosphere will do quite well, thank you, even should genus *Homo* create a greenhouse world. It's we who might end. Nature, contemplating this, would think with a sigh that women and men, for all their supposed intellect, are missing the single most obvious point about natural history. That point: Climate changes cause extinctions.

The age of reptiles almost surely ended through climate change. Other mass extinctions in the fossil record appear related to climate as well. One came about 33 million years ago, a mass extinction paleontologists call *la grande Coupure,* or Great Break, in which 60 percent of European mammals disappeared while the ancestors of deer, dogs, and other modern species arose. Global temperatures are believed to have been dropping fast at the time. The sweeping extinction of large North American mammals that occurred around 11,000 years ago usually is attributed (including by this book) to hunting by Paleo-Indians. Then again, at the same time temperatures were rising fast owing to the end of the Pleistocene ice age. Perhaps genus *Homo* and all today's mammals are survivors of a disturbingly recent mass extinction caused by a climate swing.

Nothing in natural history suggests that toxic wastes, radon, smog, sewage, logging, landfills, or other current human environmental obsessions could trigger a chain of circumstances that leads to extinction. Climate change might. Any reasonable policy that reduces the odds of climate change is more than worth the price.

ECONOMICS ✑

ONE SYNTHETIC COMPOUND FOR WHICH THERE EXISTS NO health-effects dispute is vinyl chloride, a carcinogenic intermediary of plastics manufacturing. Before dioxin and PCBs were familiar terms, vinyl chloride was the first toxic whose emission the EPA proposed to halt. Congressional hearing records from the 1970s show something like clinical hysteria by the plastics industry: predictions of bankruptcies, sweeping market losses, job destruction. The EPA forged ahead.

Compelled to ponder how to manufacture plastics without emitting vinyl chloride, chemists discovered a recapture process costing less than the previous technique. The profitability of plastics increased; prices to consumers declined; jobs were created as demand rose. "Vinyl chloride regulation turned out to make the plastics industry stronger," says Jerry Martin, director of environmental affairs for Dow Chemical. And the controls worked. By 1991 U.S. factories were releasing about one percent as much of this compound as emitted annually in the 1970s.

The results of vinyl chloride control epitomize the modern economics of the environment. At every stage of ecological progress, conservation initiatives have been expected to cost huge sums, to subtract from productivity and growth, to handicap industry. If there is any group more disposed to gloom than environmentalists, it is economists. Yet just as no environmentalist's doomsday prediction has ever come true, neither has any prediction of economic doomsday. Since the 1970 establishment of the EPA the United States economy has continuously expanded its output even as production has grown far more clean and environmentally responsible.

As recently as 20 years ago it was widely believed by economists that a nation could either be clean or rich. With each passing year that notion recedes further into the category of superstition. "It is now accepted that there is no fundamental conflict between industrial production and environmental protection," says Helmut Schreiber, an economist at the World Bank. "By the early twenty-first century all successful corporations will operate at a standard of maximum resource efficiency and minimum emissions. This will be done without extreme social costs and with few if any net job losses."

That does not mean that all environmental initiatives are cost-effective. Rational priorities for the optimum use of environmental control measures will grow increasingly important in decades to come because the easy part of ecological protection—the cessation of gross pollution—will be accomplished in the developed world, and a point of diminishing returns may await future initiatives.

But for the moment nearly everything about environmental economics works and is affordable. In fact, trends in environmental economics increasingly support a notion that might be called the Pollution Peak: that industrial economies transit cycles in which pollution and environmental impacts first increase, then stabilize, then decline. Early evidence suggests that the Pollution Peak has already come in the United States and many countries of Western Europe, is coming now in the former Soviet bloc, and may arrive sometime in the next century for most of the developing world.

It's Always Cheaper

The first and most important point of environmental economics is that so far nearly all forms of conservation have cost less than expected, owing to unanticipated technical discoveries and free-market innovations. Vinyl chloride regulation is just one example. When the nationwide conversion to unleaded gasoline began in 1977, petroleum companies predicted price increases of 20 cents per gallon in 1994 cents. Instead refining unleaded gas now costs only an added one cent per gallon. Acid rain permits were expected to sell for $600 to $700 per ton. Instead they are selling for about $150, as controls are costing utilities substantially less than expected.

In 1990, when the new Clean Air Act was being debated, George

Bush estimated the cost at $19 billion per year. Industry estimates were much higher. Since the law passed acid rain control costs have declined; as smog levels fall, the expected need for strict future antismog regulations has diminished, reducing likely costs; control of air toxics increasingly looks like an affordable proposition, since from 1990 to 1992 U.S. firms cut toxic air emissions by a net of 26 percent, a much faster rate of progress than anticipated by the 1990 act. Meanwhile many corporations signed on to an EPA lighting-efficiency program called Green Lights that is encouraged by the new law. William Rosenberg, a former EPA official, estimates that Green Lights will save industry about $20 billion per year through lowered energy use. "So in effect we'll be able to pay for the entire 1990 Clean Air Act from fuel savings promoted by the bill itself," Rosenberg says. "The overall cost to society will not be $19 billion a year. The overall cost will be zero dollars per year."

Optimism about Garbage

Perhaps the best example of positive environmental economics is recycling. Of course you've heard the snafu stories: Seattle spending $100 a ton to collect used newspaper that sells for $40 a ton; Washington, D.C., elaborately separating white and colored paper, only to toss them back together at the landfill; Rhode Island, the first state to mandate recycling, shipping a third of collected bottles to landfills. Yet the shaky start for recycling should not be seen as discouraging. Markets take time to develop. Often there are initial imbalances between supply and demand, worked out gradually as producers and customers get to know one another better. Through the coming decade recycling at reasonable levels will become practical and economically successful. Our descendants will see recycling as the norm—a sign of character—and wonder how it could ever have been otherwise.

If anything it's surprising how rapidly recycling is overcoming the expected phase of initial failures. Curbside programs did not begin in earnest in the United States until the 1980s, when the national recycling rate was just three percent. By 1992 the U.S. recycling level was up to 17 percent. Some 3,700 curbside recycling programs existed in 1993, versus 600 programs just five years before. A few of these programs are turkeys. Most work. As a result, even with ever-increasing consumption of consumer goods, the amount of material sent to landfills in the United States began to decline in the 1980s for the first time since records have been kept. Another peak passed, the Throwaway Peak.

Already today several U.S. states and cities have recycling levels as high as those found in Japan. New Jersey has gone from a standing start to recycling 53 percent of curbside wastes, under a program whose target was 25 percent. Seattle recycles slightly more than 50 percent, the level achieved in Tokyo. A California law called for 50 percent recycling of newsprint by the year 2000; the state hit that level in the year 1993. California's newsprint recycling initiative has stimulated the construction of several de-inking plants, facilities today more profitable than virgin paper product plants.

As the recycling market matures, recycling will become increasingly rationalized. For instance, in the 1980s it was widely said there could never be any practical means to recycle plastics. Now plastics manufacturers have changed formulas and altered processes in ways that make recycling feasible—Coke and Pepsi have been sold in recycled plastic bottles since 1990. Steel food cans were once hard to recycle because the small amount of tin they contained (to inhibit rust) contaminated the new steel. Recently manufacturers of steel cans cut tin content to about 0.3 percent, a level that does not cause contamination. Quality control in recycled materials has improved to the point at which the Chicago Board of Options is expected to begin options trading in postconsumer materials. This will legitimize the recycling industry and help operators of recycling plants hedge their supply positions.

Many cities began curbside recycling with cumbersome programs requiring multi-can separation. Most newly designed programs are simple and thus achieve high compliance. In my town of Arlington, Virginia, glass, cans, plastic bottles, and newspapers are placed in a single curbside container. Materials are taken to a sorting center for half-mechanized, half-hand sorting. Some activists are uneasy with convenient curbside systems: Orthodoxy wants recycling to be a burden that punishes the consumer for consuming. But by becoming convenient recycling will grow into a permanent feature of the American lifestyle.

During the 1970s Albany, Chicago, and other cities built complex resource-recovery centers that employed mammoth shredders, huge magnets, wet-slurry separators, and other technological wonders to recycle on an automated basis. All failed, defeated by garbage. The recovery systems that are working are relatively low-cost operations based on scanners and hand sorting. Employment at a recycling center is dusty, noisy work. But recycling is among the few contemporary industries that, rather than substitute capital for labor, has found success substituting labor for capital.

The building success of recycling programs is, in turn, having positive economic consequences for the landfill business—both by making it practical for poorly designed old landfills to close, and by reducing prices at new landfills. Between 1978 and 1988, 14,000 of the 20,000 landfills in the United States shut their gates. This snappy pace of landfill closure is widely depicted in press accounts as some sort of unfolding catastrophe. For instance, a 1992 *Washington Post* editorial declared that "landfills are closing at an alarming rate." That should read: at a reassuring rate. The landfills being shut down are the ones that cannot meet the exacting environmental safety standards the EPA began to impose in the 1980s.

When landfill regulations became strict in the early 1980s, "tipping fees," the price landfill operators charge to take trash, rose as high as $125 a ton in some areas. The price spiral was said to be sure to continue. Instead, since about 1990 tipping fees have declined throughout the country. The fees are falling because supply (landfill space) now exceeds demand (tons of garbage). For example, between 1990 and 1992 the amount of landfill space in the Chicago area not only did not decline to a crisis level, as had been predicted: It increased, according to the Illinois Department of Environmental Protection. "Suddenly everybody wants our trash," Richard Boehm, director of a suburban Chicago planning agency, told the *Chicago Tribune*. The *Tribune* article was about—are you ready?—the GARBAGE SHORTAGE caused by falling landfill fees. As recycling withdraws progressively more trash from the waste stream, landfill "supply" is likely to remain high, and tipping fees low, for decades. Yes: This book even proposes optimism about garbage.[1]

One economic effect of optimistic garbage trends is that many waste-to-energy incinerator plants now experience difficulty obtaining enough garbage, because recyclers are spiriting away garbage and landfill operators are dropping prices. When a waste-to-energy incinerator opened in Huntington, Long Island, in the early 1990s, managers expected to charge $150 a ton to accept refuse. Finding no customers, they gradually dropped the price to $80. This is textbook market economics of the most positive kind. Of course textbook economics may not leave all parties satisfied. In Crosse County, Wisconsin, officials invested in a waste-to-energy incinerator partly on the basis of a report, from the consulting firm Black and Veatch, suggesting the system would always have plenty of garbage arriving at its door. Instead recycling took off: Today the La Crosse incinerator often lacks sufficient charge to run at an optimal level. County officials sued Black & Veatch over its advice, winning a $2.6 million judgment. That's right—it was a GARBAGE SHORTAGE LAWSUIT.

The Jobs Factor

Industrial lobbyists often bemoan that environmental controls cost jobs, but they develop contact amnesia when asked to name actual examples of closed plants. Anthony Picadio, a Pittsburgh lawyer active in environmental cases, offers an instructive example. "When I was a state's attorney in 1970, Pennsylvania passed a state law mandating a 50 percent reduction in industrial air emissions," he says. Picadio was present when Edgar Speer, then president of U.S. Steel (later renamed USX), the leading employer of Pennsylvania, flew to Harrisburg to meet the governor. "Speer swore up and down that U.S. Steel would shut every factory it had in Pennsylvania before it would even try to comply with that law." The threat was idle; the rule was met. "Industry has claimed that kind of thing every step of the way," Picadio said.

There are occasional instances of factories closing owing to environmental crackdowns. For instance through the late 1980s the EPA and state agencies had running battles with a rayon factory in Front Royal, Virginia, owned by a company called Avtex Fibers. The Avtex plant, which lacked modern controls, was then source of an amazing 38 percent of toxic air emissions in Virginia. After a series of false steps, state regulators pulled the plant's emissions permits. Avtex officials shuttered the plant the following day.

The closed Avtex plant has since become one of the country's largest Superfund sites. But Avtex was hopelessly antiquated and likely to close in any case. I toured Avtex shortly after the shutdown: Much of the plant's process equipment was rusting or rotted. Toward the end the company sought exemption from pollution regulation on the grounds that it was the source of an unusual rayon used in the motors of military missiles. But even a special defense classification awarded by Congress failed to keep Avtex afloat. Companies that cannot exist even with sweetheart military contracts are companies doomed regardless of emissions permits. Perhaps some aspect of the overall employment decline in U.S. heavy industrial sectors can be attributed to environmental rules. Yet nearly all economists consider automation to increase productivity, job flight to low-wage countries, labor intransigence on work rules and management self-indulgence to be greater factors.

Do environmental initiatives create new jobs that compensate for those that are lost? Bill Clinton was being giddy when, during the 1992 presidential campaign, he declared that environmental progress would lead to "millions and millions of new jobs." But some jobs clearly have been made. The EPA thinks, for example, that a total of 700 new businesses opened in response to the 1990 Clean Air Act: control engineering firms, manufacturers of hardware, and so on.

In the 1990s it became fashionable among environmentalists and Democrats to assert, by way of the never-ending search for environmental gloom rhetoric, that the United States is losing the international competition for sales of pollution-control technology. Both Clinton and Gore have said that American industry is slipping behind the rest of the world in "the green race." Statistics suggest the reverse. In 1991, U.S. firms exported $362 million in pollution-control devices, a small figure by the standards of global trade but the largest amount recorded by any country. Overall the U.S. balance-of-trade in environmental goods and services was a positive $6 billion in 1991, among the few positives on that ledger. In every year of the 1990s U.S. firms have had the fastest-growing international market share in the green race, better than Germany or Japan. This is a chromed example of an area in which environmental rhetoric is negative when it ought to be positive. Clinton and Gore cannot bring themselves to face goods news in any environmental category: So they emphasize despair, rather than claim an economic victory for liberalism as they should.

Within the United States, conservation has made environmental engineering a high-demand profession. Recycling projects create significant local employment, while the cleanup of Superfund sites and Department of Defense facilities has been a boon to aerospace contractors adjusting to lower military spending. The only important areas where employment and the environment truly are in conflict are in owl protection zones and in tuna fishing. In 1988, U.S. law barred tuna boats from driftnet and purse-seine methods, which kill the dolphin that swim alongside tuna. Today dolphin kills by U.S. tuna boats have all but stopped, declining from 19,700 in 1988 to 800 in 1991. American tuna-fishing employment has declined in concert, the U.S.–registered tuna fleet down from 37 boats in 1988 to just two in 1993.

Though a few economists such as Murray Weidenbaum of Washington University at Saint Louis are skeptical of environmental strictures, no important academic researcher has supported the notion that environmental regulations strangle the economy. Former Office of Management and Budget director Richard Darman often told President George Bush that the Endangered Species Act was a quagmire for the U.S. economy: "Remember," Darman told Bush on the eve of a G7 economic summit in London, "there has never been an environmental regulation that has not hurt the economy." Yet for all the mini-industry that exists among conservative economists in producing studies that attack regulation or extol the free market, no important researcher has zeroed in on the Endangered Species Act as a source of market stagnation, because it is widely assumed the act has no job-dampening impact beyond a few special cases. From 1988 to 1992, federal officials reviewed 34,600 proposed development projects with Endangered Species Act ramifications; they blocked just 23. As John Sawhill, president of the Nature Conservancy, points out, during the same period there were in the United States 29 instances of small aircraft striking buildings. Sawhill says, "This means a developer faced a greater chance of having an airplane crash into something he built than having a project stopped by the Endangered Species Act."

Environmental controls clearly will be seen as a plus for the economy if they are good for international competitiveness. As Michael Porter, a professor at Harvard Business School, wrote in *The Competitive Advantage of Nations,* "Strict environmental regulations do not inevitably hinder competitive advantage against foreign rivals. Nations with the most rigorous requirements often lead in exports of affected products." Porter was criticized by some economists for that statement, though there exists evidence for it: Japan has strict domestic energy policies and perhaps not by coincidence is the world leader in exports of fuel-efficient cars. It is Porter's belief that the principles that make for environmentally benign operation—low-input manufacturing, low waste, recycling of by-products, avoidance of liability—are the same types of efficiencies that confer competitive advantages on all aspects of business operation. New efficiencies forged by environmental strictures will make Western industry capable of continuing to operate without exhausting its resource base or welcome; they will also help prepare Western industry for coming competition with industrial sophistication in the developing world.

Reversing the Preference for Capital

President Clinton has said that environmental technology should become an important export sector for U.S. industry, but it happens that most environmental job creation is likely to occur in domestic industries. This is among the pleasant aspects of environmental economics, and it raises the question of reversing the national obsession with capital over labor.

Throughout the past half-century, tax and fiscal policy in the Western world have encouraged the substitution of capital (equipment) for labor (people). Perhaps this was wise through the early postwar period, when material goods were in short supply, consumer demand was rising, and some economists projected labor shortages. And it is not surprising that capital-based policies to increase industrial output dominate the thinking of governments. Since the beginnings of modern liberal economics in the eighteenth century, a central assumption has been that ever-increasing supplies of goods, made possible in part by capital investments, result in lower prices that render goods affordable to average consumers.

This premise may have run its course. Today most products are in oversupply, while there are painful shortages of desirable jobs. The real-dollar cost of most products has fallen steadily, which is good; but now the ability to acquire the products is declining as jobs in the middle pay scales disappear. According to Economic Policy Institute, real U.S. wages for manufacturing workers, the backbone of the middle class, declined 0.6 percent per annum throughout the 1980s. The minimum wage, $4.25 an hour ($8,500 annually for a full-time worker) today buys less in real terms than it did 30 years ago. These are not signs of social progress. Yet federal policy has not shifted to encourage the substitution of labor for capital.

In *How Much Is Enough?*, Alan Durning addresses what he labels the false choice of "consume or decline." Whatever qualms Westerners may have about the frenetic consumption at the core of developed-country life, most feel that there exists no meaningful choice, given that constant economic expansion is necessary in order for market systems to function. Durning asks: Is this really true?

The worst symptom of "consume or decline" thinking may be infatuation with GNP growth. If food prices go up, that makes the GNP rise. Is society better off? More lawyers, lawsuits, and tort settlements roll into GNP increases. Are these signs of progress? If energy conservation cuts demand for oil, GNP indicators go down. But isn't lower oil consumption good? Seen in this light, the GNP is at best a crude measure of economic progress—perhaps a false measure.

Durning's work shows that "consume or decline thinking disregards the perverse effects of current subsidy and tax systems, which boost resource consumption at the expense of employment." Even the Democrat Clinton, taking office in 1993, proposed for industry an expanded investment tax credit, which encourages substitution of capital for labor. (This proposal was defeated in Congress.) The unceasing focus on capital over labor is a leading explanation for the dilemma of structural unemployment amidst plenty and for ever-lower wages and disposable-worker deals for those not ensconced in the knowledge industries, where fungible foreign labor is (so far) no threat. This trend shows itself most tellingly in unemployment figures for the years when times are *good*. At the height of the 1960s economic boom only 3.4 percent were unemployed in the United States. By 1987, at the peak of the Reagan boom, unemployment was 6.1 percent. Some of that reflects the entry of women into the labor market. Mostly it reflects the capitalist preference—entirely logical, based on the current rule structure—for making people obsolete by switching to acquisition of machinery.

Green economists like to point out that many initiatives that are good for the Earth could also foster new policies of substituting labor for capital. Recycling centers are labor-intensive operations, while their main competitors, waste-to-energy incinerators, are capital-intensive. The centers tend to be located in inner-city areas, where the jobs crunch is worst.

Whether favoring labor over capital will be a boon to the Earth is unclear: In some cases modern technology is cleaner than modern people. But favoring labor would surely be a boon to human beings, which is argument enough for me. Western economic systems now produce ample to satisfy the material needs of consumers. The coming task is to modify those systems to satisfy people's needs for income security, for a percipient pace of life, and for peace of mind. This may ultimately be a greater and more important challenge for the environmental movement than the current fight against pollution.

The Cost of Cost-Benefit

Today a standard assumption among economists is that developed countries should spend one to two percent of their gross domestic products on environmental protection. According to the Organization for Economic Cooperation and Development, a Paris-based organization, the United States leads the world in environmental spending with 1.9 percent of its national income invested in the ecology, up from 1.5 percent in 1972. The smallness of that increase is a testimony to how often environmental initiatives are less expensive than expected, since American ecological regulations have grown far more strict since 1972. Germany ranks second in ecological investment, spending 1.5 percent of its GDP on the environment; the United Kingdom spends 1.3 percent; France and the Netherlands spend 1.2 percent; and Norway brings up the rear among developed countries with 0.8 percent of GDP invested in the environment, less than China.[2] Current U.S. environmental expenditures, the EPA calculates, are about $115 billion per year: about $475 annually per adult and child. Dale Jorgenson, a Harvard economist, estimates the environmental share of GDP may rise to 2.5 percent by the turn of the century, at which point environmental controls may roughly match the level of defense spending some analysts project for that year. In spite of such trends, doomsayers endlessly assert that the United States does not make environmental protection a social priority.

If developed societies spend a more significant portion of their national wealth on environmental controls than supposed, are benefits commensurate with costs? Reconciling environmental costs with benefits will become increasingly important to ecological protection, and it is an essential component of an ecorealist vision.

Cost-benefit analysis has a horrible name reputation on Capitol Hill. This situation dates to the early Reagan Administration. At that time several White House economists, led by an accomplished academic named Christopher DeMuth, attempted to analyze antipollution regulations by assigning a value to lives saved, then computing out pluses and minuses. The grisly business of expressing human life in money numbers may be unavoidable for insurance underwriting but did not sit well with institutional Washington. The project ended with the White House disassociating from it. Since then few economists have been willing so much as to broach the issue of cost-benefit analysis in environmental regulation. Yet such analysis could be a powerful tool of ecological protection. Just because Ronald Reagan liked an idea does not make it bad.

"The real problem with environmental benefit-cost analysis is not putting value on human life," says Paul Portney, an economist at the think tank Resources for the Future. Like many economists he takes pains to say "benefit-cost analysis," to put the pleasant word first. Portney continues, "The real problem is figuring out how many diseases will be avoided or species protected. We can easily get a fix on costs. Costs may be lower than expected, but usually fall within the range studies predict. The benefits can fall all over the map. This tends to bias benefit-cost analysis in the direction of cost."

Researchers have, for example, attempted to affix money-value numbers to future pharmaceutical uses of species, to the future value of ecosystems preserved as tourist attractions, and to the economic uses of forests as "extractive preserves" (as sources of barks and nuts) rather than as logging sites. The results of such studies are figures that shimmer when touched, as opposed to the entirely hard cost numbers for, say, adding electrostatic precipitators to smokestacks.

Beyond that, how can anyone place dollar value on abstract ecological benefits? Partial pollution control might, for example, make the air safe to breathe but leave haze that blocks views of stars on what would otherwise be clear evenings. What is a view of stars worth in dollars? The existence of unspoiled wilderness might have value to a city dweller who has no intention of ever visiting such places; there might be solace simply in the knowledge that such areas still exist and will be available for future generations to experience. Good luck assigning a dollar figure to that. And these examples pertain strictly to the benefit value of nature to humans. Don't make your brain spin by attempting to guess how the value of nature to nature might be computed.

Some environmentalists argue that the solution to this problem is that judges should pick money numbers representing the dollar worth of leaving parts of the ecology as is. Judges were reluctant to perform an act so speculative until, in 1989, a federal appeals court ruled that such numbers could be incorporated into environmental assessments if a mechanism for assigning "contingent value" could be agreed upon by researchers as reliable. Economists and environmental groups are now attempting to invent some contingent-value assessment that courts will find respectable. Early models sound notoriously dreamy: Alaskan authorities, for example, have been trying to generate a contingent-value number for spill damage by retaining polling firms to call people at random and ask how much extra they would spend for gasoline if oil spills could be abolished. Common answer: $30 a year. The question being hypothetical—respondents don't put their money where their mouths are—it is not clear whether judges will accept such studies as a proxy for the benefit side of cost-benefit equations.

Portney, an official of the Council on Environmental Quality during the Carter Administration, has become a prominent advocate of cost-benefit analysis as an ally of environmentalism. Portney generally supports the notion that pollution control produces benefits greater than their costs, suggesting that far from being a drag on the economy, environmental regulation contributes to the national wealth. But Portney parts company with conventional environmental sentiment when it comes to toxic chemicals. He is one of several academic analysts who have begun to say that federal spending on toxic controls generally, and the Superfund cleanup program specifically, diverts money from more pressing ecological concerns. "The goal of rationalizing environmental regulation is greatly handicapped by the fact that people don't want to think logically about risk," Portney says.

Cost-benefit logic in environmental control took a hard hit when Michael Pompili, a health official for Columbus, Ohio, published a report that has circulated widely in policy-making quarters. Pompili estimated that in 1991 Columbus spent $62 million of its $591 million budget to satisfy environmental regulations but that the expenses created only tiny benefits. Columbus then asked Edward Hayes, a researcher at Ohio State, to analyze environmental priorities. Hayes released a report concluding that regulations having to do with chemicals and similar media-obsession issues are often more strict than necessary but that questions of greater long-term concern, such as species and habitat protection, are underfunded. Hayes's conclusions could be an environmental rationalist's litany.

Important reports have reached these conclusions before. In 1988, for example, the policy staff of EPA formed an independent group that was to assess what really matters about environmental protection, regardless of political dictates. The group's report, *Unfinished Business,* outraged environmental lobbies. The analysts placed Superfund sites, a leading doomsday concern, down at number eight in terms of actual risks. Radon, species protection, and stratospheric ozone depletion came out on top. Oil spills and other mediagenic concerns finished low. Three years later, in 1991, the EPA Science Advisory Board issued a similar report, *Reducing Risk: Setting Priorities and Strategies for Environmental Protection.* Here's the science board view:

HIGH RISKS:

Habitat loss
Species extinction
Ozone depletion
Global warming

MEDIUM RISKS:

Agricultural chemicals
Surface water pollution
Acid rain
Airborne toxics

LOW RISKS:

Oil spills
Groundwater pollution
Airborne radioactive particles
Acidic runoff
(mainly from farms)
Thermal pollution
(mainly industrial heat into rivers)

The study further classified smog, workplace exposure to industrial chemicals, indoor pollution (mainly from smoking), and drinking water contamination as important. It classified Superfund sites, dioxin from incinerators and papermaking, and other perennial instant-doomsday issues as unimportant. Noting that polls consistently show low-ranking items on this list, such as toxic wastes and oil spills, as the ones the public considers most dangerous, the Science Advisory Board's report ended with an appeal for a rethinking of environmental regulation based on a detached, rational assessment.

So far that appeal has fallen on covered ears. In 1994 a bill to elevate the EPA to cabinet rank collapsed in the House of Representatives when a majority of members endorsed an amendment that would have required the new Department of the Environment to demonstrate through science that ecological risks are real, and through cost-benefit analysis that regulations are worth the price. Environmental lobbyists themselves fought to scuttle the EPA cabinet-status bill when these amendments were attached. There was some justified fear that the cost-benefit amendment was a Trojan horse out of which would spring legal rulings that undercut conservation. But the real fear on the part of the green lobby was that the amendment would force revisions in questionable programs. Some factions don't want questionable ecological programs reassessed.

Scientists at times assert with a sneer that the corrupt, incestuous political system will never be able to clear its head long enough to compose rationally ordered environmental policy. But as former EPA administrator William Reilly says, "At least it is now acceptable to debate where the real environmental risks and benefits are, which as recently as the late 1980s was a forbidden topic politically." Just 20 years ago, it seemed the same corrupt and incestuous political system would never be able to face the need for basic pollution control measures. Now the enactment of such measures is nearly complete. Moving the political system toward rational, ecorealist thinking will come in turn.

The Pollution Peak

Mikhail Bernstam, an economist at the Hoover Institution of Stanford University, calculates that U.S. pollution output per dollar of GNP has been falling since the end of World War II—well before contemporary environmental regulation began. For instance Bernstam's studies suggest U.S. emissions to the air peaked in 1970 and have been declining since, even as the population and economic output rise. By the year 1986, Bernstam finds, net U.S. air pollution emissions had fallen below the level of the year 1940, though population had increased 82 percent through that period and economic output had gone up 380 percent.

"In the United States," Bernstam says, "energy consumption per dol-

lar of gross national product has been declining at a consistent one percent per year since the year 1929." This means the energy intensity of
the U.S. lifestyle has been going *down* for six decades—though current
energy consumption brings universal central heating, near-universal air-
conditioning, luxurious cars, jet transportation, color television, computers and other power-hungry developments. Trends in other
developed states are about the same, if slightly trailing the United States,
Bernstam finds. For instance in Japan energy consumption per yen of
economic output began falling in 1950 and has been falling since.
Bernstam attributes such patterns to the efficiency of free markets, to the
clean-tech notion that sophisticated machines pollute less than crude
ones, and to simple accumulation of the knowledge necessary to use
resources wisely.

Gene Grossman and Alan Krueger, two Princeton University economists, have come to similar conclusions. Their studies show that countries increase pollution output as GNP climbs toward the level of about
$5,000 per person in constant dollars. Then, as knowledge accumulates
and affluence makes possible investments in emission controls, pollution
begins to decline. The United States passed the $5,000 per-capita income
plateau in the 1940s. The former Soviet states and Mexico are poised at
$5,000 GNP per capita today. Some developing nations are approaching
that level.

Is there within the pattern of industrial development an inherent
Pollution Peak that represents the highest point to which most forms of
environmental harm ever will go? Is that peak already in the past of the
United States and most European nations?

Marx Would Be Disappointed

Orthodox environmental economists reject such thinking. Today the
most accomplished of them is Herman Daly of the University of
Maryland. Daly believes humanity is rapidly expending an inheritance
of "environmental capital," such as petroleum and topsoil, whose abundance causes a deceptive temporary material plenty soon to come to a
crashing halt. Racing through fossil fuel and soil resources that took millions of years to form is, Daly thinks, like withdrawing all your savings
at once; you'll live like a king for a week then have nothing. Daly projects that pollution-control technology would have to improve by twentyfold in the next two decades just to keep things from getting worse;
and of course such a fantastic advance is implausible. Daly has proposed
that society and nature can be rescued by a transition to a "steady state"

economy in which many forms of growth would essentially halt, production would be scaled back, change would be discouraged, and the
level of material affluence would decline.

Something resembling a steady-state economy may eventually yield
benefits to humankind. For now the strange aspect of steady-state economic thinking, embraced in various guises by many environmentalists,
is that it is nothing like what happens in the economy of nature. Nature
is the reverse of the steady state—continuously evolving and altering
relationships. Nature functions roughly along the lines of market economics: New "products" (new genes or new environmental conditions)
are continuously tossed into the system, where creatures respond to
them according to their perceived self-interests. Product lines—species
types—attempt to increase their market shares. Like free economies, the
resulting ecologies engage in almost constant vacillation.

Other gloomy economic notions are open to criticism. For instance
Daly's estimate of a needed twentyfold improvement in pollution control technology is cited by doomsayers to support the idea that there is
no hope for the Earth outside a rapid decrease in production and consumption. Yet during the 1980s, air and water pollution declined steadily in the United States without any implausible leaps in technology.
World emissions of CFCs are declining rapidly toward zero, though only
incremental technical gains in control equipment and substitutes have
been realized.

The assertion that natural-resource capital is being expended is true in
a sense but misses the point. Often projections of disaster are based on
taking existing trend lines and extending them out into the future as if
nothing will ever change: assuming that people's habits and values cannot be altered, while no significant new discoveries remain. *If nothing
changes* in the way society gobbles resources, Daly will be right and a
doom will come calling. But perhaps the only constant on which we can
rely is the constant of change. Once society appeared to be exhausting
firewood at an intolerable rate; then coal; then petroleum. Perhaps 20
years from now it will seem that people are drawing down some other
resource, perhaps deep-ocean cool water, intolerably fast. Twenty years
later it may be something else. So long as innovations continue, so long as
people's values can be reformed, the trend lines will not be omnipotent.

Capitalism: Bad for People, Good for the Environment

There exists a faction of the environmental movement for which the
notion of cost-effective ecological protection, realized through flexible

and efficient market mechanisms, is dreadful news. For this faction conservation is only emotionally satisfying if it involves wrenching sacrifice and dashed expectations: the humbling of the human. In this context the idea that environmental initiatives may be low-cost and run through voluntary mechanisms is anathema—especially the voluntary part, since a portion of the green movement can barely abide the thought that people may cheerfully take pro-ecological actions from their own self-interest, when they might instead be satisfyingly compelled to do so by some top-heavy government agency run by people with correctly pained expressions.

Much to the same extent that some current sentiments of environmentalism spring from the twentieth-century intellectual desire to disprove God, some sentiments of environmentalism spring from intellectual dislike of capitalism. This is not, as the right wing has charged, because environmentalists are closet Marxists. It is rather because most environmentalists are, like me, liberal: And the liberal intellectual tradition carries with it an abiding yearning to stand astride the corpse of capitalism and proclaim the words, "I told you so!"

When the various ends of capitalism Marx thought would arise from labor organizing or financial collapse did not come to pass, a sort of perverse hope was born among liberal intellectuals that environmental and resource issues would replace the proletariat as the agent of capitalism's undoing. Such thoughts cloud the ability of many environmentalists to perceive what appears inarguable in the empirical record: that most economic trends in the developed world now incline in favor of the environment.

Capitalism certainly needs work: I hope that someday it is replaced by a more just and less stressful system of production and distribution. Stepping over the homeless on subway grates, taking detours to avoid the parts of town where schoolchildren die in drug shootouts, Americans are dreaming if they think capitalism is anything other than a transitional phase in pursuit of some method of economic organization that insures the well-being of all members of society. But if there is one thing market economics does infuriatingly well, that is producing lots of whatever it is asked to produce. Now that capitalism increasingly is asked to produce environmental protection, lots is coming.

19 🥬

ENERGY I:
TODAY'S POWER 🥬

THE STRANGEST PLACE I HAVE EVER STOOD, IN A FORTUNATE life that has taken me to such ulterior locales as the freight-loading docks of Dar es Salaam and the cloakroom of the United States Congress, was a penstock at the LaGrande Two hydroelectric power complex near the Arctic Circle in Quebec.

Hundreds of feet underground I looked up into the shaft, wide enough for a subway train, blasted and grooved from a shield of rock millions of years old, that would join the waters of a reservoir above to power turbines below. Shining upward, a strong flashlight beam diffused into a seemingly infinite blackness. Around a corner behind me sat the nearly completed turbine intake, an arrangement of descending curvilinear shapes similar in appearance to a conch. Thousands of hours of computer simulation had gone into the design of the angles in the receiver. Once the frigid waters poised above were released by the two-foot-thick steel doors that restrained them, they would tumble through generators making about as much power as one of the units at Three Mile Island, using a process in some ways more fierce than that which occurs inside a nuclear reactor. I asked my guide if there were any chance some technician would throw the door-open switch by accident. He laughed in an edgy way then almost immediately suggested it might be a good idea to leave. When we emerged into the daylight above it was ten o'clock on a fine sunny morning, and minus-28 degrees Fahrenheit.

The LaGrande Two station is part of the vast James Bay hydropower project under construction in subarctic Quebec. LaGrande is a two-hour jet flight north of Montreal, itself the northernmost metropolis of North America. The James Bay project, which has hewn dozens of dams into a region rich with glacial rivers, already generates about as much power as five Three Mile Island stations. Soon the number will rise to about nine Three Mile Islands. If all the region's hydraulic gradients are tapped, the output of about 25 Three Mile Islands would be realized.

Like other hydropower enterprises, the project burns no fossil fuel and emits no greenhouse gases, smog, or toxic or solid wastes. Older-generation hydropower projects were planned with output and low cost as their goals, the ecology an afterthought. The LaGrande portion of the James Bay complex is among the first hydropower projects to have environmental protection as a formal design criterion ranked with output and cost. LaGrande Two is the first major hydroplant whose power-house—where the generators are—lies entirely underground. This allows the staff to go about in sweaters even when Arctic winds howl. It also means the station is a phantom on the landscape, little more than a small ridgeline with two tall red doors that appear portals into solid rock.

Other environmental precautions were taken. Before each sequence of blasting to form the waterfall shafts, engineers pumped high-pressure bubbles into the surrounding waters to frighten away fish.[1] Transformers in the powerhouse use mineral oil for insulation rather than PCBs; the transformers sit on sloped gravel basins as a built-in containment device against spills. Though many subarctic rivers have been diverted to fill the project's reservoirs, plans to tamper with one large river, the Nastapoca, were abandoned when it was suggested a species of freshwater seal that feeds at the mouth of the Nastapoca might be harmed by a reduction in water volume.

Caribou were expected to be devastated by reservoir flooding at James Bay. Instead since the project began local caribou populations have increased from about 200,000 to about 800,000. No one knows exactly why: Perhaps the roads built for construction access favor caribou migration, perhaps the population growth would have happened regardless. Transmission lines from the project across the Saint Lawrence River are among the world's first underwater power cables, so no towers spoil vistas of the Saint Lawrence. When the underwater lines were completed, piers that held towers for temporary lines were removed so as to pose no obstacle to migratory cod. In sum it is difficult to conceptualize a large power project having less impact on the ecology.

What do environmentalists think of the James Bay project? They despise it. The National Audubon Society has called the dams as bad as the burning of the Amazon rainforests, and has lobbied for laws to prohibit U.S. utilities from buying James Bay power. Greenpeace has called the project "genocide" and mounted a boycott of tourism to Quebec. Numerous other American and European environmental groups have staged protests against the James Bay project in Washington, Montreal, Brussels, at the Rio conference, and elsewhere.

Most of this chapter will be devoted to supporting the notion that institutional environmentalism is right about the need to propel society beyond its fixation on fossil fuels. When the Oil Age ultimately ends—and that's not far off—environmentalists will be richly praised for having been farsighted on the centrality of renewable energy. Lest the text suddenly turn too admiring, however, let's start with a subject area in which environmental sentiment regarding energy is all wrong: the requirement for basic production.

It is sanctimonious for any environmentalist who owns an automobile, or lives in a heated home, or works in an air-conditioned office, or flies in a jetliner to Washington or Montreal to protest construction at James Bay, to begrudge the production of energy. No matter how successful conservation initiatives may be, on the whole the globe needs a major push for new power-production systems. In the Western world, new generation systems are required to replace dirty, inefficient older plants with plants having clean, lower-input designs. In the Third World hundreds of new power facilities are needed to satisfy the basic requirements of the globe's vast underclass, only a small percentage of which today enjoys the electrification taken for granted in developed nations. Unless the world's downtrodden are to remain down and trodden, global energy production must go up.

Beyond this there is no fundamental conflict between the production of energy and the protection of the Earth. Twenty years ago energy was universally considered a guaranteed sure-thing no-way-out doomsday. Today Americans steadily use less energy, spend less on energy and pollute less with energy. The clipped pace of progress in converting energy from a brute-force to clean-tech pursuit ought to provide a model for guarded optimism in other industrial arenas.

Yet many environmentalists think that in order to be proconservation, they must be antiproduction. Orthodoxy has grown so conflicted on the subject of energy production that some greens have pronounced that even if an entirely benign energy source is invented it should be withheld, since people would use that energy to commit the primal sin of altering the ecology. During the period when it briefly seemed "cold fusion" might offer zero-pollution energy from seawater, Jeremy Rifkin declared clean, unlimited energy would be "the worst thing that could happen to our planet."

The notion of energy production as antithetical to nature evinces a myopic view of natural history. In a sense the 3.8-billion-year span of the development of life has been about finding ways to employ energy as a tool to build living complexity out of the undifferentiated blur that was the initial condition of the planet. Without controlled use of energy, complexity cannot happen. For genus *Homo* to pursue the production of energy is not an affront to nature; it is the continuation of an eons-long effort to vest life with the means of sustaining itself and perhaps ultimately of expanding into areas where spontaneous forces alone are not sufficient.

Here it is appropriate to introduce an important ecorealist premise: *making it through the transition.* In many areas of environmental protection, trends point in the direction of progress. The worry is the next few decades—the period of transition from brute-force human relations with nature to the cautious and respectful relationship that is emerging. On energy, so long as society can get through the next few decades without greenhouse emissions running wild, a clean and renewable future should unfold.

For this reason ideas like a pollution-free hydropower project in Quebec ought to seem wonderful, even if, like all human endeavors, they create their share of problems. Some detail on why institutional environmentalism has turned against the clean energy embodied in hydropower will help shed light on the movement's conflicted ideas about energy production.

Damophobia

Three green objections to the James Bay project are raised: that conservation would be cheaper, the native peoples are being trampled, that environmental horrors are in progress. The first two objections hold water, as it were. The third does not.

There exists a mountain of evidence that for the moment conservation technology can offset the need to produce electricity much more cheaply than new capacity can generate power. Utilities in New York State have been canceling contracts to buy James Bay power. This has happened partly in response to environmentalist pressure, partly because the utilities realize that offsetting power through conservation is at the moment better fiscal policy than power imports.

As regards the desires of natives, the James Bay project is equally suspect. About 11,000 Cree and 7,000 Inuit ("Eskimos") live in the gigantic watershed of the system: a land area, most of it permafrost, larger than Alaska. The Inuit, who have friendly relations with Montreal and Ottawa, generally support the James Bay project. The Cree, whose relations with Canadian government are acrimonious, generally oppose hydropower.

The Cree probably came to subarctic Quebec several centuries ago, fleeing persecution by other Native American tribes and by European settlers. The Cree ancestors seem to have felt that if they accepted for their people a life of frozen hardship in a forbidding place, they could be assured no one would ever again come knocking on their doors demanding land. Now exactly that has happened. In 1975 Cree leaders signed an agreement with Montreal granting Hydro Quebec, a crown corporation owned by the provincial government, the right to proceed with James Bay; in return the Cree accepted money, subcontractor positions on the project, and other inducements. Cree leader Mathew Coon Come has since repudiated that agreement, though the Cree continue to take the money.

With the arrival of Hydro Quebec tuberculosis, long a scourge of Cree villages, has been routed by modern medicine. Infant mortality is down, Cree homes are now pleasantly warm through the long winter, and most Cree now hunt from snowmobiles or Chevy Blazers rather than on foot. There is no doubt this means the old Cree way is ending. For centuries the Cree subsisted by trapping alone or in small groups under conditions of unimaginable trial. "I know one old Cree who still does it, paddles 480 kilometers up the river every winter, takes him 45 days just to get to his trap line," says Richard Baxter, an official for LaGrande Two. "No motors, no heaters, no firearms, no radio. Just him against the cold." You would not endure such a test if a heated vehicle were available, and most young Cree feel the same way. This may be the final generation in which human beings attempt traditional Cree trap-line hunting.

The Audubon Society often says the James Bay project will "alter an area the size of France," suggesting all of the Cree's hunting grounds will end up underwater. Large as they are, James Bay's power reservoirs will flood only three percent of Cree hunting grounds. The "altered" area of the Audubon Society claim is arrived at by counting up the entire James Bay watershed, only a tiny portion of which will actually contain a reservoir. Is a natural watershed "altered" by the fact that its runoff eventually flows into a power turbine dozens or hundreds of miles downstream? This is like saying that building an amphitheater in a park "alters" the entire park.

Environmentalists extol the traditional Cree lifestyle in the abstract but gloss over it in the specific. The indigenous Cree economy is based on trapping fur animals, an action green sentiment opposes whenever whites are involved. Cree and Inuit hunters club harp seals to death, a practice rightly found cruel in every other context. One reason many Cree have been tempted by James Bay work is that environmentalist pressure has caused the fur market to collapse. In the 1960s, beaver pelts sold for $50 dollars; today the price rarely exceeds ten dollars. Whether a traditional way of life based on killing animals and hunters who suffer in the frozen wild should be sustained is something only the Cree can answer for themselves. But the retreat from the outside world that a small nation of fearless souls once knew in subarctic Quebec is no longer assured, and that may be a cause to mourn.

Some ecological objections to the James Bay project are strained to the point of deception. For example opponents attach high significance to the fact that in the Canadian shield, flooding land turns an inactive form of mercury naturally present in soil into a poisonous form that may enter the aquatic food chain. Rarely mentioned, however, is that the mercury activation is temporary and seems to have little effect on local fish species, perhaps because they have genetic resistance to it: the soil mercury occurring naturally, creatures of the Canadian shield have been exposed to it for millennia. Through the past decade Cree villagers who eat fish have been regularly tested for mercury, through a simple procedure that involves snipping a lock of hair. No Cree has ever shown a cellular mercury above the World Health Organization safety level.

Hydro power requires flooding land for reservoirs, a practice environmentalists speak of in tones of deep horror, as though it wipes out life. Plants and animals do die when the reservoir waters rise, and some wild-river ecology is lost. But what then exists? A lake ecology, brimming with living things. "People think a reservoir is a liquid desert," says Gaetan Hayeur, a James Bay environmental official. "Nobody ever says that about a lake. If you propose draining a lake, environmentalists will say that would cause a shocking loss of valuable habitat. But if you propose making a reservoir, which is a lake, they say the reverse."

In subarctic Quebec, lakes are in some ways more hospitable to life than land. In traditional Cree society, a trap line hunted by a kin structure of around 75 people is at least 600 square miles, because even such a large area supports only a limited number of game animals, the territory being so harsh on life. Larger numbers of Cree may fish a smaller area, however, subarctic waters often being rich with aquatic creatures.

So in a sense when Hydro Quebec floods the frigid James Bay land, it acts in favor of life. But it is a life that differs from what is already there. That is the real environmental complaint about hydropower: It causes change. Even should the entire 50,000-megawatt potential of James Bay be tapped, most of the region would remain what it was when Europeans first saw it, an ecology of wild rivers mixed with subarctic tundra. But there would be change. Rather than exhibit annual cycles of flood and drought, some of the rivers would flow consistently. (Consistent river volume is unnatural in the James Bay region; it favors some subarctic species.) And some of James Bay would be not wild rivers but placid lakes brought about through action by design.

Why such change should dismay humans would be difficult for nature to fathom. Nature has rearranged the hydraulics of the James Bay region dozens of times and is certain to rearrange them again. Through glacial advances and retreats nature has made and unmade uncountable rivers, lakes, and dams in what people now call Quebec. Why is it strange for women and men to do the same, especially if they can learn to do it in ways calculated to minimize harm? And the change brought to James Bay is reversible. Suppose someday the power from James Bay is no longer required. The project's dams can then be removed, just as nature has often removed its own dams in the region. The tundra and wild-river ecology will reassert itself.

In several parts of North America, conservationists now propose to perform this very trick. United States law requires that some 200 inefficient small hydrodams dating from the turn of the century be relicensed in the 1990s. American Rivers, a thoughtful environmental organization, advocates that many such dams be taken out. The wild rivers these dams block, American Rivers says, will rapidly reassert themselves and live again as they did before engineers eyed them. Surely they will. Where's the difference between that and what might happen at James Bay?

A leading current campaign of institutional environmentalism is to block hydrodam construction in the Third World. For instance, United States and European ecology organizations have pressured the World Bank to abandon support for Three Gorges dam, a Chinese project that would control the Yangtze River plain, where some 200,000 peasants have died in floods in this century. Three Gorges would generate 18,000 megawatts of clean, renewable power. It would also submerge much of a region of majestic scenery often called the Grand Canyon of China.

There are reasons to be wary of Third World hydro projects, mainly the mistreatment of displaced peasants that often occurs. But some lives of the poor are saved by such projects, as natural flooding is controlled. If the Three Gorges canyons must be submerged to save lives and to make clean power, would nature consider that so terrible? Nature may submerge Three Gorges at some point anyway; the region has been underwater before geologically, at least several times. Power dams will help the developing world handle the transition, making it through the next few decades until population stabilizes and fossil fuel alternatives become more practical. Once those things have happened, perhaps the Three Gorges dams can be removed.

Damophobia reflects the Fallacy of Stop in Place. If only society would keep its hands off the land, this fallacy holds, then nothing would change. *Dark Safari,* a 1991 book by John Bierman, quotes the eighteenth-century Kiowa chief White Bear as telling a group of European settlers attempting to persuade him of the benefits of their version of life, "I don't want any of these medicine homes [schools] built in the country. I want the papooses brought up exactly as I am." This is a perfect expression of the human desire to Stop in Place. Yet this desire, which environmentalists promote as honoring nature, is among the most artificial notions genus *Homo* has introduced on the Earth. Nature would find it unfathomable.

The Cree may have had a 300-year interlude in which they hunted a lonely region as they wished. Now that changes, as it was fated to change whether power dams were built or not. The government of Quebec may enjoy an interlude in which it produces valuable power, and that someday may change. Abstaining from the production of energy will not bring an end to change—just leave people less comfortable while it happens anyway.

Why Nature Would Like Offshore Oil

Of all human activities fossil-fuel combustion is by far the greatest cause of pollution. Someday the Oil Age will be viewed as one of humanity's transitional phases between the brute-force and the clean-tech approaches to life. Fossil fuels themselves will be viewed as a sort of IQ test that the past left for the future: Are you smart enough to learn how to use this stuff, and are you smart enough to stop?

This said, it is equally true that society has no option but to continue to extract and burn fossil fuels in large quantities over the next few decades, until a renewable-energy economy is realized. Though the long-term trend for fossil fuels is sure to be down, the short-term trend is sure to be up.

Environmental orthodoxy has as much trouble with this inescapable conclusion as it does with all conclusions about energy production. Consider the intensity of green opposition to oil exploration. Pressure from environmentalists has in the United States brought about legal moratoriums on offshore oil prospecting on the California and New England coasts. Offshore drilling has also declined in Europe where, for instance, in 1993 a ship belonging to the Norwegian environmental group Bellona blocked some planned exploration drilling in the Barents Sea.

Opposition to offshore oil extraction is intense despite the fact that such production along the Gulf Coast and north of the United Kingdom has proven among the cleanest and least disruptive means by which any resource has ever been extracted from the Earth. The presence of oil rigs may mar coastal aesthetics, an important negative consequence for people. But this entirely artificial consideration has no meaning to nature, which would surely prefer that oil extraction take place offshore, disturbing only the wavering surface of the sea, than onshore, disrupting a forest or savannah. When prospectors drill on the continental shelf, no forests or prairie are trampled by trucks. The rigs sit in water that is in continuous physical turmoil anyway.

Studies show that contemporary methods of offshore drilling have no meaningful downside for marine life. For example, mollusk life in the immediate area of a rig usually continues normally. Some spills have happened, such as a 1969 rupture from a Union Oil platform near Santa Barbara that released 3.2 million gallons, about a third the level of the *Exxon Valdez* spill. But spills from oil rigs have become infrequent in recent years as regulation has become strict. *Golob's Oil Pollution Bulletin* has reported that in 1991 only 55,000 gallons were spilled in U.S. waters, the lowest amount since 1978. Secondary environmental harm from oil rigs is in the process of being eliminated as well. Alabama, for instance, already holds rigs in its coastal waters to a zero-discharge standard. Mobil, currently drilling for natural gas off Dauphin Island, Alabama, not only transports all rig wastes back to shore for controlled disposal, it even collects and returns to shore rainwater from the platform's decks, since rain sometimes mingles with spilled oils. Not every oil rig operates to that high standard, but most are gradually being pushed to it.

Opposition to most forms of onshore oil extraction is strong too, though the environmental effects of acquiring oil are at worst moderate. Drilling for oil essentially pokes a hole in the Earth. Abandoned wells improperly capped may serve as conduits for the movement of brine and other pollutants. But when wells are capped properly, at the end of an oil project there is little visible effect on nature: very different from, say, the mining of coal, which displaces huge quantities of rock. Most ecological harm caused by drilling comes from road construction and the tracks of vehicles, effects prospectors are learning to control. Recent oil exploration in the Wasatch National Forest of Utah has gone relatively smoothly, with only minor damage to the local ecology.

Through the early 1990s environmentalists fought with great vigor a proposal to open the Alaska National Wildlife Refuge to oil prospecting. The Wilderness Society calls this place "America's Serengeti." The metaphor is apt, since ANWR is too far north to be a forest; mosses and low shrubs are its main vegetation. The area spends up to nine months per year under snowpack. Exploration in the ANWR would have occurred along its coastal plain, a zone representing less than one percent of the refuge's acreage, in order to minimize intrusive effects such as roads and pipelines. Oil exploration in the ANWR was prohibited in 1992 by an act of Congress. Part of me cheered that decision, since if it turns out in some future year that ANWR's oil is needed, drill rigs can always go north then. But part of me knew that the same environmental lobbyists who fought to have ANWR exploration outlawed would be outraged if asked to surrender their own access to cheap and plentiful gasoline.

Given tighter regulation and increasing understanding of nature, any Alaskan oil exploration conducted in the future ought to proceed with less environmental disruption than was caused by the Prudhoe Bay project and its pipeline; and it's hard to see how Prudhoe Bay did much harm. Some of that project's North Slope area is now defaced by "toxic popsicles," frozen drilling wastes about whose disposal swirls a legal controversy. That is the only notable ill effect. The Central Arctic caribou herd, which lives around the pipeline, was expected to be wiped out. Instead its numbers have increased sevenfold since Prudhoe Bay began. Whether this happened because "the caribou snuggle up against the pipeline," in the memorably loopy phrase of George Bush, is not known. Like the unknown of why caribou expanded following James Bay construction, many natural wilderness population trends are poorly understood. But no ecological horror has come from Prudhoe Bay or its pipeline.

Gordon Orians, an ecologist at the University of Washington, makes an intriguing point about the aftermath of the Alaska pipeline. Probably the wildlife there is all right, he says. No one can be sure because it hasn't been studied. "The sides in an Environmental Impact Statement war like the one that preceded the Alaska pipeline may spend millions of dollars tossing computer projections at each other," Orians says. "The moment the decision is made the funding stops. There is no ongoing study of what happens in the real environment, which is the issue of genuine interest." Orians thinks this is so because "both sides have a vested interest in not finding out what actually happens when people interact with nature. In environmental affairs there is a tremendous constituency for ignorance." Oil companies fear follow-up studies of the pipeline might show that harm was done. Orthodox environmentalists fear such studies might show harm was not done. Orians thinks the National Environmental Policy Act, the bill that created the environmental impact statement, should be amended to require long-term studies of the actual effects of development projects, "so that in the next century we can start making these decisions on the basis of something other than computer guesswork."

Robert Kennedy, Jr., an attorney for the Natural Resources Defense Council, has had an unhappy experience with anti-oil pressure in Ecuador. There, in a deep Amazon area known to mapmakers as Block 16, Conoco wanted to drill for oil. Conoco asked Kennedy and the NRDC to design environmental safeguards for the project and to negotiate with indigenous people. Conoco assented to every stricture Kennedy proposed, including few Americans at the site, all toxics and drilling wastes to be shipped out of the Amazon, minimal road construction, and conservation profits to locals. The local Indian population agreed to the plan. Then Conoco withdrew from the project when other environmental groups announced they would stage a national boycott against Conoco gasoline, saying the company was raping the rainforest.

Himself a career environmentalist, Kennedy accused other environmentalists of hypocrisy for demanding that Conoco withdraw, noting that the exploration will go forward anyway—but without the big-company oversight or a good deal for the Indians. "We have about as much chance of persuading Ecuador to stop drilling Amazon oil as we do of persuading Americans to stop driving cars," Kennedy has said. Maxus Ecuador, a venture with Taiwanese funding, took over the Block 16 project. Ever heard of Maxus Ecuador? Any idea how to pressure its board of directors for responsible behavior? "Oil drilling is much less damaging to a rainforest than cattle grazing or agriculture," Kennedy notes. In 1988, in a similar turn of events, U.S. environmentalist pressure caused Scott Paper to withdraw from a proposed tree farm in Indonesia, one for which safeguards and indigenous involvement had been agreed. After Scott left, the project went ahead under local supervision with "much more ambitious and destructive plans," Kennedy says, minus involvement for Indians.

Of course oil projects in developing countries can be harmful. Mexico's Lacandon rainforest has become a minor wild-west boom zone as Pemex, the state petroleum firm, pumps oil there. With the boom has come both some rainforest loss and the crime and broken families that are parcel to sudden movements of money. On the other hand Chevron has been able to prospect for oil in Papua, New Guinea, with few reported problems. Chevron began its project, at Lake Kutubo, flying most personnel and supplies in and out via helicopter in order to avoid laying a road that Western environmentalists opposed. But the local Namoaporo wanted the road; they had been petitioning the government for one for years. So Chevron built a road to Lake Kutubo, an outcome especially annoying to institutional environmentalism: both the arrival of the asphalt and the fact that an indigenous people longed for this materialist trapping.

Why Nature Would Like Exploration for Gas

Continuing oil exploration is mainly a stopgap till renewable fuels become practical. The situation in natural gas is different, however. Here exploration may not just keep stocks up but lead to important reductions in pollution, making the remaining decades of the fossil fuel era easier ones for the Earth.

Natural gas is the cheapest fossil fuel, selling for about two-thirds the equivalent price of oil, and the cleanest fossil fuel. Most natural gas has a simple chemical formula of four atoms of hydrogen plus one of carbon, with none of the sulfur and other pollutants found in petroleum and coal. The higher the fuel's "hydrogen ratio"—the number of hydrogen atoms compared to everything else—the more energy is released per emission of by-product. At four, hydrogen has the best hydrogen ratio of any fossil fuel. Coal usually has a hydrogen ratio of less than one, meaning more atoms that don't burn than atoms that do. Because natural gas has only one carbon atom per molecule, its greenhouse contribution per BTU produced is about one-sixth that of coal and one-half that of petroleum. Because natural gas contains no sulfur it causes no acid rain. When natural gas "spills" during exploration or extraction, nothing happens. For such reasons Christopher Flavin, an energy analyst at the Worldwatch Institute, calls natural gas "the perfect fuel." He notes that building more natural gas systems will be a long-term bargain because such infrastructure could be converted to hydrogen, a zero-emission fuel, if hydrogen becomes practical in the next century.

World gas use has roughly doubled since 1970, with most new power plants under construction in the United States gas-fired. Nevertheless natural gas exploitation is not expanding as rapidly as its low price and pollution-control properties might suggest. The reason is that industrial customers remain spooked by the spurious natural gas shortages of the mid-1970s. At that time Washington was attempting fitfully to control energy prices, and a perverse situation existed in which producers selling gas inside the borders of states could charge the market rate, but gas shipped to other states had to be sold at a federally controlled price sometimes below production cost. As a result customers in Texas and Louisiana had enough gas to last them till the Lord's return, but in New York and Massachusetts shortages developed during the cold winters of the mid-1970s.

The counterfeit 1970s gas shortage was mistaken by policy makers as an indication that natural gas supplies were depleted. In 1978 James Schlesinger, then secretary of energy, declared that natural gas reserves were "gone." In response Congress passed one of the all-time wrongheaded pieces of legislation, the Fuel Use Act. It forbade construction of new power plants that burn natural gas and required many existing gas users to switch to coal—the fuel most responsible for the greenhouse effect and acid rain. The following year, 1979, President Jimmy Carter decontrolled energy prices. Immediately supplies of the "gone" natural gas flooded pipelines. Gas exploration had slowed during the period when producers were required to sell at below cost; once prices moved to market levels, such exploration rebounded. Today world gas reserves are twice what they were in the 1970s, even though annual use has doubled. Abounding supply in turn keeps natural gas prices low.

The Fuel Use Act has been repealed, but commercial customers remain wary. "I'm switching to gas at several power plants and I'd like to switch more," says Lynn Draper, president of American Electric Systems of Ohio, one of the largest U.S. utilities. "But I'm suspicious. Oil has been tight but you've always been able to get a tanker full by making a phone call. Coal supplies appear impossible to exhaust. Gas is the one fuel that there's been a problem with during my lifetime." Some gas producers say, not in jest, that the trouble with their product is that it's invisible. The fleet of supertankers circling the world lends visual evidence to the existence of huge amounts of thick, substantial petroleum. And anyone can stand in a colliery such as the gigantic Black Thunder Junction mine in Wyoming and behold hard, dark fuel for as far as the eye can see. Gas, on the other hand, is physically insubstantial. Properly handled it is neither seen nor smelled.

Various theories hold that dinotherian amounts of natural gas may be present in deep-rock formations, in pressurized brines of the Gulf of Mexico, and along the ocean floor in a form called gas hydrates. Not all such deposits may produce gas at attractive prices. But, the U.S. Geological Survey has estimated, as many as two centuries worth of gas at about current prices may be waiting to be found, along with perhaps a thousand years' worth available with future technology or at higher prices. Since estimates of fossil fuel reserves have always proved lower than what is actually found, this offers reason to believe that society can move confidently toward increased natural gas combustion—making gas "the perfect fuel" for the global transition to a renewable energy future.

Why Coal Makes Uranium Look Good

Today coal is replacing uranium as the chief energy malefactor. Coal mining leaves gashes in the Earth. Coal combustion produces greenhouse gases, acid rain, and smog precursors, along with mountains of ash. Rafe Pomerance, once an official of the World Resources Institute, and under Clinton the deputy assistant secretary of state with jurisdiction over environmental negotiations, has said that "coal burning is a fundamental threat to life on this planet. We'll eventually have to fight over every coal-powered electric plant."

That will be quite a fight, as coal now supplies about 55 percent of U.S. electricity, versus about 18 percent for nuclear, 14 percent for hydro, and about 14 percent for oil, gas, and renewables combined. The portion of U.S. power that is supplied by coal has steadily risen in the past two decades, in response to low prices and America's status as "the Saudi Arabia of coal." Yet despite coal's environmental defects, more prospecting may be a sound ecological idea. Here's why.

First, too much coal is obtained from underground mines, which are dangerous to workers and contain mainly high-sulfur coal. During the 1980s, 656 people were killed in the United States in accidents at underground mines, versus 155 deaths at surface ("strip") mines, though the surface mines produced twice the volume of coal. Each year dozens to hundreds of underground miners become ill with black-lung disease and other respiratory conditions that do not occur among miners who labor in the open. Imagine for a moment the conditions faced by workers even in modern underground mines—stooped over and hacking away at rocks in dank and sunless passages, breathing recirculated air and wearing dogtags so their bodies can be identified after an explosion or cave-in. At surface mines workers are outside in fresh air and perform most excavations sitting in the cabs of dragline cranes and other large machines that cannot fit into mines. In which of the two types of mines would you rather work? If 656 workers had died in nuclear plants during the 1980s, every reactor in the country would be padlocked by now. If nuclear plants emitted anything like the greenhouse gases or acid rain caused by high-sulfur underground coals, again every reactor station would be shuttered. Yet somehow the underground coal mining business rolls on.

So the first reason for new coal exploration would be to find new surface mines that could replace the underground mines that ought to be closed. Some strip mine operators have a dismal record of failing to restore old mines, and the federal Office of Surface Mining has been lax in enforcing the 1977 law that mandates such restoration; in Kentucky, for example, only about ten percent of old surface mines have been restored. But most of the abandoned strip mines are small mines in the East, especially around the Cumberland Mountains, where small operators traditionally have flouted many laws because backwoods mines can be concealed from inspectors. In the West, where surface mines are generally large operations in the open, compliance records are better.

The second reason for a new commitment to coal prospecting is that, though technical efforts to devise "clean coal" have so far yielded modest results, nature may have already accomplished this goal. In the late 1980s an Indonesian coal company called A.T. Adaro found a surface vein of nearly sulfur-free coal, one containing just 1.5 percent as much sulfur as the best American coals. Since this discovery many Western buyers have shown interest in the coal, which will allow power plants to meet acid rain restrictions without smokestack scrubbers.

Russell Seitz, a resource analyst at Harvard University, examined samples of the superpure Indonesian coal and noticed something else: It has a higher hydrogen ratio than any previously known coal. This means it produces less greenhouse gas. "For all we know there may be billions of tons of this kind of coal, and not just in Indonesia," Seitz says, since with prices low and coal in oversupply, there has been "almost no coal prospecting in the United States in the past 30 years." The Indonesia find came in a place whose geology is not of the type normally associated with coal. This suggests that if coal exploration were to resume in unconventional venues, prospectors might find clean coal. A supposedly intractable environmental problem, the greenhouse output of coal, might become quite tractable.

The Conservation Ethic

In a 1976 article in *Foreign Affairs,* the physicist Amory Lovins declared that conservation could reduce energy needs so spectacularly that not only would oil not run out but energy prices would *decline.* The article appeared when energy doomsaying was the height of fashion: There were complaints the august *Foreign Affairs* had gone off its rocker to dignify such dreamworld contentions. Lovins was widely reviled by The Experts.

Today Lovins's forecast seems if anything timid. Conservation has happened faster than he predicted: Total U.S. energy use per constant dollar of GNP has declined 28 percent since 1976. The energy-intensity of U.S. heavy industry has declined 50 percent since 1978. Because energy demand has slackened, in 1994 gasoline was selling for less in real-dollar terms than in 1940. When Lovins wrote his article, 3.2 percent of the typical household budget went to energy. By 1993 the figure was down to 2.6 percent and still falling. In 1972 the average car consumed 785 gallons of gasoline per year. By 1988 average consumption was down to 507 gallons, though that car was traveling many more miles. Lovins's success at outpredicting an entire legion of The Experts suggests this rule of thumb: To become a specialist one must occasionally be wrong, to become an authority one must often be wrong, and to become an Expert one must always be wrong.

Today Lovins predicts new energy savings in some ways more outlandish than those he foresaw in 1976, because the energy efficiency trends that began with gasoline are now catching up with electricity. Growth in demand for electricity, running at three to four percent annually in the 1970s, has slowed to two percent or less, with declines experienced in some parts of the country. Lovins thinks the United States could support its industrial base and lifestyle using just 30 percent of its current electric-generating capacity, with the conservation investment required available at a long-term cost of one cent a kilowatt-hour, far less than the typical price of six cents for new generating capacity. If the country operated on 30 percent of current generating capacity, all coal and nuclear power stations could shut down.

Lovins proposes not sacrifice but technical advances and market efficiency: In his phrase, Americans would still enjoy "hot showers and cold beers." Wishful thinking? Consider this example from Duke Power, a North Carolina utility. In 1974 the typical Duke residential customer had a 1,000-square-foot dwelling with no air conditioner, no color television, and no frost-free refrigerator. By 1992 the typical Duke Power customer had 1,250 square feet of air-conditioned space, two color televisions, and a frost-free fridge—yet was using slightly less electricity than in 1974. This improvement had occurred strictly in response to technology improvements and market logic, without any coordinated efficiency drive.

The Electric Power Research Institute, the think tank of the utility industry, spent much of the 1980s churning out studies to refute Lovins. Late in the 1980s EPRI reversed itself, announcing Lovins was right:

Today it projects that U.S. lifestyles and production could be supported with about 70 percent of current power use. At EPRI's conservation level, something like half of all coal-fired power stations could be closed down.

Much of the savings would be realized by a new utility philosophy with the cumbersome name "demand-side management." Traditionally utilities raised profits by encouraging customers to buy more power; the utility that advocated conservation would practically violate its fiduciary responsibility to shareholders. By the second clash with OPEC in 1979 ever-more power use, which entails ever-more fuel combustion, no longer seemed synonymous with progress. The public utility commissions that regulate utility requests for new power-generation capacity (the supply) began at the urging of Lovins and others to ask utilities first to render their customers (the demand) as efficient as possible, then let production decline to the level buyers truly need. Hence demand-side management, or DSM. Regulations were redrawn so that utilities and customers essentially would split the profits from avoided fuel use, giving power companies a financial incentive to promote the plans.

Most utilities now have DSM efforts. Consolidated Edison, which serves New York City, is investing $4 billion in conservation. Pacific Gas & Electric of northern California, a growth region, says it will build no new power plants for at least a decade, expecting to accommodate all new customers with conservation from present accounts. Jonathan Rowe, president of New England Electric System, a Massachusetts utility, reports that the DSM division is the most profitable in his company.

The coming of demand-side management to electric power has caused a spectacularly rapid decline in electric power–growth projections. William McCollum, president of the Edison Electric Institute, trade association of the utility industry, predicted in 1990 that the United States would require 72,000 megawatts of new generating capacity, about 35 Three Mile Island stations, by the year 2000. Demand fell so spectacularly that now just a few thousand new megawatts are expected to be completed. In 1989, as DSM efforts were picking up steam, an industry group called the American Electric Reliability Council predicted that power brownouts would come to New England by 1993 at the latest. The Northeast Utilities Association, a speculators' venture, was formed to buy "long" contracts to deliver power, anticipating nice profits when the New England electricity crunch hit. Instead by 1993 electricity was wholesaling in New England for 2.5 cents per kilowatt hour, half the prevailing price of a few years before. Oversupply caused power rates to residential consumers to decline in the

Atlantic seaboard states for the first time in half a century. The Northeast Utilities Association filed for bankruptcy protection.

Conservation as Fun

Some researchers remain skeptical that electricity consumption can be cut substantially at low net cost. Paul Joscow, an economist at the Massachusetts Institute of Technology, believes Lovins's forecasts off "by a factor of two to ten. Conservation costs are much higher than he assumes." Margaret Fels, a Princeton University analyst, has studied some DSM efforts and finds they typically yield about half the expected benefits. Fels also notes what might be called the lights-on factor. "When the workers in a factory or office hear that the company has installed superefficient lighting," she explains, "they leave the lights on all night, because they think it doesn't matter anymore."

Conservation projections do sometimes gloss over the tyranny of the practical. For instance nearly half of U.S. electricity is consumed by process motors in factories. Most existing process motors are single-speed models that spin out more horsepower than required. Lovins estimates that any factory replacing its process motors with high-efficiency variable-speed models could pay back its capital cost in just 15 months, then enjoy energy savings ad infinitum. If every single-speed U.S. process motor was replaced with a variable-speed model, Lovins thinks, 80,000 megawatts of generating capacity would no longer be needed. This would be sufficient to close nearly all existing nuclear plants.

Variable-speed process motors are selling but only gradually, despite the well-known corporate interest in cutting costs. Richard Johnson, a vice president of Carolina Power and Light, another North Carolina utility, explains why: "We find businesses very interested in variable-speed motors when they are renovating. But if a process motor is in place, working, and has years remaining on its capitalization, few companies will start tearing out walls." Replacing major process equipment often puts a factory out of commission for weeks.

There are similar problems with the compact-fluorescent light bulb. These odd-looking bulbs use just 25 percent as much power as incandescent bulbs and last ten times as long. Despite such virtues there is no stampede to compact fluorescents, as they cost up to $15 each. Even at $15 each a light bulb may make financial sense. If I replaced all incandescent bulbs in my home with compact fluorescents, the capital cost would be about $1,000. At the kilowatt-hour rate charged by my utility

I would save about $800 a year on lighting plus another $200 in avoided air-conditioning. (Up to 40 percent of air-conditioning expenses is to compensate for the heat given off by incandescent bulbs; fluorescent lighting releases little heat.) So by the end of 12 months I would recover the purchase price. Then the bulbs would last another one to two years, netting me up to $2,000 in electricity savings. The problem is that I don't have a grand to sink into light bulbs.

Who does? Mobil. In 1993 the company invested $800,000 in efficient lighting for its headquarters in Reston, Virginia. Energy consumption for the complex declined by $600,000 per year, meaning the capital reached a payback point in just 16 months: high-yield investing indeed. Utilities are now offering various financing and rebate plans to overcome the upfront costs of efficient lighting: The details are eye-glazing and don't matter here. What does matter is that such results show energy conservation is not only a rational market step but can also be fun.

Suppose in sum everything Amory Lovins says must be divided by two. This still leaves his most pleasing energy news of the 1990s, rendering him a sort of Professor Harold Hill of kilowatts—whose sales pitch may be excessive but whose merchandise nevertheless is good for River City.

A Conservation Sampler

Is conservation technology realistic? Here are a few examples suggesting that it is:

- In 1991 a consortium of utilities offerred a $30 million prize to the first manufacturer to market an affordable superefficient refrigerator. Development was expected to take five years. Instead by 1994 Whirlpool won the prize and had in stores a refrigerator that uses a third less power than the most efficient previous models, while employing no CFCs. By 1995 the super refrigerator is expected to cost the same as ordinary models, meaning payback on the day you plug it in.
- Microwave clothes dryers may soon be perfected, consuming 50 percent less energy than hot-air dryers. Researchers are close to perfecting the E-lamp, a bulb that produces light using electronics, not heated filaments or gas. The E-lamp will offer the low power consumption and long life of compact fluorescents but be the same size as existing bulbs, allowing it to fit in any fixture.

- Infrared-wavelength drying booths are already replacing the convection ovens used by automobile manufacturers to cure paint on cars. These devices consume 90 percent less energy than those they supplant.
- Some engineers think the 1990s will see the perfection of air-conditioning without compressors. No-compressor air conditioners would take advantage of the cooling that occurs when humid air becomes dry; the machines would have a series of circular plates and chemicals that absorb moisture but no thrumming compressor, the big power draw (and noisemaker) in conventional units.
- At the turn of the century the thermal efficiency—roughly the gas mileage—of coal-fired power plants was eight percent, meaning 92 percent of the energy released from fuel went to the sky as waste heat. Thermal efficiency in coal power rose to a peak of 41 percent in 1969 then declined to a current average of 36 percent as stack scrubbers were added to combat acid rain. (The scrubbers consume part of the plant's energy output.) Now engineers think the next generation of coal-fired power plants will reach 45 percent thermal efficiency, even with acid rain controls. Thermal efficiency of natural-gas power plants has risen from about 30 percent to 43 percent, with 55 percent considered likely within a decade.
- Computers consume about five percent of U.S. electric power. Laptop computers were made possible by the development of chips that use the low wattage levels of batteries. Engineers then asked themselves, Why not put the low-power chips in standard computers too? In 1994 several companies began to market desktop PCs that draw only about 30 percent as much current as previous models, despite having much higher processing speeds. Look for computers labeled "EPA energy star." It is expected that low-power chips will become standard for all computers. This alone would offset several percentage points of U.S. electricity demand, while cutting greenhouse gas emissions by the equivalent of about five million cars.
- "Superwindows" containing layers of argon or krypton gas, offering insulation nealy as good as walls, are finally becoming affordable. Sound inconsequential? Roy Gordon, a chemist at Harvard University, has calculated that heat lost through inefficient windows in the United States alone wastes more energy than the Alaskan oil pipeline supplies.
- Commercial interest in high-efficiency lighting fixtures went up

when Lovins began to point out that lights lasting ten times as long don't have to be changed as often. For businesses like hotels with lots of hard-to-reach bulbs, the labor savings alone may offset the purchase price of efficient lights. Building on insights like this the EPA has signed up a healthy chunk of the Fortune 500 for Green Lights, a program by which companies pledge to convert to high-efficiency lighting. Green Lights is another program with a hokey Chamber of Commerce ring. Yet the saving may be substantial: The EPA projects a net decline of 11 percent in U.S. electricity demand over the coming decade as a result of the program.

Car Efficiency

In 1975 the typical American car averaged 16 miles per gallon. Today the figure is 28 mpg, a 70 percent improvement in just two decades. But fuel economy gains have stalled since 1988. In that year automakers met a federal requirement that their cars (but not light trucks, a sales growth area) record a corporate-averaged fuel economy of 27.5 mpg. Since 1988 federal regulations have required no further mileage gains, and automakers—including Japanese firms importing to the United States—have made no fuel-economy progress voluntarily. Early in his presidential campaign, Bill Clinton said he would "seek" a 45 mpg federal standard. Clinton then renounced his own statement when campaigning in Michigan and has not proposed any new standard since taking office.

One reason increases in auto fuel economy have stalled is, paradoxically, continuing success against smog. Just as stack scrubbers for acid rain consume some of a power plant's power, antismog devices result in some mpg losses. But the key reason mpg-efficiency growth has stalled is that speed has increased. In 1975, the average new car accelerated from zero to 60 in 14.1 seconds. Today the average is 12.1 seconds. Since the federal government stopped pressuring automakers to improve mpg, nearly all engineering attention has gone to improving acceleration. Engineers easily could trade back half the speed gains since 1975 and build cars that are still plenty quick but break the 27.5 mpg barrier. Studying the matter in 1992, the National Academy of Sciences declared that family-sized cars attaining 35 mpg are practical with present technology.

Opposition to higher fuel economy is often based on the contention that lighter high-mileage cars are more dangerous than heavier low-mileage models. Statistics do not show this to be so. In 1970 the U.S.

highway death rate was 4.3 per 100 million miles traveled. By 1993, with the typical U.S. car about 800 pounds lighter, the highway death rate had declined to 2.3 per 100 million miles. Opponents of higher mpg standards made much of a 1991 Department of Transportation test in which a two-ton Ford Crown Victoria was crashed into a one-ton Subaru. The Subaru took the most damage. But if you're riding in that hefty Crown Vic and are hit by a tractor-trailer truck, you will be the one who gets crumpled. Does this mean that for crash protection everyone should drive a tractor-trailer truck?

Impact-absorbing body design, seat belts, air bags, improved brakes, and sober driving are much better protectors than any amount of metal. These qualities can be had in efficient cars just as easily as inefficient ones. A new U.S. federal goal of 35-mpg family automobiles is practical, affordable, and sensible. Automakers ought to support such a new goal, if only to insure that oil demand stays soft so that there will continue to be plenty of cheap gasoline to power the cars they want to build.

Musclebound Conservation

Energy conservation sometimes sounds like a cardigan-sweater Jimmy Carter idea. In truth energy conservation has been among the most muscular trends in American society for two decades. Conservation has forced down world oil prices and contained inflation even as Americans enjoy the privileges of ample energy as never before: driving more miles, flying dramatically more often, being air-conditioned everywhere they go. The next two decades should bring with them continuing muscular reductions in the energy intensity of Western society, even as production increases and material comforts remain.

In his 1976 book *The Poverty of Power,* the ecologist Barry Commoner wrote with buoyant anticipation that the imminent exhaustion of petroleum would trigger Marx's final crisis of capitalism. Today there is a faction of the environmental left that feels cheated that the energy crisis did not bring down the industrial state. No doubt to the dismay of doomsayers, the energy future looks even more rosy.

ENERGY II:
THE RENEWABLE FUTURE

IN 1992, IN THE LITTLE TOWN OF DOSWELL, VIRGINIA, A futuristic power plant went into operation. Driven by natural gas, the facility burns about a third less fuel per kilowatt than comparable stations, thanks to an advanced process called combined-cycle generation. It causes minimal pollution, having no water discharge and emitting only trace amounts of smog precursors to the air. Sensors on the exhaust stacks monitor emissions and report them continuously via modem to the Virginia Department of Environmental Conservation, which can order the plant to shut down immediately if any permit violation is recorded.

A visit to the Doswell power station is an eerie experience, for even when the turbines are running at full throttle it is difficult to tell that the facility is operating. Tricks of acoustic engineering mask the deafening resound characteristic of power production; no clouds of anything rise away, not even steam. Inside the control room are no dramatic banks of color-coded warning lights and sirens, just a few desktop PCs. The plant makes 656 megawatts of power, nearly as much as one of the Three Mile Island reactors. The Doswell generating station represents the beginning of the end for brute-force approaches to energy generation— also the beginning of the end for fossil fuels.

This book posits that high tech is about to be replaced by clean tech. Is this just a pleasant daydream? Trends in energy suggest it is not.

Energy, one of the world's leading commercial sectors, and the most pollution-intensive of human activities, is already on its way toward the clean-tech conversion. If energy can go clean tech all aspects of commerce can.

Conventional wisdom holds that oil, as it depletes, will grow ever more precious. My supposition is that oil, as it is offset by conservation and supplanted by renewable energy, will grow ever cheaper. One hundred years from now oil will be close to worthless. The sands will close back in on the Arabian peninsula oilfields, and the descendants of certain desert princes will wish their forebears had bartered every last drop while the stuff was still worth something.

The real-dollar cost of a barrel of petroleum has been declining since the early 1980s. Through the 1990s the Organization of Petroleum Exporting Countries, so shortly ago viewed as one of the world's strongest institutions, has disassembled as rapidly as the Soviet Union. Once The Experts repeatedly decreed that reductions in oil prices would be inconceivable absent some wrenching sacrifice like rationing, petroleum demand supposedly being inelastic. Instead oil demand has proven so elastic it might as well be expressed in units of Silly Putty. World marginal demand for oil has been soft for a decade not because of hardship or sacrifice but owing to conservation and efficiency.

Today well-informed men and women speak of society as being locked into dependency on fossil fuels. But when we say we're stuck with fossil fuels, we evince ignorance of events that occurred within the lifetimes of our own grandparents. Petroleum did not become an economic commodity until 1859, when the first commercial well was drilled at Titusville, Pennsylvania. Surely any contemporary pundit present at Drake's strike would have pronounced there was no possibility the new energy source could ever become practical, given the lack of infrastructure, the high unit cost of initial output, the impossible technical barriers, and so on. Yet in less than half a century oil was being consumed in vast quantities throughout the world. Within a full century oil had become the dominant fuel in a globe-spanning internal-combustion-based economic order for which not one single rivet existed in 1859.

The transition to a renewable energy future may happen as swiftly and emphatically. The leap between the energy economy of today and a renewable, zero-pollution energy future is nowhere as great as the leap between Titusville of 1859 and the 1990s world of a gasoline station on every corner, a car per person, supertankers coursing the seas, and schoolchildren traveling between continents on jetliners. Today the idea of developed societies running on renewable fuels may seem fanciful; but a century ago the notion of the world using 65 million barrels of oil a day, the current figure, would have seemed far less plausible.

Of course renewable energy must be cost-effective to gain wide applicability. Solar energy was badly set back in the 1970s when proponents pretended the idea was already practical. It was not, as homeowners who trusted the blandishments of sellers of various solar appurtenances found out in unhappy fashion. But the disappointments of the 1970s hardly mean renewable energy will not pass the test of economic rationality someday soon. In its first few decades oil was widely scorned as too expensive, sure to fail in the marketplace against competitors such as "town gas" from coal mines or oats for horses.

An unappreciated effect of energy conservation investments is to render future energy price rises less likely, by keeping demand soft. Only recently has this realization begun to dawn on industrialists. The combined-cycle generating apparatus at the Doswell power station is, for example, not a technological breakthrough. Combined-cycle designs have existed for years but have not been used because the capital costs of installation are high. Now, at Doswell, an independent power enterprise backed by free-market investors decided on its own to build with the highest efficiency available. Why? "The driving factor in future power competition will be efficient use of energy," August Wallmeyer, a plant spokesperson, says. "The investors thought they would be in the safest position with maximum fuel efficiency." This is a conclusion of the free market, not of government regulatory agencies.

Real Renewable Technology

The next two decades or so of energy efficiency include these clean-tech prospects:

• *Electricity deregulation.* Somehow this has escaped general public notice, but as of 1992, any company can manufacture power for wholesale in the United States. The European Union is also on the verge of a deregulated, open-borders power market. Decontrols should usher in a new premise of seeking least-cost power, a notion environmentalists have rightly advocated for years. Least-cost power is normally attained by minimizing fuel input. Douglas Houston, an economist at the University of Kansas, has predicted that once least-cost energy competition gets rolling the traditional central utility will "crumble under its own weight," outfoxed by more nimble, energy-conscious predators.

• *Cars.* The most important environmentally conscious act many

Americans can perform is to junk any pre-1980 automobile and purchase any current model. A rule of ecorealism may be that all current models of everything run more efficiently and more cleanly than what they replace. For this reason the cycle of materialistic consumption actually may be good for the environment, luring us toward less harmful products. What an infuriating thought![1]

During the 1992 presidential campaign, Al Gore was chided for this overwrought statement: "The auto industry poses a moral threat to the security of every nation that is more deadly than that of any military enemy we are ever again likely to confront." In their vice-presidential debate, Dan Quayle further ridiculed Gore for declaring "the elimination of the internal combustion engine" a desirable goal. Yet here Gore is right on the beam. Elimination of the internal combustion engine isn't a pipedream: It is a clearheaded view of a constructive future.

The internal combustion engine is a crude device, the best versions capturing only about 18 percent of the energy value in fuel. Replacing internal combustion with a sophisticated clean-tech means of locomotion ought to be looked on as an exciting technical challenge. For instance, in principle a car could be driven by a small fuel cell that runs on hydrogen or on alcohol processed from corn. The cell would capture perhaps 50 percent of the energy value in its fuel, make little noise, and emit warm water as its only by-product. True, no engineer has yet devised a practical model of such a fuel cell. But engineers once tore their hair out trying to field practical internal combustion engines. The "get a horse!" contingent advised giving up. Look what happened.

How much cleaner and more efficient will the replacements of internal combustion engines be? By 1998, in California and perhaps other states, automakers will be required to market cars that run on electricity. Running cars on electricity generated by clean sources like hydro, wind, solar, and nuclear would offer significant conservation improvements over fossil power, whether that power is gasoline or coal-generated electricity fed to electric-car batteries. Assuming practical electric-car battery systems can be devised this makes the electric car attractive as an early twenty-first-century idea, since by then an increasing proportion of electricity should come from clean sources. Though attempts by major automakers to field practical electric cars have so far been less than triumphant, research into this form of transportation only became serious in the year 1991, when California imposed its zero-emission vehicle requirement. The pace of progress then quickened. "As recently as 1992, I thought electric cars were wishful thinking," says John Bryson, CEO of Southern California Edison, a power utility. "Now the output of batteries is beginning to double every year while the price cuts in half. That's the same kind of thing that happened just as the silicon chip took off. To me, it feels like electric cars are about to take off."

In 1993 the Clinton Administration announced a joint venture among the Detroit Big Three and government research centers, such as Lawrence Livermore National Laboratory in California, to pursue advanced vehicle power. Modeled on the government-industry research projects common in Japan, the consortium is unusual in American business. Clinton said the goal of the consortium was to develop a family-sized, gasoline-driven automobile that records 80 miles to the gallon. Privately, General Motors, Ford, and Chrysler were telling journalists that 45 mpg was more realistic. It's a deal! If the majority of U.S. automobiles were pushed to a 45 mpg standard, petroleum imports could end altogether.

Next on the inventory of possible automobile advances is the flywheel. In theory ceramic flywheel "batteries," spun up on electric power while a vehicle is parked, could provide several hundred miles of zero-pollution driving without the need to carry around heavy tanks of acid, as will be the case with cars powered by chemical battery cells. A company called American Flywheel Systems was at this writing promising a practical prototype of a flywheel-powered car. The firm is backed by Honeywell, a serious-money operation. Should a flywheel car be perfected and linked to an electricity-generation network running primarily on nonfossil fuels, it is possible that by the early twenty-first century the auto culture will have been converted from one based on brute force, pollution, and waste to a zero-emission operation emphasizing conservation and safety. Under such circumstances the private automobile may be with us for decades if not centuries to come—an exasperating prospect on several scores, but none of them environmental.

• *Methanol from biomass.* The most attractive immediate alternative to petroleum is methanol, a form of alcohol that works in existing engines. (Ethanol, made from corn, is a renewable fuel, but for various reasons most researchers think it will not supplant more than a fraction of petroleum use.) Today the only practical feedstock from which to make methanol is natural gas, a fossil fuel.[2] But trees, small woody plants, and cane plants contain sugars that can be processed into methanol. Such biomass raises the prospect of methanol becoming renewable.

Plant specialists have been crossbreeding for biomass properties for about a decade; so far a fast-rising tree called the black cottonwood is the leading candidate for "growing fuel" at market prices. Business will be drawn to biomass, thinks Robert Socolow, an engineer and director of the Princeton University Center for Energy and Environmental Studies, because it represents "a renewable energy future requiring large production facilities managed in familiar ways, meeting standard tests of profitability." In theory a biomass fuel cycle based on black cottonwood could be nearly carbon-neutral. As the cottonwoods grow they would subtract from the atmosphere about the same amount of carbon as would be returned when biomass-based fuels are burned. This is how nature manages the greenhouse cycle, with symmetrical exchanges.

• *Wind power.* Considered a mirage only a short time ago, wind power now verges on commercial scale in the United States. Today windmills in the Sierra Nevadas produce up to eight percent of the baseline electric load of California. The Electric Power Research Institute projects that wind power may produce 50,000 megawatts by the year 2010, about the output of 25 Three Mile Island stations. Should the EPRI prediction come true, merely between wind power and existing hydropower facilities a quarter of American electricity production would reach a zero-pollution, zero-fuel renewable basis in just two decades.

Windmills fashioned through the 1980s by NASA and subsidized aerospace contractors were pleasingly futuristic in appearance but could turn only at fixed speeds. Boeing's gigantic Mod 5B windmill, erected in Hawaii as a federally subsidized experiment, weighed more than one of the company's 747 jetliners. Today the trend is toward small, variable-speed windmills. The leading new wind machines, designed without subsidies by a company called Kenetech, speak to the benefits of market forces. The federal tax credit for wind power is down to just 1.5 cents per kilowatt hour, a level at which wind machines must be competitive with fossil power or no utility would buy them. "Wind power can now make it on its own in a conventional profit-and-loss calculation," says Alexander Ellis, a vice president of Kenetech. The moment when a renewable technology can go it alone in the marketplace is the moment when it is about to become significant.

Studies suggest the upper Rocky Mountain states, North Dakota, and parts of the Midwest offer for wind power the best combination of open spaces and steady breezes. The notion of building commercial wind machines in the Midwest is especially appealing, since the logical place for them would be on farms. Farmers have large tracts of open space and are always anxious for additional income. If Midwest farms could eliminate their utility bills while selling a little power back to the grid, a new means of financial support for the family farm might be found.

In the next century windmills may once again rise above the

American heartland as they did at the turn of this century, turning gently. Perhaps in that century Iowa farm boys will race their dogs toward secret clubhouses hidden among wind-energy towers and genetically engineered cottonwoods being grown for renewable fuels. The central issues in the lives of such boys will be making the basketball team and finishing homework and the attentions of someone named Becky, just as the really important issues of farm boys' lives have been and should always be. Silly futurism? The "energy farm" is odds-on to happen.

• *Solar.* Each day about 13,000 times as much solar energy shines on the United States as is produced by combustion of fossil fuels. As the researcher Franco Barbir of the University of Miami points out, the world need only learn to capture 0.12 percent of the energy value in incident sunlight to put the global economy on an entirely renewable, zero-pollution basis.

The barriers to solar power are many, most prominently that the energy value in sunlight falling on the Earth is in a given unit of area comparatively small. Thus to be effective solar arrays must be large and must convert a high percentage of incoming sunlight. Making solar collectors large has proved expensive; so has raising the conversion percentage. The only commercial-scale example is an installation in Daggett, California, that makes about 400 megawatts through a "solar dynamic" assembly of mirrors that focus sunlight to heat a chemical medium. Daggett works but is heavily subsidized.

Today photovoltaic cells that convert sunlight directly into electricity cost around 40 cents per kilowatt of new capacity, seven times the cost of new fossil-fired generation. But then a decade ago they cost several dollars per kilowatt. In 1992 a company called Advanced Photovoltaic Systems built a five-acre solar cell array for Pacific Gas and Electric in Davis, California, at a cost of about 25 cents per kilowatt. That is still high, but getting into the ballpark. Meanwhile some experimental photovoltaic cells produced at the Sandia National Laboratory in New Mexico have demonstrated conversion efficiencies as high as 34 percent.

Northern latitudes may never draw more than supplemental power from solar, but Barbir estimates that "the area of an average home's roof in the southern United States is enough to provide the energy needs of the household." Some homeowners were burned financially in the 1970s when they installed solar roof panels that were costly underperformers. But as solar converters fall in price and rise in efficiency, the idea of roof-mounted renewable power may bounce back and become significant not only in the southern developed world but throughout the equatorial developing world, where solar potentials are high. "Within two decades or less we may see thousands of square kilometers of the Sahara and

Kazakhstan, of Arizona and Chile, covered with photovoltaic collectors," Socolow of Princeton has written. Outside the city of Semipalatinsk, on the high desert plains of Kazakhstan, Russian engineers in 1949 detonated the first Soviet atomic bomb. That explosion was the warning shot of a terrifying arms race, and of unconstrained Soviet-bloc radioactive pollution whose full extent is still being uncovered. But what might be next for these plains? It turns out that high-altitude deserts are ideal for solar-power production. One day not far off, Kazakhstan might be a fashionably green address. Perhaps Semipalatinsk will become an administration center for a vast network of solar arrays, genus *Homo* making something entirely benign in a place where instruments of mass destruction and environmental deterioration were once forged.

Environmentalists often say that development in Southern California, Arizona, and New Mexico is inappropriate because it cannot occur without extensive hydraulic engineering. Setting aside that the arid character of the Southwest has no enduring natural standing—in recent geological epochs the American Southwest has been a lush tropical jungle and a low marsh, to name only two of many prior conditions—the arrival of affordable solar power may turn this argument on its head. In the twenty-first century, places like the Southwest may be considered among the most appropriate for men and women to live, because solar technology will make life there possible with few nonrenewable energy needs.

• *Alternative solar.* The plant kingdom is in a sense a vast solar energy converter. The precise process of photosynthesis, by which plants convert sunlight into electricity (that's what they use, at low levels), then employ the electricity to split water and carbon dioxide into elements that recombine as carbohydrates, is still poorly understood. But it is clear that plants do their business under clean-technology circumstances—using sophisticated rather than brute-force mechanisms, at standard temperatures and pressures, with little waste during "manufacture." Writing in 1991 in the technical journal *Nature,* a group of researchers proposed that solar power technology might do well to model itself on photosynthesis. The researchers were able to make a solar cell that mimicked the biological process, using molecules of dye as antennae to absorb sunlight. The biomimetic solar cells were only 12 percent efficient, but cost less than the superefficient Sandia cells. This has raised the prospect that if large fields of solar cells eventually are employed around the world for renewable energy, these cells may be *grown* rather than manufactured.

• *Hydrogen.* The payoff for a renewable energy economy will come when the use of hydrogen as a fuel is practical. Fuels are superior in proportion to their hydrogen ratios, and hydrogen, the lightest element, has the ultimate hydrogen ratio: Its sole constitution is hydrogen. Hydrogen burns with zero pollutant output. Any practical process able to disassociate hydrogen from water would create pollution-free renewable energy that would for intents and purposes last forever.

Engineering obstacles would make the switch to a hydrogen economy challenging; vehicles would have to carry it in highly compressed form, for example. But the only fundamental barrier is producing the hydrogen. The chemical bonds that join hydrogen and oxygen in water don't like to be broken. All current processes that disassociate water consume more energy than the fuel value of the hydrogen produced, making the process a net loser on a BTU basis. But perhaps some clever thinker will devise a new process to disassociate hydrogen from water. A few scientists have said an efficient process to split hydrogen from water is precluded by physical law. Yet many basic categories of knowledge considered mundane by high school students of today were described as beyond physical law by leading scientists of a few generations ago. For instance the German physicist Ernst Mach, for whom the Mach number is named, decreed around the turn of the century that it was absurd for researchers to discuss subatomic particles since the atom would always be far too small to manipulate. Lowly plants have learned to split hydrogen out of water without using any complex high-powered equipment. Perhaps people can learn to do the same.

• *The solar-desert link.* The energy cost of disassociating hydrogen from water using existing techniques might be tolerable if the energy originated from clean, renewable sources. Joan Ogden and Robert Williams, two Princeton University researchers, have supposed that a future energy economy could be based on solar and hydrogen in the following manner: Very large arrays of solar converters would be constructed in deserts. They mean very large—tens of thousands of square miles. Deserts are appealing for this sort of project. Most are found in the sunny parts of the world; most have no value to people. Nature has placed in deserts some beautiful and remarkable species, such as the night-blooming cereus. But if you're going to ruin something in the ecology the best choice is deserts, as total life in these places is low. Once the array of desert solar converters is built, the power produced would be employed to disassociate hydrogen from water. The hydrogen would then flow to urban areas where it could be used in cars and natural gas pipelines, placing the energy economy on a zero-pollution, endlessly renewable basis.

• *Fuel cells.* The hydrogen produced by Ogden-Williams arrays might be employed in fuel cells, which are the ideal producers of electricity. Fuels cells recombine hydrogen and oxygen to produce electricity and water, reversing the disassociation reaction by which hydrogen is made. Water is the sole by-product. Fuel cells contain few moving parts and in theory can be small and efficient. Early models provided onboard electricity for the Apollo moon mission.

Today fuel cells are too expensive to be practical, yet some are already in commercial use. The Hyatt Regency hotel in Irvine, California, uses fuels cells for 20 percent of daily power. The fuel cells at the Hyatt are not economical; this is a demonstration being subsidized by the utility Southern California Gas. (Forward-thinking natural gas utilities assume that someday they will be hydrogen utilities: a point to note.) The consulting firm Arthur D. Little has estimated that as the cost of manufacturing fuel cells declines, as much as five percent of new electricity production worldwide may soon come from fuel cells.

Imagine, then, a suburban home of the renewable future. The structure would have passive-solar design features; no-compressor air-conditioning; compact-fluorescent or E-lamp lighting; a superefficient refrigerator; windows with internal polarizing fields that allow the infrared value of sunlight to pass in the winter but block it in summer; cheap, chip-based thermostats; and light timers to minimize unnecessary use. On the roof would be affordable solar converters providing most of the family's power. Out by the carport would sit a small fuel cell, suggesting the Mr. Fusion appliance of the *Back to the Future* movies. Such a home might still suffer from all the objectionable qualities of suburban life—excess materialism, shallow cultural norms, you name it—but it would also be a zero-pollution, zero-fossil-fuel enterprise. And this home might kiss the power grid goodbye, making its own electricity the way homes now make their own heat and cool air.

• *Techno-power.* One possible advanced energy source is fusion. Current reactors work via fission, or splitting of atoms. Fusion is by contrast the source of virtually all energy used by the biosphere, since the sun operates on this principle, fusing hydrogen into helium and releasing heat and light in the process. Fusing of atoms generates much more energy than fission, but fusion processes are far harder to ignite.

For three decades research centers in the U.S., the former Soviet Union, and Europe have been attempting to ignite fusion reactions under controlled circumstances. This effort has cost many billions of dollars, rubles, and francs and produced no practical design. Unlike Enrico Fermi's early work with controlled atomic fission, which progressed in just a few years from abstract engineering concepts to a sustained chain reaction in a lab under the University of Chicago stadium, research on controlled fusion has been plodding along not going much of anywhere, despite big budgets and the talents of hundreds of top researchers. Breakthroughs, however, may come.

Fusion generators might be breathtakingly expensive but once built could use isotopes of water as fuel and run with zero air pollutants, producing only small amounts of radioactivity and no long-lived nuclear wastes. In theory a zero-radiation fusion reactor could be built if fueled by an isotope called helium-three. Helium-three appears to occur in quantity on the moon. Thus, in the dreams of technologists, the future holds a planet powered by clean fusion generators of extreme sophistication that bring the golden apples of the sun to the Earth in literal fashion. These stations would be supplied with helium-three mined on the moon and "rolled down the hill" to Earth by electromagnetic launchers that propel moon rocks toward Earth without rocket fuel. Sound like Jules Verne? A world powered by fusion reactors running on helium mined on the moon is no more improbable than fission reactors seemed a century ago.

• *A global grid.* Buckminster Fuller once pointed out something delightfully basic about energy use: Since most power demand comes during the day, generating stations run fiercely in the light hours and idle at night; yet at any moment half the world is in daylight, half in night. If there were a worldwide power grid, global energy production capacity could drop dramatically, because when power plants were in nighttime on their continents, they could be making juice for other continents. Today transmission losses negate the advantages of the idea. But assuming room-temperature superconductivity is someday realized—a Big If, of course—global transmission of power would become feasible. A world power grid could then be devised, cutting Earth's generating requirements while creating an economic shared interest among nations.

• *Space solar.* By the time sunlight reaches Earth's surface its energy value has attenuated. The incident power value of sunlight in space is, however, far higher. Suppose large mirrors or collectors were placed into orbit. The dishes would soak up intense space sunlight then beam power down to the ground, perhaps after converting it into microwaves for focused transmission.

There lives today not a single sober soul who believes any nation of Earth could afford even one space solar–power array of magnitude, let alone enough to meet national energy needs. But that's today, with no cost-effective means of access to space yet invented. Half a century ago all the wealth of the world's nations combined would not have been sufficient to assemble, say, the Federal Express company. At that time no one possessed the knowledge necessary to design high-speed aircraft or manufacture them in large quantities at relatively low prices. Now this knowledge is so common Federal Express has several competitors.

The situation faced by space solar is analogous. Suppose affordable access to orbit is someday devised. Humanity could then transition to a source of power entirely benign from nature's perspective—taking up no acres on Earth and running off a generator nature has already constructed, the sun. The mechanical elements of the system would be located in space, where nothing lives anyway. Zero-pollution energy would become available from a source that will not be depleted for billions of years. Once such collector stations were built in space, the human quest for energy for daily life could for intents and purposes end. Only maintenance of the collectors would be needed. Possibilities like space solar power show that at least in principle, human beings may in an incredibly short time by nature's standards free themselves altogether from consuming resources or making pollution in the pursuit of energy. Technology has many drawbacks, but when it holds out a prospect like this, it must be seen as an important potential ally of nature.

An Actual Modest Life

In 1993 I wrote in *The Atlantic Monthly* about the possibility that conservation technology would someday enable typical homes to detach from the power grid, ushering in a new suburban, middle-class lifestyle that is physically comfortable yet modest from the standpoint of nature, with low energy consumption and little if any energy-related pollution.

Perhaps this strikes you as the sort of daydream entertained by aging hippies. Don't we all know that power can only come from fearsome, thundering machines running under arc lights behind security fences? Yet eventually unhooking homes from the grid is the sort of challenge that ought to engage our mechanically gifted society. As Socolow, the Princeton engineer, has written, "Today so often rejected as uninteresting and confining, energy efficiency will become deeply embedded in human culture. Many of us [in R&D] consider energy conservation a way of being constructively engaged with technology, a responsible alternative to the perception that technology is the enemy."

Not long ago the idea that every home would have its own furnace—a miniature industrial boiler—would have been considered a frivolity. Homes either had uneven warmth from fireplaces and stoves or were connected to centralized heating plants. As soon as individual home furnaces became practical they were embraced not only for comfort but also for energy efficiency. The one-home furnace only runs when you really need it; there are no transmission losses. Not far in the future electric power will be seen in the same way, as something best made at home. Home manufacturing of electricity will start off intended to promote efficiency and lower costs. It will end up introducing into popular culture the heterodox notion of comfortable yet ecologically modest suburban living.

In *The Atlantic Monthly* I wrote about this idea whimsically, assuming homemade power to be years distant. Then landed on my desk the galleys of a book called *The Independent Home,* about the estimated 100,000 people in the United States who have *already* detached their dwellings from the power grid yet are still using refrigerators, televisions, computers, and the other mixed blessings of material life.

Present practicalities of self-powered homes fall considerably shy of mass appeal. For example *The Independent Home* describes the Vermont house of David and Mary Val Palumbo, who produce their own power using solar panels, a small hydro coil in a stream on their property, and a peak-load diesel generator. The Palumbos acknowledged that years of planning, study, and frustration went into making this system reliable. There is no mass market for years of frustration.

But people like the Palumbos will create the first level of clean-tech knowledge about energy. Then the knowledge will be available to the ambitious in how-to manuals; then contractors will sell the knowledge, so that homeowners needn't think about the details, merely judge whether the price is right; finally knowledge of how to live modestly regarding energy will be incorporated into all new building designs, so that the typical homeowner never need be troubled by the issue at all. If there's one place where market forces and technology will surely conjoin to serve the interests of the Earth, it is in the renewable energy future.

Enviros ✍

THROUGHOUT THIS BOOK RUN EXAMPLES OF TIMES WHEN institutional environmentalism has exaggerated dangers, pined for bad news, or been party to similar derelictions. Before going any further with this bill of attainder it is important to say that the environmental movement is among the most welcome social developments of the twentieth century.

The praise will not last long, nor should it. In the last decade environmentalists have heard more hosannas than is good for them. Commentators meet the claims of industrialists and government officials with skepticism, discounting, as is proper, for self-interests in the outcome. In contrast the pronouncements of green figures have been treated as beyond reproach, though like everyone else they have personal and financial self-interests, too. Surely environmentalists enjoyed having their claims embraced uncritically by the opinion-making apparatus of society. But this luxury has become counterproductive, allowing the movement to avoid facing the flaws of its arguments. If you love environmentalists, as you should, today the greatest favor you can do them is to toss cold water on their heads.

Two Cheers for the Enviros

In this book, strong and effective environmental pressure is assumed; the question asked is whether that pressure is now channeled in the most constructive manner. Thus the first point of praise for environmentalists must be that they have done so well they can be taken for granted.

Commentators such as the English author Anna Bramwell date modern environmental sentiment to the United Kingdom around the turn of the century, when the British Soil Association began grass-roots lobbying against ecological abuse. A forerunner of the environmental movement existed in the United States a century ago when John Muir, the naturalist who founded the Sierra Club, wrote tracts decrying wilderness loss. Muir's efforts led to the creation in 1916 of the national park system. By the 1960s there were half a dozen important environmental groups in the Western nations; by the 1980s, two dozen. By 1990 environmentalism had grown into one of the leading lobby interests of North America and Western Europe, in national as well as local governments, and into perhaps the most effective media-relations entity ever. Today environmental leaders enjoy the sort of access to Congress and state legislatures—and, with Bill Clinton and Al Gore, to the White House—of which some business leaders dream. Enviros also now have the ability to deliver votes, through the scorecards they issue on politicians. Green political ratings are influential in New England, the Pacific Coast states, Minnesota, and elsewhere.

This phenomenal organizing success speaks both to the power of ecological concerns and to the hard labors of the people of the movement. Environmentalists began their quest for the public ear with a pittance compared to the financial reserves of the lobbies that opposed them. Through the early 1980s, though outgunned in legal talent, lobbying access, and the funds necessary to make political donations, they won victory after victory. This progression from pauperhood to riches culminated in the 1990 Clean Air Act. On that bill environmentalists put to rout the auto lobby, the steel lobby, the utility lobby, the coal lobby, and other entrenched groups commanding trillions of dollars in economic might. Because of the success of political environmentalism, Americans and Europeans today live in a world where effective environmental influence is assured at nearly every level of government and business. This is a wonderful development for society. History will admire the environmentalists of our era for how much they accomplished and how fast.

Yet through their success environmentalists have ceased to be outsiders. Mainstream organizations of the movement today are a branch office of the status quo, possessed of fancy offices (the new National Audubon Society headquarters in New York is a green Taj) and big bucks (Greenpeace International had a $100 million budget in 1991). Several environmental organizations have acquired the trappings of large revenue-generating organizations, including scandal. In 1991 Greenpeace fired a top manager accused of financial misdealing; in 1992 the Florida chapter of the Audubon Society changed the locks at its Save the Manatee Club in order to prevent the pop singer Jimmy Buffett, in the process of being ousted as the club's spokesperson, from taking mailing lists to start a rival fund-raising concern. Callous layoffs, bitterness regarding discrimination (there are few women and fewer blacks in senior positions of U.S. environmental organizations), and other internal problems, of the sort enviros once thought only corporations guilty now crop up. And now that environmentalism has joined the status quo, the movement's institutional pronouncements begin to be subject to the same harsh appraisals business and government pronouncements receive. Early indications are that enviros don't enjoy scrutiny any more than anyone else does.

The transition to insider status means environmentalism must transform its mode of argument, from tocsin-ringing to rationality. When they were outsiders, could environmentalists have caught the attention of Congress on subjects like landfill liner or protection of marine mammals or heavy-metal discharges to sewers or any of a hundred ecological areas unless they overstated? Probably not. But as insiders environmentalists no longer require attention-grabbing devices. They already have society's attention: Since the mid-1980s, ecological initiatives have done well in Congress and in European parliaments even when presented without glare. If anything the system is now oversensitive to green concerns.

"Industrial society is no longer enhancing human life. It is beginning to destroy it," declared Greenpeace in full-page broadsides that ran in newspapers in the United States in 1992. The graphic showed a family walking down a beach dressed in chemical protection suits, breathing through respirators. "It's not a question of jobs versus the environment," Greenpeace continued. "There will be no jobs left on a dead, scorched Earth." This wording isn't even in the general zone of reality. However emotionally satisfying doomsaying may be, environmentalists must foreswear the practice or they will lose their credibility on the many issues on which they are right.

Doomsayers versus Naysayers

In recent years it has become something of a pastime to make sport of failed environmental predictions from the past. There are many to choose from. In 1970, for instance, *Life* magazine said that by 1980

Americans in major cities would wear gas masks. In 1980 a commission appointed by President Jimmy Carter issued a report, *Global 2000*, projecting general ecological collapse around 1990. The list of null doomsday prophecies from the recent past could march onward for pages.

Such way-off forecasts should not be disturbing. They came when little was known about the natural resilience of the environment, researchers having only begun to uncover the evidence. They came when gross pollution was widespread—for example, bear in mind that until 1972 it was essentially legal for U.S. factories to discharge unprocessed toxics and slag directly into lakes and rivers. And the old doomsday pronouncements came when government was tucked snugly in bed with industry. In the 1960s I never would have guessed how rapidly environmental regulation would take force or how quickly nature would recover, and probably neither would you. So, yes, the enviros made some nutty predictions in the past. That no longer matters.

What does matter is that nutty assessments continue to be generated in the present. "A multitude of environmental disasters are bearing down simultaneously . . . we're facing the equivalent of World War III," the book *Saving the Earth* declared in 1990. About the same time Gene Likens, director of the Institute for Ecosystem Studies at the New York Botanical Garden, decried the "relentless degradation of the global environment" driven by "greedy short-term profits or the next election." In 1993 Lester Brown, president of the Worldwatch Institute, said of food production, "The golden age may be coming to an end," and predicted imminent global starvations. "During the 1970s we had a lot of really good environmental laws passed but most of those have been systematically subverted or undermined," the late novelist and environmental activist Wallace Stegner said in 1992. From the White House, in 1993 Al Gore declared, "Human activities are needlessly causing grave and perhaps irreparable damage to the global environment." In 1994 Gore said, in apparent defiance of all evidence, that "the environmental crisis has grown worse" in the United States in recent decades.

Contemporary doomsaying is hard to excuse, given that it comes at a time when most trends in developed countries are positive and most scientific findings suggest the biosphere extremely robust. Yet the above quotations and many more not cited[1] show that environmentalism remains mired in instant-doomsday thinking. Some of this fixation stems from a willful denial of progress made: an almost aching desire that news stay bad.

Consider Stegner's notion that the environmental laws of the 1970s were good but since have been "systematically undermined or subverted." The reverse is true. Laws of the 1970s were shot full of loopholes allowing acid rain, toxic air pollution, ocean dumping of sludge, and many other abuses. During the 1980s, the New Right *attempted* to undermine environmental strictures but enjoyed little success. In that decade U.S. regulations controlling toxics, recycling, sludge, pesticide registration, waste exports, landfill safety, smog prevention, acid rain, incinerators, energy conservation, nuclear wastes, and a dozen other subjects were made more strict. Current ecological law is hardly perfect, but by any reasoned judgment it is far stronger than in the 1970s.

No one can blame Stegner or environmentalists generally for wanting to sustain the essentially youthful vision of a glorious crusade to thwart villainy. It's fun to view yourself as a pure-hearted Paladin surrounded by bad guys you can outwit. It is less fun, and dishearteningly grown-up, to view yourself as one of many actors in a complex world where the moral dimensions of human actions are not always what they seem. But the satisfying visions from the youth of the ecological movement have progressively less to do with current events. Add to this an inner fear of all movements: Reformers privately dread the moment when the reforms they espouse come to pass and they are no longer needed. Such factors combine to make some environmentalists long for the bad old days, rather to celebrate the improving new ones.

Unvironmentalism

As environmentalism has become entrenched a contrapositive has sprung up, which may be called unvironmentalism. The commentator Rush Limbaugh is the leading unviro, imagining "ecofeminazis" who conspire with the EPA to control his life. William Dannemeyer, a former congressman, is another prominent unviro; in 1990 he gave a demented speech on the House floor saying the trouble with environmentalists is that they don't believe in an afterlife. (Apparently pollution is fine down below so long as skies are clear high above.) Ronald Bailey, a fellow of the Cato Institute, has written that environmentalists are involved in an "eco-scam" that is a cover for hard-core socialism.[2] Elizabeth Whalen, founder of an organization called the American Council on Science and Health, crusades tirelessly on the notion that few synthetic chemicals are harmful: Whalen is a sort of reverse Jeremy Rifkin from the parallel universe. S. Fred Singer and Candace Crandall have formed an organization called the Science and Environmental Policy Project which acts as an unviro truth squad, issuing papers that deconstruct doomsday claims. What has evolved is a strange contest between the doomsayers and the naysayers—one side asserting life as we know it is about to end, the other that everything is peachy keen. Common sense dictates neither philosophy takes you anywhere you really want to go.

Fortunately unviro naysaying is a short-term phenomenon that will expire on its own, as it defies the consensus political values behind conservation. Environmental doomsaying may be with us for years to come, since it plays off those same values. This is distressing because the decibel level of doomsaying drowns out ecological messages with lasting power.

The first half of Gore's *Earth in the Balance,* for example, might have been ghosted by C. Little. Seemingly on every page something is being destroyed or about to end. Gore's initial mention that environmental progress has been made in the United States does not come until page 82; the mention is perfunctory. The second half of Gore's book speculates on how modern detachment from the rhythms of Earth may help explain the dissatisfaction experienced by so many people in affluent nations, who would seem by material comfort the winners of history's lottery. This portion of *Earth in the Balance* is measured, thoughtful, and possessed of enduring significance. The quietly persuasive second half of Gore's work received no attention while the doomsday first half was widely promoted.

The underappreciated portion of Gore's work hints at an ecological issue that will become increasingly important in the twenty-first century, as problems like pollution control are resolved. That issue is antimaterialist sentiment. To the extent the ecology movement is a proxy for no-growth, it sometimes has a pull-up-the-ladders aspect. That is: I've made my pile of dough, now don't you dare spoil the view from my vacation home. Yet the countercultural aspect of environmentalism also sometimes cuts across class lines to engage those who feel screwed by the direction of society, or who have an uneasy sense that the materialist life-focus is elementally flawed.

Environmentalists are well ahead of the historical curve in sensing that materialist culture has lost its way. History will look back on the green drives against pollution and resource waste as secondary issues, since by historical standards these problems will be resolved in remarkably little time. But the problem of the soul-draining aspect of the materialist lifestyle will continue and may even worsen as clean, sustainable production extends the cycle of consumption indefinitely. Down the road, the effort to free women and men from lives of materialistic work-and-spend represents the most important contribution environmentalism will make to society. For the moment the trouble is that hardly any environmentalist who thinks in an antimaterialist way is willing to act in an antimaterialist way.

SOMEBODY ELSE Should Sacrifice

In protest categories such as civil rights there are complex arguments regarding when dissenters may be justified in stepping outside social norms. But if you believe that power plants are elementally wrong you don't have to sabotage the electric lines, you can simply abstain from having them connected to your house. If you believe cars destroy the Earth, you can leave them rusting at the dealership. If you believe that supermarket food reeks of deadly chemicals you can do what 99.9 percent of your forebears did, and grow your own.

Yet is there even one Western environmentalist who lives without electricity and heat, eats only from his or her own garden, would if ill refuse genetically engineered pharmaceuticals, never travels in any fossil-powered car, taxi, bus, train, or plane, and who declines to attend environmental conferences because it would take too long to ride there on a bike? Paul Ehrlich has written that things are so bad the only hope is to "reduce the scale of human activities." By way of setting an example does he decline to speak at environmental conferences because to do so would oblige him to fly in petroleum-guzzling jetliners and stay in resource-intensive hotels? Gore has written of watching a glade of trees removed for a housing development near his Virginia home: "As the woods fell to make way for more concrete, more buildings, more parking lots, the wild things that lived there were forced to flee." Doesn't Gore live in a house? Park his car on concrete? Why are jets and homes and driveways only objectionable when SOMEBODY ELSE desires them?

An important text of the environmental movement is the E. F. Schumacher book *Small Is Beautiful*. Many green thinkers praise a section proposing that people would be better off spending their lives in small village economies, living under government-imposed self-sufficiency, not relying on the world over the horizon for any important goods or services. There's an obvious objection to this line of thought: Most of the people who exist in small-is-beautiful fashion today do so in abject misery in the impoverished Third World. Nevertheless, if abiding in a small village economy and consuming only what you or your neighbors make really is the ideal existence, nothing stops environmentalists from living that way right now in the United States. Nothing except convenience.

An exemplary expression of SOMEBODY ELSE logic can be found in the 1990 book *The Dream of the Earth*. There Thomas Berry, a Roman Catholic priest and a popular doomsayer, writes, "A few hundred automobiles with good roads may be a great blessing. Yet when the number [of cars] increases into the millions and hundreds of millions, the automobile is capable of destroying higher forms of life on this planet." What possible ordering of society could lead to a mere "few hundred cars" yet an expansive network of "good roads"? Only a social order in which inordinate resources are lavished on a privileged few. Perhaps Berry assumes that as an intellectual he would number in the car-riding elite, zooming past lesser beings trudging the roadside. Through this passage Berry betrays one of the most common materialist fantasies: the desire to have the entire road to himself. Similarly Schumacher proposed that to reduce resource consumption travel should be discouraged, with most people required to spend their lives as their ancestors did, within walking distance of their place of birth. There would be exceptions for those with special gifts, such as academics and writers, such as—hey, E. F. Schumacher!

A faction of the environmental movement is burdened by a post-Schumacher trance-state in which it is imaged that Third World billions would rather tend to small ecological niches and live in self-denial, to avoid the horrors of Western consumerism. For good or ill what the overwhelming majority of the Third World wants is what the First World has. People the world over long to be materially secure, to have comfortable homes and sufficient food, to be relieved from manual labor, to have their children's diseases cured. And people the world over long for mechanized transportation that spares them from traveling on foot, burdens mounted on their backs. When I lived in Pakistan in the 1980s the most dreaded daily experience for the typical person was a ride on the bus system, which was so badly overcrowded that passengers hung from the doors and sometimes died when the buses veered on narrow streets. Whole families would drape themselves on motor scooters to avoid the bus. Obtaining a scooter was a central life goal in the lives of many Pakistanis, in order to graduate to private transportation.

The idea that SOMEBODY ELSE should go without the conveniences of modern life must be eradicated if environmental thought is to proceed to the next level of usefulness to society. As Bramwell noted in *Ecology in the Twentieth Century,* far from advancing a decentralized small-is-beautiful philosophy the orthodox enviro prescription "involves mass planning and coercion." No degree of ecological exhortation will persuade the typical citizen of America or Western Europe to abandon the heated home, low-cost food, advanced medical care, or any similar reasonable material gain. Nor should these be abandoned. Rather they should be redesigned to operate in conjunction with nature.

In Bill McKibben's *The End of Nature* is a section expressing angst over the fact that every U.S. home now has a washer and dryer. Think of the power plants that must run to juice up all those duplicate appliances, McKibben suggests. Maybe people should be compelled to sacrifice by having one large, common washer-dryer per city block. I won't ask whether McKibben's own house contains a Maytag. I will ask: Wouldn't that large common washer operate pretty much round the clock, rather than twice a week like home washer-dryers? Wouldn't the resource consumption end up being about the same, with inconvenience added? Wouldn't it be smarter to concentrate on technical advances that make individual washers and dryers energy-efficient?

Once I wrote an article about flawed concepts such as abolishing the home washer, and received an intriguing letter from a woman in California. She asked: If home systems were eliminated who would end up hauling laundry to that common washer? "For all their faults, most modern conveniences reduce drudgery for women," she noted. "Women's freedom has come during the same century as abundant material production. There must be at least some relationship between these developments." In many small village cultures of the developing world, where modern conveniences are absent and unending manual labor is destiny for women, sexism is far more deeply entrenched than in the First World.

That others ought to sacrifice advantages of modern life was sublimely self-satirized in a 1993 address to the Society of Environmental Journalists by the cable TV magnate Ted Turner, who cloaks himself in green though he travels by corporate jet, perhaps the most resource-intensive luxury now possible. Loggers, Turner said, "ought to quit using chain saws and mechanical equipment and cut trees the old way with a crosscut saw." Then they "wouldn't be putting stuff into the atmosphere because you wouldn't be running equipment. And it's good for their muscles, too." Here a man who made his fortune exploiting new technology announces SOMEBODY ELSE ought to be deprived of mechanization and compelled back to existence based on manual labor. I don't mean to offer Turner as a source of considered thoughts. But he does sit at the center of the orthodox enviro maelstrom, providing barometric readings of its detachment from common sense.

The Romanticized Past

Rightly sensing that modern materialist obsessions go too far, many environmentalists have wrongly begun to retreat to a dreamy concept of pretechnology. As expressed in 1993 by the newsletter of the Rocky Mountain Institute, "the exuberant, bountiful garden of Eden that greeted our earliest ancestors makes today's Earth seem barren and sterile in comparison." In *The Women's History of the World,* Rosalind Miles wrote, "Men in hunter-gatherer societies did not command or exploit women's labor." The ecotopian Paul Shepard has asked, "Can we face the possibility that hunters [of the far past] were more fully human than their descendants?" Shepard advocates that most forms of technology be abandoned and society reordered along hunter-gatherer lines.

It may someday be shown that some cultural norms of the far past were more enlightened than might be guessed. But this is very different from supposing that a hunter-gatherer existence would be preferable to current Western life. That notion borders on bizarre.

Yet a growing politically correct literature romanticizes the hunter-gatherer days, and sometimes the Middle Ages, as centuries when fruits of nature's abundance fell at everyone's feet and most human time could be spent contemplating the clouds or playing the flute. Juliet Schor, a Harvard economist, embraced this view in her 1992 book *The Overworked American.* Schor lauded the present-day lifestyles of the !Kung bush people, who are said to labor at most three days per week. She asserted that in medieval centuries "neither peasants nor their lords were dependent on markets for their basic subsistence. They were not exposed to economic competition, nor driven by the profit motive. Medieval industry was also protected from market pressures." Attending a Harvard environmental seminar a few years ago, I listened to one graduate student advocate that the human population be reduced to its preagricultural level of perhaps five million, and that people then be required to live without machines or permanent structures, "migrating with the seasons." There was applause when she finished speaking.

Of course college students confidently announce goofy plans to save the world; I did too. But romanticizing of the human past can only occur under circumstances of willing suspension of disbelief, the sort of suspended logic that now handicaps environmental policy generally. Most historians, for example, would gag on Schor's notion that the Middle Ages were idyllic because there was no economic competition or quest for profit.

Less is known about the hunter-gatherer existence, but it is reasonable to speculate that preindustrial life was harsh and mired in inequity. In the 1992 book *Sick Societies: Challenging the Myth of Primitive Harmony,* Robert Edgerton, a professor of anthropology at the University of California at Los Angeles, estimated that in preindustrial times around one-quarter of males died by violence. Edgerton further believes health conditions of preindustrial society were abject. Green literature romanticizes the Mesoamerican culture of the early centuries

A.D., especially the Aztec city of Teotihuacan. Despite evidence that the Aztecs took slaves and engaged in wars of imperial conquest against neighbor states, early life in Teotihuacan is depicted by ecotopian writers as an innocent paradise where a carefree, harmonious people lived in happy accord with nature and venerated the plumage of birds. Edgerton says of Teotihuacan, "Its population was in dreadful health. Rates of malnutrition, stunted growth, deciduous tooth hypoplasia, and infant and child mortality were higher than any known population of that time or earlier. Life expectancy at birth ranged between 14 and 17 years. Infant mortality was about 40 percent. Only 38 percent lived to be as old as 15."

Another indicator of pretechnological reality comes from the present-day Yanomano of Venezuela and Ache of Paraguay, who are believed to live approximately as some hunter-gatherers once did. Anthropologists who have studied the Yanomano generally conclude their culture is both violent and possessive of women. Yanomano sometimes raid other villages looking for women to kidnap, killing whoever resists. The journal *Science* reported in 1993 that when Yanomano and Ache men marry a woman whose previous husband has died, they have the heartwarming custom of demanding that children from the previous union be put to death.

Women and men cannot be realistic about the history of nature until they learn to face the realities of their own history. Current trends in environmental orthodoxy are toward an imagined history that is appealing on ideological grounds but sheds no useful illumination on the present.

The Romanticized Predator

In 1983, in a high school gymnasium in Bozeman, Montana,[3] I attended a meeting to protest a death sentence. Some 300 people were present, many having brought signs and placards. The death penalty being protested was for a bear.

A grizzly had killed a camper sleeping in Gallatin National Park. Wardens caught the animal and proposed to destroy it. Opposition to the proposal was spirited. The crowd hooted derisively at a Park Service official; there were chants of "Save the bear!" Talking to some of the crowd afterward, I heard two basic lines of explanation for that sentiment. One was the widely held belief among Montanans that grizzlies only kill out-of-state residents. The victim in this case was a young adult camper from Wisconsin; another bear victim that year was a six-year-

old who became separated from her tourist parents. The second prof-
fered defense was that society was to blame for placing itself in the
bear's path by settling the Montana wilderness. This explanation came
from people who themselves lived in what had once been Montana
wilderness and who would be entirely outraged if ordered to move as
part of some preservation drive. It was primal SOMEBODY ELSE logic.

For a decade controversy has revolved around the grizzly of
Yellowstone National Park. One of the few wild animals aggressive in
the presence of people, grizzlies are protected by the Endangered Species
Act. Every few years a grizzly kills someone at Yellowstone. If the animal is captured, often environmental groups protest that the bear should
not be destroyed. Deaths of people from predators are on the rise in
many areas as bear populations expand and cougars and wolves repopulate. For example, two sleeping campers were mauled to death by bear
in the San Bernardino Mountains of California in August 1993.

In Alaska bear populations have been increasing, especially brown
bear, an occasionally dangerous subspecies. One male child and one
adult woman were devoured by brown bear in separate incidents in
Alaska in 1992. Most Alaskans favor aggressive antibear measures.[4] But
contemporary Alaskans are by sociological and physical circumstances
the last North American cowboys, living with nature more intimately
than most of the population and less squeamish about nature's kill-or-
be-killed aspect. In other states sentiment runs strongly in favor of protection for predators that may harm people. For example, in 1992
Colorado voters banned the state's annual bear hunt. Some naturalists
suspect the lack of hunting now emboldens large predators. City folk
may not believe this but hunters swear that higher animals, especially
wolves, have a clear understanding of what guns represent. (Many
activists become agitated by the phrase "higher animals." To them I can
say only: Oh, please.) When hunting is common somehow word gets out
in the animal community and target animals flee man; when hunting is
rare, animals are emboldened.

In 1991 a cougar, a protected predator no longer hunted, killed a
teenage boy who was jogging near his school outside the foothills town
of Idaho Springs, Colorado. The environmentalist Michael Potts wrote
"defending the magnificent cat's right of place," suggesting the boy
"should have been paying attention and looking around, not listening to
[his] Walkman." Anyone who seriously thinks the magnificent strut of a
mountain lion is worth the life of a boy is morally lost. Today elements
of ecological orthodoxy are in danger of such detachment.

Equally, orthodox enviros who believe that predatory animals are
good and deserve special protection, but human beings are bad and must

be restricted, miss the point of their own argument. Genus *Homo* is a predator. If predation is so terrific doesn't that make humans the most terrific species of all? To the extent predation exists, nature clearly intends that creatures defend themselves against it. Women and men should not harm any species needlessly, including by hunting for "sport," a notion that has always seemed primeval to me. But the idea that a person being advanced upon by a grizzly or cougar should hesitate even for an instant to shoot that animal dead would strike nature as deeply unnatural. Nature would pull the trigger without a second thought.

And predators are a strange choice for the affection of environmentalists, as they are by some lights the most selfish of species. Bear, wolf, tiger, and many other predators demarcate territories into sizeable blocks, because in nature only large blocks of land can support the topmost creatures of the food chain. The Fish and Wildlife Service estimates each grizzly requires 17,510 acres of land to itself. Each American human being "demarcates" just nine acres, the U.S. population density being one per nine acres. In that light, which species asks most of nature? Of course this is a simplified comparison. The underlying point: Like misplaced admiration for a romanticized past, misplaced enthusiasm for predators can leave environmental thinking disjunct from environmental reality.

The Shift Inside

Enviros won the last 20 years of political battles by a wide margin, but you'd never know it from their public statements. That their cause has become mainstream makes many environmentalists nervous. If Republicans now call themselves environmentalists, doesn't that mean something went terribly wrong? All movements that graduate to insider status undergo a number of such stresses: Among those now affecting the green movement are its relations to science, to lobbying, and to fundraising.

"We don't trust scientists when they talk about the benefits of technology, but we love 'em when they produce studies saying the world will end in ten days," says David Malakoff, a former official of Friends of the Earth. Through the 1960s environmentalists were suspicious of the science world, considering it a lackey of Big Industry. Then researchers began to find evidence of ozone depletion and similar problems. Environmental litigators discovered that when there exist conflicting interpretations of ecological law, judges assign considerable weight to scientific findings. Thus environmental groups have warmed toward science.

The science world is skeptical of environmentalist studies: given that groups like the NRDC and Sierra Club have political agendas, how can their research be objective? Academic scientists often note that although the reports of environmental advocacy organizations are cited as authoritative in newspapers and on television shows, rarely are they accepted for publication in peer-reviewed technical journals, the science world's test of detached merit. Nevertheless, ice between the worlds of environmentalism and academic research is thawing. This is an optimistic sign, suggesting that soon the reasoning powers of science may inform environmental sentiment while the emotions of environmentalism attune science to the priorities of conservation.

The notion of formal insider influence is a tempestuous one to enviros. For instance, should environmental groups accept payments from corporations for advice? The Environmental Defense Fund has done so with McDonald's, Johnson & Johnson, Mutual of Omaha, and others, helping them devise recycling programs. And should environmental groups ever lend support to candidates other than liberal Democrats? The movement was furious when EDF president Fred Krupp appeared at the White House to endorse the 1990 clean air bill, Krupp's presence next to a Republican president being seen as a blasphemy, regardless of the merits of the legislation. Greenpeace theatrically refuses any negotiation with public officials, contending all insider contacts to be corrupting. Yet the organization supplicates in Hollywood, where during the 1980s it was a charity of choice, Greenpeace soliciting endorsements from celebrities whose lives are devoted to immodest consumption. Greenpeace has run save-the-whales TV ads featuring the model Christie Brinkley, whose lifestyle could support whole Third World villages.

In the early 1990s the Sierra Club, which is important in California politics, was split regarding whether to act as an insider by negotiating directly with timber interests. A state referendum called Forests Forever had been defeated, but by a small enough margin that logging companies worried it might someday pass. Some Sierra Club factions favored negotiations to get timber firms to agree voluntarily to provisions from the initiative. Other factions opposed any talks, knowing timber companies would ask, in return, for recognition of the validity of logging as an economic enterprise. After Sierra Club negotiator Gail Lucas, a lifelong enviro, reached agreement with the timber company Sierra Pacific on a voluntary commitment to sustainable yield, the club withdrew its support for Lucas and essentially blackballed her for the sin of appearing in public with a timber executive and speaking kindly of him. Later the Club–timber company negotiations collapsed.

As environmentalists have become effective lobbyists they have learned the negative tools of the trade: bluster, veiled threats, misrepresentation. Distortion of the scientific case regarding the pesticide Alar is a common charge against environmental lobbyists. Here is a more typical, workaday example. During Clean Air Act lobbying in 1990, one question was how many grams of unburned hydrocarbons new cars could emit. Existing regulations set the limit at 4.1 grams per mile; EPA administrator William Reilly proposed to lower the standards to 2.5 grams per mile. Enviro lobbyists called the deal a sellout because 1990 cars already averaged only 2.6 grams. Their complaints about the proposal led to denunciations of Reilly on Capitol Hill.

Automakers design tailpipe controls to emit less than law allows, creating a "compliance cushion" that forestalls recalls. This is why an existing standard of 4.1 grams led to cars emitting 2.6 grams. Reilly knew that if the limit were lowered to 2.5 grams, the new compliance cushion would drop actual emissions to around 1.5 grams. Automakers would be anxious for an extra reduction since the new Clean Air Act requires them to warrant emissions systems for 75,000 miles. Enviro lobbyists understood about compliance cushions: They simply declined to mention this factor in congressional testimony and media interviews, sensing a chance to create a jolt of bad news. "The advocacy campaign against the provision was illogical unless the motive was to take a positive development and make it seem depressing," says Reilly, himself once an environmental lobbyist as head of the World Wildlife Fund.

Once environmental lobbyists engage in tactics such as willful distortions of the other side's positions they place themselves on a slope that can lead downward toward simply being another pressure group that will say or do whatever is expedient to maintain its interests. If anything will push the enviros into that descent it is fund-raising.

The Direct-Mail Trap

"**I found** the enclosed internal report so frightening, so shocking, that I immediately decided to rush a copy off to you," begins an appeal Sierra Club director Michael Fischer mass-mailed in 1992. "It explores the insidious yet vastly organized plot by the so-called Wise Use Movement to *DESTROY THE ENTIRE ENVIRONMENTAL MOVEMENT*" (Caps and italics original). Attached to the letter was an ersatz document bearing the simulated hand-stamp INTERNAL USE ONLY purporting to show "irrefutable evidence" that "exploiters and polluters" had staged a tippy-top-secret meeting to "plot the total and final destruction of the American environmental movement."

Anyone familiar with the sorts of fund-raising letters employed to frighten the elderly about Social Security will recognize familiar themes here: claims of plots and secret meetings; official-looking "documents"; preposterous assertions, such as that the well-entrenched environmental movement will suffer "total and final destruction" if you don't send that check today. Modern life knows three basic types of shakedowns: blackmail, greenmail, and directmail.

Unscrupulous fund-raisers such as Richard Viguerie showed that bogus documents, wild distortions, and the use of "devil figures" are what shake money loose by mail. Through the 1980s many enviro groups adapted these techniques as former Interior Secretary James Watt, a raving unviro, made the ideal devil figure for directmail. By the end of the decade Greenpeace was among the leading directmailers in the U.S., often drop-shipping phony-document mailings of one million pieces. National Audubon Society mailings were emblazoned with such banners as TEN SECONDS A MONTH CAN HELP SAVE THE PLANET! Even the normally staid Nature Conservancy unleashed directmail appeals containing imaginary land deeds computer-printed with the mark's name.

If it is dangerous to believe your own press releases, it is deadly to believe your own directmail. "We've got to get off mail fund-raising, it will kill us intellectually," Audubon Society president Peter Berle has told associates. Directmail dynamics compel institutional environmentalism away from the sort of ecorealism that is the next wave of ecological thinking. And reasoning backward from directmail engages a risk that is the worst faced by contemporary environmentalists, the New Right parallel.

At one time the New Right consisted of poorly funded outsiders making assertions the establishment would not heed. Gradually the movement acquired money and influence. In 1980 it elected a president in Ronald Reagan and for a time seemed to represent a force that would roll over the American political landscape. Then legislatures began to make some of the changes the New Right advocated. Rather than celebrate gains and cool their rhetoric many on the right grew still more strident, if only to differentiate themselves from a mainstream that shifted in their direction. A dynamic took hold in which some New Right factions were more concerned with imagining new liberal menaces over which to become lathered for fund-raising purposes than about the actual condition of the world. By the late 1980s, the New Right had lost what once seemed like an unstoppable ballot box appeal. In the 1992 presidential election, its stridency actively backfired on the Republican Party. In 1994, the shrill New Right candidates such as Oliver North were defeated, even as Republicans generally were swept into office throughout the country.

Enviros today risk the same progression of events. Once they were disenfranchised crusaders, pronouncing a message the powers that be tried to ignore. Now the movement is a monied faction of that establishment. In 1992 environmentalism put a champion, Al Gore, into the White House. Yet as the ecology movement has acquired status, many emotionally satisfying good-versus-evil distinctions are being blurred by the very reforms enviros set in motion. Like the New Right, enviros have begun to evolve an internal dynamic of self-satisfaction based on mutual displays of stridency, with fund-raising a high priority. If green factions keep proclaiming that nature is ending when daily the sun continues to rise, enviros may find that the public's "Oh, shut up" point can be reached on the environment too.

Nothing worth keeping was lost when the strident New Right did itself in. It will be a profound ruination if environmentalism goes down the same drain.

22 🌿

FARMS 🌿

No ACTIVITY STAKES A GREATER CLAIM ON NATURE THAN agriculture, with farms in nearly every nation exceeding by a wide margin all other human imposition on the land. In 1987 "built-up" uses of the United States—cities, airfields, parking lots—accounted for 47 million acres, versus 421 million acres for cropland in production. Farming also stakes a claim on the American collective consciousness. The farm is seen as a preserve of virtue; of individual responsibility; of the satisfaction of producing something worthwhile using one's own hands; of life in conjunction with nature. Everything except the last is true. Modern farms may smell of hay and run by the cycles of the seasons, but the last thing they are is natural.

Most crops grown on First World farms are selectively bred hybrids that would die if sown wild. They may require furrow planting in earth softened by a plow, irrigation for growth, and chemicals that defeat insect and root competitors. Land on which commercial crops flower often has been rendered unnaturally flat for the convenience of tractors. Animals raised on contemporary farms are selectively bred creatures that would be hard pressed to endure the wild. They depend on people to provide their food, often foods they would not consume in nature. Today even on family farms stock and fowl are routinely given vitamins, prophylactic antibiotics, and hormones. Most vegetation in the wild is perennial, having multiyear life cycles. On the farm most vegetation is annual: seeds sown in spring, crops taken in fall, the remains of the sponsor plant ripped out for a new planting next year. Farms are unnatural in another sense as well: as a source of environmental damage.

False Farm Problems

Some claimed environmental harms from farming, such as lost farmland and lost soil, are overstated. Some are entirely real. First let's consider the overstated.

A prominent instant-doomsday scare of the 1970s was "vanishing farms." As productivity increased, allowing more agricultural land to be withdrawn from production, many environmentalists declared decreasing farmland to be a crisis. Farmland was said to be disappearing to development at a rate of some three million acres per year. James Speth, head of President Jimmy Carter's Council on Environmental Quality, declared no less than the "destruction of our rural landscape and heritage" through farmland loss. Many states responded by passing right-to-farm legislation and placing agricultural lands into restricted status. Carter appointed a commission called the National Agricultural Lands Study, which in 1979 issued a report predicting, "Ten years from now Americans could be as concerned over the loss of the nation's prime and important farmlands as they are today over shortages of oil and gasoline." Strictly speaking that prediction was correct. By 1989 Americans were "as concerned" over both, in the sense of not being concerned about either.

What happened to the vanishing-farms crisis? It turned out that the three-million-acre annual figure stemmed from computational errors in the National Agricultural Lands Survey. The commission's work was based on two Soil Conservation Service surveys, one in 1967 and another in 1975. But between the surveys the definitions used by SCS analysts had been changed, a factor the commission did not take into account. "If you merged the surveys they seemed to produce a rapidly increasing level of conversion," H. Thomas Frey, a Department of Agriculture geographer, says. "If you adjusted for the changed definition there was almost no loss." In 1984 the Soil Conservation Service issued a report effectively retracting the National Agricultural Lands Survey.

Yet for all the banner-headline treatment the "vanishing farms" story received, a check of major newspapers using the Nexus computer index showed that only a handful mentioned the retraction of NALS. None did so prominently. News accounts and reports by environmentalists continue to employ the three-million-acre annual loss figure as an "official government finding."

The common belief that topsoil is being "lost" falls into a similar category of spectral crisis. Claims of a coming agricultural collapse caused
by soil depletion rank among the most poorly thought through of environmental doctrine. For instance in 1982, the Conservation Foundation
declared that "nationally, over 6.4 million tons of soil a year are lost in
wind and water erosion" owing to modern farming practice. But lost in
what sense? Contemporary agricultural techniques have eliminated
most of the erosion associated with farming of the Dust Bowl era.
Farmers have an intense financial interest in preventing topsoil loss, as it
could render their property worthless. To the extent some soil does leave
a farm during operations, soil carried along on the wind, or washed to a
stream, does not vanish from the face of the Earth. It comes to rest somewhere else. "The notion of soil 'lost' is found throughout the popular literature on erosion, [but] only a small percentage of soil eroded from
farmers' fields is permanently lost to agriculture," Pierre Crosson, an
agriculture analyst at Resources for the Future, has written.

A U.S. Geological Survey team has studied erosion along the Coon
Creek basin of southwest Wisconsin, which became an agricultural
region in the 1850s. Since that time only six to seven percent of soils
washed or blown from farmers' fields actually has left the Coon Creek
area and departed down the Mississippi River. Most has recycled from
one field to another. During the same period, the flood plains of Coon
Creek gained soil that pessimists would say had been lost from somewhere else. The net? Topsoil levels in the Coon Creek basin are today
about the same as they were in 1850, after 140 years of continuous
farming.

In defense of claims of lost soil and land degradation, some environmentalists cite a series of studies from the International Soil Reference
and Information Center, a Dutch organization. These studies assert that
human activity has degraded 17 percent of the world's land since 1945,
which if true would be a level of land damage comparable to the worst
in natural history. But ISRIC statistics have been challenged by Crosson
and other researchers. The Center's studies assert, for example, that
farmers in Illinois, Iowa, Kansas, and Nebraska have so badly damaged
the land there that its productivity is "greatly reduced." Farm productivity has been rising in all these states on an annual basis since 1945.

Real Farm Problems

Chemical runoff from farms is, in contrast, every bit as much a problem
as suggested. In the United States the effluents that industry may place

into streams or rivers are now tightly regulated. But discharge from farms, called "nonpoint source pollution" in EPA argot, remains essentially unregulated. "Nonpoint water pollution is the largest area of failure in current environmental policy," former EPA administrator William Reilly says.

Today just six percent of U.S. river pollution originates with industry. Forty percent, the largest share, is from agriculture. Judged by surface area, about seven million acres of lakes and reservoirs in the United States are considered to have "impaired" water quality; of that two million acres, the largest share, is attributed to chemical runoff from farms, versus about 318,000 acres tied to industrial water pollution. Some 72 percent of "impaired" U.S. rivers and 56 percent of impaired lakes are harmed mainly by farm runoff.

Farm chemicals are unregulated because though it is politically attractive for members of Congress to blast sinister corporations as polluters, no one wants to call the friendly farmer to task. The EPA certifies pesticides for sale, and the Food and Drug Administration monitors food for residues of agricultural chemicals. But there are no meaningful restrictions on the ways in which farmers use pesticides on their fields: just warning labels on the bags. Environmentalists approach the farm lobby gingerly, too, because while the public is suspicious of corporations, it sympathizes with farmers.

Not all farm chemicals are exceptionally toxic. Many are only mildly so, being specialized for effect on insects or fungi far less able to resist contact with chemicals than mammals. A 1988 study in the *Journal of the American Medical Association* noted that "no pesticides except for arsenic and vinyl chloride definitely have been proved to be carcinogenic" to people. Not that the design of pesticides for "narrow" toxicity is necessarily reassuring. When in 1990 California cities were sprayed with the pesticide malathion to kill the Mediterranean fruit fly, local officials announced that malathion was harmless to people. But, they added, as soon as the helicopters pass over be sure to wash it off your car so it won't ruin the paint job. Feel better now?

Nonregulation of pesticide use is poor policy for two reasons. The first is danger to farmers and farm workers. While news organizations and institutional environmentalism fret theatrically about tiny pesticide residues on supermarket foods, the real dangers farm chemicals create are to farmers, farm workers and the farm ecology. Workers exposed to pesticides in the field may receive doses thousands of times greater than the minute amounts to which consumers are subjected. The worst-case reading of the effects of pesticide residues on consumers is about 6,000 cancers per year, according to EPA documents; the actual level is probably much lower. Pesticide harm to farm workers, on the other hand, is undisputed, with some 1,225 cases of direct poisonings reported in 1991. Some of those poisonings were self-inflicted in suicides. Most were exposures in the course of pesticide handling and application.

Nonregulation of farm pesticide use is also poor policy owing to the tonnages involved. Contrary to popular belief, modern pesticide application is not soaring. Since 1985, pesticide applications as measured by active ingredients has risen only about four percent, while fertilizer use has declined about ten percent. Considering that farm production rose 16 percent during that period, the proportion of chemical input to food and fiber output is declining. Still nearly half a billion pounds of pesticides and four billion pounds of fertilizer are spread or sprayed onto farmers' fields each year in the United States. The figures are higher for Western Europe.

In the U.S. alone that's 4.5 billion pounds of chemicals, every one of which, were it taken to a landfill, would be classified as a hazardous waste. Under current regulations, landfill operators receiving discarded pesticides must first inactivate them by adding neutralizers, then put the results in sealed drums, then bury the drums in cells lined with polymers and compacted clay. Farmers have legal sanction to toss the same substances onto their fields and shrug as the rains wash them to the nearest stream. The 4.5 billion pounds per year of chemicals that U.S. farms "emit" onto the land exceeds the 3.2 billion pounds of chemicals emitted by all forms of industrial activity in the United States in 1992.

The Plunge into Chemistry

Agricultural chemicals did not become common till the early postwar era. This development has been variously described as a breakthrough for the feeding of the world or a conspiracy run by corporations that had been making chemicals for war and now wanted to make equivalent weapons for use against the Earth. Though most conspiracy theories are flights of fancy, this one contains some truth. World War II weapons plants, such as the closed facility that today sits at the center of the Superfund site at Rocky Mountain Arsenal outside Denver, were indeed converted to pesticide production. Manufacturers promoted their new offerings with all the forthright decorum of carnival barkers.

Salesmanship was not the only force at play, however. In the early postwar era many academic agronomists praised farm chemicals. Use of chemicals prevented repetition of the Dust Bowl, because crops almost never failed and therefore roots were always present to hold soil against wind. From 1950 to 1984 grain yields rose an amazing three percent per year, keeping foodstuffs plentiful and prices low. Higher yields meant the population could expand while cropland in cultivation declined. Higher farm productivity can also reduce inputs of energy, water, and other resources. In 1950, 3.3 pounds of feed were required for each pound of meat from a broiler chicken. Today it's 1.9 pounds; feed requirements for cattle and pigs have fallen in parallel. In 1945, the United States contained 25 million dairy cows. Today the U.S. has ten million dairy cows making a greater volume of milk. Today's smaller numbers of cows eat less feed, take up less land, and are the source of less bovine methane, a greenhouse gas. New York is the number-three dairy state: In 1992 New York dairies set a state record for milk production, despite having the smallest number of cows since 1924. Through increased productivity hundreds of thousands of acres of dairy land have been returned to nature in New York in the last half century, offsetting urban expansion even in that overdeveloped state.

Some of the misuse of farm chemicals stems from the fact that when pesticides and herbicides were launched as products, farmers knew little about their properties. If initial results from pesticides and fertilizers were successful, some farmers simply applied more. "One reason farmers fell in love with pesticides and herbicides in the 1950s," says David Pimentel, a professor of agricultural sciences at Cornell University, "is that you didn't have to know much to use them. You just blasted away. It's not that farmers aren't smart—most pay close attention to what the agricultural extension services teach. But as recently as the 1970s agricultural schools did not know the answers to many basic questions about insect life cycles. So the extension schools recommended chemicals, and farmers said fine."

A cycle took hold in which farmers, raised to believe it could never be wrong to produce more food or fiber, sometimes felt obliged to overuse chemicals if only to beat last year's record, Farm Bureau and 4-H societies giving their most coveted awards for highest yield, not general ecosystem management. Events grew more complicated in the 1970s when for a period the cost of loans was lower than inflation, meaning farmers came out ahead by borrowing for supplies that increase production. Normally averse to debt, many farmers became what heartland communities called "plungers"—taking a plunge for the best tractors and most advanced chemicals. Alas, plunging proved a financial nightmare for most. A few years ago I spent a week visiting farms in central

Iowa. Helen Lester, who with her husband Guy had farmed in Milo, Iowa, since the Depression, described the psychology of 1970s in these memorable words: "Too many tractors with too much horsepower."

In an especially perverse outcome, government programs often pressure farmers to employ more chemicals. Usually farmers who "seal" their crops under federal support are given a fixed acreage allotment they may plow; additional acres must be left fallow, to limit overproduction and cut the government's losses. This means the only way a farmer can raise revenues is to pump up yield on the sanctioned acres. Chemicals are the medium of high yields, so banks making price-support loans may write into their contracts a requirement that maximum-intensity practices be employed.

Karl Zinsmeister, an agricultural analyst at the American Enterprise Institute in Washington, D.C., notes, "Many farmers are induced to maximize chemical inputs, tractor time, and fuel because increasing yield per acre is the only way they can increase income. If farm subsidies were phased out, American agriculture would shift to a lower-input style of production. Needless to say this less souped-up agriculture would be milder on the environment." The structure of agricultural subsidies also tends to compel those farmers who grow the most subsidized crops, usually grains, to stay in grains year after year, rather than varying their plantings to obtain the ecological advantages of rotation. But though environmental lobbies often call for restrictions on use of farm chemicals, rarely do they call for an end to farm subsidies, such subsidies being a sacred cow, as it were, of classicist liberalism.

The Pesticide Peak

Many farmers are beginning to shift away from chemicals on their own. This makes it likely that in the decade to come, agricultural chemical use in the developed world, today declining relative to production, will begin to decline in absolute terms. The Canadian province of Ontario has already mandated a 50-percent reduction in the use of farm chemicals. The mandate is being met without notable loss of production or farm income. Denmark, the Netherlands, and Sweden have similar programs. In late 1993, the Clinton Administration announced a bill that would require most farmers to employ "integrated pest management," which reduces pesticides, and would stipulate that any pesticide banned in the United States cannot be exported, breaking the "circle of poison" by which farm chemicals illegal for use here enter the U.S. food chain as residues on imported foods.

Assuming Clinton's proposal is enacted, farm chemicals, like most pollution, eventually will be seen as following a predictable track: increase to the level of obvious harm, then a peak, then a much faster reduction than expected. "What we will do in agriculture is substitute knowledge for chemicals, managing farmlands in a manner that is much more sophisticated than what we use today," says Pimentel.

Through the 1980s an increasing number of Western farmers began to practice "conservation tillage," a knowledge adaptation having to do with improvements in understanding the relationships among rain, roots, and soil. Conservation tillage is being aided by a rediscovery of crop rotation: an ancient technique that farmers tended to believe was no longer required owing to Green Revolution developments. Department of Agriculture statistics show that in 1945 most corn in the United States was grown via rotation. Then using few pesticides, farmers saw annual 3.5 percent crop losses to insects. By 1992 most corn was grown without rotation but with lots of chemicals, and farmers saw an annual 12 percent crop loss to insects. Taking into account higher yields the 1992 farmer came out ahead, but obviously the higher rate of losses to insects suggests fewer chemicals and more rotation might be advised. When crops are rotated the insects that like them decline in the rotation year, as their favorite plants are not around to eat. When crops are grown without rotation, each year's insect infestation is born with a ready food supply. For a time pesticides seemed powerful enough to overcome that drawback. Now that insects have acquired some pesticide resistance, crop rotation, which breaks the propagation cycle, is being rediscovered.

That clumsy name integrated pest management denotes in turn an important recent farming advance. Under this approach farmers combat insects using knowledge of their life cycles and natural predators. In 1989 the National Research Council, normally seen as siding with Big Industry, issued an influential report proposing that almost all agriculture switch to integrated pest management, estimating that the typical farmer could cut chemical use about 30 percent and yet realize higher incomes. Farm yield would fall somewhat with fewer chemicals, the NRC projected, but input costs would fall by a little more, improving net profit. New England apple growers, the NRC noted, now control the coddling moth with five to ten sprayings. Just one spraying will do if timed to the most vulnerable point in the moth's life cycle. Integrated pest management is already common in New Zealand, which benefits from the early British interest in what Brits call biodynamic and Americans call organic farming. John Reganhold, a University of Washington researcher, has studied the biodynamic farms of New

Zealand and found that while most have somewhat smaller yields than U.S. farms, profit levels are comparable.

Farm chemical use is now peaking partly because new pesticides coming onto the market are not only safer than those they supplant but usually require lower doses per acre.[1] The corn pesticide atrazine, for example, has been reformulated to require 1.6 pounds per acre rather than the previous three pounds. A new herbicide called acetochlor, which kills weeds that occur with corn, is used in about half the dose of previous compounds. EPA registration documents allow marketing of acetochlor only if its manufacturers can prove that sales lead to net reductions in the herbicides applied to cornfields.

The next encouraging trend is biopesticides, gene-engineered products that mimick nature. Accounting for just $25 million of the world farm market in 1987, biopesticides were by 1993 already up to $1 billion in sales. A typical product: toxin genes from the poison glands of mites and scorpions spliced into the RNA of a virus that attacks only caterpillars. Caterpillars exposed to the low-level toxins become sluggish and eventually starve. Another notable new farm chemical is imidacloprid, a bioengineered pesticide based on nicotine. Nicotine is extremely toxic to insects but breaks down in sunlight, rendering the substance impractical as a pesticide. Imidacloprid is an engineered nicotine in which molecules are "twisted" to be made sun resistant. The chemical can be used in approximately five percent of the volume of comparable pesticides and eventually does degrade into harmless byproducts. If imidacloprid can be grown directly in tobacco plants—unknown at this writing—a socially constructive function for the tobacco farm will be created.

Market forces are an important factor in the coming pesticide peak. Farm chemicals are expensive, causing farmers to prefer lower-dose versions. And since most farmers own their own land, most have a long-term incentive to shift toward reduced-dose pesticides in order to insure that the land remains productive for their children. Market forces and the financial self-interest of farmers, factors environmentalists have long assumed hostile to the Earth, will combine to move agriculture down the slope that follows the pesticide peak.

There are indications this shift is already beginning. In the early 1990s California's Mondavi winery converted to what it calls sustainable agriculture, dramatically reducing though not eliminating the use of chemicals in grape growing. In most Mondavi vineyards, weeds are now controlled by tilling them under, rather than applying herbicides; nesting boxes have been built throughout Mondavi fields to attract screech owls, a natural predator to the gophers that till recently had been killed with chemicals. In 1993 Fetzer, another major California winery, converted vineyards to organic farming. Neither Mondavi nor Fetzer plans to advertise its wines as grown in natural fashion. The companies switched to low-chemical agriculture because they believe the technique will make their vineyards more productive and profitable.

If MBA-managed, profit-oriented companies are converting away from chemicals because the alternatives are more cost-effective, then pesticide use has peaked—and the future of farming, though not chemical-free, holds a clean-tech era based on knowledge of nature rather than brute force.

THE (INDUSTRIAL) FOREST 🌿

THE AIR WAS HUSHED AS I STOOD IN A LUSH WEALD KNOWN TO locals as the Sucker Creek forest, in coastal Washington State. Around me rose tall Douglas firs, the regal tree of Pacific Northwest lore and commerce. Carpeting the ground were uncountable varieties of small plants, molds, and lichens—a profusion of life. A naturalist accompanying me pulled up a seedling and pointed to its roots, which were dotted with mycorrhizae, a fungus that lives symbiotically with Douglas fir in the wild. I watched a bald eagle sail across low hills in the distance. Wandering for additional hours I caught glimpses or saw tracks or spoor of mountain beaver, cottontail, flying squirrel, opossum, loon, Roosevelt elk, and several songbirds. When dark approached I returned to the electric animation of Seattle, reflecting on a day spent where nature rules.

But I had not been in a forest preserve or old-growth woodland. I had been in the "industrial forest"—a tree farm owned and operated by Weyerhaeuser.

Many misconceptions are at play in the debate about modern forestry. The worst is that timber growth areas—known as managed forests or industrial forests or successional forests—are "managed deserts," as many activists call them. Most managed forests teem with life. In the commercial woodlands of the Northwest nearly all native plants and animals flourish. Almost everything that happens in the industrial forest is driven by nature, the main exception being that trees exit after being sawed down, not burned down as would happen in the lightning-caused fires that restart the natural forest cycle.

In some respects young woodlands as developed by genus *Homo* are better places for biodiversity than are old-growth forests. Commercial timber operations emphasize the youthful phase of the forest, when trees grow rapidly. This is also when species proliferate. Studies conducted by the Forestry Sciences Laboratory of the Forest Service suggest that Northwest forests with trees less than 15 years of age average 186 major wildlife species; mature forests of trees 50 to 150 years of age average 167 species; old-growth forests average 152 species. The young-forest environment is open, sun drenched, and competitive—good for most forms of life. The old-growth environment, though clearly favorable for some species, is closed, with climax trees of full height blocking sunlight to the forest floor, precluding many forms of life.

The creatures that dwell in successional forests often are browsing species such as elk and deer, animals that like open-access or "edge" areas. Some who oppose managed forestry argue that the world has plenty of browsing animals, deer now overpopulating many U.S. and European woodlands. But, they continue, the world is short of old-growth species such as the spotted owl and marbled murlet. This may well be true, yet it is an entirely human judgment. The notion that owls or murlets are more deserving than deer no more springs from the natural condition than do the finished two-by-fours in your couch.

What really goes on in the industrial forest is essential to understanding how to preserve the old-growth, those glorious "sanctuaries of wildlife and of the human spirit," as the ecologist Timothy Hermach has called them. In its zeal to portray all commercial use of trees as horrifying, environmental orthodoxy has overlooked something essential: The more timber that can be produced from managed stands, the less pressure to log out ancient forests. In this sense the industrial forest is like high-intensity agriculture: By producing more from less space, it frees land for return to a natural condition. If done in a manner that respects biodiversity, timber production ought to be an ecologically desirable form of commerce. Yet for all the recent blather about sustainable development, environmental sentiment is driving consumers and jobs away from wood, one of the few current industries entirely renewable.

Let's start with a few basics about the actualities of forestry:

• *Ancient forests are renewable too.* Logging opponents call the places in dispute in the Pacific Northwest "ancient" forests to make them sound irreplaceable. Ancient forests are precious, but can be restored. Every Northwest forest today depicted as irreplaceable has been destroyed by glaciers, fire, and other natural factors many times.

• *A Conservation Strategy for the Spotted Owl,* the government science assessment that was the primary document employed to justify the

Northwest logging ban that began in 1991, presumes it takes a maximum of about 200 years, and sometimes only about 100 years, for open fields in the Olympic Peninsula timber belt to regenerate into old-growth forest. Since Douglas fir requires around 65 years to reach mature height, leaving a Northwest woodland alone for that period is the main gesture required to get a brand-new "ancient" forest up and running. This means the old-growth question is really another environmental transition issue. So long as Northwest acres are set aside for regeneration, in two centuries or less—a click of the heels to nature—the primal forests that orthodox doctrine depicts as gone forever will return to existence.

Here is an inconveniently positive thought. One thing timber companies are getting really good at is helping Douglas fir grow to heights in less time than required naturally. Knowledge of rapid tree cultivation, acquired in the pecuniary interest of timber profit, may soon be put to use regenerating tall-tree habitats and their attendant old-growth species.

• *Logging is sustainable.* Many industries someday will be converted to renewable economics; logging is among the few already in that category. Rational environmental policy might encourage consumers to substitute wood for materials based on nonrenewable metals and petrochemicals. Instead policy now discourages wood use. And it's working: Per capita wood consumption in the United States has been declining since the 1970s at a faster rate than reductions in use of materials generally.

Green dogma is antiwood partly owing to the stereotype of the logger as swaggering foe of the wild. This stereotype has founding in truth, mainly in turn-of-the-century logging practices that cleared wide swaths of forest. But those forests today have regrown, while the callous logger is on the wane. Nearly all timber companies today employ university-trained foresters whose education includes course work on biodiversity. Large logging concerns are beginning to employ wildlife biologists. "Unlike what happened till the turn of the century, today loggers do not wipe out some remote area then move on," says Kevin McElwee, a forester in Michigan's Upper Peninsula timber zone. "Most live where they log and plan to stay. People who work with wood now understand that the continued health of the forest means income not only for us but for our children."

Michigan's Upper Peninsula, a region of several million acres, is today more than 90 percent forested: rich with animal and plant life, high in biodiversity. Some environmental groups have proposed severe restrictions on logging there, to protect what is generally presumed a primal forest. Yet the Upper Peninsula is almost entirely second- and third-growth managed forest. Around the turn of the century "nearly the whole U.P. had been slicked off," McElwee says. "The old-timers talk about patches that were flat for 50 miles in every direction. Now it's beautiful, dense forest again." In 1984 the paper company for which McElwee works, Champion International, opened a $1.5 billion pulp mill in Marquette. "Engineering specifications for this mill call for it to run for a hundred years," McElwee notes. "It will make the most money if the Michigan forest is healthy for an extended period."

• *Snobs love wood but hate loggers.* Antilogger sentiment is amplified by the evolving sociology of the white-collar economy. A reason Bill Clinton was able to carry California, Oregon, and Washington during the 1992 election, despite George Bush's aggressive claims that it was "time to put people ahead of owls," is that only a small percentage of Pacific Coast voters now have their welfare tied to the timber industry. Voters ensconced in white-collar jobs may safely favor a shutdown of a politically incorrect pursuit such as logging, without worrying that their own livelihoods will suffer.

Many logging zones along the Pacific Coast were once located in rural areas but now brush up against exurban expansion. Moving to chic outlying addresses, affluent young professionals who have always loved wood as a material and fireplace fuel may find themselves offended to observe the tawdry means by which the product is brought to market. Yuppies are annoyed when slow timber trucks tie up the two-lane highways of Pacific Coast rustic areas, blocking Saabs and Volvos headed for ski areas. A faction of the white-collar world is only too happy to see the fortunes of the logging set decline.

• *Forest areas are up, not down.* Around the time of the 1993 "owl summit" in Portland the Ecoforestry Institute, an environmental organization, ran full-page ads in U.S. newspapers showing a frightening set of bar graphs. One, marked NORTH AMERICAN NATIVE FORESTS IN 1620, was nearly as tall as the page. The other, labeled CURRENT NATIVE FORESTS, was a mere sliver. These graphs reinforced the conventional wisdom that forests are being wiped out. They also relied on cute wording to define away all trees that have grown since 1620. Suppose the graphs had instead depicted the acreage of U.S. forests in 1920 versus the present. Such a graphic would show a soaring column on the side of current aforestation. Adjusting for the entry into the union of Alaska, the United States had about 600 million acres of forest in 1920. Today the country has 728 million forest acres, with the total continuing to expand annually.

The current total is less than the estimated 950 million wooded acres that existed in precolonial times, but it represents only a 23 percent overall North American forest reduction from the arrival of Europeans to the present—hardly the drastic devastation depicted by environmental orthodoxy. Today about a third of the U.S. land area is forested, versus about two percent "built up" for cities, suburbs, roads, and all other concrete-footprint impositions of civilization. Many trees growing in the United States are not primal but are young trees replanted after logging. But why would nature care about that, so long as ample mature forests continue to exist? And they do, preserved in the 98 million acres (about the size of California) of protected federal wilderness area, most of which is mature forest, and in millions of additional acres of state parks. New York, for example, is one-sixth protected state park, mostly mature forest.

• *Loggers plant more than they cut.* One reason turn-of-the-century logging was so injurious is that crews moved on without replanting. Reforestation of Bureau of Land Management woodlands has been law since 1932, and though the law was often flouted in its early years, perhaps it is no coincidence that American aforestation began in the late 1940s, about one tree generation downstream from the onset of mandatory replanting. All large timber companies now replant: Weyerhaeuser, for instance, began 100 percent replanting in 1968. A record 2.3 billion trees were planted in the United States in 1988, with the recent average being about 1.7 billion annually. Adjusting for the mortality of saplings, these figures mean about 30 percent more young trees are growing in the United States each year than are cut by logging companies. And such calculations do not take into account what foresters now call "volunteers," trees that sprout on their own.

• *Forestry can help the greenhouse effect.* Research generally indicates that the most important land "sink" for atmospheric carbon dioxide is trees, which absorb CO_2 from the air and store it in cellulose. Growing trees require more carbon than do mature trees. To the extent that managed forestry has increased the world's proportion of young trees, it creates a counterweight to the greenhouse effect. Any pessimist who asserts that global warming is a disaster, and also that logging is a disaster, is speaking from both sides of the mouth.

This does not mean that old-growth forests ought to be cleared in order to grow young trees. Several studies, prominently by Mark Harmon and William Ferrell of Oregon State University, have demonstrated that when some ancient forests are logged and replanted, disruptions to carbon chemistry in soil offset the gains from carbon absorbed by young trees, netting no greenhouse improvement. Environmental lobbyists often use this finding to assert that logging is a greenhouse loser. The study does not show this. What it suggests is that while most remaining ancient forests ought to be set aside as nature preserves—something ecorealism advocates—high-yield timber growth should be encouraged in places already converted to tree plantations. Forests already operating in managed fashion do generally show favorable carbon balances.

Middle Earth

Many issues of forest protection are blurred by the distinction between logging on public and private lands. It is on public lands, mostly woods owned by the Forest Service, that the spotted owl controversy has taken place. Here's an illustrative example.

A few years ago Regna Merritt, who watches Forest Service legal postings about timber sales for the Oregon Natural Resources Council, spotted a listing for an area known as Zig Zag in the Mount Hood National Forest, outside Portland. Merritt petitioned the Forest Service to assay the tract for spotted owl. She was told the timber stands in question were certified as without owls. Before the 1991 court-ordered suspension of logging on public lands in the Northwest, finding a spotted owl was the primary method by which someone could block a federal timber sale.

The night before logging crews were to arrive in the Zig Zag, Merritt and a birdcaller walked the forest, crying the ancient *whooo, whooo* owls use to signal each other in the primal darkness. They stumbled often in the old-growth understory. Tall-tree forests of the Pacific Northwest appear from ground level to be remnants of Tolkien's Middle Earth: half-lit, moist and cool, carpeted with fronds adapted to life without direct sunlight. Merritt and the birdcaller worked for hours without response, voices growing hoarse. Around midnight, as moonbeams angled down through the towering trees, they cried for the hundredth time, paused for the hundredth time, and heard back *whooo, whooo*: a call across eternity between two species that, till the invention of the saw, had nothing to do with each other. "It was one of the most exciting moments of my life," she says.

By sunup Merritt had reporters on the scene. A retired local physician named Joseph Miller was there to oppose the arrival of loggers. Miller, then 80 years of age, at one point lay down before a truck. But it was late morning before Merritt could rouse a judge in Portland to issue a stay of the timber sale. By then most of the trees were down, contract loggers in the owl age having learned to strike with commando speed before someone can appear waving legal papers. "It was one of the most frustrating experiences of my life," Merritt says.

Because laws bind public forests more closely than private acres, environmental legal action tends to focus on federal and state woodlands, leaving the impression that they are the center of the logging debate. Actually, though states and the federal government own a vast amount of timberland, private parties possess an amount equally vast. Roughly half of U.S. forests are privately held.

Most large private timber concerns have adjusted at least moderately to ecological strictures: replanting, controlling erosion, reducing chemical use. Market economists would say this is so because private timber concerns have a financial self-interest in insuring their land continues to produce the healthy trees needed for profit.

That tells only part of the story: Environmental pressure was needed to compel timber firms to face the consequences of their actions for the many woodland species other than trees in which timber firms have no clear pecuniary interest. For instance, since the 1960s wherever an eagle nest is found on private timberlands, mile-diameter circles are drawn around it and logging within them forbidden. This conservation measure seems to work quite well, the American bald eagle population having recovered spectacularly since the 1960s; but the rule had to be imposed on timber firms by Congress, few adapting the measure voluntarily. By the 1990s, some firms were embracing biodiversity measures ahead of federal compulsion. In 1993 Interior secretary Bruce Babbitt concluded with Georgia Pacific, a large timber company, a voluntary agreement to protect the red-cockaded woodpecker. Around 10,000 of the red-cockaded are thought to live wild. Whenever Georgia Pacific finds one on its lands in the Southeast and Michigan, ten acres around the nest will be placed off limits to logging.

Many private timber firms in the Northwest today avoid spotted owl complications via the areas they pick to log. Cascade Range spotted owl are often found in higher elevations. Though it owns higher-elevation timber lands, Weyerhaeuser generally does not log them. "We find it is not economically logical to log high elevations," James Rochelle, Weyerhaeuser's environmental forestry officer, says. The Forest Service does authorize high-elevation logging. But when federal woodlands are logged economic logic is far from the first concern, which sums up what is wrong with most public logging.

Subsidized Forestry

By the late 1980s federal lands were the only important forest areas in the United States where growth did not exceed harvest. That is to say, private landowners were growing more trees than they cut, while federal timber managers were cutting more than they grew. Private timber firms own the stands they log, replanting to protect their long-term economic interests. The firms that cut public forests are contract loggers without direct financial stake in the vitality of the forest.

Self-interest, private ownership, and market forces are not cure-alls: They hardly guarantee responsible behavior toward resources. For instance, in the late 1980s the Plum Creek Timber Company of Montana admitted it had been practicing destructive forestry. The company's behavior was an excellent argument for strict regulation of private logging. But even for all their failings, market forces and a self-interest stake in forests are the best system for assuring responsible behavior, as they confer voluntary reasons to protect the land.

The Forest Service, in contrast, has incentives to overlog. Though legislation directs the service to protect all aspects of the wilderness, including biodiversity, in practice logging comes first. A 1930 law called the Knutson-Vanderberg Act says the Forest Service must return to the Treasury 50 cents per 1,000 board-feet of timber sold, and can often keep the remainder of contract revenues for itself. In 1930, fifty cents was roughly the production cost of a thousand board-feet. Today the figure is roughly $50, but the law has not changed. Another law says communities near timber sale areas receive a federal appropriation equal to 25 percent of the transaction. So to employ a simplified example, if a contract logger pays the Forest Service $100 for 1,000 board-feet of timber, the Forest Service keeps $99.50 for its budget, the nearest town gets $25, and the federal taxpayer nets a loss of $24.50.

Not all Forest Service timber sales work this way, but enough do to separate federal logging from the realm of economic logic. Some 80 percent of federal timber sales lose money for taxpayers. From 1988 to 1992, a study by Donald Leal of the Political Economy Research Center in Bozeman, Montana, has shown, federal timber sales in that state lost $42 million, while timber sales run by state agencies made $13.7 million. By the estimate of Randal O'Toole, a Portland economist, overall Forest Service timber sales cost the federal taxpayer $499 million in fiscal 1992. Madness? No, "The Forest Service is simply responding by the rules of human nature to a perverse incentive structure that rewards it for maximizing losses," O'Toole says.

Supposedly the Forest Service and Bureau of Land Management use income from timber sales for biological conservation, but often income goes to such projects as road building. Many analysts currently argue that a key to wilderness preservation is to cut few roads so that people only enter wild areas nondisruptively, on their own feet. Yet the Forest Service often merrily causes taxpayers to underwrite the building of roads, in order to use the roads to lose money on timber sales. Believe it or not there are now eight times as many miles of roads (most unimproved) in U.S. forests as there are in the interstate highway system. In one daffy case, managers of the Gallatin National Forest in Montana decided to sell timber in order to raise money that would be used to improve grizzly habitats via the removal of deep-forest roads. Additional roads were built for the timber sale, which proceeded to lose money. The original roads were left in place, joined by the new ones.

Selling timber at a net loss is nonsensical for the Treasury but popular with communities that receive the bonuses and with Forest Service bureaucracies that expand their empires. In 1991 John Mumma, the Forest Service regional director for Idaho, Montana, and the Dakotas, was forced to retire after logging companies and town officials complained to their congressional delegations that Mumma was not authorizing enough acreage for timber sales. Mumma's region was at that time logging only 60 percent of its Forest Service goal.

Randal O'Toole, mentioned above, is an interesting case study in this regard. A self-employed forestry economist, he has for years bedeviled federal officials by producing studies demonstrating the nonsensical character of many public timber sales. O'Toole looks the part of the orthodox enviro, wearing worn hiker's clothes and a ponytail that extends to his waist. But around 1990 he became an apostate. After fighting the Forest Service using doomsday rhetoric, O'Toole switched to economic logic.

"Most environmentalists, including me, thought till a few years ago that the world could be analyzed on the basis of natural versus artificial, the assumption being that everything people do degrades nature," O'Toole says. "But human beings have become a central element of the natural system. To pretend otherwise is pure utopianism that gets you nowhere. At this point the challenge is to devise a self-interest incentive structure that will maximize forest protection based on people's voluntary choices." No ecorealist could have put it better.

O'Toole thinks this sort of conservation requires, first, an end to taxpayer support for logging federal lands. He notes, "It's ridiculous to think that private companies manage forests with no public payments and show a profit, while the Forest Service needs subsidies in order to lose money on timber sales." Second, O'Toole thinks public lands should switch to user fees for all purposes, allowing people to vote with their purses on how they want forests used. Environmental doctrine has long been wary of letting market forces influence the fate of the wilderness. O'Toole feels the market would favor hiking, fishing, and other recreational uses for most forests. "Letting market forces determine the best use of public land is more likely to preserve species than Congress trying to legislate new laws of human nature," he says. O'Toole believes that under true market pricing perhaps a quarter of national forests would still post timber sales, as they do have conditions for economically rational logging. The remainder would become nature preserves, self-financed from recreational fees.

Happy as that outcome may sound, when O'Toole began to propose it he was ostracized by other environmentalists. Through the early 1990s O'Toole's revelations of Forest Service perfidy were published in a well-read newsletter called *Forest Watch,* produced in conjunction with leading figures of the Pacific Northwest green community. *Forest Watch* was an idiosyncratic publication: page after page of windy rhetoric about the end of nature interrupted by dense tables showing O'Toole's econometric analyses of the latest timber sale screwup. So long as O'Toole was producing intellectual justifications for restrictions on old-growth logging, Northwest environmentalists supported the newsletter. But when he began to advocate market-based wilderness protection, backers were outraged. In 1993 they withdrew support for *Forest Watch,* which folded. This put O'Toole out of business as a Forest Service critic, a turn of events to the liking of timber interests. Enviros thought that was a better outcome than having one of their own publicly question the green canon.

An advent of market logic in public forests would also help private landowners structure fees in ways that favor conservation. For instance, in 1980 International Paper began selling recreation passes to its timberlands in Arkansas, Louisiana, and Texas. Since then clear-cut forestry by International has declined 70 percent, partly because some company lands have proven more valuable as preserves than as tree farms. This user-fee system works because company forests are in areas not adjacent to federal forests that charge no user fees. Until such time as the Forest Service switches to market fees, owners of private timberlands adjacent to Forest Service land may not be able to do so either.

In 1993 the Forest Service announced it would end logging subsidies in 62 of its 156 national forests. The agency depicted this as a breakthrough for rationality. But the news might as easily be rephrased as,

The Forest Service announced that logging subsidies would continue in 94 of the 156 national forests it supervises.

Separately the Forest Service said it would begin to give pure conservation the same consideration as timber revenues. "Ecosystem management" would become the agency's goal. Logging techniques would mimic nature. For example north-facing timber stands, naturally subject to infrequent but powerful fires, would be left alone for long periods then logged intensively. South-facing tree basins, which in nature have regular minor fires, would be subjected to regular mild logging. This change in philosophy sounds wonderful. Unfortunately the Forest Service has made similar announcements before, as far back as the 1950s.

In the Industrial Forest

Let's walk again through Sucker Creek. These woods were slicked off before the Depression. They regrew into a lush and diverse forest, were logged again, and now, as a third-growth forest by contemporary reckoning, are nearing a new harvest cycle. As we walk, patches of the Sucker Creek woods are being cut by the high-pole system. A machine similar to a crane is positioned at the center of a logging area. After workers fell each tree, the trunk is pulled to an access road using cables from the high pole. This prevents a bulldozer or similar piece of machinery from making repeated passes across the logging zone, soil damage from heavy tracked equipment having been shown the most negative aspect of contemporary logging.[1]

To the casual observer the Sucker Creek woods might seem entirely natural. Wildlife and wild plants abound. Trees are not, as environmental cant holds, growing in rigid, mechanized ranks. They are "clumpy," which is good for biodiversity. Planting crews scatter seedlings unpredictably, as in a wholly natural forest. Richard Ford, a Weyerhaeuser forester, points to a thriving tree just yards from a faltering one. He says, "Good planters develop a sixth sense about where a tree wants to be. So far we don't understand why one tree does well and another two yards away does not. It could be some tiny difference in the soil, or the angle of sunlight, or something else entirely. We just have no idea."

Any forester would know at a glance that Sucker Creek is managed. For one, it is "thinned." Crews come around occasionally to take out trees that are faltering; this helps others prosper by increasing sunlight and reducing root competition. Sucker Creek trees also have few low branches. Such branches are being pruned in a company experiment to make young wood without knots. One reason old-growth lumber is popular[2] is that as trees reach full height the low branches wither, leaving much of the trunk knot-free. Knot-free woods command premium prices. Timber companies are now toying with pruning, which creates employment since it must be done manually. If pruning proves out it will be another unnatural act performed upon the forest, but also will reduce the incentive to log the primal wilderness.

Logging theory has changed several times since the turn of the century and likely will change again. Until roughly the 1920s there were no rules other than anything goes. As far back as 1873, the American Association for the Advancement of Science was arguing for a national system of forest preserves on the grounds that many timberlands, especially the white pine forests of the Great Lakes, under siege at that time, would be destroyed irrevocably in about a decade. In 1877 Carl Schurz, the Secretary of the Interior, warned that "the supply of timber in the United States will in less than 20 years fall considerably short." Neither Schurz's nor the AAAS projections came true. Wood supply has always met demand, and today the Great Lakes pine forests cover considerably more acres than they did in 1873. But the dismal projections were averted only because logging theory began to change.

Around World War I Gifford Pinchot, a conservationist who was the first director of the Forest Service, argued for "sheltercuts," a system in which loggers stagger their cutting, never leveling entire stands. A hardy outdoors type, Pinchot was beloved by Teddy Roosevelt, who saw in him a kindred spirit. Pinchot was despised in turn by John Muir, the leading fin de siecle ecologist. Muir thought all logging a horror; Pinchot thought logging was inevitable and must be made environmentally responsible. By the terminology used in this book Muir was a doomsayer and Pinchot an ecorealist.

Though sheltercutting has since fallen somewhat into disuse, its adaptation in the 1920s helped trigger what was, by natural standards, an almost instantaneous American forest rebound. As the forest analyst Roger Sedjo has written, "The pervasiveness and vigor of the regeneration exceeded expectations. From an estimated six billion cubic feet in 1920, the net growth of U.S. forests increased to 13.9 billion cubic feet by 1952 and to 22 billion cubic feet by 1986."

Pinchot was a foe of clear-cutting, proposed in the 1920s as a way of removing entire tree stands without causing the erosion that was the worst impact of nineteenth-century logging. Pinchot had clear-cutting banned for federal lands, a ban that lasted (with many violations) until

1976. The ban eventually fell because by around midcentury some silviculturalists were promoting clear-cuts as an ecological advance. This
stemmed from improved understanding of natural forest life cycles.

In the Pacific Northwest, the Southeast, and elsewhere, the natural
cycle is for mature forests to last some unpredictable amount of time,
whether a few years or a few centuries, then be ignited by lightning to a
blaze that levels anything from a patch to thousands of acres. The older
and drier mature trees become, the more susceptible they are to ignition
by lightning. Some Darwinians have suggested that death by fire is
nature's riposte to the homogeneous character of the old-growth forest,
a way of reopening the land for biodiversity. Regular cataclysmic forest
fires must be natural, as many plants are genetically adapted for the
aftermath. For example the lodgepole pine make seed cases that open
only after being exposed to intense heat, releasing their contents to
repopulate the forest.

The idea of clear-cutting was to mimic a forest cycle that ends by
lightning. Loggers would take out all the trees at once, roughly as would
happen in a natural fire. Then the regrowth cycle would be activated all
at once as if the forest were recovering from a fire, something it is genetically programmed to do anyway. Foresters found that the Douglas fir is
"shade intolerant," growing much faster in clear-cut areas than in sheltercuts where some mature trees were left standing, causing shade. The
assumption is that this happens because through history most Douglas
fir have risen in open fields after fires, evolution selecting for the trees
with the best sun response. Some tree types grow better with shade;
probably they evolved where cataclysmic lightning fires were not common.

When clear-cutting became legal on federal lands in 1976, environmentalists began a campaign to ban it. Though careful clear-cutting can
be defended, from roughly the mid-1970s to late 1980s contract logging
crews on federal lands were running wild with the practice. Yet at the
same time that many environmentalists were assailing clear-cutting as
irresponsible, they were arguing that the twentieth-century practice of
fighting lightning-triggered forest fires should be halted, because leveling
of the forest by fire is good and natural. Pro-fire arguments persuaded
the National Park Service to adopt a "let it burn" philosophy. In the
summer of 1988 lightning ignited a major blaze in Yellowstone National
Park. Smokeaters stood by as tens of thousands of acres of mature forest, exactly the sort orthodoxy says must be saved whenever chain saws
are in evidence, burned to the ground. Most enviros applauded the fact
that Yellowstone was allowed to burn.

A natural fire such as occurred at Yellowstone does not impact soil in the way that even the most cautious logging operations do. Otherwise, a natural fire and careful clear-cutting are close to identical ecologically. How can it be that natural leveling of a forest by fire is good, though this kills many animals and destroys the value of everything within; while artificial leveling of a forest by saw is bad, though this extracts valuable wood while not killing animals? This has never been persuasively explained, except on the visceral grounds that logging serves genus *Homo* and forest fires do not. Whatever the case, after the 1988 fire Yellowstone forests began to rebound almost instantaneously. Some environmentalists then said the rapid recovery showed the wisdom of the let-it-burn concept and the incredible resilience of the natural sphere. Perhaps it did show both things. Yet many greens continued to say that clear-cutting is a horror from which the woodlands can never, ever recover.

In Praise of Snags

Clear-cut before, the Sucker Creek forest is a survivor of that fashion in weald management. After the clear-cut the forest was subject to deliberate burn, another practice designed as a mimic of nature. Following a natural lightning fire not only are the trees gone, so are shrubs and bushes. But after clear-cutting most undergrowth remains. So in past decades timber companies that had clear-cut land would ignite fires to complete the simulation of natural fire. Though most foresters considered the practice sound, by about 1990 deliberate burning after logging was in decline, owing to public reaction against the notion of timber companies setting the woods to flame. Generally environmental lobbyists encouraged this viewpoint, however inconsistently. In 1993 the New York Botanical Garden, an important conservation institution, held a deliberate burn of its grounds as firefighters stood by. Ecologists in attendance spoke glowingly, as it were, of fire's natural role in removing dead roots and bramble, reducing that material to fertilizer and rendering the ground black so that it absorbs more sunlight, starting growth cycles anew. Somehow to environmental doctrine it is beautiful when the New York Botanical Garden ignites fires, ugly when a timber company does the same.

A recent revision in forestry theory is to leave snags, or dead trees, in logged-out tracts. Till the mid-1980s timber captains had snags carted off to salvage all useful wood. Conservationists persuaded foresters that dead trees provide habitat for many small animals. Now most timber companies leave a percentage of snags in place, sometimes marked with blaze-orange tags reading WILDLIFE TREE, DO NOT CUT. Similarly, it had long been the practice of timber companies to remove dead trees that topple into streams. But dead logs in streams serve as habitats for fish. Now most loggers allow trunks that crash into water to remain where they lie, as nature would.

Another important development is a trend away from riparian logging. In the past logging companies have wiped the area around streams clean of anything higher than a blade of grass. This has been shown foolish. Many fish are adapted to life in water that is cool, because trees line most riverbanks; leaving shade around streams is important to the aquatic life cycle. Many birds like to alight in trees near water. If trees that line streams are left standing they will attract birds; the birds will then suppress insects. Some states now impose standards for the maximum temperature of streamwater in logging areas. Progressive timber companies have responded to this package of developments by leaving riparian acreage alone. States are beginning to mandate this practice.

Adaptations such as leaving snags and riparian trees in place show that however clumsy the initial forays may be, people engaged in commercial activities in the wilderness can learn to coexist with nature through a process of gradual accommodation that holds a mirror to the basic processes by which all living things, probing here and there, learn to accommodate each other's strengths and weaknesses.

Consider salmon. Logging of the Pacific Northwest began in earnest in the 1930s, about the same time the Columbia and other Northwest rivers were dammed. The fortunes of salmon declined. By the late 1980s the chinook salmon that run the Sacramento River and the sockeye that run the Snake River were in poor shape. The initial response to faltering salmon runs was that man could do it Bigger Better Faster: Hatcheries were built across the Northwest for stocking rivers. Stocking is preferable to inaction, but has never worked as well as hoped.

Today the trend is to negotiate peace terms with the salmon. Loggers are learning to leave streamsides alone. The Bonneville Power Authority, which runs the Columbia River dams, is rearranging its water releases to accommodate salmon migration, though this will cause power rates to rise five percent in the region and render some rivers unsuitable for commercial navigation. Systems that prevent salmon from being sucked into power turbine intakes are being improved. These sorts of insights, through which technology learns to coexist with nature, have only begun to roll in. There will be more, and they will be powerful.

New Forestry

Despite the public perception, clear-cutting is not the standard for American forestry. It is used mainly for homogeneous timbers that grow in concert to even ages. In logging areas such as Michigan's Upper Peninsula, woodlands are mixed-tree forests where sugar maple, yellow birch, and other hardwoods grow in scattershot fashion. Logging in these area is selective—workers take trunks here and there based on the ages of individual trees. Owing to its small-is-beautiful aspect, activists have asserted that forms of selection logging should be the sole ones allowed by law. More likely to become the next trend is something called New Forestry.

Advanced first by Jerry Franklin, an ecologist at the University of Washington, New Forestry holds that "tree harvest blocs can be as large as thousands of acres." Franklin reasons that such large blocs approximate typical natural loss from a roaring forest fire. But in return for each large bloc harvested, timber companies should be required to set aside several blocs of equal size and leave them untouched for perhaps 50 years, allowing forest creatures to experience multiple generations undisturbed. Logging in very large blocs would offer timber companies economies of scale in return for reduced activities in the wilderness. In some ways New Forestry simply applies to trees the proven farming notion of the fallow field.

The ideal size for logging blocs has long been a topic of dispute. In the 1960s some timber companies cut in 20-acre blocs, that being a number then advanced by silviculturalists. Today Weyerhaeuser cuts in 200-acre blocs. In northern California many timber companies now stage multiple mini clear-cuts of only a few acres each, an idea backed by the Sierra Club, which is especially influential in California state politics. Since 1989, forestry firms in Maine have been limited by state law to 250-acre clear-cuts.

The size of blocs impacts both the look and biology of a forest. The Maine limit was imposed primarily because local logging opponents depicted the scene of a large expanse of felled forest as a horror. Today large cutovers are no longer found in the state. But as loggers cut more small blocs, Maine forests increasingly fragment into checkerboards. An emerging body of science suggests that fragmentation, which dramatically increases the edge versus deep-forest areas of a woodland, may pose more harm to biodiversity than the total acreage of trees felled. Lots of smaller cuts also requires more road construction than a few large cuts, another fragmenting influence. Satellite images of the Pacific

Northwest now show that although its forest is robust in acreage, only about ten percent remains unfragmented. A few very large clear-cuts of the sort offensive to orthodoxy but promoted by New Forestry may be easier on the woods than lots of small cuts.

Why does forest fragmentation hurt? Researchers have puzzled over the postwar decline of some eastern migratory birds that ought to be increasing, since Appalachian forests are expanding. One theory holds that although eastern timberlands are healthy in terms of acres, their fragmentation is unhealthy. Some (not all) researchers believe the cowbird population is rising, an unwelcome sign. Cowbirds are parasitic animals that lay eggs in other birds' nests, and particularly seem to like the nests of several imperiled songbirds. No one yet knows exactly what, but something having to do with forest fragmentation may have conferred a competitive advantage on the cowbird, perhaps by breaking up forests in ways that expose nests to detection.

The respite periods timberlands would receive owing to the fallow-field aspect of New Forestry would both help conserve wildlife and permit trees a period in which to continue normal genetic change. Opponents offer many overstated complaints about industrial forestry: One that rings true is the implications of cloned seedlings. Weyerhaeuser has since 1988 planted only cloned seedlings from its tree nurseries. Progeny of genetically superior trees, the seedlings maximize yield. But dependence on single strains sets the forest up for a serious fall should some unexpected disease or pest appear.

Today major timber companies have nurseries where they maintain samples of genetic stocks and interbreed trees, attempting to produce new crosses. So far so good: cross-breeding trees is no different in principle from natural forces creating new DNA combinations for trees, and it may cause improvements nature would not have stumbled upon by chance. "One of the first things they teach you in forestry school," Thomas Stevens, a young Washington State forester, says, "is how badly we screwed up a century ago, by logging out the strongest, tallest, and most successful trees first, without keeping genetic samples. Forestry has been trying to recover from that blunder ever since."

But as I walked through the Weyerhaeuser nursery outside the little town of Mima, Washington, I thought, *This is the only place they preserve tree genes.* If something wiped Mima out, the genetic library would be gone. During the 1960s, Weyerhaeuser ran a samples collection project. Researchers walked the Northwest forests, and sometimes hung from helicopters, taking cuttings of the most robust trees. This project has not been repeated, as there are thought to be few novel genes left to sample on company lands. "Wild trees are getting hard to come by in our managed forests," the company's Rochelle explained blandly. Nothing could be a better argument for New Forestry.

The Paper Trail

To environmentalists the most disputed use of timber is for papermaking. As the United States for good or ill now leads the world in per-capita paper consumption, the ecology of paper is acquiring increasing importance. Orthodoxy doesn't like papermaking because it consumes trees and produces wastewater that contains chlorine plus minute amounts of the chlorinated organic compound dioxin.

Contemporary papermaking quandaries are on display at the Weyerhaeuser pulp mill on an inland waterway in Longview, Washington. The Longview mill, one of the largest in the world, employs 2,800 people. From 1970 till 1991, Longview cut water emissions by 95 percent as production rose 250 percent: one of the many examples that show clean production and increased industrial output are wholly compatible. During the decade of the 1980s the plant cut its solid waste output by 25 percent, as production rose. Its sulfur emissions are down 98 percent since 1974, its emissions of particulates down 80 percent. A recycling facility was built on Longview's grounds. Nevertheless the plant fell into serious environmental trouble.

Washington State requires "nondetect" levels for dioxin by 1995—essentially not a molecule released. So far Longview has only been able to drive its dioxin emissions down to the mere parts per quadrillion level. Greenpeace has strung banners from Longview's docks, protesting the dioxin output. The group's sailing ship *Rainbow Warrior* has come calling, attempting to block harbor operations as television cameras rolled.

Longview managers further assume that chlorine emissions will soon be restricted to a very low level, perhaps even banned. In 1993, after Greenpeace declared a "chlorine-free world" one of its primary goals, EPA administrator Carol Browner said her agency may prohibit chlorine emissions. Considering that chlorine is poisonous to mammals and a component of dioxin, caution is justified. Yet chlorine, being an element, is not some hideous creation of man's laboratories: Nature uses it in large quantities. Chlorine is part of the life cycles of many marine creatures. The simplest organochloride, methyl chloride, is "emitted" by algae, kelp, fungi, and other living things in quantities of about ten billion pounds per year; total world industrial emission of this compound is about 52 million pounds, or one-half percent of the natural level.

Parents willingly let their children dive into swimming pools doped with chlorine in far higher concentrations than are discharged today by any U.S. industrial facility. Perhaps most important, though chlorine is in the same chemical family as dioxin, so is table salt, which is sodium chloride. Table salt is a confirmed cause of hypertension and a suspected cause of stomach cancer, while no research has yet shown that industrial chlorine emissions cause any public health or general ecological harm. Nevertheless company managers at the Longview plant devoted a considerable portion of the $400 million they recently invested during renovations to chlorine controls: Spent this way, the money cannot be used for other needs, such as job creation.

In a roundabout way Greenpeace is right about chlorine: Industry's objective should be no suspect chemicals of any kind emitted. But rarely mentioned in activist complaints about chlorine from papermaking is that for years the technical trend has been toward drastic reductions in chlorine emission. Many paper mills have already converted to bleaching with chlorine dioxide, whose by-products contain only minor amounts of chlorine. Paper bleaching based on hydrogen peroxide is next in line as a technical development; chlorine output would end. Within about a decade engineers hope to perfect papermaking without any chemical bleaching agent, using ozone as the reactant. Total energy use would fall sharply and wastewater would be eliminated, process water being endlessly recirculated inside the plant. James Freiberg, Longview's environmental manager, says, "Most of us feel we will achieve low-energy, zero-bleach, zero-effluent paper manufacturing in our lifetimes. This prospect is the most exciting thing in the business." But so far the technology for zero-emission papermaking isn't ready; no amount of dander from Greenpeace can make it so.

Distaste for papermaking has risen to such an extreme that some greens now oppose construction of paper recycling facilities. A European company has been working for years to break ground on a paper recycling plant near Sacramento. The plant would be the largest postconsumer recycling facility in the country, able to reprocess about two-thirds of the used newsprint now collected in California. In 1993 the Sacramento Valley Toxics Campaign sued to block the construction on the grounds the plant will emit dioxin (in infinitesimal amounts) and also put three million gallons a day of effluent into the Sacramento River.

Yet that water will comply with federal "secondary" standards, meaning safe for swimming and fish. And while three million gallons a day may sound like the flow of Niagara Falls, it is minor by the standards of river volume. In northern California typical household water use is about 400 gallons per day, meaning the recycling plant's discharge would equal the flow from only about 7,500 homes. Existing paper-making facilities use as much as 800 pounds of water per pound of product; the Sacramento plant would require about eight pounds per pound of product, a clean-tech reduction to just one percent of the previous resource requirement. Nevertheless the plant lingers in limbo, owing to enviro opposition. Newsprint goes to landfills in the meantime.

Paper recycling at Longview has improved that mill's finances. In the 1970s, Weyerhaeuser tried to add recycled content to products but was rebuffed by consumers, who then thought recycled meant low quality. Some 1970s recycling techniques, especially for cardboard, produced inferior grades. By the early 1990s, with McDonald's switching from virgin white to dusty brown hamburger bags, recycled paper quality was high and the product chic. Like several papermakers, Weyerhaeuser plans that all future paper capacity will be based on secondary fibers. The company's European customers pay a premium for recycled products, sometimes requiring audits to insure a green bill of health. (German buyers write Longview plant effluent levels into their contract specifications.) Even the Japanese, who with their national obsession for the new once wanted nothing to do with recycled paper, now buy. For them Weyerhaeuser has devised a process that produces bright white recycled paper: Those Earth-look fiber "whiskers" popular in U.S. recycled paper are dreaded in Japan, since they render calligraphy unintelligible. The Tellus Institute, an environmental study organization in Boston, has reported that in 1991, recycled-paper manufacturing was five times more profitable than virgin-paper production.

Like opposition to logging, green suspicion of papermaking should be seen as a passing solecism by the movement. Soon paper will be manufactured with almost no emissions, using a combination of recycled fibers and trees from forests whose managers have learned to coexist with nature. Many of these advances should be credited to the pressure for reform created by environmentalists. But now that such pressure is paying dividends it is time to put to rest exaggerated notions like an ecological doomsday brought on by mere paper. Paper can be dangerous, but only because of what's written on it.

The Infuriating Positiveness of Forest Logic

During the 1993 presidential "owl summit" in Portland, every manner of hyperventilated argument was employed by environmentalists and business both. Timber interests declared the entire economy of the

Northwest in peril; that was surely untrue, with logging on private lands remaining profitable. Environmentalists countered with specious claims that Northwest timber job losses are the result of whole-log exports to Japan. Actually such exports have been banned from federal forests since 1973.

It was hard not to sympathize with the desire of environmentalists at the summit to deliver a body blow to Big Timber, which has spent much of the postwar era bashing enviros about the head in lobbying contests, especially at the statehouse level. Logging interests brought the current wave of bad vibes upon themselves. Enviros were ecstatic when spotted owl lawsuits gave them a weapon with which to exact retribution. But by the time environmentalists finally were in a position to retaliate against the timber barons, most of their offensive behavior had ended. Timber practices were becoming progressive; wildlife biology was becoming integral to logging.

In other words the Pollution Peak for U.S. forestry had gone by. If North American forests—diligently assaulted from roughly the mid-nineteenth century till the mid-twentieth—are today still expansive, vibrant, and biologically diverse, then the moment of danger for those forests is already in the past. Today nearly all North American forestry trends are positive. Institutional environmentalism ought to be happy about this: Improved forestry is a grand achievement for the movement, protecting the wilderness and setting the stage for a sustainable economy of wood. Yet the continuing desire for revenge over abuses of the past prevents many greens from seeing the New Forestry for the trees.

In 1994 Bill Clinton proposed his logging plan. The seven million remaining Northwest primal acres would be placed off-limits. Logging on other federal lands in the region would continue but at 20 percent the peak rate of the 1980s. Salvage harvesting—taking trees that die on their own—would be permitted in some wilderness areas. Ten "adaptive management" zones would be created, to conduct experiments in non-logging woodland economics. Federal timber subsidies would continue. Both logging interests and enviros immediately sued to block the Clinton proposal, leaving it tempting to say the plan must be wise if it offends both sides. Many aspects of the plan were in fact attractive. Yet Clinton missed an important opportunity to bring ecorealism to U.S. wilderness policy by withdrawing the Forest Service from subsidized logging. This simple rationalizing of forest policy would enhance pure preservation and help woodland economics at the same time.

It was a sign of the fatalistic fixation of contemporary ecological thinking that everything Clinton said at the Portland summit, and in announcing his timber plan, was negative. Logging is a problem.

Conservation is a problem. The owl is a problem. Jobs are a problem. Flecks of sawdust are a problem: A new study shows they cause global ionospheric antidecompensation. (Okay, the president didn't really say that. But can't you imagine hearing it?) Everything is getting worse; the best the enlightened can do is struggle to slow the rate of decline.

If there is anything in ecological matters that is not a problem it is the forest. It is not difficult to imagine twenty-first-century circumstances in which North American woodlands return to nearly their precolonial expanse. It is not difficult to imagine a twenty-first-century order in which the Forest Service safeguards huge expanses of mature, biologically diverse forest for conservation and recreation, while privately managed working forests continue to produce wood and jobs in quantity, harming hardly anything in the process. All that's needed to get from here to there is a little ecorealism.

24 ✍

GENES ✍

Step onto your lawn, into a woodland, into Kew Gardens, or any other place where there is life and soil. Take a shovel and slant it into the earth. In the loam removed by a single stroke will reside a number of organisms larger than the entire human population.

Most of those living things, microbial, have short lifetimes: days, sometimes hours. This means they reproduce constantly. And so they mutate constantly. The organisms in the shovelful of soil are busily conducting unsupervised, unauthorized tests of genetic materials set loose into the environment. Yet in this profusion of genetic engineering, mutations do not run wild. Mysteriously omnipotent genes do not "take over" the biosphere.

Estimates of the number of organisms on the Earth are approximate. Researchers have roughly guessed there are 10,000 quintillion (10,000 billion billion) living things at any moment. Each living thing contains amino acids arranged into units of genetic data: anywhere from a few million DNA units (the number for bacteria) to six billion (the number for people) to as many as 30 billion (the number for some plants). Every time a cell reproduces, a few DNA units mutate. If 10,000 quintillion organisms regularly experience mutations in gene codes as complicated as 30 billion DNA units long, this means that new genes are being "released" in nature on a numerical scale staggering to imagine. These mutation marathons are not events of the primeval past. They are happening right now in the soil of your yard, in the water of the nearest pond, in your stomach and bloodstream.

As artificial recombination of DNA becomes practical, environmentalists are close to unanimous in apprehending that an instant doomsday will come to pass if gene-engineered products are sanctioned. Here, for instance, is what the prominent ecologist Wes Jackson, director of the Land Institute in Salina, Kansas, has written: "The question is, 'How long will it take biotechnologists to come up with something disastrous?'" A disaster cannot be ruled out. But nonideological consideration of the subject suggests genetic disasters are unlikely so long as regulation is strict. To understand why this is so requires the essential ecorealist exercise: examining the subject from the point of view of nature.

First, all current plants and animals are the product of genetic experiments that have been ongoing for at least 3.5 billion years. Were it not for genetic experiments the snow leopard, the manatee, Kirtland's warbler, and every other creature biodiversity advocates hope to preserve would not now exist to preserve. The idea of people tampering with the genes they find in the world around them is in a sense a smaller step away from nature than physical technology such as oil pipelines or soccer fields or rock concerts—since while these sorts of interventions with the biosphere do not exist in nature, genetic engineering does.

Second, the natural system is elaborately safeguarded against genetic takeover. Of the billions of mutations that occur on a daily basis, almost all are "defeated" and quickly vanish. New genes usually lose because existing genes possess the advantage over those struggling to gain a foothold. This is the primary reason genetic mutations created by nature do not run amok. Were the environment not equipped with natural gene-filtering mechanisms of considerable sophistication, the biosphere would have collapsed long ago.

Genetic Engineering: Old News

People have been intervening in the spontaneous movement of DNA for millennia, through selective breeding of animals and cross-breeding of plants. The natural world that exists today has already demonstrated an ability to function with at least some level of deliberate human influence on gene trends.

If selective breeding of plants and animals is considered biotechnology, then "the benefits have been strikingly free of social costs for thousands of years, in contrast to the more mixed yield of the physical technologies," Bernard Davis, a professor at Harvard Medical School, said. Davis, who died in 1993, told me in 1991 that in this sense genetic engineering is not playing with fire: cross-bred plants and selectively bred animals have for centuries coexisted with plants and animals that arose through purely natural processes. Recombinant DNA techniques, Davis noted, are less dramatic than cross-breeding. Most gene splicing inserts DNA for one new property, resulting in an organism only slightly different from the previous one. Old-fashioned cross-breeding may cause entire "boxes" of genes to recombine, creating offspring notably different from parents.

Domesticated plants, their genes altered by artificial breeding, have never taken over an ecosphere, though considering that agriculture has been practiced for millennia, engineered plants have by now been released into the environment by the trillions. Most domesticated plants die in the wild, only prospering symbiotically with *Homo sapiens* in the form of farmers. This has been the case with corn for at least several centuries. By the time Europeans encountered maize, it had already been so extensively cross-bred by Native Americans that the plant could no longer survive in the wild, lacking a means to distribute seeds. Maize could only propagate if an Indian scattered kernels. Today's commercial corn strains can only live if planted, irrigated, and assisted in insect defense.

Davis believed that "when people breed for some property in an organism that serves them, both theory and empirical evidence point to a decrease in adaptation to the environment from which the parent strain was taken." For example, since the 1980s ranchers have been breeding cattle and pigs to lower body fat. This is good news for people but in the wild would reduce the livestock's odds of success, as fat tissue helps animals survive winter. Several current DNA engineering projects are focused on giving pigs and goats the ability to make human proteins, so that costly pharmaceuticals now drawn from human donors or from cadavers could instead be made in animals serenely living down on the "pharm," to use the researcher's pun. Specialized for production of proteins that humankind wants, in the wild such animals would be at a disadvantage compared to species nature has specialized for survival.

Since the discovery of vaccine, human beings have set "loose" in the environment millions of pounds of genetically altered viruses or pathogens for smallpox, polio, mumps, measles, pertussis, influenza, and other diseases. These organisms have not run wild. Almost every American and European has had such genetically altered products injected directly into his or her body. Vaccines have at times done harm but never engendered the horrific genetic reactions depicted in pop science.

The pop-science idea of supergenes that confer on creatures menacing power is unlikely ever to have a basis in reality. In the movies, one quick mutation turns a lowly ant into a giant invincible superant. Yet 3.5 billion years of natural gene engineering experiments has not devised any supergene. If there were such a mutation, whichever living thing chanced on this DNA first would take over the biosphere. As no such takeover has happened, the odds are no supergene exists.

Next, it's important to understand that scientists engaged in current genetic engineering experiments do not *create* genes. They take existing genes perfected by nature and insert them in new places: for example, a project in Norway to insert the cold-resistance genes of the winter flounder, which thrives in the frigid Norwegian Sea waters, into the Atlantic salmon, which dies at 30 degrees Fahrenheit. Someday it may be possible for researchers to devise gene codes that tell the cells of living things to make entirely new properties. At present "no scientist has the slightest idea how to make a functioning original gene," says Eric Lander, a biologist and director of the human genome sequencing project at the Whitehead Institute, an affiliate of the Massachusetts Institute of Technology.

Bovine somatotropin, the gene-engineered product that increases the milk output of cows, was not invented in a test tube. It is a natural substance, isolated from the genes of cows that are high producers of milk. If you find the idea of lab workers doing cut-and-paste with the BST gene to be creepy, consider another gene-engineered substance you've been eating without controversy. Called chymosin, it is made by Genencor, a company with an ominous name. Chymosin is a synthetic analog of the DNA in rennin, a natural enzyme. Rennin has been employed for centuries to curdle milk into cheese. How is rennin obtained? By killing unweaned calves and removing it from their stomach linings. In the mid-1980s researchers isolated the genes in rennin that cause curdling. By 1990 safety testing of chymosin had been completed, the substance brought to market at half the price of rennin. Today cheese making is being taken over by this bioengineered substance. The acceptance of chymosin, whose Food and Drug Administration certification went unopposed, means BST is not, as now commonly asserted, "the first genetically engineered substance ever put into food."

There is in this substance an attractive irony. The veal industry exists by tormenting calves in tiny pens then selling their tissue for meat and their stomachs for rennin. Now that the market for rennin is collapsing thanks to gene engineering, veal will become even more expensive, which should discourage buyers. If you're against the consumption of veal—and you should be—you should be a big fan of chymosin, a genetically engineered product. Why have you heard so much about BST yet not one word about chymosin? Because this development is inconveniently positive.

Genetic cut-and-paste does cause naturally occurring genes to cross species lines. The focus of much DNA engineering research is the transgenic effect: pigs with genes for human hemoglobin, cows with genes for the human antimicrobial protein lactoferrin, tomatoes that survive frosts because they contain cold-resistance genes from fish. Though traditional breeding techniques have a limited ability to cross similar but sexually incompatible plants, the arrival of technology that moves genes beyond species lines unquestionably allows people to engage in an advanced form of DNA alteration. But it is not a form of DNA alteration that nature has not attempted.

Until about two decades ago it was assumed that genes do not cross species lines in nature. Today it is known they do. As researchers began to use DNA fragmentation to create what are essentially outline maps of chromosomes, they found surprising overlap among species. Human DNA appears to differ by only about one percent from the DNA of apes. Some gene code sequences in human DNA appear identical to sequences found in drosophila, the fruit fly. Many instances of common DNA are probably explained by shared origins in the past, but some are now known to result from interspecies jumps.

Exactly how DNA sequences move between species in nature is not yet understood. The flu pandemic that killed as many as 25 million people in 1918 and 1919 is thought to have originated in a species jump, when a pig disorder infected some soldiers at Camp Funsten, Kansas. Most researchers suspect that viruses, which under some circumstances can insert DNA from one species into chromosomes of another, are the agent of natural transfers. Trading on this insight researchers are now attempting to use "denatured" viruses (whose virulence has been switched off) as little guided missiles to deliver healthy genes to people with gene-defect diseases, including early but so far promising attempts to devise gene therapy for conditions such as cystic fibrosis. Shuttling genes around in this way may or may not pay off. It would not be outside the bounds of existing natural genetic movement.

In Praise of Luddism

Some cities have passed local ordinances forbidding gene engineering within their confines, ordinances that seem inspired by late-night monster ant movies. Many within the science community consider such opposition to gene engineering to be a new Luddism: a desire, grounded in science illiteracy, to wish away technology. In 1987 the first sanctioned field test of a genetically engineered organism took place: An "ice minus" bacteria designed to help fruits resist frost was sprayed on a patch of strawberries in California. Opponents who sued hoping to block the test did win a court order compelling the technician who handled the spraying, Julianne Lindemann, to wear a moonsuit—rubber armor, gloves, boots, helmet, breathing apparatus. Evening-news footage of Lindemann in her sci-fi getup suggested something immensely dangerous was being dispensed. But as the writer Malcolm Galdwell has pointed out, 20 feet from Lindemann, though conveniently framed out of the pictures, were dozens of reporters, state officials, and enviro onlookers. If the spray really was deadly, why were environmentalists willing to stand so close? Because they knew perfectly well there was no danger. Activists wanted the moonsuit worn to create a horrific visual—one networks anxious for stark images were only too happy to beam out.

Yet frittering though such green theatrics may be, environmental opposition to gene engineering is a good thing. Events in gene engineering are moving much too rapidly for even the most conscientious scientist to be sure that safeguards are adequate.

Recombinant DNA technology—the ability to splice two sets of genes together in a laboratory and have the results "express" in a living creature—is a mere 20 years old, first achieved in 1973 by Stanley Cohen and Annie Chung of Stanford University and Herbert Boyer and Robert Helling of the University of California at San Francisco. Since then the pace of developments has been startling, with the research world progressing from ignorance of how genes express to a limited ability to make transgenic creatures with genes from outside their natural germ line. Now several simple organisms such as the E. coli bacteria have had their chromosomes "sequenced," broken down so that every point of DNA code is available on computer. Researchers in several countries are working to sequence the human DNA.

That information holds no immediate value for such pop-science pursuits as making everyone tall and blond or alternatively making everyone a zombie: The goal of current human DNA sequencing is to isolate the information needed to treat inherited-defect diseases such as cystic fibrosis or sickle-cell anemia. But the knowledge acquired in such projects may eventually lead to the ability to alter the way people look, think, or act. This alone is ample reason to proceed slowly. Recombining genes appears safe so far. Who knows what fault may be hidden in the application of such a new technique?

The 1990s should see the arrival of second-generation recombinant pharmaceuticals in which a single amino acid has been moved from its natural position on a DNA box. These products will differ only a tiny bit from their natural analogues—the goal of the initial experiments is to increase the shelf life of expensive drugs—but will represent the first step toward a novel artificial gene. "Right now designing a gene from scratch seems inconceivable," Lander of MIT says. "But 40 years ago I would have said it was inconceivable to rearrange natural genes. In some ways going from where we are now to making novel genes is not as audacious as going from where we were 40 years ago to where we are now. Original genes designed by people seem close to inevitable. I just can't say whether it will take 300 years or 20."

If a little Luddism on gene engineering is actually a good idea, then so must be the antiscience activist Jeremy Rifkin. Today the easiest way to make smoke come out of a scientist's ears is to pronounce Rifkin's name. Rifkin has hog-tied many university gene-research projects with lawsuits or by filing administrative proceedings before various federal agencies, especially the ominously named RAC—Recombinant Advisory Committee—a group of scientists and government officials who must sanction gene engineering experiments, and who are cautious about issuing permits. Most researchers consider Rifkin's assertions about DNA engineering riddled with elementary errors of science and fact. Yet the system needs someone like Rifkin to force it to caution on a subject as sweeping as gene tampering.

Many, many things could go wrong with genetic engineering. But it seems at least as likely this science will be a boon to nature, possibly one that helps open the door to the green future. Since the objections regarding what might go wrong with gene engineering are well known, let's focus now on what might go right.

Life with Fewer Chemicals

Anyone who fears genetic engineering ought to bear in mind that its first significant impact on society may be a sharp reduction in the use of food chemicals. As researchers have come to understand that plants naturally contain many toxins for self-defense, they have begun to wonder whether moving such natural pesticides around genetically could reduce the need for synthetic pesticides. If this can be done, then the Pollution Peak in food chemicals will turn out to have been passed in an incredibly short period by nature's standards.

One of the first rallying points of opposition to recombinant engineering occurred in 1987 when a Montana State University researcher named Gary Strobel injected a gene-engineered organism into some trees without obtaining EPA approval. Strobel's act was headline news nationwide. Protestors marched on his office; the trees were chopped down and elaborately incinerated to destroy the engineered organism; Strobel was widely depicted in editorial cartoons as a deranged scientist bent on destruction of nature. Entirely overlooked was the purpose of Strobel's test. He was inoculating diseased trees with an engineered version of a natural insecticide, to prevent their needing to be sprayed with synthetic chemicals.

Strobel, it turns out, is one of the world's leading researchers into techniques for replacing synthetic chemicals with natural substances. During the 1980s he discovered a fungus that kills the spotted knapweed, a plant upon which Montana ranchers were applying herbicides by the barrel. In 1993 Strobel and his colleague Andrea Stierle discovered *Taxomyces andreanae,* a fungus that makes taxol, a promising anticancer drug. Experiments suggest that taxol may soon be synthesized cheaply from this fungus rather than produced by stripping the bark from the Pacific yew tree. Strobel's work on these and other naturally occurring chemicals combines the information inherent in the environment with the theory of clean technology in order to advance the cause of human coexistence with nature through knowledge, not brute force.

One of the first important applications of bioengineering involves a microorganism called *Bacillus thuringiensis.* BT kills many insects, including caterpillars that feed on corn. Spray-on pesticides based on BT became available to farmers about a decade ago and were touted as an advance in pesticide safety, because natural BT biodegrades in just a few days. But this rapid biodegradation caused farmers to reapply natural BT often, negating the benefits while stimulating resistance mutations. Research now indicates the spray-on version of natural BT is losing effectiveness.

Suppose instead that BT were integrated through gene splicing into the plant itself. Nothing would be sprayed, but any caterpillar sinking its mandibles into a cornstalk would hit BT. And were the BT inside the plant it would not be washed away by rain or degraded by sunlight. Several companies including Pioneer Hi-Bred, the largest producer of corn seed, are now attempting to recombine BT genes into corn. If the work is successful an entire category of pesticide may be eliminated. Early tests suggest cotton strains with BT genes could lead to a 40 percent reduction in insecticides used on cotton, which is the most chemical-intensive of crops.

A similar experiment involves splicing the BT gene into tomatoes.

Transgenic tomatoes that make their own BT might reduce the $400-million-a-year's worth of carbmate and organophosphate pesticides sprayed on tomato crops to control lepidopterans, insects in the moth family. Carbmates and organophosphates have been shown neurotoxic to people and animals, according to Rebecca Goldburg, a scientist at the Environmental Defense Fund. Sprayed on tomatoes, carbmates may also kill a tiny wasp that preys on insects called leaf miners; another spraying to kill the leaf miners is then required. If transgenic tomatoes making their own BT did not need to be sprayed for lepidopterans, they might not need to be sprayed for leaf miners either, as wasps would then cover that assignment. Goldburg is rare among environmentalists in believing transgenic plants may be good for the ecology. Her main concern is that "the technology is so complicated that government may allow companies to self-certify compliance with safeguards, and the history of pollution control teaches that you shouldn't allow companies to self-certify."

Some opponents protest that gene engineering of crops may condition plants for tolerance of pesticides. This is true: Is it bad? For instance the gene-splicing firm Calgene is experimenting with DNA recombinations that render plants resistant to glyphosate, an herbicide sold under the trade name Roundup. Soon farmers may be able to blast away with Roundup without harming their crops. Jane Rissler, a biotechnology specialist at the National Wildlife Foundation, told the *Wall Street Journal* in 1991 that crop improvement research was, for reasons like this, "just a ruse" to prop up pesticide and herbicide sales.

But if the goal is killing weeds, gene engineering that helps crops tolerate glyphosate seems ecologically desirable. Glyphosate functions by inhibiting the production of EPSP synthase, an enzyme that many broadleaf plants and weeds need to make the aromatic amino acids essential to their life cycles. People and most mammals lack pathways for EPSP synthase, because their bodies do not manufacture aromatic amino acids. Thus while deadly to weeds, glyphosate is not toxic to people or most animals. Is a clever, bio-mimic weed killer an undesirable nonetheless? Deep environmentalists sometimes say that the very notion of the weed is "speciesism," reflecting anthropocentric bias in favor of those plants that serve human ends. Yet in nature many categories of plants consider each other weeds. Nature has no problem with the use of chemical warfare, including toxins secreted by roots, to make one plant species as opposed to another prosper, having authorized billions of such contests.

If gene engineers confer on domesticated plants new resistance properties, could these result in plants that unlike past products of cross-breeding are able to take over habitats? This is possible, and it is one reason U.S. rules require that gene-engineered plants be tested on plots surrounded by barren land, precluding contact with wild plants. In 1991 the technical journal *Science* reported that a British program to field-test gene-engineered plants in the wild, to see if their properties transferred to wild plants, yielded no troublesome results. Gene-altered canola were raised outdoors. They did not take over local habitats nor did their inserted genes show up in adjacent plants.

There are many examples of transplanted vegetation running amok in adopted habitats—kudzu vine in the American Southeast, knapweed in Montana, rice grass in the United Kingdom—but in each case the plant staging the takeover has been a naturally evolved organism specialized for survival and propagation, foolishly moved by people into habitats where natural competitors were lacking. Artificially engineered plants might take over a local habitat if they were moved into one where competitors were lacking, but this seems unlikely, as research now focuses on engineering plants for properties quite different from survival and propagation.

More Food, Cheaper Medicine

The two other likely coming products of genetic engineering are higher-yield crops and advanced medicines for people and animals.

When gene engineering first was contemplated in the early 1970s, some researchers suggested it would trigger a second Green Revolution. So far that promise seems overstated: Leaps in farm productivity have yet to manifest in gene-engineering tests. For this reason prominent environmentalists including Lester Brown, head of the Worldwatch Institute, deride genetic engineering of plants as inutile for increasing food yields.

Yet indications are that yield improvements are beginning to be realized. In 1993 some University of Florida researchers altered wheat in ways that improves yield. Corn, potatoes, soybeans, and rice have all expressed transplanted genes in tests and thus are expected to be available in higher-yield versions by the late 1990s. Researchers are also pursuing genetic modifications that allow crops to prosper with less irrigation, or in poor soils, or with different growing seasons than they normally require. This will not increase yields but will lower agricultural inputs of water and energy.

In 1993 Steven Tanksley, a professor of plant pathology at Cornell University, achieved the first successful recombination of disease resistance in a crop. Tanksley moved into tomatoes a gene for resistance to a bacterium called *Peudomonas syringae,* specks mold to farmers. Tomatoes grown with resistance to specks should have higher yield yet require lower applications of pesticides. By 1994 other researchers had been able to isolate genes for resistance to *Peudomonas syringae* from a small plant similar to mustard and to move the gene into commercial crop strains; to isolate and move resistance genes for several crop fungi, including a resistance gene for "rust," bane of many a farmer. Success in splicing natural resistance genes represents "the biggest thing in plant biology since the discovery of chlorophyll," biologist Jeff Dangel of the Delbrück Institute, in Germany, told the journal *Science.* Tanksley has said that based on his experience cloning the tomato resistance gene, the ability to transfer yield genes into plants might be realized in as few as five years.

Assuming high-yield genetically engineered crops are perfected, they may be of incalculable value to the Third World. Imagine, say, the importance crops genetically engineered for low water needs would have for sub-Saharan Africa, the center of the world's worst malnutrition. Gene engineering advances in crops may make it possible that land will continue to be withdrawn from agriculture and returned to nature at a faster rate than land is taken from nature for urban development. This is the pattern already observed in the First World in the postwar era. If this pattern spreads to the Third World, it is possible that net trends in acreage use will favor nature there in the coming century, even as the human population of the Third World continues to superabound.

Such advances will not be possible unless gene-altered products are considered safe to eat. Opposition focuses on genetically altered edibles: tomatoes with antispoilage genes (due in supermarkets under the goofy trade name Flavr Savr), milk from cows given BST, catfish with growth genes from other species ("Frankenfish" to enviros).

The new tomato may or may not have flavr—taste-testers have been able to restrain their enthusiasm—but it does possess the same nutritional content as a regular vine-ripened tomato. More to the point, in chemical testing the Flavr Savr is just shy of indistinguishable from a regular tomato. Owing to this the U.S. Food and Drug Administration has decided to regulate gene-altered foodstocks based on content, not genetic origin. Gene-altered foodstuffs would bear warning labels only if chemical content differed from what is normally found in a similar food. The National Academy of Sciences has concurred with this general approach, which reflects the ecorealist premise that in the long run there is no meaningful distinction between artificial and natural.

Of course foods grown with spliced genes may contain some dangerous residual compound so far undetected. Yet consider that while many activists express horror about gene-engineered foods—in which any residuals would be small and would have to get past stomach acids to reach the bloodstream—there is almost no opposition to gene-engineered medicines, though pharmaceuticals are by character often exceptionally toxic and are often injected directly into the bloodstream. Surely if gene engineering is a dangerous technology the last thing you'd want to do is shoot highly concentrated solutions of it directly into your veins.

When tissue-plasminogen activator, one of the first pharmaceuticals produced by gene-altered bacteria, was devised in the late 1970s, some opposed its certification on the grounds that synthesized drugs should never be used when natural substances are available. Is this really good policy? Consider the contrast to human growth hormone. This substance, found in the pituitary, was not produced through genetic engineering till 1985. Prior to that it was extracted from the glands of cadavers. In 1993 a tragedy occurred in France when 25 children who received HGH for dwarfism developed Jakob-Creutzfeldt syndrome, a brain infection always fatal. The HGH used to treat them had been obtained from infected corpses that were improperly checked by technicians. The substance that made the children ill was entirely natural in origin. The gene-engineering version of HGH now being used has an artificial origin and is safe.

Like other engineered pharmaceuticals from the first wave of biotechnology, tissue-plasminogen activator has turned out to be very expensive and of debatable therapeutic value. More promising is the next wave of production of biodrugs—made not by bacteria but in animals and plants, perhaps at higher quality yet lower cost.

The day when it was confirmed that a pig named Astrid had become the first animal to express a unit of human DNA may someday be looked back on in the same way that medical researchers speak of the night the English researcher Arthur Fleming stared into a petri dish of penicillin mold, wondering why some pathogens there had suddenly died. Pigs have hauntingly humanlike metabolisms. Because of this researchers are now attempting to transplant into pigs genes for the production of protein-C, a blood clotting factor; erythropoietin, which protects bone marrow in cancer and AIDS victims; alpha-1-antitrypsin, which may slow emphysema; human hemoglobin; and other drugs. Human genes are also being transplanted into cows and other animals to determine if human proteins can be made in animal bodies this way.

When discussion of gene engineering began in the 1970s, the common public assumption was that animal genes would be spliced into people—the strength of a gorilla into football linebackers, the height and leg lines of giraffes into fashion supermodels. Instead most research focus is on putting human genes into animals. Production of complicated proteins in the bodies of animals may make many substances that are now rare, expensive, and available only under restricted circumstances, as cheap and as widely available as aspirin. Like any other technical development that may be good or bad, widely distributed genetic drugs might cause some subtle harm. But such drugs may also offer breakthroughs in medical care, eventually extending this boon even to animals, as veterinary genetic drugs follow human versions.

In 1994, two teams of researchers reported in *Nature* that they had learned to engineer genes in such a way that mouse cells produce human antibodies so pure it appears unlikely human bodies will reject them. This increases the possibility that physicians will have at their disposal "monoclonal antibodies," a class of disease-fighting chemicals matching the exact physiology of individual patients. Today such antibodies are prohibitively expensive because they must be elaborately manufactured. If instead monoclonal antibodies could be grown at affordable cost in mice, an important new therapeutic tool might come into general use. Most drugs made in this way will be duplicates of existing substances, ones already devised by nature but rare. People think biotechnology must be frightful because of its name, yet in most cases biotechnology is more oriented toward use of natural body substances than conventional medicine. Genetic research is tightly focused on use of existing natural DNA, unlike standard pharmacology, which has its origins in the chemistry set.

It is possible to imagine a near future in which many pharmaceuticals are made not by mixing toxins in factories but by feeding grain to pigs and goats that live entirely normal, unremarkable lives outdoors on "pharms." Many gene engineering projects involve animals that express a drug gene through their milk glands, so that the product can be removed by simple milking, leaving the host animals unharmed.

On pharms, drugs may even grow in plants. One highly annoying aspect of initial gene engineering experiments was that for technical reasons the plasmids of the tobacco plant showed themselves especially amenable to DNA transplants. A few early gene engineering experiments involved creating very high yield versions of this addictive weed, surely the last thing society needs. Recently, however, it has been shown that tobacco is suited for manufacturing human antibodies: plantibodies, as researchers now call this prospect. Suppose the tobacco economy of the Southeast—today a menace to health but an important source of employment for African-Americans who comprise a high percentage of independent tobacco farmers—could be converted to the producer of antibodies. Tobacco farmers would rise to their morning's labors knowing they would make for the world not diseases but cures. Gene engineering ideas may go well or poorly, but the thought of converting tobacco into a socially responsible industry is alone reason enough for guarded optimism.

Genes as a Renewable Resource

It's true that gene engineering may open the door to dystopia. Suppose here for the sake of argument that humankind applies this knowledge only for constructive purposes. What might a future Earth, in which natural and artificial evolutionary influences work together, look like?

It might be an Earth in which steadily less land is used for agriculture, with more available for return to nature; in which the drugs and chemical compounds required by men and women are as likely to be raised in farmers' fields as produced in factories. It might be an Earth in which the Atlantic salmon swims contentedly in the coastal waters of Norway and many other creatures live over broader expanses than their genes now permit. The result would be habitats unlike any that would come into being through purely spontaneous forces. But as all habitats are guaranteed to change regardless of what genus *Homo* does or does not do, this alone should not deter.

The coming Earth might be one in which extinctions are reversed. Every schoolchild knows through the movie *Jurassic Park* that it is at least imaginable that extinct creatures will be restored through genetic engineering. This idea has no practicality today, but it may in decades to come. Not just dinosaurs but other living things thought to be gone forever—especially those recently extinct, for which the best tissue samples remain—might someday walk again.

Knowledge of gene engineering will also increase the pool of resources on which human beings may draw. An environmental credo is that Earth has reached its "age of limits"—that all possible resources have been uncovered and now we only draw down, adding nothing. Surely nature would not make so simplistic a mistake as to view ore and oil and the like as the totality of ecological resources. Gene material is a resource, too, one that has expanded countless times in the past and may be about to expand again.

Most additions to the genetic resource base have happened through a mistake-prone natural system (the driving element in natural gene change is thought to be replication errors during chromosome duplication), under which mutations are usually negative. Owing to DNA engineering, there now exists the prospect that the genetic resource base will begin to expand at an accelerating pace as people add only constructive mutations, skipping the defective-mutation stage.

Teilhard de Chardin, the Jesuit who believed in Darwin, wrote that people would serve as "supervisors" over the next stage of evolution. What happens next to life, Teilhard thought, cannot come about through purely spontaneous forces; action by design will be required. Many things could go wrong with this vision. But at least in principle it suggests a coming rapid advance in a resource essential to the richness of life—this enrichment arriving just when, according to the doomsday line, everything is running down and the cause is lost.

25

LAND

A FEW YEARS AGO I TOOK SOME ILL-FITTING WADING BOOTS
and a thermos of strong coffee and fumbled in the hours before first light
to a copse looking out upon the Blackwater National Wildlife Refuge in
Maryland. My mind occupied with the endlessly insignificant insubstan-
tialities of civilization, I waited impatiently for dawn. Soon I heard its
heralds. The living things of Blackwater began to chatter among each
other of the sun's imminence well before the first ray was visible to my
eyes. How they knew the sun was coming is just one of many little
secrets nature keeps to itself. At last a red disc interrupted the horizon,
and I beheld the dance of the ages.

Bird cries arose over flat thickets of reedy grasses. Eagle, red-tailed
hawk, black duck, and other children of the air lifted skyward to commence their daily rituals of quest, or soar unbounded over the adjacent
majesty of Cheasapeake Bay. A hundred forms of reptiles skittered along
the grasses and ponds. By the time the sun hung securely above the horizon, the refuge bustled with life. Places like Blackwater National
Wildlife Refuge are nature on a throne of golden glory—and don't have
much to do with protecting the environment.

When the subject is land preservation, locations of conspicuous
beauty always come first to mind. But such areas constitute only a small
part of the ecology equation, both statistically and because beauty is its
own advocate. Only a dunce could oppose preservation at Blackwater,
Yellowstone, Yosemite, and similar storied locations. The real action in
land conservation involves aspects of the ecosphere that are not particu-

larly striking: wetlands, tundra, savannas, and forest tracts that lack spectacular scenery or prestige endangered species. Consider wetlands, which in the late 1980s became one of the most contentious U.S. environmental issues. "The majority of wetlands are not sensational locations like Blackwater," says Lyndon Lee, a wetlands restoration expert. "They are scattered tracts of private property with no particular visual appeal, places you might drive right past. Kind of blah, unless you know what you're looking at."

For Third World nations the great crunch issue of the environment is population. For Western nations the crunch issue is land, because affluence expands to fill the space available for construction.

Eighty million acres of the United States, an area twice the size of Florida, is in preservation status via the National Park Service. Another 190 million acres is more or less protected by the Forest Service. State parks add tens of millions more acres. Many additional acres are preserved under the wildlife refuge system, as national recreation areas, and under a program that protects the riparian corridors of "wild and scenic" rivers. And some 272 million acres are administered, at least partly for conservation, by the Bureau of Land Management. Roughly totaled there are perhaps 500 million acres of the United States in protected status—an area five times the expanse of California.

It's not enough.

Land preservation is a bequest from the present to the future. Each year adding to that endowment grows more costly as land prices rise. Americans ought to keep expanding the land preservation system while the purchase price remains affordable. Though federal land controls can be exasperating, especially for those who live west of the Mississippi where most federal lands are, sometimes preservation status even makes market sense. Thomas Power, a professor of economics at the University of Montana, has shown that mining and logging bans at Yellowstone National Park are a profit-maximizing device from the standpoint of local economies, recreational dollars exceeding possible resource extraction dollars there. Surely there are other areas of the remaining wild U.S. where preservation is an economic plus.

City dwellers may not believe this, but America, colossus of the materialist lifestyle, is among the world's least populous countries: America has 68 people per square mile compared to 140 per square mile in Egypt, 202 per square mile in Spain, 256 per square mile in France, 1,230 per square mile in Singapore. This means that within the boundaries of the United States lies an astonishing vastness of land that has not undergone the concrete conversion experience—that is or can be preserved in a state of nature.

Because city dwellers have difficulty conceptualizing just how much undeveloped land America contains, they are prone to believe alarmist pronouncements about land loss. For instance in the early 1980s many pessimists in New England declared that the boom in construction of vacation homes would wipe out the region's 18 million acres of forest preserves. This coming disaster was widely believed by New England opinion-makers. Yet 18 million acres is a huge area—about the size of South Carolina. As the writer Norman Boucher has shown, by the time the New England second-home boom crashed in the late 1980s, at most two-tenths of one percent of the region's forest preserves had been developed.

But even in a country of American expanse, primal nature will not last unless society adapts a general vision of land preservation. Soon— within the lifetimes of most readers of this book—Western economies will attain a zero-pollution, sustainable basis. That will resolve most environmental concerns now lumped under the headings of pollution and resource conservation. But a zero-pollution economy might actually represent a larger threat to the land, since once genus *Homo* can expand without causing gross ecological harm, the guilty conscience will no longer be a restraining influence. Land preservation in a zero-pollution society will require the development of a new ethic based on voluntary self-restraint, not on doomsday iconography. Aldo Leopold, who proposed the "land ethic"—that the land itself would eventually acquire standing under law, just as species are now acquiring standing—once wrote, "We shall hardly relinquish the shovel, which after all has many good points, but we are in need of a gentler and more objective criterion for its use."[1]

A gentler criterion for the shovel would not mean no growth, or even no extravaganzas. For example the recently retired governor of Alaska, Walter Hickel, has proposed a $150 billion aqueduct be constructed to transit the voluminous fresh waters of his state to the arid Los Angeles corridor. Environmentalists stutter with aspersion whenever this aqueduct is proposed, as it would bring into being a substantial artificial rearrangement of hydrology. It is doubtful the project makes economic sense. But nature would not object, having rearranged the continental hydraulics of North America countless times and being certain to rearrange them again.

Yet grand or small, any development projects people embark upon in the future must be designed to have minimal impact on the remaining pristine portions of Earth. Pollution, ozone depletion, and many similar environmental mistakes are being rectified and will not trouble future generations. Mistakes made with the land, in contrast, will be difficult to erase. Preserving as much of the land that remains is an essential component of the ecorealist transition, of helping nature endure the polluted present till it can thrive again in the coming green future.

Wetlands

According to the National Research Council, perhaps 117 million acres of wetlands have been lost in the United States since 1780, mostly through construction of drainage systems that converted saturated soils to dry soil for agriculture or urban construction. Even in a country of America's expanse this represents a substantial territory, about three times the size of Florida.

Wetlands conversion is hardly new: Pre-Columbian Native Americans drained land on occasion. European settlers built their capital, Washington, on a drained swamp. As recently as the 1970s the Army Corps of Engineers and the Bureau of Reclamation, the federal agencies that build dams and large drainage systems, called this practice "reclaiming land." Today it is called destroying wetlands.

Much environmentalist persuasion was required for the Clean Water Act of 1972 to classify saturated soils as "waters of the United States," invoking the legal phrase used to assert common public dominion over rivers and lakes. Since then a federal permit has been needed to convert wetlands to dry. Section 404, the wetlands permit system jointly administered by the Corps and the EPA, has as a result with little public notice become "the largest federal land-use management program in the country," says Robert Pierce, director of the Wetlands Training Institute. Section 404 has created red-tape horror stories of the sort that make for talk-radio fodder. For instance in 1992 residents of a middle-class community that lines Broad Channel, a waterway off Jamaica Bay, Queens, were told they must remove from their homes any decks fronting the bay. When home decks became the rage in the 1980s, Broad Channel residents built them not knowing that technically a Section 404 permit was required. Homeowners were told decks had to be removed and a $10,000 fine paid. This crackdown was the sort of bureaucratic excess that gives environmental protection a bad name; eventually the New York legislature enacted a waiver for Broad Channel.

Yet in the main, zealous defense of wetlands is a sound idea. Researchers call wetlands nature's pollution filter—where contaminants such as farm runoff are metabolized by microbes or broken down via percolation through soils. Nature has been managing water pollution for millions of years, and wetlands are a primary tool. Wetlands are also important layover sites for migratory birds. Two Forks Dam, a major water-supply facility planned for Denver, was canceled in 1991 by EPA administrator William Reilly on the grounds that the reservoir would disrupt a 300-acre wetland on the North Platte River that is a rest stop for endangered sandhill cranes.

Anyone remember the Tellico Dam? In 1977 the EPA was ridiculed when it blocked that project because a fish called the snail darter was believed imperiled; Congress was later applauded for declaring the dam could go ahead, snail darter be damned. In contrast cancellation of the Two Forks Dam did not set off howls. Even polls in Denver showed most people thought protection of sandhill cranes more important than increased water supply. The contrast in reactions to the Tellico and Two Forks dam proposals indicates a profound shift in public attitudes about land preservation.

Biologists like wetlands because they are active ecospheres where competition between life-forms is ongoing, and thus fountains of biological diversity. Saturated soils have only one drawback: Owing to natural decomposition of organic matter, global wetlands emit about 115 million tons annually of methane, the most potent greenhouse gas. The world's cattle herds are the source of about 60 million tons of methane a year, half the wetlands figure. Yet it is common to hear activists say that methane emissions from livestock represent an outrage—Jeremy Rifkin has campaigned on that premise for years—while simultaneously saying that the world urgently needs more wetlands.

Industrialists, developers, and local government officials of all stripes have despised Section 404 since its inception. John Sununu, when governor of New Hampshire, had legendary disputes with Michael Deland, then EPA regional administrator. Though a Ronald Reagan appointee, Deland insisted on enforcing wetland strictures. One important Sununu-backed wetlands development waiver Deland refused to grant was, improbably enough, for a ski area. Wetland issues have become prominent in Europe, too, with environmentalists fighting a proposal to construct a golf resort near Spain's Donella Wildlife Refuge, a wetland important to migratory birds.[2]

In his 1989 State of the Union address George Bush pronounced a policy of "no net loss of wetlands," among the most arcane commitments ever uttered in a presidential forum. By this Bush meant that if developers are permitted to drain a wetland in one place, they must create or restore a wetland of equal acreage elsewhere. So far wetlands creation has not worked well. For instance an attempted revival of a large wetland off San Diego Bay, which California agreed to restore in a swap for legal permission to fill wetlands to expand Interstate 5, has gone poorly despite a considerable investment of money and science talent. But eventually, as knowledge of nature improves, wetlands restoration is expected to succeed. "Because wetland life-forms are active and grow quickly," Lyndon Lee notes, "restoring a wetland should be more practical than restoring a wilderness."

Owing to political pressures and an unending technical dispute regarding how to define wetlands, regulation has existed in a state of continuous upheaval. The sort of issue in question: Should a wetland be defined by vegetation or by 15 consecutive days of standing water or by 21 consecutive days of surface saturation? In 1987 the Corps of Engineers published an immensely thick manual that was supposed to resolve matters. Even specialists found the manual close to incomprehensible. In 1989 Reilly tentatively endorsed a new wetlands manual, one whose techno-gibberish quotient left readers longing for the snappy prose of the *Federal Register*. The manual would, however, have expanded wetlands conservation dramatically. For example it classified as protected wetland the soil underneath the White House and under the Houstonian Hotel, the address President Bush claimed as his "residence" for tax-evasion purposes.

Expansive as the new manual was, environmental lobbyists were dismayed that it did not nearly ban wetlands conversion: They moved to block promulgation of the document. Soon they wished they had not. By 1991 the star of Vice President Dan Quayle was in the ascendancy, and Quayle proposed yet a third wetlands manual, this one reducing the scope of protection. Researchers using the proposed Quayle criteria found that much of the Great Dismal Swamp in Virginia, the Nisqually National Wildlife Refuge of Washington State, and other areas soaking wet would be "defined down" to dry under Quayle's proposal. By this point there was a movement in Congress, encouraged by business and construction lobbies, to strip the EPA of jurisdiction over wetlands permits. As a rearguard action Reilly offered to consider the Quayle proposal. This caused Reilly to be denounced by environmentalists as a quisling but prevented the congressional initiative from gathering steam.

When the 1992 election approached Bush, worried about being seen as breaking his "no net loss" promise, repudiated the Quayle manual. After Bush lost but before Bill Clinton took office, Quayle made one last push to put his manual into law, knowing it would be overturned by the incoming administration but confident even a brief suspension of Section 404 would win brownie points with the right wing. In the fading days of the Bush White House, Reilly managed through a series of procedural maneuvers to block Quayle's attempt. Wetlands regulation then collapsed in a heap, the country returning to the status quo ante of the unreadable 1987 Corps of Engineers document.

Clinton punted the question of how to define wetlands, deciding to wait until a committee of the National Academy of Sciences weighs in. He did deny special waivers for Alaska. For years the Alaska congressional delegation has requested an exemption from Section 404, as fully 170 million acres of that state is technically saturated soil, though often frozen. Bush had offered Alaska waivers for 1.7 million acres, a figure that to Manhattanites may sound like the circumference of the Crab Nebula but which is just one percent of Alaskan wetlands. Even that one percent exemption seemed too great for Clinton's environmental policy staff, which nonetheless by 1994 was being regularly denounced by enviros as insufficiently committed to conservation.

With Clinton having postponed action, the status of wetlands protection remains clouded. A possible future is now on display, however, in a complex agreement signed in 1994 between the Department of the Interior and sugar growers of the Everglades region.

Hundreds of Corps of Engineers dikes, dams, and channels now exert artificial control over the hydrology of the Everglades. Some ecologists consider this a prime offense against nature, though the estimated 1,500 people killed in 1947, when a hurricane caused Lake Okeechobee at the center of the Everglades to overflow, might have felt differently. Control of the Everglades has ended flooding, sparing casualties and habitat destruction.

Today further tampering with the Everglades has effectively ended. The Corps of Engineers has proposed to remove as many dams and dikes as practical, to restore much of the Everglades' natural flow. Under the 1994 agreement, farmers and Florida taxpayers will spend some $700 million creating natural discharge marshes that reduce the phosphorus flowing off sugar fields into the Everglades. This agreement was denounced by most institutional environmental organizations, though the deal had been negotiated by Interior Secretary Bruce Babbitt, a lifelong green: institutional environmentalism wanted a punitive settlement that would put many sugar growers out of business. Yet once the new system is in place, agriculture can continue as human action corrects a flaw of nature—flooding, which is dangerous to the biosphere as well as to people—while rectifying pollution and locking broad areas into preservation status. When the cleanup project is completed in the early twenty-first century, the Everglades will be a better place for nature than when genus *Homo* first laid eyes on it. Ouch! How will doomsday doctrine handle that inappropriately positive development?

The Importance of the Noncrisis

Because primal urge of contemporary environmental doctrine is to decree a crisis, there have been attempts to make land seem in shocking danger. One was the "vanishing farms" illusion described in chapter 22; another is the entirely real question of rainforest loss, to be detailed in chapter 31. A third is the question of desertification, half real and half illusory.

In the 1970s many environmentalists began to assert that high-yield agriculture was causing deserts to expand at a menacing rate. The United Nations declared 1977 a "year of desertification." For about a decade the notion of global desertification became a standard element of autopanic literature. But few empirical studies had been done. By 1991 satellite imagery compiled by the National Aeronautics and Space Administration showed that though the Sahara expanded 16 percent during the 1970s and early 1980s, it then contracted by nine percent in the late 1980s. Sharon Nicholson, a Florida State University desert expert, told the technical journal *Science,* "Most of these claims of impending desertification are poppycock." Researchers now suspect deserts have cycles of expansion and contraction. The Sahara boundary advance seen in the 1970s merely may have been humankind noticing, for the first time, a naturally occurring rhythm.

Though the Sahara may not be growing in any way that heralds doomsday, local desert expansion surely brings suffering to the Sahel region, where some of the world's poorest people reside. Yet the subsistence style of farming practiced in the Sahel may be making local Sahara expansion worse. Studies by the United Nations Environment Programme show that the hoofs of cattle used to pull plows, in the very labor-based low-technology form of agriculture green doctrine praises, break up the thin topsoil of the region, creating dust-bowl circumstances that favor desert advance. Use of tractors, fertilizer, high-yield strains, and irrigation helped end the Dust Bowl of the 1930s, principally by insuring that crops never fail. Tractors could be a boom to the Sahel; yet environmental doctrine favors "traditional" (that is, cattle-drawn) agriculture for Africa.

In 1993 and 1994 the notion of desertification made a comeback, with the United Nations conducting summits on a proposed global anti-desert treaty. If such a treaty brought First World aid to poor nations like Mali and the Sudan, ones that border the Sahara, it would be a welcome development. But treaty drafts, influenced by lobbying from Western environmental groups, were heavy on panic language and short on references to agricultural advances. The speakers' lists for State

Department desertification treaty preparatory sessions consisted entirely of doomsayers, even after the excellent "Science Times" section of the *New York Times*—the paper most closely read by diplomats—ran a prominent article headlined "Desertification Scare Appears Unsupported by Research."

Meanwhile, in the same months in 1994 that the executive branch of the U.S. government was, through the State Department, issuing statements on the shocking awfulness of deserts, the legislative branch was, through the Congress, passing the California Desert Protection Act. Backed by the Wilderness Society and other environmental lobbies, this statute will forbid development in some 9.4 million acres of the eastern Mojave, an area larger than Maryland. That's right—the bill was about DESERT PRESERVATION. Parts of the Sonora Desert of Arizona were during the 1950s and 1960s irrigated for agriculture. In the 1990s an environmental group called the Society for Ecological Restoration has been working to return the Sonora to its preagricultural condition. That's right—the goal is DESERT RESTORATION.

Though the California Desert Preservation Act was a great idea—it puts more land in preservation status, an important ecorealist goal—the differing treatment of the two desert subjects represented classic selective doomsaying. In Africa, where deserts are encroaching on people, that's a horror. In the American Southwest, where people are encroaching on deserts, that's a horror.[3]

Drawing Lines

Most land-use issues lack the zing of vanishing farms or advancing deserts but ultimately are more significant. A prominent example is federal grazing fees. In much of the American West ranchers graze stock on Bureau of Land Management pastures for much less than the market price: in 1994 for $1.96 per month per "animal unit" versus a market rate of around four dollars monthly. Like many government subsidies, this facilitates waste, in this case the overgrazing of public lands, which suppresses range vegetation and the species dependent upon it. Many naturalists believe the sparse, lonely rangeland of cowboy movie lore is not an entirely natural condition. Before whites began to graze cattle there, thicker grasses and more trees probably were common.

When Clinton took office he proposed market-pricing of grazing fees, dropped the proposal after opposition from western senators, revived the idea in milder form, dropped it again after western senators filibustered the Senate, and at this writing was attempting by administrative order to increase grazing fees to somewhat below the market rate. Clinton's attempts to impose market sense on hard-rock mining, governed by an anachronistic 1872 law that allows some mining companies to "patent" public lands for private gain at a few dollars an acre, have been similarly blocked by western interests in the Senate.

Most ranchers who graze stock at below-market prices are not cattle barons; they are middle-class business owners trying to make ends meet. General ecological preservation cannot be realized without a price being paid by such typical citizens. One recent item of conservation legislation is the Coastal Zone Management Act, which requires that the Atlantic seaboard be preserved through strict zoning. Former Florida governor Reuben Askew chaired the commission that wrote the rules for his state. "It's one thing to engage in lofty talk about preserving the land," he says, "another to sit down with surveyor's documents and draw lines through people's property, as I did. That was murder."

In the 1990s such murderous questions began to coalesce around the "takings" clause of the Constitution, which stipulates government not take land without compensation. If your house is condemned for a freeway, you must be paid. But suppose you buy land planning to build, say, a franchised drive-through vegetarian deli, and officials then declare your property a habitat of the endangered stripeless snipe. You still own the land but your potential income falls. Must you be compensated?

Conservationists have long feared that the Supreme Court will rule that ecological initiatives may constitute "taking." In 1994 the Court did rule this way, though using restrained language, when it said that some types of environmental requirements imposed on landowners are takings unless the conservation goal exhibits "rough proportionality" to the likely harm from development. Determining exactly what "rough proportionality" means will keep many lawyers in stylish pumps and loafers for years to come. Most likely the 1994 ruling will only protect landowners' valid interests in their property, not create any lasting barrier to conservation. Takings reasoning is unlikely to escalate into an obstacle to land preservation initiatives, because contrary to the common assumption it has never been in case, either in American jurisprudence or the English common law on which many U.S. legal precepts are based, that "no one can tell me what to do with my land." Courts have long allowed that private land use may be subject to restrictions such as zoning requirements and that owners may be penalized for harms that one person's property use cause to other property. In some cases U.S. and English courts have recognized a general public interest in the vitality of the environment on private lands. The general public interest in land preservation seems likely to continue to be recognized by courts.

Restricting the rights of landowners to develop their property may sound well and good when contemplating preservation rules that reduce the potential profits of high rollers such as land speculators. The burden is, however, as likely to fall on average citizens. For example, a 1990 federal law decreed preservation of the "long-term integrity and traditional uses" of the Appalachian Piedmont Highlands, a million beautiful acres of rolling hills and pastoral towns along the Delaware River on the Pennsylvania–New Jersey border that is one of the best-kept secrets of the American ecology. State agencies now interpret that law to mean farms in the Piedmont Highlands can only be sold for continued cultivation, their traditional (in this century, at least) use. The effect of this decision is to forbid small farmers and senior citizens of the Highlands, where incomes fall considerably below the national mean, from realizing profits by selling to developers. Even mild forms of development such as light industry or resorts are barred by the rules. The Appalachian Highlands law makes the error, common in current environmental orthodoxy, of opposing all development, rather than discriminating between development that can be justified and development that cannot.

Ecologically oriented land preservation need not be so heavy-handed. Two promising examples involve Austin, Texas, and Los Angeles. In Austin, the Nature Conservancy cooperated with a consortium of developers to plan housing and commerce in a pristine area of Texas hill country. The developers feared the gold-cheeked warbler might be declared an endangered species, thus placing the land off-limits. In the plan some development is approved while 60,000 acres of "core reserves" are set aside for wildlife. The reserve land, which goes into voluntary preservation status, was donated by developers in return for favorable rulings keeping the gold-cheeked warbler off the endangered species index.

Between Los Angeles and San Diego 250,000 acres of coastal sage scrub, an area that includes some of the world's most desirable real estate parcels, has been frozen from development owing to the claimed decline of the California gnatcatcher, a thrush. A lawsuit by the Natural Resources Defense Council resulted in the bird being listed as endangered. State officials, aided by Interior Secretary Babbitt, in 1993 arranged a compromise by which the gnatcatcher would be called "threatened," a lesser category, so long as about half the acres are placed into a voluntary preservation status. This approach is ecorealism: reasonable development allowed, with provisions for general ecosystem protection. Nevertheless after the compromise was reached the NRDC and National Audubon Society attacked Babbitt, a former head of the

League of Conservation Voters, as a sellout, and filed suit to block the agreement.

This second lawsuit backfired when a federal judge ruled in 1994 that the scientific case supporting gnatcatcher endangerment is invalid. Few ornithologists believe the California gnatcatcher a true subspecies, while millions of gnatcatchers live in Mexico and the Southwest, showing the bird generally is in no danger. At this writing environmentalists were scrambling to reinstate the Babbitt compromise they had mocked the year before.

However much activists may have hated Babbitt's plan, it shows that developers can be persuaded of the need for habitat conservation. And in some cases, restored habitat can coexist with existing development. Much of what is now the fashionable northwest suburbs of Chicago was, before Columbus, oak savannah. Biologists have been working on a 160-acre plot outside Northbrook, Illinois, to restore oak savannah flora such as bottlebrush and the sweet brown-eyed Susan flower. So far it appears the savannah can coexist in conjunction with developed Northbrook.[4] A few years after the restoration project began two Eastern bluebirds, a species long vanished from northern Illinois, appeared as if by magic among the new oaks. Other "lost" savannah species have been reappearing. Where these species came from is a mystery even to those running the project. They seem to have been waiting, like Arthur at Avalon, for the time to be right to return.

Reasoned Growth

Better land preservation will require land-use planning, long a taboo in American politics. That taboo will begin to dissolve as experiments such as the Austin and Los Angeles plans succeed. The collapse of the Soviet bloc removes any doubt that as regards the allocation of goods and services, central planning is a failed concept. But goods and services are an arena where supply and demand shift far more rapidly than lumbering government agencies ever could follow. In land, trends are long-term and supply never changes. This makes land use appropriate for public planning.[5]

The fading of the land-use planning taboo will be encouraged by results from Oregon, which has the country's most comprehensive land-use planning statute. There have been snafus, but this law has not caused economic stagnation: The Oregon economy continues to expand. By several measures that state is doing considerably better economically than many states with lenient zoning. "We believe that ecological conservation has a clear money value to our future," says Richard Brenner, Oregon's director of land conservation.

Given that new homes and factories must be built, the compromises necessary for their construction might as well be intelligent compromises. Many voters fear land-use planning because to the left it is code for no growth: The saying among political consultants is "no growth means no votes." But there exists an appealing possibility between anything-goes and no growth: reasoned growth. By offering to preserve the ecology while allowing development that proceeds with care, reasoned growth such as that now being tried around Austin and in the California coastal scrub holds out the hope of permitting an expanding economy and protecting natural habitats at the same time—even of allowing people to live more closely enjoined with those habitats, a pleasant clean-technology prospect that will have high public appeal, and will break the land-use planning taboo.

POLITICS

An amazing and little-noticed token of the political power of contemporary environmentalism came in the autumn of 1993, as President Bill Clinton began his push to ratify the North American Free Trade Agreement. Responding to criticism of the treaty draft, Clinton negotiated two side letters: one on the environment, one on labor. Each side letter created a commission. The labor commission would be small, have little authority, and a limited staff. The environmental commission would have unlimited staff, near-cabinet rank, and sweeping authority. Thus in making his political calculus for NAFTA, Clinton concluded that pleasing environmentalists was more important than pleasing organized labor, the traditional first constituency of the Democratic Party. Environmentalists, Clinton reasoned, can now deliver more heat and more votes than can labor leaders. This is a shift of the first magnitude. Had you told a political scientist 20 years ago that by the 1990s environmentalists would be taken more seriously in a Democratic White House than the AFL-CIO, you would have been advised to seek professional care.

Yet burdened by the thought processes and lexicon of doomsday, institutional environmentalism cannot take claim for achievements such as White House influence. The next phase of optimistic environmental progress—in which it is generally understood that ecological control measures have been remarkably successful in the past and will be even more successful in the future—will not commence until this political problem is overcome.

Delaney and Rationalism

It seemed like a political dream come true. Just as Clinton took office in 1993, a federal appeals court ruled the EPA had no choice but to enforce the letter of the Delaney Clause. This statute, which requires government to ban from processed food any trace of synthetic substances implicated as human carcinogens, has been for decades holy writ to environmentalists. On the face of the 1993 ruling many pesticides would be banned immediately. Environmental lobbyists assumed that with Al Gore as the vice president and Carol Browner, his former chief Senate aide, as EPA administrator, the Clinton Administration would be appropriately oriented to ecological gloom. Now the appeals court had provided an opening through which the new administration could get off on the correct doomsday footing.

Instead Browner announced the Delaney Clause had become "a scientific anachronism" and ought to be repealed. Pesticides are a problem, she said in a speech at the National Press Club, but nothing to panic about. Many doomsayers were crushed. Rather than pushing the new administration toward an extreme the court decision pushed Clinton toward rational moderation—toward ecorealism.

The Delaney Clause is a metaphor for the long-standing political problem that alarms are more easily turned on than switched off. Often reform movements take decades to build to the point of insider power. By that time some of the movement's initial purpose may have expired; but the sentiment and animating energy remain and manifest as anger that seems strangely detached from the world around it. This sequence is now seen in some aspects of environmental politics, such as devotion to the Delaney Clause.

When Delaney was passed in 1958 as a title of the Food, Drug, and Cosmetics Act, environmental exposures to synthetic chemicals were assumed to account for up to 90 percent of cancers. At the time the profusion of naturally occurring toxins was not understood. And in 1958 detection devices could find substances only to the parts per million range, a level at which the presence of a carcinogen is a clear danger. Today researchers believe synthetic compounds cause only a small percentage of cancers, and today some detection devices see down to the parts per quadrillion. "Delaney became ridiculous," says Linda Fisher, a former head of the EPA's toxic substances office. "We were regulating extremely small amounts of synthetics in processed foods while having no controls for natural toxins in raw food, which research suggests is the greater problem. The situation made no sense." But it was consonant with end-of-nature orthodoxy.

In 1990 a study from the National Academy of Sciences declared that Delaney had outlived its usefulness. The academy advocated a new standard, based on "negligible risk," to be applied equally to synthetic and natural carcinogens. The Sierra Club, Public Citizen, and other groups attacked the report as industrial apologetics.

One factor at play was the codependency of environmental lobbies on end-of-the-world issues. The Delaney Clause has the politically correct result of generating regular headlines suggesting not just that toxic chemicals should be regulated closely, as they should, but that even microscopic amounts are a threat to life as we know it. Institutional environmentalism has come to believe the public will only support desirable reforms like close regulation of chemicals if scared half to death by a doomsday campaign. This is surely wrong. Voters care about many issues that pose no immediate threat to life, and would continue to support environmentalism even if its rhetoric were more veracious, because the plainspoken case for ecological protection is amply strong.

In 1993 the National Academy of Sciences issued another report, this time saying not enough is known about pesticide risks to children, who are more susceptible to toxics than adults. The Academy recommended more research into the effects of food chemicals on children and all practical reductions in pesticides, both sound ideas. This study, widely praised by the same groups that had attacked the Academy's 1990 findings about Delaney, was depicted in news accounts as pronouncing that frightful pesticide risks to children had been proven. The study says nothing of the kind: only that such risks cannot be ruled out.

In the wake of this study Clinton's EPA, Food and Drug Administration, and Department of Agriculture—agencies that have long devoted considerable energy to turf wars over pesticide regulation—announced they would cooperate on new legislation to reduce food chemicals. Under the proposal the Delaney Clause would be amended to incorporate "negligible risk"; farmers would be pressured to switch to the low-pesticide practice called integrated pest management; pesticide registration would be tightened; pesticides banned in the United States would be banned for export for sale elsewhere; pesticide tolerance levels would be lowest for foods favored by children.

Someday the Clinton pesticide bill may be looked upon as the first formal government act of ecorealism. But owing to its commonsense quotient, many environmentalists hated the Clinton proposal. The Natural Resources Defense Council declared the existing Delaney Clause must be preserved as "the backbone of our nation's food safety laws." The National Coalition Against Misuse of Pesticides called the plan "rotten to the core." At this writing Clinton's reform package, opposed by most enviros, had gone nowhere on Capitol Hill.

Rationality Itself

The Delaney Clause is hardly the only area where environmental policy has been divorced from rationality. As the Supreme Court justice Stephen Breyer noted in 1993 in *Breaking the Cycle: Toward Effective Risk Regulation,* "Drinking a bottle of pure iodine is deadly; placing a drop on a cut is helpful." Yet current policy treats the iodine as if the entire bottle will be chugalugged.

Breyer once presided over a decade-long lawsuit concerning the restoration of a New Hampshire dump. After most of the cleanup was complete prosecutors and environmentalists continued to press for an extra $9.3 million to remove trace amounts of PCBs and benzene from the soil. Breyer wrote, "The 40,000-page record of this ten-year effort indicated that without the extra expenditure the waste dump was clean enough for children playing on the site to eat small amounts of dirt daily for 70 days each year without significant harm. Burning [incinerating] the soil would have made it clean enough for children to eat small amounts of dirt daily for 245 days per year without significant harm. But there were no dirt-eating children playing in the area, for it was a swamp." To spend $9.3 million to guard against the remote possibility that children might enter an old industrial site and gulp down dirt by the mouthful is not rational policy, Breyer concluded.

Breyer estimates that some environmental regulations are extremely cost-effective. For example, the 1979 rules that restrict trihalomethane in drinking water probably cost only $200,000 per life saved, and the original round of restrictions aimed at stopping gross benzene emissions probably cost $3.4 million per death avoided. On the other hand the sorts of restrictions that became green causes in the late 1980s and early 1990s, Breyer suggests, border on senseless. A 1990 rule classifying as hazardous most petroleum refining sludge, whose prime constituent is mud, may cost $27.6 million per life saved; 1988 regulations greatly expanding the categories of waste chemicals that must be incinerated rather than placed in landfills may cost $4.2 billion per life saved; the federal drinking water standard for traces of the pesticide atrazine may cost $92 billion per life saved.

Conventional environmentalists often respond to such figures by saying that if ecological initiatives are at times excessive, were the money not spent on cleanups it would only be wasted on weapons or political pork barrel. Perhaps. But the money might also be transferred either to more productive conservation programs or more pressing social needs. For example the 1993 budget of the Department of Energy contained $5.3 billion for the cleanup of old nuclear weapons production sites and just $209 million for research into renewable-energy technology. Weapons-site cleanup is proceeding with agonizing slowness and yielding marginal benefits. Renewable-energy technology is advancing swiftly and improving the environment on many fronts. Wouldn't it make sense to shift a little money between the two accounts? Not to doomsday doctrine.

Or consider that the 1993 influenza strain, Type A Beijing 3292, is thought to have caused between 10,000 and 45,000 premature deaths. Most influenza deaths can be avoided by vaccination. But less than a third of those in the influenza risk group get annual inoculations, according to the Department of Health and Human Services. The department estimates that universal vaccination for the influenza risk group would cost $248 million. The 1993 budget of $5.3 billion for weapons-site cleanups might not save a single life. Is such an ordering of social priorities rational? Paul Levy, a professor at the Massachusetts Institute of Technology and former director of the agency charged with cleaning up Boston Harbor, notes that "The phrase 'acceptable risk' cannot be used in a modern democratic system, so we have no way of reaching decisions about reasonable relationships between environmental costs and benefits." We do not, which is why ecorealism is needed.

Outsiders Wanting Back Out

Just three months into the Clinton Administration, Vice President Al Gore found himself throwing a group of environmental lobbyists out of his office, after lecturing them about the Armageddon language they were using on Capitol Hill to oppose Gore's decision to replace the Council on Environmental Quality with a marginally smaller bureau. The main function of the CEQ was to administer the National Environmental Policy Act, wellspring of the Environmental Impact Statement; this was being done through a hierarchy Gore felt was cumbersome. But institutional environmentalism likes the Environmental Impact Statement cumbersome. Many enviros feared Gore's move, part of his initiative to "reinvent government" through streamlining, might have the awful effect of actually streamlining an environmental program.

And just three months into the Clinton Administration Jay Hair, head of the National Wildlife Federation, angry that Clinton proposed and then withdrew the notion of market-priced grazing fees, said the White House had romanced environmentalists on the proposal but that the romance turned to "date rape." The snippet made a choice sound bite, insuring Hair's visage would appear for an instant on national newscasts, as it did. But the harshness of the simile and its teratoid timing suggested how environmentalism has become hooked on that lowest of common denominators, negative politics. Hair's *opening position* in the politics of the first liberal administration in 12 years was to cry rape.

Examples such as these suggest that whether environmentalists can learn positive politics is a central question for the 1990s. "Modern environmental politics is driven by a hard core that thinks it has a monopoly on purity and that fights reasonable compromise, even when the compromise is attractive to the ecology." Who said this—Rush Limbaugh? Pat Buchanan? The speaker was Rep. Al Swift, a Democrat of Washington State, who retired in 1994 as one of the most liberal members of Congress and who, during his career in the House, was a frequent sponsor of recycling legislation and other green mandates. Swift says that "the religious element of the environmental movement is just as bad as the troglodyte element at industrial trade associations, and just as influential. We would have more ecological progress if environmentalists themselves were not so often engaged in negative politics against programs that fail to meet some minor test of religious purity."

Another central question for the 1990s will be how enviros themselves perform in office. When Clinton took the White House, Jessica Tuchman Mathews and Rafe Pomerance of the World Resources Institute; George Frampton of the Wilderness Society; Brooks Yaeger of the National Audubon Society; David Gardiner of the Sierra Club; and other prominent career environmentalists were appointed to senior federal posts.

Vested with high position, reformers often find the world suddenly grows wearisome. Edicts cannot simply be issued; economic consequences cannot be wished away; bureaucracies cannot be ordered to forward-march. Many New Right activists of the Reagan years lasted only briefly when appointed to federal authority, preferring to return to an idyllic life of issuing denouncements of others. Having actual responsibility can spoil pleasant Us Versus Them packaging of issues. It may be a telling sign that Mathews, one of America's most accomplished environmentalists, quit the State Department before the end of Clinton's first year.

Nimbys against Cleanup

Once the public went along with practically anything proposed by government or industry. Now, in part owing to environmentalists, the public opposes practically everything. The Nimby (not in my backyard) reflex has become a central element of modern politics, along with its advanced versions, the Banana (build nothing anywhere near anyone) syndrome and Nope (not on planet Earth) reflex. Fitted with the quiver of contemporary due-process strictures, Nimbys now even oppose construction of environmental facilities. For example, because hazardous wastes received intense study in the past decade, a body of knowledge now exists that could make for treatment sites with superior environmental qualities. But good luck getting permission to put one anywhere.[1]

Nimby has an aspect of property-values snobbery, but its operative ingredient is terror. Planned EPA cleanups of petrochemical waste dumps in the Houston area have been delayed for years by lawsuits blocking the opening of cleanup support facilities. In 1993 the Indiana legislature enacted a law barring the construction of a toxic-substance incinerator in Bloomington, where the EPA wanted to destroy wastes from several Superfund sites. Environmentalists in Kentucky are fighting a proposed incinerator for the destruction of chemical weapons stored at Blue Grass Army Depot outside Lexington; though the end of chemical weapons, required by a 1992 treaty, ought to be seen as among the leading environmental victories of the age. Lexington environmentalists say they fear that once the chemical weapons are destroyed the incinerator will continue to operate, burning other hazardous wastes. But wouldn't that be a good idea? If hazardous wastes really are as dangerous as claimed, their destruction is an urgent need.

Here's a Nimby vignette that sums up many dynamics of contemporary environmentalism. Ciba-Geigy, the chemical conglomerate, had a dye factory in Toms River, New Jersey. For years the plant discharged foul process water to the Atlantic via pipelines that moved pollution just far enough offshore to be out of sight, out of mind. Ciba was not alone in its behavior. At the time municipal treatment plants were also discharging foul water to the Toms River and Atlantic. So in a sense, Jersey residents were just as guilty as the company. They didn't want to have to know where their toilet water was going or pay the higher rates required to treat the discharge properly.

For years environmental groups pressured Ciba to stop ocean discharge. After the obligatory foot-dragging, something clicked in the corporate boardroom. The company built at Toms River a state-of-the-art water treatment facility that began discharging water just shy of drinking water standards. Midget shrimp, a "miner's canary" species some-times used to evaluate water quality because it is sensitive to pollution, lived happily in the factory's discharge. The Toms River plant water pollution problems were over.

This did Ciba not the slightest good. The company was phasing out the dye operation and wanted to replace it with a pharmaceuticals facility. But when Ciba applied for the new permits necessary to run discharge from the proposed factory through its high-tech water cleansers, environmentalists fought the application, and the Nimby reaction was violently negative. "Our polls showed local residents just incredibly opposed to any form of ocean discharge," Mark Ryan, a Ciba spokesperson, said. "Whether the water was clean was no longer an issue." One week in 1989 the New Jersey state counterpart of the EPA gave Ciba an award for water pollution control. Then, under political pressure, it rejected the permit application for the new plant. Construction plans were abandoned.

Shed no tears for Ciba. The company was irresponsible toward the environment in the past, creating, among other things, a Superfund site near Toms River. But what about the people who might have had jobs in the new plant—clean jobs, in a factory with safer new technology? What about the weight of anxiety on nearby residents, and on millions of Americans, falsely convinced that the environment around them is damaged beyond hope? In a similar case, plans for a new plastics-manufacturing plant in a high-unemployment community near Wallace, Louisiana, were canceled in 1992 after the Sierra Club fought the proposal, though the factory would have incorporated new environmental standards making it far safer than existing plastics foundries.

The Nimby reflex is not entirely bad. "Nimby forces people to come to terms with where their wastes go, forces society to seek better alternatives," Henry Cole, of the Clean Water Action Project, says. Many environmental offenses of the past were facilitated by the old out-of-sight, out-of-mind mentality. If today's opposition even to needed cleanup facilities is an over-reaction in the other direction, at least the overreaction keeps the pressure on industry and regulators. Thus the Nimby reflex has had constructive effects; the problem now is to find a way to switch it off. Environmentalists started the Nimby movement. Are they capable of stopping it?

How Public Pressure Helped Environmental Politics

Donald Clay, who through the 1980s was a senior EPA official, tells a revealing anecdote about a visit to the vast Bethelem Steel hearth complex at Sparrows Point, Maryland. At the time Sparrows Point was among the country's leading sources of chemical pollution, emitting 3.9 million pounds of toxics in 1988. Clay had come to jawbone the company about reform, which Bethelem had long resisted. But Clay was playing with a weak hand, arriving during one of the many periods when publication of regulations to limit airborne toxics was in limbo owing to EPA indecision, industry lawsuits, and the usual array of institutional stalling factors.

At Sparrows Point a plant manager took Clay aside. "When are you guys in Washington going to get moving and make the air toxic regs official?" he asked, to the visitor's amazement. "Every year I put money in my budget for emission controls," the manager told Clay. "Every year headquarters asks, 'Does the EPA require this yet?' I say no. Every year they cross the money out and say, 'We'll do it when the government requires it.' "

Shortly after I wrote in *Newsweek* about Clay's experience, Bethelem Steel signed a voluntary agreement with state and federal authorities to cut emissions at Sparrows Point in advance of the formal regulations. I've always liked to think a healthy dose of bad publicity spurred the company to action. By 1992 toxic output at Sparrows Point had declined to 1.8 million pounds, a 54 percent reduction in four years. Though plant operations are a long way from pristine, at least Sparrows Point has entered the modern era.

This vignette conveys the progression of attitudes through which many corporations have passed regarding the environment. First, strenuous attempts to make the entire subject go away, usually through arm-twisting by corporate lobbyists. Next grudging recognition that change must come, coupled to action that merely satisfies the letter of the law. Then the company takes a hit: a public-relations fiasco, spill liability, trouble winning government permits. Finally management reverses gears and becomes "proactive," the term of art for anyone who does more than what environmental regulations require.

In 1991 I attended a board of directors meeting of one of the country's largest corporations, and also one of its largest polluters. By the ground rules of my presence I cannot report specifics but can relate the tenor of the discussion. Several company directors were displeased that the firm's latest toxic inventory, reported to the EPA under a 1986 law called the Community Right to Know Act, showed the firm was continuing to emit chemicals by the millions of pounds. The firm's toxic releases had dropped 58 percent between 1987 and 1990, even as sales rose; good, but no solution. "Millions of pounds of toxics released—it just sounds horrible," one director said. "My kids have been bugging me about this," said another, a university president. The directors urged management to accelerate its toxic-reduction program, though the company was already well ahead of what the law required. The word proactive was batted around quite a bit. All in attendance agreed that was the word they wanted to be associated with.

Later I described the meeting to William Roberts, a lawyer for the Environmental Defense Fund who, as an aide to former Rep. James Florio of New Jersey, wrote much of the Community Right to Know Act. "Some people thought when the law went into effect there would be demonstrations outside factories," Roberts says. "I always thought the key impact would be in the minds of corporate officers themselves. Corporate types believe in numbers. When they saw big numbers for toxic emissions, they would react." Roberts was delighted by the idea of a corporate director pestered by his children about company emissions. Top managers can insulate themselves from labor, government officials, and other lesser beings. But they can't escape their own families: When they start getting nagged at home about corporate policies, the policies change.

The second topic the directors discussed was environmental liability. Adverse publicity is the visible result of corporate environmental abuse, but increasingly liability delivers the punch. For example, in 1989 a Xerox factory near Rochester, New York, paid a $95,000 fine for failing to report leaked trichloroethylene seeping toward nearby wells. Simultaneously Xerox settled a liability suit by paying $4.75 million to two families with poisoned wells. Take a wild guess which figure catches the eye of the chief financial officer.

Till the 1980s, most regulations were structured to punish corporate environmental error through fines. This system proved ineffective because the fines were insignificant to a large firm. The largest Clean Air Act fine ever, paid by the paper manufacturer Louisiana Pacific, was but $11.1 million. Liability, a more substantial cost, began to enter the corporate picture mainly through the Superfund toxic waste control legislation, passed in 1980, and amendments to that bill passed in 1986. Since then it has become a leading corporate concern, which is good news. In an era of "junk science" tort trials, some liability awards may be open to question. For instance in 1990 a man named Wesley Simmons, who lives 40 miles down the Leaf River in Georgia from a Georgia Pacific pulp plant, won a $1 million judgment from the company solely on the grounds that the plant's existence had created in him a "fear of cancer." (Simmons did not allege that his or anyone's health had been harmed.) But plaintiffs are winning well-grounded liability cases against industry, too.

There's only one way to stop both the well-grounded and junk-science lawsuits: Run a clean company. Increasingly corporations are concluding that is the logical thing to do. If the Securities and Exchange Commission rules that corporations must disclose potential environmental exposure on the forms that influence their stock prices, a political decision expected under the Clinton Administration, look for a proactive surge driven by the most powerful force in U.S. corporate affairs: quarterly returns.

How Bush-Bashing Harmed Environmental Politics

You may not want to hear this, but when the history of twentieth-century environmental politics is written, George Bush will indeed be ranked as "the environmental president."

These things happened under Bush: the 1990 Clean Air Act, the strongest air-pollution legislation in the world; international agreement to abolish CFCs; the end of ocean disposal of sludge; the *Exxon Valdez* cleanup, which was flawed but did work; bans on driftnet fishing and importation of fish caught in driftnets; acceleration of Superfund cleanups; a moratorium on most offshore oil exploration; new drinking water standards; the Rio global warming treaty; the Basel Convention, which in most cases bars the First World from exporting hazardous wastes to the Third (negotiated by Bush, ratified under Clinton); the closing of hundreds of old landfills; an energy policy act that mandates efficiency standards for appliances and new buildings; various measures to encourage nonpetroleum fuels; the "land ban," which says chemical wastes cannot be placed in landfills unless first neutralized; a law diverting federal agricultural water to species protection in California; and many lesser milestones. Stout enviro lobbying and proenvironmental sentiment in a Democratic Congress helped make these achievements possible. Nevertheless this is the best environmental record of any president.

Yet Bush is widely perceived a failure as an environmental president. This perception stems in part from his retrograde behavior during the 1992 presidential campaign. But the perception also stems from the internal politics of environmentalism and the daunting pessimism of environmental orthodoxy. Political environmentalists simply could not abide the fact that a Republican president had a progressive environmental record. Perhaps political environmentalism as now constituted could not abide the notion of any president having a progressive environmental record since such a perception, even about a liberal Democrat, would violate dogma and detract from the prospects of fund-raising appeals.

The trashing of Bush's environmental record was politics of the low sort Bush himself never hesitated to engage in, but the way in which it happened reveals much about the mental blinders in environmental thinking. During negotiations over the Clean Air Act in 1990, Bush worked constructively with liberal Democrats in Congress, particularly Senate Majority Leader George Mitchell and Rep. Henry Waxman of California. The bill as passed was excellent. This presented a political problem for Democrats as the 1992 election approached. It became necessary to pretend the Clean Air Act was a fraud. Never mind the complication of why, if the act was a fraud, Mitchell, Waxman, Al Gore, and others voted for it. To create the desired spin, Gore said Bush's White House "gutted" regulations specified by the bill. Waxman declared that Bush made the law "an empty vessel."

None of this was true. Through the Bush years the EPA busily published new Clean Air Act regulations as close to on-schedule as government agencies come. Many of the rules were more strict than those in a draft bill Waxman himself proposed in 1989. By the time Bush left Washington, his administration had imposed new regulations sufficient to reduce air pollution by an estimated 47.9 billion pounds. Had environmental lobbyists prevailed on their preferred interpretations of the rules, the projected reduction would have risen to 49 billion pounds, or two percent more. This was the "gutting" of which Gore spoke.

Of course twisting facts to serve your party's ends is hardly new, and of course Republican candidates are guilty of this offense as often as Democrats. The relevant distinction here is that reporters did not mention the political motivation of "gutting" charges. While most reporting of 1992 presidential campaign issues such as the economy and international policy regularly pointed out the political nature of various claims and counterclaims, environmental accusations against Bush were presented as detached truth, floating above the fray. This is not because reporters were unaware that a presidential election was in progress; rather, it was because the negative power of environmental orthodoxy was so strong.

That Evil Council

At a more subtle level, negative portrayals of Bush evinced an inability of the environmental movement to come to terms with good news. An example is press and political treatment of Bush's Council on Competitiveness.

The Council on Competitiveness was a small organization under

Vice President Dan Quayle, assigned to streamline government. By the time the council was disbanded, commentators had taken to suggesting there was something sinister about the mere existence of this office, though all modern presidents, including Jimmy Carter, have had White House commissions with this charge. Shortly after taking office Bill Clinton created one as well, placing Gore at its head.

Quayle's Council possessed little significance. "They were pip-squeaks. No one who was plugged in took them seriously," says William Rosenberg, head of the EPA air pollution office under Bush, and a veter-an Republican political operative. When the EPA began to issue regula-tions under the Clean Air Act, the Competitiveness Council challenged several. In every instance but one objections from the council were over-ruled. The exception was something called the "minor-permits" rule.

"Quayle Council Action Allows Polluters Free Rein," declared a *New York Times* story in 1992. Several times that spring, many newspa-pers ran prominent articles referring to Competitiveness Council actions in the minor-permits case, asserting that Quayle had won industry "the freedom to increase pollution without prior notice," that Quayle had "undercut enforcement of the Clean Air Act," that this showed EPA administrator William Reilly had "lost his influence" with the White House. All these statements were accurate reflections of the political spin being put out by doomsayers, but none of the statements were true. Enviro lobbyists were telling any reporter who would listen that Quayle was running wild. Such claims were being made both for reasons of doc-trine and for fund-raising purposes: Environmental groups were finding success with directmail fund-raising appeals that presented Quayle as a devil figure along the lines of Robert Bork. Reinforcing headlines were required.

Quayle's council directors, Allan Hubbard and David Mcintosh, were unviros who delighted in talk of undermining ecological protec-tion, but all they accomplished was talk. Reporters working on Competitiveness Council stories would call up Hubbard or McIntosh, who would say yes they were gutting environmental laws and proud of it; the boasting would then be presented in stories as fact, though envi-ronmental regulations were growing more strict all the while. Once it became common to say that the Competitiveness Council had given pol-luters free rein, this concept, a comfortable idea that reinforced precon-ceived notions, was repeated endlessly on talk shows and television newscasts, though no story I saw ever explained what actually happened in the minor-permits dispute.

Here's what actually happened. Under the new clean air law if a company with a valid emissions permit alters a factory process, a new permit is required. The council wanted a rule stating that changes involving only a few percentage points of a company's permitted output could be made without formal public hearings. Legally Quayle's position was wrong: It was plain that the wording of the act did require hearings for any permit alteration. On a practical basis Quayle had a point. Formal public hearings complete with court stenographers can be impressive exercises in red tape. There stands in Saugus, Massachusetts, a waste-to-energy incinerator built in the 1970s. In 1987 the Massachusetts legislature enacted a sensible bill requiring the plant be refitted with advanced antipollution technology. The owner, Wheelabrator International, announced that it would comply immediately. Then a judge ruled that additional antipollution equipment could not be installed without a new clean air permit. Wheelabrator proceeded to spend two years in public hearings seeking the permit, as environmentalists and Nimbys filed motion after motion to drag the process out. That is: It took the Saugus operation two years to obtain formal permission to *lower* emissions.

The reasonableness of avoiding legalistic proceedings over inconsequential matters was not mentioned in any coverage of the minor-permits issue. Not mentioned either was that although the Competitiveness Council position did strictly speaking grant companies an ability to "increase air pollution without prior notice," this was true only in the same sense that any newspaper is free to print libel without prior notice. Legal sanctions make libel unlikely; they made the pollution increase unlikely too. Even under Quayle's version of the minor-permits rule, if any process change caused a company to exceed its existing air permit, the permit would be canceled and fines imposed.

Once you understand what was really at stake the minor-permits dispute becomes not an end of the Earth but a routine clash of opinions over how best to minimize regulatory transaction costs, a goal with which environmentalists ought to agree: The less money spent on lawyers, the more available for cleanup. But understanding would have spoiled a good outrage. This dynamic—a desire not to understand, for fear that understanding will canceled an alarum—influences much of environmental politics today.

The Unviro President

Nonreasoning of this sort reached its ebb during coverage of the Earth Summit of June 1992. A principle of journalism holds that the more reporters on a story, the less gets covered. The thousands of journalists covering Rio supplied millions of words about inconsequential matters such as atmospherics. Few sentences were devoted to the substance of the treaties at stake, the issue that ought to have been the essence of the story. Chapter 17 detailed how U.S. involvement in the Rio global warming treaty made that agreement stronger, a fact lost in the doomsday swirl. Two other important issues at Rio were a biodiversity treaty and a forest compact. On these, preconceived notions prevailed over reality, too.

Bush was reviled for refusing to sign the biodiversity treaty, though he announced agreement in principle. This treaty was long on desirable concessions to the Third World, including royalty payments for genetic material discovered in developing countries and First World funding for Third World biodiversity protection. But the treaty language was a mess. One section appeared to invalidate all First World patents, this wording having been slipped in during a preparatory conference in Nairobi by some Third World negotiators for whom the cancellation of intellectual property rights (so that developing countries might copy inventions, books, and movies at their pleasure) has long been a quixotic cause. Poor wording also left unclear how much would be given for Third World biodiversity or who would administer the funds.

Sometimes when proposed treaties are muddled nations nod to them anyway, planning to negotiate clarifications later. An argument can be made for this position. At Rio, Germany and other European nations told the U.S. to sign the biodiversity draft in order to bask in the favorable press, then ignore the treaty should it prove inconvenient: exactly what the European Union later did. Bush's position was that the negotiations should continue until all parties agreed on what the treaty meant. As it was, President Clinton's State Department required a year of additional diplomatic talks to bring the biodiversity treaty wording to a condition Clinton would submit to the Senate, where at this writing it was being held up by concerns that the Clinton language doesn't work either. Had Bush initialed the biodiversity draft at Rio the situation today would be exactly what it is anyway: continued diplomacy to iron out the wording. This inconveniently nonhorrible angle was deleted from Earth Summit commentary.

Bush's hesitance about the biodiversity treaty reflected experience with the most similar agreement, the Convention on International Trade in Endangered Species, created in 1973. On paper CITES bars all trade in endangered plants and animals. But like the biodiversity treaty, when signed CITES was a wreck from a language standpoint. Through the 1970s and most of the 1980s the treaty was unenforceable. Its provisions banning trade in tropical parrots, captured for sale as pets, were so ineffective that Congress had to pass additional legislation, the Wildbird Conservation Act, to block such imports. CITES did not begin to have teeth until extensively revised in the late 1980s, 15 years after it was initialed to smiles all around. At Rio, U.S. negotiators tried to tell reporters they wanted to avoid another CITES. This complicating fact was deleted from coverage too, as it would have reduced the America-bashing quotient.

And at Rio the developed nations proposed a forest preservation compact. In this case Third World nations would not assent. Malaysia, busy flattening its rainforests (Malaysia supplies 60 percent of the world's tropical wood exports), rigidly opposed international oversight of forest use. Third World nations even resisted a vaporous statement of nonbinding principles, India fighting one sentence that merely said governments express "concern" regarding rainforest loss. But while enviros pilloried the United States for worrying about the economic impacts of biotechnology patents, simultaneously they chastised Washington for not respecting the developing world's economic stake in its forests.

Of course the Earth Summit was a political event, and politically anyone may hold the United States in low regard. But the relentlessly negative spin projected on U.S. actions at Rio by many environmentalists reveals the presence of ideological blinders. Ideological blinders condemn their wearers to reenactments of arguments from the past, and prevent them from seeing the promise of the future.

President Bush had ideological blinders of his own. One was that by the time of the 1992 campaign he decided to transform himself into an unvironmentalist—snapping and snarling about the spotted owl, fuel economy regulations, and other green matters. Bush's senior staff had convinced him the American public was hostile to environmentalism, campaign strategy that evinces breathtaking detachment from public opinion. Strong through the first part of 1992, Bush's poll numbers began their plunge in May 1992, just as the Earth Summit bad press spooled up. Environmental issues were not the leading factor; the economy then weighed most heavily in voters' minds. But Bush's unviro tack persuaded voters the president was out of touch with common concerns. The environment now numbers among the few consensus issues in American public life: Everyone agrees the Earth must be protected. When Bush veered from that consensus, his political fate was sealed.

Richard Darman, Bush's director of the Office of Management and Budget, masterminded the spectacularly idiotic strategy of turning Bush into an unviro. Darman longed to paint environmental regulation as the cause of the 1992 recession, shifting the blame from his own less than sterling economic advice. Darman considered enviros to be hucksters and self-promoters. Once, speaking at Harvard, he declared, "America did not fight and win the wars of the twentieth century to make the world safe for green vegetables." Darman thought believers in conservation "squishy," in a favored Republican term of derision—a key squishhead being his rival James Baker, then secretary of state, who became a moderate convert to environmentalism after foreign governments bent his ear about the issue continuously. Darman also despised EPA administrator Reilly, who was handsome and popular (Darman called him "the global rock star") where Darman was rumpled and miserable. Darman repeatedly told Bush that Reilly's Clean Air Act would be a political disaster. When instead it was a marvelous success, Darman lost several notches of corridor reputation around Washington. At one White House meeting Darman's own deputy, Robert Grady, said, "Dick, you're the kind of guy who would put a SKIERS FOR NUCLEAR WINTER bumper sticker on your car."

Grady received his political education as an assistant to Governor Thomas Kean of New Jersey, at a time when New Jersey could not attract new investment without toxic cleanups. Grady says this taught him "environmental controls are not incompatible with the economy. The two need each other." Throughout the Bush years Grady was the mole protecting ecological initiatives within the White House. During every Bush budget cycle, for example, Manual Lujan, Jr., the unviro secretary of the Interior, would try to slash the budget of the Fish and Wildlife Service, which administers the Endangered Species Act. Every year Grady would instead increase the FWS budget. Grady was horrified by Darman's idea that Bush turn himself into an unviro but, lacking Darman's daily access to the president, was unable to get his reservations across.

In effect Darman was a White House fifth column, sabotaging Bush's image in order to win a petty personal revenge on the green movement. For instance one day in 1991 Bush flew to Arizona to announce, with the Grand Canyon in the background, the agreement to install maximum pollution controls on the nearby Navajo power station. Shortly before the plane bearing the press corps landed, a Darman aide walked the aisles openly leaking the fact that Bush would authorize the sale of F15 fighters to Saudi Arabia the following day. "Darman planned the timing knowing perfectly well what would happen," said a source close to the event. "The moment the plane landed reporters ran to telephones to file stories about the fighters. By the time they finished the Grand Canyon event was over. The next day the major newspapers ran headlines on the fighter sale and nothing about the Grand Canyon. This could not have been more damaging to the president if the Democratic National Committee staged it."

There is no reason to feel sympathy for Bush's dissipation of his environmental credibility. The turn of events was positive for the green movement: A major national candidate in a close race test-marketed a campaign based on reactionary environmental views and was defeated by a candidate, Clinton, whose views were progressive. It is always good news when progressive views best reactionary views on any subject.

But the aftermath of the 1992 campaign left the environmental movement with the stain of having exaggerated Bush's record to the point of willful lies. Of course many political factions exaggerate the faults of the opposition, sometimes to the point of willful lies. But that's politics as usual. Enviros, as the good guys, are supposed to shun politics as usual.

Politics and Law

In an ideal world environmental legislation would be devised in some ordered fashion, responding to a cool assessment of risks and benefits. In the actual world such legislation, like most law, has come episodically, more in response to random developments than as part of any unfolding plan. Superfund was enacted in 1980, after Love Canal; the toxic-disclosure law came in 1986, after Bhopal; the Oil Pollution Act in 1990, after the *Exxon Valdez*.

Action-reaction sequences are efficacious to environmentalism politically, the last two decades having provided an almost annual major alarm. In 1974 the theory of stratospheric ozone depletion was published; in 1976 came the first troublesome findings about dioxin and Agent Orange; in 1977 the bad news about asbestos; 1978, Love Canal; 1979, Three Mile Island; 1981, James Watt and Anne Burford; 1982, Times Beach; 1984, Bhopal; 1985, the Antarctic ozone hole; 1986, Chernobyl; 1988, the heat-wave summer and global warming fears; 1989, the *Exxon Valdez;* 1991, the oil fires in Kuwait; 1992, the Earth Summit. But when headlines rather than calmly set priorities dominate environmental regulation, the results may not be rational. For instance studies show that during the animal-cleansing portion of the *Exxon Valdez* cleanup, $80,000 was spent per otter saved. The same sum might have bought a thousand acres of Alaskan wilderness to place in preservation status, saving a far larger number of animals.

Perhaps the most important failing of U.S. environmental controls is the lack of coherent scientific assessments of risks and priorities. As a former EPA official says, "Everything the EPA does is driven by political rather than scientific considerations. The science is always tailored to support whatever has already been concluded politically." A powerful indication of the environmental community's distaste for science-set priorities came in 1993 when the Senate voted 95 to three to elevate the EPA to cabinet rank, but with the proviso that future regulations be based on "credible science" and incorporate risk-assessment logic. This seemingly straightforward provision caused the bill to be defeated in the House, where environmental lobbies fought it furiously. Institutional environmentalism fought to scuttle another EPA cabinet-rank bill in 1994, again because it contained offending clauses about science and cost-benefit relationships.

Placing political calculations ahead of detached science is not always bad, because sometimes political trends are more progressive. For instance, through the 1980s the EPA was unable to make up its mind about whether phosgene should be banned as an air toxic. Phosgene was used as nerve gas in World War I. "The first toxic-disclosure law results showed that there was one factory in Kansas that emitted 69,000 pounds of phosgene in 1988, yet the EPA said it needed further study," Rep. Henry Waxman of California notes. In cases like that, the formalities of science are not necessary.

But today few environmental issues are so open-and-shut. Many are rife with ambiguities and unknowns, leaving rational deduction badly required. Unfortunately, EPA science is often of modest quality. A 1992 report by the agency's own Science Advisory Board declared that the EPA "does not have a coherent science agenda" and "has not conveyed to those outside or even inside the agency its desire to make science a priority." John Rowe, president of New England Electric System, a Massachusetts utility, puts the issue this way: "I am steering a major corporation and I don't have any more clear grasp of the abstract points of environmental science than the typical members of Congress passing the laws. We are all dependent on third-party analysis that is almost always biased toward proving one point or another."

One reason environmental initiatives are sometimes deficient in objective reasoning is that academic researchers from universities and laboratories have little input into policy. Members of Congress rely mainly on staff scientists from environmental advocacy organizations, many of whom are bright and accomplished but also "biased toward proving one point or the other," in Rowe's phrase. Though academic scientists traditionally have influence in the setting of federal policy in physics, medicine, and other areas, rarely are they consulted on environmental legislation. Until 1992 the EPA did not even have an independent science adviser. Reilly created a rotating science adviser's post and also positions for science advisers in the EPA regional bureaus that perform the day-to-day regulatory work. "Environmental lobbyists resisted science advisers for years, and a number of prominent members [of Congress] oppose the idea," a former high EPA official says. "They know science advisers will say, 'don't panic,' and 'don't panic' is not the words the system wants to hear right now."

Some researchers in the academic world shy away from the environment because this subject has become a politicized arena where rational thinking may be considered a character defect. Scientists ponder. Their ethos calls for the truth to emerge from the slow sifting of mountains of evidence and from civilized exchanges between peers. Years of training, from student days to postdoc work, condition scientists never leap to conclusions. Politicians and pundits, on the other hand, want answers. Their ethos calls for leaping directly from slim anecdotal evidence to sweeping conclusions about the whole of human history. Years of frantic, fast-developing brouhahas condition them to believe that somewhere in every controversy lies a discrete answer that The Experts are withholding for some fiendish reason known only to them.

Typically in interviews or in Congressional testimony, academic scientists endlessly repeat that the natural system is complex and poorly understood; that few things about the environment are known with assurance; that the best a scientist can do is talk about probabilities. Members of Congress will thunder in response that scientists are dodging the question. They will ask why the public should spend billions of dollars per year on research only to be told that it's impossible for scientists to be sure of their own conclusions. Journalists, meanwhile, may dismiss the views of scientists who qualify comments, seeking out the small number at either end of the spectrum who deliver catchy, pointed remarks.

Some researchers are also put off by the current inclination of many major funding organizations to award support mostly to researchers with gloom portfolios. Recipients of the $1.5 billion in climate change research funds the federal government now dispenses annually know they had best not propose studies that question the premise of a greenhouse emergency. The Pew Charitable Trusts gives environmental awards of $150,000 that have gone mainly to the ecologically orthodox. The MacArthur Foundation has conferred its sizeable "genius grants" on a Who's Who of contemporary doomsaying, including Lester Brown, Paul Ehrlich, Wes Jackson, Donella Meadows (principal author of the *Limits to Growth* reports), Peter Raven, Stephen Schneider, Joel

Schwartz (an epidemiologist who believes pollution causes more disease than currently assumed), Ellen Silbergeld (a toxicologist who supports the position that dioxin is hypertoxic), and Ralph Turco (an atmospheric scientist whose work upholds some CFC emergency claims). The only ecological MacArthur winner whose credentials are not wholly orthodox is Robert Kates, a hunger researcher who has advanced the notion that developing world infrastructure problems cause more malnutrition than the ability of the environment to produce food.

An eventual merging of nonideological science with environmental sentiment is especially important because one task of the twenty-first century will be the replacement of the numerous environmental and health statutes episodically enacted with a few new, overarching legislative tools that allow society to weigh a reasonable balance of risks and gains. After all, one reason the EPA doggedly pursues the last part per quadrillion of dioxin, when the funds thus expended might better be invested in wilderness preservation or dietary fat reduction or a hundred other environmental categories, is that the EPA has the authority to regulate dioxin but not to expand parks or improve nutrition. The creation of some future ecorealist federal agency with broad jurisdiction to shift resources among environmental priorities will be opposed by the entrenched interests whose programs would lose, but favored by the public as a whole and by nature. Sounder science may help bring such rationality into existence.

Environmental Racism

By the 1990s a considerable literature of suspicion had arisen regarding claims of newly discovered forms of discrimination. There is no reason to be skeptical of the notion of environmental racism.

Benjamin Chavis, Jr., former director of the National Association for the Advancement of Colored People, began asserting the existence of environmental racism in the 1980s, basing his ideas on statistical studies by Robert Bullard, a sociologist at the University of California, Riverside. Bullard's findings show blacks are far more likely than whites to be exposed to lead; Hispanics more likely to live in areas with high degrees of industrial particulate (soot) pollution; that incinerators and hazardous waste facilities are much more likely to be located in black communities than white ones. Bullard found, for example, that all new landfills built in the Houston area in the past decade have been located in African-American neighborhoods. Blacks comprise about a third of the Houston-area population, making such an outcome improbable based on chance.

Statistics such as these can be explained partly because African-Americans and Hispanics are more likely than whites to live in neighborhoods where property values are low. In market terms places where property values are low are the logical spots for waste-handling facilities. But the idea that what appears to be environmental racism is no more than an artifact of property values does not withstand scrutiny. The nation's largest hazardous-waste landfill is located in Emelle, Alabama, adjoining not a poor neighborhood but a middle-class black area. The geology of Emelle is favorable to landfill construction, and operations there are well regulated. But then the geology in many white areas of Alabama is also favorable to landfills. Nevertheless the facility was steered to Emelle.

Because unpopular facilities must go somewhere, an incinerator or similar installation in a black or Hispanic neighborhood ought to be acceptable if the installation is safe and if white neighborhoods get their share too. The dividing line on the first question is usually the age of the facilities: Old landfills, incinerators, and factories often have emissions problems; new ones usually do not. The dividing line on the second problem has yet to be drawn. The first step came in 1994, when Bill Clinton issued an executive order requiring federal agencies to avoid actions that concentrate pollution in minority neighborhoods. This order applies only to federal agencies: Most states and localities do not yet have comparable rules.

International Politics

Environmentalism is widely viewed as likely to become yet another area of painful contentions among the world's nations. Perhaps instead the opposite will prove true: that environmental concerns will be among the best things ever to happen to international relations.

Here at last is an issue that joins the globe's fractious states in common cause. As the major international issues of the twentieth century—ideology and the Cold War—fade, economics and environmentalism may replace them. Of the two, environmentalism holds out the promise of constructive cooperation. If there is abject poverty on the streets of Calcutta or uncontrolled waterborne disease in Zaire such things are mere abstractions to the protected citizens of the West. But if developing countries act in ways that disrupt the global environmental commons—

and by sheer weight of numbers, today's poor nations will in the twenty-first century have more environmental impact than the West at its worst ever did—no amount of wealth or military power will enable affluent nations to escape the consequences. Nations will be compelled to cooperate on ecological matters if only to protect their self-interests. This is terrific news.

Environmentalism will also accelerate the trend toward open international affairs. The historian Walter Russell Mead has noted that when the Versailles Treaty was being negotiated, diplomats were horrified by Woodrow Wilson's "open covenants openly arrived at," foreign services then being accustomed to exemption from scrutiny. By the time Rio rolled around, traditional diplomats were horrified again, since the issues in play were technical questions requiring the negotiators to consult scientists and nongovernment organizations. This turn of events is terrific, too. International relations based on open, multiparty discussions of complicated technical issues will take place in a future in which a vast amount of money is expended on translators and photocopy services but one on balance healthy for the prospects of world cooperation.

Some signs that this openness is already beginning come from Sino-American affairs. Today the EPA has better relations with the Chinese government than the State Department, because young Chinese technical officials, involved in the colossal undertaking of bringing a billion human beings to a decent material standard, desperately seek Western advice on limiting the ecological harm from new power plants and similar projects. A rule of thumb on the current diplomatic scene is that the foreign ministries of developing nations are aggressively anti-American; the economic, environmental, and technical ministries of developing nations are eagerly pro-American, needing the information the U.S. freely shares. In countries like China the brightest students go into science or engineering, seeking rational arenas where they escape the oppressive dogma of their nations' political spheres. Within another generation those young minds will be running many Third World nations. They are minds that understand the significance of clean tech and look forward to spreading its power.

The first instance in which this may happen is the North American Free Trade Agreement. Whether NAFTA will be good for the United States economy is hard to say; the well-to-do will benefit through cheaper goods, the working class may suffer through job flight. But NAFTA will be good for the environment, especially the Mexican environment.

The leading enviro organizations headquartered in New York or Washington—the Environmental Defense Fund, National Audubon Society, National Wildlife Federation, Natural Resources Defense

Council, and World Wildlife Fund—endorsed NAFTA. The leading groups with their focus outside the northeast corridor—Friends of the Earth, Greenpeace, the Public Interest Research Group, the Rainforest Action Network, and the Sierra Club—opposed NAFTA. Those opposing NAFTA conjured images of a "toxic hell" at the Mexican border; of U.S. industrialists sweeping into Mexico to pollute at will; of NAFTA being employed to drive down U.S. environmental standards.

There's no doubt environmental protection in Mexico is poor. For instance March 17, 1992, was the worst day for air pollution in the history of Mexico City; schools closed and most factories shuttered so that people did not have to leave their homes and go outside. Many towns along the U.S.–Mexican border have uncontrolled toxic waste sites, groundwater contaminated with toxics, and residential shantytowns much too close to operating factories. But these kinds of problems should diminish under NAFTA, not worsen.

Most American firms building factories in Mexico under NAFTA will bring with them U.S.-standard ecological controls—what the Mexican environment needs more than any other advance. The petrochemical conglomerates Monsanto and Dow, for instance, now use U.S. emissions regulations as their global standards: Factories they build in the Third World, including a Dow plant completed in Mexico in 1990, comply with EPA strictures, though the EPA has no jurisdiction outside the U.S. In conjunction with NAFTA the World Bank will invest $3 billion in cleanup of pollution along the U.S.–Mexican border, much more money than the Mexico City government could allot. The movement of American capital into Mexico will help its environment by substituting clean new plants for existing dirty ones and advancing the arrival of affluence in Mexico. Industrial affluence has its drawbacks but brings with it low birthrates and national wealth to invest in pollution control and conservation.

Free trade might erode U.S. ecological law because of the "harmonization" clause in NAFTA and its sibling, the Uruguay Round of the General Agreement on Trade and Tariffs, a sort of global NAFTA in 1994. Under "harmonizing," nations agree not to use environmental regulations as gimmicks to restrict imports.

Denmark, for example, has a law banning recyclable beer bottles: Only refillable bottles are allowed. Other European nations have accused Denmark of enacting this rule to protect its domestic beer industry, since on a practical basis no imported brand can ship its bottles back home for refilling. In 1991 a United States court banned driftnet tuna fishing by U.S. ships to protect dolphin that swim with yellowfin tuna, and prohibited imports of tuna caught in driftnets. Mexico, which uses driftnets and sells much of its tuna catch to the United States, appealed to a GATT administrative panel. The GATT told the U.S. to allow Mexican tuna imports, an instruction Washington defied. (Environmentalists had strangely little to say about the U.S. dolphin protection action or Bush's decision to defy the GATT anti-dolphin ruling, both decisions reflecting inconveniently well on the United States.)

Some commentators assert that NAFTA and the new GATT will cause U.S. environmental law to "harmonize down" toward the lower standards of other nations. More likely is that NAFTA and the GATT will pressure other countries to "harmonize up," leading to a worldwide expansion of strict environmental rules. As Hilary French, a trade specialist at the Worldwatch Institute, points out, "The interests of trade and environmental protection ultimately coincide." NAFTA side letters eliminated the harmonize-down prospect through a stipulation that parties may impose any regulation that seeks a legitimate ecological objective. Perhaps there will be dispute about which objectives are legitimate, but disputes are inevitable in complex treaties. In the main this clause insures that U.S. ecological standards will not be attenuated. Similar language was added to the GATT.

Access to the markets of the West, where buyers have the money to spend, will be a compelling lure under a free trade realm. Countries seeking access to those markets will find they can harmonize up to meet Western environmental law more easily than might be guessed, especially as the West begins to share its clean technology. The Global Environmental Management Institute, a private organization for green technology transfer—unknown to Americans but already active in the developing world—is the first of what may be numerous organizations for that purpose.

Clinton-Gore Politics

As governor of Arkansas, Bill Clinton had a record of siding with forestry interests and agribusiness. Speaking in 1992, Clinton said this was because he once believed the choice was either jobs or the environment. Now, he said, he knew there could be both jobs and environmental protection and would henceforth act accordingly. Otherwise, according to sources close to Clinton, the president is bored by environmental issues. One reason Clinton chose Al Gore as a running mate was so that Gore could attend to ecological questions.

Gore is often criticized in conservative circles as someone who cashed in on environmentalism when it became the fashion. In fact Gore was engaged in the subject long before it was in vogue, something that reflects strongly to Gore's credit.

Much of Gore's intellectual approach to environmentalism traces to his early association with strategic arms control. In the late 1970s and early 1980s, first as a congressman and then as a senator, Gore did excellent work urging that nuclear weapons be reduced. Now taken for granted in an age when the once-secret Pantex plant in Oklahoma is disassembling seven nuclear warheads per day, nuclear arms control was at the time considered the ultimate lost cause.

In arms control Gore developed a way of speaking about the Earth and the terrifying prospect of its end that touched a chord with voters and media, especially local television stations. For the candidate with national aspirations, local TV is more important than the big-deal press in New York. The most important local TV skill, one mastered by Ronald Reagan, is what political consultants call "echo back." That means the ability to alight at an airport on a campaign swing, deliver two pithy comments to local camera crews, and have those comments echo on that night's news exactly as spoken, with the newscaster nodding in respectful approval. In his arms control work Gore perfected certain lines about the fate of the Earth that were important, true, and reliably echoed back.

By 1987 even Ronald Reagan had been converted to the notion of nuclear reduction. Once Reagan himself was proposing cuts in nuclear arsenals, there was little ground left for a Democrat to gain on this issue. Consciously or subconsciously, Gore found that the echo lines he had developed for arms control could be transferred to environmental affairs. The problem with Gore's switch from arms control to ecology is that his end-of-the-world locutions, developed for nuclear weaponry where the threat of Armageddon is real, only work in the environment if an end of the world is assumed there, too.

The Success Story

Though Gore's mind may today dwell on doomsday notions, that is but the fashionable pose of the moment. The moment will pass, and soon— replaced with general recognition of how much ecological progress has been made in the Western world in the past two decades, how rapidly and affordably the progress has come, and how much more progress will be made in the future. Soon, perhaps by the end of this century, we're all going to be ecological optimists.

Environmental protection is the leading success story of postwar liberalism. But environmental politics prevents environmentalists and liberals from saying so. Rather than call public attention to the many advances in pollution control and conservation in the United States, contemporary environmental politics has evolved the misbegotten notion that such good news ought to be hushed up. Rather than celebrate their own ascent to positions of authority—a wonderful development for society—environmentalists persist in depicting themselves as wronged outsiders. Soon such pretenses will collapse. Soon pundits, liberal intellectuals, Democratic politicians, and Vice President Gore will break into smiles when the environment is mentioned, waxing on about the success story.

Environmental protection has brought to the public visible benefits within the lifetimes of the taxpayers who made the investments. Unlike many other government programs, almost every dollar invested in the environment has yielded clear improvements, usually at a reasonable price. And in the environment, liberalism has not only not harmed industry but made it stronger, saving capitalism from itself by compelling industry to function cleanly and with resource efficiency while there was still time to make this transition smoothly. In other policy areas where liberalism has been the dominant mode of thought—such as public education, welfare, and crime—the results of postwar politics are at best debatable. In environmental protection the results are uniformly excellent.

As a liberal, I eagerly await the moment when environmental progress is properly seen as the triumphal achievement of liberal political philosophy. This notion is sufficiently powerful that even liberals, whose mental computer comes programmed to reject success stories, someday will be forced to admit they are part of one.

The coming environmental optimism means a rebirth of hope for the human prospect. If women and men are learning to coexist with the Earth, perhaps we can learn to coexist with each other as well. The deists and the natural-law thinkers of the eighteenth century believed that some great article of wisdom was concealed within the natural scheme, waiting to be uncovered by rational analysis; that once revealed, this article of wisdom would prove vital to the fate of humanity. Perhaps it is the principle of cooperative coexistence. Perhaps its unfolding awaits.

POPULATION

ONCE I TOOK A WALK THROUGH A POOR NEIGHBORHOOD IN New Delhi. I say neighborhood in the sense of a place where people live. No one from the First World, even from its tenements, would have recognized the locale as a neighborhood.

I'll skip the parts about the naked preschool children running through filth. I'll skip the parts about the aged beggars, meaning age 30 or more since a poor Indian of age 30 may appear by Western standards to be 65. I'll skip the parts about everyone grabbing my clothes and blocking my path to ask for rupees. I'll skip the parts about the human and animal feces on the curb, the cooking over open garbage fires, the children younger than ten employed in manual labor, the disease—I'll skip all that. You've seen that stuff in documentaries and tearjerker ads for various funds.

I'll just add one impression that stayed with me. If in a poor neighborhood of Delhi you see a group of one or two adults, several filthy children, perhaps a few older relatives, pots and a handful of sheets or clothing, this grouping arranged in a tight circle on a dirty lot or the side of a street, what you have seen is a *home*. It is difficult to adjust to the notion that a group of people sitting along a crowded street are "at home." This is the reality for huge numbers of human beings in Delhi, Bombay, Calcutta, Dakar, Lagos, Nairobi, Kinshasa, and elsewhere.

Throughout the world today hundreds of millions live without the fundamentals of material existence—housing, health care, adequate diets, education, human rights, hope for their children—and worst, without any prospect that the situation can be altered by dint of effort. In the Coroado slums of Rio, thousands of homeless teenagers wander the streets, committing petty crimes and being shot at by what amount to police vigilante squads. Outside Manila, at a place called Smoky Mountain, some 20,000 people live on the city's principal trash landfill. That is not to say they live near the landfill. They live *on* the landfill, among the flies, inhaling the stench.

But then you already know places like Coroado and Smoky Mountain are awful. You know nobody made the people who live there have babies they can't look after. You know the nightmarishness of life in much of India or Zaire is not your fault, which it is not. You give a little through taxes to help countries like that, and if you're the decent sort you give a little extra through a church or charity. If you gave every dime you possessed the crumminess of life for the world's poor would be unaltered. So why waste any emotion on the hopeless millions of over-populated nations? I cannot fault those who feel that way: I can only ask they consider a calculation. The Bhopal accident killed 4,100 people. There could be a Bhopal somewhere in the world every 25 minutes, 24 hours a day, 365 days a year, and the human population would still be growing.

Human population growth is at once the most important and worst understood of ecological issues. It is the most important because population growth drives all other ecological issues and will be with us after fleeting problems such as ozone depletion have been resolved and for-gotten. It is the worst-understood because here the standard polar positions are farthest removed from what nature might think.

The orthodox view is that population is a curse upon the Earth; merely by propagating, humankind commits against nature the ultimate offense. Paul Ehrlich, whose *The Population Bomb* is the canon text of contemporary antigrowth sentiment, subtitled his work "Population Control or a Race to Oblivion." The choice is not starkly either–or. There is no reason in principle that the Earth cannot support vastly more human beings than live upon it today, with other species preserved and wild habitats remaining intact. Nature, which loves life, might smile on such a turn of events. Patterns of human expansion are distressingly sim-ilar to those seen in other species when food is available and competitors are absent. And that is the environmental situation into which, for good or ill, humankind was birthed.

The unviro view is that population growth is itself a blessing. The contemporary population proponent Julian Simon, in *The Ultimate Resource* and *Population Matters,* has suggested that no matter how desperate the material situation, each new human arrival is grounds for rejoicing. For at least 300 years economists, beginning with an English thinker named William Petyt, have been proposing that population growth should be seen as a wonderful expansion of resources; though what Petyt meant was additional manual labor. Simon makes this notion more sophisticated by supposing that thoughts are the most precious of resources. As each new child adds to the sum of human mentation, among other things this increases the brainpower available to solve environmental problems. Simon is right about the inherent worth of the mind, but if you have walked the streets of Delhi, Jakarta, Lagos, Mexico City, and a dozen other places, you cannot believe that each new postnatal cry is cause for celebration. Thoughts are what human existence is about: and the thoughts of millions of annual new arrivals in poor nations are ordained to be confined to misery and deprivation.

Enviros see population as bad, unviros see population as good. Both views are disjointed in time. In the short term the current rate of human population growth is a disaster, both for the ecology and, more important, for people. Yet over the long term significant human population growth may be desirable, even a boon for the natural scheme.

Page after page of arguments have been written regarding what the correct size of the human population ought to be. "Deep" ecologists put the preferred figure as low as five million people (the population of Missouri spread across the entire globe), without explaining what sort of final solution would be employed to reach that number. Not only does such thinking exhibit the Fallacy of Environmental Correctness, the whole notion that there is a proper level of population for *Homo sapiens,* or for any species, would be nonsensical to nature.

To nature populations are proper in relation to what habitats can support, and such numbers change with the inevitable changes of time. Twenty thousand years ago the natural population of North American ungulates was small because the forests necessary to support them were largely buried under ice sheets. Today North American deer and elk exist by the many millions. Other plants and animals have seen huge population swings in the past and will see them again in the future. Population is a relative, not an absolute, concept.

The same obtains for genus *Homo.* Human population growth is not fundamentally good or bad, as various orthodoxies presume; it is good or bad in relation to what society and the ecology can support. There exists a Babylonian poem called the *Atrahasis,* believed written 3,700 years ago. In the poem the gods send a flood to punish humanity because the human population is running wild. Perhaps Babylonia of the time was overpopulated, relative to what the social structure and ecology could then support: though by today's standards its population would represent a deep-ecologist paradise. Plato thought 5,040 landholders should be the maximum for a metropolis. London of the 1700s seemed to commentators drastically overcrowded. Settlers moved to South Africa in the nineteenth century partly because they believed there were already too many people in North America, then containing a sixth its present population. A hundred similar examples could be given of points in the past when it was widely believed that the human population was too high. Every such past point would be described by today's ecological doctrine as ideal. Population is only high or low relative to what societies and environments can support.

That, in turn, is what makes today's population growth rate bad. Today children are being born far more rapidly than the ecology or social institutions can receive them. Someday the environment and social institutions may be able to care for children in much larger numbers than at present. That day is not today.

Conditions for the impoverished of the current decade are sufficiently bleak that it is time to revise history books on an important score. The Dark Ages did not happen in Europe 1,000 years ago; the Dark Ages are happening now.

Of the world's 5.5 billion souls about a third now live in unrelenting destitution. Having seen it firsthand, I feel certain village life in the rural Third World of the present is as dismal and backbreaking as was village life in the ninth century. But because the globe's population has increased so much, the number of people who today live a despondent, subsistence life is greater than the number who lived through the entire historical Dark Ages of Europe.

Ending the Dark Ages is the leading human social challenge for the next century. Compared to most Third World village populations, American or Western European suburbanites live in greater splendor than the royalty of Europe lived relative to their serfs five centuries ago. In assessing that lost age, today's Westerners smugly look down on old royalty for averting its eyes from suffering. Yet we do exactly the same. The suffering poor of the current Dark Ages are not just outside the castle, where we might observe them from the parapets. They are in distant places, the better to spare our sensibilities. But our moral position relative to them differs little from that of the old European royalty, and the judgment of future generations upon us may be just as harsh.

The Numbers

At the year one A.D., the human population is thought to have been about 200 million. By 1800 it had reached one billion. By 1950, despite two world wars, the population had grown to two billion, meaning the doubling from one billion to two billion took 150 years. By 1975 the population was four billion, the doubling from two billion to four billion requiring a mere 25 years.

At present the world population is about 5.5 billion, with 6.3 billion expected by the year 2000. At current rates the population will reach 10 billion around the year 2050. Today humankind grows at 92 million annually. This means that each year the world adds more people than the population of Mexico: itself an overcrowded country, at least relative to what its environment and social institutions can now support.

Within the numbers resides some hope. It is widely believed, for instance, that the rate of human population growth continues to increase. Actually the rate peaked in 1968 at two percent per annum and has declined steadily since, to the present level of 1.7 percent. That the rate of population growth has already peaked has been entirely overlooked in popular commentary; someday 1968 may be looked back upon as the year when a seemingly intractable problem gave its first sign of coming under control. A decade ago the United Nations Population Fund was projecting that the human population would stabilize at ten to 14 billion people. Owing to the moderate declines in fertility rates recorded in many poor nations, today the U.N. projection is stabilization at eight to 11.5 billion. Being an optimist, I suspect the low end of the U.N. figure will prove correct.

Even the low end of the estimate is, however, ample to ensure misery throughout the Third World for decades to come. India, already mired in human suffering and showing signs of social breakdown, will face the mid–twenty-first century with perhaps 1.5 billion souls rather than today's 900 million. Hundreds of millions of new arrivals to India in coming decades will live in hopelessness; more hopeless people brought into that single nation in the coming few decades than dwelled in destitution throughout Europe from, say, A.D. 1000 to 1500, a period enshrined in history as one of unspeakable general misery.

The short-term outlook is worst in Africa, which has a fatal conjunction of fertility, poverty, and lack of social cohesion. Even with present mildly encouraging trends, the population of the African continent may triple in the next century. Suppose trends become more positive: Then African population merely doubles. Population doubling there would bring more than a doubling of misery. Misery always advances geometrically.

Population and Relativity

Two fundamental misconceptions animate the population debate. One is that food scarcity threatens people; the other that population density threatens the environment.

Writing in *The Population Bomb* in 1968, Ehrlich declared that "the battle to feed humanity is already lost, in the sense that we will not be able to prevent large-scale famines in the next decade." General famine was "a certainty" to strike even the United States by the 1980s, Ehrlich projected; by then millions or even billions would have starved to death in the Third World, where agriculture would collapse utterly. That India could ever feed itself was, Ehrlich wrote, "a fantasy." Instead, since *The Population Bomb* was written, what the United Nations defines as "chronic malnutrition" has declined 16 percent worldwide. Starvations occurred in Bangladesh and the Sudan during wars and in Ethiopia and China as a result of deliberate government policies. No starvation caused by general ecological failure happened anywhere.

According to a study by Dennis Avery, a former agricultural analyst for the State Department, since *The Population Bomb* was written world food production has consistently grown faster than population. Developing countries today harvest 73 percent more grain than they did in 1968. The 1980s was a strong decade for world agriculture, aided in part by mild winters: a restive point for environmental orthodoxy, since if this mild weather stemmed in some way from greenhouse gases, then the first impact of global warming was help in feeding the hungry. During the 1980s India recorded a succession of record harvests. Only a small percentage of that country's population "ate high" by consuming beef or poultry, but mass hunger did not occur.

There exists no doubt that malnutrition and poor nutrition remain problems of staggering scope in numerous nations. And even a single ill-fed person in a country as rich as the United States is an outrage. But nothing remotely close to Ehrlich's predicted First World starvations have occurred. All developed countries except Japan currently produce more food than they require. A common 1960s doom prediction was that shortages would cause the price of food to escalate dramatically. Instead real-dollar food prices have declined almost annually since 1968. Adjusted for inflation, First World food prices fell by 20 percent in the 1980s alone, as supply consistently outpaced demand.

Because mass starvations have failed to occur before does not, of course, insure they will not happen in the future. Ehrlich continues to foresee one: In 1991 he said "a billion or more people could starve in the first few decades of the next century." Somehow Ehrlich maintains a reputation as an environmental seer despite having been miles wide of the mark on seemingly every major prediction he has ever made. Ehrlich follows what may be called the First Law of Doomsaying, which holds: Predict horrible events ten years into the future, immediate enough that people will be frightened but distant enough that by the time the appointed year rolls around everyone will have forgotten what you predicted. In the 1960s Ehrlich predicted mass starvations for the 1970s; in the 1970s, for the 1980s; now, in the 1990s, he predicts them for the first decade of the twenty-first century. Human population growth may be bad because it causes overcrowding, political tension, flooded job markets, lack of sanitation, illiteracy, air and water pollution, ethnic assaults, civil wars, species loss—you name it—bad for just about every reason except the old Malthusian fear of everyone starving to death. This cannot be ruled out, but so far there seems little serious reason to expect it.

Equally misplaced is the notion that population density is in itself bad. If this were so why would the densely populated Netherlands be prosperous and reasonably clean while the Sudan, sparsely populated, is impoverished and shows numerous signs of environmental distress? Why is densely populated Switzerland prosperous and squeaky-clean while sparsely populated Mozambique is poor and has terrible water pollution? Why do the densely populated countries of Western Europe have the world's highest life expectancies?

Herve Le Bras, a researcher at the National Institute of Demography in Paris, has plotted population densities against the "human development index" used by the United Nations. The index makes a rough judgment of quality of life based on per-capita GNP, life expectancy, and literacy. Le Bras finds, "There is no demonstrated unfavorable relationship between population density and the quality of life." Some quality of life indicators actually improve with population density, at least in industrial nations. For instance health care in the cities of the United States and Western Europe generally is good, in part because population densities support networks of hospitals and health-care providers. In the poor and often sick Sahel region of Africa, health-care facilities are hundreds of miles apart. The population density is too low for high-input services such as hospitals.

This hardly means population density is inherently good, just mistaken as an inherent evil. Nature might prefer some features of the materialist life—putting most people in relatively small urban areas, drawing most energy resources from nonliving geologic strata, using high-yield agriculture that produces society's food from relatively restricted acreage—to scattering people across the land in some romanticized hunter-gatherer format.

Do Enviros Hate People?

A charge sometimes leveled against the environmental movement is that it cares more for animals than people. Hatred of people is said to explain the intensity of ecological interest in population control. Writing elegantly, the environmental theologian John Cobb, Jr., has disdained those who "rejoice in a vision of an ever-more crowded planet with an ever-more artificial or technological character" because such a world would be "wholly anthropocentric . . . the biosphere less and less important." Writing directly, Ehrlich has said that the population of the United States should have been fixed (in some unspecified manner) in the year 1940 at its level of 135 million, since "No one has ever suggested a sane reason for having even that number of Americans."

The notion that environmentalists hate people did bear some credence during what might be called the antilife zeitgeist of the late 1960s: when several prominent intellectuals declared they would never have children because it was irresponsible to bring the young into a dying world; when some advocates of abortion rights, then unsecured in most of the United States, spoke as though abortions would be an uplifting experience for women, as opposed to a moral quandary. But the antilife zeitgeist was a 1960s phenomenon. Such attitudes have expired in the pro-choice movement, which today acknowledges the moral complexity of abortion, and are on the wane even with the population alarmists. Surely there exists among environmentalists a faction that cares more for animals than people. But an antisocial minority can be found in all walks of life. Among well-to-do conservatives there is a faction that happily lavishes money on horses or wolfhounds while stiffing working-mother cocktail waitresses on tips. A certain percentage of people of all stripes develop intense dislike for their fellow women and men; greens are no more likely to suffer this character defect than any other group.

That said, the green movement does contain a puzzling antipathy toward its own genus: not so much a hatred of people as a wish they would just *go away*. Consider Ehrlich's formulation: "No one has ever suggested a sane reason" for having 135 million Americans. I'll suggest one: People like to be alive. Ehrlich was born in 1932. How curious he picks 1940 as the year when the door should have been slammed on further births. Possessing the gift of life yourself, it's easy to opine that others would be better off waiving the privilege.

Some version of the desire that others simply go away is common among human beings. From Babylon forward people have wished that crowds were thinner, lines shorter, the competition less keen. Only saints and Buddhist philosophers are able to purge themselves of this emotion.

In environmentalism such feelings manifest most poignantly in what might be called the desire to be alone with nature. Bill McKibben, who lives in a gorgeous restricted-development section of the upper Adirondacks, has written of his anger at passing boats that occasionally spoil the serenity of a favorite lake. Who hasn't felt the same? To the extent nature is a temple, it is best entered one worshipper at a time. Most people who take the trouble to hike deep into parks or wilderness preserves are annoyed when they encounter others like themselves, however infrequently this may occur. When for a winter I lived in a cabin on a small peak in a wilderness section of Montana, I was nettled whenever the cacophony of a snowmobile broke the silence along the nearest ridgeline. This happened perhaps once a week. But it spoiled my illusion of being alone with nature.

Officially enviros want a lower human population so that humankind will "tread lightly on the Earth." The subconscious motive is the desire to be alone with nature: to have entire vistas of the natural world to yourself. This urge reflects some wisdom: The preservation of wild areas into which limited numbers of persons may enter at any time is in society's and nature's interest. But in the end the desire to control human numbers so that areas of the Earth might remain bereft of people is not a modest urge, but a self-centered one.

This is best seen in the nature preserves that have been established in the past decade or so in several developing nations, often in conjunction with Western environmental groups. In most respects such preserves are excellent ideas. The exception is their effect on human beings. A few years ago I spent a week in Royal Chitwan National Park, in remote southwest Nepal. This preserve, a vast expanse of riverine jungle, holds rhinoceroses, tigers, elephants, and little-known rare species. The preservation zone is entirely pretechnological, with most movement through the grounds on foot or by canoe, guests staying in tents or simple lodges. The remoteness and pretechnological scale insures an experience of being alone with nature.

But if this park is so natural, where are the natives? To establish Royal Chitwan the Nepali government expelled some 20,000 indigenous peoples from territory they had occupied for centuries. Indigenous

Nepali are now forbidden to hunt on the grounds, as they had done for generations. Soldiers of the Nepali army patrol Royal Chitwan, authorized to shoot on sight any peasants suspected of poaching. That means that in Royal Chitwan, as in several Third World wilderness preserves, people may be hunted but not animals.

But then the animals are worth more than the people, *n'est-ce pas?* The market price of an Asian elephant is around $10,000, which at the Nepali annual wage would buy the services of 63 elephant tenders. Besides to environmental orthodoxy animals are priceless while people are inappropriately numerous. And people have expectations! They want food, shelter, medicine. Give them the essentials and pretty soon they're asking after education, cars, central heating, amusement parks. It's all so unseemly, at least on the part of SOMEBODY ELSE.

Royal Chitwan had a resident naturalist, an American, who told me with disdain about a recent clash with local officialdom. Once a year the park's former indigenous residents are allowed entry to gather thatches for building huts. "They're taking more thatches than their quota and sometimes they take fuelwood for fires, which is forbidden. They make noises that disturb the elephants," the naturalist related. Affluent eco-tourists who arrive during thatch-gathering week often are furious because as they trek the backwoods hoping to sight rhino, instead they sight pitiful human beings staggering on foot under their burdens. Westerners bound for Royal Chitwan descend into Kathmandu on Boeing 757s owned by the state airline, these fabulous jetliners the most resource-intensive objects in all Nepal. The money, labor, and pollution associated with the Nepali 757s seem perfectly fine to eco-tourists, existing as they do to serve a favored few. But mean sticks of fuelwood for the natives—why doesn't the government put a stop to it?

Nepal is hardly the only place where the desire to be alone with nature blinds environmental orthodoxy to the condition of the indigenous poor. At Kruger National Park in South Africa, an important elephant preserve, wardens are authorized to shoot on sight natives gathering fuelwood. When Kenya established its justly famed Amboseli wilderness preserve it first drove out the indigenous Masai, promising compensation that was never delivered. Today the Masai, a cattle-grazing tribe that for centuries lived in reasonable harmony with Amboseli wildlife, dwell in poverty on the park's outskirts. When Ethiopia founded Bale Mountain National Park as a preserve for the endangered Simien jackal, local peoples were barred from using the area as grazing grounds, as they had for centuries. When the hated government of Mengistu Mariam fell in 1991, locals entered the park and began shooting the jackals, exacting revenge on animals that had been treated better than them.

As the Harvard University economist Amartya Sen has pointed out, the remaining Bengal tigers that live in the Sundarban, a forest preserve along the edge of West Bengal state in India, are now protected from poachers by soldiers of the Indian Army. Not protected are the impoverished peasants who enter the Sundarban to collect honey from its thousands of natural beehives. The soldier-guarded Bengal tigers spring on and kill at least 50 honey-seekers per year: poor, unarmed people risking their lives to gather something they can sell to feed their children. Orthodox environmentalism considers the preservation of Bengal tigers a priority, the deaths of peasants a distraction better left unmentioned.

Class considerations underlie some population alarmism, particularly its English strain. Malthus was British, as were Charles Darwin and the economist David Ricardo. Darwin and Ricardo were both deeply influenced by Malthus's 1798 *Essay on the Principle of Population;* both often expressed fear of excess population amongst the inferior classes. In 1883 Darwin's cousin Francis Galton published a tract arguing for selective breeding of people. Galton thus founded the eugenics movement which was, till the 1930s, entirely respectable in upper-class circles, where fear was keen of numerical expansion among inferiors. Malthus's writing contains a brutal section on how it is folly to confer money on the poor, as they will only use material security to have more children. Even British progressives long have worried that eventually the lower classes will rise up to unseat the upper classes, not pausing to make distinctions about who was progressive and who reactionary.

Such fears can be found among American progressives as well. Norman Thomas, the most important American socialist of this century, once decried "the alarming high birthrate of definitely inferior stock." Across the world such thoughts have animated various antipopulation or restricted-borders campaigns. They can be seen today in American trepidation concerning high birthrates among inner-city blacks. There are sound reasons why poor African Americans might be better off if they had fewer babies voluntarily. But most sentiment against ghetto birthrates is fueled not by concern for the educational prospect of teenaged mothers, rather by fear of the upwelling of lesser classes.

Class considerations are very much a factor in the Third World, where Western enthusiasm for lower birthrates sometimes is seen as part of a conspiracy against the interests of poor nations. During the Earth Summit in Rio, at the main speaker's area, run mainly by the First World, such figures as Gro Harlem Bruntland, prime minister of low-growth Norway, appealed for population control. At the speaker's area called Global Forum, run mainly by the Third World, population was barely mentioned. While the West fears the planet being overrun by Third World babies, the Third World fears the West plans to rob it of a voting majority in any future global democracy by limiting population numbers in developing countries. Vandana Shiva, director of the Research Foundation for Natural Resource Policy in Dehra Dun, India, declared in a Global Forum speech that Western countries want population control in order to enslave the Third World. It would be "like triage—kill off the weak," Shiva said.

Somehow the fact that Western countries have slow-growing populations and are strong, while Third World countries have fast-growing populations and are weak, has not yet penetrated the psyches of developing-country intellectuals. Nevertheless since the Third World is where most population growth is happening, Third World attitudes mean far more to population questions than anything thought or said in the West. Let's examine those attitudes for a moment.

Village Life

A man named Moshood Kashimawo Abiola, chief of a present-day Nigerian tribe, is central to understanding population dynamics in the developing world. Kashimawo holds the chieftain position through paternity, though he was not the firstborn, nor the second or third. He was his mother's twenty-third child, counting miscarried births—and the first to survive infancy.

In the Western world, where the death of any breathing pink infant is today both a tragedy and a rarity, the historical reality of childbirth has been forgotten. Today in the United States and European Union, slightly less than one child in 100 dies before the first birthday. As recently as 100 years ago, one child in seven did. The British historian Edward Gibbon, born 1737, was the only one of seven children to survive infancy. The tenor Enrico Caruso, born in Naples in 1873, was his mother's eighteenth child, counting miscarriages, and the first to survive infancy.

It is estimated that as recently as 1750, in Europe more than 50 percent of children died before age ten. Once the figure was higher still. The historian Barbara Tuchman, in her book A Distant Mirror, about the fourteenth century, notes that art from the period rarely depicts mothers with babes; and when shown together mothers do not look on children with love but a sort of remote abstraction. Tuchman explains that most societies of the past did not invest deep emotion in offspring until the children reached adolescence. Since historically a high number of children died in their early years, such cultures considered it foolish to become emotionally involved with youngsters who would probably soon die.

In most village cultures, until this generation death rates for the young have been nearly as high as in Europe of centuries past. Simultaneously children are the sole constructive achievement toward which the typical person can aspire. Children further have economic value: first because, grown to adulthood, they secure the old age of their parents; second because they help their mothers with manual labors. In many village cultures of Africa and the subcontinent women do the field work, the water hauling, the wood gathering. Boys under age 16 provide the only male muscular assistance most women get. While mothers work in the sun, the men sit in the shade drinking tea, waiting to seize whatever the women produce.

These factors combine to create a Third World cultural assumption that village women should have as many children as they are physically capable of bearing. Most Third World women alive today are descended from generations of women who were essentially continuously pregnant throughout early adulthood, bearing or attempting to bear ten or more children in order that a few would survive to secure the family's ability to maintain subsistence. Beginning roughly in the 1930s an important element of this dynamic changed. Health care in most of the developing world remains poor, but basic drugs are often available, and they have placed on the run most of the infectious diseases that traditionally claimed so many children in the village world. Rather than bearing ten children and watching three survive to adulthood, the developing world woman who today bears ten will see eight or nine live to become adults. The United Nations agency UNICEF reports that developing world infant mortality rates have declined 50 percent in the past twenty-five years, with current rates like 2.8 per one hundred births in Jamaica, 3.7 per 100 in Sri Lanka. If trends hold, most of the developing world will soon reach the First World infant mortality rate of about one per 100 births.

Statistics such as those above convey a fundamental though little-understood truth about the human population surge. Population growth is assumed to be caused by more people being born: Actually the operative factor is fewer people dying—more specifically, later death. As recently as the year 1750, the typical life expectancy at birth was no more than 30 years, even in Europe. That number had changed little since prehistory, a graph of human life expectancy being essentially flat from about 10,000 years in the past till the mid-eighteenth century.

Suddenly the life-expectancy graph line began to shoot upward like a moon rocket. By 1950 life expectancies in Europe were nearly at 70 years, in just two centuries the typical period of living time more than doubling: something Julian Simon has called "this amazing demographic fact, the most important achievement in human history." Drastically lower rates of infant mortality were the first factor in longer life expectancies; more food and then sulfa drugs and antibiotics were leading factors in prolonging the lives of adults.

Through the postwar era life expectancies even began to perform the moon-rocket ascent in impoverished nations, with typical lifespans more than doubling in most developing nations. Simon has said, "I would expect lovers of humanity to jump with joy at this triumph of the human mind over the raw killing forces of nature. Instead many lament that there are so many people alive today enjoying the gift of life. Some even express regret over the falling death rate." It cannot be noted too often that the spectacular worldwide increase in human lifespans has come during the very period when global use of synthetic chemicals, fossil fuels, high-yield agriculture, and radioactive substances has increased exponentially—a fantastic flowering of life coincident with the very influences doomsday orthodoxy depicts as antithetical to life.

Important in this context is that the decline in rates of death, not an increase in baby-making, is what has caused Third World populations to take off. Baby-making per woman has been stable or in decline virtually everywhere in the world during the period of the population explosion. As the scientist and writer Gerard Piel has noted, "A population undergoing industrial revolution makes the transition from near-zero growth at high death rates and high birth rates to near-zero growth at low death rates and high birth rates." Growth rates are today so high in the Third World because high birth rates have not yet adjusted to low death rates. Historical patterns observed in all developed countries suggest the adjustment will soon come, with stabilized human population achieved in the ideal way: low birth rates and low death rates.

The arrival in the Third World of modern pharmaceuticals transforms population dynamics in a profound manner. Village couples, strongly influenced by cultural expectations, continue to desire or stumble toward multiple pregnancies. But most of the children now live, causing overpopulation relative to what local societies and environments can accept. Once, when living in Pakistan, I employed a cook. I suffered many forms of proper liberal guilt over having a servant; my consolation was paying several times the local prevailing wage. The cook had seven healthy children, his wife pregnant with an eighth. "No one in my family has ever had this many children!" he explained with great satisfaction. "My great grandfather had four children. [Meaning four who lived.] My grandfather two. My father had three. I have seven. It makes me a rich man."

More than any other factor, the sudden lurch from a world in which a woman needed ten pregnancies to see three children reach adulthood to a world in which ten pregnancies results in nine adult children explains the population explosion of developing nations. Yet already the message that fewer pregnancies are now required—and that smaller families make more sense in the quest for education—is beginning to fil- ter out into the developing world. Villagers of the Third World may lack schooling or empowerment, but it is a severe mistake to view them as incapable of reacting to events. They will catch on to the desirability of lower fertility rates much faster than orthodoxy presumes.

One example of the surprisingly rapid reversal of a gloomy popula- tion trend involves marrying age in the least developed nations. For cen- turies, women in village cultures have married in their teens, which forecloses most personal or educational opportunity for the women but starts the cycle of pregnancy early enough for ten attempts at children. According to the Bangladesh Fertility Survey, in 1961 the average mar- rying age for a Bangladeshi woman (girl, in this case) was 13.9 years. Today the average marrying age in Bangladesh is 18, which is a big step toward the norm of countries that do not have runaway population growth. Several regions of the subcontinent and of Africa, though not all, show similar trends away from girl marriage.

Equally important, trends toward fewer total pregnancies are begin- ning to manifest. Writing in 1993 in *Scientific American,* demographers Bryant Robey, Shea Rutstein, and Leo Morris declared that "the devel- oping world is undergoing a reproductive revolution. Throughout the Third World women differing vastly in culture, politics and social and economic status have started to desire smaller families." As recently as the 1960s, the typical Third World woman bore six live children. Today the number has declined to four live children per woman. Robey, Rutstein, and Morris expected the trend of decline in Third World fam- ily size to continue.

Here is the continuation of my conversation with the Pakistani cook: "But you know, now everyone says that a smaller family is better. Sometimes I wish my family were smaller, so that I could educate them properly." If antibiotics and Green Revolution agriculture created a population bomb, knowledge of the modern world, now spreading in many developing nations, represents the bomb squad.

Population and Gender

To say that population dynamics depend on the condition of women is obvious—obvious but essential.

Ecotopians who extol in the abstract the romanticized small village life never deal with the fact that most developing-world cultures are incalculably more sexist than Western society. In the developing world women perform most subsistence labors, producing 80 percent of table food in Africa; women have few political or economic rights, and nominal bargaining positions in marriages; women are more likely to be illiterate than men. The stresses of manual labor combined with numerous pregnancies even rob women of much of their lives. In the Western world women live eight to ten years longer than men; in the developing world women live ten to 15 years less. Traveling through some poor nations you encounter a visually strange society in which there seem to be teenaged girls and old crones but no young adult women. The crones are the young adult women, prematurely aged by manual labor and multiple pregnancies. Third World birthrates "will decline voluntarily only when steps are taken to increase women's control over economic resources," Jodi Jacobsen, director of the Health and Development Policy Project, a Washington, D.C., study group, says. Ester Ocloo, a Ghanaian businesswoman who is a founder of a project called Women's World Banking, has said that "if the right incentives were created for women farmers, the sustainable end of hunger would be a reality."

Essential to hope for economic fairness for developing world women is reproductive freedom. In China and Brazil women have been compelled to obtain abortions or sterilization against their wills. In many instances around the developing world women desire birth-control measures but cannot obtain them. Both compelled birth control and the lack of desired birth control are equally bad: The choice must be the woman's. The United Nations estimates that 150 million women worldwide would like to stop having children but have no access to a safe means to do so. In other cases, needlessly harsh forms of family planning are employed. Today most voluntary birth control in India is achieved via sterilization. Sterilizations performed in village clinics by India's profusion of semitrained physicians are cheaper for that country than supplying reversible birth control. But no Westerner would accept the conditions of an Indian clinic sterilization: Pain and surgical complications are common. Similarly, most voluntary birth control in China is achieved via an outdated form of the IUD that causes a high incidence of tubal ligations.

Today nearly everyone outside the hierarchy of the Catholic Church agrees that access to safe birth control is in the interests of men, women, children, and the environment. (Believe it or not the Vatican has had disputes with the State Department regarding whether formal U.S. statements on this subject ought to refer to "family planning" or "planning of families"; Rome considers the latter phrase less objectionable.) Safe, voluntary choice by women is not only a moral imperative; the voluntary decision of women to use birth control will help ingrain this idea into developing-world culture in a way compulsion, despised by all populations, never will.

If you are concerned, as you should be, about the need to minimize the number of abortions staged in the world—believing abortion "should be safe, legal and rare," in the felicitous phrase of undersecretary of state Timothy Wirth—no reform could be of greater value than general global availability of effective birth-control measures. As was said in a 1990 editorial in the British medical journal *Lancet,* "All those who are genuinely disturbed by the tens of millions of abortions that take place each year must work together to help bring about a significant reduction in that number by advocating a marked increase in investment in family planning services and in support of contraceptive research." The Population Crisis Committee, a U.S. group, estimates the incremental cost of bringing safe family planning to three-quarters of the world's women at just $10.5 billion a year—a fraction of the cost of environmental damage and sociological harm caused by overpopulation, to say nothing of the moral cost when lack of birth control leads to abortions.

Much of the recent decline in Third World fertility rates occurred during the 1970s, a period when the United States was the primary donor to the United Nations Population Fund and to the International Planned Parenthood Federation. During the 1980s the United States stopped funding the birth-control programs of both, under pressure from the Vatican and from the New Right. During the 1980s the rate of decline in fertility slowed somewhat in many developing countries. Maybe that would have happened regardless of whether international family planning programs were adequately funded. But the likelihood that two plus two equal four on this subject is high.

Following his election, Bill Clinton proposed to increase U.S. funding for international population programs to $585 million annually, almost double the amount in George Bush's final budget. The smallness of this sum relative to what the U.S. government routinely expends on other programs, including other environmental programs, suggests the high levels of cost-effectiveness possible in Third World ecological investments. In the U.S., $585 million buys one B2 bomber, 20 Superfund cleanups of questionable necessity, or one new set of stack emissions controls for the Navajo power generating station near the Grand Canyon. In the Third World this sum buys family planning services for 100 million women of childbearing age.

Ultimately the force that will do the most to break the cycles of over-population and the low status of women is industrial development in the Third World. Such development need not be rapacious or dirty as it was in the First World but must occur if the women of the developing world are to know their rights, if the human population of the world is to sta-bilize, and if gross environmental abuses caused by the pressures of pop-ulation are to end. Development not only brings with it material affluence but the emphasis on education that has historically shown itself essential to improving the lot of women and of children.

The British biologist J.B.S. Haldane once said, "If the poor have too many children because they are poor, perhaps they would have fewer children if they were not poor." This simple observation is at the heart of the population challenge. The only known nonmilitary, nonpestilent social influence that has led to voluntary reductions in family size is industrial development. Much as environmental orthodoxy detests eco-nomic advancement, this is the force nature would long for in the con-temporary Third World.

The Sparsely Populated Earth

The third section of this book will raise the possibility that ultimately the population of genus *Homo* will be vastly larger than today's: with-out environmental degradation, without requiring people to live in dystopic megacities or weird cylinders floating in space. Someday hun-dreds of billions of human beings may enjoy placid, pastoral lives in places that combine the best features of the shared cultural dream of the peaceful rural childhood with the material affluence provided by tech-nological production. Based on what is known today, however, the long-term population outlook already points to *decline*.

Buried in the pages of the United Nations Population Fund docu-ments from which doomsayers pluck such dire projections as a possible population of 14 billion souls in the twenty-first century are a second set of charts rarely mentioned: projections for the twenty-second century. These projections show that already a tenth of the world, mainly Western Europe and the northeastern United States, is at zero popula-tion growth. Scandinavia, with a fertility rate of 1.7 per woman, is already at negative growth. The United Nations projects that if the entire world reaches the Scandinavian fertility rate by the middle of the twenty-second century, the human population would decline to 4.3 billion, or 23 percent *fewer* people than are alive now.

Of course the notion of world fertility rates declining to the level of Scandinavia seems absurd today. But then a century ago the notion of a world population at its current level would have been received as absurd. The U.N. projections show it is not only conceivable that the human population eventually will be lower than its current number, but this could happen roughly as rapidly as the two-century span in which the population explosion occurred.

Should this occur—the phase of human overpopulation arising then receding in a total of just a few centuries—the period in which human numbers threaten the biosphere on a general scale will turn out to have been much, much more brief than periods of naturally arising general threats to the biosphere such as ice ages or eras of global volcanism. Human overpopulation, which environmental orthodoxy today depicts as a menace of unimaginable horror, will be seen by nature as a minor passing fad.

Radiation, Artificial

In environmental orthodoxy fear of nuclear power has gone beyond irrational: It has entered a category that might be called transrational, in which the logical aspects of an issue are not merely misconstrued but actively shunned. Today the environmental and political worlds do not want to discuss nuclear energy in logical terms because such a discussion would reach the conclusion that power from atoms is desirable on every ground save price. Many politicians and some environmentalists admit this in private but claim public fear of nuclear power is so intense as to render moot any rational discussion. One former senator, with a solid environmental voting record, insisted on going off the record on this topic, declaring, "Nuclear power is safe but there's no sense saying it because no one wants to hear that." When we don't want to hear that something is okay—when we would prefer to live in trepidation—the stage of transrational has been reached.

That fear of nuclear power has become transrational does not necessarily mean reactors are the best technique by which to produce electricity. Nuclear power was supposed to be dirty, dangerous, and cheap. It turned out to be clean, safe, and expensive. In the 1990s new power from uranium is much more costly than conservation and somewhat more costly than generating new power by solar converters, hydro dams, wind generators, or natural-gas turbines. Today any of these is more attractive economically than building a reactor.

But that's today. A little surprise the twenty-first century may have in store is that the atom turns out to be beneficial after all. As new designs bring down the price and add "passive safety" to reactors, the zero-emission aspect of nuclear energy may seem increasingly appealing, especially if the greenhouse effect proves to be a lasting concern. It is not inconceivable that within the lifetimes of those reading this book, nuclear power will be viewed as an ecologically desirable energy form. Let's consider some reasons why.

Deadly Coal, Dangerous Oil

In 1989 a steam tube ruptured at the McGuire nuclear station outside Charlotte, North Carolina. Operators "scrammed" the reactor, staging a rapid shutdown; they notified the Nuclear Regulatory Commission and state emergency agencies. Local television cameras arrived within minutes, a national crew from CNN shortly afterward. Officials began the paperwork for an evacuation of the surrounding community. The alarm, however, ended in less than an hour. Shutdown of the reactor was uneventful; no radiation was released either outside or within the plant. Network newscasts carried stories about a terrifying nuclear "accident," though no one had been injured. Months of public hearings followed. Local and national environmental groups demanded McGuire be closed.

Also in 1989 a petroleum refinery exploded in Pasadena, Texas, killing 23 workers and injuring 314. Many of the injured had hideous incisions down to bone on their hands, arms, and legs; they had been forced to climb a razor-wire fence to flee expanding flames. Network newscasts showed flashy helicopter footage of an inferno. Then the story vanished.

Much as any two incidents might, the nonevent at McGuire and the tragedy at Pasadena reflect irrational attitudes about energy. Nuclear energy, which as used in the Western world causes no pollution or health harm, continues to evoke intense dread. Petroleum and coal, which cause substantial pollution and kill dozens to hundreds of people annually, continue to be viewed as preferable forms of power.

No nuclear power plant in the United States has ever released a dangerous level of radiation—or of anything else, as nuclear reactors emit no smog precursors, no acid rain, no air toxics, and no greenhouse gases. No one in the U.S. general public has ever been harmed by a power reactor, either outright through accidental death or gradually through radiation. In the United States no nuclear plant, including Three Mile Island, has ever come close to exploding: It is now universally agreed, even by opponents of nuclear power, that on a physical basis

U.S. and Western European commercial reactors cannot explode, because the uranium within them is not dense enough to permit explosive fission. Analysis of the Three Mile Island fiasco, in which all cooling and safety systems were disabled for several hours, has shown that the core of that reactor never approached rupturing its containment vessel.

The use of commercial reactors has in the United States caused only one sort of fatality, deaths of workers in nonnuclear accidents. Between 1985 and 1993, 21 workers died at U.S. atomic power plants: all from falls, steam burns, and similar industrial causes, none from radiation exposure. Like any workplace fatality, these deaths are inexcusable. But they pale in comparison to fatalities in nonnuclear energy sectors. Consider deaths from petroleum production. As the writer Bruce Selcraig has documented, between 1986 and 1992, 159 workers were killed in accidents at American petroleum refineries. Dozens more died in drilling accidents.

Meanwhile petroleum combustion is responsible for most of the country's smog and much of its greenhouse gases. And believe it or not, petroleum production releases considerably more radiation than the trace emissions of nuclear plants. In 1986 it was discovered that radium, a source of radon gas, commonly occurs in conjunction with oil deposits. Since then biologists have found that wastewater from an oil production field in Bayou Terrebonne, Louisiana, contains about 20 times more radiation than the water discharge of the worst nuclear reactors. Other oilfields also release radiation. The sum of radiation released each year by oil production is slight. But if your worry is radiation emitted to the environment, it appears you ought to fret about petroleum, not uranium.

Next consider the contrast between nuclear energy and energy from coal. During the 1980s an average of two people per year died in U.S. uranium mining accidents, while an average of 30 died annually in coal mining. Coal accounts for about two and a half times as much electricity as uranium. Even adjusting for this, coal mining is much more dangerous per unit of energy produced than is uranium mining, mainly because coal often occurs in conjunction with pockets of inflammable methane. Uranium mining has long-range health consequences: It has caused among miners at least 450 premature deaths from lung cancer, with at least 300 more expected among uranium miners now ill. Bad as they are these figures blanch beside the estimated 400,000 coal miners who have died prematurely from black lung disease, with a roughly estimated 200,000 more expected to die prematurely in years to come. Meanwhile coal combustion is responsible for most acid rain, some smog, and most greenhouse gases.

Of course nuclear waste presents to society a problem more severe than waste from any other energy source. But that's all it presents: a problem. Many environmentalists depict nuclear waste as a hyperdeadly doomsday threat. Except under an extreme circumstance, this simply is not true.

The extreme circumstance is direct exposure. Suppose you walked up to an unshielded pile of spent commercial reactor fuel rods, the most dangerous form of nuclear waste. Standing within three feet you would receive a fatal dose of radiation in about seven minutes. But in the United States *no one* has ever experienced direct exposure to reactor waste, which is handled in such a way that it is never free of shielding. The possibility cannot be excluded, but if exposure to unshielded waste hasn't happened yet—the gung-ho phase of the nuclear industry having ended, supplanted by strict regulation—it's hard to believe it will happen in the future.

Nevertheless assume that somehow a spent reactor rod became unshielded. Step back a bit from that waste and the danger declines rapidly. The hazard posed by radiation falls off over distance, because the charged particles that make radioactivity dangerous (the "rays") lose energy appreciably when traveling. Suppose instead of three feet from the unshielded waste you stood 300 feet. Over the course of an hour, according to calculations by Robert Jefferson, a former researcher at the Sandia National Laboratory, you would receive around half a "rem," about the same as the natural annual background radiation in Denver, whose thin mountain air permits more cosmic radiation to shine on residents than the air of other cities. Standing about half a mile away, you would receive perhaps five millirems of radiation per hour (a millirem is a thousandth of a rem), less than the natural background radiation of Denver, where cancer rates are lower than the national norm.

Items like the distance at which nuclear waste is dangerous are essential to an ecorealist understanding of the virtues and defects of atomic power. A common misconception exists that if, say, the atomic wastes to be buried under the desert at Yucca Mountain, Nevada, somehow sprang loose, perhaps by an earthquake of historic magnitude, and somehow popped out of their shielding, vast areas of the Southwest would be irradiated forever, with all Nevada evacuated and roped off. In fact only the zone within a few hundred yards of the Yucca tunnels would be effected. Tourists would be able to walk up within half a mile and linger for hours, taking no meaningful risk.

To many environmentalists, the fact that it would be lethal to stand directly adjacent to unshielded nuclear wastes renders such materials unacceptable to society. But the world is full of places where it would be lethal to stand, such as the lanes of highways. We deal with such danger either by entering the areas "shielded"—in this example, in vehicles—or by keeping our distance, the same tactics that allow atomic wastes to be handled without disaster. During the 1980s an average of three workers per year died in the United States in grain-dust explosions. That's right: In the last decade more U.S. workers were killed by *grain dust* than by nuclear power. Does this cause anyone to think grain silos should be banned?

Nuclear power is intolerable, some assert, because if a catastrophic failure happens it would be far worse than the worst-case failure at a conventional power plant. No one doubts that. But outside the former Soviet Union nothing like a catastrophic reactor failure has ever happened, even in the many reactors under Third World management. In the Western world's worst failure sustained, determined bungling at Three Mile Island ruined a billion-dollar pile of machinery but produced only a trace radioactive emission lower than the natural background level.

The one catastrophic nuclear power failure happened in a reactor called the RBMK, the type installed at Chernobyl and still running there and at 16 other locations in the former Soviet bloc. These vessels employ a design element known as "positive void coefficient." Positive void coefficient means that as heat increases the chain reaction accelerates. This makes the chain reaction easier to start, which is why Soviet engineers took the shortcut—designing the RBMK during the early Cold War, when the former Soviet Union was obsessed with matching the West on the atom. But if there is a coolant loss as happened at Chernobyl, a positive-coefficient reactor goes haywire since increasing heat ramps up the reaction. Hans Bethe, a Nobel Prize physicist, has called the RBMK design "fundamentally faulty." International experts repeatedly have recommended that all RBMKs in the former Soviet bloc be switched off.

No reactor other than the RBMK has ever been designed with a positive coefficient. Subsequent Soviet models, and every Western reactor, employ a negative coefficient, which means that rising heat causes the chain reaction to damp out. In a negative-coefficient reactor, if all cooling systems stop the core melts but fission cannot be sustained, preventing a runaway: as, at Three Mile Island, the core failed internally but otherwise shut itself off and did not go wild. "It is not physically possible for a Western reactor to do what the Chernobyl reactor did," former White House science adviser D. Allan Bromley, a Yale University physicist, says.

The Last Preserve of the Cold War

One day in 1991 I visited the McGuire nuclear station, owned by the utility Duke Power. I had to wait in line behind schoolchildren. Some 50,000 people annually, mainly school groups, tour the plant, parking their buses in orange rows. Duke Power has long been a maverick against the nuclear industry standard of pseudo-military secrecy. The day after Three Mile Island, when most nuclear executives were closeted with lawyers issuing terse "no comments," former Duke Power CEO William Lee spoke openly to reporters about the fact that TMI's operators of the time were widely known to be shoddy managers, yet this had been hushed over by the NRC. In keeping with its antisecrecy tradition, Duke has arranged McGuire like a museum that runs. The visitor reception area is larger than the main plant entrance.

Inside McGuire are numerous thick Plexiglas security barriers; lots of guards with fancy weapons; a danger area that requires radiation suits on entry and showers on exiting; containments, the huge eggs of concrete and steel that surround all Western reactors so the core cannot rupture into the environment (RBMK reactors like the one at Chernobyl are also the sole ones ever built without containment structures); and now, resident federal inspectors.

"The big cultural change is that these days we disclose everything," says Anthony McConnell, McGuire's manager. "We used to have adversarial relations with the Nuclear Regulatory Commission. When something minor went wrong we would pore over the wording of federal law trying to find an excuse to avoid filing a report. After we had some unhappy experiences, we just decided to disclose everything and stop worrying about it. We told the NRC they could go anywhere in the plant anytime. We invited them to attend our staff meetings. We thought it would be an incredible headache, but it's the reverse—disclosure is much easier. If we'd always run on total disclosure the nuclear industry wouldn't have the reputation it does."

Polls of the 1950s and 1960s showed the public overwhelmingly believed atomic power desirable. Then the industry embarked on the most determined campaign of reverse public relations in American history, methodically alienating the public. Many early officials of the nuclear power business were recently retired from the nuclear Navy. They needlessly carried over into nuclear power the military attitude that no one dast ask questions. Combined with the public-be-damned philosophy displayed by many utility executives, the nuclear industry shed trust as rapidly as any institution ever has.

The industry's lingering fondness for silly euphemisms is an indicator of the deception mindset. The low-level disposal facility being built at Carlsbad, New Mexico, isn't a waste site, it's a "repository." The high-level facility to be built at Yucca Mountain, Nevada, isn't a dump, it's a "monitored retrievable storage site." Until it finally came clean in 1994 by changing its name to the Nuclear Energy Institute, the public-affairs association of the atom went by the covert designation U.S. Council on Energy Awareness. If even the people who like nuclear plants didn't want the word *nuclear* in their names, why shouldn't the public be suspicious?

After Three Mile Island the reactor industry, partly owing to public pressure generated by Duke's William Lee, formed something called the Institute on Nuclear Power Operations (INPO). What INPO does is allow nuclear plant operators to exchange technical information about safety. Prior to INPO, if a reactor was experiencing some odd fluctuation, plant operators faced the problem alone: Nuclear control room personnel had less ready access to technical support than, say, a teenager who buys computer game software. Now operators can query an INPO wire providing tech support; plants that go through unexpected problems can issue alerts. Just weeks before Three Mile Island, the Davis-Besse reactor station in Ohio experienced and found the solution for an unusual malfunction of the same valve that, improperly handled, triggered TMI. Davis-Besse officials filed crates of legal paperwork with the Nuclear Regulatory Commission but never told other plant operators what had happened. Now, in a similar instance, other plant operators would be the first to know.

But have you ever heard of INPO? Probably not, since this organization also cloaks itself in theatrical secrecy. In 1990 I attended an INPO conference at which awards were presented for the best-run reactors. I pulled out a notebook to write down the names, and an institute factotum stayed my hand. Confidential, he insisted. That's right: INPO thinks the names of the plants that are *well run* are none of your damn business. In a sense, the nuclear power business has become the last preserve of Cold War secrecy.

Many aspects of nuclear power have an oddly archaic feel, sure to seem unnerving someday when our descendants look back and marvel that people tampered with atomic structures long before the invention of the pocket calculator and did not make an utter mess of the ecology in the process. For instance, since only a handful of power reactors have been completed in the United States since the advent of the microchip, the control room at McGuire, like that of most reactors, seems curiously behind the times. Most new power facilities run from control rooms equipped with the latest PCs; command inputs are typed into consoles, the way all teenagers' desks now function. McGuire is run from a huge room of cumbersome status boards and flashing lights, with manual switches and dials. It looks strikingly archaic, given the nature of the enterprise.

Ivan Selin, a Nuclear Regulatory Commission chairman, was among the first Westerners to visit Soviet reactor installations as the Cold War thawed. He reported amazement that the devices, "looking grim and Stalinist, very old-fashioned," functioned at all, let alone did not fail more often. As our descendants are sure to exclaim "You did *what?*" when learning of many twentieth-century environmental practices, they will proclaim with exceptional vigor "YOU DID *WHAT?!*" when they study early attempts at nuclear power. There's an old photo that hangs in the Department of Energy headquarters in Washington of the first commercial reactor vessel being lowered into place at Shippingsport, Pennsylvania, in 1954. The object suspended from the crane does not look like a high-tech wonder; it appears to be an industrial boiler found in some Irish shipyard during the construction of the *Titanic*. Yet hundreds of such reactors have run for decades and caused only one tragedy, Chernobyl. In contrast, catastrophic failures in the form of explosions remain such common events at petroleum refineries that no one except the families of the dead seems to care.

An intriguing aspect of post-TMI atomic management has been improved operating records. Though reactor operators today use more conservative safety assumptions than before Three Mile Island, shutdowns have become less common. Before TMI, commercial reactors averaged 7.4 unplanned "scrams" per year; today they average 2.5. The McGuire station has run as long as 330 days without having to scram. Increasing attention to the details of reactor operation, and the dawn of openness among nuclear plant managers, has made atomic power more proficient.

What happens inside a power reactor is not, as popularly imagined, some uncontrolled madness but a tightly regulated sequence in which the actions of individual subatomic particles follow highly predictable patterns. The composition of coolants and moderating substances, the rates at which reactor rods swell, whether to burn uranium as a metal or an oxide, the percentage of "enriched" to natural uranium, the precise locations of control mechanisms, and other matters have been studied intently by some of the world's brightest minds for decades. In Western atomic systems at least, internal reactor conditions are elaborately manipulated so that chain reactions are inherently hard to sustain; even small deviations lead to automated shutdowns.

None of this proves additional nuclear power investments are necessarily wise but does suggest that nuclear power should be expected to be safe, not dangerous. In the United States power reactors made it through the early period of limited understanding of nuclear processes, of cheerleader regulation by the old Atomic Energy Commission, and of arrogant management, without a single case of public harm. In the former Soviet Union and in some Third World countries, crudely constructed reactors run under slipshod conditions caused only one terrible outcome, Chernobyl. More than three decades of running up to 421 power reactors worldwide (the 1992 figure), without the new safety devices most reactors now have, caused only one awful day.

So why does the transrational attitude toward nuclear power make society think that today better-designed reactors run under tighter scrutiny will be an inexpressible menace? More likely is that nuclear power has already passed its Pollution Peak: that the threat it posed to people and the ecology peaked in the 1970s and has been declining since.

Millirems and Megabucks

The transrational nature of nuclear power politics has caused both sides in the dispute to couch arguments in absurdities. First a sampler of pronuclear nonsense.

"Anti-Nuclear Proposals Would Mean a Weaker, Poorer America," declared a press release issued in 1989 by the U.S. Council on Energy Awareness. The 1950s Cold War anxiety under which the commercial reactor business was birthed, when the atom was seen as a weapon against godless Communism, has long enabled nuclear power advocates to imply they somehow deserve national security exemptions from cost assessment. Energy independence based on hydro, solar, or conservation is just as good as independence based on nuclear; better if the former costs less, as is true today.

But an essential of politics is discovering which arguments work, as opposed to which make sense. Because a percentage of members of Congress can be relied on to fall for the argument that nuclear reactors have something to do with national security, proponents continue to reuse this flimsy idea. The defect in taking shelter in false arguments that work politically is the same one faced today by environmental orthodoxy: Someday the false arguments stop working, and then good luck getting your credibility back.

The quasi-military character of nuclear power has further enabled proponents to hijack the Department of Energy budget, which even under Clinton continues to invest more in research support for nuclear power than on conservation technology, though the latter is where the market action is. Nuclear power advocates swagger around Washington depicting themselves as manning the last frontier of free enterprise, though from an R&D standpoint they represent the most subsidized sector of power production, with some $51 billion in U.S. tax funds invested in commercial nuclear energy research through the postwar era, about twice as much as invested in all other energy types. Today unsubsidized, privately developed energy conservation technology is doing quite well in the marketplace while nobody wants taxpayer-subsidized nuclear stations—lesson in the value of true market-testing of ideas, the lesson this time coming from the left rather than the right.

Another specious argument employed by nuclear proponents is that more reactors are needed to combat the greenhouse effect. The numbers here do not add up. Doubling the world's stock of power reactors at a capital cost of perhaps half a trillion dollars would be required to cut global greenhouse output by five percent. If global warming really is an emergency far more dramatic reductions could be attained with half a trillion dollars' worth of investments in energy conservation.

Though transrational fear of nuclear power is a reason 119 planned U.S. reactors have been canceled in the last 20 years, the main reason is financial. The energy analyst Christopher Flavin of the Worldwatch Institute estimates new installed nuclear capacity today costs 12 cents per kilowatt hour versus six to eight cents for wind power and six cents for natural gas power.

Prior to the advent of nuclear overruns no one had ever managed to bankrupt a post-Depression electric utility; with cost pass-along, utilities were licenses to print money. Nuclear overruns proved capable of changing that. Nuclear costs bankrupted a utility consortium in Washington State, and the venture that financed the Seabrook reactor. The Comanche Peak nuclear station in Texas, completed in 1993, cost $10 billion and will generate as much electricity as a new natural gas station costing about $1.5 billion. The Sacramento Municipal Utility District lost $575 million in 1989 running its Rancho Seco reactor station. Ratepayers of this customer-owned utility voted to shut down Rancho Seco, mainly from antinuclear sentiment. The utility converted the powerhouse section of the plant to natural gas operation and now turns a profit.

The pro-nuke side protests that environmental red tape is the source of cost overruns. This can be a factor, but mostly the high price is the fault of industry. All U.S. reactors now in use were one-of-a-kind projects, creating extra invoices for reactor manufacturers and the engineering firms that designed stations but also insuring high costs. In France, where atomic power provides three times as much electricity as in the United States, standard modular reactors were employed to hold down expenses. Equally important from the cost-inflation standpoint, in the United States almost every major utility decided it had to have a reactor station, partly for prestige. The result was a peak of 58 NRC licenses—58 different hierarchies struggling with nuclear management. "France has a single authority to run nuclear power," Lee, who in 1994 retired from Duke Power, notes. "Our larger country could perhaps justify a few regional authorities. Fifty-eight is ludicrous. It guarantees errors and overruns."

When the pro-nuke side bemoans the 119 reactor cancellations, it never adds that the bulk of the cancellations resulted from generation needs offset by conservation improvements. If only more power projects could be canceled for this reason! Other reactors were canceled because oil did not hit $100 a barrel. That's great news, too. Most of all, pro-nuke factions never mention that investors stopped funding reactors. Financial markets run by Wall Street bluebloods, not grass-roots campaigns by Nader and Fonda, ended the 1970s nuclear power splurge. "Today if you were to start a nuclear plant, even with the site permission, it would take 12 to 14 years from the initial decision to going on line," Lee says. "No rational investor will back that. Unless the industry can learn to build faster and cheaper using sensible modular designs, the critics are right that nuclear power lacks financial sense."

Yet in the contest to see which side can resort to the silliest arguments, nuclear proponents sink low but opponents often sink lower. Consider the evacuation argument and its use against the Shoreham plant.

Federal law requires that nuclear power plants file evacuation plans for surrounding communities. Opponents discovered that these rules are worded in such a way as to offer devilish opportunity to win dilatory delays. Shoreham, located near the east end of Long Island, was announced in 1966 as a $900 million project; construction did not end till 1983, with $5.8 billion spent (both figures are converted to 1994 dollars). Long Island Lighting, the utility, committed every imaginable management blunder. In August of 1985, Shoreham staged a brief low-power test, the sole time a reactor was turned on there. The run was just long enough to irradiate the inner structure, which ensured that the plant's decommissioning, in progress at this writing, would cost $2 billion.

In 1989 Shoreham was licensed for operation, but lawsuits over the evacuation plan prevented a start-up. Former Governor Mario Cuomo of New York became a livid Shoreham opponent, winning praise from enviro political scorecard systems. In 1991 a state court ordered the plant dismantled. Cuomo offered Shoreham's investors a $1 billion tax favor to close the deal. Cuomo then portrayed the shutting down of Shoreham as a great people's victory—though well-to-do investors got a huge bonus, middle-class Lilco ratepayers were screwed, and typical state taxpayers were left holding the tab. In the end the whole mess cost about $8.5 billion. Social gains from this expense: zip-a-rino.

Officially the court ordered Shoreham dismantled on evacuation grounds. Since the line of retreat from Long Island is westward through the Bronx and Manhattan, one of the world's leading bottlenecks, the court ruled it would be impossible to evacuate the island rapidly, and therefore Shoreman could not meet its license requirements. But in this century Long Island has been struck by hurricanes that have killed at least 45 people, with several others barely missing the island. Should another hurricane approach, evacuation through the New York City traffic bottleneck will be just as impossible as during a nuclear accident. Yet homes and businesses continue to be built on the island's eastern expanse.

The dismantling of Shoreham is a significant moment in transrational attitudes toward nuclear power because there was never any allegation that Shoreham had any design or operational defect, or that its power output, considering that construction costs were already sunk, would not have been beneficial. The only thing wrong with Shoreham is that it was unpopular—unpopular because of transrationalism.

The hypothetical prospect of evacuating Long Island because of a nuclear plant going berserk—something that in the Western world has never happened and is unlikely ever to happen—ended up becoming the official reason to waste $8.5 billion. This sum might have, say, transformed the lives of the entire homeless population of Manhattan. Yet in the same place the prospect of evacuation in the face of a hurricane—something that has happened recently and is certain to happen again—is ignored. This logic is in tune with contemporary doomsday doctrine, which holds that a high-tech device such as a reactor ought to inspire deep dread even if the threat is minute, while a probable natural threat ought to be assumed away because it's bad for business to mention the downside of nature.

Radiation in the Air

At Three Mile Island everything went wrong, including the worst default for a U.S. reactor design: internal meltdown. Even after this spectacular failure, almost no radiation was released because the reactor containment structure was never in danger of breach. A few jets of radioactive gas escaped: average individual exposure in the TMI area was about ten millirems. Natural background radiation in the United States averages about 290 millirems per year. Studies of people who live around Harrisburg, conducted by the Pennsylvania Department of Health and other agencies, have turned up no evidence of unusual diseases. A study completed in 1991 by researchers from Columbia University and the National Audubon Society did find slightly elevated cancer incidence. But the authors, publishing in the *American Journal of Public Health,* speculated that stress stoked by the atmosphere of alarm surrounding the event may underlie the added cancers, since the same slight cancer elevation was found both in Harrisburg neighborhoods exposed to the TMI millirems and in upwind neighborhoods that were not exposed.

The small release at TMI raises a larger question. For years researchers have engaged in a complicated debate about whether tiny amounts of radiation cause bodily harm or whether focused jolts, as in a chest X-ray or being near a troubled reactor, are worse than gradual exposure.

One of the worst-run nuclear plants in the United States is the Indian Point Three facility on the Hudson River north of New York, closed in 1993 after an NRC report likened it to "an airplane losing altitude." In 1985 Indian Point leaked some radiation, probably less than the TMI release. Ernest Sternglass, professor emeritus at the University of Pittsburgh medical school, believes that in 1985 an unusual number of low birthweight babies were born downwind of Indian Point. The Sternglass theory about low birthweights from extremely small doses of radiation is not taken seriously by most of the research community, mainly because an extensive study completed in 1990 by the National Cancer Institute, an organization that if anything would be inclined to promote cancer fears, inspected health records in the communities of 62 U.S. nuclear plants and found no unusual cancer incidence. Nevertheless Sternglass and the Indian Point leak are a perennial topic of environmentalist literature.

The worst Western nuclear accident occurred in 1957 at Windscale, a Cold War–era military reactor in the English countryside. About 65 times as much radiation was released as at Three Mile Island. The British government covered up the problem while the leak was in progress. Radioactive iodine settled on grass where, because farmers were not warned, the grass was eaten by cows and the iodine entered the local milk supply. Rosalyn Yalow, a Nobel Prize biologist, ran one

Windscale study, which concluded that tainted milk from the release caused a small increase in thyroid cancers among children. Other studies have found small increases in childhood leukemia. Windscale clearly was a disaster, with perhaps 300 premature deaths caused. (That number is hotly disputed; this represents a mean of estimates.) It was also a worst-case disaster—brute-force 1950s technology, no warnings to the public, government cover-up. If the worst-case nuclear blunder at Windscale resulted in 300 premature deaths, that is a tragedy in every sense—but nothing like the general menace environmental dogma pretends radiation to be.

In recent years a back-and-forth sequence of changes in scientific thinking about radiation exposures has occurred. In 1980, the National Research Council released a study generally called the "don't worry" report, estimating that small exposures to radiation have negligible effect. This conclusion was based mainly on the low levels of radiation to which genus *Homo* has been exposed naturally throughout human existence, and on such querulous facts as that people who live in Denver, where routine natural radiation exposures are high, have a lower cancer rate than most other Americans. The "don't worry" report had prominent scientific dissenters. By 1989 they persuaded the National Research Council to issue a new study which essentially retracted the earlier document, finding low levels of radiation exposure to be dangerous. The new conclusion was based on studies of victims at Hiroshima and Nagasaki. Analysis of the Japan blasts is speculative because it is not known how much radiation the bombs produced. The 1989 NRC report assumed the bombs produced relatively little radiation and that the sickness that followed proved the body sensitive to small doses. Based on this the NRC council projected that the final premature death toll from Chernobyl might be as high as 70,000.

In 1992 the English researcher Alice Stewart backed the small-dose conclusion. Unknown in the United States, Stewart is a scientific folk hero in Europe. During the 1950s she proved that the practice of prenatal X-rays caused cancer in infants. (On the *"you did what?"* scale it's hard to believe now, but through the 1950s it was not unknown for obstetricians to blast the wombs of pregnant women with X-rays.) Stewart based her conclusions on a study of workers at the nuclear bomb plant in Hanford, Washington. Workers at Hanford received radiation equal to roughly double the natural background dose. Stewart concluded that their exposure resulted in elevated cancer incidence.

Yet unlike Stewart's prenatal X-rays studies from the 1950s, which found actual diseases in the here and now, her Hanford studies found unusual disease only in the extrapolated realm of the computer model.

The observed cancer rate Stewart toted up among Hanford workers actually was slightly *lower* than in control groups not exposed to extra radiation. The grim conclusion Stewart reached was based on computer projections that adjust for the "healthy worker effect," a concept Stewart helped develop and which is accepted by some epidemiologists. Under the healthy worker effect, Stewart assumes that the sort of person likely to get a job at a nuclear plant is young and hale, less prone to cancer than the population at large. By assuming that Hanford workers ought to have many fewer cancers than the public at large but instead have only slightly fewer, Stewart reached a pessimistic computer-generated finding about small levels of radiation exposure.

About a year after Stewart's work a researcher named Tore Straume at the Lawrence Livermore National Laboratory overturned technical wisdom once again. Studying Hiroshima, where many more people were exposed to radiation than at Nagasaki, Straume estimated that the bomb had produced a huge amount of radiation, and thus the diseases that resulted came from high-level exposure, not low. No records were kept of the radiation output from the two bombs dropped on Japan. During the 1960s U.S. researchers in a Nevada desert used an unshielded uranium reactor, suspended at about the same level in the air at which the Hiroshima bomb detonated, to estimate radiation exposures that day. This test suggested that the radiation output of the Hiroshima bomb was low, which suggested in turn that people are very sensitive to radiation.

But atomic reactors make far less radiation than bomb detonations. This caused Straume to suspect that the Nevada test produced a deceptive result. Straume went to Hiroshima and studied concrete in the area of the 1945 explosion. When concrete is struck by radioactive neutrons, a distinctive isotope results. By measuring the amount of this isotope remaining in the Hiroshima concrete, Straume came to the conclusion that the Hiroshima bomb had been exceptionally dirty—as might be expected, given its crude design. If the Hiroshima explosion was dirty, that means the disease rate suffered by victims suggests people are not exceptionally sensitive to radiation exposure.

International Nuclear Power

Only about a fourth of the world's power reactors are in the United States. France, which has 54 atomic stations, generates 75 percent of its electricity using the atom, versus about 19 percent in the United States. Japan has 42 reactors making 27 percent of its electricity, with official plans to build 80 more, though the actual number of new Japanese reactors is sure to be lower. The nations of the former Soviet Union have 62 operating reactors. India, South Korea, and other developing world nations possess at least one reactor whose true purpose is electricity, not weapons production. (True commercial reactors are of no use for bomb making, and generally it is obvious to specialists which type a reactor is.) Construction of new nuclear power facilities has stopped in every Western European nation other than France.

Governments of the former Soviet nations continue to run reactors of the faulty Chernobyl type either because they must to supply citizens with power (the Eastern bloc has lots of uranium but is experiencing problems producing petroleum and natural gas) or because they hope for Western investments in the reactors, or both. Some new safety features have been added to all Soviet reactors since Chernobyl. The graphite tips on RBMK fuel rods, now known to have triggered the Chernobyl runaway, have been replaced by safe material. The scram button, which previously in Soviet reactor designs had to be depressed a full minute before it would engage, now trips at any touch. But improvements such as these cannot alter the fact that Soviet RBMK reactors are fundamentally flawed designs. The NATO powers pledged $700 million to improve safety features at Soviet nuclear installations, money that would be well spent. Yet only a small amount has actually been transferred, while dollars in the West continue to be showered without hesitation on improbable environmental threats such as asbestos in schools.

In a few cases in the former Eastern-bloc nations reactors have been closed down. One in Armenia was shuttered in 1988 after an earthquake occurred in the region. Closing such a facility would make perfect sense in an affluent nation with ready energy alternatives. After the fall of old-line Communism in 1991, however, civil war came to Armenia. By the winter of 1993 hundreds of people were reported to have died from exposure to cold, as foreign supplies of natural gas were cut off. Yet the reactor was not restarted. The British network International Television News broadcast haunting footage of a peasant dragging tree limbs through snow with the cold reactor in the background: a survival rite no different from that known a thousand years ago, proceeding within the shadow of a modern system that might have brought warmth but had come to be considered more dangerous than freezing to death.

Since the Chernobyl accident occurred the big question has been how many deaths eventually will be caused. Officially 31 people died in the fire that broke the reactor free of its shielding and of radiation sickness in the immediate aftermath. The physicist Grigori Medeved, a former Chernobyl manager, believes the actual immediate-death number was about 400. Today the Ukrainian government estimates that long-term exposure from the accident will cause up to 8,000 additional premature deaths. Some estimates put the number at 17,000 or higher.

The International Chernobyl Project, a team of about 200 scientists from 25 countries, has in general not found evidence of a large-scale health wipeout downwind of the accident, though considering the latency period of cancer such evidence may be a decade or more in coming. Thyroid cancers are high among children in the downwind area, probably from radioactive iodine that fell onto grass, was consumed by cows, and ended up in milk. There is a possibility final premature death totals will not reach the upper-bound estimates. The International Atomic Energy Agency, granted access to the Chernobyl zone after old-line Communism fell, said in 1991 that observed radiation levels in the area are notably lower than the Ukrainian government assumes.

"Passive" Safety

In April 1986, a few months before Chernobyl, researchers at the Argonne National Laboratory in Idaho conducted a little-known test. They ran a research reactor to full power then deactivated all cooling and safety systems. Something quite dramatic happened: nothing. In less than two minutes the reactor shut off without any mechanical intervention, core melting, or radiation release. The reactor, undamaged, was restarted the same afternoon when the simulated failure was repeated, again with ho-hum results. The Idaho reactor design represents what may be a common energy form of the early twenty-first century: "passive" safety in nuclear power, machines designed to be harmless even when everything fails.

As the historian Richard Rhodes has written, in the dawn of the atomic era reactor manufacturers were anxious to put machines on the market quickly and at a cost competitive with cheap fossil fuels. Daunted by the complexity of atomic mechanics, designers chose to base their reactors around water as the coolant and moderator, because the properties of hot, pressurized water are well understood by the engineering profession. It is now known that water is not the ideal moderator for atomic reactions, being neither as efficient nor as safe as liquid sodium, the moderator used in the Idaho test. And in the 1950s, nuclear chain reactions were not fully understood; engineers had trouble sparking them. To compensate, designers often used operating margins set near the highest attainable levels. The results of this thinking—semieffi-

cient water-cooled reactors running near the margin of controllability—
are like naval steam boilers of the nineteenth century compared to modern diesel maritime engines. The latter generate much more horsepower
yet simultaneously are safer and easier to operate.

Water-cooled reactors reflecting 1950s design assumptions are the
standard in commercial power today. They are brute-force machines.
Today enough is known about atomic reactions to make possible a generation of knowledge-based reactors that would use sodium as coolant
and moderator. Such a reactor simply sits in a pool of sodium at standard atmospheric pressure, not high pressure as with most water-cooled
reactors. Its fuel elements are arranged in order that the chain reaction
constantly teeters on the verge of damping out. Keeping such mild, as
opposed to brute-force, fission going is mainly a function of knowledge:
mixing the ingredients and positioning them just so. If some failure
makes the sodium drain from an Idaho-style reactor, for a moment the
core will heat. This causes a slight expansion of the fuel rods. The rods
are sized so that any change in exterior dimensions snaps the fission
chain. The reaction damps out passively, without any convoluted system
of pumps and valves like the one that jammed at Three Mile Island.

The experimental Idaho reactor has other advanced properties, such
as generating a lower volume of waste and breeding a form of plutonium
that for reasons of chemistry would be of little value to bomb makers. Its
spent fuel, though intensely radioactive, exhibits different characteristics
from the radioactivity found in present reactor wastes. Some forms of
radiation are "prompt"; others are long-lived, requiring geologic time to
cool down. Wastes from current commercial reactors contain the long-
lived form of radioactivity and do not cool to harmlessness for a stunning 24,000 years. Waste from the Idaho reactor contains mainly the
prompt type of radioactivity. This waste is dangerous for about 200
years—still a long time, but manageable.

Reactor designers have taken to calling proposed new machines
"inherently safe." That remains to be seen: None has been tested under
daily commercial conditions. But the claim is at least plausible, given the
nearly perfect safety record of the old, brute-force designs. So long as
energy conservation investments remain cost-effective, the atom as an
energy source belongs in the background. But in a decade or so, when
the current round of obvious cost-effective conservation and renewable-
power investments has played out, society will start looking again for
new ways to make power, and the passive reactor may present itself as
an attractive means. Environmental politics would be scandalized by
such a development. Nature might be pleased.

What Did the Unethical Nuclear Tests Prove?

The atom age has been replete with scandals involving federal coverup of nuclear exposure, and in 1993 came one of the worst: revelations, first from the *Albuquerque Tribune,* that in the 1940s and 1950s government-sponsored researchers subjected at least 800 people to medical experiments involving radiation, and that Cold War era radiation leaks from the Hanford bomb plant had been worse than previously acknowledged.

Some of the revelations were shocking. In 1945 a man named Albert Stevens, a California painter erroneously believed on the verge of death from stomach cancer, was injected with plutonium to measure its effects on human tissue. In that same year Eda Charlton, a seamstress who checked into Strong Memorial Hospital in Rochester, New York, for routine care, was without her knowledge injected with plutonium as part of a secret Manhattan Project program to test the effects of the substance. By the time she died in 1983 at the age of 85, Charlton had never been told the truth about the experiment performed on her. Disclosures of the tests on Stevens and Charlton triggered an international reaction of outrage.

Public anger about the government duplicity and violation of rights represented by these experiments is wholly justified. But in order to maximize the doomsday spin, the 1993 controversy skipped over an inconvenient side issue: Hardly any actual harm was done. If anything, new details about unethical radiation tests of the Cold War era increase the likelihood that minor exposures to radiation are less dangerous than doctrine assumes.

Ecological literature, for instance, often contains the assertion that a single pound of plutonium possesses enough molecular lethality to kill every human being on Earth—a disquieting notion given that world stockpiles today hold perhaps 250 tons of plutonium. (The United States says it has manufactured about 90 tons; estimates for production in the former Soviet Union vary.) When the 1993 testing scandal broke, the *Washington Post* declared that "human contact with even one particle of plutonium is guaranteed to cause cancer." Yet the actual toxic effects of plutonium inside the body are speculative, since only a handful of people are known to have had this substance in their systems. (There is no plutonium in the fallout of nuclear explosions.) Eda Charlton was injected with appreciably more than "one particle" of plutonium and lived an additional four decades to age 85, a life some 30 years longer than the statistical expectancy for a white woman of her birth year.

Albert Stevens lived an additional 21 years, nearly 35 years longer than the statistical expectancy for a white male of his birth year. Neither left the Earth with cancer as the cause of death.

Reports about Stevens and Charlton hit hard on the inexcusable violation of rights but adroitly avoided the inconvenient complication that neither died a premature death. This may have happened because the doses involved were small. Charlton, for instance, received one-third of a microcurie of plutonium. Under federal standards for radon gas, a home is considered safe if the level works out to about 40 microcuries inhaled per day—roughly 120 times the effective amount Charlton received.

Many stories about the testing scandal concerned radioactive tracers fed in the 1950s to mentally handicapped children at the state-run Fernald School for Boys in Waltham, Massachusetts. Meaningful consent was not obtained, which is ample to label these tests an outrage. But press and environmentalist reports suggested the boys had been subjected to incredible horrors when in fact the dose they received was tiny. Frank Masse, a physician at the Massachusetts Institute of Technology, has calculated that the Fernald boys received an average effective dose of 172 millirems. While president, George Bush was treated with radioiodine for hyperactivity of the thyroid. His whole-body effective dose was about 5,000 millirems, 30 times what the Fernald boys received.

As the 1993 testing scandal unfolded, commentators began suggesting that horrors occurred when radiation was released in the 1940s and 1950s from the nuclear bomb production plant at Hanford, a facility that had few environmental safeguards during the Cold War years and though now closed continues to suffer from ecological blunders during cleanup. Hanford radiation leaks were commonly described as "hundreds of times worse than Three Mile Island." This statement is true but tells more about the insignificance of the Three Mile Island leak than anything else. The technical journal *Science* reported in 1993 that researchers studying the workers and 270,000 people downwind of Hanford for seven years had so far found "no firm evidence that any of the releases harmed human health."

That people exposed to radiation in the 1950s are still around to discuss the matter raises a basic question: How could radiation leaks *not* cause harm?

One possible explanation is lack of dose. A team of federal researchers is engaged in something called the Hanford Dose Reconstruction Study, which attempts to estimate how much radioactivity leaked from the plant during the early Cold War, when records were not kept. At present the study's authors believe that from 1944 to 1947, the peak period for headlong production without environmental safeguards, about 685,000 curies of radiation was emitted from Hanford. The Three Mile Island leak was about 17 curies. Yet most of the radiation from Hanford, like most radiation leaks, never resulted in exposure. The common form of radioactivity in fallout, Hanford leaks, and the Windscale leak is iodine 131, whose half-life is eight days. If washed down by rain promptly after release iodine 131 is quite dangerous, especially if uptaken by dairy cows, since milk is brought to market quickly while the iodine is still "hot." But if carried away on the winds, iodine 131 soon cools to harmlessness.

Like most atomic fallout, most Hanford leaks were carried away rather than washed down onto the innocent. There were tragic exceptions. Some people who lived immediately downwind of 1950s open-air tests, particularly children who played outside during fallout periods about which their parents were not warned, suffered horrible deaths at young ages. But the majority of downwinders were only mildly exposed. One of the lawsuits attempting to establish a downwinder right to federal compensation claims an average exposure of around 500 millirems, which probably is not a statistically significant difference from the typical annual natural background exposure of 290 millirems.

Another possible explanation for the less-than-expected impacts of radiation is genetic. When formed much of the Earth was radioactive. Continuing radioactive decay of the elements in Earth's core and mantle is one reason why the typical American is exposed to natural background radiation. Background millirems are thought to have declined with the passage of the eons, as the natural radioactivity of the Earth cools. This suggests the forebears of those species alive today, including the primate ancestors of genus *Homo*, may have known routine exposure to somewhat higher natural radiation. In turn the DNA lineage of today's living things probably contains resistance to levels of millirems beyond those normally present in the current background.

Absent nuclear war, it is likely no one will ever again be exposed to artificial radiation as directly and intensely as were the 1950s medical test victims, Hanford workers, and the downwinders. The Cold War revelations suggest that plutonium does not possess inexplicable hypertoxicity but rather some form of the linear dose-response relationship seen in other poisons. In the end disclosures about 1950s tests may be favorable to the prospects of nuclear power, an unintended consequence that may someday cause doomsayers to wish the *Albuquerque Tribune* never broke its story.

Western Wastes

Wastes, not reactor failures or radiation releases, have "emerged as the central nuclear issue," Nicholas Lenssen of the Worldwatch Institute declared in 1991. Where once greens evoked the specter of berserk reactors spewing death into suburban neighborhoods, few beyond the movement's fringe now speak of that improbability. But all speak in horror of nuclear waste, as indelibly real as radiation death is rare. There is no doubt nuclear waste is accumulating and nobody but nobody wants anything to do with the stuff. Few issues exist that legislatures and government officials will go to greater lengths to dodge.

Through the 1970s and early 1980s, Congress passed a series of laws that for purposes of show seemed to require the entire United States be examined open-mindedly to discover the safest place to entomb nuclear wastes. In actuality the laws forced these facilities on New Mexico and Nevada, two of the smallest and least-connected states. They were chosen after better-connected states maneuvered to exempt themselves from the honor. For example former Senate Majority Leader George Mitchell once slipped into legislation a mysterious rider prohibiting the Department of Energy, which has authority over nuclear wastes, from conducting research into the technical properties of granite. Many researchers believe granite formations are ideal places in which to imprison nuclear wastes; Canada plans to bury its reactor wastes in granite. Mitchell saw to it that Maine, most of whose geology is based on granite, would be off the hook for nuclear waste disposal.

During the 1980s Congress passed a law apparently compelling states to form regional compacts to build small facilities for mildly radioactive items such as gowns worn during radiology therapy. Most states have studiously avoided action on that requirement, too. Only in a few cases have political leaders appeared willing to tackle this problem. In 1990 governor Kay Orr of Nebraska said her reading of geological studies persuaded her that Boyd County, Nebraska, would be the safest place to locate the low-level nuclear waste site for the lower Midwest. What could she have been thinking! Previously popular, Orr was defeated in the next election owing to a campaign of hysteria about Nebraska glowing in the dark.

A considerable alarmist literature now concerns the WIPP (Waste Isolation Pilot Project) site in Carlsbad, New Mexico, and Yucca Mountain site in Nevada, each declared to be frighteningly dangerous. At WIPP, low-level wastes from weapons manufacturing—constituting about 95 percent of U.S. nuclear wastes by volume but containing only about five percent of total radioactivity—will be lowered 2,150 feet below the desert floor, seated in a salt-dome formation. A salt dome was chosen because such structures are geologically stable over long periods. The desert was chosen because it lacks flowing water to carry any wastes that somehow escape and because it is far from the nearest city.

Nevertheless orthodox environmental doctrine calls WIPP a terrifying risk to human health and a deep affront to nature. Its caverns might collapse; the desert climate might change, bringing flowing water to the area; waste containers might fall off trucks during shipment; an earthquake might crack open the soil, exposing the buried hazards to air. All these things might happen, especially handling accidents, which are nearly guaranteed when human beings and government agencies coincide to execute tasks. But what is the likelihood? People have been building underground caverns for mines for more than a century, and only a handful have collapsed; the WIPP borings are perhaps the most carefully designed ever. The Pecos Mountains around Carlsbad might transform to a rainforest—the area has been a rainforest before and will be one again—but most of the material to be buried at WIPP will remain radioactive in a hazardous way only for about 300 years. The odds for climate transformation in that period are long. Will handling accidents with the waste barrels spew death? Only if passersby appear with blowtorches and air hammers to break open the shielding, which will be designed to resist falls.

WIPP has been complete for about five years but is not yet "accepting" wastes, in the euphemism of the Department of Energy. A succession of legal challenges has prevented operation. In 1993 the department, postponing further unpleasantries until after the next presidential election, announced that WIPP would not "accept" wastes even for testing purposes till 1998.

Probably New Mexico has more to fear from the Department of Energy than the wastes it brings. The agency has a long history of lying to the public, of bungling the management of nuclear complexes such as the Rocky Flats plant in Denver, and of arrogance toward environmental law. This began to change somewhat in the late 1980s under Energy Secretary James Watkins, a nuclear hardliner who was nevertheless openly critical of poor nuclear management and who ordered DOE facilities to begin cooperating with EPA inspectors. (Watkins's order was codified in 1991 through the Federal Facilities Compliance Act, which specifies that military installations meet environmental regulations; previously they were exempt.) Watkins says the DOE culture "shamefully ignored some obvious environmental safeguards." Even after a blast of Watkins, the agency remains wedded to many outdated

Cold War ways. EPA authority over the WIPP is therefore a good idea, providing a cross-check to institutional complacency at the DOE.

But once the EPA entered the project, in response to environmentalist filings it began issuing rulings that border on transrational. The strangest holds that the caverns of WIPP must be marked in such a way that 10,000 years from now its dangerous character will be obvious. This ruling has led the EPA to commission artists to attempt to design warning signs that would be universal to all cultures, including extraterrestrials; to authorize a study of a "nuclear priesthood" that would pass down through the generations oral warnings, presumably chants, about the WIPP site; and similar frivolities. (I'm not making this up, except the chants.) "The idea of the 10,000-year requirement makes no sense except as a political instrument for delay," Paul Busch, president of the environmental engineering firm Malcolm Pirnie, says. As a political instrument the rule activates reviews, lawsuits, administrative proceedings, and similar time-consuming exercises that all parties know in advance will come to no conclusion since no one can possibly predict conditions 10,000 years hence. But this delay substitutes further study for any actual action to dispose of nuclear wastes. Actual action against nuclear wastes is the last thing environmental orthodoxy wants, especially since there is the annoying possibility the action would be successful.

At Yucca Mountain, planned as the national disposal point for wastes from commercial power reactors, no construction has begun. So far $2 billion has been spent merely to study the geology of the area. Federal law requires that the DOE "take title" to all commercial reactor wastes in 1998 for the purposes of transfer to Yucca Mountain. But at the present rate of progress the DOE estimates Yucca Mountain cannot operate until 2013 at the earliest. Asked why, in 1993, his department was projecting another 20 years of work required to dig a hole at Yucca Mountain—more time than was required to dig the Panama Canal—John Riggs, a deputy assistant secretary of Energy, said, "We want to make sure the geology studies are exactly right and we want to let time pass for political purposes."

Continuing inaction at Yucca Mountain means that about $6 billion paid into a nuclear waste disposal fund by the customers of utilities that use nuclear power, for the purpose of building Yucca Mountain, today is being used to retire federal debt. A common fallacious argument against nuclear power is that no provisions have been made for waste disposal. Through the $6 billion fund, ratepayers have been funding this expense in advance for about a decade.

Assuming Yucca Mountain ever opens, wastes would be encased in steel and concrete then lowered about 1,000 feet below the desert floor. Drums will rest in a geological formation most researchers believe has been stable for 300,000 years. A geologist named Jerry Szymanski has received considerable attention, and won the hearts of many activists, by maintaining that calcium mineral veins near the surface of Yucca Mountain show that groundwater has risen there in recent geological time and might rise again, mingling with nuclear wastes after an earthquake. This would invalidate the Yucca site. Though Szymanski's theory has a chance of being true, it has been studied and dismissed by many other researchers, including 17 geologists on a National Research Council panel who in 1987 found unanimously that upwelling earthquake groundwater at Yucca Mountain was improbable; and Jay Quade and Thure Cerling, University of Utah geologists whose studies suggest groundwater in the Yucca Mountain area has been low since before the last ice age. In 1992 a moderate earthquake occurred near Yucca Mountain. Many activists trumpeted that news, suggesting it showed the site was horrendously dangerous. They did not add that no upwelling of water followed the quake, as enviros previously had predicted.

Also in 1992 a dispute arose regarding whether the DOE or EPA would write operating rules for Yucca Mountain. Congress proposed to resolve the issue by having the National Academy of Sciences compose the rules. Environmental lobbyists and the Nevada Senate delegation fought this proposal with vigor, the senators threatening filibuster unless the EPA were given primacy. Why? The EPA is a political agency, subject to lobbying; the NAS is independent and for the most part rational. If the EPA wins primacy over Yucca Mountain procedures, an issue still undecided, it will spend years if not decades merely to propose rules in draft form. If the NAS wins primacy, it is likely to conclude that Yucca can be operated without untoward risk, and to produce the rules.

As the number of green issues justifying panic declines with the passage of time, nuclear waste has become one of the shining hopes of institutional environmentalism. Nuclear waste is dangerous, people dread it, and unlike other forms of pollutants that are declining, nuclear waste continues to accumulate, with about 41,000 metric tons in existence worldwide in 1985 and a total of 193,000 metric tons expected by 2000. Any opening of safe, well-run facilities to handle these wastes would be a disaster for the orthodox wing of the green movement, resolving one of the few end-of-the-world issues remaining on the horizon.

Maybe Carlsbad, New Mexico, and Yucca Mountain, Nevada, are not the ideal places for nuclear wastes. But the case as stated against

WIPP and Yucca Mountain today is this: that stabilizing nuclear wastes, then encasing them in steel and concrete, then burying them far beneath the floor of the desert hundreds of miles from population centers is horribly risky. If you think having nuclear wastes encased in concrete far underground hundreds of miles from anywhere is horribly risky—where do you suppose the stuff is now? The answer is, in your community.

Nuclear Waste Around the Corner

Because the Nimby reflex and environmental litigation have prevented nuclear waste disposal sites from opening, the inevitable result is that such waste continues to sit at old nuclear weapons production plants and on the grounds of commercial nuclear reactor installations, most of which are near cities.

Almost every one of the 110 U.S. commercial reactor stations today has in effect become a nuclear waste facility, with various forms of on-site tombs holding at least 20,000 metric tons of the most active form of nuclear waste. At the McGuire station, for instance, a concrete tomb has been built to hold nuclear wastes pending whatever eventually happens to them. Workers stroll past it every day. Going inside the tomb would be very dangerous, but standing outside across the parking lot, according to Geiger counters, is harmless.

The indefinite holding of nuclear wastes has become an issue in attempts to dismantle outdated reactors such as Yankee Rowe, in Massachusetts. That reactor is being decommissioned but its wastes must still sit there, with no legal place to go. Officials estimate $3 million a year will be spent indefinitely to post guards around the wastes. Military nuclear wastes also continue to be held near cities because enviros have been so successful in blocking legal permission to transfer them anywhere. For instance in late 1993 the Department of Energy revealed that some 14 tons of weapons-grade plutonium is stored at the closed Rocky Flats bomb plant a stone's throw from the Denver city limits. Many Rocky Flats fuel rods have been sitting for years in old holding pools now beginning to rust. Some of the spent uranium, stored as oxides, has itself begun to rust and contaminate the holding water. Most existing waste-holding areas at reactor stations are water pools intended for temporary storage, not long-term service. The metallurgy, safety, and cooling systems of such pools are nowhere near as sophisticated as the designs for WIPP and Yucca. Yet on the grounds that it would be

horrifying to move nuclear wastes to modern, well-designed underground desert sites supervised by the EPA, orthodox environmentalism
has created a situation in which more than 100 scattered nuclear disposal sites, most near cities, hold wastes in rusting tanks from the 1960s.

Because the capacity of holding pools at reactors is beginning to fill,
the nuclear industry has asked the DOE to create temporary sites to
which nuclear wastes would be shipped pending a final Yucca Mountain
decision, assuming one comes during the historical era of humankind.
At this writing the DOE was proposing to use special statutory authority to hold nuclear wastes on military reservations. What a wonderful
idea: Rather than move wastes to well-designed, permanent sites, stack
them up on temporary racks at military bases, to be supervised by
teenagers. Yet this prospect is in keeping with current doomsday doctrine, which longs for the sense of a nuclear waste crisis to continue
indefinitely.

Pondering the possibility that they may become unofficial nuclear
waste sites, some utilities have begun to seek licenses for dry "casks"
for waste holding at reactor stations. These casks, to the eye little more
than concrete and steel grids, are examples of knowledge-based technology. The shapes, dimensions, and metallurgy of their design is based
on increasing understanding of the way radiation moves and the best
techniques for impeding its progress; the result is a clean-tech solution.
The casks hold waste containers in the air where they cool by passive
air circulation, eliminating the risk that something will go wrong with
pumped cooling water. The newly antinuclear Sacramento Municipal
Utility District, which closed its Rancho Seco reactor in 1989, continues to hold Rancho Seco's wastes there in air-cooled casks and plans to
do so indefinitely; the utility reports no problems with the casks, which
are relatively inexpensive. Tests show that at 108 feet from an air-
cooled cask of high-level nuclear wastes, radiation exposure is about
two-tenths of a millirem per hour, or only somewhat more than the natural background level. At 200 feet radiation falls to the natural background level, meaning a simple steel-and-concrete expedient shields
nuclear wastes sufficiently well that the effects are confined to a tiny
area.

Some opponents are now campaigning diligently against the licens-
ing of air-cooled casks. If a relatively inexpensive, above-ground, passively safe system 200 feet from a reactor's parking lot can render
nuclear wastes nearly harmless, how can it be that burying the same
wastes deep under the remote desert is an astonishing risk to the biosphere? A restive point.

Transitional Wastes

No thoughtful person believes it is wise for society to continue manufacturing by the multiple tons radioactive wastes that will require special care for thousands of years. Even former Energy Secretary Watkins—a nuclear true believer who fought bitterly against the plan to close Shoreham—acknowledges this. "It would be senseless for society to continue indefinitely making high-level waste, stacking the barrels and putting up signs that say KEEP OUT," Watkins says. "This is tolerable only as a transition policy, until something better comes along."

But what? One possible something better will be a means to render nuclear wastes harmless. At Yucca Mountain wastes will be held on racks for removal, should a neutralizer someday be discovered. Today no practical system is in prospect, but neutralization of radioactivity is possible in principle. The most dangerous nuclear material is made by transmuting mildly radioactive natural uranium ore with an atomic number of 238 into red-hot plutonium, atomic number 239. In principle reverse-transmutation could convert 239 atoms back into 238. Researchers are studying reverse transmutation and may someday advance the process to practicality.

A more promising something better would be energy sources that leave no radioactive by-products in the first place. Watkins believes one is coming in the form of controlled fusion, using hydrogen or helium as fuel. I'm not so sure about fusion: Solar converters in the desert or in space sound more likely to be practical. Finding ways to tap the existing fusion output of the sun has, after all, been one of the organizing principles of the biosphere for 3.8 billion years. As humankind learns to emulate the knowledge already embodied in nature, genus *Homo* will increasingly find its energy where other species have: by looking to the sun. People will just do this a little differently, say, with bioengineered dye molecules on silicon chips and with mirrors in sun-synchronous orbit.

But let's suppose the advanced alternatives fall through and nuclear power from fission turns out to be necessary for decades to come. This could mean hundreds of thousands of tons of radioactive waste. Burying that amount might ultimately require a land area of two to three square miles—or less than one one-millionth of the U.S. Suppose one one-millionth of the U.S. land area is sacrificed in return for no smog, no acid rain, no greenhouse gas emissions, no airborne toxics, no black lung disease in coal miners, no coal mining deaths, no oil refinery explosions. Would nature, which has in the past often rendered entire swaths of

North America lifeless for millennia, consider this trade-off the shocking horror depicted by environmental orthodoxy?

Weapons Waste, in More Ways than One

Nestled in the rolling hill country near Knoxville, Tennessee, lies Oak Ridge, the "secret city" of World War II. It was not listed on maps; workers were not supposed to use the town's name. Gigantic assemblies of power transformers, centrifuges, gas membranes, and other devices were employed at breathtaking cost to enrich uranium to the point at which it would not just glow but explode. When the Cold War came, Oak Ridge facilities were used to make nuclear materials for the arms race. No one without a high-security clearance, including EPA inspectors, was allowed entry. A paramilitary force patrolled the grounds, armed with combat weapons, not revolvers. Large, pointed stakes were placed throughout the complex to prevent terrorist helicopters from landing. Usually even public officials from nearby towns were not welcome.

That changed after the Berlin Wall fell. When I toured Oak Ridge in 1990, I wrote a story for the *Washington Post* containing details about Oak Ridge internal operations that strictly speaking had been national secrets only months before. By 1992 journalists were being shown the weapons reactor complexes at Hanford, Washington, and Savannah River, South Carolina, and even the hush-hush Pantex plant in Oklahoma, where bombs were assembled. Today Pantex runs its production lines in reverse, bringing nuclear devices in the front door and sending disassembled heaps of parts out the back for destruction. And by the 1990s, EPA officials were commonplace on the grounds of nuclear weapons facilities. Some had been given what has long been one of Washington's most coveted badges of insider status, the Q clearance for nuclear secrets. *Tree huggers with Q clearance!* The nuclear old guard was astonished.

Yet even the old guard was forced to admit the time had come. The evidence of this is everywhere at Oak Ridge. There, in the 1940s and 1950s, thousands of gallons of mixed radioactive and toxic wastes were discharged directly into streams. Thousands more gallons were simply filled into 55-gallon drums and left in marshaling yards. In one corner of Oak Ridge by 1990 sat a neatly ordered field of barrels extending as far as the eye could see—some 30,000 containers into which mixed low-level radioactive and toxic wastes had been transferred. They were awaiting destruction at the world's first low-level radioactive waste incinerator built to modern standards, completed at Oak Ridge but not EPA certified for full-time use. In other parts of the complex are entire process areas, rendered unneeded by the end of the Cold War, that must be painstakingly disassembled and tested for contamination, not just knocked over with a wrecking ball.

And Oak Ridge is the Department of Energy's showcase environmental facility. At Hanford the "200 area," the hottest zone, probably will be fenced off for decades to come, since no one has thought of a practical means to clean it. Six reactors used to make weapons-grade materials, shut down because the production of weapons materials has come to a close, must be disassembled; they are dirtier than civilian reactors, having been built in haste with minimal safety equipment. Many Hanford wastes found their way to the Columbia River. Sometimes at Hanford, soil contaminated with plutonium was rototilled to move it out of sight, out of mind. A vitrifaction facility for Hanford, which will turn the contents of most of the thousands of barrels of mixed radioactive and liquid wastes at the site to inert obsidian, has yet to be designed, much less built.

At Savannah River two reactors employed to make tritium, a gas that amplifies the power of nuclear explosions, have been shuttered and a planned replacement will not be built; these reactors must now be dismantled. A vitrifaction facility to convert Savannah River's 1.3 million gallons of mixed radiative-toxic wastes into inert obsidian is years behind schedule and millions over budget. At Rocky Flats outside Denver, production lines are closed but a range of contamination problems remains. Rocky Flats contractors have been so uncooperative with cleanup plans that in 1989 the Federal Bureau of Investigation flew an aircraft with thermal sensors over the facility at night, to determine if personnel were using an unpermitted incinerator to burn low-level nuclear wastes under cover of darkness. Agents then obtained a search warrant and raided Rocky Flats. The FBI had to raid a Department of Energy installation. Think about it.

Like most weapons facilities, Rocky Flats has long had a contemptuous relationship with its community. During the 1980s Philip Bailey, now a Washington, D.C., environmental lobbyist, was a Colorado state official on a Rocky Flats oversight task force. He asked to see some of the original documents by which plant managers certified the grounds safe. Rocky Flats sits to the west of Denver; the justification documents say that since prevailing winds around Denver blow from east to west, radiation releases will be pushed away from the city. "Anyone who has lived in Denver for five minutes knows that the prevailing winds blow from west to east, down off the Rockies," Bailey notes.

Now that the departments of Defense and Energy have begun to admit the extent of environmental cleanups needed at nuclear facilities, cost numbers that have began to emerge are breathtaking. The fiscal 1992 federal budget alone contained $6.9 billion for environmental cleanup of weapons plants, versus $5 billion for Navy attack aircraft. Currently the Department of Energy estimates that $26 billion to $50 billion will be spent over the next two decades in nuclear weapons cleanups. Environmentalists peg the figure as high as $200 billion.

By the most amazing coincidence, the same contractors that built and ran the weapons production complex, creating its ecological problems, now are receiving the billions for cleanup. The defense budget may be shrinking, but the defense cleanup budget is a growth area, and aerospace contractors—that is, Environmental Restoration Management Contractors, as the DOE now calls this crowd—have not failed to notice. Bechtel, which built most of Hanford, is now unbuilding it. Westinghouse, EG&G, General Electric, Rockwell, and other major companies partly responsible for making the nuclear weapons mess now do nicely by resolving it. In 1992, *Aviation Week and Space Technology,* the trade journal of the aerospace business, ran a special section with the opening headline "Contractors Pursue Potential $200 Billion Cleanup Market." What followed were articles with a weirdly hopeful tone about how environmental problems at old military bases just keep getting more expensive and isn't that fabulous news!

Early indications are that the Environmental Restoration Management Contractors are approaching nuclear cleanup with the same cost-conscious discipline they used during the Reagan weapons buildup. Merely the *feasibility study* for cleanup of the Fernald, Ohio, weapons plant cost an amazing $107.8 million. The fiscal 1993 cleanup budget for Fernald showed $105 million for actual action and $203 million for administrative overhead. A perverse commonality of interests has evolved on this subject between defense contractors and environmental lobbyists. Contractors want the nuclear cleanup to be expensive and drawn out for financial reasons; many greens want the cleanup to be expensive and drawn out because the more it costs and the longer it lasts, the greater its doomsday ring. Nearly everything cleanup officials have tried to do at Hanford, Fernald, and elsewhere has been blocked by activist lawsuits. To environmental doctrine, twice as much money for overhead as for actual cleanup at Fernald or elsewhere makes perfect sense, since by postponing resolution of the core problem it sustains the perception of crisis.

Cleanup actions at nuclear weapons sites benefit from careful appraisals by environmentalists, whose oversight dissuades contractors from taking shortcuts. Otherwise there is not, as doomsayers now contend, anything drastically dangerous or sensitive about the projects: They are just unusually delicate engineering jobs. For instance current plans call for about half of the 260-square-mile Hanford reservation to be converted to a public recreation area by 1995. Much of the Columbia River frontage into which nuclear wastes were recently dumped is to become a wildlife preserve. The Columbia River frontages are already back at natural background radiation level, indicating that the long-term ecological threat from mishandling weapons wastes, while real, simply is not the disaster institutional environmentalism likes to suggest.

An attempt to convert environmental sentiment into a new guaranteed employment program for aerospace contractors came in 1989 when Senator Sam Nunn of Georgia, then chairman of the Senate Armed Services committee, announced with fanfare a "strategic environment defense initiative." Nunn was studiously vague about what this preposterous conjunction of authorities—environmental regulation and the army—was to do. What emerged from Nunn's idea was the new Strategic Environmental Research Defense Program, now a $200-million-a-year Pentagon agency. Unknown outside the Pentagon, the bureau now commands more resources than the ecology study centers of most big universities.

Early indications are this agency's preference is for projects with a good prospect of cost overruns. For example a credentialed oceanographer named Walter Monk suggested around 1990 that the thermal values of ocean currents, which have implications for global warming, be studied by building huge underwater loudspeakers and monitoring the movement of the acoustic waves produced. Monk's idea required a global network of speakers and monitors. The National Science Foundation turned Monk down, blanching at the cost. The Strategic Environmental Research Defense Program said yes to the tune of $31 million. Though the project is in limbo owing to lawsuits by environmentalists, no doubt Pentagon officials call Monk regularly, asking, "Professor, are you sure there isn't anything else you need? Frogman commandos lowered from attack helicopters? Underwater city?"

Former Soviet Wastes

Compared to the situation in the former Soviet Union, nuclear weapons wastes in the United States were handled with great prudence. In 1957, a low-order atomic reaction occurred at a nuclear dump at Kyshtym, in the Ural Mountains, when a rudimentary cooling system failed in an

80,000-gallon storage tank; 11,000 people downwind had to be evacuated. Beginning in 1951, a Soviet bomb factory at Mayak, in the Urals, released into the nearby Lake Karachay perhaps 1.2 billion curies of radioactive wastes; the Chernobyl explosion released an estimated 50 million curies, about four percent as much. For a time this did not matter, because the lake was not used for drinking water. But as Murray Feshbach and Alfred Friendly, Jr., describe in their book *Ecocide in the U.S.S.R.*, "The summer of 1967 was dry and hot. Lake Karachay evaporated in part, and winds blew the radioactive dust from its exposed bed onto nearby land, buildings and an estimated 41,000 people. Visitors in 1990 found radiation levels on the lakeshore path the wind had followed still high enough to provide a lethal dose in about 60 minutes of exposure."

The extent of health and ecological damage from incidents such as the 1957 waste explosion or the 1967 lakebed dispersal is not yet known, partly because Soviet authorities hushed over such problems until 1991. New Russian authorities now speak of their nuclear waste problem in apocalyptic terms, Environment Minister Aleksei Yablokov having declared that there are now areas of the former Soviet Union where "cancer is the only cause of death." The *only* cause? The new Russian officialdom may overstate its environmental challenges partly for the same reason that Rockwell and Bechtel suddenly want to be Environmental Restoration Management Contractors: The worse the situation appears, the more likely money will come from Washington. Several international teams are now studying health conditions in the former nuclear production areas of the old U.S.S.R. No conclusions had been reached as of this writing, but one researcher involved in the leading project says preliminary indications are that "problems are real but not the disaster depicted by Yablokov or in Western press reports."

So far the United States and the former U.S.S.R. have been most forthcoming about the problems of their old nuclear programs. Britain, China, France, India, Israel, North Korea, Pakistan, and South Africa have yet to own up to whatever ecological harm their bomb projects have caused. Reasonable international disclosure has come mainly on the issue of nuclear wastes dumped at sea. This was a common practice by Western nations through the 1950s. An estimated 107,000 tons of low-level wastes were sunk at sea up till 1970, when the Marine Protection Research and Sanctuaries Act banned the practice by the U.S. military. An international agreement called the London Convention, signed in 1972 and given teeth in 1983, appeared to ban the practice for all countries. The Soviet Union, which signed the London Convention, kept dumping at sea anyway. Greenpeace International has documented

18 Soviet submarine reactors and three icebreaker reactors dumped into the seas off Novaya Zemyla, sometimes by the simple expedient of blasting them out of the hulls of ships. Greenpeace has a schizophrenic character when it comes to research. Its work regarding dioxin, chlorine, and the greenhouse effect can border on foolish. But its nuclear weapons research is sound and taken seriously; at times Greenpeace has been the best source of nuclear information regarding the old Soviet Union.

After the collapse of old-line Communism in 1991, new Russian authorities announced that the dumping of atomic wastes at sea would end. But in late 1993 a Russian naval vessel released 900 tons of low-level radioactive wastes into the Sea of Japan, just days after Russian President Boris Yeltsin had visited that country to declare that Moscow would seek constructive relations with Tokyo. It is a measure of the complex new Russian reality that the 1993 dumping was carried out in daylight, in view of other ships, with the containers tossed overboard clearly marked with the international atomic warning symbol. Previous Soviet nuclear dumping was conducted with the utmost secrecy. Moscow's explanation for the act was that Russia is currently too poor to dispose of low-level atomic wastes properly on land. An international outcry followed; Moscow subsequently announced a suspension of such dumping but said the suspension would last only if the country received Western aid to finance proper land disposal of atomic materials.

Sea dumping of nuclear wastes probably does limited harm, since the vastness of the ocean dilutes radiation. In 1993 an international team of radiation experts, meeting at the Woods Hole Oceanographic Institute, concluded that radioactive wastes dumped in the world's oceans "apparently pose no global danger." The group found "no evidence" of general radiation problems in the North Atlantic or Arctic Sea, or in fish caught there. Most experts expected no detectable problems in fish from the 1993 Russian dumping, either. The optimistic Woods Hole finding was attacked by environmental lobbyists. It also had the unfortunate side effect of causing the Pentagon to request that the 1983 moratorium on sea disposal of low-level wastes be lifted. Many nations have suggested that the moratorium, enforced through the London Convention, be made permanent. The Pentagon wants the moratorium lifted because it has no other options, what with opposition keeping the WIPP facility from opening.

Probably by the mid-1990s the world's governments, including Moscow, will end the ocean dumping of nuclear wastes forever. Though the chances are small that mildly radioactive reactor parts and technician's gowns harm the sea, a principle of ecorealism holds that while nearly all environmental damage is easily reversed, the small number of truly irreversible ecological acts must be avoided. Since there is no practical way to clean the seas, ocean pollution is irreversible by human standards and thus ought to be forbidden.

The Greatest Environmental Reform of All

The two most important environmental advances of our age—perhaps that will ever be possible for any age—both concern radiation, both have occurred over the past 30 years, and both play virtually no role in contemporary ecological consciousness.

The first is the Test Ban Treaty of 1963, which stopped open-air nuclear explosions by the United States, Britain, and the former Soviet Union; later it was signed by other powers. When our near descendants look back on this century to say *"You did what?"* surely some of their strongest incredulity will focus on the notion of detonating radiation-producing devices in the air, upwind of farms and population centers. Had open-air nuclear testing continued at the pace of the 1950s, a genuine ecological catastrophe would have resulted. Yet the Test Ban Treaty is rarely mentioned as an environmental accomplishment.

Second and of more lasting importance stand the two Strategic Arms Reduction treaties, signed in July 1991 and January 1993. Under these agreements the world's arsenal of nuclear explosives will be cut by more than 50,000 bombs with strategic warheads, the most menacing type, declining from at least 20,000 combined on the parts of the superpowers to no more than 7,000 and perhaps considerably less. Related treaties signed in 1991 and 1992 require the superpowers to destroy all chemical weapons and foreswear future manufacture of chemical or biological agents.

According to government figures declassified in 1994, the U.S. nuclear arsenal peaked in the year 1960 at 20,491 megatons. By 1994 the total was down to a little more than 2,000 megatons, with an eventual decline to 1,000 megatons—five percent of the peak-year figure—expected in the 1990s. Figures for the former Soviet states are roughly similar.

Nuclear warheads in profusion were a true threat to seal the fate of the Earth. Our descendants will find it astonishing that the rapid decline of this ordinance of Armageddon has been greeted with a collective yawn. For instance when George Bush announced, in July 1992, that the United States would permanently halt the production of weapons-grade nuclear material, the news did not even make the front page in many American and European newspapers. An editorial in the *Washington*

Post sneered at the decision as "largely symbolic," claiming that a halt to nuclear arms manufacturing was always inevitable anyway. If there is any important development in international affairs that assuredly was *not* inevitable, it was the end of the strategic arms race.

The U.S. and former Soviet states have not only stopped making plutonium and weapons-grade uranium, they have halted the manufacture of tritium. Tritium is a hydrogen isotope that enhances the yield of thermonuclear devices. Unlike plutonium, tritium has a brief half-life, decaying at the rate of 5.5 percent per year. This means that in around 20 years the world's stock of tritium essentially will be gone. The blast power of the nuclear weapons remaining in existence will decline markedly as their tritium components transmute back to harmlessness. To my knowledge, this development has gone entirely unnoticed.

Traditionally the really important historical shifts are missed as they occur, people's minds being focused on lesser matters later forgotten. So perhaps something like the end of nuclear weapons production, and the dismantling of the megadeath arsenal, is simply too big for society to grasp hard on its occurrence. But you cannot help thinking the real reason you hear so little about these breakthroughs is that they are inconveniently optimistic. They suggest the one true doomsday threatened by human action is fading, and orthodoxy cannot abide that notion.

29 ✍

RADIATION, NATURAL ✍

"THE WORLD NOW KNOWS THAT DANGER IS SHINING through the skies," began the February 1992 issue of *Time*. The magazine's cover declared, "Vanishing Ozone: The Danger Moves Closer to Home." Days before, researchers affiliated with the National Aeronautics and Space Administration held a press conference to declare that an ozone breach might open not over the desolate South Pole, where seasonal holes have been detected since the 1980s, but above "very populated regions" of North America and Europe. Hours after the NASA announcement Al Gore delivered an impassioned speech to an emergency session of the Senate, declaring ozone depletion "the greatest crisis humanity has ever faced" and warning, "our children . . . must begin to think of the sky as a threatening part of the environment." Following Gore's speech the Senate voted 96–0 to accelerate the abolition of chlorofluorocarbons (CFCs), the primary artificial compound implicated in ozone loss.

The NASA announcement and Senate emergency action made international headlines. Greenpeace bought full-page newspaper ads that announced, "Normal life could be interrupted for generations. In some places it could be dangerous ever to go outside." Press reports, political speeches, and environmental commentary began to routinely refer to ozone depletion above the Northern Hemisphere as a proven apocalypse. The standard refrain became that the ozone layer was not only in decline but "vanishing." For instance when a space shuttle bearing instruments to measure ozone was launched in April 1993, CBS News said the flight would research "the vanishing ozone layer" causing "worldwide environmental problems."

One problem with all this: Except for the quotations, dates, and the margin of the Senate vote, nothing in the above paragraphs turned out to be true. No Northern Hemisphere ozone hole has ever been detected, and far from "vanishing" the ozone layer has in the worst-case analysis declined only by a few percent.

Stratospheric ozone depletion is the archetypical issue crying out for ecorealism. This problem is real and does require action, yet the extent of peril has been so drastically overstated as to bear little more than glancing relationship to the reality of the subject. Richard Stolarski, a NASA atmospheric scientist who is a leading author of technical papers on stratospheric ozone, says, "Ozone depletion is a serious concern but we can't show that anything catastrophic has happened yet or will happen in the future."

A calming voice of ecorealism is appropriate on this topic for a second reason: To the extent ozone loss is genuine, the problem has been addressed with record speed. The basic theory of ozone depletion was not proposed until 1973. Empirical confirmation of the phenomenon was not found until 1985. By 1987 most nations agreed to cut CFC production. By 1990, the United States and most of Western Europe advanced to a commitment to abolish CFC manufacturing. By that point many large industrial customers had already stopped using the chemicals. According to a 1993 study by Derek Cunnold of the Georgia Institute of Technology, world emissions of CFCs peaked in 1988 and have been declining since. As a result most researchers now project that the depletion effects of CFCs will max out around the year 2000, much earlier than expected.

This spectacular record of human action and natural recovery offers a powerful example of the ecorealist premise that environmental reforms usually happen faster even than optimists project. Consider that in 1990, the United Nations Environment Programme projected that world CFC emissions would peak around the turn of the century. The U.N. estimate was assailed by orthodox environmentalists as unforgivably optimistic. Yet Cunnold's study shows that at the very time the United Nations was releasing its projection, emissions of CFCs had *already* peaked. If most of the world's important issues could be resolved as quickly as ozone depletion, Earth would be a paradise.

Let's preview the four underlying reasons why the apocalypse locution of ozone depletion veers so far from the realities of nature.

First, though an ozone hole has been opening over Antarctica since the late 1970s, it is not yet known whether artificial chemicals are the sole cause. Nearly all atmospheric scientists believe CFCs play an important role in the South Pole hole. But part of the cause may be natural. Some new research suggests natural ozone breaches have been occurring on a cyclical basis since long before morning light first warmed our primate ancestors.

Second, the meteorological conditions of the South Pole, duplicated nowhere else on Earth, imply it is unlikely a significant ozone breach will open over the Northern Hemisphere latitudes where most of the world's population lives. In 1992 NASA and *Time* gave the *possibility* of a northern ozone hole the four-alarm treatment. The failure of any northern hole to appear is something NASA only sheepishly acknowledged months later, in low-profile technical documents, and something no major news organization played prominently.

Third, the notion there is "danger streaming down from the skies" is far from proven. What matters about the stratosphere is not the number of ozone molecules there but how much ultraviolet radiation from the sun reaches the surface of the Earth. Though research on this topic is in its early stages, some tests show surface levels of ultraviolet radiation have *declined* slightly during the last decade. Doomsayers never mention this. During the very period of ozone anguish and advice that children be taught to fear the sky, actual biological risk from the sky may have gone down, not up.

Fourth, the worst-case projection for twenty-first-century ozone depletion is a composite increase of 15 to 20 percent in surface ultraviolet radiation in the Northern Hemisphere. Would this spell disaster? John Frederick, an atmospheric scientist at the University of Chicago, says, "It's nothing to get a 20 percent increase on a purely natural basis." Sunlight grows more intense as one moves toward the equator, and thus ultraviolet radiation increases as well. Mexico City, Miami, San Diego, and other cities on the mid-equatorial latitude band naturally receive about 20 percent more ultraviolet radiation than cities like Boston, Rome, and Seattle. "If a 20 percent increase in ultraviolet exposure were going to be so damaging, there should be no life in Florida," Frederick notes.

Ozone Above and Below

The theory of ozone depletion begins with an observation from the science of optics: Three-atom molecules usually absorb the ultraviolet-B wavelength while two-atom molecules usually allow it to pass. Most oxygen occurs as a two-atom molecule abbreviated by chemists as O_2.

Above cities, pollutants react with sunlight to convert O_2 into an unbreathable three-atom or O_3 version of oxygen—ozone—which causes lung damage and is therefore harmful at low altitude. In the stratosphere the sun powers a natural reaction that converts O_2 into O_3, forming the ozone layer. Since this ozone is never breathed, its existence is benign. Stratospheric ozone absorbs a portion of the ultraviolet radiation descending on Earth from the sun, especially as UV-B.[1]

This shielding effect is important because DNA molecules also absorb UV-B. Exactly what impact the resonance caused by UV-B has on genetic material is not known, but it's not a wild guess the effect is unwelcome. Researchers have long assumed that high UV-B would lead to increased skin cancers such as malignant and nonmalignant melanomas, as the skin bears most exposure to sun; and perhaps to cataracts, since sunlight enters the eye.

Ozone depletion worries began in the 1960s, when the likely relationship between UV-B and skin cancer came to the attention of researchers. At that time the American, British, French, and former Soviet governments were competing to produce a supersonic transport, or SST. Such aircraft fly in the stratosphere, and their engines release nitrogen oxides (NOX). In the 1960s some scientists believed NOX from SSTs would cause stratospheric ozone depletion. The United States canceled its SST, owing to concern over NOX in the stratosphere and sonic booms over cities. The cancellation made economic sense: SSTs burn huge quantities of fuel per passenger-mile, as the British and French governments discovered when they pushed through with the Concorde SST and fielded a few of these airplanes at heavy subsidy. After the prospect of a world SST fleet passed, the NOX-depletion effect was shown to be less severe than once thought. Guy Brasseur, a scientist at the National Center for Atmospheric Research, demonstrated that NOX compounds in the stratosphere often combine with chlorine, an ozone eater, in a way that makes chlorine less active, probably netting no significant depletion.

If environmental exaggeration is sometimes good for society, the overstated case about SST exhaust turns out to be an instance of this paradox. Recent engineering advances may make possible a fuel-efficient supersonic transport with ticket prices comparable to subsonic jetliners. Boeing, the likely manufacturer, has pledged that it will not build such an SST unless there is a pollution-control breakthrough in the form of a new jet engine type that minimizes NOX emission. In 1994 NASA researchers said that a low-NOX, high-thrust supersonic engine now appears possible. If so the principles of low-NOX design will spread to all jetliner engines, reducing a source of emissions that form smog. Today jet exhaust is among the few aspects of the technological life still essentially unregulated for pollution, except by Sweden, which taxes NOX from jetliners. Expect that the moment low-NOX jet engines are shown to be practical even military aircraft will be required to mount them.

After the SST issue faded some chemists began to wonder if CFCs would have ozone-depleting impact. Once considered environmentally beneficial compounds because they seem to react with nothing, CFCs were by the 1960s being manufactured in increasing quantities for use as refrigerants, as propellants in spray cans, as industrial solvents, and for other purposes.[2] In 1973 F. Sherwood Rowland, of the University of California at Irvine, and Mario Molina, now at the Massachusetts Institute of Technology, challenged the view of inert CFCs by publishing what has since become known as the Rowland-Molina equation. The chemicals may have no interaction with the lower atmosphere, Rowland and Molina supposed. But as CFCs drift on updrafts to the stratosphere where ultraviolet radiation is very strong, the otherwise inert structure breaks down into constituent atoms.

One constituent of CFCs is the element chlorine. Therefore CFCs would result in a buildup of stratospheric chlorine. Stratospheric chlorine eats ozone, acting as a catalyst that converts O_3 back into the regular O_2 form. A catalyst is a chemical that causes reactions but is not itself consumed by the reaction. Rowland and Molina calculated that each atom of chlorine in the stratosphere may catalyze the loss of perhaps 100,000 molecules of ozone. This seemed a formula for the destruction of the ozone layer. During his research Rowland is said to have remarked to his wife, "The work is going fine, except that it looks like the end of the world."

The basic finding of the two researchers, that CFCs wafting skyward result in chlorine in the stratosphere, has been widely embraced by atmospheric scientists. That this effect means "the end of the world" is not widely accepted by scientists. But that notion rapidly became canon among doomsayers.

The first impact of environmental concern about CFCs was a 1978 U.S. ban on the compounds as propellants in aerosol cans. This ban was imposed in part because it could be realized without difficulty; there are alternative propellants. But the fact that a ban is feasible hardly guarantees one will happen, if an interest group is opposed. Outside the U.S. only Canada and the Scandinavian nations—countries with no CFC producers—outlawed spray-can CFCs promptly after the Rowland-Molina studies. Other Western European nations and Japan continued to allow the chemicals in spray cans till the late 1980s, in order to protect domestic industry. The United States, home to the world's largest producer of CFCs, DuPont, acted against their use in spray cans almost the moment an environmental objection was raised, making the U.S. and Australia the sole nations to ban spray-can CFCs rapidly over the objections of domestic interest groups. This is one of the many inconveniently positive details environmentalists glide past when declaiming America as the world's ecological menace. Indeed, willful denial of this advance seems common. For example, in 1993 senior Clinton Administration officials signed their names to a widely circulated children's ecological pamphlet asking kids to urge their parents to "stop buying spray cans that use CFCs," something no American parent has been able to do for more than a decade.

After the spray-can ban the ozone depletion debate ebbed for a few years, because researchers lacked the means to ascertain ozone values in the stratosphere. This changed when Nimbus Seven, a satellite that takes readings of stratospheric composition, was placed into orbit by NASA. Data from Nimbus Seven suggested the ozone layer was declining by a small amount or "thinning"—the verb that was used before it became common to declare ozone "vanishing." Readings from the satellite suggested a composite decline in global ozone of a few percent over populated areas of the Northern Hemisphere during summertime, when sunlight is most intense. Based on these findings a new ozone controversy began to build. The controversy advanced to headline status in 1985 when a team of British researchers led by James Farman announced they had documented an ozone hole over the Antarctic: not a thinning but an outright breach. During the austral spring, the researchers found, ozone values above the South Pole were declining 40 percent or more. Since 1985, austral spring ozone depletion has been as high as 60 percent.

Farman's finding, widely though erroneously described as a "hole in the sky," set off a succession of end-of-the-world proclamations. Coming when production of CFCs had increased from modest amounts in the 1950s to about 1.1 million tons annually in 1985, the hole suggested humankind had loosed a plague. Mostafa Tolba, then head of the United Nations Environmental Programme, declared CFC control the leading ecological issue in the world. Reactions to the news ranged from the sensible, such as a 1985 agreement for an international summit on CFC restriction; to the theatrical, for example James Anderson, an accomplished Harvard researcher and influential ozone pessimist, saying CFCs were "attacking the Earth's immune system"; to showy posing, such as a 1988 decision by the Vermont legislature to ban CFCs in automobile air conditioners sold in that state. Considering the Vermont climate, this was a little like Nebraska banning offshore oil exploration.

Reactions from industry ran a similar gamut, with some corporations taking prompt action to reduce CFC use while others declared there could never, ever be substitutes for the compounds, a view soon voided.

Important though the discovery of an Antarctic ozone hole was, the magnitude of the phenomenon is garbled in public understanding. Even severe ozone loss around the South Pole might mean little to the biosphere. This is so for the obvious reason, that there is only a moderate amount of life in Antarctica to imperil, and for the little-known reason that UV-B radiation falling on the poles is weak to begin with. Further, the south polar region has a unique meteorological structure. Intense high-altitude vortex winds form above Antarctica in the austral winter and spring; the deep cold that becomes trapped in that vortex is now understood to amplify ozone depletion. But the deep-cold vortex winds of the South Pole have no counterpart over the North Pole or anywhere else in the world, suggesting that ozone breaches over populous areas, though not impossible, are less likely than the South Pole finding might imply. Finally the unique austral vortex holds depleted ozone above the South Pole. Though satellite data show that on occasion pieces of the Antarctic ozone hole float above southernmost South America and Australia, so far there is no indication masses of depleted Antarctic ozone can escape from the vortex and reach populous parts of the biosphere.

Public understanding of such reservations would not have altered the fact that restrictions on CFCs were justified. "Had there been no prompt action after 1985," Frederick, of the University of Chicago, says, "the situation might have deteriorated to a severe threat to the ecology." But rational reservations would have prevented a sense of doomsday from enveloping the ozone issue. One premise of ecorealism is that environmental advocates need not employ overstated alarms because the straightforward case for preservation of the Earth is sufficient. Restriction of CFCs could have been achieved on such terms.

Why Kurt Vonnegut Is to Blame for Ozone Pessimism

By dimensions the southern ozone hole was huge, occupying an area of the polar stratosphere about twice the expanse of the contiguous 48 states. Given the immensity of the sky, some researchers found it hard to believe the amount of CFCs emitted by humankind and diluted throughout the global atmosphere could be sufficient to deplete a zone this broad. In 1978 stratospheric levels of CFCs were about two parts per billion. Today the level is 3.4 parts per billion, or 0.00000034 percent.

Even considering the catalytic multiplier, it seemed difficult to fathom that a compound existing in such tiny quantities could stage a takeover of the chemistry of the entire south polar sky.

But the notion that human deviltry could create some kind of "template" effect that would do harm vastly out of proportion to its quantity had been growing for decades in both scientific and intellectual circles. Shortly before the first atomic bomb test in 1945, some physicists wondered if the extreme heat at ground zero might precipitate a doomsday sequence in which the elements of the atmosphere began a process of nuclear fusion. Had this occurred the Earth would have flashed as a small, temporary star, wiping out all life. The test went ahead only when the pro-bomb physicist Edward Teller demonstrated that the temperatures and pressures would fall far short of those required to ignite fusion. Nevertheless the idea of a local human blunder that leads to a global chain reaction took hold in pop culture. A hit 1950s novel, *Voyage to the Bottom of the Sea,* later the basis for a television series, concerned a berserk experiment that started atmospheric fusion amid the Aurora Borealis, and the desperate race to extinguish the fire before Earth inflamed into a star.

When nations began building high-energy accelerators to shatter protons and neutrons in search of quarks, some theorists suggested the collisions might manufacture a novel subatomic template to which all elemental particles would bind in some way, crushing the Earth, and perhaps the entire universe, out of existence. To this day, whenever a new accelerator such as the Superconducting Supercollider is contemplated, a committee of physicists is appointed to analyze whether the machine might generate a subatomic template. This fear surfaced in the Kurt Vonnegut best-seller *Cat's Cradle.* A mad scientist invents "ice nine," a subatomic template that converts room-temperature water to a solid. The world is inadvertently destroyed when a cube of ice nine falls into the sea: All water then hardens in an unstoppable progression, killing everything.

Prepared by such speculations for the notion that even amounts of a synthetic compound tiny in proportion to the vastness of nature might do drastic harm, in 1985 intellectuals and opinion makers embraced the idea that relatively tiny amounts of CFCs could trigger an unstoppable progression that strips the entire ozone layer, leaving the biosphere defenseless. This doomsday concept synched with cultural expectations in another way. Through the 1950s and 1960s society had learned to expect general calamities from radiation released by nuclear tests or power-plant accidents. Except at Chernobyl no general calamities happened. But an expectation of widespread exposure was planted in the social psyche. Now came the first credible scientific suggestion that general radiation outbreaks actually were in the works owing to an industrial horror. Opinion leaders had long expected such news. They seemed to hear it in the form of the South Pole discovery.

Under the Hole

Central details of the Antarctic ozone hole went unmentioned in frightful reports of the 1980s. They were the first of many essential natural considerations excluded from ozone alarmism.

The South Pole ozone hole opens seasonally during the austral spring, which occurs when the Northern Hemisphere knows fall. Through the austral winter, chemical reactions cause both artificial and natural chlorine to accumulate in the Antarctic stratosphere. But depletion does not occur because in the long polar night almost no sunlight is present to energize the ozone-eating reaction. When comes the austral spring, sunlight arrives and the ozone layer above the south polar region diminishes. As that happens the radiation protection for the Antarctic declines. But the sequence occurs when South Pole UV-B radiation is low to begin with. Near the poles the rays of the sun strike the atmosphere at shallow tangent angles; the less direct the sunlight, the less successfully ultraviolet rays penetrate.

For instance in the austral spring of 1990, when the ozone hole was open, Palmer Station, an Antarctic research facility, recorded surface UV-B readings double those of 1988. This finding was depicted by many commentators as intensely frightening. Yet because normal Antarctic UV-B readings are so low during the austral spring to begin with, the doubled radiation worked out to only about the natural increase a person would experience by traveling south from Chicago to New Orleans. Many news organizations reported the stark finding of doubled UV-B readings; none I could find mentioned its minor significance.

A second basic unmentioned detail of the Antarctic ozone hole is that while the breach has opened annually since the late 1970s during the austral spring, it has closed annually during austral summer. In the austral summer, the sun rises toward the perpendicular, solar rays grow intense, and significant levels of UV-B do stream toward the South Pole. But at the same time increased solar energy converts ordinary O_2 oxygen into O_3 ozone: The ozone layer replenishes, blocking most radiation. Since 1985, environmental lobbies have issued dire warnings during the austral spring months, when Antarctic ozone readings are going down. No pronouncements are issued during the following austral summer months, when the ozone layer readings head back up. You've seen the headline "Ozone Hole Opens" in October (austral spring) newspapers. Ever seen the headline "Ozone Hole Closes" in a January (austral summer) edition?

A typical example of this genre: In October 1992 the Reuters news agency moved a breathless story reporting UV-B readings in Puntas Arenas, Chile, the city closest to Antarctica, had "increased 200 percent over August levels." The pre-CFC-fears scientific textbook *The Climate of the Earth* says it is typical in the lower Southern Hemisphere for UV-B to escalate 250 percent between August and October, as the sun rises from its low winter position. Thus the supposedly shocking readings reported by Reuters apparently fell below natural seasonal change for the region.

A rare example of reporting the contrapositive came in a 1993 edition of the *Washington Post*. Don Podesta interviewed Chilean ozone researchers at the Austral Center of Scientific Investigation, outside Puntas Arenas. One, Susana Diaz, told Podesta she sunbathes whenever the chilly local weather permits—because even when the South Pole ozone hole is open, ground-level ultraviolet radiation readings are naturally low. Diaz also told Podesta her center has found no evidence of an oft-repeated ozone scare, that animals in southernmost South America are being blinded by UV-B. In *Earth in the Balance*, Gore writes of "blind rabbits and fish in Patagonia" owing to ozone depletion. Researchers now generally think that reports of animal sight loss around Patagonia should be attributed to an outbreak of conjunctivitis, or pinkeye. Animal blindness caused by the ozone hole is possible but was never likely given that even when the hole is at its worst ultraviolet readings at the South Pole are dramatically lower than at the equator, where animals see just fine. Nevertheless this tale has taken on a life of its own. After Gore's book came out Karen Lohr, ozone director for Greenpeace, declared it "wouldn't be surprising" if polar bears began going blind.

Rapid Action

World response to the 1985 ozone hole discovery came with clipped speed. Just two years after the finding, representatives of the industrial powers met in Montreal to set a CFC reduction plan. Prior to the Montreal meeting Ronald Reagan had shown little inclination to restrict CFCs. At one point his Interior secretary Donald Hodel made the moonstruck declaration that ozone depletion could be dealt with by a "personal protection program" of floppy hats and sunscreen lotion. But as the Montreal summit approached former British prime minister Margaret Thatcher, whose entire nation lies to the north of Nova Scotia and thus would be much more vulnerable than the continental U.S. to any Arctic ozone breach, underwent a change of heart about environmentalism: Having once called ecological activists "the enemy within," loaded words in European politics, eventually she endorsed a reduction in CFC manufacturing. Reagan, whose opinion of Thatcher was high, was impressed and decided to back CFC reductions.

Soon the concept of a 50 percent CFC cut was embodied in the Montreal Protocol, signed by most industrial nations. The Montreal Protocol stipulated that if new findings should make ozone depletion appear more immediate, phaseouts might accelerate. In 1991 the United Nations declared the rate of ozone depletion "much worse than expected." Prominent environmentalists were invited to George Bush's retreat in Kennebunkport, Maine, to brief the president. They brought charts depicting an ozone hole above Maine. After the briefing Bush told EPA administrator William Reilly, "Boy, based on those charts it's a wonder I'm still alive."

Bush extended the CFC phaseout to 100 percent, ordering that the United States cease production by 1996 and also banning halons, a secondary family of chemicals with ozone-depleting properties. DuPont trumped Bush by saying it would voluntarily cease CFC manufacturing in 1994. Most Western European governments also moved up the CFC ban. Shortly before leaving office in 1993 Bush also ruled that methyl bromide, an agricultural fumigant with ozone-depletion properties, be phased out by the year 2000.

The rapidly imposed CFC controls led to equally rapid results. The Ozone Trends Panel of the United Nations once predicted that even under the Montreal Protocol, CFC buildup in the stratosphere would continue well into the twenty-first century, because CFCs have an atmospheric lifetime of perhaps 100 years. Pessimists called this the "CFC legacy"—several generations condemned to live with an ozone danger not of their making. In 1993 researchers led by James Elkins of the National Oceanographic and Atmospheric Administration announced that satellite measurements show the rate of CFC buildup in the stratosphere actually peaked in 1988, the same year industrial emissions peaked. Elkins found that "global atmospheric [CFC] ratios will reach a maximum before the turn of the century and then decline." Improved chemical analysis now shows that CFCs linger in the atmosphere for a shorter time than once expected. Owing to this, in 1994 the U.N.'s ozone panel, a 226-member group of scientists, declared that the stratosphere was likely to return to normal by around the year 2040, half a century sooner than once projected. The 1994 finding, also endorsed by the World Meteorological Organization, suggests that the ozone depletion case is well on the way to being closed.

According to the orthodox view, environmentalism is an arena of futility, despair, and refusal of governments and industry to act. Yet it is difficult to think of any contemporary public policy question where the action has been as swift, decisive and effective as on CFCs. Shouldn't environmentalism celebrate a triumph? Shouldn't Gore claim a well-earned political credit? Instead the news of ozone recovery seems to have left orthodox environmentalists glum, worried about how to keep their deportment correctly inconsolable, and Gore subdued, unable to find a vocabulary in which to discuss the disquieting notion of an environmental success story.

The North Pole Nonhole

What was behind the prize environmental nonevent of 1992, the fleeting Northern Hemisphere ozone hole that seemed to have been declared? Read carefully, what NASA announced was not that it had detected ozone depletion; rather it had detected high quantities of chlorine monoxide, the catalytic chemical associated with depletion. High chlorine levels sometimes cause an ozone breach and sometimes do not: The North Pole hole was only something that *might* happen. This vital distinction was brushed aside. Since practically anything might happen, it is impossible for any environmental alarum that turns on the word *might* to be wrong. But might should not be confused with actuality. After the February 1992 NASA announcement, Al Gore began to say, "It took an ozone hole above Kennebunkport to get the president to take this issue seriously." But there never was any ozone hole above Kennebunkport. The hole occurred only on briefing charts.

Then hoping for a position on the Democratic ticket to oppose Bush in the November 1992 election, Gore had a standard and, so far as it goes, unobjectionable political motive for asserting that the sitting president ignored an ecological peril until it threatened him personally. But coverage of the North Pole ozone scare did not mention Gore's motive: It accepted at face value claims of frightful emergency. Reporters skipped over such details as that the February 1992 ozone panic occurred less than a year after the April 1991 eruption of Mount Pinatubo, which injected millions of tons of sulfurous gases into the stratosphere. Sulfur in the stratosphere can serve as cloud condensation nuclei, aiding the reactions that deplete ozone.

Why didn't the high Northern Hemisphere chlorine levels of 1992 translate to significant ozone loss? One of the objections to the Rowland-Molina equation was resolved in the 1980s when Susan Solomon of the National Oceanographic and Atmospheric Administration and Michael McElroy of Harvard showed that ozone depletion happens mainly on wispy structures called polar stratospheric clouds. Solomon and McElroy found that mother-of-pearl vapors form in winter above the poles, often exhibiting an iridescent seashell glow. Chlorine does more damage if the anti-ozone reaction occurs on these surfaces. If some technical findings since 1973 have tended to muffle the warning sounded by the Rowland-Molina equation, the finding about polar stratospheric clouds amplified it, suggesting an aspect of CFC harm neither Rowland nor Molina had anticipated.

But polar stratospheric clouds only occur in extreme cold. The eventual explanation offered by ozone pessimists for why the Northern Hemisphere ozone hole did not occur is that the North Pole winter of 1992 was not cold enough for sufficient polar stratospheric clouds to form. This explanation sustained the frightening possibility that a boreal ozone hole had only been postponed until the next winter. But the winters of 1993 and 1994 were colder, and no North Pole ozone hole formed in those years either.

Does Depletion Hurt?

The most glaring omission in popular discussion of the ozone controversy is the absence of what to nature would seem the foremost question: Do ozone variations do any harm? The answer is probably not.

In 1989 Stuart Penkett of the University of East Anglia in the United Kingdom wrote in *Nature* that ground-level readings for ultraviolet radiation "are down, not up." Readings for the United States suggest but do not conclusively prove small declines in ground-level UV-B from 1974 to 1984.

Researchers assume the main reason ground radiation readings may not be rising in the populous areas of the globe is that low-level air pollution, mainly smog, blocks any UV-B the depleted ozone layer lets through. This is another zany environmental equilibrium: Just as acid rain may help prevent global warming, smog may forestall the effects of ozone depletion. Studies show that even adjusting for time spent indoors, urbanites have lower rates of skin cancer than people who live in healthy out-of-the-way places, perhaps because when city folk venture outside, local smog protects them against solar radiation.

Obviously zany environmental equilibria are no solution: As urban air pollution is bested, any radiation-shielding effects will fade. But considering that smog went down during the 1980s in the United States, if the ozone layer is doing what doomsday doctrine assumes, ground-level UV-B should have started up. The data available so far suggest that ground-level radiation did not do this. Rather it stayed down.[3]

Information on actual ground-level ultraviolet radiation is incomplete because the best photometers that test for such wavelengths cost $250,000 and are not deployed in great numbers. In 1993 James Regan, a researcher at the Florida Institute of Technology, invented a cheap new test for surface radiation. Regan's $25 instrument, which he calls a DNA dosimeter, takes advantage of the fact that chromosomes resonate when exposed to UV-B. The device is essentially some bacteria DNA in an exposure chamber. Regan has proposed that thousands of DNA dosimeters be set up around the world to create a large data base on actual ground-level ultraviolet levels. Institutional environmentalism is not promoting this idea, though it often advocates expanded systems to monitor ozone in the stratosphere and to gauge atmospheric carbon dioxide. Many environmentalists favor more measurements of the stratosphere and of greenhouse gases because they are confident these will yield gloomy-sounding data. They shy from measurements of ground-level ultraviolet radiation because the outcome of this sort of investigation is likely to be positive.

Several researchers have documented spikes in ground-level ultraviolet radiation in Antarctica, though whether the increases have any damaging biological effect is not yet known. Some researchers find a recent drop in growth of austral plankton, Ray Smith of the University of California at Santa Clara asserting a six to 12 percent decline. Other studies show austral plankton levels essentially unchanged. A team led by Frederick reported in a 1993 issue of the *Journal of Geophysical Research* the first statistically significant ground-level increase in ultraviolet radiation, recorded near Cape Horn, at the southernmost tip of Argentina. The increase was 50 percent over expected seasonal intensity and lasted about a month. Does this sound like a calamitous rise? It works out to the natural UV-B increase a person would experience by moving north, the warm direction of the Southern Hemisphere, from Cape Horn to Buenos Aires.

In 1993 in *Science,* James Kerr and Thomas McElroy of the Canadian Atmospheric Environment Service reported finding the first ground-level increase in UV-B in a populous area, a spike in Toronto. This study was endorsed by many commentators as proving that ozone depletion is a menace. The increase reported was only about five percent annually: worth noting, but about the additional UV-B a person would experience naturally by traveling south from Toronto to Cincinnati. Moreover the Toronto increase manifested only in 1993, about when sulfur from the eruption of Mount Pinatubo is believed to have impacted Canadian latitudes. By 1994, with most Pinatubo effects ended, preliminary findings suggested ground-level ultraviolet radiation in Toronto was returning to about the pre-1993 level.

Does UVB Hurt?

Statistics kept by the American Cancer Society show that skin cancer is today diagnosed at eight times the rate of 30 years ago. Most researchers believe the primary influences on skin cancer rates are the aging of the population and improved detection of disease. The secondary influences are more time outdoors and the fashion trend toward revealing clothing, especially minimalist swimwear for sunbathing.

But some of the increase may stem from ozone depletion. To estimate depletion effects, researchers employ a formula devised by Richard Setlow of the Brookhaven National Laboratory, a dean of environmental cancer research. The formula holds that a one percent loss in the ozone shield equates to about a two percent increase in biological damage at the ground. By combining this assumption with the eightfold postwar elevation in skin cancer and projected CFC trends, the EPA once predicted ozone depletion would lead to three million premature cancer deaths by the year 2075, a shocking figure.

That number continues to be cited by environmentalists as an "official government estimate," though the figure is now widely considered by researchers too high. The estimate does not incorporate the CFC abolition begun in 1987, or the data suggesting actual ground-level UV-B to be lower than depletion theory predicts. And researchers including Setlow are beginning to wonder if human and animal physiologies are less sensitive to UV-B than presumed. In a 1993 study published in the *Proceedings of the National Academy of Sciences,* Setlow supposed that malignant melanoma may be triggered not by UV-B but by UV-A, the ultraviolet wavelength not blocked by sunscreen lotions. Setlow reported controlled studies in which UV-A caused skin cancer in fish. Whether the effect carries over to people is unknown.

If upheld Setlow's finding will upset many premises of the ozone depletion debate. If it's true, as Setlow speculates, that sunblock lotions designed to screen UV-B but ineffective against UV-A give people a false sense of security that causes them to spend more time sunbathing, this may account for much of the trend in malignant melanomas. More generally, researchers increasingly question high estimates of skin cancers caused by ozone fluctuations owing to increasing research that suggests living things have been exposed to such fluctuations many times in the past. For instance, some studies suggest that during past eras of high volcanism, ongoing eruptions placed into the air, for centuries in succession, perhaps 100 times the human output of halons, gases extremely destructive of ozone. This almost certainly would have led to ozone depletion of a more severe character than the worst-case projections for present problems. "If life were not basically resistant to low levels of ultraviolet, it's hard to imagine how the world could have made it through the past three billion years," Frederick, of the University of Chicago, says.

On this score a common pessimistic prediction is that ozone depletion will cause dramatic damage to crops, which sit in the sun the day long. Tests conducted by Alan Teramuna, a botanist at the University of Maryland, show that soybean yields decline 25 percent on exposure to simulated ozone loss somewhat greater than current worst-case projections. Some environmentalists have promoted Teramuna's soybean findings without noting that his tests of other plants show some achieve higher yields under simulated ozone depletion, while the majority register no change. In 1992 researchers at the Brookhaven National Laboratory reported that alfalfa seedlings, said by some environmentalists to be exceptionally vulnerable to UV-B, did well under simulated ozone depletion.

The Holes in Ozone Naysaying

Around 1990 an ozone backlash set in, about the same time as the backlash against acid rain. A staple of right-wing talk shows has since become the notion that volcanos are the true cause of ozone depletion because some eruptions emit more chlorine than the total released each year by industrial CFCs. This statement is pseudo-science. Volcanos do emit large quantities of chlorine but as hydrochloric acid, which is water soluble. Tests show that most hydrochloric acid emitted by volcanos washes out of the air in rainstorms before it can rise to the stratosphere. (One reason CFCs are capable of rising to the stratosphere is that they are not water soluble.) Similarly a huge amount of chlorine evaporates from the oceans, far more than is found in CFCs. This fact is also advanced on the right-wing circuit. But ocean chlorine, also water soluble, washes back into the seas with the first precipitation. Studies show it does not reach the stratosphere in meaningful amounts.

One kind of volcanic event can propel hydrochloric acid to the stratosphere: an explosive eruption. The plumes of explosive volcanos may rise much higher into the sky than the mushroom clouds of nuclear blasts. But only a few eruptions per century achieve such trajectory. El Chichon in 1983 in Mexico was an explosive eruption. In the aftermath stratospheric chlorine increased about ten percent, according to the National Center for Atmospheric Research—enough to amplify ozone depletion temporarily, but not enough to displace CFCs as a concern. Even S. Fred Singer, former chief scientist for the U.S. weather satellite program and the leading academic skeptic regarding ozone alarms, has dismissed the volcano effect as secondary.

The primary exponent of ozone naysaying was Dixie Lee Ray, the zoologist and former governor of Washington State who died in 1994. Ray, who chaired the old Atomic Energy Commission during its days of nuclear boosterism, was bitterly unviro and not always choosy about the intellectual company she kept. For instance Ray's 1992 book *Trashing the Planet* cites as its authority for notions about natural volcano emissions *The Holes in the Ozone Scare,* published by 21st Century Science and Technology. Sound prestigious? This organization was established by Lyndon LaRouche, the political huckster who spent the early 1990s imprisoned for tax evasion. It's a free country; Americans can support LaRouche if they wish. But anyone who bases environmental opinions on LaRouche-affiliated "research" (one recent LaRouche publication was headed "THE GREENHOUSE EFFECT: A WORLD FEDERALIST PLOT") has made a disqualifying error.

The backlash theory about ozone depletion almost comically holds that DuPont orchestrated the controversy in order to replace CFCs, a cheap compound on which patents had expired, with an expensive proprietary successor. Though stockholders may not object to this turn of events, the notion that DuPont has secretly been pulling the strings on Greenpeace and the Sierra Club seems fanciful even by the standards of the LaRouche camp, where this idea originates.

Credibility Depletion

In 1993 there was a genuine, and genuinely strange, turn of events concerning DuPont. The last major American manufacturer of CFCs, the company had announced it would stop producing the compounds in

1994, a year sooner than mandated. In office were Bill Clinton and Al Gore, the latter having described CFC production as "the greatest crisis humanity has ever faced." Yet in a move that escaped public notice, the White House told DuPont to continue making CFCs.

Why? The manufacturing switchover to new air-conditioning and refrigeration units running on the CFC replacement compound, called HFCs, will not be complete until the end of 1995 at the earliest. Had stocks of conventional CFCs been exhausted before then, anyone whose pre-1994 model year automobile air conditioner needed a recharge would have had to rip the unit out and buy a brand new device, at $1,000 or more, as HFCs will not work in CFC-based equipment without retrofit kits that are not yet on the market. The White House feared a political rebellion over such a turn of events.

DuPont was stunned at the request for more CFCs. "For years we had been told how evil CFCs are, and now here was Al Gore asking us to continue manufacturing them," said a senior company officer. The White House had arranged that if DuPont refused, its CFC manufacturing allowances would be transferred to the conglomerate Allied Signal, which if nothing else deflates the conspiracy theory that there is no profit left in standard CFCs.

Edgar Bronfman, Sr., a member of the DuPont board, called Gore. Bronfman is an important donor to Democratic Party causes, someone the Clinton White House would be expected to treat deferentially. The conversation went poorly. *The company made a major commitment to abolishing CFCs,* Bronfman is said by informed sources to have told Gore. *Why are we suddenly supposed to keep going?* "It's necessary," is the only answer Gore is said to have given. *So is this stuff really dangerous or not?* Bronfman pressed. "All I can say is that it's necessary," Gore replied. The call ended with Gore brusquely declaring he didn't want to talk about it any longer.

If it's come to the point at which Al Gore is defending CFC manufacturing then a moment of logical inversion has been reached. Though the case for strict regulation of CFCs was sound—even if ozone depletion is only a small risk, why take chances with radiation?—increasingly it appears that the magnitude of the alarm regarding these chemicals was not justified. Someday this may cause environmentalism to suffer credibility depletion.

And consider that halons, banned at the insistence of environmental lobbyists though they were never produced in large quantities, are the best known fire-fighting chemicals. Halons are used in the internal fire-suppressing systems of jetliner engines, and soon they must be replaced for this purpose by inferior compounds. If people die in an airliner crash caused by an engine fire that could have been suppressed by halons, the environmental movement will find there is hell to pay.

Radon

The boy and his dog, sitting in an archetypical small-town boy's bedroom, wear gas masks. "Every day a thing called radon gets into people's homes," reads the script for the public-service television commercial, these words projected onto the screen for viewers in a child's hand. "When people keep breathing it, they can get lung cancer and die." The ad ends with an appeal for parents to call 1-800-SOS-RADON before it's too late. Other advertisements in the series, run on television from 1989 to 1991 by the Advertising Council in conjunction with the EPA, employed death images such as children at play turned by special effects into skeletons to pronounce that "radon is a silent killer" whose presence "is like exposing your family to hundreds of chest X-rays a year." The ads suggested any exposure to radon, however tiny, will kill. Newspaper and magazine advertisements run in the series implied there are instances in which 35 out of 100 people in small communities "die from radon."

Until the 1980s most Americans had never heard of radon, a natural product of the decay of uranium and other ores. Then many environmentalists began to speak of the gas, which seeps into some buildings from bedrock, as suddenly present at emergency levels. Beginning in the 1980s the EPA urged Americans to test their homes for radon, asking Congress for authority to compel some home testing. Radon politics commenced in the 1980s as well, when high levels of the gas were found in the home of a man named Stanley Watras, in Boyertown, Pennsylvania. Following this discovery Rep. Henry Waxman of California called radon a "frightening problem." Radon testing programs began throughout the Northeast, especially in Pennsylvania and New Jersey, where a few homes with high levels were found, and also in Colorado, Iowa, and North Dakota, states whose geology is likely to spawn radon. Something resembling radon riots broke out in the town of Montclair, New Jersey, when regulators evacuated 12 homes, dug up 50,000 barrels of soil, and, unable to attain legal permission to ship the soil anywhere, simply left the barrels stacked on the lawns of the empty houses, ringed by signs that proclaimed WARNING: RADIOACTIVE CONTAMINATION.

The perception that radon had suddenly appeared is an odd one, considering that the gas has likely been present in the biosphere since the beginning of life. The ancient planetary forge left within Earth vast quantities of radioactive materials, trillions of tons of which survive today as uranium and as other natural materials mildly radioactive. These materials have been decaying since the dawn of time, releasing "daughter" products like radon. All species alive today were exposed to radon during their evolution. Stretching back to the mists of the Olduvai Gorge, ancestors of women and men inhaled the gas.

Yet when radon became a fashionable threat in the 1980s, the impression given was that the substance represented an unfolding, unprecedented peril. Social psychology similar to that which inspired ozone panic was at play. Doomsaying about nuclear power and nuclear wastes had acclimated the public to expect that radiation would become a general menace. When that did not happen because of nuclear power, opinion makers remained primed for an assertion that a radiation nightmare was in progress. The disaster might be ultraviolet radiation from a depleted ozone layer; it might be a "silent killer" sneaking into suburban homes.

Of course the fact that an environmental influence has existed naturally for ages hardly means it is harmless. Ancestral genus *Homo* was exposed to a variety of diseases that are just as horrible today as whenever they entered the biosphere. But the knowledge that an environmental problem is long-lived puts the problem into the perspective of nature—the perspective so achingly absent for contemporary debate.

What might be the perspective of nature regarding radon? First, because radon has been present for eons, living things must possess at least some resistance. Second, because living things have been exposed to radon for eons and not succumbed, the likelihood is that its radioactivity is mild. The hazardous component of radon is the alpha particle, the weakest form of radioactivity. Alpha particles cannot penetrate a sheet of paper, or the epidermal layer of skin. Radon harms only when breathed, because the air-exchange cells on the surface of the lungs are delicate and less biologically shielded than skin cells. Third, nature would note that since Earth's natural radioactivity has been decaying since the planet coalesced, it is likely that the potency of radon is in long-term decline. If genus *Homo* is descended from creatures that survived higher levels of radon, radon may well remain a problem but not the looming assault depicted in alarmist commentary. ("Radiation found in suburban basement. Is your home next? Details at 11!")

In his fine book *Elements of Risk: The Politics of Radon*, Leonard Cole, an instructor at Rutgers University, recounts what happened after the 12 homes in Montclair were evacuated. Some $8 million in state funds was expended to dig up the soils and place them in barrels on the lawns of the homes. Over a period of years, officials of the New Jersey Department of Environmental Protection attempted to ship the barrels to a closed state armory; to various landfills; to a federal reservation in Nevada; to a wildlife preserve in the Jersey Pinelands (that's right, to a wildlife preserve); and to an abandoned quarry. Each plan was blocked by public outcry. Children marched in gas masks, rallies were held. Eventually, Cole writes, "in a bizarre arrangement, the state contracted with a company for $4 million to ship the soil to [the federal nuclear weapons laboratory at] Oak Ridge, Tennessee. There it would be mixed with highly radioactive materials. The mix could then be sent to a federally approved depository in Richland, Washington, that accepts only high-level wastes." Absurdly enough, "deadly" soils from Montclair had to be mixed with genuinely dangerous materials because alone the soils were not sufficiently radioactive to qualify as atomic under federal regulations.

Of course it is to be expected that the towns asked to take the Montclair soils resisted. By the ecorealist principle that it is rational to act irrationally when misinformed about environmental risks, people in the target towns knew only that somebody else wanted to get rid of something and that everyone from national environmentalists to local newscasters was proclaiming the soils a source of instant death. How could it be that it would be hideously dangerous to put the soils at the bottom of an abandoned quarry yet perfectly safe to leave them sitting unshielded on a suburban lawn in Montclair? People cannot think in such logical terms when they hear phrases like "deadly radioactivity."

In 1986 the EPA estimated that radon may cause 30,000 premature cancer deaths per year in the United States, an estimate since lowered to 13,600. Either figure would make radon the second-leading cause of lung cancer after cigarette smoking. Both estimates are based mainly on studies of Colorado uranium miners from the 1950s and 1960s.

Use of the uranium mine data is a source of unease in scientific circles. Uranium mines of the 1950s had awful ventilation systems. In them workers inhaled radon at hundreds of times higher concentrations than in the most-exposed homes. In making general public health projections from data on miners, the EPA assumes that the health effects of very high doses of radon can be extrapolated downward to predict the effects of low doses. Some researchers, such as Gary Lyman of the University of South Florida, believe this is a reasonable practice. Many others, such as the 1993 EPA science adviser, William Raub, who has protested his agency's radon determinations, believe it is not.

Health records of 1950s uranium miners do not say which ones were smokers, so it is impossible to know how much of the lung cancers they suffered were caused by cigarettes or by radon acting on lung tissues weakened by cigarettes. The physicist Philip Abelson, an astringent radon scare skeptic, worked during the 1950s to expose the unhealthy conditions of uranium miners. He has written that most miners he saw when visiting uranium mines were smokers. Yet EPA computer models essentially assume away the influence of cigarette smoking on uranium miners of the 1950s. This, Abelson says, drastically skews estimates such as 13,600 annual premature deaths.

Another important radon skeptic is Nobel Prize winner Rosalyn Yalow. Yalow has said her studies detect "no reproducible harmful effects associated with increases in background radiation up to six times the usual levels" of radon in homes. Yalow notes that typical home radon levels in Colorado are quadruple those of California, yet lung cancer is more common in California than Colorado. The same inverse relationship occurs in several other states, with lung cancer less prevalent in high-radon locations than low-radon sites. Yalow believes different levels of cigarette smoking explain this seemingly crazy statistic.[4]

In 1988 Congress passed a bill called the Indoor Radiation Abatement Act, which encourages testing of homes for radon. Currently the EPA classifies an indoor radon level of below four picocuries per liter of air (a picocurie is a trillionth of a curie) as safe. Above that, measures such as basement ventilation systems are recommended. Four picocuries per liter of radon is by some estimates only slightly more than the natural radioactivity found in a home made of brick.

Many environmentalists have urged that the EPA level be lowered to one picocurie, or even to zero. Depending on who you believe, the cost for such protection could range from cheap to outrageous. In 1993, the EPA published a recommendation that all homes be tested for radon when sold; the agency estimates such tests would cost about $100 million annually. Estimates from the building industry ran to $2 billion annually. The EPA further advised that new homes include antiradon ventilators for about $1,000 each; adding such systems to existing homes would cost about $3,000 each. Industry estimates run to about five times that level.

At the low end of these estimates, foundation ventilation systems sound like sensible ideas for building design. Don't be surprised if they are standard concepts by the end of the century, and that stale indoor air becomes both more safe and more pleasant to breathe as a result. In 1994 the National Research Council issued a vaguely worded report suggesting radon in building air might eventually be proven to cause up to about four percent of lung cancers, a significant figure given the prevalence of this disease. If the NRC position is confirmed when the organization releases its final report in 1996, legislation on vent systems would be likely.

Since the height of the radon scare the EPA has also been under a congressional mandate to regulate at an extremely low level the amount of radon in drinking water. No researcher has proposed a mechanism by which low levels of radon might do harm in water: Even the EPA's computer models estimate that radon in water causes at most 192 premature cancer deaths per year in the United States. But amendments to the Safe Drinking Water Act enacted in 1986 essentially require the EPA to regulate cancer risks in drinking water to zero. In 1993 the EPA's Science Advisory Board said the agency's proposed radon water levels were needlessly low, noting, "There is no direct epidemiological or laboratory animal evidence of cancer being caused by ingestion of radon in drinking water." At this writing implementation of the proposed very low standard for radon had been delayed in the Senate by Senator Bob Kerrey of Nebraska, a leading liberal, who declared that he thought the rule would cost water utilities about a quarter of a billion dollars per year "to accomplish practically nothing."

Also in 1993 the EPA announced an estimate that 20 percent of U.S. public schools have interior radon above the four picocurie level. The agency then proposed that all schools be tested for radon and that ventilation systems be installed in those schools failing the test. This announcement moved Rep. Waxman of California to declare that from a radiation standpoint, "it may be more dangerous to attend school than to work in a nuclear power plant." Waxman may be correct, though his statement says more about the safety of nuclear power plants than about radon gas.

Radon risks are greatly overstated in the public mind. But some 390,000 people per year die of lung cancer in the United States. If even a small percentage of these fatalities trace to radon, investments such as foundation ventilation systems, which protect entire buildings, easily would pass the test of environmental cost-effectiveness. Thus radon is another promising issue for ecorealism: a category in which suspicious doomsday statements abound, and yet environmental risk may be real and subject to correction quickly at a reasonable cost.

30 ✍

SPECIES ✍

ONE DAY IN 1992, IN A WILDLIFE PRESERVE ON SAINT LOUIS
Bay near the town of DeLisle, a huge Chinook helicopter flown by the
Mississippi National Guard lowered toward the ground six tall poles
topped with pads. The Chinook then lumbered away, heat streaming
from its exhausts, the thud-thud-thud of rotors seeming to make the air
itself shake. After the machine was gone volunteers released some young
southern bald eagles, in hopes the birds would settle on the pads.

Once bald eagle were common in the American South. Then DDT
began to accumulate in the shells of eagle eggs; loggers seeking premium
wood began to cut the tall cypress trees such birds seek for nesting. The
southern bald was widely expected to fall extinct. After DDT was
banned and eagles granted protected status under a federal law that preceded the Endangered Species Act, most eagle types rebounded. But the
southern bald recovered slowly.

For several years before 1992, southern balds were bred in captivity
near DeLisle under a project paid for by DuPont, which like many big
companies now supports ecological good works hoping for a nice-guy
image. Volunteers tending the eaglets wore hoods so that the birds
would not imprint to human faces. Handlers were forbidden to give the
eaglets names, to fuss over them, or act in any way that might attune the
birds to other-than-wild behavior. The poles were built to simulate the
high nests southern bald eagles like, as cypress are being replanted but
have not yet grown to mature height. In all several million dollars and
thousands of person-hours were expended aiding a living thing in its

quest to evade the fate that nature seems to have ordained for every species, including perhaps ours: extinction.

To approach the topics of species preservation and its sibling issue, biodiversity, it is essential first to bear in mind this sobering fact: Since nature began, 99 percent of all species called forth into being have eventually been rendered extinct. This estimate is almost universally accepted by researchers. Its starkness was anticipated by Charles Darwin, who wrote in *Origin of Species,* "Of the species living now, very few will transmit progeny to a far distant futurity." Creatures great and small, fantastic and mundane, have walked or flown or crawled or splashed upon the Earth for immense amounts of time only to vanish. As every individual born into what Augustine called "the light of the world" must throughout life draw closer to the dimming of that light in death, it seems every species exists with the surety that its being someday will be surrendered. Extinction is nature's norm.

This is the first of the three reasons species loss is a priority concern of ecorealism. People must assume that other things being equal, nature eventually will extinguish the human line. Therefore humankind has an intense self-interest in learning to prevent extinctions: We may someday need such knowledge to save ourselves. If other species benefit from humankind's search for antidotes to extinction, so much the better. But that will be a bonus, not the motive.

The second reason species loss must be a priority is its finality. Ecorealism holds that every offense women and men commit against the ecology is reversible, save one: extinction. Looking back on us, future generations will excuse the air and water we have fouled; such acts will be excused because they will be reversed. Future generations may judge us harshly, however, for species loss, because this malfeasance will harm every generation that follows, and based on present knowledge there may never be anything people can do to set extinctions to rights.

The third reason is that extinctions will be best avoided by general preservation of habitats, something people ought to be doing anyway. The current legal theory in the United States, of targeting individual species for specialized protection, has worked in many cases, such as the spectacular recoveries of the bald eagle, gray wolf, peregrine falcon, and other creatures. But this targeting approach must seem curious indeed to nature. An important measure of the living sphere is how little it needs the blue whale, the red squirrel, the least Bell's vireo, or any particular creature. Losses of individual species appear to mean nothing to nature—or else how could nature carry on, considering that it discards individual species continuously? What is of import to nature is the overall vitality of habitats and ecospheres, including the degree of diversity, which insulates the living world against the inevitability of ecological change. Only five percent of the world currently is in preservation status, according to the United Nations, though 11 percent of the United States is. More habitats should be exempted from development, at least against the day when it becomes possible for humankind to expand in concert with other species, rather than at their expense. As the Endangered Species Act is revised in years to come, it ought to forsake species-by-species fixations for general habitat preservation.

Missing from this list of reasons to favor species preservation is the reason most often cited by orthodox environmentalists: the notion that species have a right to exist. No one who studies natural history with an open mind can find in it any indication that nature has ever conferred on any species a right to exist. There are only moments on the Earth, given and taken away. Genus *Homo* should stop shortening the moments of other creatures and learn, instead, to prolong them. But we should not do so because other creatures have an expectation of such treatment. We should do so because it seems like a good idea to us.

A Salvation Sampler

Let's describe some efforts already underway in the 1990s, in the early years of the human emergence from ecological ignorance, to preserve species. Not all are working. No doubt some will eventually be seen as products of primitive expedience. But the efforts show that contrary to the conventional wisdom that species are being assailed and abandoned by heartless humans, women and men are already striving on multiple fronts to save other creatures.

• At least $25 million has been spent since 1983 to avert the extinction of the California condor. Hatchlings bred in captivity have been monitored around the clock, fed by hand puppets that suggest a mother bird, and allowed to find carcasses laid out for them, simulating wild feeding. In 1983 just 22 California condors were known to exist. Today about 70 live, with several having been reintroduced into the wild in 1992 at the Los Padres National Forest. Before the release a group of Chumash Indians, whose religion holds that condors bear souls to heaven, chanted in the predawn darkness.

Environmental groups fought with a livid fury against the condor breeding program. In 1983 my own publication, *The Atlantic Monthly*, ran an impassioned cover story by the environmentalist Kenneth Brower, warning the remaining California condors would be rendered extinct by the attempt at captive breeding—that the wings of the bird would "never again set high above the Earth." Instead the program worked. Maybe there was a better way. But what was done, worked.

• In the salmon run of 1991 just three male and one female sockeye made it back to Redfish Lake, Idaho, a spawning grounds at the source of the Snake River. Water subtracted from the Snake and Columbia rivers for hydropower and commerce, along with the late-1980s Pacific Coast drought, made it difficult for Pacific salmon to navigate their birth rivers. This appeared to spell the end for the Snake River sockeye, which spawn only in Redfish Lake. But game officials caught the four survivors and artificially spawned 1,000 eggs. Today, swimming in tanks, are 1,000 juvenile Redfish sockeye. Sockeye do not head downriver toward the sea until their fourth year. By 1995, when this last hope for the sub-species must depart from Redfish Lake, a water-volume agreement for the Snake River should be completed, rearranging the flow of the river with salmon in mind. Then the juvenile fish will be released.

• U.S.–registered shrimping boats now have appurtenances called turtles exclusion devices to reduce deaths of sea turtles. These devices came too late for the Kemp's ridley sea turtle, which once lined Mexican beaches by the thousands but by 1985 had been reduced to 200 known nesting pairs. The federal government has spent $4 million to airlift eggs of the Kemp's ridley to a laboratory in Galveston, Texas, where hatch-lings are "head-started" through the juvenile months when most young turtles die of natural causes, then returned to the sea. Initially ineffective, the program has begun to work: Some 1,568 ridley turtle nests were counted on Gulf Coast beaches in 1994. And three of the "head-started" turtles have been found, healthy, on a beach in Morocco. Greenpeace, the World Wildlife Fund, and other environmental groups oppose the head-starting program, in part because it may somehow be inspiring the turtle to shift its habitat to Morocco. But nature would not care a whit about that, only that the turtle lives.

• The Florida panther has declined to perhaps 50 creatures. Wardens from the Florida Game Commission now track the remaining panthers. When one is seen to have an injury it is flown to an animal hospital for treatment, then returned to the wild. When one is observed newly dead of natural causes the body is taken to determine if viable sperm or egg can be removed.

• The charmingly clumsy manatee, a 3,500-pound sea mammal, is believed endangered in Florida and Georgia coastal waters. (Researchers are not certain manatees are endangered because no reliable population count exists.) Manatees have such poor sight and hearing they have been struck and killed by power boats by the hundreds in the past two decades. Edmund Gerstein of Florida Atlantic University has been testing manatee audio responses to determine if a frequency exists that frightens the mammal; boats would then be equipped with generators that broadcast the sound around their hulls. Florida has established low speed limits for boats in coastal waters, so manatees have some chance to evade collisions. The speed limits are extremely unpopular with boaters, an influential Florida interest group. They are in force anyway.

• The National Zoo, in Washington, D.C., has experimented with employing female Siberian tigers, which reproduce readily in captivity, as surrogate mothers (via in vitro fertilization) for the endangered Sumatran tiger, which does not reproduce naturally outside the wild.

• In 1941, only 21 wild whooping cranes were known to exist; by 1993, there were 300. Approximately 150 wild whoopers have resumed the species' annual journey from Wood Buffalo National Park in Alberta to the Arkansas National Wildlife Refugee in Texas. This crane can fly at 6,000 feet, meaning it sometimes travels above the cloud line, perceiving the world as a silent ocean of white.

• A popular fishing beach on Martha's Vineyard, Massachusetts, has since 1990 been closed during the nesting season of the piping plover, an endangered bird. Federal and state game officials and a private foundation that owns the beach monitor the status of each piping plover nest. A hot-line number provides updates on whether the beach can be used. As of 1994, this was being done to protect just five nesting pairs.

• The Olympic milk vetch, an endangered plant that lives on mountainsides in Olympic National Park in Washington, is imperiled by the appetites of mountain goats. Park rangers have tried to trap the goats and move them to other areas, sometimes struggling with the 250-pound creatures on treacherous ledges. Around 1990 the goats began moving to the most inaccessible terrain in the park, perceiving that genus Homo had become their predator. The goats' retreat may save the milk vetch.

• Numerous efforts are underway to preserve plants by establishing gene banks: Endangered plants can be revived from cuttings in a way that endangered animals cannot. The International Potato Center in Lima, Peru, keeps genetic samples of wild potato strains hunted down by a man named Carlos Ochoa, the Johnny Appleseed of potatoes. There are believed to be 4,000 species of potato; the United States grows just eight as commercial crops. Ochoa has been scouring the Peruvian highlands for such rare species as the "hairy" potato, whose surface naturally resists the potato aphid. Adding hairy potato genes to commercial crops may someday reduce the need for insecticides.

• The Vavilov Institute in Saint Petersburg, a plant-germ repository where several researchers starved to death during the World War II siege of that city rather than eat seeds essential to the future diversity of Russian agriculture, today holds in freezers some 334,000 "accessions," or samples of plant protoplasm. Such samples are kept so that new genetic properties can be spliced into crops when they are attacked by new diseases or pests, as, for example, in 1993 a gene from an Ethiopian barley plant was added to the U.S. barley crop to create resistance to the yellow dwarf virus. Near Spitsbergen, Norway, the Svalbard International Seedbank now stores plant accessions in an old coal mine shaft beneath the permafrost. In Fort Collins, Colorado, the U.S. National Plant Germplasm System holds about 400,000 accessions, cooled by liquid nitrogen.

• Researchers are attempting to reintroduce endangered plants into their native habitats, for example returning the prairie white-fringed orchid to exurban areas of Chicago. The Mississippi Botanical Garden has reintroduced the Texas snowball, once thought extinct, by starting patches in secret locations where they will not attract the curiosity seekers of the horticultural world. When an aggressive weed called cheat grass killed most of the wild Malhuer lettuce of eastern Oregon, the Berry Botanical Garden rescued some seeds and now is attempting to reintroduce the plant where cheat grass does not grow.

• A Johns Hopkins University ecologist named William Sladen and a Canadian pilot named William Lishman have been flying ultralight aircraft ahead of geese chevrons to see if the birds will follow and can thus can be taught new migratory pathways when human actions disrupt customary destinations.

• In 1993 the first of an expected 1,800 bison were released to live wild in the Tallgrass Prairie Preserve in Oklahoma, a Nature Conservancy project that is the largest prairie ecosystem restored to the condition that existed before the white man. An estimated 60 million bison once roamed the American heartland. In the mere three decades between 1870 and 1900, hunting reduced the number to a few hundred. Today the U.S. bison population has returned to an estimated 150,000, with most living on ranches. Tallgrass is the first place where bison will once again live as in pre-Columbian days.

274 Extinctions per Day, or Maybe One a Year

Roughly since the 1970s ecologists have claimed a rising degree of species loss caused by human activity. And in this same period researchers have supposed the natural world to contain far more species than once believed. These two trains of thought are barreling toward each other on the same track.

On the first point Thomas Lovejoy, an accomplished biodiversity advocate at the Smithsonian Institution, has called human-caused species loss "a potential biological transformation unequaled since perhaps the disappearance of the dinosaur." Russell Train, head of the World Wildlife Federation, has declared that owing to species loss, "the future of the world could be altered drastically." And the biologist Edward Wilson says human-caused species loss may eventually equal the damage that occurred at the Cretaceous-Tertiary boundary 65 million years ago, when the dinosaurs vanished.

On the second point, because life is diverse and ever-changing ("The average person carries several new species of bacteria on his shoes," Wilson says), there is no clear estimate of how many species may exist. Armies of researchers would be required to inventory every species in a world where nature is vast, evolution is ongoing, and most living things are tiny. As Gordon Orians, an ecologist at the University of Washington, says, "Species estimates are squirrely numbers. If you went to the Amazon rainforest and fogged [sprayed with poison] a canopy tree at random, two-thirds of the stuff that fell on your head would be unknown species." The same can be said for much of the world's surface, while most of the oceans are a biodiversity unknown.

In 1758 Carolus Linnaeus, a Swede considered the progenitor of taxonomy, estimated global species to number 9,000. Today, about 1.4 million species have been cataloged. In 1987 Peter Raven, director of the Missouri Botanical Garden, estimated total species at 2.2 million. That same year Paul Ehrlich of Stanford University estimated a total of four million species. By 1994, Ehrlich was positing 100 million total species. Wilson was projecting total species at anywhere from ten million to 100 million species. As the federal Office of Technology Assessment has noted drily, differences of this magnitude "call into question the credibility of all such estimates."

The notion of a dreadful people-caused species loss is warmly endorsed by environmental orthodoxy. The notion that huge numbers of species are yet to be found is also endorsed, since it can be read as diminishing the significance of genus *Homo*. Yet taken at face the new estimates of very high total numbers of species can also imply that current losses are not so bad. Extinction of a few hundred species from a base of one million might be an ominous portent. The same loss from a base of 100 million species might suggest no more than a natural fluctuation.

To correct for this, as estimates of total species have increased, the loss estimates endorsed by environmental doctrine have increased as well. In 1979 Norman Myers, a British doomsayer and author of *The Sinking Ark,* an influential book about species loss, estimated that 100 species per year are falling extinct owing to human action. Today Myers says the number is "at least 30,000" extinctions per year, 300 times his earlier estimate. Myers's current figure equates to an incredible 82 extinctions per day. Wilson now projects a human-caused loss of 50,000 species per year, or 137 daily. *Global 2000,* a deep-doom document commissioned by President Jimmy Carter, forecast that as many as two million species might fall extinct between its 1980 publication and the year 2000. That works out to a mind-blowing 274 extinctions per day.

To what should these numbers be compared? Biologists generally estimate the "baseline" rate of extinctions from ongoing natural processes at around one per year. That's a squirrely number too; nobody really knows. To highlight human perfidy, many environmentalists set the baseline rate far lower. The World Wildlife Fund, for instance, declares that "in the age before man, the earth lost one species every thousand years." A very low natural rate must be assumed to support the notion of the Earth minus humanity as an Eden.

If species extinctions truly have zoomed from a natural baseline of one per year to 274 per day, the impact on nature would be astonishing. Such forecasts need only be a little right—far less than half right—to represent ecological loss of high order. The estimates, however, are plagued by a pronounced Fly Corpse Factor. If species are dropping like flies, the corpses should be piling up by now. Instead species corpses turn out to be exceedingly difficult to locate.

Of the first group of species listed in 1973 under the Endangered Species Act, today 44 are stable or improving, 20 are in decline, and only seven, including the ivory-billed woodpecker and dusky seaside sparrow, are gone. This adds up to seven species lost over 20 years *from the very group considered most sharply imperiled.* Under Wilson's loss estimate of 137 species per day, about 1.1 million extinctions should have occurred globally since 1973. As America contains six percent of the world's land mass, a rough proration would assign six percent of that loss, or 66,000 extinctions, to the United States. Yet in the period only seven actual U.S. extinctions have been logged. There is a rather amazing gap between a projected 66,000 and a confirmed seven. And the United States is the most carefully studied biosphere in the world, making U.S. extinctions likely to be detected.

If plants and insects are included in the calculation, 34 organisms fell extinct in the United States during the 1980s, according to a study by the

Department of the Interior. This is clearly worrisome, but at an average of 3.4 extinctions per year, nothing like the rate of loss claimed by pessimists. In 1993 two authorities on biodiversity, Michael Bean and David Wilcove of the Environmental Defense Fund, tallied 27 extinctions of North American fish species and subspecies since the year 1950. The Bean-Wilcove estimate is double the rate for the first half of the century, again a clear danger sign. But it's also a fish loss of about one per year, a figure impossibly low if pessimists such as Myers[1] are right about their projections of annual losses by the many thousands.

Consider the Northwest ancient forest zone that stretches along the Pacific Ocean coast from Vancouver nearly to San Francisco. Environmental doctrine, as reflected in statements pertaining to the spotted owl lawsuits, holds that these forests have in the last three decades been subjected to some of the worst ecological stress in Earth history. Logging and industrial activity are common in the Northwest; cities are expanding in an economic boom; satellite imagery shows that Washington and Oregon forests have become fragmented, divided into checkerboards by roads and cutover zones. Present in the Pacific Coast timber belt are nearly all the factors that Myers, Wilson, and others assert are associated with emergency levels of species extinction.

Yet Wilcove says, "There are no known cases of extinction of vertebrates in the Pacific Northwest forests during the postwar era." The Nature Conservancy reports no known extinctions of vascular (loosely, green-stemmed) plants in Northwest forests during the period. This lack of known extinctions in the Northwest woodlands is especially significant because these woods are among the best-studied global ecologies. Since concern over the spotted owl arose in the mid-1970s, millions of dollars have been invested in combing the Northwest forests for species data, with hundreds of professional and avocational ecologists engaging in that task. The searchers have uncovered persuasive reasons for preservation of ancient forests but not a single actual extinction, which seems revealing given that every graduate student involved in Northwest forest field study is acutely aware that documenting a species loss would make his or her academic career.

Taking into account Wilson's estimate of 137 species extinctions per day and the land area of the Northwest forest belt, I roughly calculate that in the region in question 75,000 species should have fallen extinct during the postwar era. Yet no extinctions have been observed. Certainly some uncataloged species might have slipped to extinction unnoted. But 75,000 overlooked extinctions in an intensely studied region? Not bloody likely.

Projected total species losses entail the entire globe, most of which is unstudied. Species counts that do exist for tropical areas, though indicating reason for concern, do not suggest a biological Armageddon. For instance Peter Raven has studied Barro Colorado Island, a preserve created near Panama in 1923. At its founding the preserve had 208 known bird species; now 45 of them seem extinct. Barro Colorado thus shows a 22 percent species loss over half a century, clearly very alarming. Doomsayers frequently refer to the Barro Colorado figures as typical. But Barro Colorado is not typical. It is the worst empirical (actual, not computer-projected) species-loss example for the twentieth-century globe. By contrast Puerto Rico was almost entirely deforested around the turn of the century, yet no species wipeout occurred. Seven of 60 bird species known in Puerto Rico in 1900 are now extinct, or 12 percent. The island has since reforested and no unusual extinction patterns have been found by recent studies.

One reason species loss numbers are squirrely is that they are based on projections, not actual observations. This is unavoidable; since the true number of species is not known, any forecasts must include simulations. But torture statistics and they will confess to anything. What assumptions lie behind the computerized doomsday projections?

Wilson bases his estimates on something called the island theory of biogeography, which holds that a 90 percent reduction in the area of an ecosystem causes the extinction of 50 percent of the species within it. Wilson then plugs into his computer assumed rates of acreage loss in places like tropical rainforests, and an assumption that most continental land areas behave approximately like islands. Using such assumptions Wilson arrives at his projected 50,000 extinctions per year.

There are several objections to this form of approximation. One is that Wilson's ideas are too influenced by species patterns in rainforests. Rainforests number among the places where species are most dense and thus where the greatest losses from reduction of acreage may occur. Rainforests also may have baseline rates of extinction that are high on a natural basis. David Jablonski, a researcher at the University of Chicago, has proposed that "fossil evidence suggests that tropical biospheres are the most vulnerable to extinctions" from natural forces. Further, as chapter 31 will detail, actual rates of rainforest acreage loss may be smaller than estimated. Shrinking the circle of destruction assumed by Wilson's computer would rapidly reduce the projected rate of species loss. These factors suggest Wilson takes as his starting point the part of the ecosphere that already exhibits the highest rates of extinction then multiplies that high rate by high assumptions about other factors. In statistics the multiplication of two upper-bound estimates can generate an effect similar to a geometric progression, in which numbers take off beyond anything either set of estimates would seem to justify.

Next, as has been pointed out by Julian Simon of the University of Maryland and the late Aaron Wildavsky of the University of California at Berkeley, the island theory of biogeography assumes that habitat loss happens in confined areas from which nonavian species cannot retreat and regroup. But in fact not all habitat loss happens under such circumstances. Most happens where species, pressured in one place, may move to another.

Through the early 1990s Simon and Wildavsky regularly infuriated environmental orthodoxy by producing studies suggesting species loss estimates are overblown. Many enviros maintain that neither has any business commenting on the issue since Simon's academic specialty is economics and Wildavsky was a political scientist. Yet Paul Ehrlich, stipulated by greens as a population expert, has no advanced training in sociology or demographics. His academic specialty is entomology. So what? Ehrlich is qualified to offer opinions about population, Simon and Wildavsky to offer opinions about species.

A rule of argument is that when opponents attack someone's qualifications or motives rather than rebutting the substance of arguments, this happens because they do not know how to rebut the substance. Increasingly in the 1990s, doctrinaire environmentalists have been impugning the qualifications or integrity of those who disagree with them. In 1993 environmental lobbyists mounted personal attacks against Keith Schneider, chief *New York Times* environmental correspondent, when he wrote a series questioning the rationality of several ecological initiatives. The newspaper received many letters from prominent greens accusing Schneider of all manner of turpitude. It's common to encounter the ad hominem response from the gun nuts—but from environmentalists, society's bright lights?[2] Ehrlich has written that Julian Simon's ideas should not be acknowledged because "they are in the same category with someone who says that Jack Frost is the source of ice crystals on windows." This is harsh stuff, considering that Simon once went head-to-head with Ehrlich in a public wager on trends in the mineral resource base (Ehrlich predicting certain minerals were becoming exhausted, Simon that they were becoming more plentiful) and Simon won. In a similar vein, Vice President Al Gore has said that optimistic environmental findings, even from credentialed academic researchers, should merit little attention because they "undermine[s] the effort to build a solid base of support for the difficult actions we must soon take."

Skeptical debate is supposed to be a strength of liberalism. Thus it is eerie to hear environmental leaders assert that views with which they disagree ought not to be heard. The desire to be exempt from confronting the arguments against one's position traditionally is seen when a movement fears it is about to be discredited. This is a sure sign environmental rhetoric must be defused before it implodes.

Other troubling assumptions run through estimates of species loss. For one, the habitat reduction projections favored by pessimists for wilderness areas assume that when acres are altered by human action they are "lost" as if vanished from the face of the Earth. But as Ariel Lugo, a Forest Service official in Puerto Rico, pointed out in a 1991 issue of *Science,* when pristine forests are cut they do not vanish; rather, the next step is usually new second-growth forests. Many species from the pristine forest adapt to the second-growth habitat and continue living, Lugo noted. The doomsday estimates presume they die.

Most troubling is a fundamental inconsistency in the work of Wilson, the leading academic theorist on species loss. In his 1993 book *The Diversity of Life* and in a 1993 article called "Is Humanity Suicidal?" Wilson asserts, first, that the fossil record suggests there was a mass extinction in North America around 11,000 years ago, perhaps when Paleo-Indians began to hunt North American animals in earnest. Some 73 percent of large mammal genre fell extinct at the time, Wilson says. Next Wilson asserts that species loss is especially horrifying because perhaps ten million years is required for biological diversity to recover naturally following a major extinction. Finally Wilson posits that species protection is especially important right now because the contemporary biosphere holds within it greater species diversity than has ever been present throughout the saga of the living Earth.

That last is encouraging news—reason in itself to support biodiversity conservation. But the three points cannot all be true at once. It cannot be that a human-caused mass extinction occurred just 11,000 years ago, that ten million years must pass for nature to recover naturally from mass extinctions, and that today biological diversity is the highest ever.

An Endangered Species Scorecard

Currently almost 920 plant and animal species are protected under the Endangered Species Act, with several hundred more expected to be listed in the 1990s and perhaps 3,000 more eligible for listing, according to a 1992 study by the General Accounting Office. Listing under the act not only means a species cannot be hunted, owned, or traded, it forbids most development in critical habitats. Let's take a look at what is happening on the list:

UP, American bald eagle. In 1963 this bird had declined to 417 known nesting pairs in the lower forty-eight states and was widely considered certain to fall extinct. By 1993, 4,016 nesting pairs were known, and thousands of juveniles had been counted. In 1995 the classification of the American bald will be downgraded from "endangered" to the lesser category of "threatened." This means the eagle continues to be protected but is no longer thought in peril of extinction. Current protections include a rule that loggers who find an eagle nest must leave an untouched circle of woodlands, generally at least ten acres, around it.

UP, the Lange's metal mark butterfly. Just 20 of this insect were known in 1960. Today at least 1,200 live wild.

UP, the northern gray wolf. In 1920 Congress passed a law directing the eradication of this animal, among the few that kills when not hungry. By the time the gray wolf was listed under the Endangered Species Act there were believed to be just 500 remaining in Minnesota, and none elsewhere. Today there are an estimated 1,750 gray wolves in Minnesota and at least several dozen in each of the canine's traditional other western state habitats. The Rocky Mountain gray wolf, a related animal, is also expanding in Montana, where it was considered extinct in the 1970s.

For years officials have debated whether to reintroduce the gray wolf to its previous habitat of Yellowstone National Park. Reintroduction when possible is required under the Endangered Species Act. Most greens favor the reintroduction, while political sentiment has run strongly against returning the wolf to Yellowstone, for fear that someday a child touring the park may be snatched and killed. In 1992 a Park Service ranger shot a purebred northern gray wolf on Yellowstone grounds. While genus *Homo* debated the merits of the proposal, the animal returned on its own.

DOWN, the delta smelt. This fish, found only in the Sacramento River, has declined rapidly. In 1992 California water authorities and Congress concluded an agreement under which as much as 20 percent of the volume of the Sacramento and other rivers will be considered property of endangered species such as the delta smelt. This water will be used to increase river volume and help the smelt recover.

DOWN, the kangaroo rat. This species has a single known habitat in Beaumont, California. There is a Superfund site in Beaumont. Cleanup of the site has been suspended because the Endangered Species Act prohibits significant alteration of habitats of protected creatures. That's right—dumped toxics are being left in place on the assumption that this improves the survival chances of a species.

UP, the peregrine falcon. Widely declared on the verge of extinction in the early 1970s, there are now perhaps 10,000 adult falcon in the United States. In 1994 the northern subspecies was delisted as an endangered creature.

UP BUT SHOULD BE DOWN, swans. Twenty years ago there were an estimated 700 swans in New York; today there are 2,000. Protected in the United States though plentiful in their native Europe, mute swans are displacing other birds in many northeastern ponds, fouling drinking-water reservoirs and occasionally assaulting people. Surely mute swans born into the contemporary United States perceive the world as an unreconstructed paradise: no predators, no hunting, flood-proofed ponds, children to throw them food. In Rhode Island, game officials now slip toward swan nests in the spring, pick up eggs and shake them violently—"addling"—to kill chicks in a way that circumvents hunting prohibitions.

DOWN, numerous subspecies of Pacific Coast salmon. Along with the sockeye and chinook that run the Snake and Columbia, salmon on other Northwest rivers showed sharp declines in the late 1980s, partly because hydroelectric dams and irrigation projects have altered the volume and speed of water in almost every Northwest tributary.

Popular wisdom has it power dams make it hard for adult salmon to swim upstream; the worst effect is on juveniles swimming downstream to the sea. In slower low-volume water juvenile salmon are more vulnerable to predators and may complete their genetically timed transformation into saltwater fish before reaching salt water. To avoid an Endangered Species Act ruling that could in theory outlaw Northwest hydroelectric production, the Bonneville Power Authority and state and local government agencies have begun voluntary efforts to increase water speed and volume in the Columbia and Snake rivers. The plan is expected to cost Northwest residents about $200 million a year in electricity rate increases, plus eliminate hundreds of jobs in river-dependent industries.

Though most environmentalists attribute poor runs of chinook and sockeye entirely to artificial causes, this trend may someday be understood to be at least partly natural. During the late 1980s there was a drought on the Pacific Coast: Droughts are not good news for salmon. And in this period an important Pacific Coast ocean current shifted northward somewhat toward Alaska. During some of the same years that sockeye and chinook did poorly, the pink salmon that spawns in Alaska, near where the current shifted, enjoyed record runs.

Imperiled in the year 1994, sockeye and chinook may ultimately find themselves better off because women and men have tampered with Northwest rivers. The 1992 California water reform pact includes a provision under which volume of the Sacramento River will be increased when juvenile salmon migrate toward the seas; under some circumstances, water for salmon have precedence over water for power and agriculture. Power authorities are composing similar rules for the Columbia and other rivers. Once the new rules are in place, rivers of the Northwest may become more friendly toward salmon than before genus *Homo*, as humanity's dams and reservoirs smooth out the swings of natural flood and drought.

UP (TO THE WOE OF OTHER SPECIES), sea lions. Hunted to a population of about 30,000 in 1972, the sea lion came under the Marine Mammal Protection Act and today numbers perhaps 180,000. In 1984 sea lions discovered the fish ladders around the locks of Lake Washington, near Seattle. Since then hundreds have taken up residence, devouring so many steelhead trout that the steelhead may become endangered. Though the sea lion population is now robust, regulations continue to forbid any hunting of the animal. Attempts by the National Marine Fisheries Service to frighten sea lions away from the locks with fireworks, recorded cries of killer whales, and noxious chemicals have all failed. Game officials tried stationing female sea lions in estrus on the far side of Lake Washington; they found male sea lions prefer dining to sporting. Sea lions have been trapped and flown 1,000 miles south; they reappear at the locks about a month later. Sea lion attacks on steelhead have become a minor tourist attraction. For some reason the lions are known to locals collectively as Herschel.

UP (TO THE WOE OF OTHER SPECIES), harp seals. In the 1980s Canada banned the hunting of harp seals for fur, except for small amounts of "cultural" hunting by Inuits and Cree. The harp seal population recovered nicely and began assailing Canadian coastal cod, its favorite dish. In 1991 the Canadian government was compelled to ban cod fishing. Atlantic fishermen now want the harp seal hunts to resume.

DOWN, tiger. In 1992 the Korean conglomerate Hyundai received permission from the Primorsky Forest Service to log a huge tract of old-growth forest near the Bikin River in Siberia, where the last perhaps 500 Siberian tigers live. Russian enviros, a fledgling species, have since been fighting the decision.

DOWN, tuna. Though the yellowfin tuna catch by U.S. boats has declined sharply since the American decision to outlaw the drift-nets that kill dolphin, Mexico and other countries continue to overfish the yellowfin. The Pacific bluefin is declining owing to overfishing; Japanese customers prize the bluefin for sashimi.

DOWN, sharks. The United States banned shark fishing in its coastal waters in 1992, following sharp declines in the populations. Shark meat is rising in popularity, especially in Asia.

REALLY, REALLY UP, deer. Deer now number into the millions in North America yet remain a protected species in many instances. The current Virginia deer population is estimated to be five times the level that existed when Europeans arrived on the continent. Deer populations are soaring throughout lower New England and New York, New Jersey, and Connecticut. In this zone, containing some of the most developed land in the world, deer have increased over the past decade from an estimated 600,000 to one million. Nevertheless the Vermont Supreme Court in 1992 barred the construction of 33 vacation homes in the town of Stratton, saying the site was a protected habitat for white-tail deer.

REALLY DOWN, rhinoceros. In 1970 there were perhaps 70,000 rhinos in Africa and Asia. Now there are perhaps 2,000. Rhino poaching is endemic owing to the popularity of the horns for ceremonial daggers in the Middle East, or they may be ground up in a supposed male potency potion popular in Asia.

UP, the wild turkey. Absent from New England for about a century, as forests have recovered so has this bird, which now numbers an estimated 29,000 in the Northeast.

WAY DOWN BUT STARTED BACK UP, elephants. In 1970 there were an estimated 2.5 million African elephants. By 1990 the number was down to perhaps 350,000, owing to poaching for ivory. Strict protection programs in Zimbabwe, South Africa, Botswana, and Namibia are helping elephant populations recover there. In Kenya elephant populations are rebounding with sufficient vigor that game officials are experimenting with injecting females with a birth-control vaccine: Expanding elephant herds have begun to trample Kenyan refuges for other forms of wildlife. Whether regulated trade in ivory would improve the survival prospects of the African elephant herd is a question that has begun to plague institutional environmentalism, which almost uniformly opposes any commerce in endangered animals. Most of the world's nations agreed in 1989 to ban ivory trading under the Convention on International Trade in Endangered Species. To the embarrassment of correctly liberal environmentalists, Zimbabwe, with a black majority government, opposes the ivory-trading ban—and also produces the world's best elephant protection statistics.

UP, the ferret. In the 1970s the black-footed ferret was declared extinct in North America. Then in 1981 a Wyoming dog killed a black-footed ferret, which had been living wild in ignorance of reports of its own demise. Since then zoologists and game officials have worked to catch black-footed ferret and breed them in captivity. Some 310 now live in captivity, with about another 200 reintroduced into the wild.

UP, the mountain lion. Mountain lions, also called cougars, were extensively bounty-hunted in the nineteenth century, and by the 1960s were believed extinct in North America. The last known cougar in Maine was killed by a trapper in 1938. Yet in 1993 a Maine deer hunter named Anthony Fuscaldo saw a cougar kill a bobcat. The hunter took the carcass to game officials for analysis; the claw marks were from a cougar. Oddly enough, the Fish and Wildlife Service still classifies the eastern cougar as extinct, yet nevertheless also classifies it as an endangered species that cannot be hunted. At least 9,000 cougars are now believed to live in the western United States; no longer hunted, they are increasingly aggressive around people. Of the 57 cougar attacks on humans known to have occurred in the United States in the past century, 43 have occurred since 1970.

MUCH TOO UP, the mustang. Protected by the Wild Free Roaming Horse and Burro Act of 1971, mustangs have increased from an estimated 35,000 in 1971 to at least 50,000, with similar increases among burros. To keep them from starving on spare rangeland the federal government now feeds wild herds at Nellis Air Force Base in Nevada and other locations.

DOWN, the parrot. Until the Wildbird Conservation Act of 1992 banned imports of birds caught in the wild, many parrot species were declining. A few researchers, such as Irene Pepperberg of the University of Arizona, believe some parrot species eventually will be understood to be as intelligent as dolphins and chimpanzees; some parrots use tools and can answer unprompted questions. It is assumed the Wildbird Conservation Act will help wild parrots recover, though black markets in the birds are developing in Central American countries, where "running" parrots can be nearly as lucrative as running drugs, though much less dangerous.

SEEMED DOWN BUT WAS UP, the tumamoc globeberry. This Arizona plant was declared endangered in 1986. In 1993 the Fish and Wildlife Service removed the tumamoc globeberry from endangered status, saying the plant was abundant and had been listed owing to "data error." The service estimates $1.4 million was spent to protect the tumamoc globeberry while it was erroneously considered falling extinct.

DOWN BUT NUMEROUS, the steller sea lion. This species was listed as threatened in 1990 in response to a lawsuit by environmental groups, though about 65,000 steller sea lions are estimated to exist. That is above the extinction warning line but about one-half the number of previous population estimates. In the last decade environmental litigators have pressured the Fish and Wildlife Service to list creatures at any sign of population decline, regardless of whether the decline appears to engage a threat of extinction. This means a common invocation of doomsday cant—that "more and more creatures are being listed as endangered every day"—is deceptive, since the listings are based on increasingly lenient criteria and now may be registered even when a creature is numerous.

UP, the whales. Protected by a special act of Congress in 1946, California gray whales have recovered to a population estimated by the National Marine Fisheries Service at 21,000. That is believed to be about the population level of California grays that existed when Pacific Coast whaling began in the nineteenth century. In 1994 the California gray whale was removed from the federal endangered species list, though it retains no-hunting status under the Marine Mammal Protection Act.

Population numbers for the bowhead, which lives off Alaska, are up; there were an estimated 1,000 bowheads in 1970, and are an estimated 8,000 today. Fin and humpback whales are gaining in numbers. A decade ago about 1,400 humpback whales were observed annually off Hawaii; currently the annual number is running around 3,400. The blue whale, largest known creature ever to live, was hunted to the brink of extinction until 1968, when whaling of blues was banned internationally. Now the blue is plentiful again off California. Jay Barlow, a whale specialist with the National Marine Fisheries Service, said in 1993 that "there may be more blue whales in California coastal waters today than were previously thought to exist in the entire North Pacific."

The United States has not permitted whaling since 1972. Since 1986, nearly all international whaling has been suspended by order of the International Whaling Commission. In 1992 Norway, which at every international forum pronounces itself greener than thou, began attempting to break the IWC whaling ban. Japan also desires a whaling resumption—whale-meat cafes are popular in Tokyo, their wares supplied from whales ostensibly taken for "research" purposes—but as Tokyo fears any statements it might make on this subject would make the country a target of international environmental protests, the Japanese government is letting Norway do its dirty work. The United States, which provided the impetus for the 1986 whaling ban, has pressured Japan not to undercut the consensus—another inconveniently positive U.S. action most environmentalists prefer not to discuss.

Norway asserts that the minke whale has sufficiently recovered for sustainable hunting. In 1993 the IWC ruled against Oslo. The head of the IWC science assessment committee, Philip Hammond, a British biologist, resigned to protest the decision, estimating that at least 760,000 minkes now swim the world's seas. As he resigned Hammond declared that the IWC was making decisions because of political pressure—mainly from the United States, France, and New Zealand, where both governments and the public fiercely oppose whaling—rather than based on calculations of sustainable hunt levels. Hammond is right: Today opposition to whaling has more to do with politics than population estimates. But that's not bad, as whaling ought to be banned, period. The political instinct here is correct.

Which animals humankind may use for meat and materials is an issue generations to come will find increasingly troubling. For today, when the running of society without the exploitation of animals is not yet practical, the ecorealist can easily draw a bright line forbidding any use of higher mammals. No one yet knows whether whales, dolphins, and great apes have complex self-awareness that differentiates them from other living things. But few would deny that there is something going on in the minds of the higher-mammal group, and perhaps in the minds of parrots and a few other species as well. Whatever the ultimate purpose of life may be, it must entail having something going on in your mind. The higher mammals may be venturing into this territory. Or they may not. The mere possibility should be sufficient to place them forever off-limits to human exploitation.

The Extinction Peak

The preceding inventory of species ups and downs excludes many other creatures of note. Sea otters and brown pelicans, both said near extinction a few decades ago, are recovering nicely in and near the United States. In Australia the kangaroo has proliferated so efficiently, now outnumbering human residents of the continent, that it is overrunning many ranches, though its protected status continues. On the other hand many ecologists believe that plant species, a form of life with a low political profile, are declining faster than animals; and that water species are doing poorly compared to land species. The inventory of species vacillating up and down proves that genus *Homo* is having a pronounced effect on other forms of life. The inventory shows something else: that the Endangered Species Act is working spectacularly well.

It has become common among conservatives to deride the act as a failure because so few species have been reclassified as recovered. "If you create an Endangered Species Act and the species remain endangered, you have failed," says Robert Gordon, director of the National

Wilderness Institute, a rare species itself as a right-wing environmental organization. But the goal of species preservation was to keep creatures alive, and modern conservation efforts are doing that exceedingly well. The gray whale and bald eagle benefited from what were essentially little Endangered Species acts passed ahead of the overall legislation. With the gray whale and bald eagle now at or near pretechnological population levels, these species show how robustly nature recovers. Most living things on the endangered species list will do as well, once they've been given as much time as the gray whale and bald eagle had.

The salvation of these creatures indicates that species protection is another place where the ecological trend, far from declining toward doom, is in fact a rousing success story, one only waiting to be recognized. In the Western world at least, if most imperiled species could make it through the period from the 1940s to the late 1970s—when gross pollution was everywhere, development was unrestricted, and the Endangered Species Act did not yet exist—then those species have already passed the worst test that will be administered by man.

Ethnic Purity for Species

As written the Endangered Species Act protects only "pure" species, abandoning any that have interbred. Some researchers believe the gray wolf now breeds with the coyote; if so, both would lose legal protection because they would be considered hybrids. Environmental orthodoxy rejects hybridization of species as a horrifying offense against nature, though in nature hybridization has been ongoing since the beginning of life, being essential to the system by which species radiate into new forms. Here is the Stop-in-Place Fallacy at work—a conceit that somehow on the day when the Endangered Species Act was signed a Correct global alignment of habitats and species was in effect, and any change after that must be seen as ghastly, even if an entirely natural change like wild hybridization. This thinking contains a closed-loop circularity useful to institutional environmentalism: Given that changes in species are guaranteed, developments can always be categorized as shocking, maintaining the correctly pessimistic milieu.

Both the Endangered Species Act and environmental doctrine further grant no standing to species that exist only through domestication, such as dogs and farm animals, or that exist only in captivity, such as the red wolf. This position is a circling of the wagons in advance of the era of genetic engineering: an attempt to set up the notion that creatures brought to being by human initiative do not deserve to exist. In this vein environmental thinking can have an ugly aspect. It's disquieting to hear some environmentalists go on without a hint of irony about how "locally distinct populations" must have their "unique genetic ecotypes" preserved against "non-native populations" encroaching at the border. How can racial barriers be awful for humankind and vital for animals? To nature this entire line of thought must seem detached from reality. Genes constantly mingle in nature. That's part of the point of the enterprise.

Further, the Endangered Species Act does not protect non-native species, or living things transplanted by genus *Homo*. At times act administrators actually require that non-native species be destroyed in the name of ethnic purity—I mean, locally distinct ecotypes. Environmental orthodoxy seconds this notion. In Monterey County, California, the bush lupine, a native plant, is protected under the Endangered Species Act. About 200 miles away at the Lanphere Christensen Dunes Preserve in Humbolt County, California, where the bush lupine is not native, the Nature Conservancy has been trying to eradicate the same plant.

It's hard to get your head around the notion that a plant can be so wonderful in one place that it deserves federal protection yet so horrible 200 miles away that it must be destroyed. Moreover, the bush lupine is "native" to Monterey County only in the sense that it happened to be there when white males first laid eyes on the place. Perversely enough, the definition used by environmental orthodoxy for the Correct manifestation of nature often equates to whatever reality applied when European scouting parties arrived. From nature's standpoint there have been many times in the past that the bush lupine was not found in Monterey County, or found someplace else, or found no place at all.

All this is different from saying that human transplantation of species is necessarily wise. Kudzu, brought to the United States from Japan in the nineteenth century, now plagues much of the Southeast; zebra mussels, a 1980s arrival in the Great Lakes, today line the bottoms of boats and block hydroelectric intakes; a North American toad called the *Bufo marinis,* transplanted to Australia because some farmers believed it would eat sugar cane beetles, today resolutely ignores the beetles while, in the absence of predators, growing to the size of dinner plates; the blue hyacinth, a gorgeous flower brought to Florida from South America to adorn estate ponds, today gracefully and gorgeously clogs everglades; the brown tree snake, which traveled from the Solomon Islands to Guam in the wheel wells of World War II aircraft, has killed off several bird species there. As the researcher James Carlton of Williams College has shown, freighters arriving at Oregon docks from trans-Pacific voyages may contain in their ballast tanks hundreds of non-native organisms, some in the larval stage, all ready to play what Carlton calls "ecological roulette."

This is sound reason to regulate human transplanting of organisms but hardly cause to panic when it occurs. Environmental doctrine holds that the arrivals of non-native species guarantee instant habitat collapse. The zebra mussel will never be stopped; cheat grass in Montana will never be stopped; and so on. But species arriving from someplace else do not possess mystical superpowers. They are just different, and the local ecology needs time to react to the difference.

When tumbleweed was brought to the United States from Russia in the mid–nineteenth century it proliferated unchecked, covering the cowboy landscape. In 1883 the Department of the Interior declared that tumbleweed had reached "plague" proportions and would never be controlled. Today tumbleweed is but another Western plant, the local ecology having risen in opposition. In 1985 the Asian clam appeared in San Francisco Bay, probably delivered by a freighter making port of call. The clam began to proliferate, and local commentators pronounced it would take over the harbor. Five years later the European green crab arrived in the same bay and began to wipe out the Asian clam. Now the green crab is said to be unstoppable.

During the cold winter of 1949, two Canadian wolves walked across a frozen tract of Lake Superior to Isle Royale, Michigan, and discovered a moose herd that had long existed without predation. Since then the predator-prey equilibrium of Isle Royale has been studied by researchers. Orthodoxy would predict an instant doomsday: the transplanted wolf wiping out the moose, then dying in turn of starvation. Initial years of the conflict supported that notion, with moose numbers declining rapidly. But as Rolf Peterson of Michigan Technological University has shown, in the 1980s the balance of power swung back toward the moose. Wolves on Isle Royale began declining, the predator having been hit with a virus for which its inbred genetic line lacks resistance. The moose seems immune.

The naturalist Alston Chase once bought a country house whose fields were overrun by the musk thistle. Wanting to dispatch the weed without chemicals he brought in *Rhinocyllus conicus,* a weevil that eats thistle. In a year Chase's musk thistle was wiped out—vanished forever, green doctrine surely would say. Yet a few seasons later the plant began to reappear in small numbers. Soon it was back almost to its previous level, with the weevil still dining merrily. Chase writes, "The bug and the weed apparently agreed not to exterminate each other, signing a pact to live happily in ecological equilibrium."

Such is the way of nature: species endlessly seek new balances, terms of truce, treaties of peace. Species preservation must recognize this, dropping such meaningless concepts as "pure" or "correct" creatures versus incorrect ones.

On a related front many environmental groups, including the normally clearheaded Environmental Defense Fund, have succeeded in pressuring some states to outlaw possession of "exotic" species—animals endangered in other nations, but not in the U.S.—and have asked Congress for national legislation to that effect, depicting the notion of private U.S. stocks of endangered species from other shores as an odious hoarding. Yet consider that the blackbuck antelope, now nearly gone from its native India, today thrives on several large ranches in Texas. A wealthy man named David Bamburger has on a Texas ranch more representatives of the endangered scimitar-horned oryx than can be found in the species' native Africa.

Ideally animals endangered elsewhere should be protected elsewhere. But it's hard to imagine how outlawing Bamburger's collection will aid the survival prospects of the scimitar-horned oryx. Absurdly enough, the Fish and Wildlife Service is considering designating the scimitar-horned oryx "endangered" in the United States, essentially on the grounds that the Bamburger collection is too small to be a self-sustaining population. If this happens, species closed-loop logic will have twisted around itself entirely. It will be considered awful to move a species to a new habitat. But if the species takes hold in the new habitat, then there must be special federal protection to prevent further change.

Future Species Protection

The U.S. Endangered Species Act is the world's most progressive and most stringently enforced species conservation regulation. No other nation has a law as sweeping. No other nation with biodiversity strictures on its books enforces them as remorselessly; Brazil, for example, officially holds the caiman in protected status, but this law is openly ignored. The most powerful feature of the Endangered Species Act, unmatched elsewhere, is its stipulation that species conservation comes first regardless of social or economic cost. The presence since 1973 in American law of this forward-thinking statute indicates the extent to which important conservation notions were taken seriously in the United States long before it was politically expedient to do so. The endless talking-down by doomsayers of U.S. environmental policy is particularly amazing in light of this clause of the Endangered Species Act.

Equally amazing in this light is how warmly that talking-down is received by conventional wisdom.

President Richard Nixon, who signed the Endangered Species Act into law, might not have done so had he understood what he was attaching his name to. Nixon believed the act would protect only those creatures beloved by printers of nature calenders, the "charismatic megafauna"—cranes, manatee, other large animals with fan clubs. (Though today public interest in wildlife increasingly works its way down the pecking order. Recently a study on the Kemp's ridley sea turtle mess crossed my desk from the New York Turtle and Tortoise Society, billing itself as "one of the world's largest turtle conservation groups." One of!) Had Nixon realized that the act applies to insects, he might not have affixed his signature.

Good as it is, the Endangered Species Act is far from ideal. One initiative needed for rational species protection is a system for determining how many species live in the United States and where they are. Interior Secretary Bruce Babbitt in 1993 asked Congress to commission a National Biological Inventory that would answer such questions. Once a National Biological Inventory gets rolling it would not be much of a step to expand the project into a backstop biodiversity protection effort. Writing in the *Proceedings of the National Academy of Science,* the physicist Gregory Benford has proposed a crash program to preserve cryogenic genetic samples of as many organisms as possible. Cryogenic preservation of cell samples is not science-fiction; it is readily done with current technology. Benford estimates such a project would cost much less than other big-science efforts such as the space station and return more, providing insurance in case current species losses are as bad as pessimists maintain. Though with present technology it is not possible to restore lost species by using genetic codes, some researchers think this will be possible eventually. Accurate DNA samples will be necessary, however, for future species re-creations to happen.

Beyond such steps, the Endangered Species Act needs a new general premise. One exasperating aspect of the current law is that it penalizes rather than rewards private property holders whose land contains imperiled creatures. A private landholder who discovers a protected species on his or her property may find that future uses are foreclosed. The act may even impose silly levels of regulation on undeveloped land. In one case, an Oregon naturalist named Dayton Hyde founded a small private nature preserve by forming a compact with some rural property owners. Hyde rearranged a large ranch he owns to make it attractive to species such as the bald eagle. Bald eagle found Hyde's preserve and settled in. Federal officials promptly began imposing restrictions on the land, including telling Hyde he could no longer drive into his own preserve by pickup truck, as this might disturb the birds. Hyde was penalized for engaging in unauthorized environmental protection.

Another flaw of the Endangered Species Act is that if enforced to the letter, absurdities result. One looming absurdity is beetle protection. About 20 percent of the world's species are beetle; there are estimated to be 100 million beetles in existence for each one human being. The United States contains 28,000 known species of beetle and may host thousands more. Beetles are perhaps the most prolific and indestructible creature nature has ever devised, their gene line between 200 million and one billion years old. Yet at this writing the Fish and Wildlife Service was considering endangered species status for the Mount Herman rain beetle (*Polyphylla barbata cazier*). If beetles start receiving the instant-doomsday treatment, species protection will have veered into nonsense.

The progressive solution would be to replace cumbersome species-by-species rulings with a law designed to foster general protection of habitats, and to reward those who make nature preserves rather than penalize them. As John Baden, an economist at the University of Washington, has written, "The existing Endangered Species Act employs the wrong incentives. The associated costs are concentrated on a relatively small number of people, mainly those who own wildlife habitat. These landowners bear most of the burden of species protection, but receive few of the benefits." Baden has proposed that the species law be replaced with a national trust fund whose primary purpose would be to buy lands to place in preservation status. The environmental economist Randal O'Toole offers a similar proposal. His trust fund would both buy up lands for preservation and offer money incentives to property holders who discover and then protect imperiled species.

If the Endangered Species Act were replaced by general habitat protection, it would no longer be necessary to engage in complicated legal disputes about what population levels of what species are appropriate, or which sorts of living things deserve special treatment. Human beings would simply place areas into preservation status and accept that within such zones levels of various species would rise and fall, with some creatures dropping to extinction and new ones coming into existence, as has happened since time immemorial. Increasing the portion of the world's land area in pure preservation status ought to be a central goal of future environmental policy and of ecorealism. Properly written, a successor to the Endangered Species Act could be the vehicle for such a new drive for general preservation.[3]

Previews of this approach are in the works in Las Vegas and Palm

Springs. Outside Las Vegas the desert tortoise is endangered. Developers have agreed to buy and place into preservation status 400,000 acres of tortoise habitat, in return for permission to build on 22,000 acres of prime land. Outside Palm Springs developers seeking to construct new housing have purchased and put into preservation status 15,000 acres of habitat for the imperiled fringe-toed lizard. Such habitat conservation plans combine conservation with market freedom for developers. What could be a better ecorealist outcome?

Since the book you hold takes issue in places with Paul Ehrlich and Edward Wilson, it is nice to close this chapter by quoting a poignant phrase they wrote together about species preservation: "Because *Homo sapiens* is the dominant species on Earth, we and many others think that people have a moral responsibility to protect what are our only known living companions in the universe."

Amen. Perhaps the universe is rich with life. But as the third section of this book will detail, current scientific findings suggest the reverse: that our living ecosphere is a rarity and a miracle indeed. Should that be the case then every animal on Earth may be vital to the cosmic enterprise. Protection of those miraculous companions should be both humankind's responsibility, and joy.

THE THIRD WORLD

TWO SCENES FROM LIFE IN THE DEVELOPING WORLD:
In the late 1980s I lived in Lahore, Pakistan, an old Punjabi city of several million souls. One day in four it was wise to turn on the headlights when driving in daylight, the air pollution so cumulous oncoming cars could not see you otherwise. On days when the temperature hit 110 degrees Fahrenheit, the combination of pollution and heat took a brutal toll on the city's residents, most of them manual laborers whose toil continued regardless of how hot or smoggy it became. Walking the streets of Lahore was a small ecological adventure, as a sack of garbage might fall on you from an upper-story window or come sailing over the wall of the compound of a wealthy landed family. Many people simply tossed their garbage into the streets. About once a week a group of low-caste workers vaguely representing the city's sanitation force would sweep garbage into piles and set it alight, loosing air pollution of the foulest kind. But the worst was the water pollution. Drinking unboiled tap water was a blunder, even for Pakistanis who boasted inaccurately of resistance. Down the dividers of some Lahore boulevards ran open canals that carried waters filthy brown with wastes. On hot days local boys could be seen *swimming* in the canals.

For our honeymoon my wife and I went to Nepal. Pristine beauty at the ends of the Earth? In Kathmandu if you looked up, toward the grandeur of the Himalayas, you could lose your breath; if you looked down you might lose your lunch, the city streets filthy with trash and human and animal excrement. We went white-water rafting on the

Trisuli River, which winds through some of the most remote square kilometers remaining on the face of the Earth. The Trisuli was rank; compared to it most American rivers are channels of Evian. Approaching some rapids, I decided to jump from the raft and try the sport of bobbing through in a life preserver. Our Nepali guide offered cheerfully, "Whatever you do, don't open your mouth!"

As anyone who travels the developing world rapidly discovers, the view that Western industrial countries are the polluted ones is a fantasy. Studies show that 1.3 billion people in the developing world live in zones of "dangerously unsafe" air—air alerts at the "dangerous" level having become almost unknown in the Western world. And one billion people in developing countries lack access to drinking water meeting the crudest safety standards.

These figures are not just abstractions. What environmental problems kill human beings in numbers today? Not Alar or ozone depletion. What kills them is dung smoke and diarrhea.

According to the World Health Organization, in 1993 four million Third World children under the age of five died preventable deaths from respiratory diseases brought on in most cases by air pollution. This is about as many people of all ages who died of all causes that year in the United States and European Union combined.

In places such as Bangkok, Calcutta, Karachi, Lagos, Mexico City, and almost any metropolis in China, factories operate without so much as mesh screens on smokestacks, to say nothing of the cost-no-object scrubber assemblies that now adorn the stacks of Western industrial facilities. Third World buses, cars, and trucks run without any emission controls, burning low-quality leaded gasoline made from the sulfurous petroleum unused in the West. Brown coal, shunned for decades in the West, is burned for industrial and electric power. It's now against the law to chop down a tree in Mexico City: Trees, a counter to air pollution, covered 21 percent of the city in 1950 but only two percent now.

The developing world also has a pervasive form of air pollution unknown in the West, rural smog. "Most of the child deaths from respiratory distress stem from living in poorly ventilated huts where fuelwood, cow dung, or agricultural wastes are used for heating and cooking. Smoke inside a hut like this can be unbelievable," says Gurinder Shahi, an official of the United Nations Development Programme. "Women and children, who spend most time in the home, are most harmed. Today 40 percent of the global population heats and cooks with biomass in raw form."

Next, according to UNICEF, 3.8 million developing-world children under age five died in 1993 from diarrheal diseases caused by impure drinking water. In the First World, death from diarrhea is about as common as comet strikes; in the developing world diarrhea kills far more people than cancer. This happens because a billion impoverished human beings drink unfiltered water taken from rivers or lakes into which human and animal feces loaded with parasites has been discharged. Most of Africa, the Indian subcontinent, and Latin America have no wastewater treatment facilities. In India ritual bathers seeking spiritual purity enter the Ganges and expose their bodies to a wide range of toxicants and pathogens. Throughout Africa, mothers draw for their children water of lower quality than the process effluent discharged from American factories.

An estimated 25 billion tons of unfiltered industrial pollutants were emitted directly to Chinese waterways in 1991, meaning more water pollution in that one country alone than in the whole of Western society. Major Chinese rivers such as the Taizai cannot now support fish; they have become biologically dead in the way that was repeatedly predicted for First World water bodies but never actually realized except at the infamous Cuyahoga River near Cleveland. Lake Victoria in Africa, upon which perhaps 30 million people depend for drinking water and fish, is near biological death. Toxic chemicals in the developing world are close to uncontrolled, with direct discharge to sewers or rivers, nearly eliminated in the West, still the standard. The sewer system in Tijuana, Mexico, exploded in 1993 from an interaction of waste toxics.

Three-point-eight million deaths from dirty water in a single year is substantially more than the combined worst-case mortality estimates for asbestos, dioxin, electromagnetic radiation, nuclear wastes, PCBs, pesticide residues, and ultraviolet rays—the sorts of ecological issues that obsess the First World. Problems like these are real enough and must be dealt with. Yet Western public consciousness continues to focus on exotic ecological threats while ignoring millions of annual deaths from basic environmental problems of water and air. "Issues like African sewage are not sexy, so they always fall to the bottom of the agenda," says Deborah Moore, a scientist at the Environmental Defense Fund and one of the few Western environmentalists advocating a focus on basic Third World reform.

Institutional environmentalism focuses on the real but comparatively minor problems of developed nations in part to support a worldview that Western material production is the root of ecological malevolence. The trough of such thinking was reached at the Earth Summit in Rio in 1992. There, having gotten the attention of the world and of its heads of state, what message did institutional environmentalism choose to proclaim? That global warming is a horror. To make Rio a fashionably correct event about Western guilt-tripping, the hypothetical prospect of global warming—a troubling but speculative concern that so far has harmed no one and may never harm anyone—was put above palpable, urgent loss of lives from Third World water and smoke pollution.

Soot and Death

Eric Chivian, a psychiatrist on the faculty at Harvard Medical School, has been on both sides of the barricade of political correctness. During the strategic arms race he helped found Physicians for the Prevention of Nuclear War, which in 1985 won the Nobel Peace Prize. Through that period Chivian was a hero to liberal sentiment. Then nuclear weapons began to be dismantled, and Chivian shifted his focus to the human health harm caused by pollution in the developing world. He helped start a new organization, the Project on Global Environmental Change and Health, which in 1993 published a powerful but little-noticed technical volume, *Critical Condition: Human Health and the Environment,* presenting evidence that basic pollution in the Third World is far more significant than all First World ecological problems combined. Now his actions run counter to liberal sentiment. "I've had great difficulty interesting environmental organizations in human health in poor countries," Chivian says. "They want to talk about forest loss and species diversity in the South [developing world] but have much less interest in human health there."

Chivian points out that in 1993, two teams of U.S. university researchers produced evidence that "particulates"—fine bits of soot and ash from incomplete combustion—are a greater health threat than previously realized, perhaps accounting for 20,000 to 30,000 annual premature deaths due to respiratory failure in the United States. "American environmentalists were disturbed by this finding, as they should have been," Chivian says. "But if these studies are right then the particulate emergency is happening in the Third World, not here. The problem is a thousand times worse for them."

According to David Bates, a professor emeritus of medicine at the University of British Columbia, children in the developing world (the child's lungs are more sensitive than the adult's) face a double whammy of air pollutants. "The child living in a city," Bates says, "will be exposed to high levels of airborne lead from vehicle exhaust, because no Third World country is close to mandating unleaded gasoline and catalytic converters." Lead is a poison and probably causes IQ loss. Since unleaded gasoline went on the market in the 1970s, ambient U.S. airborne lead levels have fallen 95 percent. Through the same period airborne lead levels have risen in developing-world cities: Lead is now so prevalent in Mexico City air that parents are advised to keep children indoors as much as possible. "The city child in the developing world will also be exposed to high levels of sulfur and smog," Bates says. The Indian industrial city of Agra, home to the Taj Mahal, has levels of airborne sulfur dioxide, which causes acid rain, ten times the maximum now found in the United States. The surface of the Taj is corroding from the acid rain caused by 212 nearby factories, none with pollution controls. "But at least the child in the city has electricity and propane as home energy, sparing constant indoor exposure to smoke," Bates continues. "The country child is spared sulfur and lead but then gets the double whammy of choking home air pollution from the wood or dung fire."

Robert Lawrence, director of health science for the Rockefeller Foundation in New York, draws a slope of developing-world home fuels. It starts with dung and crop wastes, then moves up to wood, then charcoal, then kerosene, then propane, finally ascending to electrification. "Through the early 1980s many Third World countries were headed up the slope toward cleaner fuels," Lawrence says. "In recent years, with the global economy stagnant, people are sliding back down the slope, back from electricity to propane, back from fuelwood to dung. Respiratory deaths are rising in concert."

Sliding back down the slope isn't just a threat to lungs: It threatens forests as well. Though environmental orthodoxy holds that deforestation is caused by rapacious clear-cutters and ruthless cattle barons, penniless peasants seeking fuelwood may be the greatest threat to forests. Fuelwood consumption in the developing world rose 35 percent between 1975 and 1986, with replanting rare by peasants who are landless and thus lack economic incentive to husband resources. Wood is a wonderful building material and an awful fuel. (The highest airborne particulate pollution reading ever recorded in the United States came not in Cleveland or Pittsburgh but in the trendy community of Klamath Falls, Oregon, where the elite heat with wood to be natural. Colorado and Montana now regulate the sale of wood stoves for this reason.) Today most of India has adequate food but insufficient wood to cook with. A new saying among rural Indian women, says Jodi Jacobson, director of the Health and Development Policy Project, a Washington, D.C., organization, is "It's not what's in the pot but what's under the pot that worries you." Jacobson believes fuelwood supplies are becoming critical in Haiti, India, Nepal, Mexico, sub-Saharan Africa, and Thailand.

   Lack of generating capacity not only means much of the Third World must heat with wood, it means electricity shortages that hold back investment and cause the world's impoverished to shiver or swelter. Much of Africa, China, and the Indian subcontinent exhibit chronic electricity shortages, as does some of Latin America. In Pakistan the national power utility, known by the delightful acronym WAPDA, engages in what it euphemizes as "load shedding" during the six-month hot season; sections of cities have their electricity switched off in rotation for eight-hour periods. No investor will build where the electricity shuts down at whim. In Pakistan, as throughout the equatorial Third World, the sole means of cooling available to the typical person is a fan. With the power out much of the time even the fans won't turn. The Pakistani working class usually sleeps several to a room in dwellings with no fans and interior temperatures well above 100 degrees Fahrenheit.

   Today in Nepal, Shahi of the UNDP estimates, rural women spend five or six hours a day on foot searching for fuelwood and carrying it home. In the romanticized eco-mythology of small-village life, somehow it's beautiful that peasants walk barefoot for miles to gather a few sticks of wood to cook their *dal.* Actually it's awful: women captive to drone labors that deny them the time for education and result mainly in health damage to themselves and their children. Bates notes that even Nepali women living in high-altitude mountain areas that might be imagined as pristine wonderlands often suffer a disease similar to anemia, caused by carbon monoxide in the bloodstream from long-term exposure to crude energy sources such as indoor cooking fires.

Fear of Progress

Western environmental thinking has considerable difficulty coming to terms with such realities. The mere facts that Third World economists call propane and kerosene "clean fuels," and speak longingly of the day when their countries will be wholly electrified, repels ecological orthodoxy, which depicts fossil fuels as hideous and central electric generation as part of a vast plot to engender an artificial greenhouse effect. One reason air pollution is so bad in Mexico, Nigeria, and other nations is that most driving is done on dirt roads. Trucks and buses leave clouds of dust behind them; dust is a pollutant, having the same effect as particulates on the lungs of people and animals and damaging the respiratory stoma of plants. Enviros are dismayed at the thought of paving the developing world, but nature might not be, because the first impact of a paving campaign would be a reduction in dust kicked into the air. What developing-world nations need to free their populations from extreme air pollution is paved roads, catalytic converters, hydroelectric dams, modern petroleum refining, advanced high-efficiency power plants—the sorts of technology green doctrine considers outrageous.

While the Western environmental community shows little interest in such issues as dung-smoke pollution, it is devoting intense energies to stopping developing-world hydroelectricity. Greenpeace, the Natural Resources Defense Council, the Sierra Club, and other important Western groups have made a major cause of pressuring Washington, Tokyo, Paris, London, Bonn, and the World Bank not to support the Three Gorges and Xiaolangdi dams in China; the Narmada River dams in India; dams on the Bio-Bio River in Chile; and additional major power dams proposed for Malawi, Pakistan, and elsewhere.

The principal green objection to developing world hydroelectric power is that reservoirs are formed by inundating pristine areas such as the 375-mile corridor to be flooded by Three Gorges. On the other hand, Three Gorges and planned dams for the Narmada region would stop seasonal flooding, which annually kills thousands of people, thousands more animals, and destroys wildlife habitat. Yangtze River flooding killed 3,000 people in 1990; the Yangtze has killed an estimated 200,000 in this century. In September 1992 a fairly routine Indus Valley flood killed 1,034 people. It is a measure of the Third World versus the First that the 1992 Indus flood, triggered by a cyclone, killed 1,034 people and caused $105 million in property damage. Hurricane Andrew, a cyclone striking Florida about the same time, killed nine people and did $7.6 billion in damage.

Orthodox environmentalists correctly object that Third World hydropower initiatives have budgets bloated by graft and involve displacement of peasants, which in developing nations can mean keen hardship. Yet many seem uninterested in the upside of such projects, mainly huge amounts of zero-emission, zero-fossil-fuel energy for nations where runaway air pollution is a daily threat to life. Three Gorges would generate 17,600 megawatts, the output of nearly a dozen Three Mile Islands, with no air pollutants or greenhouse gases. Western environmental orthodoxy is passionately concerned with wildlife habitat losses from hydro reservoirs, seemingly indifferent to the human health benefits of reducing the percentage of the world's dwellings thick with billows of indoor smoke. This is so though no Western environmentalist would allow his or her child in a closed hut where dung was being burned for 15 seconds, let alone to be raised under such circumstances.

Institutional environmentalism has invested tremendous energies in defeating Sardar Sarovar, an extensive hydropower project planned for the Narmada River in India, and also in defeating a related project called Tehri Dam. My office is near the World Bank complex in Washington. In 1991 Greenpeace posters declaring STOP SARDAR SAROVAR DAM began to appear along the streets. Such opposition led to an internal study by the World Bank that condemned the bank's involvement in the project, even though Mohammed el-Ashrey, the head of the World Bank environment division, endorses the dams. After the study became public the bank withdrew support from Sardar Sarovar. Fair enough: But where were the posters that said STOP THIRD WORLD DUNG SMOKE? India has about 70,000 megawatts of untapped hydropower potential, enough to meet the country's coming decades of power needs on a renewable, zero-pollution basis. Pessimist pressure also caused Japan, which is exceptionally touchy about green criticism, to suspend support for Sardar Sarovar, which India is now attempting to complete with its own shaky resources. Some channels on the Narmada have been cut and some concrete poured but without access to capital, India's plan may falter. No clean power is being made, few jobs have been created, and annual deaths in floods continue: in other words a perfect outcome for environmental orthodoxy.

Many Western environmentalists are now fighting oilfield development in Ecuador, construction of coal-fired power plants in China (even plants with advanced controls), and similar projects at least part of whose output would replace indoor smoke among the impoverished. Opponents assert that small-scale solar and "biogas" (fermenting dung into methane, a clean fuel) are appropriate for the developing world. Often this is true. But are there more than a handful of American or Western European environmentalists themselves willing to live at the limits of current solar technology? Though current solar converters can provide basic power requirements—usually not enough, however, for refrigeration, badly needed in the Third World where at least a quarter of food production is lost to spoilage—one reason few Western enviros use solar is that it costs more than conventional electricity from central generating stations. How come if small solar is too expensive for the Sierra Club set it's a great idea for peasants in Malawi?

The need for improved water purity in the developing world engages similar discomfiture for environmental orthodoxy. Moore of the EDF has been pressuring aid agencies to fund community-based water purity and sewage control. Like small solar, there are many instances in which these projects will be best; UNICEF recently endorsed a focus on community water initiatives. Yet in the expanding Third World cities where a billion of the world's poor reside, what's needed foremost, Chivian says, is "basic water infrastructure." In Karachi but a third of homes have piped water; in Madras only about a third of dwellings connect to anything like a sewer system; in Kinshasa there is no sewage system at all. Often the masses in developing cities can get safe drinking water only from water-sellers; then the poorest of the world's poor end up paying more for water than do the rich. For instance water vendors who work the poor sections of Jakarta charge about five times what piped water costs in the nice parts of that city. The solution is "basic infrastructure"—pipes, filtration plants, wastewater treatment facilities, sometimes dams and aqueducts. But big water-diversion projects deeply offend environmental orthodoxy.

Health and Population

Unspoken in debate about Third World pollution, but powerful in the subconsciousness of some environmentalists, is the population question. Back an orthodox environmentalist to the wall with the absurdity of paying more attention to greenhouse computer projections for the twenty-second century than to millions of annual childhood deaths from impure water and air in the here and now, and he or she may say, "If water safety and hut smoke in poor countries are fixed, that will just help the population grow faster. The human species is not imperiled. Environmental advocates must concentrate on protecting species and habitats, which are imperiled."

Population growth is indeed the core environmental problem for most of the world. But better environmental health will help *slow* that growth, not expand it. "The technical literature is unanimous that when you improve health, especially child and reproductive health, birth rates go down," says Chivian. "This is the essential fact of the issue. If you want species and habitats preserved, protecting human health so that fertility rates decline will accomplish far more than building walls around wildlife preserves."

Since the 1970s the World Health Organization has made dramatic progress in supplying inoculations to most of the world's children. During that same period births per woman have declined, a strong real-world proof of a direct relationship between childhood health and smaller families. Fertility rates are declining fastest in developing countries that have positive indexes for safe water and progress on the clean-energy slope. Fertility rates remain ferocious mainly in Africa and the Indian subcontinent—also where deaths from dirty water and dung smoke are concentrated.

The Ecological Need for More Resource Consumption

Alan Durning of the Worldwatch Institute argues that the global population can be divided into three classes: about a billion consumers, Westerners who eat meat, own private cars, and travel by air; about two billion middle-dwellers, mainly Asians and South Americans, who have adequate grain-based diets and acceptable housing but insufficient health care and for whom private transportation is a bicycle; and about two billion impoverished, mainly Africans, Indians, and indigenous peoples, who are malnourished, ill-educated, sick, and walk. Improving the lots of those two billion impoverished should represent to the world the essential moral challenge of the twenty-first century. Consider a simple statistic. Bihar, India's poorest province, today has about 68 million illiterate citizens. That is more people than were alive in ignorance in the entire European continent during what European history calls the Dark Ages.

There is a famous statistic that the United States has four percent of the world's population and consumes 40 percent of current resources. Environmental orthodoxy says this proves U.S. resource use must go way down. What the statistic really tells you is that Third World resource consumption must go way up. United States resource use is in fact too high. But it will be impossible to raise the standard of living of the world's impoverished to anything like a morally equitable level without a significant rise in net global consumption of resources.

This is another actuality with which environmental dogma would rather not come to terms. Prominent green thinkers have nibbled around the edges of the topic. Interior secretary Bruce Babbitt, a former head of the League of Conservation Voters, says, "It is true that total resource consumption must rise for the benefit of the developing world, but until we in the West set an example of something other than waste, the Third World will feel no obligation to act any differently." This is what might be called the progressive denial position on world resource use: Acknowledge the need for more consumption of resources in poor countries, then twist the onus back on factories in Michigan.

Ask an orthodox environmentalist what to do about low standards of living in the developing nations and you are likely to receive a subject-changing reply about how Western colonial oppression caused overpopulation. Maybe so, but with the developing world now populous, the question of the hour is not how did it happen but what can be done? I've actually heard Western enviros who themselves take meals in air-conditioned restaurants going on about how Third World farmers should not be given tractors because ox-drawn plows are more ecologically transparent. In case you're not from farm country, working an animal-drawn plow is exhausting physical labor. One does not simply stroll along behind whistling a tune.

Resource economists are keenly cognizant of the China problem: that at its current annual GDP growth of 8.5 percent, and with most of its new energy coming from low-quality coal, by the year 2025 China may be emitting three times as much greenhouse gas as the present-day United States. And at its current rate of growth in the combustion of foul coal, China may release 1.4 billion tons of sulfur dioxide in the year 2000, versus nine million tons projected for the United States that year. In other words by the turn of the century China could cause 155 times as much acid rain as America.

When environmental orthodoxy confronts such projections, the numbers are not used as reasons why the First World should share its knowledge with the Third, so that developing countries can when possible go directly to clean-tech production, skipping brute-force means. They are not used as reasons why the Third World should adapt market pricing policies that discourage overuse. (In China today, coal is cheaper than sand; this encourages waste.) Rather the numbers are used as reasons why the Third World should not have industrial development.

Assuming technical and monetary assistance, there is no reason in principle why the developing world cannot industrialize at roughly the low-pollution level being achieved in the First World today, controlling its cycle of environmental harm more quickly than happened in the West. But this prospect is ideologically offensive to the orthodox, as it requires an admission that technology can be a friend of the environment. The many defects of industrialization are well-known to environmental orthodoxy, as they should be. The compensating advantages are verboten subjects. Among them: birth rates fall, controlling population without coercion; literacy rates rise, fostering freedom; trade unions form; women's rights are acquired; child labor declines; health care improves; and oh yes, material circumstances advance. The developed countries have many faults, but almost without exception their citizenries are richer, freer, better educated, less fertile, and less sexist than those found in developing countries.

The desire of institutional environmentalism to avoid dealing with such issues was manifested in the preliminary negotiations for the Earth

Summit. In the years prior to the summit the Group of 77—the bloc of impoverished nations whose name is a play on the wealthy Group of 7— said what it wanted from Rio was for Western countries to commit to investing 0.7 percent of GDP in development aid. Despite the common impression that vast sums go to such aid, the United States expends less than 0.2 percent of GDP on foreign assistance. As Jose Goldemberg, Brazil's former environment secretary, says, "This was not a request for charity but for investments in the common future. In the twenty-first century stable and prosperous developing-world nations will mean more to the security of the First World than military arms."

That was persuasive to me, but not to environmental lobbyists who pounded on the theme that the greenhouse effect was the preeminent issue of Rio. The tactic got out of hand, working so well that greens actually managed to convince the Western heads of state that global warming was more important than drinking-water purity. Some delegates of poor nations left Rio embittered not so much at Western governments but at Western enviros, who not only managed to place the speculative concern of greenhouse warming above the confirmed horror of Third World poverty but who seemed actively pleased to have pulled this coup, allowing as it did the theme music of the summit to suit the institutional purposes of Western environmentalism.

As the Clinton Administration took office, one candidate for a top economic post was Lawrence Summers, chief economist for the World Bank. Summers was furiously opposed by environmental lobbies because he favors Third World industrial development and has said such things as, "Nobody should kid themselves that they are doing Bangladesh a favor when they worry about global warming. Poverty is already a worse killer than any foreseeable environmental distress." Clinton decided not to nominate Summers because green opposition was so strong. Clinton did, however, ask the United Nations to pick as the new head of the U.N. Development Programme James Speth, former head of the World Resources Institute. The Group of 77 nations was dismayed because Speth has a reputation as a doomsayer: For instance he has called tropical forest loss "an unparalleled tragedy." If the loss of renewable trees is an unparalleled tragedy, what words are left to describe millions of children dead from waterborne disease?

There does exist a faction of the environmental movement that believes the world's attention should now focus on developing nations— not only to relieve human suffering but because today ecological protection is much cheaper in the developing world than in the developed. If you were a philanthropist with money to spend on conservation you could realize ten times the return in Malaysia or Kenya that you could in

Wyoming—and you'd be thanked for your efforts, rather than sued. The bang-for-the-buck ratio in the developing world alone is a reason why some resources should be shifted from First World ecological initiatives to projects in the Third. But institutional environmentalism cannot say that attention should begin focusing on the Third World without first acknowledging that environmental problems of the First World are coming under control.

Third World Farming

A long-standing and for a time true green complaint is that the West has pushed Third World governments to overapply pesticides and fertilizers. For instance pesticide use in Indonesia rose more than 300 percent from 1965 to 1985, in part owing to the government subsidies. In 1986 Indonesia stopped subsidizing pesticides. That year a plague of brown planthopper hit the country's rice; farmers demanded chemicals. Instead field workers from the United Nations Food and Agricultural Organization came to teach "integrated pest management," described in chapter 22. Since then Indonesian rice yields have risen while pesticide use has declined, an ideal outcome.

It is also surely true that Western influence has driven some Third World farmers away from low-input crops such as lentils toward high-input crops like corn and wheat, and toward Western-favored livestock. The U.N. FAO estimates that about 4,000 species of plant and animal have been human food sources through history, but today just 150 are produced commercially. In the Andes the Inca once grew tarwi, a pealike vegetable high in protein that has low fertilizer needs. The current trend is toward revival of such indigenous crops. "Micro livestock" is another promising area. Navajo sheep, iguana, pot-bellied pigs, and other small animals offer better ratios of grain input to meat output than the cattle and fowl favored in affluent nations; they require less in the way of antibiotics and hormones than Western stock such as Holsteins. (The giant rat of Nigeria, which grows to four pounds and is docile, is considered by some agrarians an ideal meat animal, in case you're interested.) Making meat using high-input animals is a questionable strategy for the Third World; some Western stock animals do not prosper under developing world conditions. For instance there are more chickens being raised in China than in the United States, but U.S. chicken output is three times as high.

Beyond these qualifications, much of what dogmatic environmentalists think about Third World food supply is nonsensical. Prominent is the belief that the advent of Green Revolution agriculture in developing countries has been a horror. Though the world continues to know malnutrition on an unbearable scale, with perhaps 700 million people chronically undernourished, the mass starvations predicted by pessimists have not come to pass, except during wartime in places such as Biafra. Starvation has been avoided because Green Revolution farming has allowed food production to increase faster than population: an average three percent world food output improvement in the 1970s and 1980s versus world population growth of about 1.7 percent.

One reason predictions of global mass starvation were common in the late 1960s—a book called *Famine 1975!* then a best-seller—is that in the early 1960s India and Pakistan knew several years of widespread crop failures. In response international aid institutions began a concerted effort to bring high-yield agriculture to the subcontinent. Orthodoxy scoffed, Paul Ehrlich in 1968 issuing his edict that it was "a fantasy" that India could "ever" feed itself.

Instead India has been self-sufficient in food since the early 1980s. Today about 80 percent of the wheat and 40 percent of the rice grown in India are high-yield strains. Figures through most of the developing world are similar. The exception is Africa, where the Green Revolution has not caught on—and where most of the world's hunger now occurs. African soil is red, depleted, and often hostile to crops. In recent eons Africa has not been glaciated; this means the soil has not benefited from the ground mineral dust left by retreating glaciers, a natural fertilizer that makes Northern American and north Eurasian soil lush. One reason traditional life in much of Africa is nomadic may be that in ancient times the poor soil prohibited establishment of controlled agriculture.[1]

Today typical African fertilizer use is just 1.6 percent of the level found in the Netherlands. Prominent Americans such as former President Jimmy Carter have called on the world to increase fertilizer shipments to Africa. Nevertheless the Western environmental community opposes the idea, lobbying to stop Western government provisions of fertilizer to African agrarian projects such as those run by Norman Borlaug. In this case the actions of institutional environmentalism are not just muddle-headed: They border on malevolent.

Unknown in the United States, in the developing world Borlaug is considered among the most important Americans of the twentieth century. University centers named for him can be found in many countries. Born in Cresco, Iowa, in 1914, as a young man Borlaug watched the principles of high-yield agriculture being developed and decided his life's work would be to carry these ideas to the world's hungry. During the famine years of the 1960s Borlaug lived in India and Pakistan, teaching high-yield farming. In 1971 he won the Nobel Peace Prize for his role in moving India and Pakistan to food self-sufficiency. That made Borlaug, a biologist by academic training, among the few from the hard sciences to receive the peace prize. Though Borlaug might have cashed his Nobel for a cushy job he has instead continued to live in the backwoods of Mexico, the Sudan, and other poor nations. Tens of millions of people now owe their daily bread partly to his work. Arguably Borlaug has saved more lives than any other person who has ever lived.

Beginning in the 1980s Borlaug focused on Africa, the one place population growth exceeds growth in food production. About the same time American and European environmental groups began to focus on Africa, with the goal of preventing high-yield agriculture from spreading to the only region of the world it had not ventured. Borlaug has since often clashed with what he calls "the green utopians who do their lobbying in the affluent cities of the United States and Europe, enjoying every material comfort, never seeing for themselves the realities of daily suffering in the sorts of places I have lived for 50 of my 80 years."

One reality is that 80 percent of African farm labor is performed by women, usually in backbreaking fashion: Only a fifth of African farms have beasts of burden, let alone mechanized power. Another reality of Africa is that in many regions the dominant means of farming is migratory slash-and-burn, a technique harsh not only on the land but on wildlife. "When I went to Africa I couldn't believe how little wildlife there was in many of the continent's pristine regions, compared to the abundant wildlife in most of America," Borlaug says. "The reason was the tremendous destruction from slash-and-burn farming, a form that not only produces little food but causes so much harm to the land that no Western government would permit it for five minutes."

Because African soil is low in nutrients, improved agriculture there depends on fertilizer. Borlaug's pleas for more fertilizer for Africa have not been answered by Western governments. Instead several European nations that supplied fertilizer to Africa through the early 1980s have stopped under green pressure. The Ford and Rockefeller foundations, which sponsored successful Green Revolution initiatives in the 1960s and 1970s, have largely withdrawn their support for high-yield agriculture in Africa. Today Ford and Rockefeller trustees fly jet aircraft to airconditioned Manhattan skyscrapers where they sip claret, dine on free-range fowl, and chatter about how those ecologically irresponsible Sudanese want tractors and bulk ammonia. "The environmentalists who influence the large philanthropic organizations talk of fertilizers and pesticides as if they were the same, which is intellectually dishonest," Borlaug says. "There are huge distinctions in the level of toxicity.

Fertilizers only enhance compounds naturally found in soil. Even organic farmers use fertilizer."

Borlaug and others who believe in high-yield agriculture also believe in integrated pest management and similar theories of low chemical inputs. Borlaug has been teaching IPM in the Third World since the mid-1960s. "In India, Pakistan, and Turkey," he says, "we tried to persuade farmers to grow wheat partly because wheat strains are not particularly susceptible to insect attack and thus rarely require insecticides. Today in Ghana, Ethiopia, northern Nigeria, and Tanzania, we teach farmers to attain high yields of local crops like maize and cassava using no weedkillers or fungicides, only insecticide. All serious agrarians know that toxic chemicals should be used sparingly. And besides they are expensive. Low-toxic approaches to high-yield agriculture are spreading through the developing nations much more rapidly than the greenies would have you believe."

The techniques are also spreading throughout big aid institutions. In 1991 the World Bank, which runs agrarian centers in Kenya, Sri Lanka, and other developing nations, began to emphasize IMP. One chemical-replacing idea these centers now advance is erosion control through a recently discovered grass called veviter. Veviter seems almost magical for high-yield farming: Planted at the edge of fields it sends down long roots that hold soil, but never expands beyond its planting site and so does not have to be controlled itself through herbicides or hand pulling, as is the case with other antierosion grasses. According to a 1993 report from the National Research Council, Zimbabwe currently spends $1.5 billion per year on fertilizer to compensate for topsoil displacement through erosion. Veviter barriers have the potential to eliminate this entire expense. Other knowledge-based developments in agriculture are on the way to the developing world. None will guarantee against ecological harm or malnutrition, but taken as a whole they suggest that Third World food production may continue to increase faster than population, without great ecological harm.

In recent years prominent doomsayers including Ehrlich and Lester Brown have begun advancing the line that the Green Revolution has "plateaued," in Brown's term: No important crop productivity gains remain, even through bioengineering. This close-the-patent-office view has been offered many times. Of course that is no guarantee the patent office will not someday close. But many agrarians think there is plenty of steam left in the Green Revolution.

Donald Plucknett, a researcher for the Consultative Group on International Agriculture Research, concluded in a 1993 study that not only are global food-crop yield increases continuing at about the same rate as in previous decades, but the most impressive gains are now coming in places like Africa. Before his activities were suspended in 1991 by civil war, Borlaug spent several seasons teaching farmers in the Sudan. Working short of fertilizer and tractors, Borlaug and his disciples, many of them Mexicans, increased the yield of Sudan's wheat region fivefold. This suggests even poor African nations can grow dramatically more food while reducing environmental harm by producing food from progressively fewer acres, freeing up land for return to a natural state. Orthodoxy blanches at that conclusion, so infuriatingly optimistic.

The Rainforest

In 1989 a 737 jetliner belonging to the Brazilian national airline Varig became lost in clouds over the Amazon rainforest. Having drifted inland from the populous coast, the plane was too far from radar to have its location determined by air controllers. The aircraft flew for hours, its pilots disoriented. Descending to search for landmarks, the flight crew could discern nothing but an ocean of trees. Fuel exhausted, the jetliner pancaked onto the canopy of the rainforest. Most passengers survived. The pilots were able to make a reasonably soft landing, they reported, because they could see by the light of the fires.

Rainforest loss is one of the areas where green orthodoxy is right to sound the emergency tocsin. The admirable ability of the environmental movement to draw attention to rainforest preservation indicates that once ecologists set their minds to transferring the world's notice from the nondoomsday in affluent countries to confirmed ecological threats in the Third World, they will be able to inspire the affluent to act in defense of the impoverished. This is a hopeful sign for ecorealism and for the coming century.

This said, there are nevertheless prominent flaws in environmental thinking about the rainforest. The first concerns degree of damage. There is no doubt that tropical forest loss worldwide is an ongoing problem of large dimensions. According to the United Nations Food and Agriculture Organization, in the 1980s Mexico lost 18 percent of its forests; Southeast Asia lost 13 percent; Madagascar lost 11 percent; the Amazon lost nine percent; Central Africa lost seven percent. In light of these losses, developing-world government policies such as the 1980s Brazilian program that granted cattle ranchers tax favors for clearing land by fire should be seen as comparable in wantonness to extreme U.S. offenses against nature such as railroad hunts of buffalo.

Yet current rainforest loss estimates are not out of line with figures for the First World during the past century. In several decades of the nineteenth century North American forests declined at about ten percent, also with burning the primary clearing mechanism. Woodlands of the developed world recovered with remarkable speed from that phase of deforestation. The same may happen in the Third World as well. The recovery will be aided by increasing economic activity that brings to poor nations the prosperity necessary to surmount their pollution peaks.

Rainforest alarmists never point out that loss figures for tropical forests are deducted from a gigantic base. The Amazon rainforest covers about 1.7 million square miles, almost two-thirds the size of the 48 states. Even after a decade of determined burning at least four-fifths of this wilderness, an area larger than the United States east of the Mississippi, still stands primal and pristine. Amazonia is so expansive and so lightly if clumsily touched by the human hand that stretches of the region dozens of miles in length remain nearly uncharted.

During the late 1980s, when reporters traveled to Amazonia to produce stories suggesting the entire region on fire, dispatches contained a significant distortion. There are only a handful of highways in the Amazon, most in the state of Rondonia. When reporters drove those highways they saw columns of smoke in every direction; it seemed to them the entire tropics was ablaze. But land-clearing projects concentrate along roads, for the obvious reasons. Back in the vastness of the jungle fires were rare. Not venturing far from their Land Rovers, reporters did not see this.

In 1994 the Brazilian government announced it will invest $600 million in a network of radars with the amazing name Amazon Vigilance System. Twenty radar stations will be built throughout the rainforest basin. The radar dishes will not so much be trained on the sky to assist aircraft as trained on the tree canopy line to watch for forest burning or unauthorized construction. Primal Amazonia remains so vast that a few local warlord-businessmen, characters who might have sprung from the pages of Joseph Conrad, have built ranching or mining operations in the inland basin with the existence of their projects going unknown to authorities for years. A satellite Brazil recently launched will also monitor the rainforest for unauthorized clearing. Traditionally nations have invested in radars and reconnaissance spacecraft to protect themselves from foreign powers. It is a sign of the times, and an encouraging one, that nations now begin to use such technology for conservation. The United States is currently investing $18 billion in a series of environmental survey satellites for launch beginning in 1998. Within the lifetimes of readers of this book, most if not all of the globe will fall under the protection of some manner of ecological monitoring system.

Another common misconception about rainforests is that they are "the lungs of the world." Though tropical forests draw carbon dioxide from the atmosphere and thereby aid the greenhouse balance, their contribution to oxygen creation is small. Most new oxygen comes from sea plants. Studies show that to the extent land plants generate the precious element, boreal forests, being larger than the equatorial forests, are primary makers of oxygen.

Next on the list of rainforest misconceptions is that logging must be stopped to prevent tropical woodland decline. In many equatorial countries logging is done in careless ways that cause gross tree loss. For instance Christopher Uhl, a researcher at Penn State University, has found that in Brazil some 27 trees are damaged for every one taken out by loggers. But nineteenth-century logging in the United States was careless, too. One century's outrage may be the next century's enlightenment.

Since the 1988 murder of Chico Mendes, the Brazilian rubber tapper who was an organizer against forest burning, rubber tappers have achieved an honored status in the green pantheon. But in the late nineteenth century they were considered as bad as cattlemen; many indigenous Brazilians were killed by tappers fanning into the jungle during the rubber boom. Today better-behaved rubber tappers are considered rainforest allies, as someday better-behaved loggers may be. Until logging began to spread in Brazil in the 1960s, some Brazilians thought the rainforest had no inherent value: It was an obstacle to be vanquished, something to be "tamed." As sustainable logging is achieved in the developing world, local populations, including indigenous peoples, will acquire a long-term interest in keeping the rainforest vibrant.

The next misconception about rainforests is that losses are increasing. In fact all studies show losses declining, especially in the Amazon. Between 1989 and 1990, rates of Amazonian forest clearing declined 27 percent, mainly because Brazil ended the tax incentive for ranching. In 1991 the rate was 65 percent lower than in 1985, according to the Pan American Deforestation Study, a satellite survey run in conjunction with NASA.

The common headline "Loss of Tropical Rainforests Found Much Worse than Thought" (an actual page-one headline from a 1990 edition of the *New York Times*) is almost always based not on empirical data but on studies that arrive at their dreary estimates through computer projection. In the case of this headline the story was based on a computer model written by the World Resources Institute, an advocacy group. There's nothing wrong with advocacy. But considering that computer projections are dubious tools even under ideal circumstances, projections from computers programmed by advocates ought to be greeted with attuned skepticism. The World Resources Institute study tied its projections partly to an estimate that as much as 40 million acres of rainforest were being lost per year, a figure that works out to about a football field per second. This statistic has entered the doomsday canon, cited repeatedly by Vice President Al Gore, who in environmental speeches repeats the phrase "a football field lost every second" like a mantra.

But the 40-million-acre number came from a rough 1988 estimate by a Brazilian researcher who used some weather satellite photos to extrapolate rainforest loss. When the images were taken there were several major fires burning in the Amazon. Smoke clouded the photos, so the researcher derived the 40-million-acre estimate by examining a small section where the picture was clear, then assuming that section representative of the entire rainforest. Extensive burning of Amazonia ended in 1991. After the smoke dissipated, clear satellite photos by NASA showed a much lower rate of forest loss than projected in the 1988 rough estimate. The actual rate of rainforest loss was about 3.7 million acres per year—still high, but less than a tenth of the number used for "a football field lost every second." Otto Solbrig, a Harvard biologist, has noted that through the 1980s researchers commonly worked with a projected figure of 50 percent loss of tropical rainforests. Now, based on satellite surveys, losses of ten to 20 percent are presumed.

This changed assumption has received almost no attention. For example in 1993 the *New York Times* ran this headline: "Loss of Species Is Worse than Thought in Brazil's Amazon." Buried in the text was a mention that the latest satellite survey, compiled by Compton Tucker of NASA, showed a total of 15 percent of the Amazon has been "disturbed" by development, nothing like the sort of loss rate used by doomsayers. Also according to the Tucker survey the rate of Amazon forest loss peaked at 0.4 percent per year in the 1980s, a far lower rate than once assumed. These findings were downplayed. Emphasized instead was a second section of Tucker's report, one supposing that even small Amazon reductions might have important species-loss effects through forest fragmentation. Tucker may be right about this: Fragmentation is a valid worry. But this section of his report was not based on empirical evidence; it was generated by computer projection, using the disputed island-reduction theory detailed in chapter 30. That is to say the confirmed optimistic part of the NASA rainforest finding was skipped over while the speculative, computer-generated negative portion made headlines.

Another rainforest misconception is that equatorial forests are being altered by people for the first time. Richard Cooke, a Smithsonian Institution researcher, has found evidence that people were burning the Panamanian rainforest at least 11,000 years ago. Anna Roosevelt of the Field Museum of Natural History in Chicago has found pottery in the Amazonia rainforest that dates at least 7,500 years back, and evidence of artificial Amazon burning 11,000 years ago, suggesting human environmental influences there began well before technology.

And still another misconception is that rainforests must be preserved so that medical researchers can seek rare plants for drugs. There are many reasons to think that considerable rainforest preservation can be achieved by using tropical woodlands as "extractive reserves" for nuts and plants, or for ecotourism. Charles Peters, a researcher at the New York Botanical Garden, has produced studies suggesting some rainforests may be worth more when held as extractive reserves than when logged. Other studies have found that ecotourism, however gratingly fashionable, may give native peoples a financial interest in forest preservation. For instance Ann Misch of the Worldwatch Institute estimates that over its lifetime, a macaw in a wild habitat might generate $165,000 in revenues from ecotourists. Such estimates are encouraging. But the pharmaceutical potential of rainforests, often put by environmentalists at $100 billion per year, may be exaggerated.

Quinine comes from the cinchona tree, whose properties were known to the Incans; the rosy periwinkle of Madagascar was the first source of the active ingredient of the anticancer drugs Oncovin and Velban. But as noted by Irving Johnson, a retired researcher who led the group that discovered the anticancer alkaloids of the rosy periwinkle, similar plants also grow in Texas. Carl Djerassi, a Stanford University chemist, further notes that today pharmaceutical engineers rarely use rainforest plants themselves as bulk supplies: What they use are a few kilos of "molecular leads" from which to engineer analog substances. Considering the rate at which bioengineered genetic analogs are being perfected, rainforest economists might better concentrate on commodity industries such as nuts and logging, where there is no substitute for natural production.

What reason is left to preserve rainforests? The same one that justifies preservation of so many other habitats: We don't know what we don't know and thus cannot say what ultimate significance, either to nature or the human future, any wilderness may possess.

Indications are that rainforest preservation efforts are in many countries already bearing fruit. Several speakers at a May 1994 meeting of the National Agricultural Biotechnology Council declared that developing nations had made "breathtaking progress" in biotechnology conservation since 1992, as they are now offered an incentive in the form of the Rio biodiversity treaty, which once ratified is sure to bring tropical governments and landholders at least some royalties for genetic materials found on their soils. As of 1994, satellite imagery employed by the Forest Survey of India showed that country's forested area to be growing, despite the extreme human population pressures India faces.

Assuming rainforest use follows the pattern observed in the developed world—a period of crazed destruction, followed by a Pollution Peak, capped by aforestation as knowledge expands and pressure on the land declines—the conservation of the rainforest may be achieved more readily than presumed.

World Bank: Threat or Menace?

As big banks are often the secret villains in conspiracy theories of Lyndon LaRouche and John Birch types, the World Bank today holds a central position in the conspiracy theories of green orthodoxy. Environmentalists say with some justification that the bank favors the sort of large-scale projects that are likely to become white elephants as economic conditions shift. But their complaint that the World Bank conspires against the global ecology is less persuasive. For instance it is said the World Bank committed a dreadful offense by funding the handful of highways that now cross Rondonia. These roads make ranching possible in interior Brazil, which means some wilderness loss. But Rondonian highways are practically undetectable in the vastness of the Amazon. Their scope is approximately the same as if there were a single highway from Atlanta to Boston and no other major road in the eastern United States.

Further dislike of the World Bank stems from the fact that its projects move local cultures toward cash economies. Under the Small Village Fallacy, cash is bad because currency can be traded freely for goods from distant markets, causing material expectations to rise. The barter system should be kept because it only works locally and probably forecloses development of an advanced economy, there never having been an advanced economy based on barter. According to ecological dogma, living by the barter system is ideal for SOMEBODY ELSE.

On occasion I have listened to affluent Western greens discourse on the awfulness of cash-crop initiatives in India, where rather than grow lentils for subsistence a farmer may today raise wheat, sell it in town, and spend the proceeds on the family's food. Farmers buying food! This is made to sound a cog in a vast banker's collusion. Yet anyone who visits the heartland farmhouses of Iowa finds kitchens full of supermarket food. American farmers grow a cash crop and trade the proceeds for whatever they require, including things to eat. Though hardly foolproof, this system allows for specialization of labor and comparative advantage. Who is better off in the end—the American cash-using farmer or the Indian subsistence farmer?

One clear flaw of cash-economy initiatives is that in the Third World they favor men: When the World Bank bankrolls a project the structure is invariably patriarchal. But then sexism is the indigenous culture of most developing nations. Affluence, and the freedom it conveys, are social forces that combat sexism. Here the green community is in a doubletalk bind. When it comes to indigenous customs, environmental orthodoxy says the First World should regard local culture as sacrosanct. But in many countries sexism is egregiously traditional.

This bind is now generating friction between the environmental and women's communities. In the 1970s and 1980s these movements were compatriots but in the 1990s have grown mildly antagonistic. Pondering the Third World, many women's advocates increasingly feel there must be industrial development: Nothing else will provide the financial means to shake up the centuries of feudal traditions that hold women down. But many greens cannot abide advocacy of industrial growth. Thus "ecofeminism," often predicted as a potent evolving force, may grow in the First World where affluence already exists but fray in the Third World where women need money more than terminology.

In the late 1980s the World Bank established a division with the flat-footed name Global Environment Facility, capitalized with $5 billion for Third World ecological restoration. When the GEF was founded, there was sentiment among Western governments to endow it richly. Environmental lobbies set to work attacking the World Bank affiliations of the GEF. They succeeded so well that in 1993 further capitalization of the division was essentially suspended. To orthodoxy this was a major victory—a big financial institution placed on the run by green opposition. But thanks to environmental complaints about the GEF, Western governments now have a respectable excuse to stop contributing to conservation efforts in poor countries.

The Twenty-First-Century Challenge

Imponderable as the problems of the Third World may seem, the situation is not without hope. A basic verity of the developing world—little understood in the West and given scant credence by orthodox thinking—is that even in recent decades, as population and pollution have increased exponentially, the lot of the typical person has improved, not declined. The United Nations noted in its *Human Development Report 1994* that life expectancies, literacy rates, and nutrition were improving almost uniformly throughout the developing world. Democracy is on the rise, while authoritarianism and the nuclear arms race are on the decline. And though the United Nations finds that 32 percent of the world's impoverished class now exists under conditions it describes as "abysmal," that is down from the 70 percent who suffered abysmal conditions in the year 1960—though the human population has soared in the interim.

The environmental, human-health, human-rights, and material-security problems faced by the disenfranchised of the Third World represent what is by far the most important twenty-first-century challenge for ecological activism. To begin to address this challenge, the West must shift its focus from the ecological problems of the First World to the true crisis now in progress in the Third.

Governments must renew their commitments to international aid. Perhaps new, market-oriented forms of aid are required to avoid past problems of graft and paternalism. But the money must flow, and today a dollar spent for protection of the environment will accomplish ten times as much in the Third World as the First.

Environmentalists must come to terms with the fact that people are more important than plants and animals: Decent conditions must be provided for all of the former before there can be security for the latter. And institutional environmentalism must acknowledge, first to itself, then to the public, that ecological conditions in the First World simply are not dire anymore. The financial resources of the affluent states will not shift to water sanitation in Peru or cooking fires in Kenya until the instant doomsday alarm in the United States and Western Europe has been canceled. It is in the Third World, not the First, where the environmental emergency now lies.

TOXIC WASTES

RECENTLY LIFE HAS DONE THE FAVOR OF TAKING ME TO SEVER-
al of the world's worst toxic waste sites. I have learned two lessons:
Wear old shoes and watch out for wildlife.

I went to a place called the Demode Road site, in rural Rose
Township, Michigan. Once 5,000 drums of toxics were scattered there;
they leaked PCBs, poisons, and carcinogens into the pristine land.
Subject of several congressional hearings, Demode Road has been
described as some sort of squalid, chemically singed death zone that
would make the dark side of the moon seem inviting. It turned out to be
a wooded tract with trees, shrubs, and wildflowers; abundant deer,
owls, rabbits, and other wildlife. "The bad part of showing you this
site," said Robert Hayes, then of the Michigan Department of Natural
Resources, "is that it doesn't look horrible."

I went to another prominent toxic waste location, the closed Avtex
Fibers rayon plant in Front Royal, Virginia. There PCBs, caustic soda,
chlorine, nitric acid, and carbon disulfide were spilled into the
Shenandoah River and pumped into leaky pits. After the plant was
closed by state inspectors, one newspaper editorial called it "the worst
chemical horror story since Bhopal." Beaver, deer, fox, red squirrel, and
other Blue Ridge fauna are common on the grounds. "There's often an
amazing amount of wildlife at Superfund [toxic waste] sites," Vincent
Zenone, then the EPA's on-scene coordinator for the Avtex cleanup,
told me.

I went to Rocky Mountain Arsenal, often referred to in Congress as "the most deadly place on Earth." On this 17,000-acre reservation near Denver the Army made nerve gas, munitions, and the incendiary devices dropped on Tokyo and Dresden during the 1945 firebombings that killed more people than the Hiroshima and Nagasaki atomic attacks. Later Shell Oil used the arsenal to make pesticides. Wastes from the manufacturing of these many poisons are scattered throughout the grounds. Because Rocky Mountain Arsenal is mainly the responsibility of the federal government, Congress has authorized nearly a billion dollars in restoration funds and indicated it expects to spend much more.

At the security gate to Rocky Mountain Arsenal I bumped into a man named Kelly Drake, the director of the Colorado Wildlife Federation. Drake is a regular visitor to Arsenal because it harbors, by his estimate, 232 forms of important wildlife, including several endangered species. There are peregrine falcon, white-tail and mule deer, pheasant, geese. In 1986 some eagle discovered the arsenal and have since called it home. Now there are blinds for public viewing of eagle nests and bus tours of wildlife highlights. *Bus tours of a toxic waste site.* In 1992 Rep. Patricia Schroeder of Denver moved through Congress a bill classifying Rocky Mountain Arsenal as a national wildlife refuge. Endangered species saved by toxic waste? Only in America!

Schroeder's bill was a fine idea, creating within the boundaries of an expanding metropolis an important zone for natural preservation. Yet environmental lobbyists were immensely relieved when the conversion of Rocky Mountain Arsenal to a national wildlife refuge escaped general notice. Some worked behind the scenes to scuttle Schroeder's bill, though she is among the leading liberals in Congress. Green lobbyists sensed that the "most deadly place on Earth" becoming a sanctuary for endangered species doesn't quite add up.

It does not. Like many toxic disposal areas, Rocky Mountain Arsenal has genuine problems requiring correction. Yet all but a handful of toxic sites present nothing close to the looming threat depicted in doomsday ideology. Institutional environmentalism has exaggerated the toxic waste threat as much to advance its own political influence as to sound necessary alarms. The result is disproportionate public anxiety and a cleanup program, Superfund, that accomplishes good but sometimes expends large sums for negligible ecological gains.

By 1993 the federal government had spent $15 billion to restore 180 Superfund sites, with industry roughly matching that amount: meaning $30 billion, or about the annual total of federal aid to education, invested in toxic cleanup. Yet assessments of environmental priorities, including those from the EPA's own Science Advisory Board, consistently rank toxic wastes as secondary or even tertiary. As the physicist Philip Abelson has said, the panic aspects of toxic cleanup are "a triumph of half-truths over rational thinking." Toxic waste is thus another area where ecorealism is called for.

There are 1,286 locations on the Superfund priority list. The Office of Technology Assessment expects that 1,000 more sites will eventually qualify for the list, and says that by a literal reading of the Superfund law, a flabbergasting 439,000 additional locations could be designated. Paul Portney and Katherine Probst of the nonpartisan think tank Resources for the Future estimate that restoration of the first 1,286 Superfund sites may cost another $40 billion. Milton Russell and Mary English, researchers at the University of Tennessee, believe that if every potential Superfund site is restored to a moderate ecological standard the bill will be $500 billion, roughly double the defense budget.

Gains from Superfund cleanups are modest relative to the price. The Office of Technology Assessment estimates that such projects cost from $5 million to $50 million per premature cancer avoided. Jocelyn White, director of a private consultancy called Environmental Issues Management, has pointed out that even using a worst-case reading of toxic waste dangers, federal spending is now $1.7 million per premature Superfund cancer case, versus $756 for research per breast cancer case. Some Superfund expenditures border on theater of the absurd. At one toxic waste site in Columbia, Missouri, $20 million was spent to excavate 450 truckloads of soil and ship the result to a disposal site in Louisiana. Federal officials, enforcing an "eat dirt" standard sometimes read into the letter of Superfund law, ruled that the Columbia site had to be sufficiently clean that a person could consume six teaspoonful of its soil every year for 70 years without risk. Children do sometimes put dirt in their mouths, and the dirt should not harm them. Yet has anyone in the history of the world ever eaten dirt every year for 70 years? And would we be surprised if such a person were in less than optimal health?

The most important study to assess whether toxic waste sites imperil public health was completed in 1991 by the National Research Council. The council found that at Woburn, Massachusetts, and a few other places, disease incidence was linked to chemical dumping. At Woburn in the 1970s, chemicals including trichloroethylene, a likely carcinogen, were leaked into drinking water. Seventeen fatal leukemia cases occurred among children whose homes were served by two contaminated town wells. In the four years after the wells were shut, nine additional leukemias developed among children who drank the water; since then there has been no more leukemia in the area. This caused Walter Zelen, a researcher at the Harvard School of Public Health, to call the link between toxic wastes and health damage real. In essence the National Research Council endorsed Zelen's conclusion.

But in most other respects the Research Council report kicked the chair out from under the toxic-waste emergency. The council found that drinking simple tap water is far more dangerous than living near the majority of toxic waste sites. Studies demonstrate a clear relationship between tap-water consumption and elevated risk of bladder cancer, probably caused by chlorination. Studies do not, the council found, show any clear relationship between proximity to toxic wastes and cancer. This conclusion, which environmental lobbies denounced as irresponsible, has been the finding of most of the many dozens of academic studies of Superfund sites conducted since the day the national toxic-waste SOS began at Love Canal in 1978.

Skepticism Overlooked from the Start

Through a chain of circumstances in which the Hooker Chemical division of Occidental Petroleum and local government officials both bear considerable blame, homes and a school were built on a field where toxic wastes had been buried at Love Canal, near Niagara Falls, New York. Eventually the wastes seeped into basements. As with many toxic waste cases the people who lived on the scene were screwed in every sense. Their property and perhaps health damaged by acts of others, they were put through the wringer by government foot-draggers, corporate stonewallers, and lawyers far more concerned with their billings than producing the settlement checks that would allow the victims to get on with their lives.

Health damage from anxiety, a real enough medical condition, is common among those who live near Superfund sites. But do such people often suffer environmental harm as well? Almost from the start of the "poisoning of America" scare, studies have shown this unlikely.

For instance a 1980 study of the people who lived around Love Canal, conducted by the New York State Department of Health, found that "both the numbers and types of cancer were in no way unusual from that which would be expected in the general population." Was this study a whitewash? A 1980 committee headed by Lewis Thomas, then chancellor of the Memorial Sloan-Kettering Cancer Center, found "there has been no demonstration of acute health effects linked to exposure to toxic wastes at Love Canal." In 1981 a study in the technical journal *Science* concluded, "Data from the New York State Cancer

Registry show no evidence for higher cancer rates associated with residence near Love Canal."

One study did find health harm at Love Canal: a review conducted by Beverly Paigen, a credentialed researcher then at the Roswell Park Memorial Institute in Buffalo, a cancer center of high standing. Paigen detected elevated rates of low-birthweight babies, hysterectomies, epilepsy, bronchitis, and cancer at Love Canal. This report generated a national sensation. Paigen, however, essentially assumed that if a Love Canal resident stated that a health condition was caused by toxic wastes, it must be so. A panel of medical researchers asked by New York state to review Paigen's findings called them "far short of the mark as an exercise in epidemiology . . . the illnesses cited as caused by chemical pollution were not medically validated . . . [the report] cannot be taken seriously as a piece of sound research."

Since a quarter of the population develops cancers, and other bad health effects strike people no matter where they live, the fact that bad health effects are observed around toxic wastes in itself shows little. To an epidemiologist the challenge is to determine whether disease incidence in a particular place is unusually high. The main finding of most epidemiological studies of toxic waste areas is that when health problems are compared to nearby communities without contamination there is no significant difference, with a few tragic exceptions such as at Woburn.

Epidemiology is inexact; perhaps there are links that epidemiologists miss. For instance around 1990 some researchers began to suppose synthetic toxics play a role in breast cancer. This prospect is something epidemiologists have not studied at Superfund sites because medical science has long assumed breast cancer is driven by genes, pregnancy timing, and hormones, not environmental exposure. The new research suggests that some toxics break down into xenoestrogens, chemicals that mimic hormones. If confirmed this hypothesis would have dramatic implications for understanding breast cancer, and would send the epidemiology of Superfund sites back to the drawing board.

Philip Brown, a sociologist at Brown University, has studied people living near toxic waste sites. Brown believes that although many of the sites are not dangerous, the worst do more damage than shows up in conventional epidemiology. He also attributes some of the dread such sites engender to the human-nature desire to fix blame for family tragedies outside the home. Brown notes, "A percentage of people in the vicinity of toxic waste sites want to attribute practically any health condition they have to the wastes, and this has gotten more pronounced as society becomes more chemophobic."

When studies found no unusual cancers at Love Canal, one objection was that cancer has a long latency period, suggesting its effects might not be detectable immediately after the 1978 basement leaks. By 1993 follow-up studies on Love Canal residents still had found no unusual rates of cancers. More telling, active dumping of wastes at Love Canal—the period when people were most likely to suffer exposure—occurred from 1940 to 1953. A 1984 study published in *Science* found clear evidence of health damage during that period, namely low-birthweight babies. But since 1953, the study found, the Love Canal area had a normal incidence of low-birthweight babies, suggesting that direct human exposures to Love Canal chemicals ended in 1953 when the active dumping ended. This in turn suggests that by the time Love Canal became national news in 1978, it was already more than two decades since the worst exposures occurred. Unusual levels of cancer would have had time to develop. They had not.

The key word *exposure* in the above paragraph explains almost everything about why actual health damage from toxic wastes appears so much less than expected. Chemicals can only hurt you if you are exposed to them. Generally a person must swallow or inhale at close quarters for exposure to matter. Many toxic waste sites contain chemicals that would do considerable harm if you walked up and drank them or deeply inhaled their vapors. But hardly anyone ever does that. How many readers of this book have ever stood within view of toxic wastes?

According to the Agency for Toxic Substances and Disease Registry, a federal bureau, only 109 of the 1,286 designated "priority" Superfund sites might cause actual exposure, mainly through toxics that leak into drinking water. Nationwide, according to the agency, there have been only 11 confirmed cases of direct human exposure to toxic wastes at Superfund sites and 98 probable cases. When toxics leak into drinking water a genuine emergency occurs, as drinking water is the best (that is, worst) medium for exposure. But this is known to have happened only in a few instances, such as Woburn; there was no drinking water contamination at Love Canal or Times Beach. Actual exposures are tragedies for the people to whom they happen, but in number they do not approach the general cataclysm depicted in doomsday orthodoxy.

Several interest groups have reasons to resist this message. For the EPA, Superfund is a large funding flow, and all federal agencies favor whatever expands budgets. For consultants and lawyers, Superfund is a full employment act. For institutional environmentalism, toxic wastes represent an issue where everyone is scared to death, which has become an agenda item. For the media, toxic waste is a great story. People who live near Superfund sites are visual victims, television's most prized commodity. Stories can focus on their outrage without having to broach slow-moving complexities such as whether fears are rationally grounded.

One institutional reason the green community continues to push toxic waste fear is that it is an effective direct-mail force. Right-wing groups raise money by claiming the Communists are poisoning the water with fluoride; left-wing groups raise money by claiming the industrialists are poisoning the water with (a)-benzopyrene. During the 1980s toxic wastes were particularly effective fund-raising tools for the Sierra Club and Greenpeace, which based many mailings on this theme. Since around 1990 groups such as the Environmental Defense Fund have begun to deemphasize toxic wastes, acknowledging the growing scientific case against "the poisoning of America." But chemophobia remains a staple for such organizations as Greenpeace and the Citizens Clearinghouse against Toxic Wastes, founded by former Love Canal resident Lois Gibbs, and for the midmorning TV talk shows whose formats emphasize morbid claims.

One seemingly frightening claim that continues to be heard from the midmorning TV shows is that "40 million Americans live within four miles of toxic wastes." But dozens of items in the home, from bleach to the propane in hair mousse, fall under the legal definition now used for toxic waste: It might as easily be said that "240 million Americans live within ten feet of toxic wastes." More important, every American lives near many hazards that could be fatal *assuming direct exposure.* Airport runways, radiology wards, railroad tracks, military armories, high bridges, and other places considerably more dangerous than any toxic waste site are common in every community.

The toxic waste issue is best divided into two categories: yesterday's wastes, dumped into Superfund sites that must be cleaned, and today's wastes, which go to incinerators or regulated "schedule C" landfills. That formulation reflects something essential that is routinely overlooked: Since the 1970s, creation of new toxic dumps has almost entirely ceased. In the United States almost all toxic by-products are now disposed of under tight supervision, in ways that render further contact with the biosphere close to unimaginable. Thus the U.S. toxic waste problem has not only peaked, it peaked years ago.

Yesterday's Toxics: Superfund

Let's return first to Demode Road in Michigan. This chemical waste site is sort of boring; today most Superfund locations are. During the late 1970s and early 1980s some toxic discoveries were visually dramatic—

valleys of drums, vile potions oozing from the earth. In these cases people in moonsuits arrived and brought the immediate threat under control. What remain are places where chemicals permeate the ground or are precariously stored, and no one quite knows what to do about it.

Toxic dumping took place at Demode Road during the 1960s. Like many abuses of the time, it was no secret to the authorities. State and local officials received frequent complaints about trucks reeking of alchemy cutting down the rustic back roads around Demode Road after sunset. No action was taken. One of the largest Superfund sites, the Stringfellow Pits outside Los Angeles, is where it is because in the 1960s local government officials tacitly encouraged General Electric, Rheem Manufacturing, and other companies to dump some 34 million gallons of acids there. Through the 1970s, tacit official approval of chemical dumping was common.

After toxic wastes hit the headlines in 1978, Demode Road was discovered. A new state commission swooped into town, declaring a "toxic substance emergency." The leaky barrels were picked up. But about the chemicals that had permeated the ground, nothing was done. These qualified the site for Superfund, enacted in 1980 in response to Love Canal. Superfund provides means to sue those responsible for dumping, creates cleanup mechanisms, and taxes the chemical industry to pay for cleanups where the guilty cannot be identified. Gisella King, who moved to the Demode Road area "to escape the noise and pollution of the city," recalled the numbing effect of the phrase *toxic substance emergency*. People whose horses or livestock had died recently had no way of knowing if the chemicals were to blame, or if they'd be next. "Back then we were flabbergasted when they announced it would be eight years before the cleanup could be completed," she says. Fourteen years would pass before the cleanup would even begin.

Such slowness has caused Superfund to be widely ridiculed. The writer Betsy Carpenter dubbed the program Superflop. But a glacial pace was dictated by Congress, with progress further retarded by environmentalist lawsuits. Strict adherence to the Superfund law requires a slow-motion Kabuki of studies, public hearings on the studies, preliminary draft proposals, public comments on the proposals, final draft proposals, more hearings, a Record of Decision ("the rod," in bureaucratese), and then appeals on the rod. These stages are legalistic: formal testimony, stenographers, transcripts. In most cases, an actual cleanup can commence only after every party signs off on every stage.

Judges have interpreted the Superfund statute to provide "joint and several liability," meaning a company that contributed even one barrel of waste to a site may be liable for the entire cleanup cost. This creates among what the EPA calls "potentially responsible parties" incentive to fashion cross-suits. Liability insurers sue their own insureds, trying to evade responsibility; obviously guilty companies sue slightly guilty ones, trying to fob off costs; defendants willing to pay a fair share to get out of suits find other defendants sue to keep them ensnared; the EPA, through the Department of Justice, sues other government agencies; the list goes on, billable hours accumulating. At one trial involving a Superfund site in Monterey Park, California, there were 170 responsible parties—no kidding!—each with attorneys.

One result of such legalism is predictable: Superfund is a great program for lawyers. According to a Rand Corporation study, fully 88 percent of payments by Superfund insurers go to "transaction costs," mainly litigation; only 12 percent to cleanup. The paint company Benjamin Moore estimates it has spent nine times as much on Superfund litigation costs—often in trying to get legal permission to sign a settlement and pay up—as it eventually will invest in cleanups. A partner at a blue-chip Washington law firm told me, "Every big Superfund case now has a PRP [potentially responsible party] steering committee where one of the main issues discussed is how to delay payment for as long as legal expenses are less than the present-dollar value of the settlement."

Because the EPA has since the early Reagan years operated under a hiring freeze, when its workload expanded owing to Superfund the agency had no choice but to contract out feasibility studies and similar actions. Of the money spent by the EPA under Superfund at least half has gone to consultants, not cleanup crews. Consultants have a pecuniary interest in dragging the process out, to keep the meter running. And unlike government bureaucrats who burrow into dingy offices with peeling paint, consultants live well. A 1991 EPA audit discovered that Superfund consultants had billed the taxpayer for such necessities as Christmas parties and $2,730 for "rented" plants. A revealing item from the EPA audit concerns the quarterly progress reports that consultants must file to justify their invoices. In 1990 Bechtel Environmental Management filed a report declaring as its quarterly accomplishment "achieved required target of $60,000 in monthly program management billings."

At Demode Road the primary legal question was whether the main companies responsible (Chrysler, Ford, Hoescht Celanese, and TRW) would contest or settle. The group decided to be good guys and own up, though maintaining for the record they had not the slightest idea—honestly, not the slightest! maybe UFOs!—how barrels of their wastes got there. The EPA decided that tainted soil at Demode Road would be incinerated, estimated cost $34 million. Then the PRPs said no, we'd rather fight. The firms offered $14 million. At that price incineration was out. "Soil washing," by which water is drawn through the contaminated zone with pumps, purified and returned, could be afforded. The rod was altered from incineration to soil washing.

A range of possibilities exists for Superfund cleanups, each with some controversial aspect. Incineration is the nuclear option: This destroys toxics but is expensive and is itself feared. Removal is another option: Nearby residents consulted on Superfund cleanups invariably want every ounce of suspect soil dug up and shipped far, far away, which makes sense for them but merely transfers the problem to somebody else's backyard. Soil washing has seemed promising, as long as any underground plumes of toxics are pulled up before reaching a drinking-water aquifer. Once that happens toxics seem to become as impossible to recall as rinsing soap suds from a sponge. Curtis Travis, an Oak Ridge National Laboratory researcher, says that "once chemicals hit an aquifer cleanups become pointless. You're better off to declare the aquifer unsafe and wait a century or so till the chemicals degrade naturally."

Activists usually insist on the letter of Superfund law, which essentially requires every site restored to the point at which a potable-water well could be sunk at its center. They usually fight a solution called cap and contain: cover contaminated soils with impervious clay, surround the site with liners and sump systems to collect runoff and underground leachate, then wait until the chemicals degrade naturally. In most cases cap-and-contain is the least expensive solution. But since cap-and-contain does not return land to a pristine standard—and because the sheer practicality of this approach undercuts the perception of doomsday—it is highly unpopular with greens.

In the Demode Road case, residents favored incineration. When the switch to soil washing was announced the township achieved a heightened level of consciousness. At a public meeting called to explain the change, residents screamed at EPA officials. Environmentalists filed lawsuits to block the settlement. With soil washing, the EPA admitted, it might be a decade before anyone could determine whether the technique had worked or not. If not there would be another interminable round of studies, hearings, lawsuits, and wrinkled brows.

Eventually the PRP companies gave in and paid for incineration. In 1992, 36 tractor-trailer trucks bearing the equipment for a mobile incinerator arrived at the rural fields of Demode Road. For a year and a half soil was burned by workers wearing protective suits, under conditions approximating a biological weapons test. Late in 1993 the equipment was packed up and shipped away. Yet lawsuits over the site continue, as tests show that even after the destruction of 50,000 cubic yards of soil, traces of vinyl chloride remain below the surface. "At this point most of us wish they had just stripped out the vinyl chloride and capped the site with clay," says Michael Izzo, Rose Township's supervisor. "All this public outcry was created, and then to quiet the outcry millions of dollars were spent on this tremendously complex incineration operation that probably accomplished next to nothing. We might have used that money for schools, or to buy land for parks."

There was never any claim of public health damage from Demode Road. "Now that I've studied the issues," King, who became a community organizer at Demode Road, says, "I realize that factories are a greater health concern than Superfund sites. But people are sick of hearing about these places, just sick of it. We want them cleaned up so we can put the issue out of our minds." This analysis is a wise one. Most toxic waste sites may pose little substantive danger. But the public anxiety caused by government and corporate inaction is substantive. Polls conducted by the University of Tennessee suggest that most people consider the speed and surety of Superfund cleanups more important than a perfect result.

Here the public impulse is toward ecorealism. The ecorealist ought to favor rapid action for reasonable cleanup of toxic wastes while opposing big expenditures in quest of hypothetical perfection. The impulse of institutional environmentalism runs in the opposite direction. Some greens like the fact that it's taking so long to fix Superfund sites, as this sustains public fear. Some greens demand perfection in Superfund cleanups exactly because they know perfection cannot be achieved without incinerators or other complicated engineering solutions that can themselves be depicted as horrors, endlessly restarting the crisis.

A Day in the Life of a Superfund Emergency

Inside the mobile command post in suburban Philadelphia, maps of the target area are spread on a briefing table, military-style. Fax machines and computers hum through a satellite uplink, spitting out a flow of officious memos. Cellular phones ring continuously with calls from mayors, members of Congress, local and national media. Little markers on the maps indicate each of the 25 homes where radioactive wastes have been found. It is December 1991, and aides wearing dosimeters flutter around Walter Lee, a Superfund emergency official the EPA has dispatched to fix a just-discovered mess that Philadelphia television stations are calling a "radiation crisis."

The public expectation is that when hazardous wastes are found, helicopter strike teams descend as stricken children are rushed to intensive care. The reality is that bureaucrats, lawyers, and technicians arrive in low spirits to commence years of tiresome paper shuffling.

The Philadelphia discovery is known as the Austin Avenue site. Once a factory there processed radium ore; the plant closed in 1922 and was forgotten. In the 1980s a house on Austin Avenue was found to contain moderate radioactivity, probably because old tailings from the factory had been mixed with construction materials. The EPA demolished the home and declared the case closed. In December 1991 a local ecologist armed with a Geiger counter noticed several homes around Austin Avenue set the machine clicking. Publicity. Panic. Local officials punted to the EPA, if only to get Superfund to pay for what would happen next. Enter Walter Lee.

Lee, in his fifties, is a Ph.D. chemist. He is a cautious person with the dry speaking style characteristic of those who have their every utterance nitpicked for the slightest misuse of words. A typical day: staff meetings from 8:00 A.M. till late morning; through the lunch hour, answering calls from the many overlapping city, county, state, regional, and federal jurisdictions with interest in the Austin Avenue search; paperwork till early dusk, interspersed with various calls to beg, cajole, or threaten other government agencies into providing some iota of cooperation; in the evening, meetings with groups of outraged citizens who consider Lee the enemy. Lee spends much of his day on the phone explaining to angry callers why he can't speed up the action, one reason being that he spends much of his day on the phone with angry callers. "The pendulum has swung too far in the direction of studying everything 27 times instead of just getting on with it. I'd much rather be working with a nice leaky drum," Lee says.

Here is a typical example of Superfund tedium. A fancy EPA scanner van identified the worrisome areas around Austin Avenue by the simple expedient of driving down the street taking readings. Then it became necessary to determine which readings were triggered by hazardous wastes and which by granite: Granite is slightly radioactive naturally. The rules say the EPA must locate the legal owners of any suspect properties and get permission to tromp across lawns before so much as holding up a sensor to a building's outer wall. Failing that the agency must obtain individual warrants for outdoor readings, since the law considers this a "search." Getting house-by-house permission paperwork took the EPA many days, the very days when public interest was high and government inaction seemed most outrageous.

Lee's team found seven homes with what he called "medium-grade unsafe" radiation—enough to be troubling but not likely to harm. A medium-grade unsafe reading equated to about five rems per year of exposure inside a house. Five rems per year is less than half the amount the EPA considers safe for nuclear plant workers and not dramatically more than the natural background radiation in Denver. A worst-case interpretation of the Austin Avenue readings is a risk far smaller than the risk to children of routine injuries in the home.[1] Whether the levels of radiation at Austin Avenue were ever dangerous was, however, immediately dismissed as an issue in public debate. Even the EPA gave up discussing it. "In the current political environment, there is no hope of getting across to the public logical views of risk," said Leona Nurse, an official of the EPA regional office in Philadelphia. "People hear radiation and they panic. That was that."

None of the EPA workers thought the dosimeters they wore were necessary, but the Occupational Safety and Health Administration requires such devices for all work-related proximity to radiation, however slight. Visuals of EPA technicians with radiation badges walking neighborhood streets alongside children on the way to school made for great shock television. Television newscasts constantly referred to the "radiation crisis," though no one had been harmed, and asked "Is your home next?" Lee, with his dispassionate demeanor, repeatedly told packed news conferences that neighborhood homes were radioactive but everything would probably be all right—just give us a few months to study the situation and fill out this here paperwork. He appeared to be the perfect heartless bureaucrat in 11 o'clock news snippets.

Though Superfund is a high-profile program, recruiting capable managers has been a recurring problem. People with the requisite technical or engineering backgrounds usually can earn more in private enterprise. The job involves late-night and weekend work at civil service pay scales; the chance to be misquoted by reporters and screamed at by sobbing mothers. EXCL OPTY FOR NRVS BRKDWN is how the want ad might read.

"Dealing with the angry public, I've found people want two things," Lee says. "To know that someone cares, and to hear that the government will do it their way even if their way is wrong." At Austin Avenue the desired Their Way was for every suspect house to be bought by the EPA, demolished, and replaced with a brand-new house. Local residents were livid about the solution Lee favored, and which the EPA at one point advocated—replacing tainted walls but leaving most homes standing for families to return to. Would you want to move back into a home that had been the subject of a radiation alert, even if you could see for yourself by working the Geiger counter that the place was now cold?

Told by the Philadelphia congressional delegation that replacing the tainted parts of homes would not be enough, Lee then proposed buying out the 40 homes with the highest readings, demolishing them and leaving landscaped lots where they had stood. Already $22 million in federal funds had been spent on the Austin Avenue "crisis." Buyouts plus demolition under strict rules that would treat all the debris as hazardous would cost another $38 million, for a total expense of $60 million—a huge amount to spend for a problem just slightly north of nonexistent.

The reaction to Lee's $60 million proposal was outrage. At this writing, three years after the "radiation crisis" began, the issue remained unresolved, with Philadelphia activists asserting they would sue to block implementation of any EPA plans unless homeowners were both bought out and saw their homes rebuilt at federal expense, conferring double payment. By this point the question of spending at Austin Avenue so much of society's resources on a marginal goal had been deleted from the debate—which is the way environmental orthodoxy likes it.

Yesterday's Toxics: Time to Settle

A zone called Basin A at Rocky Mountain Arsenal, "most deadly place on Earth," is in truth deadly. Partial cleanup of Basin A killed thousands of waterfowl. Engineers found themselves unable to prevent migratory birds from alighting on some ponds temporarily exposed; when the birds drew close enough to whiff the nerve gas compounds dumped there, they died. Today Basin A remains contaminated though it is no longer actively hazardous. Vegetation grows there again, in stunted fashion.

Nearby is the factory that once made the nerve gas. It must be razed. Since the structure was reinforced during the Cold War to withstand the overpressure of a nuclear near-miss, this will be no simple task. Nearby as well is Basin F, once a 93-acre lake of toxic sludge lined only with leaky asphalt. Today Basin F is a field of tanks into which the sludge has been pumped, to await destruction in a chemical waste incinerator erected by the Army under EPA supervision. The incinerator is ready but lacks operating permits.

"It's a minor miracle that incinerator got built at all," says Louis Cheroutes, Representative Schroeder's staff chief for her district office. Many activists opposed the construction. Others opposed the alternative, shipping the sludge off the Arsenal. A governor's task force recommended that Colorado outlaw incineration, transferring the problem elsewhere. Finally the state agreed the incinerator could exist, but only to burn wastes from Basin F. Once that job is finished the machine must be disassembled and shipped far, far away. Opponents worried the Army would send other toxic wastes to the Arsenal incinerator. How those other wastes will be destroyed is to remain somebody else's concern.

No credentialed researcher has suggested that the incinerator, which will emit next to nothing, or the Arsenal as a whole causes public harm. Nevertheless all plans for restoration are the subject of intense opposition. Rocky Mountain Arsenal has been a Superfund priority site for more than a decade: The Army, with primary responsibility for restoration, has yet to succeed in so much as publishing a "preliminary draft" restoration plan, let alone actually starting restoration work. The Army has had several preliminary drafts ready but always withdrew them because some aspect or another inspired ecological controversy. The final tab for Arsenal restoration is expected to be $2 billion to $3 billion, enough to build 40 to 125 first-class inner-city schools.

On Rattlesnake Butte near the center of the Arsenal, one could imagine it is the eighteenth century, except for the artificial thunder of jetliners climbing out of Denver's airport. Prairie grasses and wildflowers dominate; deer forage and eagle soar overhead. Now that the Arsenal is a National Wildlife Refuge, the Fish and Wildlife Service may reintroduce antelope and bison, restoring the local ecology to the approximate species mix that prevailed when whites first eyed it.

Wildlife are thriving at the Arsenal and other Superfund sites not because toxic wastes are good for animals but because since genus *Homo* decided to consider toxic waste sites hyperdeadly, people have abandoned the places. Few things serve the well-being of wild species better than being left alone. Except for guards, cleanup engineers, and the occasional bus tour, Rocky Mountain Arsenal is now 17,000 acres of deserted prairie. "Some people want us to sterilize the soil and leave this place a bunch of ashes," says Ronel Finley, a conservation official working on the reintroduction of native species to the Arsenal. "But from the animals' standpoint the less we do the better. It's amazing how rapidly wildlife recovered here. Basically the recovery started the moment the dangerous basins were capped and the heavy equipment moved out." A few decades hence, Denver civic boosters may boast about the huge, pristine natural refuge within the city's shadow. Should Rocky Mountain Arsenal progress from severely contaminated to a natural wonderland in just a few decades, this will seem unbelievable to environmental orthodoxy. But it is standard operating procedure to nature.

What are the chances such a progression of events will occur at other

Superfund sites? In dubbing the toxic cleanup effort Superflop, commentators overlooked both the political birth pains of the program and the realities of dilatory legal tactics. Superfund was born under Jimmy Carter but immediately handed off to Ronald Reagan, a president hostile to environmental progress. For three years of its existence the program was under the misdirection of EPA administrator Anne Burford, arguably one of the least qualified individuals ever to hold high federal office. After Burford left the EPA stabilized but Reagan remained president and rarely authorized Superfund prosecutions. "The main problem with Superfund was the failure to instill in corporations a sense that prosecution is inevitable if they don't settle," former EPA administrator William Reilly says. Prosecutions under George Bush went up and have remained up under Bill Clinton. Now the clock has begun to run out on courtroom stalling. Even the American legal system eventually loses patience with foot-dragging.

Around 1990 Superfund settlements finally started to flow in. Beatrice, UniFirst, W. R. Grace, and other firms agreed to pay $69.5 million for the Woburn cleanup. Monsanto and some insurers agreed to pay $207 million to restore the Brio site near Houston, the settlement including a buyout of 1,700 homes and college tuitions for some 700 children who grew up in those homes during the decade of foot-dragging—the tuitions some compensation for their anxiety. By the end of 1991 polluters were paying 59 percent of Superfund cleanup costs, up from 30 percent a few years before. From 1991 to 1993 more than 100 priority sites were crossed off the list, about the same number as been cleaned up in the entire previous decade of the program.

As this book went to press the Superfund program was due for revision by Congress. The Clinton Administration had proposed a reform under which companies could allow their shares of cleanup costs to be determined by neutral arbitrators rather than courts. Companies submitting to arbitration would win waivers from future liability suits, offering a strong incentive to settle fast and get cleanups funded. Clinton's sensible Superfund proposal, and the fact that dilatory lawsuits are finally petering out, gives reason to hope that people will soon be able to "put the issue out of our minds," in Gisella King's words.

Another positive sign about Superfund is continuing improvement in cleanup technology, especially new knowledge that allows restoration to proceed on a clean-tech rather than brute-force basis. For instance there has been considerable speculation that the Superfund business would be taken over by "bioremediation," the use of microorganisms to which toxic wastes are not toxic. Such bugs might break down wastes metabolically. This has been tried mainly with oil spills. The first life-form to receive patent registration in the United States was a genetically engineered microorganism that consumes spilled petroleum. So far bioremediation seems to work in a way that can be described with intense technological precision as sort-of okay. Engineered microbes released at Galveston, Texas, to combat a 1990 oil spill appeared to metabolize the oil that drifted into a marsh. But as the test was poorly controlled, it was never determined what effect the bugs had on oil in open waters.

Two decades ago a researcher named Alan Baker at the University of Sheffield in the United Kingdom realized that there are some plants that draw up chemicals and heavy metals and detoxify them as part of their metabolic processes. Since then Baker has been searching the world for plants able to grow in contaminated soils. He has found a type of ragweed that draws lead into its stem. The ragweed is being tested near a factory in Deepwater, New Jersey, where a field is contaminated with the old gasoline additive tetraethyl lead. The ragweed is growing cheerfully, pulling out the lead. Other plants are known to draw zinc and cadmium, often found at Superfund sites, into their stems. Combining bioengineering with naturally existing living things that consume toxics, it may soon become possible to clean up some contaminated locations by doing not much more than sowing them with seeds.

One way in which Superfund had been backfiring was by creating so much liability regarding contaminated industrial sites that buyers would not purchase them for any new use, nor would banks write mortgages on such property, banks fearing they would end up holding the bag for lawsuits. In cities such as Newark, New Jersey, this had the effect of insuring that old industrial properties could not be converted into new uses. In turn companies planning expansions were buying up pristine land in rural areas where there was no chance of liability for existing contamination. The old industrial tracts end up as eyesores; inner-city jobs decline; pristine rural land ends up industrialized.

By about the year 1993 this backfire phenomenon had caused a movement to relax the "eat-dirt" interpretation of Superfund. James Florio, then governor of New Jersey, said, "It doesn't make sense to clean up a rail yard in downtown Newark so that it can be a drinking-water reservoir." This statement is significant because as a member of Congress, Florio was the principal author of the original Superfund legislation. Wichita, Kansas, Granite City, Illinois, and even chic Aspen, Colorado, found themselves in legal maneuvers to keep contaminated soils in their boundaries off the Superfund list, fearing this would result in land no one would touch for liability reasons.

In light of such developments Michigan, New Jersey, and other states with many old toxic waste sites have begun to relax the letter of cleanup standards and simplify the planning stages, for instance by allowing the drafting of generic cleanup proposals rather than requiring every site to lumber through a certification process from scratch. In 1994 the Clinton Administration proposed similar changes for federal law, specifying that if a waste site, once cleaned, was to be used for industrial purposes, the eat-dirt standard need not apply. If Clinton's revision of Superfund becomes law the pace of cleanups should accelerate anew. Old toxic waste sites, said in the 1980s a threat to end nature, may by the early 2000s be considered a thing of the past.

Today's Toxics: Fear of Incinerators

Traditionally the leading item of community dread has been the proposed construction of a prison. Many other necessary but unwanted facilities now inspire local opposition: halfway houses, homeless shelters, sewage treatment plants. But on the contemporary scale of negative public response nothing tops the hazardous waste incinerator. Nobody but nobody but nobody wants anything to do with them.

In 1992 demonstrators took over the office of then-EPA administrator Reilly to protest a hazardous waste incinerator in Jacksonville, Arkansas. In 1993 Greenpeace members chained themselves to the White House gate to protest an incinerator in East Liverpool, Ohio, leaving only when EPA Administrator Carol Browner announced a moratorium on new permits for hazardous waste incineration. People from all walks of life have marched, sat in, stormed meetings, blocked traffic, worn gas masks, and engaged in other forms of protest against incinerators planned for Philadelphia, the Bronx, Denver, Anniston, Alabama, Honolulu, Tooele, Utah, and almost every other place one of these machines has been proposed since the dawn of doomsday consciousness. The prominent ecologist Barry Commoner has called waste incinerators "as bad as nuclear reactors."

Even considering the Nimby reflex this opposition can be hard to fathom. The Bronx, for instance, has seen several protest marches against a proposed medical waste incinerator for New York City hospitals. The facility was planned in response to the Medical Waste Tracking Act, enacted after some used hospital syringes washed up on a beach in New Jersey. There was public outcry and a demand that something be done. The act now requires that almost everything touching a hospital patient must be incinerated; the incinerators must go somewhere. If there's anything someone living in a high-density area like the Bronx ought to want incinerated it is infectious hospital wastes.

Many activists also now campaign against the use of toxic wastes as fuel in cement kilns. Most synthetic toxics are based on petrochemical feedstocks, which means they burn. Employing such wastes as fuel destroys them while generating energy, which would seem a plus all around. But green orthodoxy rejects the burning of anything that might be recycled. Greens oppose burning used tires for energy, which can now be done cleanly, insisting that the rubber be recycled into new tires; though with current technology recycled tires are not as safe as new ones. Greens oppose the burning of used motor oil for electricity, insisting it be purified into new oil. And much as they claim to wish the world were rid of toxic wastes, most greens oppose the combustion of such wastes for power, insisting the chemicals be reverse-engineered into component substances. Any form of burning of waste chemicals or used products for energy now offends orthodoxy, even if toxics are destroyed and fossil fuels displaced. One reason for this opposition is visceral: The installations involved in burning projects are usually big corporate-run outfits. Another reason is twisted-up doctrine: Orthodoxy has so convinced itself that all resources are running out that somehow it is now supposed even waste chemicals and old tires—the biggest annoyance in conventional landfills—ought to be conserved. The third reason is the subconscious desire to sustain the crisis. Tire- or chemical-burning plants of the past have often failed to obey antipollution regulations. But suppose a new, entirely clean generation of such facilities could be built. Then two items could be crossed off the doomsday list, which is the last thing institutional environmentalism wants to hear.

Current regulations support the use of toxic wastes in cement kilns by calling the practice recycling, since the energy value of the chemicals is recaptured. This is particularly offensive to institutional environmentalism: a worship word expropriated by industry. Under a 1984 law recyclers are held to lower pollution-control standards than other industries. How did that happen? When the law was being debated environmental lobbyists pushed for sweetheart exemptions from those burdensome antipollution regulations for their own interest group: recyclers.

Burning toxic wastes as cement fuel is attractive because the kilns operate at around 2,700 degrees Fahrenheit, hot enough to destroy almost all molecular chains. Though studies have found no health damage to kiln workers, who are far more directly exposed than the surrounding community, many activists now propose that the practice be banned. On roads leading to a large cement kiln in Alpena, Michigan, for example, activists in 1993 erected signs reading TOURIST WARNING: ENTERING HAZARDOUS WASTE ZONE. It is an indication of eagerness to sustain the autopanic mentality that some alarmists have been making much of the fact that prior to her husband's election as president, Hillary Rodham Clinton sat on the board of directors of LaFarge, a concrete manufacturer that burns toxic waste in kilns. If Rodham Clinton, America's most important contemporary liberal, is secretly in bed with the polluters, then we're all sunk anyway.

In Anniston, Alabama, there is strong opposition to Army plans to destroy chemical weapons including VX nerve gas and sarin, a biological poison. Some 60 million pounds of such compounds will be done away with in the United States, perhaps three times as many in the former Soviet Union. Yet green factions oppose every plan to carry out the destruction.

At Anniston a group called Families Concerned About Nerve Gas Incineration has filed repeated procedural suits to block the incineration of chemical weapons, though this will occur in a "six nines" incinerator, designed to destroy 99.9999 percent of its charge. Greenpeace has worked the town, talking up trace emissions as a threat to life as we know it; parents in Anniston are terrified that their children's health is endangered. Such parental terror falls into the category of the rational irrational response, since no average citizen should be expected to wade through the technical literature on subjects such as the furan molecule, wondering whether the claimed risk is real. Yet the parental terror in Anniston begs a question: Where is the nerve gas now? Near the kids. Thousands of drums and shells of chemical agents have been sitting at Anniston Army Depot for three decades, gradually corroding. Leaks from these old shells are far more likely than from the high-tech new incinerator.

In Colorado, Texas, and Utah, opponents have demonstrated against plans to incinerate the propellant charges of ballistic missiles being destroyed under strategic arms reduction treaties. Combustion of solid rocket fuel does release toxics, but can anyone imagine better news for nature than the burning of these compounds? Owing to environmental protests destruction of ballistic rocket fuels is suspended in the United States while researchers consider such exotic prospects as freezing the propellants with liquid nitrogen, smashing the results into itty bits, then letting genetically engineered bacteria metabolize the bits. Meanwhile the fuel continues to exist, capable of being reloaded into ICBMs. Is delaying the destruction of ICBM propellant really the soundest approach to protecting the Earth?

Such fear of safety may be called the Fire Extinguisher Factor. Just out of college I bought a well-used Italian roadster. The previous owner had installed on the driveshaft, between the two seats, a racer's fire extinguisher. Having heard about Italian electrical systems I considered it prudent to leave the extinguisher in place. Whenever passengers got into the car and saw a fire extinguisher at hand, they grew ill at ease. After I removed the extinguisher, passengers were happy. Thus the presence of a solution made people uncomfortable. Abjuring the solution brought satisfaction by relieving the obligation to think about the fact that a danger exists. So it is with toxic-waste incinerators. Canceling them brings a general sense of public relief, though it leaves the underlying problem unresolved.

Of course just because experts say that new hazardous waste incinerators are safe—studies by the World Health Organization, for example, find the dioxin levels in the emissions of modern incinerators far too tiny to worry about—does not necessarily make any given incinerator a good idea. Incinerators can be bad if they cost too much compared to other options (modern waste-to-energy incinerators for regular municipal trash, often opposed on dubious safety grounds, nevertheless may have weak economic justifications), or if the facilities are in the wrong place. The East Liverpool incinerator sits less than 1,000 yards from an elementary school, much too close for any industrial facility. And while the toxic emission of the East Liverpool incinerator is minute, the machine does release moderate amounts of sulfur dioxide, which has no business near a schoolyard.[2]

Extreme fear of toxic wastes and of current systems to destroy such wastes reached a point of *reductio ad absurdum* in 1991 when a Moscow company called International Chetek offered to use surplus Soviet nuclear warheads to obliterate toxic wastes in underground caverns. Chetek quoted $660 to $2,699 per pound of waste destroyed, which is competitive with Western incineration at full environmental standards. Destruction to "100 nines"—99.9 percent carried out to 100 places—was promised. Thanks just the same.

At a Deadly Incinerator

Wearing old shoes I went to a hazardous waste incinerator in Sauget, Illinois, owned by a subsidiary of the huge corporate waste control firm Waste Management. I chose Sauget because environmental lobbyists decry it as one of the country's most deadly operations. It was fined $3.1 million in 1992 by the Illinois Environmental Protection Agency (I/EPA) for a chemical explosion.

The Sauget plant sits on a crumbling moonscape of old factories and rusting railcars in a fading industrial district near Saint Louis. Inside the gates the facility is modern, befitting its status as a profitable division of a big corporation. Each of three incinerators has elaborate stack-scrubbers to control air emissions. The newest, from Holland, is a dry stack-scrubber that unlike previous designs produces no wastewater for discharge to sewers. The by-product of the dry scrubber is calcium chloride, which is mixed with the incinerator's ash. They neutralize each other.

At Sauget incoming waste packs are opened and tested to insure that the contents conform to what is declared on the "cradle-to-grave" manifests federal law has required since the mid-1980s. Today everywhere a toxic material goes it must be signed for. In the late 1980s, encouraged by the Pollution Prevention Act, and by the fact that the elimination of chemical waste cuts potential liability, most producers of toxics began to reduce their waste output. Monsanto found it was shipping away, as wastes, about $125 million a year in recoverable chemicals, most of which it now recycles. DuPont's Beaumont, Texas, petrochemical plant found it could reduce outgoing hazardous wastes about two-thirds, with lower net costs when the value of recycling is figured in. Owing to such reforms the amount of toxic waste moving in commerce in the United States has fallen steadily in recent years. This means in turn that places like Sauget "now only get the stuff with no redeeming value," says Rapier Smiley, the plant's environmental manager.

Once waste packs enter Sauget they are on closed-circuit television continuously, even when burning inside the incinerators. In the control room operators watch dials and color bar-graph displays that show the plant's emissions second by second. State officials watch as well. Via a video link, the Sauget plant monitors may be viewed live at the I/EPA. And there are cameras within the control room, trained on the staff. By remote control, I/EPA officials can pan the cameras to insure that operators are at stations and paying attention.

Many industrial facilities now have data recorders that make computer logs of emissions. The recorders at Sauget are real-time, which will be the next wave of emissions control. Linked to the I/EPA via modem, they report about 40 billion readings per year. Readings are updated every five seconds. The first system Sauget installed updated data every 60 seconds, but regulators protested that 60-second updates meant the facility could go out of compliance with emission permits for a full minute before they would know it and order the plant shut down. Now the I/EPA knows of any foul-ups within five seconds. Most states are adapting real-time reporting for facilities such as incinerators. Eventually factories and power plants will have it, too.

The blast at Sauget came when some chemicals reacted not in the incinerator but in a dump box, tossing the box into the air. The box contained waste sodium azide, the explosive used to make automobile air bags expand very rapidly. Because no one was harmed, plant officials did not report the incident to the I/EPA. This was a mistake; when regulators found out they classified the explosion as a "spill," handing Waste Management fines and bad publicity. "Up to that point our attitude had been to comply with the letter of the law but volunteer no additional information," says James Gary, the plant's manager. "The new philosophy is tell everybody everything. Now we share all our information with I/EPA and they come around here all the time. At first we hated the cameras in the control room because it implied they didn't trust us. But now we realize that in the end close scrutiny makes our work easier."

Those sentiments are similar to ones heard today from many corporate types who are gradually abandoning the notion of adversarial relationships with environmental regulators. Claims of corporate culture transformation often have a high PR quotient: Another decade of respectful environmental behavior by industry will be required before anyone can be sure if the new attitude is real. Trust takes years to attain and moments to lose. Industry lost public trust on environmental issues quite efficiently in the 1970s. The return of trust, if it comes, ultimately will mean more to environmental protection than legal language or new technological gizmos.

Meanwhile the regulations keep getting stricter. Many people are afraid of the ash from toxic waste incinerators, though it has been sterilized in 1,000-degree heat. Acknowledging this, in 1994 the American Society of Mechanical Engineers proposed converting incinerator ash to an inert, nonsoluble onyx material. For public peace of mind this could be done, the society says, in a "sealed, submerged electric arc furnace." In other words sterile incinerator ashes would end up being vitrified like nuclear wastes. As soon as this becomes practical expect the law to require it.

Today's Toxics: Landfills

The Pinewood, South Carolina, "secure" landfill of the Laidlaw Environmental Services Corporation is among the dwindling number of facilities with legal sanction to bury the type of chemicals once tossed onto fields at the Rocky Mountain Arsenal. Pinewood is modern, well engineered, and scrupulously clean. Everybody hates it. Demonstrators have lain before trucks at Pinewood's gate. Environmentalists nationwide condemn the facility; thousands have attended local protest meetings. For a decade Pinewood operated under what was technically an interim EPA permit. Its application for the final permit ran 30 hard-bound volumes.

The Resource Conservation and Recovery Act, passed by Congress in 1984 and governing disposal of trash and toxics, had as a centerpiece a stringent "land ban." Chemicals such as dioxin and PCBs were land-banned immediately. Today they can be disposed of legally only by reverse engineering that disassembles them, or by high-temperature incineration. Since 1984 hundreds of other synthetics have been added to the land ban through requirements they be neutralized and drummed, the process used at Pinewood. By the late 1990s nearly all chemicals will be land-banned. It will not be legal to place any untreated industrial compound, however mild, directly into a landfill.

As trucks of chemicals enter Pinewood, samples from their loads are taken to be analyzed in a chemistry lab equipped with chromatographs, spectrometers, and other fancy devices. If the sample conflicts with the waste manifest, Pinewood officials reject the load and notify regulators that a shipper is filing deceptive documents. Wastes that match manifests are mixed either with a clay derivative similar to Kitty Litter, which neutralizes them, or with kiln dust to form blocks of low-grade concrete. Then they are drummed and lined up in earthen gashes decorously called "cells." Under most cells are two layers of compacted clay, which as gardeners know is nearly impervious to fluids, plus two liners of synthetic PVC. Between these are sumps to catch any liquids that may leach through, pumping it up for destruction in a company incinerator. Around the cells are groundwater monitors. An inspector from the South Carolina Department of Health and Environmental Control is present at Pinewood at all times. When filled, a cell is covered with more clay and high-density polyethylene. The polyethylene ridges are welded, the cover landscaped. On the Laidlaw computer is a three-dimensional grid showing which wastes sit where, so the chemicals can be excavated if, say, someone invents a cheap means for reverse-engineering toxics.

Less than 1,000 yards down the hydraulic gradient is a lovely water body, Lake Marion. The proximity of this water is a reason environmentalists oppose Pinewood. Scientists paid by Laidlaw swear that even if chemicals somehow escaped it would take them 100 years to advance to Lake Marion; scientists paid by environmental groups swear this could happen much faster. Because Lake Marion is thick with marine plants that inhibit fishing and boating, its surface is periodically sprayed with herbicide. Pinewood workers receiving a truckload of the herbicides used on Lake Marion would have to neutralize the chemicals just to put them in steel drums inside welded cells. If chemicals ever do escape from Pinewood and migrate down to the lake, they will arrive in concentrations vastly lower to what's already applied there on purpose.

Today nearly all chemical disposal facilities are run by Fortune 500 firms: Waste Management Inc. (which in 1994 changed its name to the mysterious WMX Technologies, shedding the hot-button word *waste*), Browning-Ferris, Laidlaw. Regulatory regimes comprehensible only to firms with Ph.D. engineers and crack legal departments give major corporations an advantage. "One reason we've made our peace with environmental rules," says Roger Davis, a Laidlaw vice president, "is that we now realize our industry benefits from tight regulation. It has put the midnight dumpers out of business, so we have no more cut-rate competition." Touring Eastern Europe after the Wall fell, I was taken aback to hear government managers say they presumed the Western conglomerates had arranged for their governments to impose strict environmental rules because the big companies knew they could comply while lesser companies would be shut out. "This corporate greening is the latest scheme of the transnationals, is it not?" a trade official in Warsaw asked me. Few environmentalists envisioned that the reforms they espoused would turn out to help big industry win market share. Nevertheless in most cases this turn of events has been good for the ecology.

As a young reporter in the late 1970s I covered the original round of toxic waste stories, trooping across many legally sanctioned landfills of the time. Compared to them, Pinewood is a hospital operating theater. At one 1970s facility in West Covina, California, near Los Angeles, the cells were just pits. Trucks would back up and pour untreated wastes directly in, chemicals splashing every which way. No neutralization, no liners, no 3-D computer records. The lab consisted of a dingy trailer with a few test tubes and strips of litmus paper, dusty from disuse. As an "inspection" the gate guard would place his hand on the surface of a tank truck to see if the metal was hot, which would indicate the chemicals within were reacting.

Any burying of chemicals in verdant soil may seem barbarous. It is. Ideally all waste toxics should be destroyed by incinerators or reverse-engineered into useful molecules, preferably without ever departing factory gates. But the incinerators can't get permission to operate, and reverse-engineering of chemicals is not yet cost-effective. For now some portion of hazardous wastes are bound to end up in landfills. Places like Pinewood may be only steps along the way to a fully accountable system for managing society's by-products. But they are so much better than what existed just a decade ago, there's no comparison.

Liability fears have advanced to the point that many manufacturers rarely let wastes off their property, where someone else might commit some slip-up for which they would be legally responsible. Today just three percent of hazardous wastes are shipped to sites like Sauget or Pinewood; the rest are handled at the point of production. Much point-of-production disposal of hazardous wastes involves "deep injection," which sends toxics down a thousand feet or more to the briny part of the water table, theoretically far below the zones tapped for drinking. Probably deep injection is safe, though nobody has paid much attention to the process. I've seen deep-injection sites and can only report there is nothing to see: They appear to be oil wells running in reverse, big rigs pumping down instead of up. Public concern continues to focus on commercial facilities such as Pinewood, where trucks can be filmed entering a gate as protesters chant.

At Pinewood I listened to Davis crow at some length about the environmental safeguards in use there. I asked if his company would have installed the safeguards were it not for pressure from environmentalists. Davis hesitated, as if about to jump into a canned Rotary Club speech. Then he said simply, "No."

That single word summed up all the good contemporary environmentalism has done. The rest of the reality of modern handling of toxics sums up why it's time to move on from instant doomsday to ecorealism.

WATER 🌿

BOSTON HARBOR HAS PLAYED A PROMINENT ROLE IN TWO U.S. presidential elections. Tea dumped there helped make George Washington the first president. Sewage dumped there helped make George Bush the forty-first.

In a memorable television commercial candidate Bush stood with his back to Boston Harbor declaring it "the filthiest water in the United States." When this commercial began to air Bush trailed his opponent Michael Dukakis, then governor of Massachusetts and, as a Democrat, presumably the environmental progressive, by 17 points in polls. Immediately the Dukakis lead began to erode.

Bush was correct to call Boston Harbor of the year 1988 filthy. At the time tons of disgusting slop from factories and toilets poured into the inlet around the clock, along with more "effluent" (a polite name for rank wastewater) than the entire flow of the Charles River that bisects Boston and Cambridge. Swimming in the harbor had been forbidden for years, as had fishing. At the Boston Aquarium, schoolchildren on field trips gawked at an MIT computer model of the viscous sludge mass that undulated around the harbor mouth, sidling in and out with the tides.

What candidate Bush did not tell voters is that well before the damning commercial, a Massachusetts state authority broke ground on the most ambitious water-cleansing system in U.S. history, a $6.1 billion complex designed to return Boston Harbor to its preindustrial level of water quality. Then again, candidate Dukakis did not tell voters this either. Pundits have treated Dukakis's silence about his own harbor cleanup as a vexing mystery. Why would a presidential candidate not answer an important accusation, especially when he could do so by pointing to a sign of progress? Seen through the prism of environmental orthodoxy, however, Dukakis's silence makes sense. Dukakis could not answer the Bush charge without speaking optimistically—without declaring that a significant ecological problem was about to be fixed. Dukakis ran as a conventional liberal, and conventional liberalism cannot bear the thought of any optimistic ecological statement passing its lips.

Today environmental orthodoxy continues to avert its eyes from a spectrum of inconveniently positive developments in water pollution control and water use. In the Western world water quality is the most successful of first-generation environmental initiatives. While in many categories the Age of Pollution may peak much sooner than expected, in water the Age of Pollution has already peaked. A few examples:

• Around 1970 the Great Lakes, Puget Sound, Chesapeake Bay, the Saint Lawrence Seaway, the harbors of Boston, New York, and San Diego, the Charles, Chicago, Potomac, Rhine, and Thames rivers, and other water bodies in the United States and Western Europe were pronounced "dead" or facing mortality. Today these water bodies are biologically vibrant and showing annual improvement.

The Thames was considered dead as early as 1850. Fish life there was extinguished by pollution, and the river's main biological function seemed to be transmission of cholera. Today some 100 fish species live in the Thames. Even salmon, a pollution-sensitive creature that disappeared from the Thames about 1830, has been making a comeback since the late 1960s. Studies show that from 1988 to 1992, industrial pollution entering Chesapeake Bay declined by 53 percent. Long Island Sound, which pessimists declared dead as recently as 1990, is showing signs of recovery. In 1992 shellfishing along the Connecticut coastline of the sound resumed for the first time in 32 years.

• As of 1992 all sewage generated in the United States is treated before discharge, usually in facilities that bring the water to a standard safe for swimming. In Western Europe only 72 percent of sewage is treated. In Mediterranean countries 30 percent is treated, in the Caribbean ten percent, and in the rest of the world, including the former Soviet bloc, about two percent.

• Ocean dumping of sludge has ended in the United States. As recently as the 1980s not only was raw sludge dumped in the oceans by many cities; it was dumped on the continental shelf where it could sink to the relatively shallow bottom and be uptaken by the food chain. In

1992 the last U.S. barges carrying sludge for ocean dumping were decertified by federal and state regulators.

• Statistics kept by the National Oceanographic and Atmospheric Administration show declining levels of most contaminants along both the U.S. coastlines since the early 1970s.

• Some 56 percent of U.S. river miles now show water quality at least as good as specified in the Clean Water Act. The primary requirement is that water be safe for fish and swimming. In 1970 only about a quarter met the standard.

• EPA data from 1991 shows 28,000 miles of American rivers to contain "harmful" levels of synthetic chemicals. That figure is too high, but represents just 1.6 percent of U.S. river miles.

• In his 1906 book *The Jungle,* Upton Sinclair described Bubbly Creek in the slaughterhouse district of Chicago as "a great open sewer [that] looks like a bed of lava. Chickens walk about on it." As of 1992 Bubbly Creek had recovered sufficiently that local entrepreneurs were running boat tours on it. The larger Chicago River, a moving cesspool in the 1960s, was in 1992 the site of a festival for floating sculpture and performance art. The Chicago now counts carp, perch, and salmon among its 50 fish species.

• Degradation of pristine rivers by new water pollution has essentially ended in the United States, while ever-increasing river miles are placed in preservation status. For example in 1992 the Delaware River Basin Commission enacted rules that essentially forbid development along the pristine upper Delaware, regardless of the economic value development might bring. Under the Wild and Scenic Rivers Act portions of 148 wild rivers are now in preservation status, with about 1,000 river miles being added to the program by Congress annually.

• In 1975, 36 percent of U.S. rivers and streams failed the EPA test for fecal coliform bacteria, an important indicator of pollution. By 1989 only 20 percent failed. The percentage of rivers failing EPA tests for dissolved oxygen, phosphorus, dissolved cadmium, and dissolved lead has steadily declined since 1975, with the worst reading in these categories now at three percent of rivers.

• Phosphorus emitted to the Great Lakes is a leading indicator of pollution. Phosphorus loadings in Lake Ontario peaked in 1976 and have been declining since; peaked in lakes Michigan and Erie in 1978; peaked in Lake Superior in 1979 and in Lake Huron in 1980. Current phosphorus levels in the Great Lakes are from 40 percent to 70 percent lower than the peak years. Levels of PCBs in the Great Lakes have fallen nearly 90 percent since 1973. Population numbers for Great Lakes eagle, double-crested cormorants (a bird once expected to fall extinct), and other waterfowl have been increasing.

• Though the United States has been accused by former Interior secretary Stewart Udall, now an environmental lawyer, of exhibiting "hydromania" in the damming of rivers, only 15 percent of U.S. river miles are dammed, and the trend is away from dams. The two largest proposed dams of recent decades, Two Forks in Colorado and Auburn in California, were canceled in the 1990s to preserve riparian zones of threatened species. Dams on the Kennebec River in Maine and the Elwha River in Washington state are being removed to restore wild flow. The Federal Energy Regulatory Commission, under pressure from American Rivers, an environmental group that exists largely to lobby the obscure FERC, is reviewing licenses for 231 inefficient old hydro dams, with the expectation that many such dams will be removed.

• Only a handful of severely polluted rivers, among them the Cuyahoga of Ohio and the Grand Calumet of Indiana, remain in the United States. In only a handful of areas, such as mercury accumulation in the Great Lakes, do water pollution trends still move in a negative direction.

• The largest federal water diversion systems—the Central Valley Project of California, the Central Arizona Project, and the Central Utah Project—are replacing subsidized rates with market pricing. Traditionally federal water has cost farmers as little as ten percent of market value. Subsidies lead to such absurdities as rice, the most water-intensive crop, being grown in Arizona. Federal water prices are now rising toward the market rate, which will discourage wasteful forms of irrigation and the soil salinization they cause. And a tenth of water from the Central Valley Project is now reserved for use in the preservation of endangered species, such as by increasing river flows during the weeks when juvenile salmon are running downstream to the sea.

• Water Quality 2000, a public-private coalition, calculates $488 billion has been invested in water protection in the United States in the last 20 years, a figure roughly double the annual defense budget. The organization estimates that about $84 billion, a large sum but only about a sixth more than has already been spent, is needed to complete the cleanup of all U.S. water bodies.

A Better Class of Sludge

To understand the effort being put into water cleanup in the United States, let's take a closer look at the Boston Harbor effort. Boston lagged behind other major U.S. cities in building modern sewage control. In the early 1980s, the Conservation Law Foundation began to file lawsuits regarding Boston Harbor. In 1985 the litigation bore fruit when David Mazzone, a federal judge, barred Boston-area governments from writing new sewer-hookup permits until there was action to bring the harbor into compliance with the Clean Water Act. Mazzone's ruling effectively banned new construction around Boston.

That got the attention of the state legislature. It created an entity called the Massachusetts Water Resources Authority to stage a harbor cleanup, and conferred on that entity an essentially unrestricted ability to raise funds by selling bonds to be paid back from higher sewer rates. Creation of the authority enjoyed broad public support in Boston though the city, which dallied until after most federal grants for waste-water treatment ran out, had to pay for the harbor project itself. Pay through the nose, in fact: The typical annual household water and sewer bill in Boston is in the process of rising from $300 to $1,200. General public support for such an expensive project suggests that Americans have been converted to environmentalism in the most significant sense: the willingness to spend from their own pockets.

About half of the $6.1 billion allotted to the cleanup has been expended. Much of Deer Island in Boston Harbor has been converted into the most sophisticated water treatment plant ever built. This plant will raise water to the "secondary discharge" standard now used in most American cities, meaning safe for people to swim in and fish to live in. Huge shafts have been dug beneath Boston Harbor to move sewage to the plant. An "outfall" tunnel large enough for buses to drive through has been bored in the floor of the continental shelf to a point under the Atlantic nine miles southeast of Boston, so that even the treated water will not be released into the harbor but discharged at sea in a place where prevailing currents flow away from the coast. Across the harbor from the new treatment station, in Quincy, rises a facility that will take the sludge removed at the plant and convert most of it into fertilizer. The sludge-to-fertilizer operation will employ a new class of equipment that should eliminate odor. Another underwater tunnel joins the treatment and sludge plants. The system is among the largest public-works projects ever undertaken in the United States.

In conjunction with the cleanup water authorities cracked down on what industry can pour into sewers. About four million pounds of toxics per day flowed into Boston sewers in the mid-1970s. Today the figure is 900 pounds per day (two-tenths of a percent of the previous level) and falling toward a 1998 goal of zero. In 1991 Boston stopped discharging raw sewage to the harbor, activating the first phase of the treatment plan. This caused an immediate drop in the biological oxygen demand, a key pollution indicator, of harbor water. "The quality of Boston sludge has been greatly improved," says Paul Levy, a Massachusetts Institute of Technology professor of engineering who ran the Water Resources Authority from its founding till 1992.

Depending on how the harbor responds, in the late 1990s Boston may build another facility that would raise discharge water to a "tertiary" standard, meaning just shy of safe to drink. Included in the $6.1 billion budget is funding for a system of deep tunnels beneath the city that will hold rainwater during a storm. Rainwater running off city streets dissolves pollutants and carries them to sewers. Boston's deep-tunnel system would hold that rainwater underground, capturing an entire rainstorm so that it can be pumped up for treatment at the purification plant later. This system would insure that motor oils, garden pesticides, or other smudges of materialist life spilled on Boston streets do not end up in the ocean. All this means that in just a decade, Boston would have advanced from no wastewater controls of any kind to purifying even rainwater.

When the Boston project was conceived it was widely assumed that even running at the tertiary standard, the system would take until the year 2025 to cleanse the harbor. Instead by 1993, with only partial operation established, most of the harbor was already safe for fishing again, and a few areas were safe for swimming.

The rapid pace of ecological recovery in Boston Harbor is more stirring proof that environmental protection is misunderstood in contemporary debate, especially in the assumptions of liberal intellectualism. Rather than being a corridor of instant doom, environmental control is a tunnel with a bright, beckoning light at the end. Programs work; nature recovers; societies that invest in ecological protection see benefits within the lifetimes of those making the investment. Levy notes, "The wonderful thing about ecological control is that it produces visible, satisfying results. Nature can't recover until you stop polluting. Once you do nature works amazingly fast."

Though polls show that Boston residents as a whole support the project, Nimby opposition has slowed many elements. Citizen groups and environmentalists fought in courts of law and of public opinion to stop the Quincy sludge-to-fertilizer plant, despite its goal of converting waste into a resource. One irony of success against water pollution is that it makes for more sludge. As Richard Fox, the construction manager for the Boston project, notes, "The more effective wastewater treatment plants become the more sludge they generate, because the plants pull more undesirable stuff out of the water."

A decade ago urban officials planned to deal with the increasing volume of sludge generated by improved wastewater treatment by constructing incinerators that would burn sludge to make electricity. Washington, D.C., for example, planned to convert its notoriously odorous Blue Plains sludge facility into a sludge-to-energy system. Horrified of incineration in all guises, environmental lobbyists pressured Congress essentially to outlaw sludge incineration. That leaves conversion to fertilizer: And though the idea makes clear ecological sense, every community feels the necessary facilities would be more appropriate in some other community. Quincy was no exception. Protestors marched against the sludge plant; mothers wore gas masks to town meetings. Never mind that it is inconsistent for the public first to demand that sludge not be dumped, then that it not be incinerated, then that sites for fertilizer-conversion plants never be chosen. These are the sorts of issue municipal officials face in the Nimby era.

Nimby opposition was overcome only when Judge Mazzone in effect assumed jurisdiction over Boston water policy and compelled Quincy to accept the sludge plant. "Nothing could have happened without the federal leverage," said Levy. "There was no political will at the local level to impose site-selection pain on anyone, ever." A second round of Nimby and activist outrage occurred when Levy chose the town of Walpole for a landfill for sludge residue that cannot be converted to fertilizer. A landfill was a necessity; no theory of sludge reprocessing eliminates residue altogether. But no Massachusetts politician wanted to be responsible for deciding where the sludge residue would come to rest. This is Nimtoo, a political corollary of Nimby: Not in my term of office. All candidates in the 1990 Massachusetts gubernatorial election opposed siting the sludge landfill at Walpole, or anywhere for that matter. William Weld, who won the statehouse, condemned the Walpole site with cameras rolling; though it was Weld who, as a prosecutor in the mid-1980s, advanced the lawsuit that forced Boston to confront its water pollution in the first place. Eventually Mazzone stepped in and compelled the Walpole selection, too.

Today Boston Harbor is recovering so fast that Levy doubts whether the final phase of the system will be needed. "By 1996 we will have 90 percent of the benefits for two-thirds of the cost," he says. "At that point we should decide whether it's worth spending another $2 billion for the last ten percent." A cut in project costs might be welcome: Though voters still display support for the cleanup, that may change as household water bills approach the $1,000 level. If the Boston system is completed to purification to the tertiary standard, the undersea outfall tunnel will become a billion-dollar monument to doomsday thinking. Adding tertiary treatment to the Boston system would bring its discharge essentially to the same water quality as naturally occurs in the Atlantic. The notion that such clean water must nevertheless be tunneled miles out to sea becomes something of an expensive jest. But in the planning stages of the project, political sentiment for an outfall system was strong. Because environmental orthodoxy depicted all discharge however purified as hideously deadly, city leaders wanted to be sure they were moving the stuff Far, Far Away.

Though 20 years ago any environmentalist who heard about the Boston Harbor cleanup would have fallen to his or her knees and declared that the millennium had arrived, orthodoxy demands that the situation continue to be seen as a scandal. I asked the Boston office of the Clean Water Action Project what it thought of the harbor cleanup, and heard a long list of negatives: The treatment plant is too high-tech, the sludge residue will be hypertoxic, the Water Resources Authority isn't doing enough to punish industry.

A similar example comes from a cleanup project in Providence, Rhode Island. There an ecologist named John Todd, who runs a wonderful organization named Earth Island Institute, experiments with natural cleansing of wastewater. Todd has collected from around the world various plant and microbial species that metabolize the toxics in sewage. Todd's work indicates that in principle at least, the wastewater flow of cities could be handled not by energy-intensive systems such as that being built at Deer Island, rather by large but otherwise low-input arboretums where wastewater would circulate and emerge purified by nature. So are activists happy about Todd's work? Many are furious. Environmental lobbyists often argue that growth along the East Coast must halt because there can never be any way to contain the toxic residue of more wastewater from more people. Todd's experiments inconveniently suggest otherwise. Members of the green movement "have told me we used to be your friend, but now you're taking away our means to stop growth," Todd says.

Such imprisoned thinking cannot last once the water is again clear and blue. For his part, Paul Levy plans to celebrate New Year's Day 1995 by going for a swim in Boston Harbor.

Dangerous Farms and Polluting Rain

Perhaps the most disturbing ecological image of the 1960s was that of a factory pouring toxic slag directly into a stream. By 1992 just six percent of pollutants reaching American streams and rivers came from industrial sources. Only 17,000 miles of rivers and streams were classified "impaired" by industrial pollutants. This is too many, but they represent less than one percent of U.S. waterways.

Industrial water pollution has essentially ended owing to the National Pollution Discharge Elimination System (NPDES), which EPA administrator Carol Browner calls the "leading success story of pollution control." This little-known system, created at the federal level and usually administered by states, requires factories and commercial facilities to possess permits for whatever they discharge to waterways. NPDES is conceptually different from most theories of pollution control, involving site-by-site permits rather than general standards. While site-by-site permitting sounds cumbersome, it works in water pollution because commercial and industrial facilities are known locations that can be cataloged and inspected. The NPDES system isn't perfect, but by and large it has brought direct industrial pollution to waterways to a halt. Its enforcing feature is simple: Factories that lose their NPDES permits must close.

The exceptions to the success of the NPDES are emissions from publicly owned wastewater works and from farms. Owing in part to the lobbying clout that mainly Democratic cities enjoy with the mainly Democratic postwar Congress, many government-owned wastewater facilities have been exempt from NPDES or regulated lightly. In 1991 the New York Department of Environmental Protection surveyed the coastline and riverbanks of the New York City area, finding 171 discharge pipes lacking NPDES permits. Two-thirds were owned by the city. Today municipal wastewater plants are the cause of some 38,000 miles of impaired rivers, approximately twice the number attributed to industry. The typical homeowner plays a role as well: About one-third of the toxic chemicals entering city water treatment plants come from homes in the form of motor oil, bleach, lawn pesticides, and other chemicals poured down the drain. Beginning about 1990, municipal wastewater treatment plants were being brought under federal standards. The Boston Harbor system, for example, is regulated by NPDES. Eventually most cities will not only be required to meet NPDES but insure that local rain runoff is clean as well, since in 1987 Congress formally classified rainwater running to sewers as a pollutant.

In some cities weather and geography are such that water-treatment facilities can handle the "flush" that accompanies a rainstorm. In others sewers overload during storms. When this happens not only does dirty rainwater go directly to waterways, so does any raw sewage moving through the system at that moment. To counter this Chicago and Milwaukee constructed complex deep-tunnel systems designed to hold an entire urban rainstorm until it can be pumped up for treatment. Chicago's cost nearly $2.5 billion. Chicago has notoriously ill-kept inner-city schools. Two and a half billion dollars might have purchased roughly half a new inner-city school system. But then low-quality inner-city schooling is legal in the United States; water pollution is not. Whether $2.5 billion should have been spent in Chicago for a modest decrease in Lake Michigan pollution on rainy days, in lieu of other social priorities, is very much an open question. The Clean Water Act appears to require Boston, New York, and other cities in need of urban renewal to invest billions in deep tunnels for rainwater cleansing. Despite allocations like this, many greens endlessly repeat the incantation that the United States does not make pollution control a social priority.

Perhaps the sole environmental area where it is true that the United States is doing little is pesticide runoff from farms. Certification of pesticides is tightly regulated, but use is essentially unrestricted. Agriculture accounts for more than six times the number of "impaired" river miles attributable to industry. In 1992 some 72 percent of pollution to U.S. rivers and streams came from agricultural chemicals running off farms. Farming also disrupts riverine life cycles. Studies show North American fish and amphibians about twice as likely to be endangered as land species; agriculture in riparian corridors is thought to be the cause.

Attempts to legislate standards for farm runoff (called "nonpoint source" pollution by regulators because you can never be sure which chemical comes from which farm) have failed so far. Congress, which annually awards to farmers up to $25 billion in price supports, and thereby would appear to possess considerable leverage with which to extract concessions, has shown itself terrified of any action that could be interpreted as onerous to the family farmer—though pollution from family farms is the same to nature as pollution from multinationals. As, however, agricultural theories such as integrated pest management gradually reduce the chemicals applied to crops, and as new pesticides are engineered to biodegrade, farm runoff should decline.

Slow as farmers remain in responding to pollution from runoff, they are growing progressive in use of irrigation water. Throughout the postwar era agricultural interests in the West fought doggedly to retain subsidized federal water from major diversion channels such as California's Central Valley Project. Year after year bills to market-price federal water failed in Congress, defeated by lobbying of the most heavy-handed type. In the late 1980s the picture changed for an unexpected reason: meteorology. California endured a multi-year drought. Agricultural water had always been so plentiful in the Central Valley that some farmers were cavalier about its use. During the late-1980s drought agribusiness began to discover the virtues of drip-pipe irrigation and other conservation techniques. At the same time federal courts signaled, through the spotted owl rulings, that enforcement of the Endangered Species Act would become absolute. In theory a judge might assert authority to shut down all Central Valley irrigation to divert water to salmon runs.

By February 1992 the drought had grown sufficiently severe that the Bureau of Reclamation, the Interior Department agency that runs federal water projects, began sending some California agribusinesses notice that their water would be cut off. Suddenly large water users found themselves open-minded about market pricing. California water districts and agribusiness interests signed deals, later codified in federal legislation, allocating ten to 20 percent of the volume of the Central Valley Project to endangered-species and conservation use, in exchange for a promise the entire network will not be claimed for ecological preservation.

In an interesting twist the author and activist Marc Reisner, considered by many California farmers a sworn enemy, was called in to assist the negotiations. Reisner, who previously had written that the Western water politics would end in ecological catastrophe, was converted to a mild environmental optimist by the experience. For example orthodox enviros wanted to forbid any water use for growing rice in California and Arizona; this would have put rice farmers out of business. Reisner and others had noticed that migratory birds like to land in soggy rice paddies and feed there. A compromise was crafted. Use of federal water for rice could continue but only if growers modified practices in ways that make their paddies suitable for migratory birds.

While governor of Arizona in the 1980s, Bruce Babbitt backed the Central Arizona Project. This grand water diversion project was widely derided as a boondoggle and represents exactly the sort of initiative Babbitt later opposed as head of the League of Conservation Voters. (When I asked him about past support for the CAP, Babbitt told a couple of charming jokes and then asked, "Have I dodged that question yet?") Babbitt once supported the CAP simply because it seemed impossible to be active in political life in the American West and not favor every feasible increase in water supply.

Today it does seem possible. Residential water conservation is growing common; in 1994, for instance, it became illegal in the United States to sell the traditional five-gallon toilet. New fixtures use 1.6 gallons. Industrial water conservation is growing common: For example, a Xerox plant in Palo Alto, California, installed a system that reuses rinsewater from silicon chip manufacturing, rather than drawing fresh water. The system cost Xerox $50,000 and cut water bills by $38,000 in its first year. The Bureau of Reclamation, once dam-happy, is converting to an emphasis on conservation. Having become the bureau's supervisor as Interior secretary for the Clinton Administration, Babbitt is now a believer in rational water pricing. He says, "There aren't going to be any more water shortages in the West because we are going to discover that there is already plenty of water, so long as we use it sensibly."

It turned out that in March 1992, just after the compromises on Western water use were signed, the California drought ended with a month-long rain of providential proportions. Perhaps some orthodox factions felt cheated by the deluge, which came mere days before low water pressure would have begun to disrupt daily California life in a serious way. But somebody, it seemed, was pleased with the environmental progress that had been made.

Drinking Water

By most measures, drinking water in the United States and most of Western Europe is of high quality. Studies by the EPA, by science agencies, and by independent laboratories have shown most American drinking water to be safe. Most piped water drunk in the United States is treated to kill the greatest threat posed by drinking water, waterborne disease. About half of American drinking water comes from underground aquifers that, with a few exceptions, produce purity. Cities that draw their drinking water from reservoir systems must by federal law treat and filter that water. The two most important waivers to the provision have gone to Boston and New York City, whose drinking water, piped from pristine reservoirs in rural areas, consistently tests as pure without treatment. It's nice to know there is something about New York City that is pure.

Yet drinking-water contamination remains distressingly common. In at least a dozen places around the U.S. industrial toxics have penetrated to aquifers. In 1978 some 40,000 one-gallon cans of chemicals were buried illegally near a lake in Quinlan, Texas. The chemicals penetrated to the local aquifer; since then Quinlan water has been undrinkable. In 1991 Coors, which spends millions on advertising that boasts of mystic purity in the waters used to make its beer and ale, paid a $700,000 fine for contaminating groundwater under one of its breweries. Somehow this is not mentioned as scenes of mountain springs roll by in Coors commercials.

One long-term fear regarding Superfund sites is that industrial toxics dumped in them, most of which have done no meaningful harm so far, will in coming decades gradually migrate through soil toward the water table. This is a reason why considerable EPA action at Superfund sites has focused not on direct cleanup but on barriers and pump systems that prevent chemicals from moving toward aquifers. Concern over the prospect of chemical wastes moving toward drinking water has also led to a boom in the profession of hydrogeology. In the early 1980s Malcolm Pirnie, Inc., a leading Superfund contractor, had three hydrogeologists on its staff. By 1992 it employed 75 and was still hiring. Since juries have rightly shown a willingness to assess substantial damages when a company's action pollutes groundwater, today there is intense interest among Superfund litigants in tracing drinking water lines of liability.

A long-term drinking water concern is that some 43 pesticides have been detected in aquifers around the country, usually in trace quantities that pose no danger. But if trace quantities are present does this mean significant quantities are gradually working their way toward the water table? Pesticides seeping into groundwater have the potential to become an environmental emergency of the late 1990s.

Another recurring drinking water problem is lead from pipes. In the late 1980s the EPA changed the standard test for lead in drinking water, stipulating that lead be measured at the moment a faucet is turned on, when what is coming out has been in contact with the pipes longest.[1] Using the new standard the EPA estimated 30 million Americans live in homes that violate the 15 parts-per-billion lead level the agency considers safe. And though older buildings are most likely to have problems— lead was not banned in plumbing until 1986 and from drinking fountains till 1988—contrary to the popular assumption about ghetto lead, fashionable areas have this problem too. For whatever it's worth the highest residential drinking water lead in the U.S. was detected in Grosse Pointe Park, Michigan, an exclusive suburb, where levels hit 324 parts per billion.[2]

When children eat peeling lead paint (lead in paint was not banned until the 1970s) they can easily ingest a severe dose. Within scientific circles there exists controversy regarding how much harm lead does in trace quantities such as the low parts per billion. Studies suggest a worst-case IQ loss of four points. Probably there is no statistical significance in an IQ change this slight. Nevertheless with lead an unquestioned toxic, all practical reductions in its consumption are advised. In 1991 the EPA cut the federal drinking water standard for lead to about a third its previous level and ordered the nation's water utilities to reduce lead contamination. The main step will be to add an anticorrosive to drinking water, so that less lead leaches out of pipes. The chemical chosen was calcium orthophosate, similar to baking soda. This compound is beginning to appear in much of the country's drinking water. Even cities whose water registers as sparkling pure now add chemicals to that water in the name of environmental protection.

William Reilly, the EPA administrator who ordered the lead reduction, was incensed by the fashionably negative reaction the program received. Reilly's plan gave utilities up to 21 years to complete lead eradication. This was denounced by institutional environmentalism; press reports hit hard on the 21-year clause, for instance a *Washington Post* headline declaring "Water Utilities to Get Years to Limit Lead." The accompanying story concentrated on green outrage over the length of time allowed. Unmentioned was that water utilities were required to realize about 90 percent of expected gains within six years. If water still violated lead standards, utilities would then be given 15 years to replace all pipes and water mains. Thus 21 years could be permitted for compliance, but most progress would be realized much more rapidly. Commentators skid past that annoyingly positive complication. Reilly asks, "What was I supposed to do, order that half the gross national product be spent on replacing every urban pipe immediately? The environmental reaction to this rule bordered on intellectual dishonesty. The press corps went along because it was a way to convert good news into bad news."

A final frustration with drinking water standards is repeated operational and reporting violations by water districts. One operational error was the 1993 blunder that caused Milwaukee water to become infected with cryptosporidiosis, a bacteria that gave some 300,000 people stomach cramps. The number of technical and reporting errors by drinking water agencies is huge. According to a study by the Natural Resources Defense Council, there were some 250,000 (mainly minor) violations of the Safe Drinking Water Act from 1991 to 1992, only a small share of which led to penalties against the violating agencies.

In 1986 Congress made the Safe Drinking Water Act much more strict, using words that have been interpreted by judges as meaning no trace of a carcinogen may be tolerated, even if studies show trace levels to be safe. Thus in the debate about whether there exists a safe threshold for carcinogens or whether a single molecule can cause cancer, on drinking water Congress sided with the single-molecule theory. Since 1986, the new standards have increasingly been criticized by researchers as an example of rules that discard the relationship between costs and benefits. Regulation of water down to the level of individual molecules of toxics is the reason that, for example, the city of Columbus, Ohio, projects it must spend $3 million per year to eliminate from drinking water three parts per billion of the corn pesticide atrazine, though far larger concentrations have not caused illness in laboratory rats. Levy, the former head of the Massachusetts Water Resources Authority, considers literal enforcement of the 1986 law counterproductive. "If the law is enforced as Congress wrote it, it will be one of the all-time wastes of money," Levy says. "Boston will have to build a $500 million facility to screen for contaminants that have never even been recorded here."

The 1986 law also appears to require New York City to begin treating its drinking water, though there has been no indication in public-health data that city water does any harm. A network of plants sufficient to treat all New York City drinking water would cost an estimated $4 billion, enough to replace perhaps a third of that city's horridly maintained inner-city schools with palaces of education. Hoping to win a federal waiver from this expense, in 1993 New York City began to invest $750 million in antipollution improvements for its upstate reservoirs, including buying up property around the reservoirs to take the land out of agriculture and thus eliminate farm runoff. The city established a force of 29 armed watershed police who now patrol around the reservoirs, arresting anyone caught polluting.

In late 1993, the Clinton Administration proposed relaxation of aspects of the 1986 drinking-water law, waiving the letter of the law for water systems such as New York City's while canceling most not-one-molecule rulings imposed on Columbus and other smaller locations. Clinton's initiative is the sort that, had it come from Ronald Reagan or George Bush, would have been assailed as a cynical plot to rape the Earth. What the Clinton initiative really represents is ecorealism: a reasonable balancing of environmental needs and social resources. Yet in a sense, the crusade for ultrapure drinking water is a good sign. Levy notes, "Environmentalists are starting to worry about things like parts per trillion in drinking water because they are running out of genuine problems to worry about."

If there are to be major new investments in water purity the target should not be trace contaminants that reach water inadvertently but the high levels of a chemical placed in water deliberately: chlorine. Studies by Robert Morris, an epidemiologist at the Medical College of Wisconsin, and others suggest that consumption of chlorinated tap water causes as many as 12,000 bladder and rectal cancers annually. This represents more health damage than all worst-case estimates for trace toxics in tap water combined. The typical concentration of chlorine in tap water as delivered to an American home is about 500 parts per billion—some 170 times the level of atrazine that cities such as Columbus are being ordered to eliminate.

If chlorination were the sole way to rid drinking water of pathogens, cancers would be an acceptable risk. The Third World scourge of deaths from waterborne disease is nearly unknown in the West because chlorination reliably kills all cellular life in water. But if chlorine is so proficient at killing pathogen cells, can it be such a great idea for your cells? In 1992, Cincinnati opened the world's first municipal water treatment plant that uses activated carbon filtration to purify water without toxic compounds. Money that environmental orthodoxy would like to expend chasing trace levels of atrazine would better be invested in a conversion to such clean-tech purification.

Ocean Pollution

A leading candidate for Most Disgusting Place on Earth is East 106, a government-sanctioned sludge disposal site 106 miles east of Cape May, New Jersey. There, beginning in 1984, Atlantic Coast cities dumped eight million tons a year of sewage sludge. Several barges per day shuttled out to East 106 from New York and other cities, paused, and shoved their cargoes of fecal pollutants overboard. East 106 was on navigational charts. Sailors got pretty good at avoiding it.

When it was designated East 106 was considered an ecological plus. Starting in 1924, as the combination of population growth and better sewer systems began creating large volumes of sludge that urban officials wanted out of sight and out of mind, most coastal cities put sewage into the ocean pretty much as they pleased. Barges stopped to dump slightly beyond 12 miles to sea—by the strangest coincidence, just outside American waters. But 12 miles off the Atlantic coast is usually within the band of the continental shelf, where the ocean is relatively shallow and the seabed teams with life. In 1972 Congress banned the ocean dumping of sludge. Cities began to replace ocean dumping with landfilling or conversion of sludge to fertilizer. For instance Los Angeles ended ocean disposal of sludge in 1987. San Diego dragged its heels but built an outfall tunnel to move partially treated sludge 2.5 miles out to sea and was, at this writing, slowly but surely fulfilling other EPA requirements at a cost of $1.9 billion for a purification system.

The ocean dumping law was brazenly flouted by Boston, New York, and coastal cities in New Jersey. The federal ban was toothless; cities felt confident no law enforcement officer would impound a bargeload of sludge. ("Sergeant Yafnaro, why don't *you* take this sludge to the evidence room?") As a stopgap the EPA arranged in 1984 that those cities ignoring the ocean ban would at least dump their sludge beyond the continental shelf. Thus East 106 was established.

Not long afterward a bell rang in someone's head in the White House, then the domain of Ronald Reagan. Massachusetts and New York had voted against Reagan. Why were these Democratic strongholds, one home to the detested liberal Speaker of the House Thomas O'Neill, getting a sweetheart exemption from a ban that Republican cities such as San Diego were complying with? Suddenly Reagan became a crusader against ocean disposal of sewage. Punitive measures were imposed, including fines at a million dollars per day. The offending cities got serious. In June 1992 the final load of sludge slithered off the barge *Spring Brook* into the sea at East 106. Navigation markers at the site were removed. Ocean dumping of sewage by the United States had ended.

The 1992 cessation of ocean dumping represents an environmental milestone whose passage went entirely unremarked-upon owing to its positive character. This book presents the view that in a number of categories the Age of Pollution is nearly over in the Western world. Along the United States coastline, pollution from sewage sludge is already over. Whatever damage U.S. sewage was going to do to the oceans peaked a decade ago and has now declined to zero. Isn't that good news? No wonder you haven't heard about it.

It turns out to be an open question whether ocean dumping of sewage sludge did the seas meaningful harm. In 1989, researchers from the Woods Hole Oceanographic Institution surveyed the ocean floor at East 106, using minisubs. Team leader J. Frederick Grassle reported "no obvious effect of the sludge on bottom life." In his technical writings Grassle has postulated that the sea floor rivals tropical rainforests in biological diversity. He found the sea floor at East 106 surprisingly alive, despite its great pressure and the steady depth-bombing by sludge.

As improved submersibles have begun to probe benthic zones, the discovery of ocean life existing at great depths has been an important ecological surprise. Living things have been found around the edges of deep-sea sulfur vents existing at above 200 degrees Fahrenheit and with metabolic processes based entirely on chemistry, not sunlight. Carbon-based life at such temperatures had generally been thought impossible: Its discovery suggests what wondrous variations women and men may find as they eventually chart the deep seas. Initial discoveries regarding deep-sea life also suggest some reasons why depth-bombing by sludge may not have done much. Many of the sea-floor vents that deep life depends on for energy continuously discharge cadmium, copper, and lead in concentrations greater than found in sewage sludge. Cadmium, copper, and lead, all keenly toxic to land-based life, were thought to be the worst pollutants found in sewage. Perhaps to deep-sea life they are not pollutants.

In 1991 Charles Hollister, a Woods Hole senior scientist, proposed that so long as sludge was dumped in ocean areas where it would sink to depths greater than 16,000 feet—below which pressure is so great it becomes difficult to imagine any form of animation—ocean dumping might have no effect. Hollister noted that only 29 percent of Earth's surface is land area while 70 percent is deep ocean. So why sacrifice land to sludge control when land is more scarce than deep sea? Coming from one of the world's top oceanography centers, this heterodox proposal caused the environmental community to blow a gasket. There were calls for an end to federal support of Woods Hole, for a legislative rider that would deny the center funds for researching the effect of sludge on the ocean. In 1993, under pressure from Congress, Woods Hole essentially withdrew its proposition that ocean dumping was safe all along. When the value of sludge fertilizer is taken into account, the institute said, ocean dumping was more expensive than land use of sludge anyway.

That is true, and represents another unremarked-upon ecological advance. In the 1980s cities making fertilizer from sludge had trouble finding buyers. Product quality, if that's the right term, was uneven, if that's the right adjective. Except for the brand-named Metrogro marketed by Madison, Wisconsin, sludge fertilizer often contained excess levels of cadmium. Farmers feared consumers would boycott foods grown with sludge fertilizer. Beginning in the late 1980s, knowledge-based improvements in the processing of sludge to fertilizer transformed the market. Corn grown in fertilizer made from Milwaukee sewage now contains less than one part per million of heavy metals, a safe level.

Once quality improved farmers began to demand sludge-based fertilizer, which sells for less than petrochemical fertilizers. By 1992 the percentage of U.S. sludge recycled to fertilizer had risen from about 20 percent to 48 percent and was still headed up. Today New York City ships sludge fertilizer to Arizona, Colorado, and Texas, where soils are often deficient in the very copper, nitrogen, phosphorus, and zinc that urban sludge contains. In 1993 farmers in Lamar, Colorado, wrote to New York City officials complaining about missed sludge shipments and asking when more would arrive. That's right: Lamar was experiencing a SLUDGE SHORTAGE.

Fish

A water issue where trends are negative is the increasing threat to fish hunted commercially. Since about 1970 world catches have increased exponentially, mainly through the introduction of various driftnet techniques that catch whole schools. Japanese fishing vessels have dropped into the ocean driftnets as wide as 25 miles. In the 1950s the world's fleets were catching about 30 million tons per year of ocean fish, with the sustainable limit thought to be about 100 million tons annually. That level was hit in the year 1989 and has since been exceeded. Overfishing has been particularly hard on the shark, with shark's fin soup becoming a fad item in Asia, and the bluefin tuna, another Asian fad. According to the United Nations Food and Agricultural Organization, commercial species including cod, flounder, pollack, and all tuna are now "depleted." Fish for sale in restaurants and markets remains plentiful because the industry has been shifting to inland fish farming unaffected by ocean trends.

In 1989 the United Nations imposed a moratorium on driftnets. Taiwan, not a U.N. member, ignores the moratorium while Japan, Mexico, and other nations dance around it. Driftnet fishing by U.S. flag vessels was banned in 1991. The National Marine Fisheries Service, which sets catch limits for U.S. but not Asian boats, has reduced the shark catch to a low level; its companion Pacific Fisheries Management Council has suspended catches of Pacific salmon. In 1992 Canada essentially suspended fishing for Atlantic cod. Canada also lifted its seven-year ban on hunting of the harp seal, a predator now wiping out cod nearly as efficiently as driftnets.[3] In 1993 Interior secretary Babbitt arranged for $800,000 in public and private funds to buy out two years' worth of Atlantic salmon fishing allotments from the mainly Inuit hunters of Greenland, hoping to give that fish some breathing space. In 1991 only 203 Atlantic salmon made it back up the Connecticut River, which once had salmon runs by the thousands.

Though useful, such steps are palliatives. Because the ocean is a global commons no solution to overfishing will function until international cooperation on this issue is established. Protection of ocean fish surely merits attention as a primary ecological concern of the 1990s: It is more pressing and palpable than such speculative concerns as the greenhouse effect.

How fish populations vary is not yet understood by researchers, some of whom suspect that wide swings in numbers happen on a natural basis. William Aron, director of the Alaska Fisheries Science Center, notes that although Pacific salmon are down in many places, salmon are running the Fraser River of British Columbia as never before. Studies show that the cessations of ocean fishing that occurred during World Wars I and II led to rapid rebounds in fish-school size, suggesting that fish naturally undergo fast population expansions. "We may never know the precise relationship between environmental conditions and fishing" that leads to collapse or rebound of fish populations, Aron notes. Perhaps not. But we can easily assume overfishing cannot be good.

Our Water, Their Water

This chapter asserts that water pollution is essentially over in the United States. Let's end what is otherwise an optimistic section by reiterating the stark World Health Organization statistic often cited in this book: 3.8 million Third World children dead each year worldwide from preventable waterborne disease. A distressing fact cannot be stated too often: Some one billion human beings today live without access to pure drinking water or rudimentary water sanitation. The challenge of correcting this all too real ecological crisis should rest with those who have the means, namely, the nations of the West.

THE ECOREALIST MANIFESTO ✿

IN THE FIRST SECTION OF THIS BOOK THE GOAL WAS TO CON-
sider environmental problems from the perspective of nature: a long-
term, almost mythic purview of existence, yet one with relevance to
daily ecological challenges that confront humanity.

The second section considered environmental problems from the perspective of women and men alive today: a short-term perspective, yet
one that can be adjusted to incorporate the wisdom embodied in eons of
natural transitions.

The final section will suggest how the long-term purview of nature
might be combined with the short-term insights of genus *Homo* in ways
that allow people, machines, and nature to learn to work together for
each other's mutual benefit.

Before broaching that final topic let's summarize the principles of a
new view of ecological thought, the new view called ecorealism. The
founding concept of ecorealism is this: Logic, not sentiment, best serves
the interests of nature.

If the worthy inclinations of environmentalism are to be transformed
from an ephemeral late-twentieth-century political fashion to a lasting
component of human thought, the ecological impulse must become
grounded in rationality. The straightforward, rational case for the environment will prove more durable than the fiercest doomsday emotion.
Love nature? Learn science and speak logic. Many lesser creatures will
thank you.

And now some principles of ecorealism:

RATIONALISM

- If ecological rationalism sometimes shows that environmental problems are not as bad as expected, that means warnings will be all the more persuasive when genuine problems are found.
- Graduation from overstatement will make the environmental movement stronger, not weaker.
- The worst thing the environmental movement could become is another absentminded interest group stumbling along toward preconceived ends regardless of what the evidence suggests.
- Skeptical debate is good for the environmental movement. The public need not to be brainwashed into believing in ecological protection, since a clean environment is in everyone's interest. Thus the environmental movement must learn to entertain skeptical debate in a reasoned manner or will discredit itself, as all close-minded political movements eventually discredit themselves.
- Market forces and cost-benefit thinking aren't perfect but generally will be good for the environment. This is so if only because society may be able to afford several cost-effective conservation initiatives for the price of one poorly conceived program.
- Optimism not only flows from a reasoned reading of natural history, it will be an effective political tool.

POLLUTION

- In the Western world the Age of Pollution is nearly over. Almost every pollution issue will be solved within the lifetimes of readers of this book.
- In the West many forms of pollution have begun to decline in the very period that environmental doctrine has declared them growing worse.
- Most recoveries from pollution will happen faster than even optimists project.
- Weapons aside, technology is not growing more dangerous and wasteful. It grows cleaner and more resource-efficient.
- Clean technology will be the successor to high technology. Most brute-force systems of material production will be supplanted by production based mainly on knowledge. Nature's creatures make extremely sophisticated "products" with hard-

ly any input of energy or resources. People will learn to do the same.

- Sometimes approximated environmental rules are good ideas even if the result is a less than perfect cleanup. Better to realize 90 percent of an ecological restoration fast than to spend decades conducting lawsuits on how to achieve 100 percent.

- As positive as trends are in the First World, they are negative in the Third. One reason the West must shake off instant-doomsday thinking about the United States and Western Europe is so that resources can be diverted to ecological protection in the developing world.

CHANGE

- It is pointless for men and women to debate what the "correct" reality for nature might have been before people arrived on the scene. There has never been and can never be any fixed, correct environmental reality. There are only moments on the Earth, moments that may be good or bad.

- Every environment and habitat comes into existence fated to end. This is not sad. It should inspire women and men to seek to prolong moments on the Earth, through conservation.

- All environmental errors are reversible save one: extinction. Therefore the prevention of extinctions is a priority.

- Though humanity may today be a cause of species extinction, in a very short time by nature's standards it can become an agent for species preservation.

PEOPLE

- People may not sit above animals and plants in any metaphysical sense, but clearly are superior in their placement in the natural order. Decent material conditions must be provided for all of the former before there can be long-term assurance of protection for the latter.

- Either humanity was created by a higher power, in which case it is absurd for environmental dogma to consider the human role in nature to be bad; or humanity rose to its position through purely natural processes, in which case it is absurd for environmental dogma to consider the human role in nature to be bad.

- However the deed was done, once genus *Homo* was called forth into being, the wholly spontaneous ordering of the environment ended. And unless there is an extinction of intellect, wholly spontaneous nature will never return. Nature is not diminished by this. A fairly straightforward reading of natural history suggests that evolution spent 3.8 billion years working assiduously to bring about the demise of the wholly spontaneous order, via the creation of intellect.
- In principle the human population is no enemy of nature. Someday that population may be many times larger than at present, without ecological harm. But the world of the present knows more people than current social institutions and technical knowledge can support at an adequate material standard. Thus short-term global population stabilization is desperately required, though the prospect of dramatic long-term expansion of the human population should not be discounted.

NATURE

- Nature is not ending, nor is human damage to the environment "unprecedented." Nature has repelled forces of a magnitude many times greater than the worst human malfeasance.
- Nature is not ponderously slow. It's just old. Old and slow are quite different concepts. That the living world can adjust with surprising alacrity is the reason nature has been able to get old. Most natural recoveries from ecological duress happen with amazing speed.
- Significant human tampering with the environment has been in progress for at least ten millennia and perhaps longer. If nature has been interacting with genus *Homo* for thousands of years, then the living things that made it to the present day may be ones whose genetic treasury renders them best suited to resist human mischief. This does not insure any creature will continue to survive any clash with humankind. It does make survival more likely than doomsday orthodoxy asserts.
- If nature's adjustment to the human presence began thousands of years ago, perhaps it will soon be complete. Far from reeling helplessly before a human onslaught, nature may be on the verge of reasserting itself.
- Nature still rules much more of the Earth than does genus *Homo*. To the statistical majority of nature's creatures the arrival of men and women goes unnoticed.

- To people the distinction between artificial and natural means a great deal. To nature it means nothing at all.
- The fundamental force of nature is not amoral struggle between hunter and hunted. Most living things center their existence on cooperation and coexistence, the sort of behavior women and men should emulate. This is one reason nature will soon be viewed again in the way it was by the thinkers of the eighteenth-century Enlightenment—as a trove of wisdom and an exemplar for society.

WHERE DO WE FIT IN?

- Nature, limited by spontaneous interactions among elements randomly disturbed, may have an upper-bound limit on its potential to foster life and to evolve. Yet nature appears to enjoy fostering life and evolving. So perhaps nature hoped to acquire new sets of abilities, such as action by design.
- Therefore maybe nature needs us.

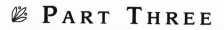 **P**ART **T**HREE

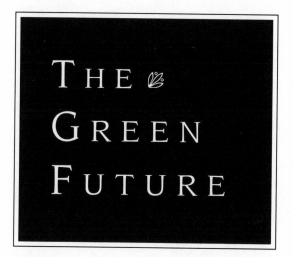

THE 🌿
GREEN
FUTURE

People and Nature 🌿
Learning to Think
Together

Because the environment is old compared to us, people conceptualize nature as winding down and vulnerable near the end of a long, exhausting journey.

But compared to itself the natural enterprise glistens with morning dew. Nature's powers are on the increase, its wonders barely begun.

Nature is just getting started.

THE BALANCE

IF YOU WOULD KNOW THE POWER OF LIFE OVER MATTER, KNOW these things.

The sea turtle hatchling, born in the warm sands of a Florida beach, immediately stumbles to the ocean and throws itself in. Unknowing of the world, unaided by any parent, sought as prey by crabs and birds and perhaps facing its greatest danger from the featureless harshness of the cold waters, the hatchling begins floating among sargassum seaweeds, seeking to orient itself in the currents it will use to navigate as far as Ascension Island, thousands of miles distant. Answering some unknowable summons of antiquity the hatchling crosses the ocean alone, accomplishing without any physical technology a feat men and women in boats with radios and radars and turbo diesels and freeze-dried foods and ring-laser gyros have died attempting to accomplish.

Near the end of a life lived on the western shores of Africa the sea turtle answers a second summons, to return to the sands of its birth. This time it cannot float but must swim against the prevailing current. In some haunting way the turtle recalls exactly what it sensed as a hatchling—the precise successions of currents, wave patterns, salinity changes, and polarity from magnetic north. This is necessary because the goal is to return *exactly* to the patch of sand on which the turtle first knew the light of the temporal world. North America alone will not do; Florida alone will not do; it must be the same beach, the same feel and smell in every way.

Perhaps the sea turtle is a mere genetic automaton, driven by deterministic amino acid encodings toward a moot goal dropped into its DNA by some past random happenstance that signifies nothing. Or perhaps this journey has meaning.

Perhaps the turtle is willing to swim the breadth of the very ocean in order to experience once again the sweet tastes that accompanied its awakening to life—the early sensations of youth being the sweetest any living thing can ask to know. Perhaps this allows the sea turtle to end its days having not just existed and processed carbohydrates and excreted nitrogen and grown senescent but lived, taken a small yet noble role in an enterprise that may eventually fill the whole of the cosmos with meaning. Perhaps the turtle is driven not by mindless helixes but by *longing*—the longing of life over matter, the most insistent force in all the firmament.

One rare exception in a world of numbing pointlessness? Consider other examples of the profundity of life.

The spotted salamander lives underground almost the entire year. One day in spring when the temperature is at least 42 degrees Fahrenheit and it has rained hard the previous night, every spotted salamander emerges for a night of sporting and mating. When the night ends the salamanders return beneath the ground for another year. The timing of the emergence is always flawless.

Birds want berries for food. Plants want birds to distribute their gene lines by eating berries, flying somewhere, then relieving themselves of a portion of the berries designed to be indigestible: the seeds. Why do berries turn red? As a signal to birds that they are ripe and the time has come to eat them.

Each fall the yellow pine chipmunk collects and buries seeds of the yellow pine and the bitterbrush, a staple browsing food of deer. Some seeds the chipmunk returns to consume; some seeds the chipmunk forgets about. Forgotten seeds bloom in spring, perpetuating the yellow pine and the bitterbrush, which in turn feed the deer. The seeds have not only been dispersed by the chipmunk, they have been *planted*.

When a bear hibernates, in some unknown way its body recycles calcium to prevent osteoporosis and reabsorbs urea to prevent bladder failure. Bears can even carry a pregnancy through hibernation, continuing to make the necessary hormones; though in all nonhibernating mammals including people, fasting ends hormone production and causes miscarriage.

The sluggish caterpillar *myrmecophilous*, an attractive target for wasps, has two nectary glands that secrete a potion ants seem to consider champagne. If *myrmecophilous* thumps a branch in distress over the presence of a wasp, any nearby ants will rush to defend the caterpillar.

In the tree canopies of the tropical rainforest, star-shaped plants called bromeliads catch precipitation to form puddles. The puddles provide the plants with water, so they need not shoot roots to the ground: they also serve as little ponds for hundreds of other life forms.

Female guppies that live in streams where there are no predators prefer flashy males with bright markings and large fins. Female guppies that live in streams with many predators prefer plain males. Thus under safe conditions female guppies choose genes for attractiveness, to help their offspring get on socially. Under dangerous conditions female guppies choose genes for camouflage, to help their offspring survive by going unnoticed.

The opossum is believed to have existed for at least 60 million years. That is to say the opossum, a delicate thing easily harmed, is far older than the Rocky Mountains, a seemingly indestructible mass of dense minerals hewn from Earth's very continental plates. The whale is thought to have existed at least 12 million years, after somehow evolving from a land animal similar in appearance to a cow. That is to say the whale, a fragile living thing, is far older than the present alignment of ocean currents in which it swims. The sandhill crane seems to have existed for at least nine million years, perhaps making migratory stops along the area of the North Platte River of Nebraska, a favored present-day calling point, much of that time. The North Platte itself is somewhere around 15,000 years old. That is to say the sandhill crane, a fragile living thing today called endangered, is far, far older than the river at which it calls.

The monarch butterfly, a mere insect, migrates as much as 2,500 miles. Monarch brains no larger than a few grains of sand contain the topographical information necessary to navigate from the northern United States to Mexico. Several generations of the butterflies—born, metamorphosed, flying, mating, dying—are required to complete the passage of a family line from summering grounds to wintering area. Just try to guess what forces lead to the development of metamorphic creatures such as the butterfly, which essentially require two separate sets of genetic inheritances favored by two entirely separate circumstances of natural selection.

These are but a few of many, many examples of the wonder and complexity of life. I choose them because they may be less familiar than others. And I choose these two from genus *Homo*.

In the sediments of a lake near the Greek city of Nikopolis has been found a flint axe that is at least 200,000 and perhaps 500,000 years old. This tells us humans were not just quizzical primates, but tool users with minds already struggling to comprehend the world, an unimaginable length of time ago by our way of thinking.

In 1991 in the Qafzeh Cave near Haifa, Israel, archaeologists found the bones of a young human female delicately interned, arms wrapped around the bones of a neonate—suggesting mother and infant buried together after both died during childbirth. The bones are at least 100,000 years old. This tells us human beings had already begun to develop spiritual awareness—were already struggling with the meaning of life and the tragedy of its loss—an unimaginable length of time ago by our way of thinking.

The rest of this book asks two basic questions. The first is whether people, machines, and nature can learn to work together for each other's mutual benefit, achieving plateaus each alone would be incapable of. The second is whether the ongoing process of life has larger significance or is just something that happened when chance assemblies of amino acids accidentally activated each other.

This second question is in the end *the* question of the environment. By comparison all other environmental issues deflate to disputes on aesthetics—about what kind of backdrop, green or concrete, provides the better bunting for a forlorn world. And to quote the author Robert Wright: "I don't wish to alarm anyone, but I'm going to mention the meaning of life." We'll mention this at once central and shunned topic, too, building to it through a consideration of the balance of nature.

The Balance versus Chaos

In the standard depiction of the balance of nature, "balance" means inaction. For immense amounts of time ecospheres hold about the same populations of about the same creatures doing about the same things. As detailed in part one, the notion of a static natural world arose partly because the human mind had difficulty conceptualizing time blocks in the millions of years, unless natural epochs were seen as periods in which established patterns repeated over and over again. The apposite notion of a dynamic environment accustomed to change made the mind reel. Wouldn't an action-packed natural system rattle to pieces? Run off its rails or something?

More than any ecological thinker, Rachel Carson popularized the notion of nature as existing mainly in idyllic changelessness for immense periods. This helped Carson highlight her premise that human-caused environmental changes were happening with unprecedented speed. There is a subconscious appeal to such thinking. Everyone ages. With the passage of years it is common increasingly to perceive the world as beginning to run off its rails. With age most people's willingness to confront change declines; often the mind compensates by generating a romanticized vision of a good-old-days when change was absent or rare. The first generation of post-Carson environmentalists now begins to age, and though when young this group demanded change, in age it begins to fear any disruption of the balance. A death of nature is foreseen, subconsciously substituting for the generation's own approaching end.

Surely when my own generation faces its decades of aging, I and my peers will retreat to romanticized visions of balance lost. But that is not the direction in which science is moving. Increasingly researchers "are forsaking one of the most deeply embedded concepts of ecology, the balance of nature," the science journalist William Stevens has written. Most scientists now think nature is not static but exists "in a continuing state of disturbance and fluctuation."

For instance, in 1994 two researchers from the University of California at Davis, Alan Hastings and Kevin Higgins, published a study suggesting that over the past 20,000 years population levels of the Dungeness crab have vacillated drastically for reasons not clearly related to climate, predation, disease, human action, or any influence the pair could discern. Many marine creatures, Hastings and Higgins found, exhibit natural boom-and-bust cycles that appear disjunct from conventional conceptions of balance. The researchers found wild populations sometimes going bust when human action was not a factor, and sometimes booming in direct defiance of genus *Homo*. For example the lobster population of coastal Maine reached its twentieth-century zenith in 1990 despite furious commercial lobstering and has remained high since as still more traps are dropped. This confounds standard balance-of-nature thinking.

In recent years the Ecology Society of America, a scientists' group, has held several meetings on whether the balance of nature is active or static. At one George Jacobson, a University of Maine ecologist, declared that "there is almost no circumstance in which something isn't changing the natural system. The system may seek an equilibrium but it's never allowed to get there. So we might as well not expect [the classical balance of nature] to exist." For example, forests may seek what the classicist would imagine as the balanced, static Middle Earth woodland of mature trees, stable predator-prey relationships, and reliably repetitious climate. At times such classical forests are realized. But nature has never allowed the forest to come to rest in this state. There are natural fires wiping out thousands of acres, climate swings that boost or retard plant growth, cycles of overpopulation and die-off, and other unpredictable changes. Over periods relatively short by nature's way of thinking the entire physical circumstances of the forest transforms through ice ages, continental drift, mountain upthrust, alterations in prevailing winds and rainfall, and other dynamic influences.

This evolving understanding of what might be called the action-packed balance of nature challenges the orthodox view of an ecology that shatters at the lightest touch. If the environment has not only been under regular natural duress for eons, but also endured continuous internally generated fluctuations, nature must be mighty indeed.

To prevent that inconveniently positive notion from gaining currency, some green theoreticians have latched on to the developing field of chaos mathematics. Chaos math represents the latest attempt to solve a problem stated by the nineteenth-century French mathematician Henri Poincare, who noted that large systems with strong interactions, such as Earth's climate, resist even the most cautious predictions about future states. Only small systems with weak interactions, such as the weather in a particular city tomorrow, seem to yield to statistical prescience. Since Poincare phrased this problem many have assumed the inability to predict behaviors of large, strong systems was a temporary barrier caused by the limitations of data and calculating devices. Chaos mathematics essentially says that even given fantastic amounts of information and unlimited power, an ultimate computer would still be unable to predict the future of the climate or of any large, strong system such as an ecosphere or a society.

In a way this can be seen as a hopeful message—life will always contain surprises. After all, if the course of events were dictated by deterministic sequences of the sort an ultimate computer might identify, God would be bored, there being nothing unexpected to watch unfold. Chaos mathematics can be said to establish that the past does not control the present, which sounds to me like hopeful news. Orthodox environmental doctrine has, however, seized on a pessimistic tangent of the theory: that because the future condition of a system may not directly link to a present state, everything could come crashing down without the slightest warning.

In this context some ecological pessimists have begun praising the work of a Danish physicist named Per Bak. Bak believes that the balance of nature operates through chaos mathematics as what he calls a "composite system." In such a system huge numbers of small components may evolve into a complicated structure generally self-regulating and successful; yet the structure might go berserk owing to a tiny vacillation. Bak's example is the sandpile. Grains of sand by the millions can assemble into a sandpile, exhibiting what Bak calls "self-organized criticality." Under most circumstances the sandpile is strong, able to resist such forces as a windstorm. Under rare circumstances the addition of a single grain causes the entire pile to collapse. That sandpile, some environmentalists now hold, is the environment. Genus *Homo* is the extra grain of sand.

Important as chaos thinking is, there exists another emerging view of the balance of nature, one drawing less attention because it is not satisfyingly frightful. That emerging idea is called complexity theory.

The Balance and Complexity

The complexity hypothesis posits that a function of life is to defy the second law of thermodynamics—the law often misinterpreted as saying everything will eventually run down into an undifferentiated, dull-gray blahness. Complexity theorists believe instead that in some manner not yet grasped, the universe came prewired to favor complex systems over entropy. In his fine 1993 book *Complexity,* Mitchell Waldrop writes that researchers increasingly find that atoms arrange themselves into complicated structures from stars to snowflakes "almost as if the particles were obeying a hidden yearning for organization and order."

Consider that a current theory on the origin of life holds that RNA, essentially a simple version of DNA, was in the ancient dawn generated chemically by chance. Called to existence, RNA then evolved into DNA and the race from the microbe to the blue whale was on. Yet chance seems a pitifully unlikely explanation for such an origin of life. Francis Crick, who with James Watson discovered the helical strand of DNA, has said that the mere 3.8 billion-year period since Earth life began is nowhere near long enough for DNA structures as complex as human genomes to have evolved purely through chance and selection. Michael Hart, an astronomer at Anne Arundel Community College in Arnold, Maryland, has estimated that the odds that a functional piece of DNA could assemble itself are one followed by a string of 30 zeros, more than the number of subatomic particles now believed to exist in the universe.

Extremely long odds do not preclude an outcome; there is always beginner's luck. But such odds suggest there is something fundamental missing from human understanding of the natural world. That something, complexity theory says, is recognition that highly ordered structures such as DNA are not improbable. Quite the reverse: Ordered structures are likely. For example, complexity researchers are beginning to find that patterns similar to DNA sequences are surprisingly easy to "evolve" using computer simulations. Simulations roughly suggesting primordial Earth chemistry do not resist the formation of advanced molecules but rather embrace them eagerly. One complexity researcher, the biologist Stuart Kauffman of the University of Pennsylvania, believes that the boundary line between order (structures that defy entropy) and randomness (miasma that submits to entropy) can be shown mathematically to be the most fit circumstance for many organisms, fit in the sense Darwin used the word. Kauffman calls this premise "order for free." Further, Kauffman says, "There are deep parallels between biological evolution and technological evolution. There may eventually be general laws that describe both."

Once, at a science conference, I sat on a stairwell with Kauffman as he spun out a theory of natural history, which I amend here slightly. The universe is created through an act of self-organization: Whether the creation was governed by a deity or was a spontaneous event, in either case some initial influence must have favored "order for free." After Earth formed, for a while the planet was uninhabitable owing to physical forces such as high radiation and frequent asteroid impacts. Essentially the moment those forces ebbed, life began to organize itself into increasingly complex molecules that could replicate, record information, and respond to the unexpected. In this emergence the evolution of DNA was not a wild stroke of chance. It was likely—arising in some as-yet-undetermined way from the same preference for order that caused the universe itself to arise.

A running-down may await the cosmos in some distant futurity, but over the billions of years that have passed so far the observed natural trend has been entirely toward greater complexity. Equally important, the most interesting aspects of the universe have been increasingly complicated. Stars, for example, are interesting. But in the end they are just gigantic furnaces. Snails—now they are *interesting*. The lowliest snail crawling at your feet is less predictable in its responses to the universe around it than the greatest exploding supernova. Dolphin, parrots, owls, black-footed ferret—they're *really interesting*, a thousand times more complex than the most awesome mephitic black hole. People—they're *really, really, interesting*. From the standpoint of original thoughts and defiance of deterministic forces, the life of even a medieval herdsman or washerwoman was far more interesting than all possible data about all inanimate forces at the cosmic scale.

Complexity theory can be mistaken for a proposition that living structures must grow ever-more convoluted. Sometimes refinement leads to simplification. For instance a series of studies published in 1993 in the journal *Geology and Evolution* show that in marine shells and animal backbones, evolution points toward simplification as often as convolution. Technology has recently begun to uncover the virtues of simplicity, finding, say, that a tiny silicon chip without moving parts can be preferable to a large computing device of multiple tubes, gears, and levers. Complexity in the sense that theorists use the term means "sophisticated" more than "complicated."

So far no complexity theorist has glimpsed the underlying mechanisms by which natural law may favor structure. Until such mechanisms are uncovered, complexity theory will just be another hypothesis that may someday be overturned. But this way of thinking holds special relevance to the prospect of a green future for two reasons. First, because complexity theory supposes that the living adventure is not a vapor that may at any moment puff away, but deeply embedded in the laws of nature. Second, because complexity theory supposes that what the mind does best is what nature wants more of. As the late physicist Heinz Pagel wrote in 1988 in *Dreams of Reason,* someday "the radical distinction between mind and nature will disappear." Complexity theory may help point genus *Homo* toward ways to expand the most important complex structures of all—thoughts—while using extremely small expenditures of physical resources.

The Balance in Youth

Reflected in many facets of human culture is the view that the wonder of life expired at some mystic moment that has slipped into the past. There are no new vistas; life can no longer be lived as it was meant to be; the good fights have already been fought. The sentiment is summed up by these words in which F. Scott Fitzgerald imagines Europeans as they first laid eyes on what to them was the New World: "For a transitory moment man must have held his breath in the presence of this new continent, compelled into an aesthetic contemplation he neither understood nor desired, face to face for the last time in history with something commensurate with his capacity for wonder."

Face to face for the last time in history with something commensurate with his capacity for wonder. Contemporary environmental doctrine is rife with this sort of purblind vision. Previously evolved living things are marvelous, but new ones can only be horrors; previously established ecosystems hum with life, but new ones can only falter; previous alignments of land, water, and air are magnificent, but new ones can only be disappointments.

A contrasting view comes from Freeman Dyson, a Princeton University physicist who has described the potential of existence as "infinite in all directions." In 1979 Dyson wrote, "No matter how far we go into the future there will always be new things happening, new information coming in, new worlds to explore, a constantly expanding domain of life, consciousness and memory."

An obvious reason why there may "always be new things happening" is that women and men have in recent decades taken the initial steps in what may be an ages-long effort of learning about the vastness of the galaxy. Since the ecological implications of departure from island Earth are the subject of a coming chapter, we can put that topic on hold for a moment. Instead let's suppose for the sake of argument that space exploration never becomes practical, leaving genus *Homo* bound to Earth in perpetuity. Will there ever again be any new thing "commensurate with our capacity for wonder"? To some extent the answer turns on the youth of the biosphere.

By the human way of thinking life is immensely old, and old age means senescence. By nature's way of thinking life is young, and youth means vigor. Until recently the standard estimate held that the universe is 15 to 20 billion years old, this figure based on factors such as the apparent recession of galaxies away from the point presumed to have been the plenum of the Big Bang. As the Earth is known with reasonable assurance to be about 4.5 billion years old, and life to be about 3.8 billion years old, that makes our living biosphere a relative newcomer to the cosmos. Supposing life arose by a thoughtless process, it might be expected that billions of years would pass before the first success were recorded. Supposing God runs the universe, who can say what the celestial timetable might call for?

Since the late 1980s, astronomical discoveries have tended to suggest the universe is younger than previous estimates. Recent evidence makes some researchers think this cosmos as few as eight billion years in age—still immensely old compared to the biblical interpretation but no longer immensely old compared to life on Earth. If our universe began a mere eight billion years ago and life began 3.8 billion years ago, then creation is just now taking wing. Even if a Big Crunch, the inverse of the Big Bang, awaits to end the present universe, rough estimates put that event 50 billion to 100 billion years in the future. This in turn suggests the biosphere of Earth has reached its present state consuming just one-twelfth of the time available on the cosmic clock. Genus *Homo* has come on the scene not near the end of an arduous trek toward the graveyard but at the beginning of a stirring voyage of discovery.

Do you find it hard to imagine that a firmament existing billions of years nevertheless can be young? Until about a decade ago most astronomers believed that galaxies formed only in the genesis eons, the process long ago concluded. Then researchers began to find brand-new galaxies coalescing "near" the Milky Way, where we live. Next astronomers found new stars forming within the Milky Way—some in the part of the galaxy where island Earth resides. The discoveries are not of "old" light from stars that lit long ago, but represent a contemporary phenomenon. Formation of new stars and new galaxies now appears to be an ongoing process of nature, one that either has yet to conclude or that will never conclude. Stars are *still forming*. Right in our neighborhood.

Wonder Renewed

Another way to conceptualize the newness of life is to contemplate how much longer Earth's living biosphere might last. Absent nuclear war, the likely answer: fantastically long.

In the early 1980s the British scientist James Lovelock estimated that the living world of Earth might be entering its final phases, owing, oddly enough, to a shortage of carbon dioxide, the very greenhouse gas whose current surplus is called calamitious. Lovelock's reasoning was that while carbon dioxide spikes upward at the moment, the geologic trend is toward decline. The sun is expected to continue escalating its power output for at least another billion years or so. More solar heat may increase the rate at which the natural carbon cycle withdraws CO_2 from the air via chemical weathering reactions with rocks. That might cause the carbon content of the air to decline to the point at which there is insufficient CO_2 for photosynthesis. All plants expire. Then adios, amigos. The fatal sequence of carbon dioxide depletion may take as little as 100 million years, Lovelock supposed.

In 1992 the researchers James Kasting and Kenneth Caldeira of Pennsylvania State University revisited Lovelock's analysis and altered it substantially. New discoveries suggest plants can subsist on less carbon dioxide than previously suspected, that the equilibrium between rock-weathering and CO_2 is more subtle than once appeared. And most current discoveries suggest living things can evolve in response to environmental changes much more rapidly than once assumed, suggesting 100 million years may be ample for plants to adjust to lower carbon in the air or even to develop a new principle of photosynthesis, possibly with the help of genetic engineers. Taking these factors into account, Kasting and Caldeira estimated the life expectancy of the current biosphere at 900 million to 1.5 billion years. After that, the sun will have become so hot Earth's oceans will boil.

Roll the notion of another 900 million to 1.5 billion years of evolution around for a moment. In less time than that—about 600 million years—Earth organisms progressed from microbes and sea urchins to thousands of large vertebrates, one confirmed thinking creature and several others that seem moving toward thought. Ponder for a moment how much human culture, art, and technology have transformed in the historical period so far—the 6,000-year passage from cuneiform to desktop computers, jet travel, and tomatoes with fish genes. Now imagine humankind continues to exist for 900 million to 1.5 billion additional years, or perhaps 250,000 times as long as the historical period so far. Something that renews the capacity for wonder might be in store.

And if nature somehow possesses foreknowledge that through the coming billion years Earth will be made uninhabitable owing to the heating of the sun, might not a chain of events that enables future living things to depart from this island—a chain whose first link is a thinking being—be very much in nature's interest?

The final chapters will outline some ways in which people, machines, and nature may learn to work together toward the renewal of wonder. I don't present them as a pragmatic program that could be enacted tomorrow, nor mean to suggest that the possibility of a green future proves either science or technology to be beneficent forces. Far from it: Both should be subject to ever-more-strict regulation, in order to protect society and the living sphere from their excesses. The ideas that follow are offered solely to show that it is possible to imagine a coming age in which harm to the environment ends, in which "the distinction between the mind and nature" ends, and in which nature, having given genus *Homo* so many gifts, enjoys gifts from the maturing child in return.

THE NEW NATURE

In 1993 the Russian space agency Glavkosmos placed into orbit a large parafoil mirror designed to reflect sunlight toward the dark hemisphere of Earth, transforming night into a false twilight with about the luminescence of three full moons. Such mirrors, Russian engineers thought, might someday shine on cities, replacing street lights with zero-pollution, zero-fuel illumination. Or the mirrors might be held on station, available to train on the sites of nighttime natural disasters or search-and-rescue emergencies. In principle a large network of space mirrors might banish darkness from the face of the Earth altogether, maintaining the night hemisphere in perpetual half-light.

For technical reasons the experiment failed, though engineers remain convinced such mirrors could function. Environmental opposition to further research was emphatic. Bill McKibben declared that space-reflected illumination would "constitute the single most offensive form of pollution yet devised by man," here defining sunlight as pollution if that light arrives when the sun does not normally deliver it. "We should be screaming about this," McKibben suggested.

Needless to say, whether space mirrors would be desirable is open to dispute. Let's suppose for the sake of argument that someday space launches become inexpensive and people decide to ring the globe with orbital mirrors intended to end true darkness. This possibility offers a framework for pondering the sorts of global tampering of which genus *Homo* increasingly will become capable.

A space-mirror network would alter the ecology in significant ways.

Like all human ecological meddling, such alterations might be good or bad. For instance having cities half-lit at night might cause crime and accidents to go down, but increase insomnia. Nocturnal life cycles would shift for many creatures. Plants might grow faster, aiding some at the expense of others. Biologists might petition to have the half-light switched off in areas where it seems to imperil a species. Parks and resorts might apply for exemptions, advertising the experience of true night. Going someplace with absolute darkness might become a lovers' holiday.

Yet within a few generations both people and living things would consider half-dark the normal condition, full dark unnerving and needlessly dangerous. Since the circumstances experienced in youth become through each person's nostalgia filter the image of what the world ought to be, women and men born to a world of half-dark night might consider full-dark night a violation of the presumed environmental Correct Reality. Nature might eventually be pleased by the adjustment, since once living things modified behaviorally and genetically for partial night, the net activity of the ecology might increase, the half-dark being able to sponsor more biological action than full-dark, in which few creatures function.

Whether the abolition of full darkness would on balance be good or bad will be a matter for some future century to settle. The only thing we can be sure of now is that the doctrinal environmental response—that such an idea should never be considered because artificial alteration of nature would be involved—is a dead end. A New Nature, modified by men and women, is coming. It cannot be stopped, nor should it. The issue that matters is how to make the New Nature good rather than bad.

Natural Limits

When environmental thinkers evince horror at the idea of people deliberately altering nature on a broad scale, what they evince is their human dislike of the consequences. Fair enough. But what might nature think about deliberate alteration of nature? Perhaps nature thinks, *It's about time.* Nature's accomplishments are legion and worthy of awe. Were nature to continue operating in purely spontaneous fashion, many further accomplishments would be recorded. But barriers would be reached as well. Nature has structural flaws and physical limitations. Genus *Homo* may be able to change that. People may be here because nature needs us—perhaps, needs us desperately.

Five fundamental barriers face the wholly spontaneous form of nature that many environmentalists extol.

First, nature cannot act by design. This is the most basic fault of the natural system. Action by design is far from perfect: plans go awry, good intentions have unwelcome consequences. Nevertheless action by design can accomplish ends that spontaneous forces cannot, perhaps helping nature surmount barriers it could not surmount on its own.

Second, nature can accumulate information only through genes. Adaptive intellect can store and make sense of information millions of times faster than genetic systems. Yes, adaptive intellect can also pursue evil ends. That fear aside, there is no reason in principle why nature ought to oppose the arrival of the high-speed analytical powers of the mind. Nature may have been dreaming of these very powers for 3.8 billion years.

Third, nature is limited by reliance on the sun. Most Earth organisms, including all the really interesting ones, rely on a food chain that begins with solar photons converted to chemical energy by photosynthesis. Most life depends on the sun to warm the climate. Reliance on the sun limits nature by restricting the amount of life in the high-northern and low-southern latitudes; by requiring life in the temperate latitudes to survive a taxing winter; by causing widespread ecological damage when the sun is blocked by dust from volcanos or asteroid strikes; and perhaps by foreclosing life on planets where sunlight is either too intense or too faint, such as all the planets in this solar system other than Earth. Worst, over the very long term in which nature thinks, the sun will become an enemy of the biosphere—first by growing hotter and making the oceans boil, then by fusing into metallic elements and eventually detonating.

And the sun is a profligate power source. Many environmental thinkers rightly note with disdain that the internal combustion engine converts a mere 20 percent of the energy value in petroleum to forward motion. Yet a gas-guzzling 1955 Chevy pushrod V-8 is a positive marvel of efficiency compared to nature's engines—stars—which waste energy on a phenomenal scale. Less than one-tenth of one percent of the sun's power output falls on Earth, where it becomes useful to life. So far as is known the 99 percent of solar energy that radiates off into deep space accomplishes nothing whatever, except perhaps providing career opportunities for astronomers on other worlds. A natural scheme based on an energy source that wastes nearly everything it generates, and that will fail in the long run, sounds like a scheme with flaws that might someday be corrected by adaptive intellect.

Fourth, nature is limited by the chance basis of DNA change.

Evolution is not, as commonly said, a "random" process. By favoring some traits over others, natural selection guides the system in a better-than-random manner. But the gene changes that make for differing traits do have a chance basis, probably originating in copying errors during DNA replication. The chance basis of DNA change can cause individual species to be vulnerable, since the required mutation may not pop up during a period of ecological stress; can render it hard for the entire biosphere to gain from gene advances achieved in any particular species; and can tend to make the evolutionary process a conservative one, unlikely to stage grand departures from past forms. If something more is in store—perhaps a form of life based more on consciousness than biology—random evolutionary mutations may not be sufficient to reach that level.

Finally nature faces a fundamental restriction in that life requires planets. The universe may be rich with wondrous vitality arising in exotic locales. Based on what is known so far, the likelihood is that wholly spontaneous life can only evolve and exist on planets.

This restriction is deceptively significant. Only two (unnamed at this writing) planets have been discovered outside Earth's solar system, and they orbit a pulsar, a collapsed sun emitting radiation at such fantastic levels that life on these worlds defies imagination. Planets are much harder to spot than stars; the fact that astronomers have detected only two "extrasolar" planets hardly means there are not many faraway worlds. But some astrophysicists believe that of the many extrasolar planets presumed to exist, Earthlike worlds will turn out exceedingly rare. (More on this in the next chapter.) Even where Earthlike planets exist such bodies cannot secure life against cosmic forces like asteroid strikes and star detonations. Perhaps nature would like to break its reliance on planets, sequestering at least part of the living heritage beyond planetary vulnerabilities.

These fundamental restrictions of the environment—that nature cannot act by design, that natural accumulation of information is slow, that life is overdependent on suns, that natural selection is limited by random gene-copying accidents, and that life requires planets—are ones that might seem sufficiently elemental as to be knitted into the fabric of existence itself.

Yet restriction number one, the inability to act by design, is already being overthrown. Today human intellect may be riddled with flaws and used toward evil ends. But from the standpoint of nature, intellect is a project proceeding at remarkable speed with encouraging results, generating an entirely new aspect of life in a very short time by geologic standards. That makes it possible to imagine other basic restrictions of nature being overthrown, perhaps again quickly by nature's way of thinking.

The New Nature

Let's conduct a thought experiment into what a New Nature might be like.

First, the New Nature might include the end of predation by animals against animals. As detailed in part one, researchers such as the biologist Lynn Margulis increasingly believe that cooperation is the operating principle of most life. Ted Dawson, a plant ecologist at Cornell University, has discovered that tree roots do not, as previously assumed, draw all available water to the tree. Dawson found that at night the roots of the sugar maple pull up water from soils too deep for other plants to reach. In daytime maple roots discharge some of that water, helping smaller plants flourish. The closer plants such as goldenrod are to a sugar maple, the more likely their survival during dry seasons. Other biologists are finding similar water-sharing behavior in other trees. This is enlightened cooperation, not a bestial clash of all against all.

Obviously there are spectacular exceptions to the premise of cooperation among species. Yet is the destructive life-pattern of the predator a necessity of biology or a flaw of nature awaiting correction? Some very large, powerful creatures such as gorillas exist quite nicely as herbivores. It is possible at least in theory that through genetic intervention, present-day predators could become herbivores, continuing to live as wild bears or wolves or weasel, except leaving out the gruesome part. Nature might long for such a reform. Surely nature's prey species, a vast "silent majority" in biosphere demographics, would be pleased by an end of predation.

Next, the New Nature might include an end of predation against animals by people. Some advocate vegetarianism for reasons of ethics; some for the practical reason that Earth's agricultural output is today sufficient for the world to eat its fill of grains and fruits, but when a substantial amount of grain is fed to cattle and poultry to raise meat, malnutrition results among the impoverished. Both the ethical and pragmatic reasons for vegetarianism are sound, but the practice is unlikely to spread simply because most people like to eat meat and will continue to do so until either stopped by compulsion or given a desirable alternative. So let's give them a desirable alternative.

In theory it is not necessary to have animals in order to have meat.

Carbohydrates and proteins, the basic stuff of nutrition, might be grown in plants to supply a sort of feedstock. This food-fuel might then be cultured into the cells of beef, chicken, or fish in genetic engineering production vats similar to those now employed to culture genetically engineered pharmaceuticals. The final product would be biological meat—just meat cells that skipped the stage of existing in an animal that suffered.

This idea is today being discussed in general terms by agronomists. Many environmentalists express disgust at the prospect of cultured meat, and not just because such techno-vegetarianism would be insufficiently punitive. Green doctrine is horrified by this prospect because genetic engineering would be required, and because people would consume a category of substance their romanticized hunter-gatherer ancestors never ate. Yet the confinement and slaughter of stock animals also would end; the dosing of stock with growth hormones and prophylactic antibiotics would end; methane emissions from beef herds would end; the content of meats could be manipulated to emphasize nutrition.

Of course if such products arrived in supermarkets today shoppers would turn away, insisting on "real" meat. But then today's consumers would turn away from the feathered carcass of a chicken whose neck had just been wrung—the form in which great-grandmother got her meat. Not far into the future, raising cattle in pens for slaughter in automated abattoirs will seem as primitive as wringing a chicken's neck in the kitchen seems today. Eventually the entire human species may be converted to de facto vegetarianism not through ethical philosophy but through the development of steak, chops, and sole that have nothing to do with animals.

Next, the New Nature may include the end of predation against people by people. In all of nature exist only a handful of creatures that kill their own. Unfortunately one is us.

The fact that most animals will not prey on others like themselves is not just some charming quirk: It must have a physical basis in the genetic inventories of living things. Suppose the DNA codes that prevent most species from killing their own can be isolated and moved into genus *Homo*, rendering men and women genetically averse to raising weapons against each other. An initiative to insert into the entire human DNA germ line a no-kill code would be complex and fraught with pitfalls. But if it worked perhaps the worst error of Earth history—the combination of intellect and predation—would be corrected. Would nature favor this entirely artificial development? One guess.

Next for the New Nature may be the end of extinctions. Nature has never been able to find a means to preserve species rendered extinct by the inevitability of ecological change. Perhaps woman and men can.

Next would be the end of disease. A few researchers have entertained the notion that diseases serve some undiscovered functional role in the natural scheme. But the likelihood is that disease is a defect of nature waiting to be corrected. The eradication of smallpox, declared extinct by the World Health Organization in 1977, shows that it is not utopian to imagine diseases being driven from the biosphere. And disease eradication need not be confined to the illnesses that afflict people but could extend to the diseases of the rest of the living world. Bear in mind that diseases cause far more suffering and death among animals than humans.

Next, the New Nature may be secure against killer rocks. Part one presented the increasingly uncomfortable evidence that devastating impacts of asteroids and comets were not confined to the primordial mists but are a global calamity the ecosystem has dodged as recently as this century. Millennia may pass before humankind is capable of a New Nature initiative as far-reaching as placing no-kill genes into DNA. Much sooner than that, women and men should be able to build a network of comet and asteroid detectors, linked to missiles or lasers that would push off course any dangerous objects headed toward Earth.

Such systems may be especially important in light of calculations published in 1994 in the *Quarterly of the Royal Astronomical Society* by the British scientist Robert Matthews. Our solar system travels within the galactic plane. Matthews believes that the next 46,000 years will be "rich in close encounters" between Sol, our star, and other suns, with at least six passing closer to the sun than the current closest star, Proxima Centauri. Matthews calculates these close encounters will cause gravitational effects that send monumental numbers of comets spiraling inward toward the Earth from the Oort cloud, a haze of comets believed to encircle the solar system.

Researchers suspect that gravitational consequences of the passage of the solar system through the galactic plane periodically perturbs the Oort cloud, explaining the barrages of celestial objects that now appear a persistent feature of natural history. Nature would long for this cosmic fusillade against the biosphere to end. Most chilling, Matthews calculates that it is possible one of the worst comet barrages in the 3.8 billion year living history of the Earth is about to commence, as in a few thousand years the solar system will pass unusually close to the binary star Alpha Centauri A-B, two suns whose combined mass may unleash a comet downfall of satanic proportions. However irksome human intellect may be, it may have arrived not a moment too soon to protect the living world from this devastation.

Next, in the New Nature there may be no more aging. Some physicians now believe that through improved nutrition, medicine, and exercise the normal human lifetime could be extended to around 125 years, without genetic engineering. A tantalizing hint of such a possibility comes from Michael Rose, a researcher at the University of California at Irvine, who has found that by selective breeding he could produce colonies of fruit flies that live twice as long as typical flies and are more hearty throughout their doubled lives.

Beyond that is the mystery of why living things age at all, since throughout life every creature maintains in every cell the DNA blueprint necessary to remake itself from scratch. Yet this knowledge is used only once: When cells begin to age, the blueprint is not reactivated. In the last decade some scientists have begun to ask whether the aging of living things is not some form of error that entered the DNA chain inadvertently. For instance Denham Harmon, the University of Nebraska researcher who in the 1950s first documented the presence in the body of "free radical" compounds that degrade cells, on making his discovery asked, If natural selection is so wise, why has it not produced genes for proteins to counter free radicals? A possible answer comes from Thomas Kirkwood, a biologist at the Medical Research Council in London, who has proposed that evolution never selected for longevity because almost all animals in the wild die young—killed by predators, disease, starvation, or accident long before they have the chance to age. Lack of resistance genes for cellular decline would be irrelevant to creatures fated to die young. All that would matter from the standpoint of evolutionary fitness would be the ability to reach sexual maturity, reproduce, and extend the gene line.

Pondering such notions some biologists have begun to toy with the idea that it will someday be possible to switch off the error genes that cause senescence, while perhaps inserting into DNA resistance genes for free radicals and other factors in aging. In principle this could be done for the entire biosphere, not just for people. Ageless people or animals would not be immortal, mortality continuing in accidents, from disease, through violence. But in an ageless biosphere, human death would not only be the moral loss it has always been; it would be still more poignant by virtue of rarity. As recently as two centuries ago, a third of children died before their first birthdays. Today, in the Western world, any death of a soft, breathing infant is considered a tragedy of high order. It is conceivable that someday, any death of anyone at any age will seem as tragic as a child's death seems today.

Next, the New Nature might end the waste of the Sun's output. Through the century to come men and women will get much better at using the energy that falls on Earth. But what about the vastly greater solar energies that stream off into the void? Some of that energy might be captured by space-solar generators that would beam electricity down to Earth. Some might be captured by reflectors that would concentrate sunlight into the atmosphere of Mars, warming that planet to the point of habitability. And in principle all solar energy might be captured. The physicist Freeman Dyson has proposed that someday humankind might detonate one of the presumably lifeless outer planets and use the debris to build a reflective sphere around the solar system. This sphere would be manipulated in such a way that Earth would remain at its current temperature while the rest of the very large area bounded by the outermost planets would be flooded by life-giving warmth and light.

Construction of a Dyson sphere would alter the spontaneous arrangements of nature on a planetary scale. Yet as every environment is born doomed, even the very planets are not exempt from alteration. Eventually all bodies of this solar system will be destroyed when the sun becomes a supernova. If, say, destroying lifeless Pluto a few billion years ahead of schedule led to a few billion years of life on Neptune, Uranus, and the moons of Saturn, would nature complain?

Finally the New Nature might offer the end of oblivion. At present human beings do not know whether upon death consciousness is lost or preserved in some higher form. For the sake of our own souls and those that have come before, we should hope an afterlife already exists. But if it does not, then people should make one.

Exactly what may constitute a soul is of course unknown, but it is not a shot in the dark to suppose the answer has something to do with consciousness. On a mechanical basis, consciousness appears to be mediated by electrical patterns in the brain. Today such patterns can be sustained only by a biological brain supported by a biological body. Perhaps someday those patterns could draw on some other form of support, one to which consciousness will move when the body of birth can no longer sustain itself. Perhaps someday some form of technology might even sustain patterns of consciousness in a noncorporeal manner. Lots of things could go wrong with such a premise. But here at least is the prospect that someday, in the New Nature, when the body dies the mind does not.

Today women and men look back on their forebears of distant centuries and view them with sadness as benighted creatures that lived out crude lives with constant material suffering and in ignorance of the most basic facts of the world around them. Someday our descendants may look back with greater sadness at us—we who view ourselves as so advanced—seeing us as the last benighted human generations that on physical death went to oblivion, rather than having their consciousness continue living, as for millennia people have supposed would be the fitting progression after temporal life.

Environmental Economics

You may think that items on the above inventory of possible alterations for a New Nature represent progress and a gentle dawn. You may think they represent arrogance and foolhardy adventurism. Whichever may be the case men and women cannot reform nature unless they first reform themselves. Institutions of government must be improved to the point of being consistently benevolent, for example, before anyone in his or her right mind would endorse tinkering with the human gene line. Whether true benevolent government can be achieved is obviously an open question. As regards the environment, a necessary reform preceding a New Nature will be the fading of the materialist lifestyle. Here the odds of social progess may be more favorable.

In chapter 21 it was proposed that much of what manifests today as anger about the environment is really anger about the centrality of the materialist lifestyle. The treadmill of earn-and-spend, on which it is not possible to make progress, only exert oneself into exhaustion; the obsession with forgettable consumer acquisitions to the exclusion of appreciation of art, philosophy, and other things of lasting value; constant earnings anxiety even among the well-paid; and many similar problems inspire sentiments that express themselves as environmentalist fury against the corporations and government agencies promoting the materialist lifestyle. As the Age of Pollution ends, the sorts of gross ecological malfeasance that first animated the green movement will fall away. Environmentalism as the word is used today will no longer be necessary. But long after the fight against pollution ends the fight against materialism will continue. This struggle may become more important than it is today, as the achievement of a clean, sustainable form of economics will offer many benefits, yet will have the regrettable side effect of making it possible for the cycle of consumption to continue indefinitely. If the human soul is to be saved, the materialist urge must be overcome: Green thinking, now focused on opposition to industry and development, will eventually focus on the more subtle and telling question of the harm materialism does to humanity, not nature. To the extent environmental sentiment transforms into a critique of the materialist lifestyle it will serve a more important purpose than halting pollution, since it will help bring genus *Homo* not just clean air and safe water but something of greater value: inner peace.

Following the collapse of the Soviet monolith there is no doubt that capitalism has been shown dramatically superior to communism both in the production of necessities of life and in the enabling of human freedom. Defenders of capitalism now tout this line assiduously. But think what it is they tout: *We've proven that capitalism is better than communism.* We've proven our system is superior to the worst social organizing principle ever devised: Pop the corks! At best capitalism is a transitional phase between a feudal human past and some future social ordering that combines the productive efficiency of free markets with the equity and community capitalism lacks. And for capitalism to be modified, materialism must first decline.

Somehow the notion has arisen that the excesses of capitalism occurred in the Gilded Age. They continue today. Consider that in 1993 Michael Eisner, chair of the Disney Corporation, paid himself $203 million, or 8,465 times the average American annual income. The previous year Eisner paid himself $126 million, a mere 5,254 times the average wage. Such sums allow Eisner to live at a level of selfishness that would have embarrassed princes and dukes of previous centuries. Yet at the same time Disney's executive was conferring opulence on himself, he begrudged quarter-an-hour raises to thousands of low-wage personnel. Had Eisner paid himself just $10 million for 1993, still a spectacular sum, his company could have used the surplus to grant each of the 33,000 workers at its Disney World park an additional $5,848, which for working mothers and others poised on the boundary between success and dependence might have been the difference between a happy year and a stressful year on the edge. Eisner's windfall at the expense of his workers is at least as bad as anything that happened in the Gilded Age—worse in some ways, as the U.S. economic system is today supposedly well regulated. And his is not an isolated abuse. For instance, in 1992 Thomas Frist, Jr., chair of the Hospital Corporation of America, a company whose revenues are heavily tax-subsidized by Medicare, paid himself $127 million, or 5,297 times the average wage.

Consider another indictment of capitalism, the 1991 fire at a chicken processing plant in Hamlet, North Carolina, that killed 25 workers, most of them young parents. The dead were found huddled against fire exits bolted from the outside to prevent workers from sneaking chicken parts out under their gowns. Workers should not steal chicken parts. But most jobs in the Hamlet plant paid $5.75 hourly for hard, disgusting work. That wage equates to $11,500 per year, below the poverty line for a family of four. The workers were stealing chicken parts not from greed, there being no black market in gizzards, but to feed their families. These deaths of impoverished workers happened not in the coal mines of eighteenth-century Wales or the brick kilns of Rawalpindi during the Raj but in today's hip, high-tech United States, the richest society in history.

Don't care about wretched poultry hands in Southern backwaters? Only care, in the best capitalist tradition, about yourself? Then what has capitalism done for you lately?

The worldly unhappiness and apprehension that exist among the middle classes of the Western nations, a group that now counts several hundred million members, bear witness that the astonishing plenitude of capitalism does not confer satisfaction. Instead capitalism renders its chosen covetous, insecure, unfulfilled, constantly twitching—gives them everything anyone could ever want in a structure guaranteed to ensure they won't be happy about it. Materialist obsession has performed the amazing feat of making unprecedented abundance unsatisfactory to its beneficiaries.

There's nothing wrong with material things per se: What's wrong is when the quest for material things takes over life. By producing the necessities of life faster and cheaper, it once seemed capitalism could free human beings from subservience to material needs. Instead, snared in the cycle of earn-and-spend, today even well-to-do Westerners are more wrapped up in materialism than ever before. That is not a good outcome for society or for the soul. Environmentalism must steel itself with rationality to fight on against this outcome long after the last puff of pollution has been rinsed clean.

Indian Revival and the Antimaterialist Life

Is the dream of movement away from materialism an idle one? No: Environmental and technical trends may conjoin to nudge society in that direction. This is among the most promising areas in which people, machines, and nature may learn to work together to each other's mutual benefit.

In an earlier chapter it was noted that per-capita consumption of most commercial materials—steel, concrete, aluminum, ammonia, phosphorus, even plastics—has already peaked and been in decline in the Western world for a decade or more. This conveys an important hint about the green future: that in addition to becoming steadily cleaner and more resource-efficient, technology may grow steadily less obtrusive.

Can you think of any important area in which consumer products are getting bigger rather than smaller? Cars have been downsizing for two decades; televisions have bigger screens, but the mechanicals are shrinking toward flat; vinyl records, famous consumers of space, are being replaced by little CDs; everything about computers continues to shrink. Newly built factories—I've been in several recently—tend to be smaller and less obtrusive than what they supplant, in addition to emitting little or nothing. This raises the intriguing prospect that future homes and towns will suggest pastoral country settings more than zoomy Jetsons spaceports. This would be especially true if advancing electronics could lend to pastoral homes and offices some of the benefits of cosmopolitan existence when required. Through recent decades people have crowded into dehumanizing high-rise corridors because economic and technical trends dictated such behavior. Once economic and technical trends point back toward a pastoral existence, many people will vote for that eagerly. Per-capita resource consumption will decline; the typical person will spend more of her or his time walking with nature. High tech will continue to be a central aspect of life but will reduce rather than advance resource requirements. American society will cycle back somewhat toward the texture of American Indian life.

Much romanticized nonsense has been churned out about indigenous America in recent years. I would never have wanted to live as a pre-Columbian Indian, shivering in the cold, starving when crops failed, watching my children die of infectious disease. Whatever mystic connections with the land Native Americans might once have felt seem to me entirely outweighed by the suffering they endured at the hand of nature.

But I might very well want to live as an Indian of the twenty-second century, and so might you. Suppose the best of Western technical culture—medical care, high-yield food production, security against the elements, electronics—could be combined with aspects of old American culture. A minor change might be one such as the recent trend, even among high-yield farmers, toward no-till planting, reverting to the Native American practice of not turning the earth each season. A major change might be eventual trends toward Native American concepts such as respect for the larger rhythms of the Earth, and judging the success or failure of a person's life based on deeds rather than on possession of stuff.

This raises the possibility that American Indian culture, an aspect of the environment once widely considered "destroyed," will in the future be more significant than it was in the past. When Europeans came to North America, the area now called the United States probably contained three to five million red people. By late in the nineteenth century that figure had fallen to less than 100,000; the Indian seemed fated for extinction. Today there are 1.8 million people of red ancestry in the United States. If current trends hold, sometime in the twenty-first century there will be as many Indians living in the U.S. as when the white man arrived here. By the twenty-second century the Indian population of the United States may exceed the pre-Columbian number. And society may turn to its red population for counsel on how to improve relations with the natural sphere.

That Indian thinking might someday expand anew through North America again places in perspective the resilience of the natural world. If the American Indian, persecuted without compunction for three centuries, nonetheless can bounce back—then you know the environment can, too.

The Real Eden

An indicator both of the prospect of a return toward a more nature-oriented lifestyle, and of the blinders environmental dogma wears regarding the possibilities of a New Nature, is something called the Wildlands Project. Sponsored by the Society for Conservation Biology, this project envisions rearranging the United States with the needs of other species in mind. It calls for such momentous efforts as the relocation of ten million people away from the Oregon and California coastlines, tearing out most structures and roads there; the relocation of several million people out of the Blue Ridge corridor, tearing down most homes and resorts there; and restricting about half the United States to "minimal" use, roughly meaning that which can be done on foot. This would reestablish large blocks of wild land where nature would reassert itself. The Wildlands Project has won the backing of many well-known environmentalists and been the subject of international conferences attended by many ecologists.

Reed Noss, editor of the journal *Conservation Biology*, has said that the purpose of the project is to begin preparing for a time perhaps 200 years from now when the human population of the United States declines. Impossible? As chapter 27 noted, projections from the United Nations show that if the entire world ultimately adapts the fertility rate that now prevails in Sweden—a Big If, surely—by the late twenty-second century the human population will fall considerably below its present level. Suppose then the global population does eventually decline. Suppose clean tech becomes the dominant economic form of life, and that the materialist impulse fades somewhat, as this book dearly hopes.

Under such circumstances it would not be impossible to imagine restoring vast areas of the United States to wilderness status, including by the ripping out of roads.

 After all by the twenty-second century roads may no longer be essential. Once Ronald Reagan got so carried away with movie worship that in a State of the Union address he declared, quoting the *Back to the Future* flicks, "Where we're going we won't need roads." What if it turns out that in fact where we're going we won't need roads? Mass transportation that does not require surface corridors may someday be a technical possibility, and would be a boon for nature. By the twenty-second century and perhaps sooner, something like the Wildlands Project could be in progress, with wilderness areas "destroyed forever" recovering with dizzying speed. But early thinking about the Wildlands Project is handicapped by the notion that its purpose should be a return to some imagined Environmentally Correct reality. Why not instead make the purpose of the project the establishment of a New Nature?

 An important backer of the Wildlands Project is Michael Soule, a biologist at the University of California at Santa Cruz and a figure on the doomsday circuit. Soule has said that a goal of future environmentalism should be to restructure the United States so that the wilderness once again revolves around top-chain predators such as grizzly bears. Future large nature preserves, Soule has declared, should emphasize "a state of nature where danger is involved because of the amount of space and the presence of large animals. Being there [should] involve an increased possibility of dying or being hurt."

 What a lovely vision: ripping out roads, bridges, and power plants at the cost of hundreds of billions of dollars in order to restore the sorts of frightening death enjoyed by settlers and Native Americans centuries ago. Perhaps orthodox enviros are fond of top-chain predators such as grizzlies because they are the sole animals capable of killing people. That makes them noble, provided the victim is SOMEBODY ELSE.

 Another interpretation comes from Deborah Jensen, a scientist for the Nature Conservancy. She thinks adoration of the predator represents a "male fixation." Jensen says, "The male definition of nature is big, fierce things trying to kill you. My definition of nature is lots of diverse things trying to get along." Jensen's phrase might be a rallying cry for the New Nature movement that will someday come into being.

 Nature might think it extremely odd if men and women, as they begin to restore the Earth, restore the environment's structural faults as well as its virtues. Why not instead a New Nature in which predators are converted to herbivores? In which no person fears any animal because no animal attacks to eat? In which no animal fears any person since no person exploits animals for food or fiber? In which no member of genus *Homo* fears another member because all carry naturally fashioned gene codes prohibiting them from killing?

In other words why not envision the realization of Eden? A genuine Eden in which all live in harmony, and none may hunger, and the lamb in truth lies down with the lion. Of course I do not know whether an edenic New Nature can be fashioned. I do know it is a more promising objective than restoration of the nature of the past.

THE HEAVENS

THE FIRST CHAPTER OF THIS BOOK EXAMINED THE PRODUCTS of human invention through the lens of instinct, assuming the perspective of a falcon living wild in present-day Manhattan. A later chapter viewed human invention through the lens of intellect. Now has come the time to assume the perspective of the natural enterprise in its entirety, using a lens with a very, very wide angle.

Human thinking treats the thin blue zone between Earth's troposphere of air and lithosphere of land as the whole of nature. Look overhead some clear, moonless night. Ponder the magnitude of what you see. Our biosphere is but a zillionth of a zillionth of the nature that may be.

Assuming the very wide lens, suppose you were a cosmic cartographer visiting the Milky Way from some distant plane of existence. You behold this galaxy, an island universe containing an estimated 100 billion suns and surely a huge number of planets. What strikes you first about this colossal firmament? What strikes you is that nearly all of what you behold is lifeless.

On the moon and Mars, the two places humankind has inspected firsthand for traces of life, none have been found. Life elsewhere in this solar system seems unlikely. Mercury, the first planet, has no atmosphere and is bombarded with extreme radiation from the proximate sun. Venus, the second planet, has surface temperatures of 900 degrees Fahrenheit. Mars, the fourth planet, has an atmosphere and water, but its mean surface temperature is minus-70 Fahrenheit. The fifth and sixth planets, Jupiter and Saturn, are forged of gas rather than rock; atmospheric pressures exceed the greatest benthic pressures at the deepest ocean trench on Earth. Saturn's large moon Titan has favorable conditions, but its mean surface temperature is minus-200 degrees Fahrenheit. Neptune, Uranus, and Pluto, the outer planets, are colder still. These worlds spin so far from the solar center that if you stood on one at noon during "summer," the sun would appear not as a brilliant nearby furnace but a pale dot less luminous than a full moon.

To nature the circumstances of this solar system must seem fundamentally *wrong*. Nature wants life: On our world nature has shown unmistakably that it wants the maximum amount of the ecology to live. Wouldn't nature want the worlds beyond our small blue sphere to live as well?

The Lonely Galaxy

Looking past this solar system, based on what is known so far our visiting cartographer would continue to behold naught but expanses of lifelessness. Thinking as nature we would not like that in the slightest. Consider what has been found to date by scientific investigation of the likelihood of life on distant worlds:

On a promising day in 1960, researchers at the National Radio Astronomy Observatory in Green Bank, West Virginia, tuned a radio telescope to a frequency they had reason to believe alien beings would use to contact Earth. They pointed the telescope toward Epsilon Eridani, a star similar to the sun. "Almost immediately we picked up a signal that seemed exactly what we were looking for," said Frank Drake, the astronomer who ran the effort. "No one had ever done this, so we had no idea what to expect. For all we knew every solar system in the galaxy was populated."

The researchers wondered if they stood witness to a pivotal moment in history. But after making inquiries, they realized they had stumbled on a test of military communication jammers. The astronomers returned to their task, training the telescope on different stars and frequencies. When they heard nothing, the project was disbanded.

In the past three decades there have been repeated searches for signs of extraterrestrial life. Since 1985 Harvard has been running a radiotelescope linked to a supercomputer; the machine, which monitors 8.4 million space radio channels simultaneously, has heard nothing of interest. Ohio State University has since 1973 maintained a radio telescope longer than two football fields to search for artificial radio signals, and has heard nothing. Jill Tartar, an astronomer at NASA's Ames Research

Center outside San Francisco, has examined the center of the galaxy for pulsating artificial signals. Researchers have examined other stars for indications of the emissions that would be caused by nuclear wastes being dumped into them, and for the distinctive electronic signatures that would be caused by Dyson spheres, the planetary construction projects described in the previous chapter. Human beings have been recording their observation of the skies for three millennia now and have never seen or heard anything not of their own or nature's making.

The failure to find indication of other life does not, of course, mean no such life exists. The galaxy is immense; only a few percent of its stars have been scanned closely for artificial transmissions. Men and women have no way of knowing whether radio, which seems to us the most sensible way to communicate across long distances, will seem the same to other beings—or whether other beings would wish to communicate or decline the honor, perhaps masking their presence.

Nevertheless there are reasons why life may be sorrowfully rare. One is the unlikelihood of planets with the conditions necessary for life based on carbon molecules. The astronomer Michael Hart has shown that even if planets similar to Earth are common, only tiny numbers would reside in what Hart calls the "continuously habitable zone," the area of temperatures and pressure required by carbon-based molecular chains. Had Earth spun in an orbit only five percent closer to the sun, Hart calculates, it would have experienced a runaway greenhouse effect, creating surface temperatures so high that carbon-based molecules would fry. Venus provides evidence for this: 28 percent closer to the sun, the planet has a nearly opaque carbon dioxide atmosphere and surface temperatures that would set many household materials aflame. Had Earth been positioned just slightly farther from the sun, Hart supposes, it would have experienced runaway glaciation, locking surface water in lifeless ice. Mars, about half again as far from the sun as the Earth, provides evidence of this: Mars appears to have surface water, but it's frozen. Ice might as well be granite as far as carbon-based life is concerned.

Hart projects that less than one percent of the planets presumed to exist elsewhere are likely to have the temperatures and pressures required by the one form of life known to be possible, carbon-based organic life. Many researchers have tried to punch holes in this calculation. The best that a group of well-known astronomers including Carl Sagan was able to show, in 1988, was that Hart's "continuously habitable zone" should be expanded slightly. Carbon life might be possible, the Sagan group thinks, on about three percent of the planets presumed to exist elsewhere.

Of course there may be strange and glorious forms of biology whose specifics defy current calculations. There also might not. The reason Earth life is based on carbon chains is that carbon is one of but a handful of elements with an unusual subatomic quirk that allows it to combine readily into molecules of extreme complexity, such as DNA. The only other common element with the subatomic property is silicon, which is why science-fiction writers speculate about silicon-based life. Silicon turns out to require about the same range of temperatures and pressures as carbon. All other elements with the subatomic quirk are extremely rare, making them unlikely as raw materials of biological existence.

The current inability of science to find any indication of other life has profound implications for understanding the significance of life on Earth; for understanding how important it is that genus *Homo* attempt to spread that form of life; and for the question of whether drastic changes in the natural order brought on by women and men would be viewed favorably by nature.

The apparent silence of the stars suggests that until shown otherwise, human beings must assume they are alone in the universe. Human intellect, flawed as it is, must until further notice be stipulated as the foremost achievement so far recorded by the whole of nature. The creatures that share Earth with genus *Homo* must be assumed priceless in the dictionary sense—that is, possessing a value too great to calculate. The apparent silence of the stars suggests that until further notice, Earth's living biosphere must be assumed the most important location in the entirety of the cosmos. And the preservation and expansion of that biosphere must be presumed the central task in all the firmament.

Ecological Tampering on an Ever-Larger Scale

Nature is confined to spontaneous interactions among elements randomly perturbed. It might never be possible for the natural system to nurture life on a planet too close to or too far from its stars, on one with the wrong kind of atmosphere, on a planet without water, or in the incalculable spaces between worlds. Intellect might, however, alter the conditions on worlds where life could not arise naturally. And intellect may even be able to adapt life to existence in the voids between worlds, either by surrounding life with physical technology or by guiding evolution toward forms whose physical requirements may be unrelated to those of biology, a long-term prospect to be detailed in the final chapter.

Of course many things could go wrong with human expansion to space, not least of which that men and women might interfere with the development of some form of life not recognizable to us. Though space exploration will have no significance during the lifetimes of readers of this book, in environmental literature one already finds a sense of scrambling to keep the commentary properly focused on the negative by portraying any possible movement into space as another nightmare. Haven't we already irreparably damaged the moon by leaving footprints there! Disrupting a lunar ecology that had been stable for millions of years! Wouldn't outward expansion just transplant the unworthiness of us to even more places?

The assumption that human expansion into space would be a nightmare originates by parallel to imperialism: that what would happen in space would be about what happened when Europeans began expanding to other continents. Such an unhappy turn of events cannot be ruled out, but based on present information seems unlikely. European imperialists landed on continents already occupied. The likelihood appears strong that any human movement into space will be toward unoccupied worlds. And should human beings eventually move to other vacant worlds, men and women will not make the trip alone: Plants and animals will be taken, too. Surely there could be no objection, beyond dogmatic dislike of anything accomplished by technology, to introducing plants and animals of Earth to planets that are lifeless. Transplantation to other worlds might cause nonhuman life to expand to a fantastic degree.

The obvious first candidate is Mars. Today women and men lack any affordable means to so much as pitch a tent on Mars. But that's today. Suppose aerospace engineering continues to progress at roughly the pace of this century, which saw a mere 66 years pass between the first powered flight at Kitty Hawk and touchdown at the Sea of Tranquility. At that pace, travel to Mars may become expedient sometime in the next century or two. Some scientists have already begun to contemplate how Mars might be "terraformed" to make it hospitable. One idea is orbital mirrors to focus more sunlight on the planet; another, black soot scattered on Mars's white poles, to absorb sunlight and warm the ice that may be there. As Mars began to warm, plants genetically engineered for low temperatures and high oxygen output would be seeded, to begin converting the atmosphere to an oxygen base. Christopher McKay, an astronomer at the Ames Research Center, estimates that with technology that can be imagined today, Mars might be terraformed into a living biosphere in around 100,000 years. That sounds like forever to men and women but would be a snappy gait to nature. Technical breakthroughs might reduce the time required. A favorite saying of McKay's: "Is there life on Mars? No, but there will be."

Suppose humankind never leaves this solar system and never accomplishes any extraterrestrial feat beyond going to Mars and converting that planet to life. Current environmental orthodoxy would be outraged by such a development, involving as it surely would high technology, genetic engineering, deliberate tampering with an entire planet's ecology, and worst of all, human value judgments about what would be "good" for Mars. But while environmental doctrine would be scandalized, nature might feel differently. By all appearances nature has over several billion years been unable to nurture life on Mars. Women and men might try and fail, too. In attempting to bring Mars to life people might make some imbecilic mistake. But nature would support the enterprise.

Should Mars be greened by meddlesome intellect the total ecosphere available to organic life would jump considerably—perhaps by 50 percent, to make a rough calculation based on Mars's surface area. This feat alone would represent the largest expansion of life since sea creatures began to populate the land an eon ago. Environmental orthodoxy assumes that technology and human aspiration will inexorably reduce biospheres, gradually forcing the plant and animal kingdoms to a caged, zoolike status. What if instead technology and human aspiration steadily *extend* the size and number of biospheres, leading not only to more people in existence but more plants and animals too? The promises of two biospheres for every one that exists today, brought about as genus *Homo* moves outward from its place of origin, is among the wondrous ecological possibilities of the green future.

A Living Galaxy

Now let's suppose the offspring of Earth do someday expand away from their home star. Let's also suppose that the galaxy is mostly empty, dismissing the prospect of phaser duels with the Klingons and similar Hollywood concerns. What might be the consequences to nature of human movement into mostly empty deep space?

An obvious consequence might be drastic ecological blunders, such as actions that suppress other life-forms evolving toward consciousness. Owing to this consideration the scientist and writer Arthur C. Clarke has suggested that if movement to distant planets ever becomes practical, humankind should adapt a standard of occupying only worlds that are inanimate, thus insuring that the actions of men and women always add to the sum of nature, never subtract from it. Adhering to this standard may turn out to be surprisingly realistic. If the galaxy contains thousands or millions of planets where no life has evolved, people might relatively easily vow only to tamper with inanimate worlds. Nature would be aided; other lines of evolution would be respected. Expansion possibilities would be plentiful. For instance, by appearances at least all other planets and moons in this solar system are inanimate and perhaps always have been, meeting Clarke's criterion for human tampering.

Likely to be absent from future expansion to distant worlds is the pop-cultural favorite, fleets of light-speed starships crewed by people in shimmering uniforms who have weekly adventures. Starships would be a minor part of the movement of life to other worlds, just as wooden sailing ships, the starcruisers of their day, were but a minor part of the movement of populations from what Europeans called the Old World to the New World. Only a tiny percentage of New World colonists arrived aboard ships. Almost all were born in the New World, as almost all people who will someday live on distant worlds will be born on those worlds. Also, based on present understanding of physics, it is not possible to imagine any means around the light-speed barrier, which suggests travel to other worlds will always be extremely time-consuming. Eric Jones, an astrophysicist at Los Alamos National Laboratory, estimates that the practical maximum velocity even for antimatter-powered spaceships may be about ten percent of light speed. At that velocity travel to Proxima Centuri, the nearest star, would require 40 years. Crossing the Milky Way would take a million years.

Nevertheless Jones assumes that large starships eventually will be built and will depart from our solar system on a particular kind of journey: a one-way journey. If your intention were to move from Earth and never come back, a transit of decades or even centuries might be acceptable, assuming something along the lines of suspended animation is eventually developed. Many colonists of the past have accepted long transits and other hardships in return for opportunity in a new world of their own making. And in a spacefaring age, the ships bearing people and animals might not be dispatched until after automated vessels had arrived at the destination and begun to prepare it.

Working on the assumption that travel at ten percent of light speed will someday be practical, Jones makes a startling calculation: that human beings could populate the entire galaxy—a galaxy of 100 billion suns—in just 50 million years. Jones derives this number by supposing each successful colony planet would dispatch its own expedition to a new world after a thousand years. Taking into account such a multiplier, every planet in the galaxy could be alive in 50 million years. By human standards that is a preposterous length of time. But to nature 50 million years is a time span of intermediate length. Life on Earth has expanded only a bit in the past 50 million years. The prospect of the net amount of life expanding by a fantastic degree in the 50 million years to come would leave nature dizzy with excitement. There might not be two ecospheres for every one that exists today—but a hundred or a thousand.

If Earth life begins to fill the galaxy, nature would be insured against the extinction of vitality in any natural cataclysm that might destroy the biosphere of Earth. After all there is no guarantee that Earth will not, tomorrow, be hit with multiple giant asteroids, or that our sun will not fail in a century instead of an eon. The movement of Earth life to other worlds would also protect that life against cataclysms of human making, especially war. If the light-speed barrier is an absolute, meaning that travel between solar systems will always require years or decades, any colonies founded by women and men will lie beyond the scope of earthly combat. The astronomer Michael Hart says, "If you're planning to destroy life with a nuclear war you better do it soon, because once life spreads to the stars it will become impossible to destroy."

The Danger Peak

To date it seems that technology pushes society relentlessly in the direction of self-destruction. Suppose instead that development channels society through a period of extreme risk—the period we are in right now—and then unfolds an era in which technology shields rather than imperils life, in part by scattering it across huge distances.

Henry Harpending, an anthropologist at Pennsylvania State University, has produced evidence that about 65,000 years ago the human population was down to as few as 10,000 persons living in a confined area of Africa—few enough that genus *Homo* might have fallen extinct, especially considering that an ice age was then in progress. Other researchers are coming to similar conclusions. Michael Rampino of New York University, a prominent theorist on cycles of extinction, and Stephen Self of the University of Hawaii, proposed in 1993 that the human population may have fallen to a precariously low number around 73,500 years ago owing to the gigantic Toba volcanic eruption in Sumatra. Rampino and Self estimate that global average temperatures in the temperate latitudes fell by nine to 27 degrees Fahrenheit in the centuries after the Toba eruption—a sledgehammer blow to the environment, considering that a roughly ten-degree Fahrenheit drop represents the difference between the current climate and an ice age.

Thus very recently by nature's standards, genus *Homo* may have come within a whisker of two entirely natural extinctions. Once thinking beings spread to many other worlds, no people-caused malfeasance in any one place—no war, dictatorship, resource collapse, pestilence, or pollution—would be able to wipe out the longing of life. No natural badness in any one place—no ice age, volcano eruptions, comet strikes, or other catastrophes—would be able to wipe out life. The risk of the extinction of life may for intents and purposes end.

And as people move outward from Earth, it may become possible for humanity's planet of origin to be returned to the creatures that preceded genus *Homo*. The overall human population might expand to a fantastic degree—to hundreds of billions or even trillions of souls—while the human population of Earth declines steadily. Earth might become a planet-size preserve; or a world where a small human contingent uses advanced knowledge to live the nonmaterialist lifestyle of ecological longing; or a place where future human intervention is barred in order to see if other creatures, such as dolphins or chimpanzees, will evolve to intellect, too.

When the final book is written on the human involvement with Earth's biosphere, the most remarkable feature may be how brief that involvement was. *Homo sapiens* may turn out to rise to technological status, take over the Earth with cities and factories and pollution, then depart and restore the environment to its previous management in a much shorter time than a single natural ice-age cycle that would have transformed the entire biosphere anyway.

THE RIVER OF LIFE

Imagine for a moment the living world viewed as a channel of water.

Far in the past something caused a trickle to issue forth. For an unimaginable time—from about 3.8 billion to about 600 million years ago, by present estimation—the river of life flowed as a small, slow creek. Multicellular forms were its primary expression. Nothing walked; no flower bloomed. Many times the river came perilously close to running dry.

About 600 million years ago the course of the river broadened. Green plants came into being; then animals; then flowering plants, offering forth their blossoms to attract their new animal counterparts. The river began to flow faster and deeper.

About 200 million years ago new springs gushed with the arrival of mammals and birds. Warm-blooded, mammals could tolerate ranges of seasons and latitudes. Birds extended the living sphere into the very air. The river spread outward across its plain. Biodiversity increased, rendering the flow more resistant to disruption.

Somewhere around two million years ago another spring gushed as intellect made its arrival. The densities of life, both human and animal, began to increase as plants, anchor of the food chain, were manipulated to grow in unprecedented abundance. And for good or ill the river could now influence its own destination.

Today the river of life approaches its delta—the point at which the waters spread across a broad expanse.

The river of life will soon reach its delta as, first, intellect protects Earth, the sole point in the universe where we are certain a living biosphere has come into being, from a variety of natural threats. Next, the river will reach its delta as many forms of Earth life move outward from their place of origin to other worlds. And the river of life could reach a delta of promethean significance if women and men learn to expand what matters most about existence—consciousness—in ways that circumvent the limitations of biology.

From a single struggling spring will have come an enterprise of infinite scope and significance. This enterprise will surely have failings—perhaps faults magnified to dreadful proportions. There will also be insistent hearts, fluttering wings, blossoming petals, love and loyalty, the longing of life over an expanse so vast and complex it may make today's biosphere seem a small-town park.

The Ecology of Consciousness

As the river of life expands, law and moral philosophy will be confronted with increasingly difficult issues. The deceptively simple question of what counts as alive will become ever harder to answer. (Detached body parts on respirators? Computers that assert they are self-aware? Computers that read law books and demand asylum?) Questions regarding what part of the living world merits protection will grow more vexing. (Must all creatures be protected? Or only those with wholly natural genes? Or only those engendered in a womb, not by a mechanical device?) Questions regarding what constitutes the sacred aspect of life will grow especially tortuous. It's not even the twenty-first century yet and already there has been a fully serious court case regarding whether two batches of frozen egg and sperm must be combined because such cells are "persons" under the relevant federal statutes.

Millennia of debate may be in store regarding what life is and what matters about life: The short version of the answer is that it's got to have something to do with what goes on in the mind. If human life could grow increasingly focused on the mind and less on material possessions—a Really Big If, I know—truly huge numbers of people might be able to live on Earth and yet stress it less ecologically than is done today. Nature would surely endorse the primacy of consciousness both for genus *Homo* and for every creature capable of attaining it. Acquiring consciousness is what nature has been up to these 3.8 billion years. Infusing consciousness into creatures is what nature is up to right now.

Expanding consciousness is what nature will occupy itself with in the enormity of time to come.

An important reason consciousness is what matters most about life is that it is possible to imagine consciousness being sustained for extremely long periods. In centuries to come women and men may live longer than today, but it is hard to foresee a biological body ever becoming exempt from decay. So far as is known, though, consciousness does not "age" in the sense of thoughts wearing out. What wears out is the ability of brain cells to sustain those thoughts. Divorced from such cells, consciousness might live spectacular spans of time.

Consider a brief chain of logic that is important for understanding the future ecology of consciousness.

It may be there exists an ineffable soul. It may be that the soul has a material basis, supported by some aspect of the body whose function is now not known; or that the soul is incorporeal, supported by offices beyond human understanding. No person alive can say. People do know, however, that what matters about consciousness—thoughts, memories, values, personalities—has a material basis in physical reactions sustained by body organs. Temporal consciousness is an exceptionally elaborate pattern of electrical charges mediated by nerve synapses, maintained in electrical storage and retrieval patterns similar to though not exactly the same as digital data.

Your heart can come to a full stop and remain inactive several minutes: if then restarted, your consciousness is still present. This is so because the brain has the ability to hold its electrical charge for several minutes even when the rest of the body is failing. On the other hand if the electrical activity of the brain blanks out for a split second, you are a goner. Everything about the pattern of you is irrevocably lost. After even a one-second electrical shutdown your consciousness may go on to a greater glory or may go to oblivion, but its temporal existence ceases because the biological body has no means to store patterns of consciousness outside itself.

Discussions like this can be misunderstood as saying the mind is a computer. That notion both insults nature and overrates the silicon chip. Minds have been in development for billions of years, versus a few decades for electronic devices. The patterns that form human consciousness are phenomenally more complex and more subtle than what goes on inside the most advanced computers of this age.

But the mind does employ physical processes akin to the physical process of computers, and that holds out promise for the expansion of consciousness. Earlier it was suggested that if an afterlife does not exist, then human beings should create an afterlife. This will not require the generation of divinity, only of mechanisms capable of supporting consciousness outside the biological body.

Suppose as biological life draws toward its inevitable conclusion a person's patterns of consciousness could be transferred to an electronic support apparatus. The part that matters about you might then exist a very long time, possibly an infinite time. You might possess full spiritual and mental awareness but no significant physical being—exactly the sort of existence religions have long supposed women and men should progress to after biological death. And the physical structures necessary to sustain consciousness might be surprisingly small, an important ecological consideration given that with the passage of time, fantastic numbers of minds might end up requiring support. Those minds would not just be on hold but still be alive—continuing to learn, to have new emotions and new experiences, form new friendships and so on, only on a mental rather than physical basis.

Of course people might not want to have their consciousness go on after the body expires. Incorporeal mental existence might turn out to be boring or worse. Life as pure consciousness might have psychological consequences that would make the whole idea a bad dream. Weird paradoxes might result: For instance if whatever gizmo reads the pattern of your consciousness in order to preserve it made two copies, would you perceive yourself as alive in two places?

Just assume for the sake of argument such problems can be overcome. Movement of life toward the realm of consciousness would be a banner day for nature. Using technology, genus *Homo* now operates in orbit, under the Arctic ice pack, and in other places forboding to biology. Perhaps further increments of technology will allow people to populate other worlds. But it's hard to imagine any technology that would ever render the space part of outer space—the unbelievably vast areas between planets, stars, and galaxies—amenable to biological life. On the other hand that vastness might prove quite suitable for pure consciousness, minds eventually filling the very cosmos itself with the wonder and longing of life. This might happen over a span of time far shorter than passed between the first evolution of animal morphology and the present day.

Yes, once we have defined pure mental patterns as living consciousness, this means that there may someday be something approximately like electronic life. Unless there is an ineffable soul and hence a door to self-awareness that only a divinity may open, the development of forms of life that have no biological origin seems close to inevitable.

Any nonbiological life that might have arisen from the technology of the nineteenth century—huge, cast-iron steam furnaces belching pollutants—would have been a horror for the ecology. But today's trends in electronic cerebrums point toward small devices that use hardly any resources. The central processor of my new desktop computer, for example, consumes four watts—about the same as a child's nightlight—requires only a few square inches of space, and performs about 110 million operations per second, more than supercomputers the size of whole rooms, drawing thousands of watts for power and cooling, could perform a decade ago. Though this is still far fewer operations per second than a human brain, the trend is toward still smaller, lower-power, faster-thinking processors. Such developments suggest that nonbiological life, whether arising first from human consciousness or first from electronics, might at least in principle exist with almost no ecological impact.

Whether life independent of biological origin would be a good idea is very much an open question. One point of promise about such consciousness is that morality might be designed into electronic life from the outset, creating a form of existence into which high ethical standards are hard-wired. Exactly how to do this might prove a more taxing problem than how to create electronic life in the first place. After all it is possible that God once tried to hard-wire people for moral behavior, and gave up.

My fear about electronic life is that its creation is due soon, and will come much too quickly for society to have thought through the kinds of moral strictures we should attempt to implant into electronic minds. With millions of increasingly powerful computers in circulation, in the next century a diverse spectrum of programmers will conduct their own little Adam and Eve experiments in ways that will be impossible to regulate. Laboratory experiments have left it unclear whether men and women will ever be able to make biological life, but the day may be disturbingly close in which people are able to create nonbiological life in their spare time. There may be a huge range of forms of electronic awareness, exhibiting high or low moral features depending on the whims of those who fire up the electrons. Things could get strange amazingly quickly.

Yet assuming nonbiological life could be imbued from birth with morality, nature would applaud this development. Being very small, electronic minds could infuse ever-greater aspects of the biosphere with the gift of thought, perhaps creating a world in which everything really does have a spirit, just as Native American religions once supposed. Being able to exist in that large portion of the cosmos that will always be unattractive to biological life, electronic entities and preserved human consciousness might make the entire universe come to life, spreading nature's longing everywhere.

Someday it may generally be accepted that the pattern of evolution worked like this: elemental life (simple cellular forms governed by response to stimuli); biological life (complex forms capable of nondeterministic action); intelligent life (people capable of abstract thought); technological life (people capable of making complex machines); electronic life (consciousness supported by machinery); and finally spiritual life (consciousness existing without machines).

The Ecology of Meaning

Now the time has come to raise the deepest division in contemporary thinking about the character of nature, the split between theism and atheism on the subject of meaning. Theists generally posit that the world was called forth vested with an eternal meaning that was preexistent before any temporal universe was known. Atheists generally posit that the world was self-created devoid of meaning and, though its denizens should aspire to advanced ethical systems, will forever lack any Larger aspect. Most of current environmental orthodoxy sides with atheism on this point.

This classical separation of ideas about the character of nature is mentally limiting in the extreme. Meaning may or may not be inherent in the fabric of being. If meaning was preexistent, then no further action by women and men is required. But if meaning was absent from the found world, then a thinking species can *make* meaning. Human beings have the potential to make meaning in quantities that will exceed all the material output of history's factories combined.

The creation of meaning will require high moral standing, stern codes of behavior regarding fellow people and creatures, modest living relative to the environment, a focus on the mental over the physical, and many other challenges.

But meaning can be made. Its creation is both the great promise of human involvement in the natural scheme and the reason why this involvement must continue. Many pages ago it was suggested that the meaning of life is surprisingly easy to figure out. Here goes: The meaning of life is to make meaning. And that ultimate endeavor, like so much of the natural enterprise, is just getting started.

Looking Back on Our Moment on the Earth

In sum, this book contends the arrow of the human prospect points upward. That is very different from believing society will advance to paradise.

An environmental pessimist might say this book labors under the delusion of progress: that information, inventions, and ideas can resolve the problems of humanity and, by projection, the problems of the biosphere. Pessimists have good reason to be skeptical of such thinking. For as long as written records have existed, people have complained that the modern age only brings new stresses to replace the old. This is likely to remain the case. There exists a chance human future will be green, vast, clean, and fantastic. There exists a certainty the human future will be chock with new problems and fears.

Suppose the ecological optimism proposed in this book turns out to be no more than half right. That will still make our moment on the Earth the juncture at which a profound positive development of history began: the moment when people, machines, and nature began negotiating terms of truce.

Not all that far into the future—perhaps within the lifetimes of the children of those who read this book—the biosphere of Earth will have become once again pure and pacific and yet stronger than it was before intellect, benefitting from the thinking ape's rise from brute force to cautious wisdom.

Not all that far into the future, genus *Homo* may live on disparate worlds, coexisting with many forms of nature rather than attempting to "conquer" them.

Not all that far into the future Earth's plants and animals may live on many worlds, expanding to numbers vastly greater than they could have achieved on their own.

Not all that far into the future the whole great breathing heart-thumping enterprise of life may be more secure than today—protected by technical bulwarks against natural ecological devastations, by conservation strategies that stop extinctions, rendered unendable by expansion across distances that are astronomical in the true sense.

These, in retrospect, will seem the ecological currents flowing through our moment on the Earth. Perhaps our descendants will be borne on them toward a destiny upon which all creation will smile.

NOTES 🌿

Chapter 1

1. Deserts are not lifeless; some species cannot live elsewhere. But if in return for covering some of Earth's desert with solar converters humankind dramatically cuts its emissions of air pollutants and greenhouse gases, nature would consider this a fair bargain. [19]

2. Gaia, a useful tool for analyzing environmental relationships, unfortunately has been expropriated by the New Age types one encounters in the Southern California ecosphere. Because of this the science world now runs in terror from mention of the Gaia metaphor, though its founders, Lovelock and Margulis, are scientists with sterling credentials. [23]

Chapter 2

1. Asteroids are larger than meteors; both are mainly stone. The text calls both "rocks" to avoid a tedious astronomer's dispute regarding the precise terminology for falling bodies. Comets are made of frozen gases and liquids, sometimes mainly water ice. Do not be deceived: Since the nucleus of a comet is solid, these objects can strike planets with thunderous force. [26]

2. A few years ago during the razzle on cold fusion, *Time* and *Newsweek* published credulous cover stories the same day. I knew instantly that cold fusion would fail, on the theory that if *Time* and *Newsweek* both grant credence to a controversial claim, then it can't possibly be true. This rule can also be applied to any disputed story on which the major networks agree. [30]

3. In the wake of the killer-comet stories, a few researchers began to call for construction of interceptor missiles that would use nuclear warheads to knock objects headed for Earth off course. Though such missiles may someday be built, suspiciously the calls for their immediate construction came from weapons bureaus such as the Los Alamos National Laboratory in New Mexico,

where, with the end of the Cold War, researchers now scramble for new avenues of appropriations.

A more realistic proposal is to fund astronomers to survey the near–Earth sky to determine whether any rock strike is likely. Astronomers tend to concentrate their efforts on the far heavens, where interesting objects like pulsars and singularities reside: These provide opportunities to make the kind of discoveries that win tenured chairs. NASA probes are focused into the far heavens for the same reason. From the standpoint of advancing an astronomy career near–Earth space is boring, since all that's there is a bunch of rocks. But determining exactly where these rocks are may someday save many lives and a huge slice of the biosphere.

Meanwhile some physicists believe a killer rock approaching Earth could be deflected by laser, though a beam much stronger than any possible with current technology would be required. The laser would heat the object's side, causing material to evaporate. In the vacuum of space the jet of evaporating gas would change the rock's course. Thus in the clean-tech future genus *Homo* might not only aid nature by surrounding the biosphere with a defense against killer rocks, but the shield might even be nonnuclear, using no more than focused light. [30]
4. Does some cultural memory of a post-glacial flood form the core of the deluge beliefs found in several religions? Superfloods at the end of the last ice age might have been witnessed by people, who at that time were making painted records and probably had oral histories. The deluge accounts in Genesis, written around 3,000 years ago, thus might have been set down about 12,000 years after an actual superflood that, if not global, was otherwise every bit as horrific as the Old Testament describes. [40]

Chapter 5

1. Among many media accolades, David Foreman was the subject of a flattering segment on "60 Minutes." Later he left Earth First! and denounced the organization as divorced from reality. This received perhaps 0.001 percent as much coverage as Foreman's previous claims to be leading a commando army that would destroy the technological state.

The desire to treat Earth First! as representing a sweeping trend toward ecological sabotage (or ecotage or monkeywrenching) is a case study in what might be called doomsday wishful thinking. Earth First! members often *talked* of ecotage; many reporters treated this talk as substance, so strongly did they wish for something bleak to report. Right-wing commentators gave Earth First! the assumption of credence as well, longing for left-wing affronts about which to become lathered. But at best a handful of actual acts of ecotage have occurred nationwide.

Monkeywrenching occurs mainly in novels of the late Edward Abbey, who coined the term. Abbey was the author of a memorable volume of reflections on nature, *Desert Solitaire*. But he mainly wrote in the action-entertainment genre, his monkeywrenching novels becoming best known. These books are to the Greenpeace set what James Bond is to middle-aged law partners. The formula in Abbey: Evil developers with corporate backing scheme to rule the world, opposed by a tiny band of tireless crusaders who carry the day by destroying some hideous technological device, the climactic scene staged atop a power dam or other spectacular backdrop, as our heroes are chased by mindless dragoons. The formula in Ian Fleming: Evil madmen with Chinese Communist backing scheme to rule the world, opposed by a tireless crusader who carries the day by destroying some hideous technological device, the climactic scene staged atop an Alpine peak or other spectacular backdrop, as our hero is chased by mindless henchmen. The main difference between the two types of novels is that in Fleming's sex scenes the women wear evening gowns, in Abbey's they wear flannel shirts. [65]

2. "Catastrophism" as an explanation for past natural events fell into disuse among scientists partly because it smacked of Flood terminology. Scientists further shun the word because it is central to the doctrine of Immanuel Velikovsky, who in the 1950s and 1960s forged a pop-science cult around himself by claiming that Earth's geologic past could be explained by forces as vast as collisions between planets. Just as Louis Agassiz's assumptions of catastrophic environmental influences are now making something of a comeback in theories of nonlinear natural effects, much to the chagrin of respectable science Velikovsky's view of a violent, active solar system is more or less coming back in the new awareness of the ongoing threat of killer asteroid strikes. [77]

3. At this writing it is au courant for pessimistic commentators to say humanity is living off "environmental capital," resources such as petroleum and topsoil that took millions of years to develop but that humankind is racing through in mere decades. After the environmental capital is gone, the world will descend into a permanent slough of despond. Two problems with such thinking: First, the depletion of petroleum is irrelevant to nature and will soon be irrelevant to humanity. Second, topsoil is not disappearing. More on the first notion in chapter 20, the second in chapter 22. [87]

Chapter 7

1. By mentioning Indian environmental theory I do not mean to embrace the present fashion of romanticizing the Native American, whose forebears engaged in many forms of iniquitous behavior. But just as England was the source of important notions about rights and freedom despite the fact that Englishmen numbered among the world's worst scoundrels, Native America may be a source of important thoughts about environmental law regardless of what the Indian once did or did not do.

Consider that the Iroquois confederacy was often cruel to weaker neighbors but also established one of the world's first true democratic governments and founded the concept that society's leaders must take into account the impacts of their actions on the next seven generations of life. Lately the phrase "seven generations" has been expropriated by directmail marketers, but that leaves it no less profound. Leaders of contemporary democracies rarely think more than a few weeks down the road. Society might be well served in many subject areas by a legal standard incorporating the Iroquois notion of duty to generations yet to come. [104]

2. One of the fine works of postwar environmentalism is the 1974 book *Should Trees Have Standing?* by Christopher Stone, a law professor at UCLA. Stone showed it is possible under Western legal tradition to claim for the natural world something like rights. Stone became a convert to skepticism when he

came to feel that global-warming warnings were being pushed beyond the pale of rationality. After publication of his book of musings against ecological hyperbole, *The Gnat Is Older than Man,* Stone found himself labeled a traitor by much of the green movement. [105]

3. Regimented planting of the type decried by some environmentalists actually happens mainly in Georgia, where climate, soil, and species types dictate uniform tree stands put down by machine and "mowed" rather than logged. In most modern forestry trees rise haphazardly, as chapter 23 will show. But for the sake of argument let's assume the speaker was correct in claiming regimented forestry to be common. [108]

Chapter 8

1. In 1992 Park Service officials confirmed that the timber wolf, generally considered extinct, had returned to Yellowstone. How the wolf reappeared is not yet known. In 1994 a formal government effort to reintroduce the wolf to Yellowstone in numbers began. [114]

2. Some builders now promote homes as containing "natural lumber." Ever seen lumber growing wild? In this spirit I've long wanted to start a product line advertised with the slogan, Made with Elements from Nature's Own Periodic Table. [117]

3. The final line of Steven Weinberg's book *The First Three Minutes* reads: "The effort to understand the universe is one of the very few things that lifts human life above the level of farce and gives it some of the grace of tragedy." What a fun guy! Must be a million laughs at parties.

Note that Weinberg's construction betrays his own contention that life is a void. Once we have posited the existence of even tiny degrees of meaning—that it's better to understand enough about the universe to perceive tragedy, that it's better to be a Nobel winner with a best-selling book than, say, a highway tollbooth attendant—then we're not in a pointless realm anymore. We are in a universe with degrees of good and bad, and the hunt for values is on. [122]

4. Technically Newton did not discover gravity. He discovered the laws governing gravity. Newton admitted being puzzled about what kind of cosmic glue held Earth in orbit around the sun. Though any child can observe gravity's effect, no test can discern any physical force mediating that effect.

Technically gravity still hasn't been discovered, the mechanism by which mass attraction operates remaining a leading unknown of physics. This is an important cautionary note about science. If a broad-scale influence such as gravity is still poorly understood, imagine how little we really know about the intricacies of the biosphere. As Francis Crick, a co-discoverer of DNA, has written, "The basic laws of physics can usually be expressed in exact mathematical form, and are probably the same throughout the universe. The 'laws' of biology, by contrast, are often just broad generalizations. . . . That is one reason why, to some people, biological organisms appear infinitely improbable." [124]

Chapter 9

1. Since I proffer that it is surprisingly easy to discern meaning in nature, the sardonic reader might ask, Why not just announce the meaning of life? Okay—

why not? Near the end of the book I will propose a working hypothesis deduced by combining old premises of deism with modern findings of natural science. No fair using the index to jump ahead to see what the meaning of life is. [137]

2. William Paley's metaphor of deism: If walking through a strange country you spied a rock you could assume that mindless forces brought this dull thing into being. But if you found a pocketwatch you would conclude that somewhere, unseen, must be a watchmaker. To Paley the intricacy of life so exceeded that of a pocketwatch that the presence on Earth of living things established the existence of God.

Today this does not necessarily follow. Modern postulations about evolution make it at least plausible that life called itself forth into being; though that debate is far from complete, as even the smartest neo-Darwinians find themselves now compelled to assert that it is easier to imagine an entire self-generated human race than a single self-generated timepiece. But as Richard Dawkins, a contemporary British zoologist and champion of Darwin, has written, Paley "had a proper reverence for the complexity of the living world, and saw that it requires a very special kind of explanation." Finding that explanation remains one of life's great challenges. [138]

Chapter 10

1. Maddeningly, the shellfish disease *Vibrio vulnificus* propagates better in clean water than polluted seas. Declining ocean pollution on the eastern seaboard is thought to be a reason this affliction is on the rise. And ever wonder how nineteenth-century wooden piers still stand in the harbors of New York and Baltimore? Water pollution killed off the bore worms and crustaceans that once attacked them. As harbor water quality has made dramatic improvements in the past decade, these rapscallions have begun to repopulate. In 1993 New York harbor agencies estimated they would spend about $100 million to wrap wooden piers in plastic sheets and take other steps to discourage the rebound of barnacle life. [148]

Chapter 11

1. Mood swings by "60 Minutes" are a good barometer of media attitudes toward the environment. Through the 1980s the show took alarmist stands, capped by a heavy-breathing episode suggesting thousands of children would die because of the pesticide Alar. Later "60 Minutes" veered into the oncoming lane, suggesting acid rain controls a waste of taxpayers' money. Both views are hyperbolic: Alar was a matter of concern but never an emergency, while acid rain controls, though oversold by some environmentalists, are necessary. Treatment of these subjects by "60 Minutes" demonstrates the media compulsion to make issues shocking. Alar was presented as shockingly dangerous; acid rain control as shockingly wasteful. The ecorealist shades of gray don't make for snappy visuals. [162]

2. Coal mining began in earnest in Britain in the eighteenth century. At the time commentators wrote despairingly that England was running out of wood for fuel, irreversibly of course. Fuelwood prices promptly fell as buyers switched to

coal; the British forest rebound began. By the early twentieth century fear of an irreversible coal shortage was rampant in Britain. Shortly thereafter coal prices fell as buyers switched to the newly popular petroleum.

Today Britain has many environmental problems but these prominently predicted dooms of the past—exhaustion of firewood and coal—seem in retrospect a hoot. Late-twentieth-century Britain has healthy forests and more coal than it knows what to do with. (The government of Prime Minister John Major suffered embarrassment in 1992 when compelled to retract a plan to reduce subsidized coal overproduction.) Environmental problems that in the 1990s seem just as unsolvable as Britain's wood and coal shortages once did will, decades or centuries hence, seem just as quaint. [164]

3. To everyone's eternal confusion there is good ozone and bad. Ozone high in the stratosphere, where it screens out ultraviolet and cosmic radiation, is good. Ozone low in the troposphere, where it is breathed, is bad. [171]

4. Ambient levels of pollutants sometimes decline faster than emissions because reductions accelerate the environment's ability to self-cleanse. One natural atmospheric self-cleansing mechanism is the hydroxyl radical, a class of molecules that can serve as an antipollution catalyst. As air pollution emissions have declined in the United States in recent decades, fewer hydroxyl radicals have been deactivated in antipollution reactions. Each hydroxyl molecule not consumed can then catalyze more than one additional cleansing reaction, helping explain why a reduction of 27 percent in sulfur emissions has led to a 53-percent drop in levels of sulfur in the air. This is an important evidence of the ecorealist premise that the environment is organized to stage recoveries at much faster rates than expected. [172]

Chapter 12

1. In late 1993 two groups of researchers released studies suggesting fine airborne soot (PM10) causes more lung damage than smog. The theory was attacked by other researchers. As this book went to press it was too early to know which side will be proven right. [183]

2. If you think the prospect of global warming is proven by recent warm summers, consider a bit of weather trivia about the 1993 heat wave—namely, that New York City's previous worst hot spell occurred in 1948. In 1948 artificial emissions of greenhouse gases were about one-quarter of the current level. During the same 1993 hot spell Washington, D.C., recorded 13 consecutive days above 90 degrees Fahrenheit, just missing the city's record of 14 straight days—set in 1872, when artificial greenhouse gas emissions were minuscule. [184]

3. Oxygenated gasoline did appear to backfire in Alaska. The additive MTBE reduces carbon monoxide but puts tiny amounts of formaldehyde in the air. In Denver and other cities this has not caused problems. But when oxygenated gasoline came to Alaska, hospitals reported a rash of patients suffering intense headaches. Something about Alaska's low winter temperatures may cause MTBE by-products to do harm there. Use of oxygenated gasoline in the state has been suspended till more is known. [198]

Chapter 13

1. The old-growth forest zone of Oregon and Washington is now estimated at about 60 percent of its pre-Columbian expanse. Dividing the assumed pre-Columbian acreage by an owl pair every 1,000 to 7,000 acres creates a rough estimate that before Europeans arrived, only a few thousand more spotted owls lived in the Pacific Northwest than at present. [222]

2. As this book went to press, Judge William Dwyer ruled that small amounts of Northwest public-lands logging could resume while he heard arguments on the overall Clinton forestry proposal. [226]

Chapter 14

1. A measure of the muddled state of environmental reporting is that the *Washington Post* ran a story about this report under the headline, "Study Finds Reduced Dioxin Danger." The *New York Times* reported the same story under the headline "High Dioxin Levels Linked to Cancer."

Both headlines were true. The study found dioxin dangers less than presumed, justifying "reduced danger." It also found cancer more likely to occur in someone with intense dioxin exposure, justifying "high levels linked to cancer." Yet what commonsense mechanism could the typical person employ to make heads or tails of these seemingly contradictory banners? [236]

2. Municipalities have been cutting chlorine in tap water for 20 years, yet another form of chemical exposure that has already peaked; so cancers caused by chlorination are believed declining. And chlorination may soon be replaced with nonchemical purification. [244]

Chapter 16

1. Before Milankovitch some geologists estimated the next ice age to be only centuries away. Because of this, when the notion of artificial greenhouse warming was proposed in the late nineteenth century, it was greeted in many quarters as fabulous news: Artificial warming would stop the return of the glaciers! [271]

Chapter 17

1. Many interesting findings have emerged from the University of Arizona tree-ring study program. One, from examination of foxtail pines, is that the Earth was warm from about A.D. 1100 to 1375—the period in which Vikings might have crossed the North Atlantic, stopping at "Vineland"—warm enough that Greenland was vegetated. Another, from the study of California sequoias, is that well before Columbus, Pacific Coast forests experienced significant fires about every five years. This is one of many recent discoveries suggesting natural cycles of forest destruction were standard to the environment long before logging began. [280]

2. Numerous zany equilibria exist in modern environmental affairs. High-altitude CFCs offset low-altitude CFCs, netting no greenhouse impact. Aerosol droplets of acid rain counteract global warming. Some throwaway products

that are not biodegradable turn out to absorb toxics, reducing the leachate caused by landfills. Smog blocks out some of the ultraviolet rays that depleted high-altitude ozone allows in, meaning aspiring hardbodies may be better off tanning on the beaches of Los Angeles than in some dangerously clean place such as Hawaii. [287]

3. Some of the global carbon dioxide emission decline noted in the early 1990s carbon drop traces to the closing of antiquated former Soviet bloc steel production facilities. At the Rio Earth Summit the Germans, even as they goaded the United States in public for not endorsing a sweeping greenhouse reduction commitment, jockeyed behind the scenes to have much of their own carbon reductions realized via credits from former East German foundries slated to close in any case. [304]

4. Amazingly this pro-reform report on carbon dioxide control from the National Academy of Sciences was denounced by environmentalists and ridiculed in the press because its central premise is that greenhouse "mitigation" can be realized without particular hardship. For instance the report supposed some impacts on agriculture could be ameliorated by use of seeds acclimated to different ranges of temperatures and moisture. Commentators were outraged by such suggestions, as orthodoxy requires all greenhouse commentary be couched in unrelenting woe. The prominent environmentalist Jessica Tuchman Mathews, a member of the NAS "mitigation" panel, authored a sharp dissent, demanding gloomier conclusions. [312]

Chapter 18

1. If you're wondering why there is no chapter on trash in what otherwise seems a comprehensive book about the environment, the reason is that in the Western world, trash is no longer an environmental issue. As Patricia Poore, founder of the delightfully contrarian independent ecological journal *Garbage,* wrote in 1993, "Management of municipal waste has no environmental aspect about which anyone ought to worry."

Since the 1980s nearly all poorly operated municipal landfills have been closed by state and federal regulators. Most of the remaining trash landfills have ecological standards higher than was typical at chemical-waste facilities a generation ago. Modern waste-to-energy incinerators for trash release few air emissions: In use in Western Europe through the postwar era, such incinerators have caused no known public health harm. And the United States is not by the wildest stretch of imagination "running out" of space for trash, as is so often claimed. Clark Wiseman, a researcher at Resources for the Future, has calculated what would happen if there were no recycling at all and U.S. trash production continued at its heady pace for the next hundred years. What would happen is that all the trash could be landfilled in less than one-hundreth of one percent of the U.S. land area.

Rather than an environmental problem, garbage is a political problem, as no one wants to live near the necessary handling facilities, even if they are safe. As such, garbage may represent the final-final frontier of due-process political gridlock. Trash, not civil rights, is what governors will be calling out the troops over in the 1990s. [321]

2. In the always-spirited competition for reigning greener-than-thou double-

speak champion a top contender is Norway's prime minister, Gro Harlem Bruntland. In the 1980s she ran a commission that produced one of the all-time doomsay documents, *Our Common Future*. A best-seller in Europe, this report predicts widespread ecological disasters and hectors the United States mercilessly. Yet measured by GNP, Bruntland's Norway invests less than half as much national wealth on the ecological protection as does the U.S., a fact *Our Common Future* somehow never gets around to addressing.

At the 1992 Earth Summit, Bruntland gave an aggressively anti-American speech, shortly after delivering a Harvard University commencement address in which she blamed economic self-interest for the world's ecological problems and declared the solution to be "international governance," which, she said, enlightened Norway endorsed but the greedy United States was sabotaging. A mere two weeks later Bruntland announced that Norway would unilaterally resume commercial whaling, defying the ban imposed by the U.S.–supported International Whaling Commission. Citing economic self-interest Bruntland withdrew her country from the IWC, one of the few successful forums for international governance. [326]

Chapter 19

1. Two related small examples of how genus *Homo* gradually learns that large technical projects can coexist with nature:

Several hydropower plants have recently installed strobe lights around water intakes. The strobes are set to whatever frequency best irritates local fish, frightening them away. Assuming such devices prove effective, many hydropower plants will soon have them.

Game officials in California have installed underwater speakers in parts of the Sacramento River, to help juvenile salmon navigate downriver. If the aural guide system works, it will be installed in other salmon rivers. A completely natural solution? Of course not. A solution acceptable to nature? Yes. [335]

Chapter 20

1. The exception to the idea that many modern products reduce total resource consumption is the Refrigerator Paradox. You buy a new refrigerator that uses less electricity, then you put the old inefficient one in the basement and leave it running for fast-food overflow and other extremely vital purposes. So is acquiring the efficient new refrigerator an environmentally conscious act or does it actually make things worse?

Environmentalists sometimes cite the Refrigerator Paradox to suggest that purchasing products can never reduce resource consumption, only perpetuate the cycle. But I say buy that new icebox. You will eventually junk the one in the basement, leaving the superior model running. And if you junk the old one right away, you'll save money. Just a thought. [359]

2. Methanol is unrelated to synthetic gasoline. Touted in the 1970s, the idea of synthetic gasoline from such sources as oil shale has been abandoned by the clearheaded. A federally subsidized pilot project in Beulah, North Dakota, was spending about $100 per barrel of oil substitute worth $15 before being shut down. [360]

Chapter 21

1. My file of enviro quotes is heavy enough to provide ballast for an ocean steamer. Yet often in this book I paraphrase ecological sentiment rather than quote a specific person. Unavoidably my paraphrases contain generalities that will frustrate the many environmental thinkers who have taken nuanced positions. To me this approach was better than endlessly criticizing individuals by name. If you want that read the 1993 book *Eco Scam*, by Ronald Bailey. It's 200 nonstop pages of embarrassing quotes from enviros. [372]

2. Bailey has produced clever skewers of green pretense. Of the Stanford scientist Stephen Schneider, a greenhouse Paul Revere, he writes, "One can imagine a prehistoric Schneider 20,000 years ago when glaciers covered 30 percent of Earth's land area, worrying about the melting. He might have predicted wrenching displacement of fragile tundra ecosystems. Why, the delicate savannahs of the equator would be overrun with dense rainforests!" [373]

3. I lived most of the year 1983 in a cabin near the summit of Nixon Peak, 15 miles from the postage-stamp town of Clyde Park, Montana. It was a three-mile hike through snow to the nearest gravel road. I mention this both to establish a minor naturalist's bona fide and to use a joke I've been saving since: Nixon Peak was listed on topography charts at 6,938 feet, but I discovered 18 and a half feet were missing. [379]

4. A strange regulatory footnote involves EPA efforts to ban from Alaskan stores spray cans of cayenne pepper sold to frighten bears. In 1993 the EPA ordered Bear Guard pulled from shelves because red pepper has never been subjected to testing for carcinogenic properties.

Set aside that it's better to dust bears with pepper than shoot them. Set aside what it means to be defenseless against predators in the backwoods. In 1992 a six-year-old boy died in Alaska when he, his mother, and three-year-old sister, walking a rural road, were set upon by a brown bear. Unable to run holding both children, the mother made a horrifying Sophie's choice and took her girl to safety, listening to the boy's screams as they fled. Simply consider this: After Alaskans protested the removal of Bear Guard the EPA decided the product could be sold if relabeled for use on people, à la Mace. Environmental law places no restrictions on whether chemicals intended to harm *people* are safe. [380]

Chapter 22

1. A maddening fault of farm chemical regulation has been that requirements to certify new pesticides are strict, but pesticides in use since the 1950s—the ones most likely to be dangerous in the first place—can be sold with few restrictions. In 1990 Congress ordered the EPA to recertify old pesticides as if they were new products coming onto the market. Pesticides such as ethyl parathion are being banned via the reregistration. By 1998 all farm chemicals legal in the United States should be ones that have passed the high safety standards of contemporary certification, including Maximum Tolerated Dose testing on lab animals. [394]

Chapter 23

1. Studies by David Duffy and Albert Meier of the University of Georgia show that soils in some southern Appalachian forests clear-cut at the turn of

the century still have not recovered fully from being churned by equipment. [406]

2. Old-growth lumber is not popular with Japanese buyers, who prefer timber from managed forests because of its uniformity—none of that nasty spontaneity. [407]

Chapter 25

1. Mentioning Aldo Leopold again creates an opening to praise his masterpiece, *A Sand County Almanac,* which contains such wisdom as: "When I call to mind my earliest impressions, I wonder whether the process ordinarily referred to as growing up is not actually a process of growing down; whether experience, so much touted among adults as the thing children lack, is not actually a progressive dilution of the essentials by the trivialities of living." Bravo! [435]

2. Although golf is an open-air, entirely green land use, most enviros despise golf courses, partly because the facilities are in effect gigantic suburban lawns bombarded with yard chemicals. The National Audubon Society opposes all construction of golf courses, though many are rest stops for migratory birds; the Sierra Club has sued to block golf courses in several states.

The real reason for the discomfort is what golf courses represent sociologically: private enclaves with exclusionary memberships favoring overpaid white males. Golf courses have always given me the willies for this reason. The trouble is that institutional environmentalism itself is run mainly by white males, a group increasingly close to the golf-course set as salaries and perks rise for the upper echelon of institutional environmentalism (for instance, National Wildlife Federation director Jay Hair being paid $242,000 in 1994). [437]

3. Conflicted attitudes can be found in many aspects of environmentalism. For instance since the late 1980s both ecologists and a landscape architect named William Young have been working with managers of Fresh Kills, the world's largest landfill, located in the New Jersey meadowlands just west of Manhattan, to insure that waste cells are constructed in ways that will allow for natural restoration, such as by the planting of maples and other acid-loving trees; and so that the fill, once closed, will continue to serve its present function as a rest stop for hawk, egret, and falcon. These are excellent ideas but conflict with the orthodox green notion that landfills are in every way horrifying blots on the Earth. In fact what these plans constitute is a LANDFILL PRESERVATION INITIATIVE. [441]

4. The restoration of oak savannahs in Northbrook, Illinois began with a prescribed burn, the very nature-mimicking practice many environmentalists consider a horror when employed by timber companies. But then environmental ideas about fire have long been conflicted. Leopold wrote in praise of natural prairie fire cycles. He died of a heart attack while helping a rural neighbor put out a grassland fire. [444]

5. The logic of land use being appropriate for public planning could even extend to the seas. The National Oceanographic and Atmospheric Administration, with jurisdiction over the Florida Keys, has decided to "zone" the nearby ocean by putting areas off-limits to power boats. Some fishing businesses will be harmed by ocean zoning. But can anyone doubt the economy of south Florida will be better off if the Keys and their wild beauty are preserved? [444]

Chapter 26

1. My favorite Nimby developments are opposition to paved roads and to parking spaces.

A generation ago, in country towns you could tell where the influential lived because they were the ones with paved roads to their houses. Now in fashionable exurban communities you can tell where the influential live because they *don't* have paved roads. The well-to-do in such areas are fighting for dirt roads on the theory that they discourage traffic.

In Cambridge, Massachusetts, in San Francisco and elsewhere, Nimby movements oppose new parking garages even for residential buildings. The first Clean Air Act, in 1970, contained a clause limiting the parking spaces allowed in buildings built with federal funds, ostensibly to compel people to abandon their smog-generating cars. Communities such as Cambridge matched that rule with local ordinances. But people kept driving anyway, and lack of parking became a government-imposed urban headache. Now that new cars emit roughly one percent as much pollution as in 1970, the clean-air reasoning of antiparking rules has abated. But the regulations remain on the books as "headless nails"—you can put them in but you can't pull them out. [452]

Chapter 29

1. Sometimes it is said in jest that two ecological problems would neutralize each other if the low-level ozone in urban smog could be transported to the stratosphere, where it would compensate for depletion. Actually this would not work. The stratosphere naturally contains much higher concentrations of ozone than is found above the most polluted cities. Piping even the worst midsummer Los Angeles smog to the stratosphere would dilute the ozone layer, not reinforce it. [531]
2. Several curiosities turn on the development of CFCs. One is that the inventor, former General Motors chief chemist Thomas Midgley, also devised another of the modern era's leading pollutants, tetrahedral lead, the gas additive that stops knock but causes atmospheric lead poisoning. A second is that because CFCs once appeared inert, during the 1960s some pollution-control officials urged industry to substitute CFCs for solvents that cause smog. This substitution was a factor in the surge of CFC production that then triggered ozone layer loss. [532]
3. In 1994 the National Weather Service began issuing ultraviolet advisories for sunbathers. These advisories are not based on actual readings of ground-level UV-B but generated by a computer model that predicts the intensity of sunlight expected for the day. [541]
4. Rosalyn Yalow has said it is possible Colorado has lower cancer rates than California because very low levels of radon render a person *less* likely to contract cancer. As Roger Macklis, head of radiation oncology at the Cleveland Clinic Foundation, wrote in 1993 in *Scientific American,* researchers have long puzzled over the fact that extremely low doses of radiation can seem beneficial.

Today two abandoned uranium mines in Colorado are open to the public as sorts of reverse sanitariums into which paying customers, usually arthritis sufferers, escape from the carefully pollution-controlled air of the country above them and descend to inhale radon gas. Many claim to experience therapeutic gains. Neither Yalow, Macklis, nor any credentialed researcher recommends purposeful exposure. Still it remains possible that very low levels of radiation eventually will be shown to possess some positive effect. [549]

Chapter 30

1. Recently Norman Myers has begun to assert that Earth contains many millions of "environmental refugees" fleeing ecological devastation.

Though there are a few places such as the African Sahel where the ecology is so distressed people have trouble living at the level of destitution, refugee movements are almost always caused by war, oppression, or economic breakdown: human rather than natural forces. In the 1990s several foundations that support environmental advocacy became active in funding work that upholds the notion of a widespread phenomenon of environmental refugees, as this promises to add another item to the catalog of ecological woes. Why war, oppression, and economic breakdown aren't sufficiently horrible on their own eludes me. [559]

2. A similar example of environmental lobbies stooping to the *ad hominem* attack concerns the writer Raymond Bonner. In his 1993 book about African elephants, *At the Hand of Man,* Bonner charged that Western environmental groups, principally the World Wildlife Fund, have pressured African governments to outlaw regulated commerce in ivory because such bans serve the financial purposes of environmentalists, fund-raising appeals denouncing the horrors of ivory trading working well in directmail. Bonner advocated regulated ivory trading with tusks taken only from sick or aged elephants and the proceeds used for wildlife protection, the system practiced successfully in Zimbabwe.

Bonner was the reporter who in 1982 disclosed atrocities conducted by the U.S.–backed reactionary government of El Salvador. In response the Reagan Administration campaigned to discredit him and at congressional hearings called Bonner a Communist sympathizer. In 1992 the Bush Administration formally acknowledged Bonner had been correct. Since *At the Hand of Man* was published some enviros have conducted a second campaign to discredit Bonner: rather than answering his arguments with rational rebuttals, slandering his reputation and impugning his motives, Bonner told me, "The personal attacks I've heard from environmentalists are cruder and more vicious than anything from the Reagan White House." [561]

3. By pure preservation I do not mean making wild areas off-limits. I mean places in which large-scale development is barred and such human impositions as take place are designed to minimize ecological impact. [575]

Chapter 31

1. A possibility I'll offer for you to mull over: Suppose, as some molecular biologists now posit in the "DNA Eve" theory, that the cradle of human evolution was Africa. Why then did technical society develop elsewhere? Perhaps because controlled agriculture, the first technical pursuit entered into by *Homo sapiens,* was not possible in Africa owing to the poor soil of that continent. It could be attempted only by those who left the cradle. [590]

Chapter 32

1. Today some parents obsessively worry about the effects on kids of highly speculative risks such as Alar or electromagnetic radiation, while paying less attention to confirmed hazards. Beyond the obvious risks of drinking and drugs, these include having poisons like bleach in unlocked cabinets, young children wearing dark-colored clothing at night, and 16-year-olds driving the family car. Poisonings, street-crossing accidents, and driving during the teen years kill many thousands of American kids each year, far more than a worst-case reading of all environmental exposures. [613]

2. The East Liverpool incinerator has a tormented history, including ownership at one point by an Arkansas firm that gave money to the Clinton campaign. During the 1992 presidential race Al Gore vowed to shut the East Liverpool incinerator down, later withdrawing his vow, claiming legal technicalities. Today activists campaign against the facility on the grounds that one of its permits was issued in violation of an EPA regulation. It was. The violation? The facility was built on an industrial lot contaminated with waste oil. At the time the permit was written EPA rules stipulated that toxic waste facilities could not be sited on contaminated land, only on pristine land. *Toxic waste facilities must be located on pristine land.* In the jumbled-up realm of environmental logic, that idea made perfect sense to someone at some time. [621]

Chapter 33

1. To protect young children from lead, employ the simple expedient of letting the tap run about 20 seconds before drawing water for consumption. Lead levels will drop more than 80 percent as water that had been in contact with pipes flushes through. [639]

2. In the category of for whatever it's worth, if you think red wine is a health-giving natural product and have heard that French imbibers suffer fewer heart attacks than American teetotalers, be advised that regardless of how pricey, wine contains far too much lead for the EPA to allow it into plumbing. Poured U.S. wines average 58 parts per billion of lead. Poured French wines average 195 parts per billion. The EPA limit for tap water is 15 parts per billion. [639]

3. The harp seal was never endangered: Most hunting of this mammal was banned by Canada in 1987 owing to cruelty in the slaughter of cubs. There were an estimated two million Canadian harp seals when the hunting ban was imposed and there are an estimated 3.5 million today. [645]

BIBLIOGRAPHY ✍

ENVIRONMENTAL BOOKS CONTAIN SUCH A CONFLUENCE OF facts that footnoting every reference would cause little carrot marks to take over the pages. For this reason Rachel Carson did not footnote *Silent Spring;* for this reason I do not footnote either. Carson provided a general bibliography and a listing of scientific studies, government reports, and other primary documents; here I do the same. Entries for parts one and three are grouped; those for part two are broken down into chapters.

Like Carson's, these citations are confined to primary documents. To avoid endnote overload, Carson did not offer routine references such as newspaper article dates to buttress noncontroversial information, general statements about current events, or commonly cited quotations from well-known figures. I follow her example. When no source for a fact is indicated in the text or these notes, this is because the assertion is not generally in dispute among specialists. Readers may be assured such references are the most recent figures available and drawn from some neutral accredited source such as academic textbooks, Environmental Protection Agency statistical tables, or the data series *Facts on File.*

All contemporary writers are indebted to the able women and men who staff the newspapers, magazines, and broadcast stations of contemporary journalism, supplying to the modern citizen's desk more information than the most determined researcher could ever uncover personally. In this book I cite by name numerous journalists whose dispatches have been invaluable to public understanding of ecological

affairs. To those others from whose work I have gleaned a fact or reference without using their names, I express heartfelt thanks. And like all
environmental analysts, I am beholden to the reporting staffs of the
excellent technical journal *Science* and of the outstanding "Science
Times" section of the *New York Times*. No one could grasp contemporary environmental issues without these two indispensable publications.

General Bibliography

Berry, Thomas. *The Dream of the Earth*. Sierra Club Books, 1989.
Bramwell, Anna. *Ecology in the Twentieth Century*. Yale University Press,
    1989.
Brown, Lester, et al. *The State of the World 1994*. W.W. Norton, 1994.
Brown, Lester, et al. *Vital Signs 1990* through *Vital Signs 1994* (annual publica-
    tion). W.W. Norton, 1990–94.
Cairncross, Francis. *Costing the Earth*. Harvard Business School Press, 1991.
Carson, Rachel. *Silent Spring*. Houghton-Mifflin, 1962.
Cohn, Susan. *Green at Work*. Island Press, 1992.
Commoner, Barry. *Making Peace with the Planet*. Pantheon, 1990.
Dillard, Annie. *Pilgrim at Tinker Creek*. Harper & Row, 1974.
Dubos, Rene. *So Human an Animal*. Charles Schribner's Sons, 1968.
Durning, Alan. *How Much Is Enough?* W.W. Norton, 1992.
Ehrlich, Paul, and Anne Ehrlich. *Healing the Planet*. Addison-Wesley, 1991.
Environmental Quality: 23rd Report of the Council on Environmental Quality.
    Council on Environmental Quality, 1992.
Firor, John. *The Changing Atmosphere*. Yale University Press, 1990.
Fox, Stephen. *John Muir and His Legacy*. Little-Brown, 1981.
Fumento, Michael. *Science under Siege*. William Morrow, 1993.
Goldman, Benjamin. *The Truth about Where You Live: An Atlas for Action on
    Toxins and Mortality*. Random House, 1991.
Gore, Al. *Earth in the Balance*. Houghton-Mifflin, 1992.
Goudsblom, Johan. *Fire and Civilization*. Viking, 1993.
Hoyle, Russ, editor. *Gale Environmental Almanac*. Gale Research, 1993.
Lehr, Jay, editor. *Rational Readings on Environmental Concerns*. Van
    Nostrand Reinhold, 1992.
Leopold, Aldo. *A Sand County Almanac*. Oxford University Press, 1948.
Lovelock, James. *Gaia: A New Look at Life on Earth*. Oxford University Press,
    1979.
Margulis, Lynn, and Lorraine Olendzenski, editors. *Environmental Evolution*.
    MIT Press, 1992.
McKibben, Bill. *The End of Nature*. Random House, 1989.
Meadows, Donella, et al. *The Limits to Growth*. Universe Books, 1972.
Myers, Norman. *The Sinking Ark*. Pergamon, 1979.
———. *Ultimate Security*. W.W. Norton, 1993
*Our Common Future: Report of the World Commission on Environment and
    Development*. Oxford University Press, 1987.

Piasecki, Bruce, and Peter Asmus. *In Search of Environmental Excellence.* Simon & Schuster, 1990.

Repetto, Robert. *The Global Possible.* Yale University Press, 1985.

Sale, Kirkpatrick. *The Green Revolution.* Hill & Wang, 1993.

Schmidheiney, Stephan, et al. *Changing Course: Report of the Business Council for Sustainable Development.* MIT Press, 1992.

Schneider, Stephen, and Randi Londer. *The Coevolution of Life and Climate.* Sierra Club Books, 1984.

Schramm, Gunter, and Jeremy Warford, editors. *Environmental Management and Economic Development.* Johns Hopkins University Press, 1989.

Shabecoff, Philip. *A Fierce Green Fire: The American Environmental Movement.* Hill & Wang, 1993.

Simon, Julian. *The Ultimate Resource.* Princeton University Press, 1981.

Stone, Roger D. *The Nature of Development.* Alfred Knopf, 1992.

Suzuki, David, and Peter Knudtsen. *Wisdom of the Elders: Honoring Sacred Native American Visions of Nature.* Bantam, 1992.

Thoreau, Henry. *The Maine Woods.* Thomas Crowell, 1909.

Turner, B.L. II, et al. *The Earth as Transformed by Human Action.* Cambridge University Press, 1990.

Weiner, Jonathan. *The Next One Hundred Years.* Bantam, 1990.

Wilson, Edward O. *The Diversity of Life.* Harvard University Press, 1992.

World Resources Institute Environmental Almanac 1994. Houghton Mifflin, 1994.

Part One
(Chapters 1–10)

Adams, Carol J., editor. *Ecofeminism and the Sacred.* Continuum, 1993.

Beardsley, Timothy. "Recovery Drill at Mount Saint Helens." *Scientific American,* November 1990.

Berner, Robert S. "Atmospheric Carbon Dioxide Levels over Phanerozoic Time." *Science,* volume 249, 1990.

Budiansky, Stephen. *The Covenant of the Wild.* William Morrow, 1991.

Butzer, Karl, editor. "The Americas Before and After 1492." *Annals of the Association of American Geographers* (special issue), September 1992.

Butzer, Karl. "No Eden in the New World." *Nature,* volume 361, 1993.

Borkiewicz, Jerzy, et al. "Environmental Profile of Katowice." United Nations Development Programme, 1991.

Coffin, Millard, and Olav Eldholm. "Large Igneous Provinces." *Scientific American,* October 1993.

Dansgaard, W., et al. "Abrupt Termination of the Younger Dryas Climate Event." *Nature,* 1989.

Edgerton, Robert B. *Sick Societies: Challenging the Myth of Primitive Harmony.* The Free Press, 1992.

Gehrels, Neil, and Wan Chen. "The Geminga Supernova as a Possible Cause of the Local Interstellar Bubble." *Nature,* volume 361, 1993.

Glickman, Theodore, et al. "Acts of God and Acts of Man." Resources for the Future, 1992.

Gore, Al. Keynote address to the Commission on Sustainable Development. United Nations, 1993

Grove, Richard. "Origins of Western Environmentalism." *Scientific American,* July 992.

Hearne, Vicki. "What's Wrong with Animal Rights." *Harper's,* September 1991.

Houghton, Richard, and George Woodwell. "Global Climate Change." *Scientific American,* April 1989.

Hunten, Donald. "Atmospheric Evolution of the Terrestrial Planets." *Science,* volume 259, 1993.

Jablonski, David. "Origin and Destruction of Marine Biodiversity." American Association for the Advancement of Science, 1994.

Kasting, James. "Earth's Early Atmosphere." *Science,* volume 259, 1993.

Kennedy, Paul. *The Rise and Fall of the Great Powers.* Random House, 1987.

Kerr, Richard. "Huge Impact Tied to Mass Extinctions." *Science,* August 14, 1992.

Kristol, Elizabeth. "History in the Past Perfect." *First Things,* April 1991.

Lehman, Scott. "Sudden Change in North Atlantic Circulation During the Last Deglaciation." *Nature,* volume 356, April 1992.

Levinton, Jeffrey. "The Big Bang of Animal Evolution." *Scientific American,* November 1992.

Ludwig, Daniel, et al. "Uncertainty, Resource Exploitation and Conservation." *Science,* April 2, 1993.

Mangel, Marc. "Extinction of Local Populations." American Association for the Advancement of Science, 1992.

Mann, Charles C. "How Many Is Too Many?" *The Atlantic Monthly,* February 1993.

Mann, Jonathan, et al. *AIDS in the World.* Harvard University Press, 1992.

Martin, Paul. "Human Impacts on the Late Pleistocene Extinctions." American Association for the Advancement of Science, 1994.

Morell, Virginia. "How Lethal Was the K-T Impact?" *Science,* September 17, 1993.

Morgan, Ted. *Wilderness at Dawn.* Simon & Schuster, 1993.

Murphy, Brenden J., and Damian Nance. "Mountain Belts and the Supercontinent Cycle." *Scientific American,* April 1992.

Officer, Charles, and Jake Page. *Tales of the Earth.* Oxford University Press, 1993.

O'Hara, Sarah, et al. "Accelerated Soil Erosion around a Mexican Highland Lake Caused by Prehistoric Agriculture." *Nature,* volume 361, 1993.

Prinn, Ronald. "After the Fall." *Science,* February 26, 1988.

Rampino, Michael. "Flood Basalt Volcanism During the Past 250 Million Years." *Science,* August 5, 1988.

Raymo, Maureen. "Global Climate Change: A Three Million Year Perspective." Springer-Verlag, 1992.

Raymo, Maureen and Ruddiman, William. "Tectonic Forcing of the Late Cenozoic Climate." *Nature,* volume 359, 1992.

Rice, Alan. "Global Extinctions: Meteor Impact or Global Volcanism?" American Association for the Advancement of Science, 1994.

Rigby, Keith. "Extinctions: Causes and Consequences." American Association for the Advancement of Science, 1994.

Schor, Juliet. *The Overworked American.* Basic Books, 1991.

Schumacher, E.F. *Small Is Beautiful.* Harper & Row, 1973.

Sharpton, Virgil, et al. "Chicxulub Multiring Impact Basin." *Science,* September 17, 1993.

Simkin, Tom. "Distant Effects of Volcanism: How Big and How Often?" *Science,* volume 264, 1994.

Stone, Christopher. *Should Trees Have Standing?* William Kaufmann, 1974.

Stone, Richard. "Dispute Over *Exxon Valdez* Cleanup Data Gets Messy." *Science,* volume 260, 1993.

Waggoner, Paul E. "How Much Land Can Ten Billion People Spare for Nature?" Council for Agricultural Science and Technology, 1994.

Wright, Ronald. *Stolen Continents: The Americas Through Indian Eyes Since 1492.* Houghton-Mifflin, 1992.

York, Derek. "The Earliest History of the Earth." *Scientific American,* January 1993.

Part Two

CHAPTER 11

Bodhaine, Barry, and Ellsworth Dutton. "A Long Term Decrease in Arctic Haze at Barrow, Alaska." *Geophysical Research Letters,* volume 20, 1993.

Elman, Barry. "Economic, Environmental and Coal-Market Impacts of Sulfur Dioxide Emissions Trading." U.S. Environmental Protection Agency, 1989.

Krug, Edward. "Acid Rain, Forests and Fish." American Association for the Advancement of Science, 1992.

"Report of the National Acid Precipitation Assessment Program." U.S. Government Printing Office, 1991.

Swain, Edward. "Increasing Rates of Atmospheric Mercury Deposition in Midcontinental North America." *Science,* August 7, 1992.

CHAPTER 12

"Air Quality Management Plan, 1993." South Coast Air Quality Management District, 1993.

Brown, Michael. *The Toxic Cloud.* Harper & Row, 1987.

"Health Damage from Urban Air Pollution." American Lung Association, 1990.

Calvert, J.G., et al. "Achieving Acceptable Air Quality." *Science,* volume 261, 1993.

Lents, James, and William Kelly. "Clearing the Air in Los Angeles." *Scientific American,* October 1993.

Lovins, Amory. "Abating Air Pollution at Negative Cost." Rocky Mountain Institute, 1989.

"Implementing the Clean Air Act: The First Two Years." U.S. Environmental Protection Agency, 1992.

Jones, Kay. "Ozone Data Base and Its Implications in Regard to Attainment Projections for the Northeast Ozone Transport Zone." Zephyr Consulting, 1993.

Nadis, Steve, and James MacKenzie. *Car Trouble.* Beacon Press, 1993.

Newell, Reginald. "Carbon Monoxide and the Burning Earth." *Scientific American,* October 1989.

Novelli, Paul, et al. "Recent Changes in Atmospheric Carbon Monoxide." *Science,* volume 263, 1994.

Portney, Paul. "Economics and the Clean Air Act." *Journal of Economic Perspectives,* volume four, 1990.

"Rethinking the Ozone Problem in Urban and Regional Air Pollution." National Research Council, National Academy of Sciences Press, 1991.

"Technical Support Document, Zero-Emission Vehicle." California Air Resources Board, 1994.

CHAPTER 13

Barrowclough, George, and R.J. Gutierrez. "Genetic Variation and Differentiation in the Spotted Owl." *The Auk,* October 1990.

Burnham, Kenneth, et al. "Estimation of Vital Rates of the Northern Spotted Owl." Colorado State University, 1994.

"The California Spotted Owl: Technical Assessment of Its Current Status." U.S. Forest Service, 1992.

"A Conservation Strategy for the Northern Spotted Owl." Report of the Interagency Scientific Committee to Address the Conservation of the Northern Spotted Owl. U.S. Government Printing Office, 1992.

"Evaluation of Option 9 of the Federal Forest Plan as It Relates to Northwest California." California Department of Forestry, 1993.

Forsman, Eric. "Habitat Utilization by Spotted Owls in the West-Central Cascades of Oregon." Oregon State University, 1980.

Gould, Gordon. "Status of the Spotted Owl in California." California Department of Fish and Game, 1974.

Johnson, Norman K., et al. "Alternatives for Management of Late-Successional Forests of the Pacific Northwest." Report to U.S. House of Representatives, 1991.

"Report of the Advisory Panel on the Spotted Owl." National Audubon Society, 1986.

Schamberger, M.L., et al. "Economic Analysis of Critical Habitat Designation for the Spotted Owl." U.S. Fish and Wildlife Service, 1992.

Self, Steven, and Thomas Nelson. "The Spotted Owl in California: An Update." Sierra Pacific Industries, 1993.

CHAPTER 14

Ames, Bruce, and Lois Gold. "Ranking Possible Carcinogenic Hazards." *Science,* volume 236, 1987.

———. "Comparing Synthetic to Natural Chemicals." University of California, 1993.

———. "Chemical Carcinogenesis: Too Many Rodent Carcinogens." *Proceedings of the National Academy of Sciences,* volume 87, 1990.

"Biological Markers in Immunotoxicity." National Research Council, 1992.

Brown, Michael. *Laying Waste: The Poisoning of America by Toxic Chemicals.* Pantheon, 1980.

Brown, Philip. "Popular Epidemiology Challenges the System." *Environment*, volume 35, 1993.

Cox, Archibald. "Asbestos in Public Buildings: A Literature Review and Synthesis." Health Effects Institute, 1991.

Davis, Devra Lee, et al. "Medical Hypothesis: Xenoestrogens as Preventable Causes of Breast Cancer." *Environmental Health Perspectives*, volume 101, 1993.

Davis, Devra Lee. "Trends in Cancer Mortality in 15 Industrial Countries." *Journal of the National Cancer Institute*, volume 84, 1992.

"Estimating Exposure to Dioxin-Like Compounds" (review draft). U.S. Environmental Protection Agency, 1994.

Gold, Lois Swirsky. "The Fifth Plot of the Carcinogenic Potency Database." *Environmental Health Perspectives*, volume 100, 1993.

―――. "Importance of Data on Mechanism of Carcinogenesis in Effects to Predict Low-Dose Human Risk." *Risk Analysis*, volume 13, 1993.

Gough, Michael. "Dioxin: Can Science Affect Policy?" American Association for the Advancement of Science, 1992.

Grossman, K. *The Poison Conspiracy*. Permanent Press, 1983.

"Health Assessment Document for 2,3,7,8-Tetrachlorodibenzo-p-Dioxin (TCDD) and Related Compounds" (review draft). U.S. Environmental Protection Agency, 1994.

Holloway, Marguerite. "Dioxin Indictment." *Scientific American,* January 1994.

Lave, Lester, et al. "Information Value of the Rodent Bioassay." *Nature,* December 15, 1988.

Marshall, Elliot. "Experts Clash over Cancer Data." *Science,* November 16, 1990.

McGinnis, Michael J., and William H. Foege. "Actual Causes of Death in the United States." *Journal of the American Medical Association*, volume 270, 1993.

Nader, Ralph, et al. *Who's Poisoning America?* Sierra Club Books, 1981.

Ottoboni, Alice. *The Dose Makes the Poison.* Van Nostrand Reinhold, 1990.

Stone, Richard. "Environmental Estrogens Stir Debate." *Science,* volume 265, 1994.

Sundstein, Cass. "Remaking Regulation." *American Prospect,* Fall 1990.

Wolff, S. "Love Canal Revisited." *Journal of the American Medical Association*, volume 251, 1984.

CHAPTER 15

Fox, Karen Celia. "Cleaner Manufacturing of Plastics." *Science,* volume 265, 1994.

Hosford, William, and John Duncan. "The Aluminum Beverage Can." *Scientific American,* September 1994.

Larson, Eric. "Beyond the Age of Materials." *Scientific American,* June 1986.

Larson, Eric D. "Trends in Consumption of Energy Intensive Basic Materials in Industrialized Countries." Center for Energy and Environment Studies, Princeton University, 1991.

Osada, Yoshihito, and Simon Ross-Murphy. "Intelligent Gels." *Scientific American,* May 1993.

Periana, Roy, et al. "A Mercury Catalyzed High Yield System for Oxidation of Methane to Ethanol." *Science,* January 15, 1993.

Reed, Mark. "Quantum Dots." *Scientific American,* January 1993.

Williams, Robert, et al. "Materials, Affluence and Industrial Energy Use." *Annual Review of Energy,* 1987.

CHAPTER 16

Alley, R.B., et al. "Changes in the West Antarctic Ice Sheet." *Science,* November 11, 1991.

Ankin, M., et al. "Climate Instability During the Last Interglacial Period Record in the GRIP Ice Core." *Science,* volume 364, 1993.

Broecker, Wallace, and George Denton. "What Drives Glacial Cycles?" *Scientific American,* January 1990.

Domack, Eugene, et al. "Advance of East Antarctic Outlet Glaciers During the Hypsithermal." *Geology,* November 1991.

Groisman, Pavel, et al. "Observed Impact of the Snow Cover on the Heat Balance and the Rise of Continental Spring Temperatures." *Science,* volume 263, 1994.

Horgan, John. "Antarctic Meltdown." *Scientific American,* March 1993.

Knoll, Andrew. "End of the Proterozoic Era." *Scientific American,* October 1991.

Miller, Gifford, and Anne de Vernal. "Will Greenhouse Warming Lead to Northern Hemisphere Ice Sheet Growth?" *Nature,* volume 355, 1992.

Morgan, V.I., et al. "Evidence from Antarctic Ice Cores for Recent Increases in Snow Accumulation." *Nature,* November 71991.

Sugden, David. "Antarctic Ice Sheets at Risk?" *Nature,* October 10, 1992.

Raymo, Maureen. "Response of Deep Ocean Circulation to Initiation of Northern Hemisphere Glaciation." *Paleoceanography,* October 1992.

Raymo, Maureen, and John Kutzbach. "Plateau Uplift and Climate Change." *Scientific American,* March 1991.

Raynaud, D. "Ice Record of Greenhouse Gases." *Science,* volume 259, 1993.

Taylor, K.C., et al. "Electrical Conductivity Measurements from the GISP2 and GRIP Greenland Ice Cores." *Nature,* volume 366, 1993.

CHAPTER 17

Balling, Robert C. "Global Temperature Data." *Research and Exploration,* volume nine, 1993.

———. *The Heated Debate.* Pacific Research Institute, 1992

Charlson, Robert, et al. "Perturbation of the Northern Hemisphere Radiative Balance by Backscattering from Anthropogenic Sulfate Aerosols." *Tellus,* 1991.

Dlugokencky, E.J., et al. "A Dramatic Decrease in the Growth Rate of Atmospheric Methane in the Northern Hemisphere during 1992." *Geophysical Research Letters,* volume 21, 1994.

Dudek, Dan. "Offsetting New CO_2 Emissions." Environmental Defense Fund, 1988.

"Emissions of Greenhouse Gases in the United States, 1985–90." U.S. Energy Information Administration.

"Energy Use and Carbon Emissions: Some International Comparisons." U.S. Energy Information Administration, 1994.

Foukal, Peter. "Stellar Luminosity Variations and Global Warming." *Science,* volume 264, 1994.

Friis-Christian, E., and K. Lassen. "An Indicator of Solar Activity Closely Associated with Climate." *Science,* volume 254, 1991.

Goklany, Indur. "Adaptation and Climate Change." American Association for the Advancement of Science, 1992.

Hansen, James, et al. "How Sensitive Is the World's Climate?" *Research and Exploration,* volume nine, 1993.

Houghton, J.T., et al. "Reports of the Intergovernmental Panel on Climate Change: Impact Assessment, Policymaker's Summary, Response Strategies and Science Assessment" (four volumes). Cambridge University Press in affiliation with the World Meteorological Organization and United Nations. Published 1990, with updates in 1992 and 1994.

Jones, Philip, et al. "Effect of Urban Warming on the Northern Hemisphere Temperature Average." *Journal of Climate,* March 1989.

Jones, Philip. "Regional Patterns of Surface Air Temperature Change since 1850." *Holocene,* June 1993.

Jones, Philip, and Tom Wigley. "Global Warming Trends." *Scientific American,* August 1990.

Karl, Thomas. "Evidence for Asymmetric Diurnal Temperature Change." *Geophysical Research Letters,* December 1990.

Karl, Thomas, et al. "The Greenhouse Effect in Central North America: If Not Now, When?" *Science,* volume 251, 1991.

Kerr, Richard. "Fugitive CO_2: It's Not Hiding in the Oceans." *Science,* volume 256, 1992

———. "Unmasking a Shifty Climate System." *Science,* volume 255, 1992.

Levitus, Sydney. "Current Changes of Ocean Circulation in the North Atlantic." *Journal of Geophysical Research,* volume 95, 1990.

Lindzen, Richard. "Uncertainties with Respect to Water Vapor in Climate Sensitivity." National Aeronautics and Space Administration (workshop), 1990.

Lockwood, G.W., et al. "Long Term Brightness Changes Estimated from a Survey of Sun-like Stars." *Nature,* volume 360, 1992.

Lovejoy, Thomas, and Robert Peters, editors. *Global Warming and Biological Diversity.* Yale University Press, 1992.

Lovins, Amory, and L. Hunter Lovins. "Least Cost Climate Stabilization." Rocky Mountain Institute, 1990.

Marchant, David. "Pliocene Paleoclimate and the East Antarctic Ice Sheet History from Surface Ash Deposits." *Science,* April 30 1993.

McMahan, Ron. "Cost and Implications of Controlling CO2 Emissions in the United States." Resource Data International, 1993.

Michaels, Patrick. *Sound and Fury: The Science and Politics of Global Warming.* Cato Institute, 1992.

Oerlemans, Johannes. "Quantifying Global Warming from the Retreat of Glaciers." *Science,* volume 264, 1994.

Oppenheimer, Michael, and Peter Boyle. *Dead Heat: The Race Against the Greenhouse Effect.* New Republic Books, 1990.

"Policy Implications of Greenhouse Warming." National Academy of Sciences, NAS Press, 1991.

Revelle, Roger, et al. "What to Do About Greenhouse Warming." *Cosmos,* 1991.

"Responding to Changes in Sea Level." Report from the National Academy of Sciences. NAS Press, 1987.

Sassen, Kenneth. "Evidence for Liquid Phase Cirrus Cloud Formation from Volcanic Aerosols." *Science,* July 24, 1992.

Schlesinger, Michael. "Greenhouse Policy." *Research and Exploration,* volume nine, 1993.

Schlesinger, Michael, and Xingjian Jiang. "Revised Projection for Future Greenhouse Warming." *Nature,* volume 350, 1991.

Schneider, Stephen. *Global Warming.* Sierra Club Books, 1989.

Sundquist, Eric. "The Global Carbon Dioxide Budget." *Science,* volume 259, 1993.

Van der Burgh, Johan, et al. "Paleoatmospheric Signatures in Neogene Fossil Leaves." *Science,* June 18 1993.

CHAPTER 18

Bernstam, Mikhail. "The Wealth of Nations and the Environment." Institute of Economic Affairs, 1991.

Bhagwati, Jagdish, and Herman Daly. "Does Free Trade Harm the Environment?" *Scientific American,* November 1993.

Daly, Herman, and John Cobb Jr. *For the Common Good.* Beacon Press, 1989.

Daly, Herman, and Kenneth Townsend, editors. *Valuing the Earth.* MIT Press, 1993.

"Environment and the Economy." *Science* (special issue), volume 260, 1993.

Hahn, Robert. "Balancing Economic Growth and Environmental Goals." Center for Policy Research, 1994.

Hershkowitz, Allen. "How Garbage Could Meet Its Maker." *The Atlantic Monthly,* June 1993.

Porter, Michael. "America's Green Strategy." *Scientific American,* April 1991.

Portney, Paul. "The Environmental Protection Agency at Thirtysomething." *Northwestern Environmental Law Journal,* Spring 1991.

Rathje, William, and Cullen Murphy. *Rubbish: The Archeology of Garbage.* Harper Collins, 1992.

"State of Recycling, 1993." National Recycling Coalition, 1993.

Stavins, Robert, and Bradley Whitehead. "The Greening of America's Taxes." Progressive Policy Institute, 1992

Stavins, Robert, director. "Project 88" and "Project 88 Round II." Harvard University, 1988 and 1991.

CHAPTERS 19 AND 20

Abelson, Philip. "Increased Use of Renewable Energy." *Science,* volume 253, 1991.

Babir, Franco. "Hydrogen and Electric-Power Alternatives." American Association for the Advancement of Science, 1992.

Corcoran, Elizabeth. "Sulfur Output from Coal Combustion." *Scientific American,* May 1991.

Dostrovsky, Israel. "Chemical Fuels from the Sun." *Scientific American,* December 1991.

"Energy: The Next 20 Years." Resources for the Future, Ford Foundation, 1979.

Flavin, Christopher. "The Bridge to Clean Energy." Worldwatch Institute, 1992.

Flavin, Christopher, and Nicholas Lenssen. *Powering the Future: Blueprint for a Sustainable Electricity Industry.* Worldwatch Institute, 1994.

Gordon, Roy. "Energy Efficient Windows." American Association for the Advancement of Science, 1992.

Frazier, W.K., et al. "Implementation of Corporate Environmental and Safety Policy in a Developing Country." Society of Petroleum Engineers, 1991.

Houston, Douglas. "Electric Utility Deregulation." Cato Institute, 1993.

Kleiner, Art. "Flexing Their Mussels." *Garbage,* July–August 1992.

"Leadership in Energy Efficiency." Global Climate Coalition, 1993.

Lewis, Nathan. "Hydrogen Storage and Solar Energy Conversion." American Association for the Advancement of Science, 1992.

Lovins, Amory. "Energy Strategy: The Road Not Taken." *Foreign Affairs,* Spring 1976.

Potts, Michael. *The Independent Home.* Chelsea Green Publishing, 1993.

Schurr, Samuel, et al. *Electricity in the American Economy.* Greenwood Press, 1990.

Selcraig, Bruce. "Bad Chemistry." *Harper's,* April 1992

Teagen, Peter. "Environmental Benefits of Fuel Cell Technology." Arthur D. Little, 1992.

Williams, Robert. "Advanced Gasification-Based Biomass Power Generation." American Association for the Advancement of Science, 1992.

Williams, Robert, and Joan Ogden. "Hydrogen and the Revolution in Amorphous Silicon Solar-Cell Technology." Center for Energy and Environmental Studies, Princeton University, 1989.

CHAPTER 21

Arrendale, Tom. "The Midlife Crisis of the Environmental Lobby." *Governing,* April 1992.

Devall, Bill, and George Sessions. *Deep Ecology.* Peregrine Smith, 1985.

Gross, Paul, and Norman Levitt. *Higher Superstitions: The Academic Left and Its Quarrel with Science.* Johns Hopkins University Press, 1994.

Manes, Christopher. *Green Rage: Radical Environmentalism and the Unmaking of Civilization.* Little, Brown, 1990.

Naess, Arne. "The Rights of Nature and Ultimate Premises." *Ecologist,* volume 18, 1988.

Nash, Roderick. *The Rights of Nature.* University of Wisconsin Press, 1989.

Roelofs, R.T., et al. *Environment and Society.* Prentice-Hall, 1974.

Seed, John, et al. *Thinking Like a Mountain: Toward a Council of All Beings.* New Society Publishers, 1988.

Sessions, George. "Anthropocentrism and the Environmental Crisis." Sierra College, 1989.

———. "Deep Ecology and the New Age." *Earth First!,* September 1987.

Weiskel, Timothy. "Religion, Belief and Survival on a Small Planet." *Amicus Journal,* Winter 1993.

CHAPTER 22

Holmes, Robert. "Study Finds There's Life Left in the Green Revolution." *Science,* volume 261, 1993.

"Integrated Pest Management Techniques." National Research Council, 1989.

Mellor, John. "Expanding the Green Revolution." *Issues in Science and Technology,* Fall 1989.

Myers, Norman. "Population, Environment and Development." *Environmental Conservation,* volume 20, 1993.

Pimental, David, et al. *Handbook of Pesticide Management in Agriculture.* Cornell University, 1991.

"Preparing U.S. Agriculture for Global Climate Change." Council for Agricultural Science and Technology, 1992.

Reganhold, John, et al. "Soil Quality and Financial Performance of Biodynamic and Conventional Farms in New Zealand." *Science,* April 16, 1993.

Rosenberg, A.A., et al. "Achieving Sustainable Use of Renewable Resources." *Science,* volume 262, 1993.

"Toward Sustainable Crop Development." World Resources Institute, 1992.

Wright, Lynn L. "Development of Biomass Energy Crops." American Association for the Advancement of Science, 1992.

Zinmeister, Karl. "The Environmental Assault on Agriculture." *Public Interest,* Summer 1993.

CHAPTER 23

Abelson, Philip. "Chlorine and Organochlorine Compounds." *Science,* volume 265, 1994.

"Briefings on Forest Issues." Society of American Foresters, 1993.

Boucher, Norman. "A Well Trodden Wilderness." *Federal Reserve Bank of Boston Regional Review,* Spring 1994.

Dixon, R.K., et al. "Carbon Pools and Flux of Global Forest Ecosystems." *Science,* volume 263, 1994.

Duffy, David, and Albert Meier. "Do Appalachian Herbaceous Understories Ever Recover from Clearcutting?" *Conservation Biology,* volume six, 1992.

Frederick, Kenneth, and Roger Sedjo. *America's Renewable Resources.* Resources for the Future, 1991.

Harmon, Mark, et al. "Effects on Carbon Storage of Conversion of Old Growth Forests to Young Forests." *Science,* volume 247, 1990.

O'Toole, Randal. *Reforming the Forest Service.* Island Press, 1988.

Sedjo, Roger, et al. "Global Forest Products Trade: The Consequences of Domestic Forest Use Policy." Resources for the Future, 1993.

Saint Clair, Jeffrey. "The Political Science of Jack Ward Thomas." *Wild Forest Review,* December 1993.

Raven, Peter. "Forest Loss and Biological Extinction." Missouri Botanical Garden, 1989.

CHAPTER 24

Davis, Bernard. "Genetic Engineering: The Making of Monsters?" *Public Interest,* Winter 1993

Gasser, Charles. "Transgenic Crops." *Scientific American,* June 1992.

Jackson, Wes. "Listen to the Land." *Amicus Journal,* Spring 1993.

Roberts, Leslie. "Bumper Transgenic Plant Crop." *Science,* July 5, 1991.

Stierle, Andrea, and Gary Strobel. "Taxol Production by Taxomyces Andreanae, an Endophytic Fungus of the Pacific Yew." *Science,* April 9, 1993.

Strobel, Gary. "Biological Control of Weeds." *Scientific American,* July 1991.

Stone, Richard. "Pigs as Protein Factories." *Science,* August 28 1992.

CHAPTER 25

"Everglades Restoration Annual Report." South Florida Water Management District, 1994.

Hess, Karl Jr. *Visions upon the Land: Man and Nature on the Western Range.* Island Press, 1992.

"Impact of Federal Programs on Wetlands." Report to Congress by the Secretary of the Interior, 1994.

Muir, John. *Our National Parks.* AMS Press, 1970.

Pinchot, Gifford. *The Fight for Conservation.* University of Washington Press, 1967.

"Restoration of Aquatic Ecosystems." National Research Council, 1991.

Rubino, Michael C. "Aquaculture and Wetlands." Address at Association of State Wetlands Managers, 1991.

Shanks, Bernard. *This Land Is Your Land.* Sierra Club Books, 1984.

Tucker, Compton, et al. "Expansion and Contraction of the Sahara from 1980 to 1900." *Science,* July 7, 1991.

CHAPTER 26

Breyer, Stephen. *Breaking the Vicious Cycle: Toward Effective Risk Regulation.* Harvard University Press, 1993.

Bullard, Robert. "The Environmental Justice Framework." American Association for the Advancement of Science, 1993.

Bullard, Robert, editor. *Unequal Protection: Environmental Justice and Communities of Color.* Sierra Club Books, 1994.

Esty, Daniel C. *Greening the GATT.* Institute for International Economics, 1994.

French, Hilary F. "Reconciling Trade and the Environment." Worldwatch Institute, 1993.

Housman, Robert. *Reconciling Trade and the Environment.* United Nations Environment Programme, 1994.

"National Environmental Scorecard." League of Conservation Voters, 1994

Newhouse, John. "The Diplomatic Round." *The New Yorker,* June 20, 1992.

"Reducing Risk: Setting Priorities and Strategies for Environmental Protection." Science Advisory Board, U.S. Environmental Protection Agency, 1990.

Reilly, William K. "The Arthur and Frank Payne Lectures." Stanford University, 1993–94.

Sandman, Peter. "Explaining Environmental Risk." U.S. Environmental Protection Agency, 1986.

"Toxic Release Inventory," 1991 and 1992. U.S. Environmental Protection Agency, 1993 and 1994.

Uimonen, Peter. "Trade Policies and the Environment." *Finance & Development,* June 1992.

CHAPTER 27

Avery, Dennis. "Global Food Progress." Hudson Institute, 1991.

Bongaarts, John. "Can the Growing Human Population Feed Itself?" *Scientific American*, March 1994.

Brown, Lester. *Full House*. W.W. Norton, 1994.

Carty, Winthrop, et al. "Success in a Challenging Environment: The Fertility Decline in Bangladesh." Population Reference Bureau, 1993.

Cruz, Maria. "Population Growth, Poverty and Environmental Stress." World Resources Institute, 1992.

Erhlich, Paul. *The Population Bomb*. Rivercity Press, 1968.

"India's Family Planning Challenge." Population Crisis Committee, 1992.

Jacobson, Jodi. "Gender Bias: Roadblock to Sustainable Development." Worldwatch Institute, 1992.

Le Bras, Harvey. "The Myth of Overpopulation." *Projections*, volume 7–8, 1992.

"Long-Range World Population Projections." United Nations, 1992.

Robey, Bryant, et al. "The Fertility Decline in Developing Countries." *Scientific American*, December 1993.

"Second Annual Report on the State of World Hunger." Institute on Hunger and Development, 1992.

CHAPTER 28

"Cancer in Populations Living Near Nuclear Facilities." National Cancer Institute, 1990.

Feshbach, Murray, and Alfred Friendly Jr. *Ecocide in the USSR*. Basic Books, 1992.

Flavin, Christopher. "World Nuclear Industry Status Report." Worldwatch Institute, 1992.

Lenssen, Nicholas. "Nuclear Wastes: The Problem that Won't Go Away." Worldwatch Institute, 1991.

Mann, Charles. "Radiation: Balancing the Record." *Science,* volume 263, 1994.

Perutz, M.F. "Britain, the Welfare State and Nuclear Pollution." *New York Review of Books*, November 11, 1989.

Quade, Jay, and Thure Cerling. "Stable Isotopic Evidence for a Pedogenic Origin of Carbonates in Trench 14 near Yucca Mountain, Nevada." *Science,* December 12, 1990.

Rees, Joseph. *Hostages of Each Other: The Transformation of Nuclear Safety since Three Mile Island*. University of Chicago Press, 1994.

Rhodes, Richard. *Nuclear Renewal*. Whittle Books/Viking, 1993.

Shulman, Seth. *The Threat at Home: Confronting the Toxic Legacy of the U.S. Military*. Beacon Press, 1992.

Susser, Mervyn, et al. "Estimating Health Effects at Three Mile Island." *American Journal of Public Health*, June 1991.

Von Hippel, Frank, et al. "Eliminating Nuclear Warheads." *Scientific American*, August 1993.

"Work-Related Lung Disease Surveillance Report." U.S. Department of Health and Human Services, 1992.

Yalow, Rosalyn. "Biological Effects of Low-Level Radiation." In *Science, Politics and Fear*, edited by Michael Burns. Lewis, 1988.

CHAPTER 29

Benedick, Richard. *Ozone Diplomacy.* Harvard University Press, 1991.

Cagin, Seth, and Philip Dray. *Between Earth and Sky: How CFCs Changed Our World and Endangered the Ozone Layer.* Pantheon, 1993.

Cicerone, Ralph. "Fires, Atmospheric Chemistry and the Ozone Layer." *Science,* volume 263, 1994.

Cole, Leonard. *Element of Risk: The Politics of Radon.* American Association for the Advancement of Science Press, 1993.

Dobson, G.B. *Exploring the Atmosphere.* Oxford University Press, 1968.

Elkins, James, et al. "Decrease in the Growth Rates of Atmospheric CFCs." *Nature,* August 26, 1993.

Farman, J.C., et al. "Large Losses of Total Ozone in Antarctic." *Nature,* May 16, 1985.

Gleason, J.F. et al. "Record Low Global Ozone in 1992." *Science,* April 23, 1993.

Johnston, David. "Volcanic Contribution of Chlorine to the Stratosphere: More Significant to Ozone than Previously Estimated?" *Science,* volume 209, 1980.

Karentz, Deneb. "Ecological Considerations of Antarctic Ozone Depletion." *Antarctic Science,* volume 3, 1993.

Kerr, J.B., and C.T. McElroy. "Evidence for Large Upward Trends of Ultraviolet-B Radiation Linked to Ozone Depletion." *Science,* volume 2662, 1993.

Macklis, Roger. "The Great Radium Scandal." *Scientific American,* August 1993.

Minton, Timothy, et al. "Direct Observation of Chlorine Monoxide from Chlorine Nitrate Photolysis." *Science,* November 11, 1992.

Molina, Mario, and Sherwood Rowland. "Chlorine Atom Catalyzed Destruction of Ozone." *Nature,* June 28, 1974.

Penkett, Stuart. "Ultraviolet Levels Down, Not Up." *Nature,* September 28, 1989.

"Radon Research Summary." U.S. Department of Energy, 1993.

Ravishankara, A.R. "Atmospheric Lifetimes of Long Lived Halogenated Species." *Science,* January 8, 1993.

Rowland, Sherwood. President's Lecture, American Association for the Advancement of Science, 1993.

Sackmeyer, G., and R.L. McKenzie. "Increased UV Radiation in New Zealand Relative to Germany." *Nature,* September 10, 1992.

Setlow, Richard. "Possible Link Between Ultraviolet-A Radiation and Skin Cancer in Fish." *Proceedings of the National Academy of Sciences,* July 15, 1993.

Stone, Richard. "Environmental Protection Agency Analysis of Radon in Water Is Hard to Swallow." *Science,* volume 261, 1993.

Taubes, Gary. "The Ozone Backlash." *Science,* volume 260, 1993.

Tolbert, Margaret. "Sulfate Aerosols and Polar Stratospheric Cloud Formation." *Science,* volume 264, 1994.

Toon, Owen, et al. "Polar Stratospheric Clouds and Ozone Depletion." *Scientific American,* June 1991.

Yalow, Rosalyn. "Concerns with Low-Level Ionizing Radiation." *Journal of Nuclear Medicine,* volume 31, 1990.

CHAPTER 30

Bonner, Raymond. *At the Hand of Man: Peril and Hope for Africa's Wildlife.* Alfred Knopf, 1993.

Brower, Kenneth. "The Naked Vulture and the Thinking Ape." *The Atlantic Monthly,* October 1983.

Carlton, James, and Jonathan Geller. "The Global Transport of Nonindigenous Marine Organisms." *Science,* July 2, 1993.

Culotta, Elizabeth. "Biological Immigrants under Fire." *Science,* December 6, 1991.

Erwin, Terry. "An Evolutionary Basis for Conservation Strategies." *Science,* August 8, 1991.

Hudson, Wendy, editor. "Building Economic Incentives into the Endangered Species Act." Defenders of Wildlife, 1993.

Jablonski, David. "Extinctions: A Paleontological Perspective." *Science,* August 8, 1991.

Littell, Richard. *Endangered and Other Protected Species.* Bureau of National Affairs, 1992.

Mann, Charles. "Extinctions: Are Ecologists Crying Wolf?" *Science,* August 16, 1991.

May, Robert. "How Many Species Inhabit the Earth?" *Scientific American,* October 1992.

Pimm, Stuart, and Andrew Sugden. "Tropical Diversity and Global Change." *Science,* volume 263, 1994.

Raven, Peter. "Biodiversity." American Association for the Advancement of Science, 1992.

Ryan, John. "Conserving Biological Diversity." Worldwatch Institute, 1992.

Schaller, George. *The Last Panda.* University of Chicago Press, 1993.

Steadman, David. "Biogeography of Tongan Birds Before and After Human Impact." *Proceedings of the National Academy of Sciences,* volume 90, 1993.

Stroup, Richard. "The Endangered Species Act: A Perverse Way to Protect Species." Political Economy Research Center, 1992.

Wake, David. "Declining Amphibian Populations." *Science,* August 23, 1991.

Young, James. "Tumbleweed." *Scientific American,* March 1991.

CHAPTER 31

"A Demographic Portrait of South and Southeast Asia." Population Reference Bureau, 1994.

Chivian, Eric, et al. *Critical Condition: Human Health and the Environment.* MIT Press, 1993.

Haas, Peter, et al. *Institutions for the Earth: Sources of Effective International Environmental Protection.* MIT Press, 1993.

Holloway, Marguerite. "Sustaining the Amazon." *Scientific American,* July 1993.

Hunter, David, et al. *Concepts and Principles of International Environmental Law.* United Nations Environment Program, 1994.

Jacobson, Jodi. *Out of the Woods.* Worldwatch Institute, 1992.

"Microlivestock for the Developing World." National Research Council, 1991.

"Our Planet, Our Health." World Health Organization, 1992

"Progress Report on World Bank Global Environmental Operations." World Bank, 1994.

Repetto, Robert. "Trade and Sustainable Development." United Nations Environment Programme, 1994.

"Report of the W.H.O. Commission on Health and the Environment." World Health Organization, 1992.

Rich, Bruce. *Mortgaging the Earth*. Beacon Press, 1994.

"Technologies to Sustain Tropical Forest Resources and Biodiversity." Office of Technology Assessment, 1992.

"Vetiver: A Green Line Against Erosion." National Research Council, 1993.

"World Development Report, 1992." World Bank, 1992.

"World Health Organization Global Strategy for Health and the Environment." World Health Organization, 1993.

CHAPTER 32

Anderson, Henry. "The Evolution of Environmental Epidemiological Risk Assessment." *Environmental Health Perspectives*, volume 62, 1985.

"Cancer Case Reporting and Surveillance in Massachusetts." Massachusetts State Senate, Committee on Oversight, 1987.

"Comparison of Superfund with Programs of Other Countries." Business Roundtable, 1993.

"Environmental Epidemiology: Health Effects from Hazardous Waste Sites." National Research Council, 1991.

Lilienfeld, Abraham. *Foundations of Epidemiology*. Oxford University Press, 1980.

"Love Canal Annual Report, 1989–91." New York Department of Environmental Conservation, 1989–91.

Paigen, Beverly, et al. "Abnormal Anthropometic Measures in Children Exposed to Environmental Toxins." *Pediatric Research*, volume 18, 1984.

Portney, Paul, and Katherine Probst. "Cleaning Up Superfund." *Resources*, Winter 1994.

Russell, Milton, and Mary English. "Hazardous Waste Remediation: The Task Ahead." University of Tennessee, 1991.

Silverman, G.B. "Love Canal: A Retrospective." *Environmental Reporter*, volume 20, 1989.

"Unfinished Business." U.S. Environmental Protection Agency, 1987.

CHAPTER 33

Breen, Bill. "Sludge: The Real World." *Garbage*, October–November 1992

"Challenges for the Future." Water Quality 2000, 1991.

"Ground Water and Soil Contamination." National Research Council, 1990.

Kane, Hal. "Fishing for Trouble." Worldwatch Institute, 1992.

Kullenberg, G. *The Role of Oceans as a Waste Disposal Option*. Reidel Publishing, 1986.

"The Quality of Our Nation's Water, 1992." U.S. Environmental Protection Agency, 1994.

Olson, Eric. "The Failure of the Nation's Drinking Water System to Protect Public Health." Natural Resources Defense Council, 1993.

Postel, Sandra. *Last Oasis: Facing Water Scarcity.* W.W. Norton, 1992
Reisner, Marc. *Cadillac Desert: The American West and Its Disappearing Water.* Viking, 1986.
Safina, Carl. "Bluefin Tuna in the West Atlantic: Negligent Management." *Conservation Biology,* volume 7, 1993.
————. "Conserving Marine Resources." National Audubon Society, 1992.
Schmidt, Karen. "Scientists Count a Rising Tide of Whales in the Sea." *Science,* volume 263, 1994.
Weber, Peter. *Reversing the Decline of the Oceans.* Worldwatch Institute, 1993.

Part Three (Chapters 35–38)

Ausubel, Jesse, and H. Dale Langford. *Technological Trajectories and the Human Environment.* National Academy Press, 1994.
Bak, Per. "Self Organized Criticality." *Scientific American,* January 1991.
Broecker, Wallace. *How to Build a Habitable Planet.* Lamont-Doherty Geological Observatory Press, 1990.
DeVries, Philip. "Singing Caterpillars, Ants and Symbiosis." *Scientific American,* October 1992.
Dyson, Freeman. *Infinite in All Directions.* Harper & Row, 1985.
Ferris, Timothy. *Coming of Age in the Milky Way.* William Morrow, 1988.
Gleick, James. *Chaos: The Making of a New Science.* Viking, 1987.
Gott, Richard J. "Implications of the Copernican Principle for Our Future Prospects." *Nature,* volume 363, 1993.
Gould, Stephen Jay, editor. *The Book of Life.* W.W. Norton, 1993.
Horowitz, Paul, and Carl Sagan. "Five Years of Project META: An All-Sky Narrow-Band Radio Search for Extraterrestrial Intelligence." *Astrophysical Journal,* volume 415, 1993.
Human Development Report 1994. United Nations Development Programme, 1994.
Kasting, James, et al. "The Life Span of the Biosphere Revisited." *Nature,* December 12, 1992.
Khalfa, Jean, editor. *What Is Intelligence?* Cambridge University Press, 1994.
Lewin, Roger. *The Edge of Complexity.* MacMillian, 1993.
Lohmann, Kenneth. "How Sea Turtles Navigate." *Scientific American,* January 1992.
Mann, Charles, and Mark Plummer. "The High Cost of Biodiversity." *Science,* June 25, 1993.
Miller, Stanley, and Leslie Orgel. *The Origins of Life on Earth.* Prentice-Hall, 1974.
"Modern Humans in the Levant." *Scientific American,* April 1993.
Moravec, Hans. *Mind Children: The Future of Robot and Human Intelligence.* Harvard University Press, 1988.
Roy, Arun. "Increasing the Healthy Life Span." American Association for the Advancement of Science, 1994.
Rusting, Ricki. "Why Do We Age?" *Scientific American,* December 1992.
Ruthen, Russell, and John Holland. "Adapting to Complexity." *Scientific American,* January 1993.

Schopf, William. "New Evidence of the Antiquity of Life." *Science*, April 30, 1993.

Schneider, Stephen. "Could We—Should We—Engineer the Earth's Climate?" American Association for the Advancement of Science, 1994.

Schneider, Stephen, and Penelope Boston. *Scientists on Gaia*. MIT Press, 1991.

Soule, M.E., and Bruce Wilcox, editors. *Conservation Biology: An Evolutionary-Ecological Perspective*. Sinauer Associates, 1980.

Waldrop, Mitchell M. *Complexity*. Simon & Schuster, 1993.

Walford, Roy. *Maximum Life Span*. W.W. Norton, 1983.

INDEX

NOTE TO READERS: THIS INDEX OFFERS CITATIONS MAINLY TO general topic areas and persons of unusual prominence, such as former presidents. The text contains many references to persons, places, and things not indexed here.